Fuzzy Techniques in Image Processing

Studies in Fuzziness and Soft Computing

Editor-in-chief
Prof. Janusz Kacprzyk
Systems Research Institute
Polish Academy of Sciences
ul. Newelska 6
01-447 Warsaw, Poland
E-mail: kacprzyk@ibspan.waw.pl
http://www.springer.de/cgi-bin/search_book.pl?series=2941

Vol. 3. A. Geyer-Schulz
Fuzzy Rule-Based Expert Systems and Genetic Machine Learning, 2nd ed. 1996
ISBN 3-7908-0964-0

Vol. 4. T. Onisawa and J. Kacprzyk (Eds.)
Reliability and Safety Analyses under Fuzziness, 1995
ISBN 3-7908-0837-7

Vol. 5. P. Bosc and J. Kacprzyk (Eds.)
Fuzziness in Database Management Systems, 1995
ISBN 3-7908-0858-X

Vol. 6. E.S. Lee and Q. Zhu
Fuzzy and Evidence Reasoning, 1995
ISBN 3-7908-0880-6

Vol. 7. B.A. Juliano and W. Bandler
Tracing Chains-of-Thought, 1996
ISBN 3-7908-0922-5

Vol. 8. F. Herrera and J.L. Verdegay (Eds.)
Genetic Algorithms and Soft Computing, 1996
ISBN 3-7908-0956-X

Vol. 9. M. Sato et al.
Fuzzy Clustering Models and Applications, 1997
ISBN 3-7908-1026-6

Vol. 10. L.C. Jain (Ed.)
Soft Computing Techniques in Knowledge-based Intelligent Engineering Systems, 1997
ISBN 3-7908-1035-5

Vol. 11. W. Mielczarski (Ed.)
Fuzzy Logic Techniques in Power Systems, 1998
ISBN 3-7908-1044-4

Vol. 12. B. Bouchon-Meunier (Ed.)
Aggregation and Fusion of Imperfect Information, 1998
ISBN 3-7908-1048-7

Vol. 13. E. Orłowska (Ed.)
Incomplete Information: Rough Set Analysis, 1998
ISBN 3-7908-1049-5

Vol. 14. E. Hisdal
Logical Structures for Representation of Knowledge and Uncertainty, 1998
ISBN 3-7908-1056-8

Vol. 15. G.J. Klir and M.J. Wierman
Uncertainty-Based Information, 2nd ed., 1999
ISBN 3-7908-1242-0

Vol. 16. D. Driankov and R. Palm (Eds.)
Advances in Fuzzy Control, 1998
ISBN 3-7908-1090-8

Vol. 17. L. Reznik, V. Dimitrov and J. Kacprzyk (Eds.)
Fuzzy Systems Design, 1998
ISBN 3-7908-1118-1

Vol. 18. L. Polkowski and A. Skowron (Eds.)
Rough Sets in Knowledge Discovery 1, 1998
ISBN 3-7908-1119-X

Vol. 19. L. Polkowski and A. Skowron (Eds.)
Rough Sets in Knowledge Discovery 2, 1998
ISBN 3-7908-1120-3

Vol. 20. J.N. Mordeson and P.S. Nair
Fuzzy Mathematics, 1998
ISBN 3-7908-1121-1

Vol. 21. L.C. Jain and T. Fukuda (Eds.)
Soft Computing for Intelligent Robotic Systems, 1998
ISBN 3-7908-1147-5

Vol. 22. J. Cardoso and H. Camargo (Eds.)
Fuzziness in Petri Nets, 1999
ISBN 3-7908-1158-0

Vol. 23. P.S. Szczepaniak (Ed.)
Computational Intelligence and Applications, 1999
ISBN 3-7908-1161-0

Vol. 24. E. Orłowska (Ed.)
Logic at Work, 1999
ISBN 3-7908-1164-5

continued on page 413

Etienne E. Kerre
Mike Nachtegael (Editors)

Fuzzy Techniques in Image Processing

With 197 Figures
and 31 Tables

Physica-Verlag
A Springer-Verlag Company

Prof. Dr. Etienne E. Kerre
Drs. Mike Nachtegael
Ghent University
Department of Applied Mathematics and Computer Science
Fuzziness and Uncertainty Modelling Research Unit
Krijgslaan 281 (S9)
9000 Gent
Belgium
Email: etienne.kerre@rug.ac.be
mike.nachtegael@rug.ac.be

ISSN 1434-9922
ISBN 3-7908-1304-4 Physica-Verlag Heidelberg New York

Cataloging-in-Publication Data applied for
Die Deutsche Bibliothek – CIP-Einheitsaufnahme
Fuzzy techniques in image processing: techniques and applications; with 31 tables / Etienne E. Kerre; Mike Nachtegael (ed.). – Heidelberg; New York: Physica-Verl., 2000
(Studies in fuzziness and soft computing; Vol. 52)
ISBN 3-7908-1304-4

Physica-Verlag is a company in the BertelsmannSpringer publishing group.

Printed in Germany

Hardcover Design: Erich Kirchner, Heidelberg

SPIN 10767329 88/2202-5 4 3 2 1 0 – Printed on acid-free paper

Preface

Since time immemorial, vision in general and images in particular have played an important and essential role in human life. Nowadays, the field of image processing also has numerous scientific, commercial, industrial and military applications. All these applications result from the interaction between fundamental scientific research on the one hand, and the development of new and high-standard technology on the other hand. Regarding the scientific component, quite recently the scientific community became familiar with "fuzzy techniques" in image processing, which make use of the framework of fuzzy sets and related theories. The theory of fuzzy sets was initiated in 1965 by Zadeh, and is one of the most developed models to treat imprecision and uncertainty. Instead of the classical approach that an object belongs or does not belong to a set, the concept of a fuzzy set allows a gradual transition from membership to nonmembership, providing partial degrees of membership. Fuzzy techniques are often complementary to existing techniques and can contribute to the development of better and more robust methods, as has already been illustrated in numerous scientific branches. With this volume, we want to demonstrate that the introduction and application of fuzzy techniques can also be very successful in the area of image processing.

This book contains high-quality contributions of over 30 field experts, covering a wide range of both theoretical and practical applications of fuzzy techniques in image processing. The chapters have been grouped into three parts: *Fuzzy Mathematical Morphology*, *Fuzzy Image Filtering* and *Applications of Fuzzy Techniques in Image Processing.*

In the first part we present four chapters on fuzzy mathematical morphology. In the first chapter the reader will find an overview of both classical and fuzzy approaches towards mathematical morphology, an extensive study of their properties, as well as a close look at the links between these approaches. The second chapter is dedicated to the important property of (generalized) idempotence. In particular, it is shown under which conditions this property holds in fuzzy mathematical morphology. Chapter 3 discusses a specific approach towards fuzzy morphology based on the fuzzification of the notion of subsethood by using inclusion indicators. Furthermore it explains in which manner binary algorithms lift to fuzzy algorithms, it provides some basic representation theorems for fuzzy morphological operations, and it shows how one can define approximate convexity in this context. Finally, the fourth chapter takes a look at fuzzy morphology and derived spatial relationships such as distance, adjacency and directional relative position. These spatial relationships are very important and lead to applications in pattern recognition.

In the second part, five chapters on fuzzy image filtering are presented. Chapter 5 gives a nice and extensive overview of already existing fuzzy enhancement and filtering techniques. The following three chapters concern specific (families of) fuzzy rule-based filtering methods: the extended adaptive weighted fuzzy mean filter is discussed in Chapter 6, Chapter 7 highlights the merits of the iterative fuzzy control based filter and its modifications, while Chapter 8 concerns the design of fuzzy rule-based image processing systems — both for noise removal and edge extraction — by optimizing a nonlinear function. In every chapter, the performance of the filters is illustrated with numerous computer simulations. To conclude, Chapter 9 discusses different kinds of filtering techniques for color images. Among other things, the advantages of the HSI color space w.r.t. the RGB color space are considered when dealing with fuzzy rules in a color environment.

The third part contains six applications of fuzzy techniques in image processing, including engineering and medical problems. Among them are linguistic color processing using fuzzy logic and its application to spot welding, discussed in Chapter 10. In Chapter 11, fuzzy decision rules are used to rank segmentation paths before feeding them to a character classifier. In the third chapter of this part, several fuzzy techniques are considered for the detection and analysis of potential breast cancer lesions on mammographic images, yielding very good results. Chapter 13 concerns the design of a fuzzy motion detector and its successful application to de-interlacing, leading to highly improved quality of originally interlaced video signals. The problem of object recognition and visual servoing is treated in Chapter 14. In particular, techniques for recognising partially occluded objects and a fuzzy control approach for the fine-positioning of a robot gripper using visual data are presented. Finally, Chapter 15 discusses topology-preserving deformations of fuzzy pictures.

The editing process was divided in two phases. In the first phase we reviewed all contributions, focussing our attention on the scientific content and the readability of the chapters. We hereby are thankful to the authors for considering our suggestions. In the second phase, we have made many efforts to produce a consistent and "good-looking" volume. This means for example that all chapters have the same lay-out details, that all reference lists have been reproduced in the same style, and that we have tried to make a good overall index. The index has around 300 entries, and there are a total of 456 references to specialized scientific literature. Furthermore, the book contains 188 illustrative figures and diagrams. Note that for technical reasons, the color figures in chapters 9 and 10 are reproduced in black and white. However, the original coloured images of these chapters are included in an appendix at the end of the book.

We are convinced that this volume presents a broad, up-to-date and state-of-the-art coverage of diverse aspects related to fuzzy techniques in image processing, and illustrates the richness and the enormous potential of these techniques. As the first of its kind, we hope this book will serve not only as an important reference for scientists and practitioners in this area, but also as an inspiration for newcoming researchers.

Gent,
January 2000

Etienne E. Kerre
Mike Nachtegael

Contents

Preface V

Contents.. IX

List of Contributors XV

Part I. Fuzzy Mathematical Morphology

1. Classical and Fuzzy Approaches towards Mathematical Morphology 3
Mike Nachtegael, Etienne E. Kerre
1 Introduction 3
2 Binary mathematical morphology 4
3 Gray-scale morphology based on the threshold approach 15
4 Gray-scale morphology based on the umbra approach 20
5 Fuzzy mathematical morphology: the general framework 27
6 Fuzzy mathematical morphology: approach of Bloch & Maître 43
7 Fuzzy mathematical morphology: approach of Minkowski addition .. 43
8 Fuzzy mathematical morphology: approach of subset inclusion 45
9 Schematic overview of the different approaches towards fuzzy mathematical morphology 54
10 Bibliographical remarks 54
References 56

2. Generalized Idempotence in Fuzzy Mathematical Morphology 58
Bernard De Baets
1 Generalized idempotence in binary morphology 58
2 Fuzzy morphology: a logical approach 60
3 Residual operators of triangular norms 63
4 Fuzzy morphology with triangular norms and residual implicators .. 66
5 Idempotent fuzzy closing and fuzzy opening operations 67
6 Open and closed fuzzy objects 68
References 73

3. Fuzzy Mathematical Morphology Based on Fuzzy Inclusion ... 76
Edward R. Dougherty, Antony T. Popov
1 Introduction ... 76
2 Binary mathematical morphology and the abstract lattice theory ... 77
3 Fuzzy morphological operations based on inclusion indicators ... 81
4 Algorithms ... 88
5 Morphological representation ... 91
6 Indicators of approximate convexity ... 97
References ... 98

4. Fuzzy Mathematical Morphology and Derived Spatial Relationships ... 101
Isabelle Bloch
1 Introduction ... 101
2 Definition of basic fuzzy mathematical morphology operators ... 103
3 Fuzzy distances derived from fuzzy dilation ... 113
4 Fuzzy adjacency from fuzzy dilation and set operations ... 120
5 Fuzzy directional relative position from conditional fuzzy dilation ... 124
6 Concluding remarks ... 130
References ... 131

Part II. Fuzzy Image Filtering

5. Fuzzy Image Enhancement: An Overview ... 137
Hamid R. Tizhoosh
1 Introduction ... 137
2 Framework of fuzzy image processing ... 138
3 Fuzzy contrast/brightness adaptation ... 140
4 Fuzzy filtering ... 152
5 Subjectivity and image enhancement ... 162
6 Future view ... 167
References ... 168

6. Adaptive Fuzzy Filter and Its Application to Image Enhancement ... 172
Chang-Shing Lee, Yau-Hwang Kuo
1 Introduction ... 172
2 Adaptive weighted fuzzy mean filter ... 174
3 Extended AWFM filter for edge enhancement ... 181
4 Properties of EAWFM filter ... 185
5 Experimental results ... 187
6 Conclusion ... 189
References ... 190

7. A Fuzzy Logic Control Based Approach for Image Filtering 194
Farzam Farbiz, Mohammad Bagher Menhaj
1 Introduction 194
2 The iterative fuzzy control based filter - IFCF 197
3 Smoothing fuzzy control based filter - SFCF 205
4 The fixed point fuzzy control based filter - FFCF 212
5 Adaptive fixed point fuzzy control based filter - AFCF 213
6 The adaptive C-average fuzzy control based filter - ACFCF 213
7 Conclusion 219
8 Acknowledgments 220
References 220

8. Fuzzy Rule-Based Image Processing with Optimization 222
Kaoru Arakawa
1 Introduction 222
2 Principles of fuzzy rule-based image processing 223
3 Fuzzy rule-based systems for noise removal 231
4 Fuzzy rule-based processing for edge extraction 238
5 Concluding remarks 244
References 246

9. Fuzzy Nonlinear Filtering of Color Images: A Survey 248
Constantin Vertan, Vasile Buzuloiu
1 Introduction 248
2 Crude or pseudo–fuzzy approaches 251
3 Fuzzy paradigm based filters 255
4 Fuzzy aggregative filters 257
5 Fuzzy inferential filters 259
6 Conclusions and comments 262
References 262

Part III. Applications of Fuzzy Techniques in Image Processing

10. Fuzzy Color Processing 267
Lars Hildebrand, Bernd Reusch
1 The human vision system 267
2 Color models 268
3 Fuzzy color processing 276
4 Example: analysis of welding points 279
5 Summary 285
References 285

11. Ranking Segmentation Paths Using Fuzzified Decision Rules 287
Zhongkang Lu, Zheru Chi, Pengfei Shi, Eam Khwang Teoh
1 Introduction 287
2 Relevant techniques 288
3 Properties of a segmentation path 296
4 Fuzzified decision rules 298
5 Defuzzification 301
6 Experimental results and discussion 301
7 Conclusion 304
References 305

12. Fuzzy Techniques in Mammographic Image Processing 308
Andreas Rick, Sylvie Bothorel, Bernadette Bouchon-Meunier, Serge Muller, Maria Rifqi
1 Introduction 308
2 Fuzzy contours and fuzzy measurements 310
3 Adaptive membership functions 313
4 Comparison measures and prototypes for image processing 319
5 Computer-aided diagnosis for mammography 325
6 3D reconstruction of microcalcification clusters 329
7 Conclusion 334
References 334

13. Fuzzy-Based Motion Detection and Its Application to De-Interlacing 337
Dimitri Van De Ville, Wilfried Philips, Ignace Lemahieu
1 Introduction 337
2 Fuzzy motion detection 339
3 Application to de-interlacing 352
4 Conclusions 367
References 368

14. Object Recognition and Visual Servoing: Two Case Studies of Employing Fuzzy Techniques in Robot Vision 370
Alois Knoll, Jianwei Zhang, Thorsten Graf, André Wolfram
1 Introduction 370
2 Recognition through fuzzy invariant indexing 373
3 Fine-positioning and object grasping: turning visual observations into action 380
4 A complete recognition-grasping example 389
5 Conclusions 391
References 392

15. Topology-Preserving Deformations of Fuzzy Digital Pictures ... 394
Akira Nakamura, Azriel Rosenfeld
1 Introduction ... 394
2 Basic definitions ... 395
3 Simple points ... 397
4 Simple deformations ... 399
5 Genus ... 401
References ... 404

Appendix: Color Images of Chapters 9 and 10 ... 405

Index ... 409

List of Contributors

Kaoru Arakawa
Meji University
Japan

Isabelle Bloch
Ecole Nationale Supérieure
des Télécommunications
France

Sylvie Bothorel
General Electric Medical Systems
France

Bernadette Bouchon-Meunier
Université Pierre et Marie Curie
France

Vasile Buzuloiu
Universitatea Politehnica Bucureşti
Romania

Zheru Chi
Hong Kong Polytechnic University
Hong Kong

Bernard De Baets
Ghent University
Belgium

Edward R. Dougherty
Texas A&M University
United States of America

Farzam Farbiz
Amirkabir University of Technology
Iran

Thorsten Graf
University of Bielefeld
Germany

Lars Hildebrand
University of Dortmund
Germany

Etienne E. Kerre
Ghent University
Belgium

Alois Knoll
University of Bielefeld
Germany

Yau-Hwang Kuo
National Cheng Kung University
Taiwan

Chang-Shing Lee
National Cheng Kung University
Taiwan

Ignace Lemahieu
Ghent University
Belgium

Zhongkang Lu
Nan Yang Technological University
Singapore

Mohammad Bagher Menhaj
Amirkabir University of Technology
Iran

Serge Muller
General Electric Medical Systems
France

Mike Nachtegael
Ghent University
Belgium

Akira Nakamura
Hiroshima-Denki Institute
of Technology
Japan

Wilfried Philips
Ghent University
Belgium

Antony T. Popov
St. Kliment Ohridski University of Sofia
Bulgaria

Bernd Reusch
University of Dortmund
Germany

Andreas Rick
Université Pierre et Marie Curie &
General Electric Medical Systems
France

Maria Rifqi
Université Pierre et Marie Curie
France

Azriel Rosenfeld
University of Maryland
United States of America

Pengfei Shi
Shanghai Jiaotong University
P.R. of China

Eam Khwang Teoh
Nan Yang Technological University
Singapore

Hamid R. Tizhoosh
University of Magdeburg
Germany

Dimitri Van De Ville
Ghent University
Belgium

Constantin Vertan
Universitatea Politehnica Bucureşti
Romania

André Wolfram
University of Bielefeld
Germany

Jianwei Zhang
University of Bielefeld
Germany

Part I

Fuzzy Mathematical Morphology

Chapter 1

Classical and Fuzzy Approaches towards Mathematical Morphology

Mike Nachtegael and Etienne E. Kerre

Ghent University
Department of Applied Mathematics and Computer Science
Fuzziness and Uncertainty Modelling Research Unit
Krijgslaan 281 (Building S9), B-9000 Gent, Belgium
email: {mike.nachtegael,etienne.kerre}@rug.ac.be

Summary. Fuzzy mathematical morphology is an alternative extension of binary morphology to gray-scale morphology, using techniques from fuzzy set theory. In this chapter we first review the basic definitions and properties of binary and classical gray-scale mathematical morphology. Next we present a general logical framework for fuzzy morphology. Finally, we give an extensive overview of other recent fuzzy approaches towards mathematical morphology, and show how they all fit into the general logical framework.

1 Introduction

1.1 Objects and tools of mathematical morphology

The objects studied by mathematical morphology are binary and gray-scale images. Binary images have only two possible pixel values, e.g. 0 and 1, respectively corresponding to black and white. White represents the foreground or the objects in the image, whereas black represents the background. Gray-scale images have more than two pixel values, e.g. in the unit interval [0,1], allowing shades of gray instead of only black and white. Consequently, n-dimensional binary images can be represented as subsets of $\mathbb{R}^n$, and n-dimensional gray-scale images as $\mathbb{R}^n - [0,1]$ functions.

The basic tools of mathematical morphology are the morphological operations. A morphological operation P transforms an image A by means of a structuring element B into a new image $P(A, B)$. The object A represents the structure we want to analyse, while B is a small object with which we want to probe the structure of A, and which has to be chosen by the morphologist. The four basic morphological operations are dilation, erosion, opening and closing. These operations employ specific sequences of neighbourhood transformations to measure useful geometric features, and have several practical applications.

1.2 Binary, gray-scale and fuzzy mathematical morphology

Depending on the nature of the object under study, one has to make use of *binary morphology* (for binary images) or *gray-scale morphology* (for gray-scale images). There are two classical approaches towards gray-scale morphology, namely the threshold approach (only allowing binary structuring elements) and the umbra approach (also allowing gray-scale structuring elements). However, quite recently several researchers have introduced alternative ways to extend binary morphology to gray-scale morphology, using techniques from fuzzy set theory. These extensions are commonly referred to as *fuzzy morphology*.

1.3 Structure of the chapter

The aim of this chapter is to give an overview of the classical and fuzzy approaches towards mathematical morphology, to show how they are linked, and to show how they can all be unified in a general logical framework.

The chapter is organized as follows. In the first part we will review the basic definitions and properties of both binary morphology (section 2) and classical gray-scale morphology (sections 3 and 4). The second and largest part of the chapter is devoted to fuzzy morphology. In section 5 we present the general logical framework initiated by De Baets, based on the notions of conjunctor and implicator. We define the fuzzy morphological operations, investigate their main properties, and show how they are linked to binary and classical gray-scale morphology. Next, we give an overview of other recent fuzzy approaches towards mathematical morphology. We will discuss the model of Bloch & Maître (section 6), an approach starting from a fuzzification of the Minkowski addition (section 7), and some approaches starting from different fuzzifications of the notion of set inclusion (section 8). In particular, the fuzzified set inclusions of Zadeh, Sinha & Dougherty, Kitainik and Bandler & Kohout will be applied. Finally, in section 9 we will give a schematic overview of the links between all these different models.

The chapter is concluded with some bibliographical notes (section 10), including references to books and papers in which the reader can find supplementary information.

2 Binary mathematical morphology

2.1 Binary morphological operations

In this section the objects A and B are binary images, i.e. subsets of $\mathbb{R}^n$. The translation $T_y(B)$ of the object B by the vector $y \in \mathbb{R}^n$ is defined as $T_y(B) = \{x \in \mathbb{R}^n | x - y \in B\}$.

Definition 1 *Let A be a binary image and let B be a binary structuring element. The binary dilation $D(A,B)$ and the binary erosion $E(A,B)$ of A by B are the binary images given by:*

$$D(A,B) = \{y \in \mathbb{R}^n | T_y(B) \cap A \neq \emptyset\}, \tag{1}$$
$$E(A,B) = \{y \in \mathbb{R}^n | T_y(B) \subseteq A\}. \tag{2}$$

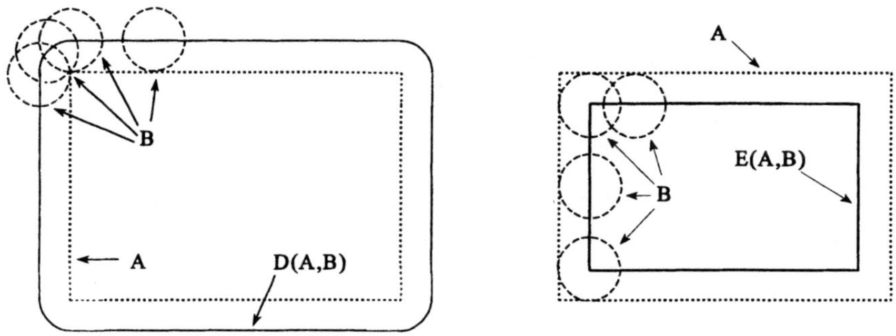

Fig. 1. Geometrical interpretation of binary dilation (left) and binary erosion (right)

Equivalent expressions for $D(A,B)$ and $E(A,B)$ are given by:

$$D(A,B) = \{y \in \mathbb{R}^n | (\exists b \in B)(y + b \in A)\} = \bigcup_{b \in B} T_{-b}(A), \tag{3}$$
$$E(A,B) = \{y \in \mathbb{R}^n | (\forall b \in B)(y + b \in A)\} = \bigcap_{b \in B} T_{-b}(A). \tag{4}$$

The binary dilation and erosion have a very nice geometrical interpretation, as illustrated in figure 1. On the one hand, the dilation $D(A,B)$ comprises all points $y \in \mathbb{R}^n$ for which the neighbourhood $T_y(B)$ hits A. On the other hand, the erosion $E(A,B)$ consists of all points $y \in \mathbb{R}^n$ for which $T_y(B)$ lies entirely in A, or alternatively, for which $T_y(B)$ doesn't hit $co\,A$.

As a consequence, the binary dilation typically will extend the contours of the objects in the image, while the binary erosion will reduce them. Furthermore, the dilation will fill up small gaps (i.e. eliminate background details) and narrow channels, while the erosion will eliminate small foreground details, enlarge gaps and broaden channels. These characteristics are illustrated in figure 3; the original binary image is depicted in figure 2. The used structuring element B is given by (the underlined element corresponds to the origin of coordinates):

$$B = \begin{pmatrix} 1 & 1 & 1 \\ 1 & \underline{1} & 1 \\ 1 & 1 & 1 \end{pmatrix}.$$

Fig. 2. Original binary image

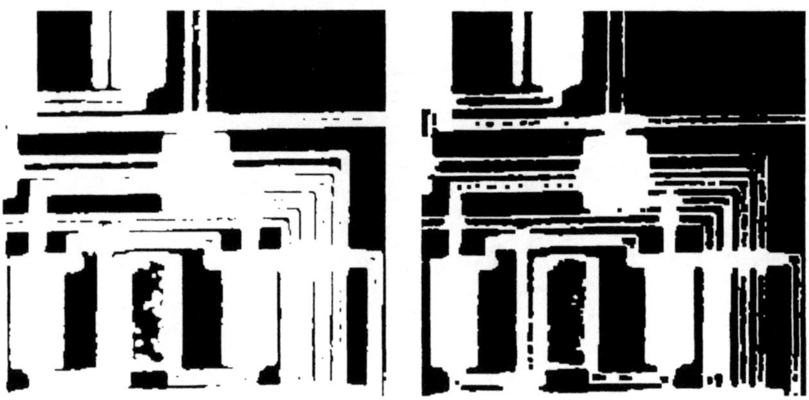

Fig. 3. Binary dilation D (left) and binary erosion E (right)

The binary closing and opening are special combinations of the binary dilation and erosion. Recall that the reflection $-B$ of a subset B of $\mathbb{R}^n$ is defined as $-B = \{-b|b \in B\}$.

Definition 2 *Let A be a binary image and let B be a binary structuring element. The binary closing $C(A,B)$ and the binary opening $O(A,B)$ of A by B are the binary images given by:*

$$C(A,B) = E(D(A,B),-B), \tag{5}$$

$$O(A,B) = D(E(A,B),-B). \tag{6}$$

The following explicit expressions can easily be derived:

$$C(A,B) = \{y|(\forall z)(y \in T_z(B) \Rightarrow T_z(B) \cap A \neq \emptyset)\}, \quad (7)$$

$$O(A,B) = \{y|(\exists z)(y \in T_z(B) \text{ and } T_z(B) \subseteq A)\}. \quad (8)$$

The previous formulas give rise to a geometrical interpretation of the binary closing and opening. From (7) it follows that the closing $C(A,B)$ consists of all points $y \in \mathbb{R}^n$ for which any translation of B that contains y has a nonempty intersection with A, whereas (8) implies that the opening $O(A,B)$ is the union of all translates $T_z(B)$ that are contained in A. As a consequence, the binary closing will fill up narrow channels and small gaps, while the binary opening will suppress small peaks and eliminate other small details (see figure 4). Note that in contrast to the binary dilation and erosion, the size of larger structures isn't really affected.

Fig. 4. Binary closing C (left) and binary opening O (right)

2.2 A note on the definitions

Scientific literature bulges out with different definitions and notations for the basic morphological operations. For example, in quite a lot of papers the binary dilation of A by B is defined as the Minkowski addition $A \oplus B$, given by:

$$A \oplus B = \bigcup_{b \in B} T_b(A). \quad (9)$$

Similarly, in some papers the binary erosion is defined as:

$$A \otimes B = \bigcap_{b \in B} T_b(A). \quad (10)$$

One easily verifies that $A \oplus B = D(A, -B)$ and $A \otimes B = E(A, -B)$. As another example, table 1 presents the definitions of some authors and indicates how they are connected to the ones we use. Note that we have chosen the definitions proposed in [25], because of their immediate geometrical interpretation. Also note that the different definitions coincide when the structuring element B is symmetric, i.e. when $B = -B$.

Table 1. The different definitions for the morphological operations

Reference	Dilation	Erosion	Closing	Opening
[25]	$D(A, B)$	$E(A, B)$	$C(A, B)$	$O(A, B)$
[14]	$D(A, -B)$	$E(A, B)$	$C(A, -B)$	$O(A, B)$
[12]	$D(A, B)$	$E(A, B)$	$E(D(A, B), B)$	$D(E(A, B), B)$
[3]	$D(A, B)$	$E(A, B)$	$C(A, -B)$	$O(A, -B)$
[29]	$D(A, -B)$	$E(A, B)$	$C(A, -B)$	$O(A, B)$

Finally, we also refer to Chapters 2, 3 and 4 of this book. Chapter 2 (*Generalized Idempotence in Fuzzy Mathematical Morphology*) uses the same definitions as here, Chapter 3 (*Fuzzy Mathematical Morphology Based on Fuzzy Inclusion*) uses the same definitions as in [29] (i.e. dilation and closing are defined in a different way), while Chapter 4 (*Fuzzy Mathematical Morphology and Derived Spatial Relationships*) uses the same definitions as in [3] (in particular, dilation and erosion are defined as in this chapter).

2.3 Properties

In this section we give an overview of the basic properties of the binary morphological operations. We will pay special attention to the interpretation of these properties, and indicate their practical importance.

Duality.

Two binary morphological operations P and Q are called dual if for any two binary objects A and B it holds that $P(A, B) = co\, Q(co\, A, B)$. One can verify that the binary dilation and erosion, as well as the binary opening and closing, are dual operations.

Proposition 1 *Let A be a binary image and let B be a binary structuring element, then it holds:*

$$D(A, B) = co\, E(co\, A, B) \quad C(A, B) = co\, O(co\, A, B)$$
$$E(A, B) = co\, D(co\, A, B) \quad O(A, B) = co\, C(co\, A, B).$$

For example, the property $D(A,B) = co\, E(co\, A, B)$ states that the dilation of an image A by a structuring element B can be obtained by eroding the complement $co\, A$ by B. This also implies that the binary dilation and erosion are strongly connected operations, i.e. they are not independent of each other. Analogous interpretations hold for the other properties.

Monotonicity.

A binary morphological operation P is increasing in the first argument if $A_1 \subseteq A_2$ implies $P(A_1,B) \subseteq P(A_2,B)$, for all $A_1, A_2, B \subseteq \mathbb{R}^n$. On the other hand, P is decreasing in the first argument if $A_1 \subseteq A_2$ implies $P(A_1,B) \supseteq P(A_2,B)$, for all $A_1, A_2, B \subseteq \mathbb{R}^n$. Similar definitions hold for increasingness, respectively decreasingness in the second argument.

Proposition 2
(i) The binary dilation is increasing in both arguments.
(ii) The binary erosion is increasing in the first, and decreasing in the second argument.
(iii) The binary closing is increasing in the first argument.
(iv) The binary opening is increasing in the first argument.

The binary closing and opening are not increasing, nor decreasing in the second argument. This is due to the fact that the dilation is increasing in the second argument, while the erosion is decreasing in the second argument.

Interaction with union and intersection.

Next, we present some interaction properties of the binary dilation, erosion, closing and opening with union and intersection. Especially the equalities can be of great importance. For example, the property $D(A, \bigcup_{i\in I} B_i) = \bigcup_{i\in I} D(A, B_i)$ implies that decomposing a structuring element into a (finite) union of several elementary structuring elements leads to another method of evaluating the dilation.

Proposition 3 *Let A, B be binary objects and let $(A_i)_{i\in I}, (B_i)_{i\in I}$ be two arbitrary families of binary objects, then it holds:*

$$\begin{array}{ll} D(\bigcup_{i\in I} A_i, B) = \bigcup_{i\in I} D(A_i, B) & D(A, \bigcup_{i\in I} B_i) = \bigcup_{i\in I} D(A, B_i) \\ E(\bigcup_{i\in I} A_i, B) \supseteq \bigcup_{i\in I} E(A_i, B) & E(A, \bigcup_{i\in I} B_i) = \bigcap_{i\in I} E(A, B_i) \\ C(\bigcup_{i\in I} A_i, B) \supseteq \bigcup_{i\in I} C(A_i, B) & O(\bigcup_{i\in I} A_i, B) \supseteq \bigcup_{i\in I} O(A_i, B). \end{array}$$

In general, an operator P on $\mathbb{R}^n$ is called an algebraic dilation if it satisfies $P(\bigcup_{i\in I} A_i) = \bigcup_{i\in I} P(A_i)$ for every family $(A_i)_{i\in I}$ in $\mathbb{R}^n$. From proposition 3 it follows that the binary morphological dilation by a given structuring element is an algebraic dilation.

Proposition 4 *Let A, B be binary objects and let $(A_i)_{i\in I}, (B_i)_{i\in I}$ be two arbitrary families of binary objects, then it holds:*

$$\begin{array}{ll}
D(\bigcap_{i\in I} A_i, B) \subseteq \bigcap_{i\in I} D(A_i, B) & D(A, \bigcap_{i\in I} B_i) \subseteq \bigcap_{i\in I} D(A, B_i) \\
E(\bigcap_{i\in I} A_i, B) = \bigcap_{i\in I} E(A_i, B) & E(A, \bigcap_{i\in I} B_i) \supseteq \bigcup_{i\in I} E(A, B_i) \\
C(\bigcap_{i\in I} A_i, B) \subseteq \bigcap_{i\in I} C(A_i, B) & O(\bigcap_{i\in I} A_i, B) \subseteq \bigcap_{i\in I} O(A_i, B).
\end{array}$$

Dual to algebraic dilations, an operator P on $\mathbb{R}^n$ is called an algebraic erosion if $P(\bigcap_{i\in I} A_i) = \bigcap_{i\in I} P(A_i)$ for every family $(A_i)_{i\in I}$ in $\mathbb{R}^n$. Proposition 4 implies that the binary morphological erosion by a given structuring element is an algebraic erosion.

If we impose the condition that the intersection of the A_i's or the B_i's is non-empty, then four of the five inclusions from proposition 4 become equalities.

Proposition 5 *Let A, B be binary objects and let $(A_i)_{i\in I}, (B_i)_{i\in I}$ be two arbitrary families of binary objects such that $\cap_{i\in I} A_i \neq \emptyset$ and $\cap_{i\in I} B_i \neq \emptyset$, then it holds:*

$$\begin{array}{ll}
D(\bigcap_{i\in I} A_i, B) = \bigcap_{i\in I} D(A_i, B) & D(A, \bigcap_{i\in I} B_i) = \bigcap_{i\in I} D(A, B_i) \\
C(\bigcap_{i\in I} A_i, B) = \bigcap_{i\in I} C(A_i, B) & O(\bigcap_{i\in I} A_i, B) = \bigcap_{i\in I} O(A_i, B).
\end{array}$$

The equalities in propositions 4 and 5 not only lead to alternative ways to obtain binary dilations, erosions, closings and openings, but also have a very important physical interpretation. Indeed, suppose that A is a binary image. From a physical point of view it is impossible to determine an exact boundary between the foreground (white) and the background (black). We can only define two disjoint sets X_1 and Y_1, each corresponding to regions where we are certain to be in the foreground or the background, respectively. The complement $co\,(X_1 \cup Y_1)$ of their union is a non-empty zone U_1 of which we know nothing, except that it contains the boundary between foreground and background. We then can try to improve the sharpness of the contour (e.g. by magnification) such that we obtain a second non-empty zone U_2, included in U_1, and so on. Note that the actual, but practical inaccessible boundary is the non-empty intersection of all the possible U_i, for U_i's becoming finer and finer. Let us further assume that the image A is modified by an increasing operator P (e.g. dilation, erosion, closing and opening by a binary structuring element). As the U_i's tend towards the boundary of the original image, it is intuitively acceptable to require that the transforms $P(U_i)$ tend towards the boundary of the transformed image. In other words, it should hold that:

$$P(\bigcap_{i\in I} U_i) = \bigcap_{i\in I} P(U_i). \tag{11}$$

Propositions 4 and 5 express that the four basic binary morphological operations fulfill this intuitive requirement (recall that $\cap_{i\in I}U_i \neq \emptyset$).

The previous discussion can be expressed in a more formal way, and is linked to the Hit-or-Miss topology on the closed subsets of $\mathbb{R}^n$ and the notion of semicontinuity w.r.t. this topology. For more details on this subject the reader is referred to [16], [19] and [25].

Invariance under translation and scaling.

Given $v \in \mathbb{R}^n$ and $\lambda > 0$, the translation $T_v(A)$ and scaling $H_\lambda(A)$ of a binary image A are respectively defined as $T_v(A) = \{x \in \mathbb{R}^n | x - v \in A\}$ and $H_\lambda(A) = \{\lambda a | a \in A\}$. Invariance under translation implies that the morphological operations are independent of the choice of the origin, while invariance under scaling means that these operations are independent of the scale used.

Proposition 6 *Let A and B be binary objects and let $v \in \mathbb{R}^n$, then it holds:*

$$\begin{aligned} D(T_v(A),B) &= T_v(D(A,B)) & E(T_v(A),B) &= T_v(E(A,B)) \\ D(A,T_v(B)) &= T_{-v}(D(A,B)) & E(A,T_v(B)) &= T_{-v}(E(A,B)) \\ D(T_v(A),T_v(B)) &= D(A,B) & E(T_v(A),T_v(B)) &= E(A,B) \end{aligned}$$

$$\begin{aligned} C(T_v(A),B) &= T_v(C(A,B)) & O(T_v(A),B) &= T_v(O(A,B)) \\ C(A,T_v(B)) &= C(A,B) & O(A,T_v(B)) &= O(A,B) \\ C(T_v(A),T_v(B)) &= T_v(C(A,B)) & O(T_v(A),T_v(B)) &= T_v(O(A,B)). \end{aligned}$$

It follows that a translation of the image *or* the structuring element always implies a translation of the dilation or erosion of the image. If both the image *and* the structuring element are translated by the same vector, then the dilated or eroded images aren't affected. On the other hand, a translation of the image or a translation of both the image *and* the structuring element implies a translation of the closing and opening of the image. Note however that the closing and opening of a binary object are independent of the *place* of the structuring element, but only depend upon the *shape* of it.

Proposition 7 *Let A and B be binary objects and let $\lambda > 0$, then it holds:*

$$\begin{aligned} D(H_\lambda(A),H_\lambda(B)) &= H_\lambda(D(A,B)) & C(H_\lambda(A),H_\lambda(B)) &= H_\lambda(C(A,B)) \\ E(H_\lambda(A),H_\lambda(B)) &= H_\lambda(E(A,B)) & O(H_\lambda(A),H_\lambda(B)) &= H_\lambda(O(A,B)). \end{aligned}$$

Remark that proposition 7 also holds for $\lambda < 0$ (with H_λ defined in the same way), and consequently is valid for all $\lambda \neq 0$. Also note that $H_\lambda(A) = H_{-\lambda}(-A)$, which implies that a negative scaling of the binary object A equals a positive scaling of the reflected image $-A$. In particular, for $\lambda = -1$ we have $H_{-1}(A) = H_1(-A) = -A$. This leads to the following result.

Proposition 8 *Let A and B be binary objects, then it holds:*

$$\begin{aligned} -D(A,B) &= D(-A,-B) & -C(A,B) &= C(-A,-B) \\ -E(A,B) &= E(-A,-B) & -O(A,B) &= O(-A,-B). \end{aligned}$$

Proposition 8 expresses that the morphological transformation of a symmetric image by a symmetric structuring element is again a symmetric image.

Extensivity and idempotence.

An operator P on $\mathbb{R}^n$ is called extensive if $(\forall A \in \mathbb{R}^n)(A \subseteq P(A))$; it is called anti-extensive if $(\forall A \in \mathbb{R}^n)(P(A) \subseteq A)$. The physical interpretation for morphological operations (using a given structuring element) is straightforward: an extensive operation enlargens the foreground of the image, an anti-extensive operation reduces it.

Proposition 9 *Let A and B be binary objects, then it holds:*
(i) if the structuring element contains the origin, then the binary dilation is extensive and the binary erosion is anti-extensive: $\mathbf{0} \in B \Rightarrow E(A,B) \subseteq A \subseteq D(A,B)$,
(ii) the binary closing is extensive, and the binary opening is anti-extensive: $O(A,B) \subseteq A \subseteq C(A,B)$.

Note that the condition $\mathbf{0} \in B$ is sufficient, but not necessary for the binary dilation (resp. the binary erosion) to be extensive (resp. anti-extensive). Neither do $A \subseteq D(A,B)$ or $E(A,B) \subseteq A$ imply that $\mathbf{0} \in B$. On the other hand, the binary closing and opening are always extensive, resp. anti-extensive, whether B contains the origin or not.

Proposition 10 *The binary closing and the binary opening are idempotent operations, i.e. for all binary objects A and B it holds:*

$$C(C(A,B),B) = C(A,B)$$
$$O(O(A,B),B) = O(A,B).$$

The idempotency of the binary closing and opening are very important properties. It means that successive applications have no effect after the first application.

Inclusion properties.

Proposition 11 *Let A, B be binary objects, then the binary dilation D, erosion E, closing C and opening O satisfy:*

$$E(A,B) \subseteq D(A,B)$$
$$O(A,B) \subseteq C(A,B).$$

Proposition 12 *Let A, B be binary objects. If B contains the origin (i.e. $\mathbf{0} \in B$), then the binary dilation D, erosion E, closing C and opening O satisfy:*

$$\begin{array}{ll} D(A,B) \supseteq C(A,B) & E(A,B) \subseteq O(A,B) \\ D(A,B) \supseteq O(A,B) & E(A,B) \subseteq C(A,B) \\ D(A,B) \supseteq O(A,-B) & E(A,B) \subseteq C(A,-B). \end{array}$$

The results of propositions 9 and 12 lead to the following conclusion.

Proposition 13 *Let A, B be binary objects. If B contains the origin (i.e. $\mathbf{0} \in B$), then it holds:*

$$\mathbf{0} \in B \Rightarrow E(A,B) \subseteq O(A,B) \subseteq A \subseteq C(A,B) \subseteq D(A,B).$$

Commutativity and associativity of the binary dilation.

Proposition 14 *Let A, B, C be binary objects, then the binary dilation D satisfies:*

$$D(A,B) = -D(B,A)$$
$$D(D(A,B),C) = D(A, D(B,-C)).$$

Although the 'commutativity' property can have some practical advantages, it doesn't have a physical interpretation. Indeed, the roles of A (the image) and B (the structuring element) are completely different and cannot be interchanged at all. The 'associativity' on the other hand states that the dilation of A by B, followed by another dilation by C is the same as the dilation of A by $D(B,-C)$. Since the computation of $D(B,-C)$ is negligible (B and C are small structuring elements), it is more efficient to compute $D(A, D(B,-C))$ instead of $D(D(A,B),C)$.

Combinations of dilation and erosion.

The following proposition implies that the order in which different binary dilations or binary erosions are carried out is of no importance.

Proposition 15 *Let A be a binary image and let B, C be binary structuring elements, then the binary dilation D and the binary erosion E satisfy:*

$$D(D(A,B),C) = D(D(A,C),B)$$
$$E(E(A,B),C) = E(E(A,C),B).$$

We also have the following properties.

Proposition 16 *Let A be a binary image and let B, C be binary structuring elements, then the binary dilation D and the binary erosion E satisfy:*

$$E(A, D(B,-C)) = E(E(A,B),C)$$
$$D(A, E(B,C)) \subseteq E(D(A,B),-C)$$
$$D(E(A,B),C) \subseteq E(D(A,C),B).$$

The equality $E(A, D(B,-C)) = E(E(A,B),C)$ is again of great practical importance. Indeed, since B and C are small structuring elements, it is much more efficient to first calculate $D(B,-C)$ and then perform the erosion of

A by $D(B,-C)$ instead of first eroding A by B and then by C. Also note that $D(E(A,B),C) \subseteq E(D(A,C),B)$ implies $O(A,B) \subseteq C(A,-B)$ (take $C=-B$).

Local Knowledge.

In general, we only have limited information about the binary image A, i.e. we only see that part of A which is contained within a binary measuring mask Z (e.g. a square frame). The local knowledge property enables us to apply a morphological transformation $P(A,B)$ in a certain mask M under this limited information. For the binary dilation and erosion we have $M = E(Z,B)$.

Proposition 17 *Let A be a binary image, let B be a binary structuring element and let Z be a binary mask. Then it holds:*

$$D(A \cap Z, B) \cap E(Z,B) = D(A,B) \cap E(Z,B)$$
$$E(A \cap Z, B) \cap E(Z,B) = E(A,B) \cap E(Z,B).$$

This property is of great importance from a computational point of view, e.g. if one wants to implement an algorithm to compute the binary dilation or erosion.

Adjunction property.

Although dilation and erosion are dual, this doesn't mean that one can freely perform cancellation on morphological equalities. In particular, the equality $D(A,B) = C$ doesn't necessarily imply $A = E(C,-B)$. However, the following proposition indicates that a containment relationship is still maintained.

Proposition 18 *The binary dilation D and the binary erosion E satisfy:*

$$(\forall A,B,C \subseteq \mathbb{R}^n)(D(A,B) \subseteq C \Leftrightarrow A \subseteq E(C,-B)).$$

Let $\mathcal{P}(\mathbb{R}^n)$ be the class of all crisp subsets of $\mathbb{R}^n$. For a fixed $B \in \mathcal{P}(\mathbb{R}^n)$ we define the operations D^B and E^B on $\mathcal{P}(\mathbb{R}^n)$ respectively as $D^B(A) = D(A,B)$ and $E^B(A) = E(A,B)$, for all $A \in \mathcal{P}(\mathbb{R}^n)$. The above property can then be expressed as:

$$(\forall A,C \in \mathcal{P}(\mathbb{R}^n))(D^B(A) \subseteq C \Leftrightarrow A \subseteq E^{-B}(C)).$$

In general, a pair (P,Q) of operators on a complete lattice $(\mathcal{L},\leq)$ is an adjunction in $\mathcal{L}$ if it satisfies $(\forall X,Y \in \mathcal{L})(P(X) \leq Y \Leftrightarrow X \leq Q(Y))$. The notion of adjunctions is extensively discussed in [16]; in [15] it is also shown how the concept of adjunctions is closely linked to the concept of Galois connections between posets. Proposition 18 implies that the pair (D^B, E^{-B}) is an adjunction in $(\mathcal{P}(\mathbb{R}^n), \subseteq)$.

2.4 Application: edge detection

Let A be a binary image and let B be a binary structuring element. If B contains the origin, then it follows from proposition 9(i) that $E(A, B) \subseteq A \subseteq D(A, B)$. In particular, the dilation $D(A, B)$ will enlarge the objects in the image A, while the erosion $E(A, B)$ will reduce them. As a consequence, the binary set $D(A, B) \setminus E(A, B)$ will serve as an edge-image of the image A. This is illustrated in figure 5.

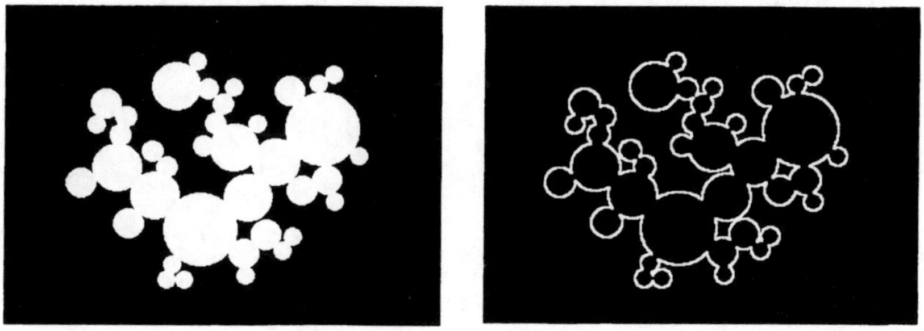

Fig. 5. Original image (left) and corresponding edge-image (right)

3 Gray-scale morphology based on the threshold approach

3.1 Introduction

Let A be a gray-scale image (represented as a $\mathbb{R}^n$-[0,1] function) and let B be a binary structuring element (represented as a subset of $\mathbb{R}^n$). Further assume that P is a binary morphological operation (based on the structuring element B), which we want to extend in order to be applicable to the gray-scale image A. The extended operation will be denoted by P_t, and will be referred to as a morphological t-operation. The threshold approach leads to the following way to obtain P_t (see figure 6):

(i) The gray-scale image A is represented as a family $(A_\alpha)_{\alpha \in]0,1]}$ of binary threshold sets, with $A_\alpha = \{x | x \in \mathbb{R}^n \text{ and } A(x) \geq \alpha\}$. In other words, A_α results from thresholding A at level α. Note that the value $\alpha = 0$ is excluded because $A_0 = \mathbb{R}^n$, which does not give any additional information regarding the image A.

(ii) The binary morphological operation P can now be applied to the threshold sets A_α, using the binary structuring element B. This results in a family $(P(A_\alpha, B))_{\alpha \in]0,1]}$.

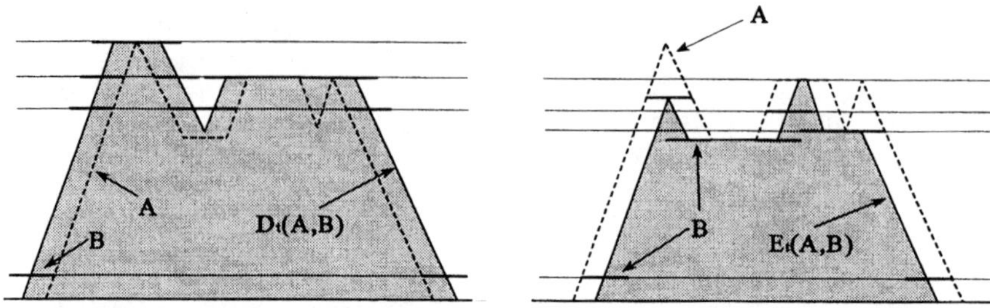

Fig. 6. Construction of the t-dilation (left) and the t-erosion (right)

(iii) With the family $(P(A_\alpha, B))_{\alpha\in]0,1]}$ of binary sets, one associates the following $\mathbb{R}^n$-[0,1] mapping, which represents the gray-scale image $P_t(A, B)$:

$$P_t(A,B)(x) = \sup\{\alpha|\alpha \in]0,1] \text{ and } x \in P(A_\alpha, B)\}, \quad \forall x \in \mathbb{R}^n. \tag{12}$$

Note that the above construction does not imply that the morphological t-operation P_t satisfies $P_t(A,B)_\alpha = P(A_\alpha, B)$ for all $\alpha \in]0,1]$, i.e. it is not a cutworthy operation. This will be the case if and only if $P_t(A_\alpha, B) = \cap_{\beta<\alpha} P_t(A_\beta, B)$ (see [23]). For example, this condition is fulfilled if A is upper semi-continuous and B is compact (see [25]). Recall that a $\mathbb{R}^n$-[0,1] mapping A is upper semi-continuous if and only if $(\forall x_0 \in \mathbb{R}^n)(\forall \epsilon > 0)(\exists \delta > 0)(\forall x \in \mathbb{R}^n)(|x - x_0| < \delta \Rightarrow F(x) < F(x_0) + \epsilon)$. Also recall that the upper semi-continuity of A is equivalent to $(\forall \alpha \in]0,1])(A_\alpha$ is a closed set).

3.2 The morphological t-operations

The domain d_A of a $\mathbb{R}^n$-[0,1] function A is given by $d_A = \{x \in \mathbb{R}^n | (\exists t \in [0,1])(A(x) = t)\}$. By definition, the t-dilation D_t and the t-erosion E_t will be respectively defined on $D(d_A, B)$ and $E(d_A, B)$.

Definition 3 *Let A be a gray-scale image and let B be a binary structuring element. The t-dilation $D_t(A,B)$ and the t-erosion $E_t(A,B)$ are the gray-scale images defined by:*

$$D_t(A,B)(y) = \sup_{x\in T_y(B)\cap d_A} A(x) \quad \text{for } y \in D(d_A, B) \tag{13}$$

$$E_t(A,B)(y) = \inf_{x\in T_y(B)} A(x) \quad \text{for } y \in E(d_A, B). \tag{14}$$

Note that we can extend the domain d_A to the whole space $\mathbb{R}^n$ by putting $A(x) = 0$ for those points x where A is originally not defined. As a result,

$D_t(A,B)(y) = 0$ and $E_t(A,B)(y) = 0$ for respectively $y \notin D(d_A, B)$ and $y \notin E(d_A, B)$, where d_A denotes the original and not the extended domain of A. We will adopt this convention in the following.

From the definitions it follows that $D_t(A,B)(y)$ is a local supremum and that $E_t(A,B)(y)$ is a local infimum of pixel values of A. This feature will give rise to the formation of small "blocks" in the transformed images. Typical for the t-dilation is that it eliminates dark and enhances light details, and that it reduces dark and enlargens light objects. The t-erosion on the other hand does the opposite: it suppresses light details, enhances dark details, reduces light objects, and enlargens dark objects. Figure 8 illustrates these characteristics; the original gray-scale image is depicted in figure 7. The used binary structuring element B is given by:

$$B = \begin{pmatrix} 1 & 1 & 1 \\ 1 & \underline{1} & 1 \\ 1 & 1 & 1 \end{pmatrix}$$

Fig. 7. Original gray-scale image

The t-closing and the t-opening are defined as the usual combinations of the t-dilation and the t-erosion. If we do not adopt the convention that $A(x) = 0$ for $x \notin d_A$, then the domain of $C_t(A,B)$ and $O_t(A,B)$ is respectively given by $C(d_A, B)$ and $O(d_A, B)$, where C and O are the binary closing and opening.

Definition 4 *Let A be a gray-scale image and let B be a binary structuring element. The t-closing $C_t(A,B)$ and the t-opening $O_t(A,B)$ are the gray-scale images given by:*

$$C_t(A,B) = E_t(D_t(A,B), -B)$$
$$O_t(A,B) = D_t(E_t(A,B), -B).$$

Fig. 8. t-dilation D_t (left) and t-erosion E_t (right)

Explicit expressions can be derived straightforward:

$$C_t(A,B)(y) = \inf_{z \in T_y(-B)} \left(\sup_{x \in T_z(B)} A(x) \right) \tag{15}$$

$$O_t(A,B)(y) = \sup_{z \in T_y(-B)} \left(\inf_{x \in T_z(B)} A(x) \right) . \tag{16}$$

As illustrated in figure 9, the t-closing typically eliminates dark details, whereas the t-opening eliminates light details. Note that the size of the objects is more or less left unchanged w.r.t. the original image.

Fig. 9. t-closing C_t (left) and t-opening O_t (right)

Finally, it is important to note that $D_t(A,B)$, $E_t(A,B)$, $C_t(A,B)$ and $O_t(A,B)$ are all $\mathbb{R}^n$-$[0,1]$ functions if the original image A is represented as a $\mathbb{R}^n$-$[0,1]$ function.

3.3 Link between the t-operations and the binary operations

It is just a matter of verification to see that the t-dilation, t-erosion, t-closing and t-opening coincide with their binary counterparts if A is a binary image (i.e. with 0 and 1 as the only pixel values).

Proposition 19 *Let A be a binary image and let B be a binary structuring element, then it holds:*

$$\begin{array}{ll} D_t(A,B) = D(A,B) & C_t(A,B) = C(A,B) \\ E_t(A,B) = E(A,B) & O_t(A,B) = O(A,B). \end{array}$$

3.4 Properties

Except for the propositions 5 (some special cases regarding the interaction with intersection) and 14 (regarding the commutativity of the dilation), all properties listed in section 2.3 for binary morphological operations are also valid in the case of morphological t-operations. The only difference in the formulation of the properties is that the first argument of a morphological t-operation is now a gray-scale image (modelled as a $\mathbb{R}^n$-$[0,1]$ function) instead of a binary image (modelled as a subset of $\mathbb{R}^n$). In the following, we list some other important remarks.

- Regarding the duality property (cfr. proposition 1), two morphological t-operations P and Q are called dual if for any gray-scale image A and for any binary structuring element B it holds that $P(A,B) = co\,Q(co\,A,B)$. The complement $co\,A$ of a $\mathbb{R}^n$-$[0,1]$ function A is defined by $co\,A(x) = 1 - A(x), \forall x \in d_A$.
- Regarding the monotonicity property (cfr. proposition 2), we say that $A_1 \subseteq A_2$ if and only if $A_1(x) \leq A_2(x), \forall x \in \mathbb{R}^n$, where A_1 and A_2 are two arbitrary $\mathbb{R}^n$-$\mathbb{R}$ mappings).
- Regarding the interaction properties (cfr. propositions 3 and 4), the union and intersection of a family $(A_i)_{i\in I}$ of uniformly bounded $\mathbb{R}^n$-$\mathbb{R}$ functions are respectively given by:

$$\bigcup_{i\in I} A_i(x) = \sup_{i\in I} A_i(x) \qquad \bigcap_{i\in I} A_i(x) = \inf_{i\in I} A_i(x).$$

- Regarding the invariance properties (cfr. propositions 6 and 7), the translation $T_y(A)$ (with $y \in \mathbb{R}^n$) and scaling $H_\lambda(A)$ (with $\lambda > 0$) of a $\mathbb{R}^n$-$\mathbb{R}$ function A are respectively given by $T_y(A)(x) = A(x-y)$ and $H_\lambda(A)(x) = A(\frac{1}{\lambda}x)$.

- Regarding the symmetry property (cfr. proposition 8), the reflection $-A$ of a $\mathbb{R}^n$-$\mathbb{R}$ function A is given by $(-A)(x) = A(-x)$.
- We already mentioned that the commutativity of the binary dilation (cfr. proposition 14) has no counterpart for morphological t-operations. Indeed, we would have to require that both arguments are binary objects in order to be able to formulate a commutativity property.
- Regarding the adjunction property (cfr. proposition 18), let us denote the class of all $\mathbb{R}^n - [0,1]$ mappings by $Func(\mathbb{R}^n, [0,1])$. For an arbitrary binary object B, we define the operations D_t^B and E_t^B on $Func(\mathbb{R}^n, [0,1])$ as follows: $D_t^B(A) = D_t(A,B)$ and $E_t^B(A) = E_t(A,B)$, for all $A \in Func(\mathbb{R}^n, [0,1])$. Then the adjunction property expresses that the pair (D_t^B, E_t^{-B}) is an adjunction in $(Func(\mathbb{R}^n, [0,1]), \subseteq)$.

3.5 Application: edge detection

Let A be a gray-scale image and let B be a 3×3 binary structuring element, with the origin at the center. From the properties of the t-dilation and the t-erosion it follows that $D_t(A,B) - E_t(A,B)$ will serve as an edge-image of the image A. This is illustrated in figure 10.

Fig. 10. Original image (left) and corresponding edge-image (right)

4 Gray-scale morphology based on the umbra approach

4.1 Introduction

Let A be a gray-scale image and let B be a gray-scale structuring element, both represented as $\mathbb{R}^n$-$\mathbb{R}$ functions (in practice we will restrict ourselves to $\mathbb{R}^n$-$[0,1]$ functions since only the interval $[0,1]$ corresponds to the set of available pixel values; the theory however considers $\mathbb{R}^n$-$\mathbb{R}$ functions). Further, let P denote a binary morphological operation which we want to extend in order to be applicable to the gray-scale image A, using the gray-scale structuring element B.

The umbra approach – introduced by Sternberg in [30]) – is based on the observation that the points on and below or above the graphs of A and B yield binary subsets of $\mathbb{R}^{n+1}$, called *umbras*, with which binary morphological operations can be performed. The resulting extended morphological operations will be referred to as morphological u-operations. Before we continue, we first give the formal definition of an umbra, a dual umbra and a top surface.

Definition 5 *Let F be a $\mathbb{R}^n$-$\mathbb{R}$ function with domain d_F, then the umbra $U[F]$ of F is the subset of $\mathbb{R}^{n+1}$ given by*

$$U[F] = \{(x,t) | (x,t) \in d_F \times \mathbb{R} \text{ and } t \leq F(x)\}.$$

The dual umbra $U_d[F]$ of F is defined by:

$$U_d[F] = \{(x,t) | (x,t) \in d_F \times \mathbb{R} \text{ and } t \geq F(x)\}.$$

The definition of the dual umbra $U_d[F]$ may not be confused with the reflection $-U[F]$ of the umbra $U[F]$, defined by $(x,t) \in -U[F] \Leftrightarrow (-x,t) \in U[F]$.

Definition 6 *Let $G \subseteq \mathbb{R}^{n+1}$ and let $d_G = \{x | x \in \mathbb{R}^n \text{ and } (\exists t \in \mathbb{R})((x,t) \in G)\}$, then the top surface $T[G]$ of G is the d_G-$\overline{\mathbf{R}}$ function defined by*

$$T[G](x) = \sup \{t | t \in \mathbb{R} \text{ and } (x,t) \in G\}.$$

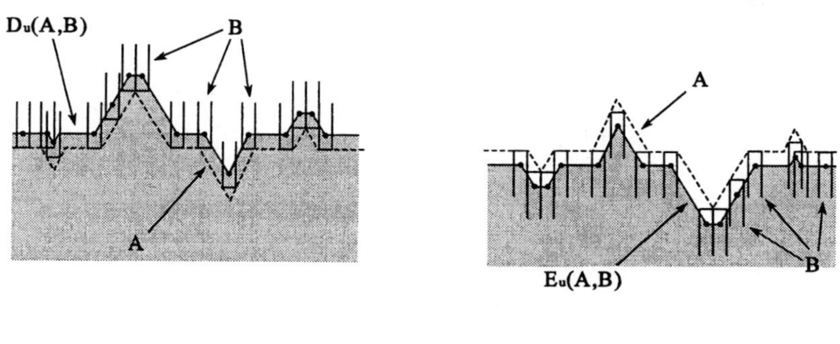

Fig. 11. Construction of the u-dilation (left) and the u-erosion (right)

Next, we will show how the binary erosion and the binary dilation can be extended to gray-scale images and gray-scale structuring elements, using the umbra approach (see figure 11):

(i) The erosion $E_u(A,B)$ is obtained by first performing the binary erosion E on the umbras $U[A]$ and $U[B]$, and then taking the top surface of the obtained result. This results in: $E_u(A,B) = T[E(U[A],U[B])]$.

(ii) For the dilation, it is clear that we have to take the dual umbra of the complement of B in order to obtain a meaningful extension (note that in this framework, the complement $co\,B$ of a $\mathbb{R}^n$-$\mathbb{R}$ function B is defined by $(co\,B)(x) = -B(x)$ for all $x \in \mathbb{R}^n$). Consequently, the dilation $D_u(A,B)$ is given by: $D_u(A,B) = T[D(U[A],U_d[co\,B])]$.

Note that in the umbra approach the morphological transformations of $\mathbb{R}^n$-$[0,1]$ functions don't necessarily produce $\mathbb{R}^n$-$[0,1]$ functions, but can generate functions with a lowerbound $m < 0$ and/or an upperbound $M > 1$. In practice we will have to transform the obtained result in order to get a $\mathbb{R}^n$-$[0,1]$ function.

4.2 Definitions

Definition 7 *Let A be a gray-scale image and let B be a gray-scale structuring element. The u-dilation $D_u(A,B)$ and the u-erosion $E_u(A,B)$ are the gray-scale images defined by:*

$$D_u(A,B)(y) = \sup_{x \in T_y(d_B) \cap d_A} A(x) + B(x-y) \quad for\ y \in D(d_A,d_B) \tag{17}$$

$$E_u(A,B)(y) = \inf_{x \in T_y(d_B)} A(x) - B(x-y) \quad for\ y \in E(d_A,d_B). \tag{18}$$

Just as for the t-operations, we can extend the domain d_A to the whole space $\mathbb{R}^n$ by putting $A(x) = -\infty$ for those points x where A is originally not defined. As a result, $D_u(A,B)(y) = -\infty$ and $E_u(A,B)(y) = -\infty$ for respectively $y \notin D(d_A,d_B)$ and $y \notin E(d_A,d_B)$, where d_A denotes the original domain of A. We will adopt this convention in the following.

The u-dilation and u-erosion have a similar effect as respectively the t-dilation and t-erosion (see figure 12): the u-dilation will eliminate dark details, enhance light details, reduce dark objects and enlarge light objects; the t-erosion will suppress light details, enhance dark details, reduce light objects and enlarge dark objects. Furthermore, the influence of the morphological u-operations highly depends upon the choice of the gray-scale structuring element. Due to the non-binary nature of the structuring element, the "block"-effect that occured with the morphological t-operations will be less prominent. In the examples we have taken:

$$B = \begin{pmatrix} 0.86 & 0.86 & 0.86 \\ 0.86 & \underline{1.00} & 0.86 \\ 0.86 & 0.86 & 0.86 \end{pmatrix} \tag{19}$$

Fig. 12. u-dilation D_u (left) and u-erosion E_u (right)

For the u-closing and u-opening, we take the same special combinations of the u-dilation and u-erosion as in the binary case.

Definition 8 *Let A be a gray-scale image and let B be a gray-scale structuring element. The u-closing $C_u(A,B)$ and the u-opening $O_u(A,B)$ are the gray-scale images defined by:*

$$C_u(A,B) = E_u(D_u(A,B), -B) \tag{20}$$
$$O_u(A,B) = D_u(E_u(A,B), -B). \tag{21}$$

Explicit expressions for $C_u(A,B)(y)$ and $O_u(A,B)(y)$ are given by:

$$C_u(A,B)(y) = \inf_{z \in T_y(-d_B)} \left(\sup_{x \in T_z(d_B)} (A(x) + B(x-z)) - B(y-z) \right) \tag{22}$$

$$O_u(A,B)(y) = \sup_{z \in T_y(-d_B)} \left(\inf_{x \in T_z(d_B)} (A(x) - B(x-z)) + B(y-z) \right) \tag{23}$$

Using the same structuring element as above, the u-closing typically eliminates dark details, whereas the u-opening eliminates light details, without resizing the large structures. This is illustrated in figure 13.

4.3 Link between u-operations, t-operations and binary operations

If the structuring element B is binary (i.e. $B(x) = 0$ or 1), then the formulas (17), (18), (22) and (23) reduce to:

$$D_u(A,B)(y) = \sup_{x \in T_y(B) \cap d_A} A(x) + 1$$

Fig. 13. u-closing C_u (left) and u-opening O_u (right)

$$E_u(A,B)(y) = \inf_{x\in T_y(B)} A(x) - 1$$

$$C_u(A,B)(y) = \sup_{z\in T_y(-B)} \left(\inf_{x\in T_z(B)} A(x) \right)$$

$$O_u(A,B)(y) = \inf_{z\in T_y(-B)} \left(\sup_{x\in T_z(B)} A(x) \right).$$

If we compare these expressions with the corresponding definitions of the morphological t-operations (cfr. (13), (14), (15) and (16)), then we immediately obtain the following result.

Proposition 20 *Let A be a gray-scale object and let B be a binary structuring element, then it holds:*

$$D_u(A,B) = D_t(A,B) + 1 \qquad C_u(A,B) = C_t(A,B)$$
$$E_u(A,B) = E_t(A,B) - 1 \qquad O_u(A,B) = O_t(A,B).$$

If both A and B are binary objects, then a similar argumentation leads to a similar conclusion.

4.4 Properties

Most properties of the morphological u-operations can be derived from the properties of the binary morphological operations on the one hand, and from properties of umbras and top surfaces on the other hand. Therefore, we will first list some of the latter properties.

In general, a subset $G \subseteq \mathbb{R}^{n+1}$ is called an umbra if $(x,t) \in G$ implies that $(x,s) \in G$ for all $s \le t$. Note that the umbra of a function is indeed an umbra.

Proposition 21 *Let G be a subset of $\mathbb{R}^{n+1}$, then it holds:*
(i) $T[U[G]] = G$ *and* $G \subseteq U[T[G]]$.
(ii) If G is an umbra, then $G = U[T[G]]$.

The foregoing proposition expresses that the top surface operation will always undo the umbra operation. In order for the reverse to hold however, a supplementary condition is needed.

Proposition 22 *Let G_1 and G_2 be umbras, then $D_u(G_1, G_2)$, $E_u(G_1, G_2)$, $C_u(G_1, G_2)$ and $O_u(G_1, G_2)$ are umbras.*

Proposition 23 *Let A and B be gray-scale objects, then it holds:*

$$\begin{array}{ll} U[D_u(A,B)] = D(U[A],U[B]) & U[C_u(A,B)] = C(U[A],U[B]) \\ U[E_u(A,B)] = E(U[A],U[B]) & U[O_u(A,B)] = O(U[A],U[B]). \end{array}$$

where D and E are respectively the binary dilation and erosion.

The following proposition concerns monotonicity properties of the top surface and umbra operations. Both are increasing operations.

Proposition 24
(i) Let A_1 and A_2 be two gray-scale objects, then it holds that $A_1 \subseteq A_2 \Leftrightarrow U[A_1] \subseteq U[A_2]$.
(ii) Let G_1 and G_2 be two subsets of $\mathbb{R}^{n+1}$, then it holds that $G_1 \subseteq G_2 \Rightarrow T[G_1] \subseteq T[G_2]$. If G_1 and G_2 are umbras, then we have that $G_1 \subseteq G_2 \Leftrightarrow T[G_1] \subseteq T[G_2]$

Next, we investigate the interaction between the umbra operation on the one hand, and the union and intersection on the other hand.

Proposition 25 *Let $(A_i)_{i\in I}$ be an arbitrary family of gray-scale objects, then it holds:*

$$U[\bigcup_{i\in I} A_i] \supseteq \bigcup_{i\in I} U[A_i]$$
$$U[\bigcap_{i\in I} A_i] = \bigcap_{i\in I} U[A_i].$$

If $(A_i)_{i=1}^k$ is a finite family of gray-scale objects, then it holds:

$$U[\bigcup_{i=1}^{k} A_i] = \bigcup_{i=1}^{k} U[A_i].$$

Finally, we give expressions for the umbra of a reflected gray-scale object and the top surface of a reflected subset of $\mathbb{R}^{n+1}$.

Proposition 26
(i) Let A be a gray-scale object, then it holds that $U[-A] = -U[A]$.
(ii) Let G be a subset of $\mathbb{R}^{n+1}$, then it holds that $T[-G] = -T[G]$.

Using the above propositions, one can verify that all the properties that hold for the binary morphological operations (cfr. section 2.3) also hold for the morphological u-operations, except for proposition 5 (some special cases regarding interaction with intersection). The only difference in the formulation of the properties is that both arguments of a morphological u-operation are now gray-scale objects instead of binary objects.

Just as for the t-operations, some additional remarks are necessary (some remarks made in section 3.4 will not be repeated here):

- Regarding the duality property (cfr. proposition 1), we recall that – in this framework – the complement $co\,A$ of a $\mathbb{R}^n$-$\mathbb{R}$ function A is defined by $co\,A(x) = -A(x), \forall x \in d_A$.
- Regarding the extensivity of the dilation and the anti-extensivity of the erosion (cfr. proposition 9(i)), the condition $\mathbf{0} \in B$ has to be replaced by $\mathbf{0} \in d_B$. The same remark holds for the inclusion properties (cfr. propositions 12 and 13).
- The commutativity of the u-dilation (cfr. proposition 14) makes sense again, since both arguments of the u-dilation are gray-scale objects. This was not the case for the t-dilation.
- Regarding the local knowledge property (cfr. proposition 17), we have to take the intersection with $E(Z, d_B)$ instead of with $E(Z, B)$.
- Regarding the adjunction property (cfr. proposition 18), we now have to work with the class of all $\mathbb{R}^n - \mathbb{R}$ mappings, denoted by $Func(\mathbb{R}^n, \mathbb{R})$. Note that we cannot restrict ourselves to the class $Func(\mathbb{R}^n, [0, 1])$, since u-dilation and u-erosion are not internal on this class.

4.5 Application: edge detection

Let A be a gray-scale image and let B be the 3×3 gray-scale structuring element given by (19). From the properties of the u-dilation and the u-erosion it then follows that $D_u(A, B) - E_u(A, B)$ will serve as an edge-image of the image A. This is illustrated in figure 14 (note that $D_u(A, B) - E_u(A, B)$ had to be rescaled to the interval [0,1]).

Compared to the result obtained for the t-operations (using a binary instead of a gray-scale structuring element), we notice that the "hard" edges are still detected very well (e.g. the person in the foreground), but that some "soft" edges are not detected any longer (e.g. the buildings in the background). Depending on the application, this feature can either be good (if we are not interested in soft edges) or bad (if soft edges have to be detected as well).

Fig. 14. Original image (left) and corresponding edge-image (right)

5 Fuzzy mathematical morphology: the general framework

5.1 Introduction

Fuzzy mathematical morphology is an alternative extension of binary morphology to gray-scale morphology, using concepts from fuzzy set theory. Note that the adjective *fuzzy* refers to the methods used to develop this alternative extension, and not to the representation of gray-scale objects as fuzzy sets. Indeed, the values of a fuzzy set should be interpreted as degrees of membership, and not as pixel values.

Both from a practical and theoretical point of view, fuzzy mathematical morphology can be of great interest.

- First, if we model gray-scale images as $\mathbb{R}^n$-$[0,1]$ functions it is preferable that the transformed images also are $\mathbb{R}^n$-$[0,1]$ functions (indeed, the unit interval $[0,1]$ represents the set of available pixel values). However, in section 4 it was pointed out that the morphological u-operations don't necessarily transform $\mathbb{R}^n$-$[0,1]$ functions into new $\mathbb{R}^n$-$[0,1]$ functions. Since a simple rescaling of the pixel values isn't always a good solution (some of the theoretical derived properties will be violated in practice), another approach towards gray-scale morphology is needed. Now, since $\mathbb{R}^n$-$[0,1]$ functions can be identified with fuzzy sets, one could try to develop a new type of mathematical morphology by using notions and concepts from fuzzy set theory. The wide variety of available tools is bound to open a whole new world of possibilities.
- Secondly, since binary morphology is based on crisp set theory, it would be interesting – from a pure theoretical point of view – to fuzzify this theory using the concept of fuzzy sets. Already a lot of mathematical branches and concepts have successfully gone through such a fuzzification process,

which gave rise to several interesting theories and applications (e.g. fuzzy algebraic structures, fuzzy relations, fuzzy topology, fuzzy geometry and fuzzy statistics).

In this section we will discuss a general framework for fuzzy mathematical morphology, which was first constructed by De Baets in [11]. In the following sections we will review the work of several other researchers that have contributed to the development of fuzzy morphology, and show how all these approaches can be treated as a special case of the general approach. We will also illustrate how classical gray-scale morphology can be embedded in fuzzy mathematical morphology.

5.2 Fuzzy logical operators

From the definitions of dilation and erosion it is clear that intersection and inclusion play a major role. The idea of De Baets was to fuzzify the underlying logical operations, i.e. the Boolean conjunction and the Boolean implication, to obtain a successful fuzzification. In the following, we introduce the notions of negator, conjunctor and implicator on the unit interval.

Definition 9 *A unary operator $\mathcal{N}$ on [0,1] is a negator if it is a decreasing mapping that coincides with the Boolean negation on $\{0,1\}$, i.e. $\mathcal{N}(0) = 1$ and $\mathcal{N}(1) = 0$.*

A negator $\mathcal{N}$ is called involutive if $(\forall x \in [0,1])(\mathcal{N}(\mathcal{N}(x)) = x)$. Note that an involutive negator always is strictly decreasing and continuous.

The standard negator N_s, defined by $N_s(x) = 1 - x$ for all $x \in [0,1]$, is an involutive negator.

Definition 10 *A binary operator $\mathcal{C}$ on [0,1] is a conjunctor if it is an increasing mapping (i.e. a mapping with increasing partial mappings) that coincides with the Boolean conjunction on $\{0,1\}^2$, i.e. $\mathcal{C}(0,0) = \mathcal{C}(0,1) = \mathcal{C}(1,0) = 0$ and $\mathcal{C}(1,1) = 1$.*

A conjunctor $\mathcal{C}$ is a semi-norm if it also satisfies $(\forall x \in [0,1])(\mathcal{C}(1,x) = \mathcal{C}(x,1) = x)$.

$\mathcal{C}$ is a t-norm if it is a commutative and associative semi-norm.

The minimum M, the algebraic product P and the Łukasiewicz t-norm W (also called bounded sum) are very popular t-norms. They are given by $M(x,y) = \min(x,y)$, $P(x,y) = x \cdot y$ and $W(x,y) = \max(0, x + y - 1)$, respectively.

Definition 11 *A binary operator $\mathcal{I}$ on [0,1] is an implicator on [0,1] if it is a hybrid monotonous mapping (i.e. with decreasing first and increasing second partial mappings) that coincides with the Boolean implication on $\{0,1\}^2$, i.e.*

$\mathcal{I}(0,0) = \mathcal{I}(0,1) = \mathcal{I}(1,1) = 1$ *and* $\mathcal{I}(1,0) = 0$. *Every implicator* $\mathcal{I}$ *induces a negator* $\mathcal{N}_\mathcal{I}$ *defined by* $\mathcal{N}_\mathcal{I}(x) = \mathcal{I}(x,0), \forall x \in [0,1]$.

An implicator $\mathcal{I}$ *is a border implicator on [0,1] if it satisfies* $(\forall x \in [0,1])$ $(\mathcal{I}(1,x) = x)$.

A model implicator $\mathcal{I}$ *on [0,1] is a border implicator that is contrapositive w.r.t. its induced negator, i.e.* $(\forall (x,y) \in [0,1]^2)(\mathcal{I}(x,y) = \mathcal{I}(\mathcal{N}_\mathcal{I}(y), \mathcal{N}_\mathcal{I}(x)))$, *and that fulfills the exchange principle, i.e.* $(\forall (x,y,z) \in [0,1]^3)(\mathcal{I}(x, \mathcal{I}(y,z)) = \mathcal{I}(y, \mathcal{I}(x,z)))$.

The Łukasiewicz implicator I_L, the Kleene-Dienes implicator I_{KD} and the Reichenbach implicator I_R are among the most popular model implicators. They are respectively given by $I_L(x,y) = \min(1, 1-x+y)$, $I_{KD}(x,y) = \max(1-x, y)$ and $I_R(x,y) = 1 - x + x \cdot y$.

Given a conjunctor one can construct an implicator from it, and vice versa. Indeed, let $\mathcal{N}$, $\mathcal{C}$ and $\mathcal{I}$ be respectively a negator, conjunctor and implicator on [0,1]. Then the operators $\mathcal{C}_{\mathcal{I},\mathcal{N}}$ and $\mathcal{I}_{\mathcal{C},\mathcal{N}}$ defined by:

$$\mathcal{C}_{\mathcal{I},\mathcal{N}}(x,y) = \mathcal{N}(\mathcal{I}(x, \mathcal{N}(y))), \tag{24}$$

$$\mathcal{I}_{\mathcal{C},\mathcal{N}}(x,y) = \mathcal{N}(\mathcal{C}(x, \mathcal{N}(y))), \tag{25}$$

are a conjunctor and an implicator on [0,1], respectively. For example, it holds that $\mathcal{I}_{M,N_s} = I_{KD}$, $\mathcal{I}_{P,N_s} = I_R$ and $\mathcal{I}_{W,N_s} = I_L$.

Finally, given a t-norm $\mathcal{C}$, the residual implicator $\mathcal{I}_\mathcal{C}$ is defined as:

$$\mathcal{I}_\mathcal{C}(x,y) = \sup\{z | z \in [0,1] \text{ and } \mathcal{C}(x,z) \le y\}, \quad \forall (x,y) \in [0,1]^2. \tag{26}$$

A straightforward verification shows that $\mathcal{I}_\mathcal{C}$ is a border implicator.

5.3 Definitions

Using the extended logical operators, the definitions (1) and (2) of respectively binary dilation and binary erosion can be fuzzified as follows. We will adopt the convention that $A(x) = 0$ for $x \notin d_A$, with d_A the set of points where A was originally defined.

Definition 12 *Let* $\mathcal{C}$ *be a conjunctor on [0,1], let* $\mathcal{I}$ *be an implicator on [0,1], let* A *be a gray-scale image and let* B *be a gray-scale structuring element. The fuzzy dilation* $D_\mathcal{C}(A,B)$ *and the fuzzy erosion* $E_\mathcal{I}(A,B)$ *are the gray-scale images defined by:*

$$D_\mathcal{C}(A,B)(y) = \sup_{x \in T_y(d_B)} \mathcal{C}(B(x-y), A(x)) \tag{27}$$

$$E_\mathcal{I}(A,B)(y) = \inf_{x \in T_y(d_B)} \mathcal{I}(B(x-y), A(x)). \tag{28}$$

Fuzzy closing and fuzzy opening are defined as in the binary case. Note that the reflection $-B$ of a n-dimensional fuzzy set B is defined by $-B(x) = B(-x)$, $\forall x \in \mathbb{R}^n$.

Definition 13 *Let $\mathcal{C}$ be a conjunctor on [0,1], let $\mathcal{I}$ be an implicator on [0,1], let A be a gray-scale image and let B be a gray-scale structuring element. The fuzzy closing $C_{\mathcal{C},\mathcal{I}}(A,B)$ and the fuzzy opening $O_{\mathcal{C},\mathcal{I}}(A,B)$ are the gray-scale images defined by:*

$$C_{\mathcal{C},\mathcal{I}}(A,B)(y) = E_{\mathcal{I}}(D_{\mathcal{C}}(A,B),-B)(y) \tag{29}$$
$$O_{\mathcal{C},\mathcal{I}}(A,B)(y) = D_{\mathcal{C}}(E_{\mathcal{I}}(A,B),-B)(y). \tag{30}$$

Explicit expressions are given by:

$$C_{\mathcal{C},\mathcal{I}}(A,B)(y) = \inf_{z \in T_y(-d_B)} \mathcal{I}\left(B(y-z), \sup_{x \in T_z(d_B)} \mathcal{C}(B(x-z),A(x))\right) \tag{31}$$
$$O_{\mathcal{C},\mathcal{I}}(A,B)(y) = \sup_{z \in T_y(-d_B)} \mathcal{C}\left(B(y-z), \inf_{x \in T_z(d_B)} \mathcal{I}(B(x-z),A(x))\right) \tag{32}$$

We have illustrated several fuzzy dilations, erosions, closings and openings in figures 15, 16 and 17, with respectively $(\mathcal{C},\mathcal{I}) = (M, I_{KD})$, $(\mathcal{C},\mathcal{I}) = (P, I_R)$ and $(\mathcal{C},\mathcal{I}) = (W, I_L)$. The structuring element is the same as in section 4, i.e.:

$$B = \begin{pmatrix} 0.86 & 0.86 & 0.86 \\ 0.86 & \underline{1.00} & 0.86 \\ 0.86 & 0.86 & 0.86 \end{pmatrix}$$

The overall characteristics of the fuzzy morphological operations are the same as in the gray-scale case, i.e. the fuzzy dilations eliminate dark details, enhance light details, reduce dark objects and enlargen light objects; the fuzzy erosions eliminate light details, enhance dark details, reduce light objects and enlargen dark objects; the fuzzy closings typically eliminate dark details, and the fuzzy openings eliminate light details.

One can derive some interesting additional properties concerning the fuzzy dilations and erosions. Indeed, the applied conjunctors satisfy the relationship $M \geq P \geq W$, while the implicators satisfy $I_{KD} \leq I_R \leq I_L$. This implies that $D_M \geq D_P \geq D_W$ and $E_{I_{KD}} \leq E_{I_R} \leq E_{I_L}$, or equivalently:

$$D_M(A,B) \supseteq D_P(A,B) \supseteq D_W(A,B) \tag{33}$$
$$E_{I_{KD}}(A,B) \subseteq E_{I_R}(A,B) \subseteq E_{I_L}(A,B). \tag{34}$$

The figures confirm these results. For example, the dilation $D_M(A,B)$ is not only lighter in general, the light details are also much more enhanced, while the dark details are much more suppressed in comparison with the other dilations. Consequently, the dilation $D_M(A,B)$ will also be less sharp (i.e. less detailed) than the dilations $D_P(A,B)$ and $D_W(A,B)$. Analogous observations hold for the fuzzy erosions.

Fig. 15. The fuzzy operations D_M (upper left), $E_{I_{KD}}$ (upper right), $C_{M,I_{KD}}$ (lower left) and $O_{M,I_{KD}}$ (lower right)

5.4 Links between classical morphology and fuzzy morphology

Links with binary morphology.

From the construction of the fuzzy dilation, erosion, closing and opening, it follows that these operations are extensions of their binary counterparts.

One can also establish other links between fuzzy morphology and binary morphology. We only mention the following decomposition properties.

Proposition 27 *Let A be a gray-scale image and let B be a gray-scale structuring element, then it holds:*

$$(\forall \alpha \in [0,1[)(D_{\min}(A,B)_{\overline{\alpha}} = D(A_{\overline{\alpha}}, B_{\overline{\alpha}})),$$

and

$$(\forall \alpha \in]0,1])(E_{I_{KD}}(A,B)_{\alpha} = E(A_{\alpha}, B_{\overline{1-\alpha}})).$$

Fig. 16. The fuzzy operations D_P (upper left), E_{I_R} (upper right), C_{P,I_R} (lower left) and O_{P,I_R} (lower right)

Proposition 28 *Let A be a gray-scale image and let B be a gray-scale structuring element, then it holds:*

$$D_{\min}(A,B) = \bigcup_{\alpha\in]0,1]} \alpha D(A_\alpha, B_\alpha),$$

and

$$D_P(A,B) = \bigcup_{\alpha\in]0,1]} \left(\alpha \cdot \bigcup_{\beta\in]0,1]} (\beta D(A_\beta, B_\alpha))\right).$$

Recall that $A_\alpha = \{x|x \in \mathbb{R}^n \text{ and } A(x) \geq \alpha\}$ (for $\alpha \in]0,1]$) and $A_{\overline{\alpha}} = \{x|x \in \mathbb{R}^n \text{ and } A(x) > \alpha\}$ (for $\alpha \in [0,1[$). Also recall that, for $\alpha \in]0,1]$:

$$\alpha A_\alpha(x) = \begin{cases} \alpha \text{ if } A(x) \geq \alpha \\ 0 \text{ if } A(x) < \alpha \end{cases}$$

Fig. 17. The fuzzy operations D_W (upper left), E_{I_L} (upper right), C_{W,I_L} (lower left) and O_{W,I_L} (lower right)

Links with gray-scale morphology based on the threshold approach.

It turns out that the t-dilation, t-erosion, t-closing and t-opening are special instances of fuzzy dilations, erosions, closings and openings.

Proposition 29 *Let A be a gray-scale image and let B be a binary structuring element. It holds that:*

$$\begin{array}{ll} D_t(A,B) = D_{\mathcal{C}}(A,B) & C_t(A,B) = C_{\mathcal{C},\mathcal{I}}(A,B) \\ E_t(A,B) = E_{\mathcal{I}}(A,B) & O_t(A,B) = O_{\mathcal{C},\mathcal{I}}(A,B). \end{array}$$

if and only if $\mathcal{C}$ satisfies $(\forall a \in [0,1])(\mathcal{C}(1,a) = a)$ and $\mathcal{I}$ is a border implicator.

Links with gray-scale morphology based on the umbra approach.

Let A be a gray-scale image and let B be a gray-scale structuring element, both represented as $\mathbb{R}^n$-$[0,1]$ functions. In general, the u-dilation $D_u(A,B)$ is a $\mathbb{R}^n$-$[0,2]$ function, and the u-erosion $E_u(A,B)$ a $\mathbb{R}^n$-$[-1,1]$ function. However, there are several ways to transform $D_u(A,B)$ and $E_u(A,B)$ into $\mathbb{R}^n$-$[0,1]$ functions. For example, we could substract $D_u(A,B)(y)$ by 1 (obtaining a value in [-1,1]), and then take the maximum of this new value and zero (obtaining a value in [0,1]). In an analogous way, we could increase $E_u(A,B)(y)$ by 1 (obtaining a value in [0,2]), and then take the minimum of this value and one (obtaining a value in [0,1]). If we denote these modified u-operations as D_u^* and E_u^*, respectively, then we have:

$$\begin{aligned} D_u^*(A,B)(y) &= \sup_{x \in T_y(d_B)} \max(0, A(x) + B(x-y) - 1) \\ E_u^*(A,B)(y) &= \inf_{x \in T_y(d_B)} \min(1, A(x) - B(x-y) + 1). \end{aligned}$$

It immediately follows that the modified u-dilation D_u^* coincides with the fuzzy dilation D_W, and that the modified u-erosion E_u^* coincides with the fuzzy erosion E_{I_L}. If, in addition, we define the modified u-closing C_u^* and the modified u-opening O_u^* as the usual combinations of the modified u-dilation and the modified u-erosion, then we have the following result.

Proposition 30 *Let A be a gray-scale image and let B be a gray-scale structuring element, then it holds:*

$$\begin{aligned} D_u^*(A,B) &= D_W(A,B) \qquad & C_u^*(A,B) &= C_{W,I_L}(A,B) \\ E_u^*(A,B) &= E_{I_L}(A,B) \qquad & O_u^*(A,B) &= O_{W,I_L}(A,B). \end{aligned}$$

Note that the modified u-operations can show a significant loss of information w.r.t. the original u-operations. For example, after the values of D_u are substracted by 1, all remaining values in $[-1,0]$ are reduced to 0. This means that *on average* 50% of the information contained in D_u is lost in the modification process. Of course, the *exact* amount of information that is lost depends upon the specific image and upon the specific structuring element employed. The following proposition gives a sufficient condition on the structuring element in order to guarantee that no information is lost during the modification process.

Proposition 31 *Let A be a gray-scale image and let B be a gray-scale structuring element. If B is normalized, i.e. if $(\exists z \in \mathbb{R}^n)(B(z) = 1)$, then it holds:*

$$\begin{aligned} D_u^*(A,B) &= D_u(A,B) - 1 = D_W(A,B) \\ E_u^*(A,B) &= E_u(A,B) + 1 = E_{I_L}(A,B) \\ C_u^*(A,B) &= C_u(A,B) = C_{W,I_L}(A,B) \\ O_u^*(A,B) &= O_u(A,B) = O_{W,I_L}(A,B). \end{aligned}$$

Under the condition of proposition 31, the fuzzy operations D_W, E_{I_L}, C_{W,I_L} and O_{W,I_L} are equivalent to the corresponding u-operations. Proposition 31 also explains why there is no difference between the pictures in figure 17 (fuzzy operations with $(\mathcal{C},\mathcal{I}) = (W, I_L)$) and those in figures 12 and 13 (u-operations). Indeed, this is completely due to the fact that we used a normalized structuring element.

5.5 Properties

In this section we will give sufficient and/or necessary conditions on the conjunctor $\mathcal{C}$ and implicator $\mathcal{I}$ in order to guarantee similar properties as in the binary and gray-scale case. The practical interpretation remains the same.

Duality.

Given an involutive negator $\mathcal{N}$, the $\mathcal{N}$-complement $co_{\mathcal{N}}\, A$ of a fuzzy set A is defined by $(co_{\mathcal{N}}\, A)(x) = \mathcal{N}(A(x))$. Two fuzzy morphological operations P and Q are called $\mathcal{N}$-dual if for any two gray-scale objects A and B it holds that $P(A,B) = co_{\mathcal{N}}\, Q(co_{\mathcal{N}}\, A, B)$.

Proposition 32 *Let $\mathcal{N}$ be an involutive negator, $\mathcal{C}$ a conjunctor and $\mathcal{I}$ an implicator on [0,1]. Then it holds:*
(i) the fuzzy dilation $D_{\mathcal{C}}$ and the fuzzy erosion $E_{\mathcal{I}}$ are $\mathcal{N}$-dual if and only if $\mathcal{I} = \mathcal{I}_{\mathcal{C},\mathcal{N}}$, or equivalently $\mathcal{C} = \mathcal{C}_{\mathcal{I},\mathcal{N}}$;
(ii) if the fuzzy dilation and erosion are $\mathcal{N}$-dual, then the fuzzy closing and fuzzy opening are also $\mathcal{N}$-dual;
(iii) if the fuzzy closing $C_{\mathcal{C},\mathcal{I}}$ and the fuzzy opening $O_{\mathcal{C},\mathcal{I}}$ are $\mathcal{N}$-dual, $\mathcal{C}$ is a semi-norm and $\mathcal{I}$ is a border implicator, then $\mathcal{I} = \mathcal{I}_{\mathcal{C},\mathcal{N}}$.

Note that the fuzzy dilations and erosions, as well as the fuzzy closings and openings depicted in figures 15, 16 and 17 are all N_s-dual.

Monotonicity.

Proposition 33 *Let $\mathcal{C}$ be a conjunctor and $\mathcal{I}$ an implicator on [0,1], then it holds:*
(i) the fuzzy dilation $D_{\mathcal{C}}$ is increasing in both arguments,
(ii) the fuzzy erosion $E_{\mathcal{I}}$ is increasing in the first, and decreasing in the second argument,
(iii) the fuzzy closing $C_{\mathcal{C},\mathcal{I}}$ is increasing in the first argument,
(iv) the fuzzy opening $O_{\mathcal{C},\mathcal{I}}$ is increasing in the first argument.

Interaction with union and intersection.

The following propositions concern interaction properties with Zadeh's union and intersection. For an arbitrary family $(A_i)_{i\in I}$ of fuzzy sets the Zadeh union and the Zadeh intersection are defined by:

$$\bigcup_{i\in I} A_i(x) = \sup_{i\in I} A_i(x)$$
$$\bigcap_{i\in I} A_i(x) = \inf_{i\in I} A_i(x).$$

Proposition 34 *Let $\mathcal{C}$ be a conjunctor on [0,1], let $\mathcal{I}$ be an implicator on [0,1], let A be a gray-scale image and let B be a gray-scale structuring element. Further, let $(A_i)_{i\in I}$ be an arbitrary family of gray-scale images and let $(B_i)_{i\in I}$ be an arbitrary family of gray-scale structuring elements, then it holds:*

$$\begin{array}{ll} D_{\mathcal{C}}(\bigcup_{i\in I} A_i, B) \supseteq \bigcup_{i\in I} D_{\mathcal{C}}(A_i, B) & D_{\mathcal{C}}(A, \bigcup_{i\in I} B_i) \supseteq \bigcup_{i\in I} D_{\mathcal{C}}(A, B_i) \\ E_{\mathcal{I}}(\bigcup_{i\in I} A_i, B) \supseteq \bigcup_{i\in I} E_{\mathcal{I}}(A_i, B) & E_{\mathcal{I}}(A, \bigcup_{i\in I} B_i) \subseteq \bigcap_{i\in I} E_{\mathcal{I}}(A, B_i) \\ C_{\mathcal{C},\mathcal{I}}(\bigcup_{i=1}^{k} A_i, B) \supseteq \bigcup_{i=1}^{k} C_{\mathcal{C},\mathcal{I}}(A_i, B) & O_{\mathcal{C},\mathcal{I}}(\bigcup_{i=1}^{k} A_i, B) \supseteq \bigcup_{i=1}^{k} O_{\mathcal{C},\mathcal{I}}(A_i, B) \end{array}$$

Proposition 35 *Let $\mathcal{C}$ be a conjunctor on [0,1], let $\mathcal{I}$ be an implicator on [0,1], let A be a gray-scale image and let B be a gray-scale structuring element. Further, let $(A_i)_{i\in I}$ be an arbitrary family of gray-scale images and let $(B_i)_{i\in I}$ be an arbitrary family of gray-scale structuring elements, then it holds:*

$$\begin{array}{ll} D_{\mathcal{C}}(\bigcap_{i\in I} A_i, B) \subseteq \bigcap_{i\in I} D_{\mathcal{C}}(A_i, B) & D_{\mathcal{C}}(A, \bigcap_{i\in I} B_i) \subseteq \bigcap_{i\in I} D_{\mathcal{C}}(A, B_i) \\ E_{\mathcal{I}}(\bigcap_{i\in I} A_i, B) \subseteq \bigcap_{i\in I} E_{\mathcal{I}}(A_i, B) & E_{\mathcal{I}}(A, \bigcap_{i\in I} B_i) \supseteq \bigcup_{i\in I} E_{\mathcal{I}}(A, B_i) \\ C_{\mathcal{C},\mathcal{I}}(\bigcap_{i=1}^{k} A_i, B) \subseteq \bigcap_{i=1}^{k} C_{\mathcal{C},\mathcal{I}}(A_i, B) & O_{\mathcal{C},\mathcal{I}}(\bigcap_{i=1}^{k} A_i, B) \subseteq \bigcap_{i=1}^{k} O_{\mathcal{C},\mathcal{I}}(A_i, B) \end{array}$$

Under supplementary conditions, some of the above inclusions also become equalities. Note that it concerns those equalities which are always valid in the binary case and the classical gray-scale cases.

Proposition 36 *Let $\mathcal{C}$ be a conjunctor on [0,1], let $\mathcal{I}$ be an implicator on [0,1], let A be a gray-scale image and let B be a gray-scale structuring element. Further, let $(A_i)_{i\in I}$ be an arbitrary family of gray-scale images and let $(B_i)_{i\in I}$ be an arbitrary family of gray-scale structuring elements. Then it holds:*
(i) if the second partial mappings of $\mathcal{C}$ are left-continuous, then it holds:

$$D_{\mathcal{C}}(\bigcup_{i\in I} A_i, B) = \bigcup_{i\in I} D_{\mathcal{C}}(A_i, B)$$

(ii) if the first partial mappings of $\mathcal{C}$ are left-continuous, then it holds:

$$D_{\mathcal{C}}(A, \bigcup_{i\in I} B_i) = \bigcup_{i\in I} D_{\mathcal{C}}(A, B_i)$$

(iii)if the first partial mappings of $\mathcal{I}$ are left-continuous, then it holds:

$$E_{\mathcal{I}}(A, \bigcup_{i\in I} B_i) = \bigcap_{i\in I} E_{\mathcal{I}}(A, B_i)$$

(iv) if the second partial mappings of $\mathcal{I}$ are right-continuous, then it holds:

$$E_{\mathcal{I}}(\bigcap_{i\in I} A_i, B) = \bigcap_{i\in I} E_{\mathcal{I}}(A_i, B).$$

If we consider *finite* families of gray-scale objects, then the four mentioned equalities are also valid.

Proposition 37 *Let $\mathcal{C}$ be a conjunctor on [0,1], let $\mathcal{I}$ be an implicator on [0,1], let A be a gray-scale image and let B be a gray-scale structuring element. Further, let $(A_i)_{i=1}^k$ be a finite family of gray-scale images and let $(B_i)_{i=1}^k$ be a finite family of gray-scale structuring elements, then it holds:*

$$D_\mathcal{C}(\bigcup_{i=1}^k A_i, B) = \bigcup_{i=1}^k D_\mathcal{C}(A_i, B) \quad E_\mathcal{I}(A, \bigcup_{i=1}^k B_i) = \bigcap_{i=1}^k E_\mathcal{I}(A, B_i)$$
$$D_\mathcal{C}(A, \bigcup_{i=1}^k B_i) = \bigcup_{i=1}^k D_\mathcal{C}(A, B_i) \quad E_\mathcal{I}(\bigcap_{i=1}^k A_i, B) = \bigcap_{i=1}^k E_\mathcal{I}(A_i, B)$$

<u>Invariance under translating and scaling.</u>

The translation $T_v(A)$ of a fuzzy set A by $v \in \mathbb{R}^n$ is defined by $T_v(A)(x) = A(x-v)$, the scaling $H_\lambda(A)$ of a fuzzy set A by $\lambda > 0$ is defined by $H_\lambda(A)(x) = A(\frac{1}{\lambda}x)$. It follows that all four basic fuzzy morphological operators are invariant under translation and scaling.

Proposition 38 *Let $\mathcal{C}$ be a conjunctor on [0,1], let $\mathcal{I}$ be an implicator on [0,1], let A be a gray-scale image, let B be a gray-scale structuring element and let $v \in \mathbb{R}^n$. Then it holds:*

$$\begin{aligned} D_\mathcal{C}(T_v(A), B) &= T_v(D_\mathcal{C}(A, B)) & E_\mathcal{I}(T_v(A), B) &= T_v(E_\mathcal{I}(A, B)) \\ D_\mathcal{C}(A, T_v(B)) &= T_{-v}(D_\mathcal{C}(A, B)) & E_\mathcal{I}(A, T_v(B)) &= T_{-v}(E_\mathcal{I}(A, B)) \\ D_\mathcal{C}(T_v(A), T_v(B)) &= D_\mathcal{C}(A, B) & E_\mathcal{I}(T_v(A), T_v(B)) &= E_\mathcal{I}(A, B) \end{aligned}$$

$$\begin{aligned} C_{\mathcal{C},\mathcal{I}}(T_v(A), B) &= T_v(C_{\mathcal{C},\mathcal{I}}(A, B)) & O_{\mathcal{C},\mathcal{I}}(T_v(A), B) &= T_v(O_{\mathcal{C},\mathcal{I}}(A, B)) \\ C_{\mathcal{C},\mathcal{I}}(A, T_v(B)) &= C_{\mathcal{C},\mathcal{I}}(A, B) & O_{\mathcal{C},\mathcal{I}}(A, T_v(B)) &= O_{\mathcal{C},\mathcal{I}}(A, B) \\ C_{\mathcal{C},\mathcal{I}}(T_v(A), T_v(B)) &= T_v(C_{\mathcal{C},\mathcal{I}}(A, B)) & O_{\mathcal{C},\mathcal{I}}(T_v(A), T_v(B)) &= T_v(O_{\mathcal{C},\mathcal{I}}(A, B)). \end{aligned}$$

Proposition 39 *Let $\mathcal{C}$ be a conjunctor on [0,1], let $\mathcal{I}$ be an implicator on [0,1], let A be a gray-scale image, let B be a gray-scale structuring element and let $\lambda > 0$. Then it holds:*

$$\begin{aligned} D_\mathcal{C}(H_\lambda(A), H_\lambda(B)) &= H_\lambda(D_\mathcal{C}(A, B)) \\ C_{\mathcal{C},\mathcal{I}}(H_\lambda(A), H_\lambda(B)) &= H_\lambda(C_{\mathcal{C},\mathcal{I}}(A, B)) \\ E_\mathcal{I}(H_\lambda(A), H_\lambda(B)) &= H_\lambda(E_\mathcal{I}(A, B)) \\ O_{\mathcal{C},\mathcal{I}}(H_\lambda(A), H_\lambda(B)) &= H_\lambda(O_{\mathcal{C},\mathcal{I}}(A, B)). \end{aligned}$$

Just as in the binary case and the classical gray-scale cases, this property also holds for $\lambda < 0$. For $\lambda = -1$, we obtain the following special case.

Proposition 40 *Let $\mathcal{C}$ be a conjunctor on [0,1], let $\mathcal{I}$ be an implicator on [0,1], let A be a gray-scale image and let B be a gray-scale structuring element. Then it holds:*

$$-D_{\mathcal{C}}(A,B) = D_{\mathcal{C}}(-A,-B) \quad -C_{\mathcal{C},\mathcal{I}}(A,B) = C_{\mathcal{C},\mathcal{I}}(-A,-B)$$
$$-E_{\mathcal{I}}(A,B) = E_{\mathcal{I}}(-A,-B) \quad -O_{\mathcal{C},\mathcal{I}}(A,B) = O_{\mathcal{C},\mathcal{I}}(-A,-B)$$

Extensivity and idempotence.

To guarantee the extensivity of the fuzzy dilation and the anti-extensivity of the fuzzy erosion we have to restrict ourselves to semi-norms and border implicators. Furthermore, just as in the classical cases, the structuring element must contain the origin.

Proposition 41 *Let $\mathcal{C}$ be a semi-norm on [0,1], let $\mathcal{I}$ be a border implicator on [0,1], let A be a gray-scale image and let B be a gray-scale structuring element. Then it holds:*

(i) if B contains the origin (i.e. $B(\mathbf{0}) = 1$), then the fuzzy dilation $D_{\mathcal{C}}$ is extensive and the fuzzy erosion $E_{\mathcal{I}}$ is anti-extensive: $B(\mathbf{0}) = 1 \Rightarrow E_{\mathcal{I}}(A,B) \subseteq A \subseteq D_{\mathcal{C}}(A,B)$;
(ii) if the following property holds:

$$(\forall(x,y) \in [0,1]^2)(y \leq \mathcal{I}(x, \mathcal{C}(x,y))),$$

then the fuzzy closing $C_{\mathcal{C},\mathcal{I}}$ is extensive: $A \subseteq C_{\mathcal{C},\mathcal{I}}(A,B)$;
(iii) if the following property holds:

$$(\forall(x,y) \in [0,1]^2)(\mathcal{C}(x, \mathcal{I}(x,y))) \leq y),$$

then the fuzzy opening $O_{\mathcal{C},\mathcal{I}}$ is anti-extensive: $O_{\mathcal{C},\mathcal{I}}(A,B) \subseteq A$.

The condition in (ii) is fulfilled for *any* t-norm $\mathcal{C}$ and its residual implicator $\mathcal{I}_{\mathcal{C}}$, while the condition in (iii) is fulfilled for any *left-continuous* t-norm $\mathcal{C}$ and its residual implicator $\mathcal{I}_{\mathcal{C}}$.

Proposition 42 *If the following property holds:*

$$(\forall(x,y) \in [0,1]^2)(\mathcal{C}(x, \mathcal{I}(x,y))) \leq y \leq \mathcal{I}(x, \mathcal{C}(x,y))),$$

then the fuzzy closing $C_{\mathcal{C},\mathcal{I}}$ and the fuzzy opening $O_{\mathcal{C},\mathcal{I}}$ are idempotent, i.e.:

$$C_{\mathcal{C},\mathcal{I}}(C_{\mathcal{C},\mathcal{I}}(A,B),B) = C_{\mathcal{C},\mathcal{I}}(A,B),$$
$$O_{\mathcal{C},\mathcal{I}}(O_{\mathcal{C},\mathcal{I}}(A,B),B) = O_{\mathcal{C},\mathcal{I}}(A,B).$$

Note that the condition in proposition 42 is a combination of the conditions (ii) and (iii) in proposition 41.

Inclusion properties.

From proposition 41 we easily derive that $E_{\mathcal{I}}(A,B) \subseteq D_{\mathcal{C}}(A,B)$ if $B(\mathbf{0}) = 1$, with $\mathcal{C}$ a semi-norm and $\mathcal{I}$ a border implicator. However, the condition $B(\mathbf{0}) = 1$ can be weakened.

Proposition 43 *Let C be a semi-norm on [0,1], let I be a border implicator on [0,1], let A be a gray-scale image and let B be a gray-scale structuring element. If B is normalized, i.e. if* $(\exists z \in \mathbb{R}^n)(B(z) = 1)$*, then it holds:*

$$E_{\mathcal{I}}(A,B) \subseteq D_{\mathcal{C}}(A,B).$$

Proposition 44 *Let C be a semi-norm on [0,1], let I be a border implicator on [0,1], let A be a gray-scale image and let B be a gray-scale structuring element. If B contains the origin, i.e.* $B(\mathbf{0}) = 1$*, then it holds:*

$$\begin{array}{ll} D_{\mathcal{C}}(A,B) \supseteq C_{\mathcal{C},\mathcal{I}}(A,B) & E_{\mathcal{I}}(A,B) \subseteq O_{\mathcal{C},\mathcal{I}}(A,B) \\ D_{\mathcal{C}}(A,B) \supseteq O_{\mathcal{C},\mathcal{I}}(A,B) & E_{\mathcal{I}}(A,B) \subseteq C_{\mathcal{C},\mathcal{I}}(A,B) \\ D_{\mathcal{C}}(A,B) \supseteq O_{\mathcal{C},\mathcal{I}}(A,-B) & E_{\mathcal{I}}(A,B) \subseteq C_{\mathcal{C},\mathcal{I}}(A,-B). \end{array}$$

Proposition 45 *Let C be a semi-norm on [0,1], let I be a border implicator on [0,1], let A be a gray-scale image and let B be a gray-scale structuring element. If* $B(\mathbf{0}) = 1$*, and if* $\mathcal{C}$ *and* $\mathcal{I}$ *satisfy:*

$$(\forall (x,y) \in [0,1]^2)(\mathcal{C}(x, \mathcal{I}(x,y))) \leq y \leq \mathcal{I}(x, \mathcal{C}(x,y))),$$

then it holds that:

$$E_{\mathcal{I}}(A,B) \subseteq O_{\mathcal{C},\mathcal{I}}(A,B) \subseteq A \subseteq C_{\mathcal{C},\mathcal{I}}(A,B) \subseteq D_{\mathcal{C}}(A,B).$$

Commutativity and associativity of the fuzzy dilation.

Proposition 46 *Let* $\mathcal{C}$ *be a conjunctor on [0,1], and let A, B and C be gray-scale objects.*

(i) if the partial mappings of $\mathcal{C}$ *are left-continuous and if* $\mathcal{C}$ *is associative, then it holds:*

$$D_{\mathcal{C}}(A, D_{\mathcal{C}}(B,C)) = D_{\mathcal{C}}(D_{\mathcal{C}}(A,B), -C).$$

(ii) if $\mathcal{C}$ *is commutative, then it holds:*

$$D_{\mathcal{C}}(A,B) = -D_{\mathcal{C}}(B,A).$$

Combinations of dilation and erosion.

Proposition 47 *Let* $\mathcal{C}$ *be a conjunctor on [0,1]. If the second partial mappings of* $\mathcal{C}$ *are left-continuous and if* $\mathcal{C}$ *is associative, then it holds:*

$$D_{\mathcal{C}}(D_{\mathcal{C}}(A,B),C) = D_{\mathcal{C}}(D_{\mathcal{C}}(A,C),B).$$

Proposition 48 *Let* $\mathcal{I}$ *be an implicator on [0,1]. If the second partial mappings of* $\mathcal{I}$ *are right-continuous and if* $\mathcal{I}$ *satisfies the exchange principle, then it holds:*

$$E_{\mathcal{I}}(E_{\mathcal{I}}(A,B),C) = E_{\mathcal{I}}(E_{\mathcal{I}}(A,C),B).$$

Note that the conditions formulated in proposition 48 are weaker than the ones postulated in [11].

Proposition 49 *Let $\mathcal{C}$ be a conjunctor and let $\mathcal{I}$ be an implicator on [0,1]. If the first partial mappings of $\mathcal{C}$ are left-continuous, the second partial mappings of $\mathcal{I}$ are right-continuous, and $\mathcal{C}$ and $\mathcal{I}$ are connected by the relationship*

$$(\forall(x,y,z) \in [0,1]^3)(\mathcal{I}(\mathcal{C}(x,y),z) = \mathcal{I}(x,\mathcal{I}(y,z))),$$

then it holds:

$$E_{\mathcal{I}}(A, D_{\mathcal{C}}(B,-C)) = E_{\mathcal{I}}(E_{\mathcal{I}}(A,B),C).$$

The conditions imposed on $\mathcal{C}$ and $\mathcal{I}$ in the previous proposition are fulfilled when $\mathcal{C}$ is a left-continuous t-norm and $\mathcal{I} = \mathcal{I}_{\mathcal{C}}$, or when $\mathcal{I}$ is the model implicator $\mathcal{I}_{\mathcal{C},\mathcal{N}}$, with $\mathcal{N}$ an involutive negator.

Proposition 50 *Let $\mathcal{C}$ be a conjunctor and let $\mathcal{I}$ be an implicator on [0,1]. If the first partial mappings of $\mathcal{C}$ are right-continuous, the second partial mappings of $\mathcal{I}$ are left-continuous, and $\mathcal{C}$ and $\mathcal{I}$ are connected by the relationship*

$$(\forall(x,y,z) \in [0,1]^3)(\mathcal{C}(\mathcal{I}(x,y),z) \leq \mathcal{I}(x,\mathcal{C}(y,z))),$$

then it holds:
(i) $D_{\mathcal{C}}(A, E_{\mathcal{I}}(B,C)) \subseteq E_{\mathcal{I}}(D_{\mathcal{C}}(A,B),-C)$,
(ii) if $\mathcal{C}$ is also commutative: $D_{\mathcal{C}}(E_{\mathcal{I}}(A,B),C) \subseteq E_{\mathcal{I}}(D_{\mathcal{C}}(A,C),B)$.

The conditions imposed in proposition 50 are fulfilled when $\mathcal{C} = \min$ and $\mathcal{I}$ is the model implicator given by $\mathcal{I}(x,y) = \max(\mathcal{N}(x),y)$, with $\mathcal{N}$ an involutive negator. Except for the left-continuity of the second partial mappings of $\mathcal{I}$ the conditions are also fulfilled if $\mathcal{C}$ is a continuous t-norm and $\mathcal{I} = \mathcal{I}_{\mathcal{C}}$ (e.g. $\mathcal{C} = P$ and $\mathcal{C} = W$ are valid choices, $\mathcal{C} = \min$ is not because the second partial mappings of $\mathcal{I}_{\min}$ are not left-continuous).

Local knowledge.

Just as in the binary case we do not see entirely the gray-scale image A, but only that part of it which is within a binary measuring mask Z. Recall that the binary local knowledge principle enables us to perform the binary dilation $D(A,B)$ or erosion $E(A,B)$ in the binary mask $M = E(Z,B)$ if we only know $A \cap Z$. Under the same conditions, the fuzzy extension of this principle will enable us to perform the fuzzy dilation or erosion in the binary mask $M = E_{\mathcal{I}}(Z, d_B)$.

Proposition 51 *Let $\mathcal{C}$ be a conjunctor on [0,1], let $\mathcal{I}$ be an implicator on [0,1], let A be a gray-scale image, let B be a gray-scale structuring element and let Z be a binary mask. Then it holds:*

$$D_{\mathcal{C}}(A \cap Z, B) \cap E_{\mathcal{I}}(Z, d_B) = D_{\mathcal{C}}(A,B) \cap E_{\mathcal{I}}(Z, d_B)$$
$$E_{\mathcal{I}}(A \cap Z, B) \cap E_{\mathcal{I}}(Z, d_B) = E_{\mathcal{I}}(A,B) \cap E_{\mathcal{I}}(Z, d_B).$$

Adjunction property.

Proposition 52 *Let $\mathcal{C}$ be a conjunctor and let $\mathcal{I}$ be an implicator on [0,1]. If $\mathcal{C}$ and $\mathcal{I}$ are connected by the relationship*

$$(\forall(x,y,z) \in [0,1]^3)(\mathcal{C}(x,z) \leq y \Leftrightarrow \mathcal{I}(x,y) \geq z),$$

then it holds:

$$A \subseteq E_{\mathcal{I}}(B,C) \Leftrightarrow D_{\mathcal{C}}(A,-C) \subseteq B.$$

The condition in proposition 52 is fulfilled when $\mathcal{C}$ is a left-continuous t-norm and $\mathcal{I} = \mathcal{I}_{\mathcal{C}}$. In fact, the left-continuity of a t-norm is equivalent to the above condition.

Under the condition of proposition 52 the pair $(D_{\mathcal{C}}^{-C}, E_{\mathcal{I}}^{C})$ is an adjunction in $Func(\mathbb{R}^n,[0,1])$. For arbitrary $B \in Func(\mathbb{R}^n,[0,1])$, the operations $D_{\mathcal{C}}^{B}$ and $E_{\mathcal{I}}^{B}$ on $Func(\mathbb{R}^n,[0,1])$ are defined as $D_{\mathcal{C}}^{B}(A) = D_{\mathcal{I}}(A,B)$ and $E_t^{B}(A) = E_t(A,B)$, for all $A \in Func(\mathbb{R}^n,[0,1])$. Also note that the class $Func(\mathbb{R}^n,[0,1])$ can be identified with the class $\mathcal{F}(\mathbb{R}^n)$ of fuzzy sets in $\mathbb{R}^n$.

5.6 Application: edge detection

Let A be a gray-scale image and let B be the gray-scale structuring element given by (19). From proposition 41 it follows that $E_{\mathcal{I}}(A,B) \subseteq A \subseteq D_{\mathcal{C}}(A,B)$, for every semi-norm $\mathcal{C}$ and every border implicator $\mathcal{I}$. Consequently, $D_{\mathcal{C}}(A,B) - E_{\mathcal{I}}(A,B)$ will serve as an edge-image of the image A. In figure 18 this is illustrated for the pairs $(\mathcal{C},\mathcal{I}) = (M, I_{KD}), (P, I_R)$ and (W, I_L).

While the hard edges are detected very well, one observes that the edge-image with (M, I_{KD}) detects soft edges better than the edge-images with (P, I_R) or (W, I_L). This can easily be explained theoretically. Indeed, from the properties 33 and 34 it follows that:

$$D_M(A,B) - E_{I_{KD}}(A,B) \supseteq D_P(A,B) - E_{I_R}(A,B) \supseteq D_W(A,B) - E_{I_L}(A,B).$$

Also note that the edge-image with (W, I_L) contains the same information as the edge-image in figure 14, which was derived from the u-dilation and u-erosion.

5.7 On the choice of the conjunctor $\mathcal{C}$ and the implicator $\mathcal{I}$

From a theoretical point of view, we want the fuzzy morphological operations to satisfy the same properties as in the binary case and the gray-scale cases. This not only restricts the choice of the conjunctor $\mathcal{C}$ and the implicator $\mathcal{I}$, but also restricts the choice of the structuring element. For example, if we review the previous section, the following conditions are sufficient for all the properties to be satisfied:

Fig. 18. Original image (upper left), edge-image with (M, I_{KD}) (upper right), edge-image with (P, I_R) (lower left), edge-image with (W, I_L) (lower right)

- $\mathcal{C}$ is a continuous t-norm and $\mathcal{I}$ is a continuous implicator;
- $\mathcal{I} = \mathcal{I}_{\mathcal{C}}$;
- $\mathcal{I} = \mathcal{I}_{\mathcal{C},\mathcal{N}}$, with $\mathcal{N}$ an involutive negator;
- The structuring element B contains the origin, i.e. $B(\mathbf{0}) = 1$.

The first and second condition are sufficient for most of the properties, the third condition is only required for the $\mathcal{N}$-duality of the fuzzy morphological operations, and the forth condition guarantees the extensivity of the fuzzy dilation and the anti-extensivity of the fuzzy erosion.

Next, we investigate whether there exist pairs $(\mathcal{C}, \mathcal{I})$ that satisfy the first three conditions. Let $\mathcal{C}$ be a continuous t-norm and let $\mathcal{N}$ be an involutive negator, then it follows that $\mathcal{I} = \mathcal{I}_{\mathcal{C},\mathcal{N}}$ is a continuous model implicator, which also implies $\mathcal{N} = \mathcal{N}_{\mathcal{I}}$ (cfr. [7]). On the other hand, the second condition states that $\mathcal{I}$ should be the residual implicator $\mathcal{I}_{\mathcal{C}}$. Now, it has been shown in [13] that the only continuous t-norms that have a model implicator as their residual implicator are the φ-transforms T_φ of the Łukasiewicz t-norm W:

$$T_\varphi(x,y) = \varphi^{-1}(\max(\varphi(x)+\varphi(y)-1,0)), \quad \forall(x,y) \in [0,1]^2,$$

where φ is an $[0,1]$-automorphism. This implies that – following the above conditions – the only choice for the conjunctor $\mathcal{C}$ is a φ-transform T_φ. The corresponding implicator $I_\varphi = \mathcal{I}_{T_\varphi}$ is then given by the φ-transform of the Łukasiewicz implicator I_L:

$$I_\varphi(x,y) = \varphi^{-1}(\min(1-\varphi(x)+\varphi(y),1)), \quad \forall(x,y) \in [0,1]^2.$$

Provided that the structuring element B contains the origin, this means that there exists an infinite family of conjunctors and implicators that guarantees the fulfillment of all the discussed properties. Note however that, from a practical point of view, the choice of the conjunctor and the implicator will also depend upon the specific problem or the specific application at hand. The same remark holds for the choice of the structuring element. We are currently doing some experiments on this topic, cfr. [24].

6 Fuzzy mathematical morphology: approach of Bloch & Maître

In [2] and [3] Bloch and Maître followed a similar logical approach to define the fuzzy dilation and the fuzzy erosion. There are however two important differences. First, they use a t-norm $\mathcal{T}$ instead of a conjunctor to define the fuzzy dilation, and secondly they use the associated model implicator $\mathcal{I}_{\mathcal{T},\mathcal{N}}$ (with $\mathcal{N}$ an involutive negator) to define the fuzzy erosion. This implies that duality is forced upon the fuzzy dilation and erosion from the beginning, whereas this is not the case in the general framework. Furthermore, several other approaches towards fuzzy morphology do not fit in this framework (see in particular section 8).

7 Fuzzy mathematical morphology: approach of Minkowski addition

7.1 Definitions

In section 2 we have seen that the binary dilation D satisfies $D(A,B) = A \oplus (-B)$, where A and B are two subsets of $\mathbb{R}^n$. Recall that the Minkowski addition $A \oplus B$ is given by:

$$A \oplus B = \bigcup_{b \in B} T_b(A) = \{y | (\exists b \in B)(y - b \in A)\}.$$

This observation suggests another way to construct a fuzzy mathematical morphology. Indeed, since the Minkowski addition is an operation on crisp subsets of $\mathbb{R}^n$, we can use Zadeh's extension principle to extend this operation to an operation on fuzzy sets in $\mathbb{R}^n$. Having a fuzzy Minkowski addition, we can define a fuzzy Minkowski-dilation based on the binary relation $D(A,B) = A \oplus (-B)$. A fuzzy Minkowski-erosion can then be defined as the N_s-dual of the fuzzy Minkowski-dilation. The foregoing chain of thoughts was originally used in [8], and leads to the following definitions.

Definition 14 *Let A and B be two fuzzy sets in $\mathbb{R}^n$, then the fuzzy Minkowski addition $A \oplus B$ is the fuzzy set defined by, for all $y \in \mathbb{R}^n$:*

$$(A \oplus B)(y) = \sup_{x \in \mathbb{R}^n} \min(B(x), A(y-x)) \tag{35}$$
$$= \sup_{x \in \mathbb{R}^n} \min(B(y-x), A(x)) \tag{36}$$

Definition 15 *Let A be a gray-scale image and let B be a gray-scale structuring element. The fuzzy Minkowski-dilation $D_\oplus(A,B)$ and the fuzzy Minkowski-erosion $E_\oplus(A,B)$ are the gray-scale images defined by:*

$$D_\oplus(A,B)(y) = \sup_{x \in T_y(d_B)} \min(B(x-y), A(x)) \quad \text{for } y \in D(d_A, d_B) \tag{37}$$
$$E_\oplus(A,B)(y) = \inf_{x \in T_y(d_B)} \max(1 - B(x-y), A(x)) \quad \text{for } y \in E(d_A, d_B) \tag{38}$$

The fuzzy Minkowski-closing $C_\oplus$ and the fuzzy Minkowski-opening $O_\oplus$ are respectively defined by $C_\oplus(A,B) = E_\oplus(D_\oplus(A,B), -B)$ and $O_\oplus(A,B) = D_\oplus(E_\oplus(A,B), -B)$.

7.2 Link with the general framework

One easily verifies that the above definitions correspond to a specific choice of $(\mathcal{C}, \mathcal{I})$ in the general framework.

Proposition 53 *Let $\mathcal{C} = M$ and let $\mathcal{I} = I_{KD}$, then it holds:*

$$D_\oplus = D_M \qquad C_\oplus = C_{M,I_{KD}}$$
$$E_\oplus = E_{I_{KD}} \qquad O_\oplus = O_{M,I_{KD}}.$$

Note that by construction $D_\oplus$ and $E_\oplus$, respectively $C_\oplus$ and $O_\oplus$ are dual operations w.r.t. the standard negator N_s. This is in accordance with proposition 32 and the fact that $I_{KD} = \mathcal{I}_{M,N_s}$. Also note that the operations $D_\oplus = D_M$, $E_\oplus = E_{I_{KD}}$, $C_\oplus = C_{M,I_{KD}}$ and $O_\oplus = O_{M,I_{KD}}$ have already been illustrated in figure 15.

Finally, note that the fuzzification of the Minkowski addition can be defined in a more general way. Indeed, instead of using the min-operator for modelling the logical 'and', we can make use of any conjunctor $\mathcal{C}$.

Definition 16 *Let A and B be two fuzzy sets in $\mathbb{R}^n$, then the fuzzy Minkowski $\mathcal{C}$-addition $A \oplus_\mathcal{C} B$ is the fuzzy set defined by, for all $y \in \mathbb{R}^n$:*

$$(A \oplus_\mathcal{C} B)(y) = \sup_{x \in \mathbb{R}^n} \mathcal{C}(B(x), A(y-x)) \tag{39}$$
$$= \sup_{x \in \mathbb{R}^n} \mathcal{C}(B(y-x), A(x)). \tag{40}$$

It immediately follows that the corresponding fuzzy dilation is given by D_C, i.e. $D_C(A, B) = A \oplus_C (-B)$. Given an involutive negator $\mathcal{N}$, the corresponding erosion can be defined as the $\mathcal{N}$-dual of D_C. From proposition 32 it then follows that this erosion is given by $E_{\mathcal{I}_{C,\mathcal{N}}}$. This implies that the construction of a fuzzy mathematical morphology starting from the generalized fuzzy Minkowski addition completely fits into the general framework presented in section 5.

8 Fuzzy mathematical morphology: approach of subset inclusion

8.1 Introduction

The binary erosion is defined by $E(A, B) = \{y | T_y(B) \subseteq A\}$, where A and B are crisp subsets of $\mathbb{R}^n$. The notion of set inclusion is of main importance in this definition. This suggests that an extension of set inclusion for crisp sets to an operation on fuzzy sets may yield alternative extensions of binary morphology to fuzzy morphology. In general, a fuzzified set inclusion can be defined as follows.

Definition 17 *Let Inc be a $\mathcal{F}(\mathbb{R}^n) \times \mathcal{F}(\mathbb{R}^n) - [0, 1]$ mapping, then Inc is said to be a fuzzified set inclusion in $\mathcal{F}(\mathbb{R}^n)$ if its restriction to $\mathcal{P}(\mathbb{R}^n) \times \mathcal{P}(\mathbb{R}^n)$ coincides with set inclusion for crisp sets, i.e. if for all $A, B \in \mathcal{P}(\mathbb{R}^n)$ it holds that:*

$$A \subseteq B \Rightarrow Inc(A, B) = 1,$$
$$A \not\subseteq B \Rightarrow Inc(A, B) = 0.$$

The value $Inc(A, B)$ is interpreted as a measure for the degree to which the fuzzy set A is included in the fuzzy set B. In this section we will review the following fuzzified set inclusions:

- fuzzy set inclusion of Zadeh
- fuzzy set inclusion of Sinha & Dougherty
- fuzzy set inclusion of Kitainik
- fuzzy set inclusion of Bandler & Kohout

Once we have defined a fuzzified set inclusion we will use it to extend the binary erosion to an operation on fuzzy sets in $\mathbb{R}^n$, as follows:

$$E_{Inc}(A, B)(y) = Inc(T_y(B), A).$$

The fuzzy dilation will be defined by duality w.r.t. the standard negator N_s, while the fuzzy opening and the fuzzy closing will be defined as the usual combinations of dilation and erosion.

8.2 Fuzzy set inclusion of Zadeh

Definition 18 *Let A and B be two fuzzy sets in $\mathbb{R}^n$, then the fuzzy set inclusion $\subseteq_z$ of Zadeh is defined by:*

$$A \subseteq_z B \Leftrightarrow (\forall x \in \mathbb{R}^n)(A(x) \leq B(x)).$$

A major drawback of this definition is that it doesn't allow any intermediate degree of subsetness. Indeed, there are only two possibilities: a fuzzy set is a subset of another fuzzy set or it is not. This also implies that the resulting "fuzzy" erosion will be crisp, i.e. a point $y \in \mathbb{R}^n$ will belong to the eroded image or it will not. In particular, we obtain the following definition.

Definition 19 *Let A be a gray-scale image and let B be a gray-scale structuring element, then the Zadeh-erosion $E_z(A, B)$ is the binary image defined by:*

$$y \in E_z(A, B) \Leftrightarrow \inf_{x \in T_y(d_B)} A(x) - B(x-y) \geq 0. \tag{41}$$

The Zadeh-dilation D_z, the Zadeh-closing C_z and the Zadeh-opening O_z are crisp as well, and are respectively defined as $D_z(A, B) = co\, E_z(co_{N_s} A, B)$, $C_z(A, B) = E_z(D_z(A, B), -B)$ and $O_z(A, B) = D_z(E_z(A, B), -B)$. For the Zadeh-dilation D_z we can derive the following expression:

$$y \in D_z(A, B) \Leftrightarrow \sup_{x \in T_y(d_B)} A(x) + B(x-y) > 1. \tag{42}$$

Similar expressions for the Zadeh-closing and the Zadeh-opening can only be derived if we restrict ourselves to structuring elements B for which the support $supp\, B = \{z \in \mathbb{R}^n | B(z) > 0\}$ contains a finite number of points (in practice this is always the case). We then have:

$$y \in C_z(A, B) \Leftrightarrow \min_{z \in T_y(-d_B)} \left(\max_{x \in T_z(d_B)} A(x) + B(x-z) \right) > 1$$

$$y \in O_z(A, B) \Leftrightarrow \max_{z \in T_y(-d_B)} \left(\min_{x \in T_z(d_B)} A(x) - B(x-z) \right) \geq 0.$$

From the expressions (41) and (42) it follows that the Zadeh-erosion and the Zadeh-dilation contain no information at all if the structuring element B is normalized. Therefore, we have illustrated the Zadeh-operations in figure 19 with:

$$B = \begin{pmatrix} 0.4 & 0.4 & 0.4 \\ 0.4 & \underline{0.6} & 0.4 \\ 0.4 & 0.4 & 0.4 \end{pmatrix}$$

Link between the Zadeh-operations and the u-operations.

The expressions (41) and (42) immediately lead to the following connection between the Zadeh-erosion and the Zadeh-dilation on the one hand, and the u-erosion and the u-dilation on the other hand.

Fig. 19. The Zadeh-operations D_z (upper left), E_z (upper right), C_z (lower left) and O_z (lower right)

Proposition 54 *Let A and B be two gray-scale objects, then it holds:*

$$y \in D_z(A,B) \Leftrightarrow D_u(A,B)(y) > 1$$
$$y \in E_z(A,B) \Leftrightarrow E_u(A,B)(y) \geq 0.$$

Link with the general framework.

The Zadeh-operations can be linked to the general framework in a straightforward way. We define the conjunctor C_z and the implicator I_z as follows, for all $(x,y) \in [0,1]^2$:

$$C_z(x,y) = \begin{cases} 1 \text{ if } x+y>1 \\ 0 \text{ else} \end{cases},$$

$$I_z(x,y) = \begin{cases} 1 \text{ if } x \leq y \\ 0 \text{ else} \end{cases}$$

The conjunctor C_z is commutative (it is however not a semi-norm, nor is it associative), and the implicator I_z is contrapositive w.r.t. the standard negator N_s (it is however not a border implicator, nor does it satisfy the exchange principle).

Proposition 55 *Let A and B be two gray-scale objects, then it holds:*

$$D_z(A,B) = D_{C_z}(A,B) \qquad C_z(A,B) = C_{C_z,I_z}(A,B)$$
$$E_z(A,B) = E_{I_z}(A,B) \qquad O_z(A,B) = O_{C_z,I_z}(A,B).$$

One easily verifies that $C_z(x,y) = 1 \Leftrightarrow W(x,y) > 0$ and $I_z(x,y) = 1 \Leftrightarrow I_L(x,y) = 1$. This leads to the following result.

Proposition 56 *Let A and B be two gray-scale objects, then it holds:*

$$D_z(A,B) = supp\, D_W(A,B),$$
$$E_z(A,B) = ker\, E_{I_L}(A,B).$$

We are now able to give an alternative description of the Zadeh-operations D_z and E_z. Indeed, given a gray-scale image A and a structuring element B, the Zadeh-dilation $D_z(A,B)$ consists of those points of $D_W(A,B)$ whose value is not zero, while the Zadeh-erosion $E_z(A,B)$ comprises only those points of $E_{I_L}(A,B)$ whose value is one.

Note that the previous observations, as well as the fact that the Zadeh-operations generate crisp objects, imply that the operations D_z and E_z contain very little information compared to earlier discussed morphological operations.

8.3 Fuzzy set inclusion of Sinha and Dougherty

As already mentioned in the previous section, the fuzzy set inclusion in Zadeh's sense does not allow any intermediate degree of subsetness. In order to avoid this drawback, several researchers have introduced other extensions of crisp set inclusion to fuzzy set inclusion. In [28] a general indicator Inc_{SD} for fuzzified set inclusion is introduced, based on nine intuitive acceptable axioms.

Definition 20 *An indicator Inc_{SD} for fuzzified set inclusion is a $\mathcal{F}(\mathbb{R}^n) \times \mathcal{F}(\mathbb{R}^n) - [0,1]$ mapping that satisfies the following nine axioms:*
(i) $Inc_{SD}(A,B) = 1 \Leftrightarrow A \subseteq_z B$,
(ii) $Inc_{SD}(A,B) = 0 \Leftrightarrow (\exists x \in \mathbb{R}^n)(A(x) = 1 \text{ and } B(x) = 0)$,
(iii) $B_1 \subseteq_z B_2 \Rightarrow Inc_{SD}(A,B_1) \leq Inc_{SD}(A,B_2)$,
(iv) $A_1 \subseteq_z A_2 \Rightarrow Inc_{SD}(A_1,B) \geq Inc_{SD}(A_2,B)$,
(v) $Inc_{SD}(A,B) = Inc_{SD}(T_\theta(A), T_\theta(B))$,
(vi) $Inc_{SD}(A,B) = Inc_{SD}(co_{N_s}B, co_{N_s}A)$,
(vii) $Inc_{SD}(A_1 \cup A_2, B) = \min(Inc_{SD}(A_1,B), Inc_{SD}(A_2,B))$,
(viii) $Inc_{SD}(A, B_1 \cap B_2) = \min(Inc_{SD}(A,B_1), Inc_{SD}(A,B_2))$,
(ix) $Inc_{SD}(A, B_1 \cup B_2) \geq \max(Inc_{SD}(A,B_1), Inc_{SD}(A,B_2))$.

Note that the axioms (i) and (ii) guarantee that Inc_{SD} is a fuzzified set inclusion in the sense of definition 17. The notation $T_\theta(A)$ in axiom (v) stands for a transformation of A induced by a permutation θ of $\mathbb{R}^n$, i.e. $T_\theta(A)(x) = A(\theta(x))$, for all $x \in \mathbb{R}^n$.

For an interpretation of the axioms we refer to [28]. In the same paper the following indicator is proposed for fuzzified set inclusion:

$$Inc_\lambda(A, B) = \inf_{x \in \mathbb{R}^n} \min(1, \lambda(A(x)) + \lambda(1 - B(x))), \tag{43}$$

where λ is a $[0,1] - [0,1]$ function satisfying the following six conditions:

(i) λ is a decreasing function,
(ii) $\lambda(0) = 1$,
(iii) $\lambda(1) = 0$,
(iv) The equation $\lambda(x) = 0$ has a unique solution,
(v) $(\forall \alpha \in [0.5, 1])(\lambda(x) = \alpha$ has a unique solution),
(vi) $(\forall x \in [0,1])(\lambda(x) + \lambda(1 - x) \geq 1)$.

Some examples of possible λ-functions are given by $\lambda_n(x) = 1 - x^n$ (with $n \geq 1$), and $\lambda_n(x) = \frac{1-x}{1+nx}$ (with $n \in]-1, 0]$).

Using the indicator Inc_λ, we obtain the following fuzzification of the binary erosion. We will refer to it as the λ-erosion.

Definition 21 *Let A be a gray-scale image and let B be a gray-scale structuring element, then the λ-erosion $E_\lambda(A, B)$ is the gray-scale image defined by, for all $y \in E(d_A, d_B)$:*

$$E_\lambda(A, B)(y) = Inc_\lambda(T_y(B), A) \tag{44}$$

$$= \inf_{x \in T_y(d_B)} \min\left(1, \lambda(B(x - y)) + \lambda(1 - A(x))\right). \tag{45}$$

The λ-dilation D_λ is obtained by putting $D_\lambda(A, B) = co_{N_s}\, E_\lambda(co_{N_s}\, A, B)$. This leads to the following expression, for all $y \in D(d_A, d_B)$:

$$D_\lambda(A, B)(y) = \sup_{x \in T_y(d_B)} \max\left(0, 1 - \lambda(B(x - y)) + \lambda(A(x))\right). \tag{46}$$

The λ-closing C_λ and the λ-opening O_λ are defined as the usual combinations of dilation and erosion, i.e. $C_\lambda(A, B) = E_\lambda(D_\lambda(A, B), -B)$ and $O_\lambda(A, B) = D_\lambda(E_\lambda(A, B), -B)$.

Link with the general framework.

It is easily verified that the λ-operations coincide with a specific choice of the conjunctor $\mathcal{C}$ and the implicator $\mathcal{I}$ in the general framework. Indeed, if we define the conjunctor $\mathcal{C}_\lambda$ and the implicator $\mathcal{I}_\lambda$ as:

$$\mathcal{C}_\lambda(x, y) = \max(0, 1 - \lambda(x) - \lambda(y))$$
$$\mathcal{I}_\lambda(x, y) = \min(1, \lambda(x) + \lambda(1 - y)),$$

for all $(x, y) \in [0, 1]^2$, then we immediately have the following result.

Proposition 57 *Let A and B be two gray-scale objects, then it holds:*

$$D_\lambda(A, B) = D_{\mathcal{C}_\lambda}(A, B) \qquad C_\lambda(A, B) = C_{\mathcal{C}_\lambda, \mathcal{I}_\lambda}(A, B)$$
$$E_\lambda(A, B) = E_{\mathcal{I}_\lambda}(A, B) \qquad O_\lambda(A, B) = O_{\mathcal{C}_\lambda, \mathcal{I}_\lambda}(A, B).$$

Note that $\mathcal{I}_\lambda = \mathcal{I}_{\mathcal{C}_\lambda, N_s}$. This is completely in accordance with proposition 32 and the fact that the λ-dilation D_λ is defined as the N_s-dual of the λ-erosion E_λ.

The conjunctor $\mathcal{C}_\lambda$ always is commutative and the implicator $\mathcal{I}_\lambda$ always is contrapositive w.r.t. the standard negator N_s. Furthermore, one can verify that $\mathcal{C}_\lambda$ is a semi-norm and that $\mathcal{I}_\lambda$ is a border implicator if and only if $\lambda(x) = 1 - x$. In that case the conjunctor coincides with the Łukasiewicz t-norm W, while the implicator is given by the Łukasiewicz implicator I_L. This also implies that in all other cases, fuzzy morphologies based on the inclusion of Sinha & Dougherty are not compatible with gray-scale morphology based on the threshold approach (cfr. proposition 29). Finally, it can be shown that the approach based on the fuzzified set inclusion of Zadeh does not fit in the framework of Sinha & Dougherty.

8.4 Fuzzy set inclusion of Kitainik

Another approach towards fuzzified set inclusion is given by Kitainik. Just as Sinha & Dougherty, Kitainik starts with a list of axioms that any fuzzified set inclusion should satisfy.

Definition 22 *An indicator Inc_K for fuzzified set inclusion is a $\mathcal{F}(\mathbb{R}^n) \times \mathcal{F}(\mathbb{R}^n) - [0, 1]$ mapping that satisfies the following four axioms:*
(i) $Inc_K(A, B) = Inc_K(co_{N_s} B, co_{N_s} A)$,
(ii) $Inc_K(A, B_1 \cap B_2) = \min(Inc_K(A, B_1), Inc_K(A, B_2))$,
(iii) $Inc_K(A, B) = Inc_K(T_\theta(A), T_\theta(B))$,
(iv) *The restriction of Inc_K to $\mathcal{P}(\mathbb{R}^n)^2$ coincides with the crisp set inclusion $\subseteq$.*

Note that axiom (iv) implies that any Kitainik-indicator Inc_K is a fuzzified set inclusion in the sense of definition 17.

In contrast to Sinha & Dougherty, Kitainik was able to characterize all fuzzified set inclusions that satisfy the postulated axioms. Let us first define the class Phi as the class of functions φ that satisfy the following conditions:
(a) φ is a $T - [0, 1]$ function, where T is the triangle defined by $T = \{(x, y) | (x, y) \in [0, 1]^2 \text{ and } x \geq y\}$,
(b) φ has decreasing partial mappings,
(c) $\varphi(0, 0) = \varphi(1, 0) = 1$ and $\varphi(1, 1) = 0$.

Proposition 58 *Let* Inc *be a* $\mathcal{F}(\mathbb{R}^n) \times \mathcal{F}(\mathbb{R}^n) - [0,1]$ *mapping, then* Inc *satisfies the axioms from definition 22 if and only if there exists a function* $\varphi \in Phi$ *such that* $Inc = Inc_\varphi$*, with:*

$$Inc_\varphi(A,B) = \inf_{x\in\mathbb{R}^n} \varphi\left(\max(A(x), 1-B(x)), \min(A(x), 1-B(x))\right). \quad (47)$$

In the following, we will use expression (47) to denote an indicator in Kitainik's sense.

Definition 23 *Let* A *be a gray-scale image and let* B *be a gray-scale structuring element, then the* φ*-erosion* $E_\varphi(A,B)$ *is the gray-scale image defined by, for all* $y \in E(d_A, d_B)$*:*

$$\begin{aligned} & E_\varphi(A,B)(y) \\ = {} & Inc_\varphi(T_y(B), A) \\ = {} & \inf_{x\in T_y(d_B)} \varphi\left(\max(B(x-y), 1-A(x)), \min(B(x-y), 1-A(x))\right). \quad (48) \end{aligned}$$

Again we put $D_\varphi(A,B) = co_{N_s} E_\varphi(co_{N_s} A, B)$, obtaining the following expression for all $y \in D(d_A, d_B)$:

$$\begin{aligned} & D_\varphi(A,B)(y) \\ = {} & \sup_{x\in T_y(d_B)\cap d_A} \left(1 - \varphi\left[\max(B(x-y), A(x)), \min(B(x-y), A(x))\right]\right). \quad (49) \end{aligned}$$

The φ-closing C_φ is defined by $C_\varphi(A,B) = E_\varphi(D_\varphi(A,B), -B)$; the φ-opening O_φ by $O_\varphi(A,B) = D_\varphi(E_\varphi(A,B), -B)$.

Link with the general framework.

Once again, the φ-operations coincide with a specific choice of the conjunctor $\mathcal{C}$ and the implicator $\mathcal{I}$ in the general framework presented in section 5. For all $(x,y) \in [0,1]^2$ we define the conjunctor $\mathcal{C}_\varphi$ and the implicator $\mathcal{I}_\varphi$ as follows:

$$\begin{aligned} \mathcal{C}_\varphi(x,y) &= 1 - \varphi\left(\max(x,y), \min(x,y)\right) \\ \mathcal{I}_\varphi(x,y) &= \varphi\left(\max(x, 1-y), \min(x, 1-y)\right). \end{aligned}$$

Proposition 59 *Let* A *and* B *be two gray-scale objects, then it holds:*

$$\begin{aligned} D_\varphi(A,B) &= D_{\mathcal{C}_\varphi}(A,B) & C_\varphi(A,B) &= C_{\mathcal{C}_\varphi,\mathcal{I}_\varphi}(A,B) \\ E_\varphi(A,B) &= E_{\mathcal{I}_\varphi}(A,B) & O_\varphi(A,B) &= O_{\mathcal{C}_\varphi,\mathcal{I}_\varphi}(A,B). \end{aligned}$$

The connection between the Kitainik approach and the general framework is much stronger than proposition 59 suggests. In order to show this, we need the following results. We will make use of the functions $\varphi_\mathcal{C}$ and $\varphi_\mathcal{I}$, respectively defined by:

$$\begin{aligned} \varphi_\mathcal{C}(x,y) &= 1 - \mathcal{C}(x,y), \\ \varphi_\mathcal{I}(x,y) &= \mathcal{I}(x, 1-y), \end{aligned}$$

for all $(x, y) \in T$, with $\mathcal{C}$ a commutative conjunctor and $\mathcal{I}$ an implicator that is contrapositive w.r.t. the standard negator N_s. One easily verifies the following properties.

Proposition 60
(i) Let $\varphi \in Phi$, then the operator $\mathcal{C}_\varphi$ is a commutative conjunctor.
(ii) Let $\mathcal{C}$ be a commutative conjunctor, then the operator $\varphi_\mathcal{C}$ belongs to the class Phi.
(iii) It holds that $\mathcal{C}_{\varphi_\mathcal{C}} = \mathcal{C}$ and $\varphi_{\mathcal{C}_\varphi} = \varphi$.

As a consequence, there exists a one-to-one correspondence between functions of the class *Phi* on the one hand and commutative conjunctors on the other hand. In an analogous way, one can show that there exists a one-to-one correspondence between functions of the class *Phi* and implicators that are contrapositive w.r.t. the standard negator.

Proposition 61
(i) Let $\varphi \in Phi$, then the operator $\mathcal{I}_\varphi$ is an implicator that is contrapositive w.r.t. the standard negator.
(ii) Let $\mathcal{I}$ be an implicator that is contrapositive w.r.t. the standard negator, then the operator $\varphi_\mathcal{I}$ belongs to the class Phi.
(iii) It holds that $\mathcal{I}_{\varphi_\mathcal{I}} = \mathcal{I}$ and $\varphi_{\mathcal{I}_\varphi} = \varphi$.

The following properties are also of main importance.

Proposition 62
(i) Let $\varphi \in Phi$, then it holds that $\mathcal{C}_\varphi = \mathcal{C}_{\mathcal{I}_\varphi, N_s}$ and $\mathcal{I}_\varphi = \mathcal{I}_{\mathcal{C}_\varphi, N_s}$.
(ii) Let $\mathcal{C}$ be a commutative conjunctor and let $\mathcal{I}$ be an implicator that is contrapositive w.r.t. the standard negator. If $\mathcal{C} = \mathcal{C}_{\mathcal{I}, N_s}$ or, equivalently, if $\mathcal{I} = \mathcal{I}_{\mathcal{C}, N_s}$, then it holds that $\varphi_\mathcal{C} = \varphi_\mathcal{I}$.

Let us now define the class *Op* as the class of ordered pairs $(\mathcal{C}, \mathcal{I})$ that satisfy the following conditions:
(a) $\mathcal{C}$ is a commutative conjunctor,
(b) $\mathcal{I}$ is an implicator that is contrapositive w.r.t. the standard negator,
(c) $\mathcal{C}$ and $\mathcal{I}$ are connected by the relationship $\mathcal{C} = \mathcal{C}_{\mathcal{I}, N_s}$ or, equivalently, $\mathcal{I} = \mathcal{I}_{\mathcal{C}, N_s}$.

The previous results imply that there is a one-to-one correspondence between the class *Phi* and the class *Op*. This is expressed in the following proposition.

Proposition 63 *The mapping $M : Phi \mapsto Op$, defined by:*

$$M(\varphi) = (\mathcal{C}_\varphi, \mathcal{I}_\varphi), \ \forall \varphi \in Phi$$

is a bijection.

As a consequence, there also is a one-to-one correspondence between fuzzy mathematical morphologies derived from the fuzzified set inclusion in Kitainik's sense and fuzzy mathematical morphologies based on conjunctors $\mathcal{C}$ and implicators $\mathcal{I}$ from the class Op. In particular, we can associate a function $\varphi \in Phi$ with each pair $(\mathcal{C}, \mathcal{I}) \in Op$, namely $\varphi = \varphi_{\mathcal{C}} = \varphi_{\mathcal{I}}$. The reverse situation – in which we associate a pair $(\mathcal{C}_\varphi, \mathcal{I}_\varphi) \in Op$ with each $\varphi \in Phi$ – was treated in proposition 59.

Regarding the links with other frameworks, the following results can be derived.

- Fuzzy morphology based on the fuzzified set inclusion of Kitainik is compatible with gray-scale morphology based on the threshold approach if and only if $\varphi(1, x) = 1 - x$, for all $x \in [0, 1]$ (cfr. proposition 29). Indeed, under this necessary and sufficient condition $\mathcal{C}_\varphi$ is a semi-norm and $\mathcal{I}_\varphi$ is a border implicator.
- The approach of Bloch & Maître fits in the framework of Kitainik, i.e. the framework of Kitainik is more general. This is due to the fact that any pair $(\mathcal{T}, \mathcal{I}_{\mathcal{T},N_s})$ of t-norms and associated model implicators belongs to the class Op, and therefore there exists a function $\varphi \in Phi$ such that $\mathcal{T} = \mathcal{C}_\varphi$ and $\mathcal{I}_{\mathcal{T},N_s} = \mathcal{I}_\varphi$ (cfr. proposition 63).
- The approach of Zadeh fits in the framework of Kitainik for the same reason, i.e. because $(C_z, I_z) \in Op$ (cfr. proposition 63).
- Finally, also the approach of Sinha & Dougherty fits into the framework of Kitainik. Indeed, since $(\mathcal{C}_\lambda, \mathcal{I}_\lambda) \in Op$ for an appropriate λ, there exists a function $\varphi_\lambda \in Phi$ such that $\mathcal{C}_\lambda = \mathcal{C}_{\varphi_\lambda}$ and $\mathcal{I}_\lambda = \mathcal{I}_{\varphi_\lambda}$. In particular, it holds that $\varphi_\lambda = \varphi_{\mathcal{I}_\lambda}$, i.e. $\varphi_\lambda(x, y) = \min(1, \lambda(x) + \lambda(y))$ for all $x, y \in [0, 1]$. Note that the reverse is not true (e.g. there exists a φ, but no λ such that $\mathcal{I}_\varphi = I_{KD}$ and $\mathcal{I}_\lambda = I_{KD}$).

8.5 Fuzzy set inclusion of Bandler and Kohout

While the approaches of Kitainik and Sinha & Dougherty are based on the postulation of intuitive acceptable axioms, the approach of Bandler & Kohout towards a fuzzified set inclusion is a logical one, i.e. they fuzzify the binary expression:

$$A \subseteq B \Leftrightarrow (\forall x \in \mathbb{R}^n)(x \in A \Rightarrow x \in B),$$

using the notion of an implicator. This leads to the following definition.

Definition 24 *Let A and B be two fuzzy sets in $\mathbb{R}^n$, and let $\mathcal{I}$ be an implicator on [0,1]. The indicator $Inc_{\mathcal{I}}$ for fuzzified set inclusion is the $\mathcal{F}(\mathbb{R}^n) \times \mathcal{F}(\mathbb{R}^n) - [0, 1]$ mapping given by:*

$$Inc_{\mathcal{I}}(A, B) = \inf_{x \in \mathbb{R}^n} \mathcal{I}(A(x), B(x)).$$

It immediately follows that the corresponding fuzzy erosion, which is defined by $E(A, B) = Inc_{\mathcal{I}}(T_y(B), A)$, is given by $E_{\mathcal{I}}$. Since the corresponding fuzzy dilation is defined as the N_s-dual of this erosion, and the fuzzy closing and opening are defined as the usual combinations of dilation and erosion, these operations are respectively given by $D_{\mathcal{C}_{\mathcal{I},N_s}}$, $C_{\mathcal{C}_{\mathcal{I},N_s},\mathcal{I}}$ and $O_{\mathcal{C}_{\mathcal{I},N_s},\mathcal{I}}$.

9 Schematic overview of the different approaches towards fuzzy mathematical morphology

In the previous sections we have discussed several approaches towards fuzzy morphology. Besides the general logical framework of De Baets, we have also reviewed the model of Bloch & Maître, an approach starting from a fuzzification of the Minkowski addition, and some approaches starting from different fuzzifications of the notion of set inclusion. It has been shown that all these different approaches fit into the general framework, and we have investigated the links between the different frameworks. The results of this investigation are schematically illustrated in figure 20. In this figure, it is also indicated which fuzzy approaches are compatible with gray-scale morphology based on the threshold approach; recall that only the case $(\mathcal{C}, \mathcal{I}) = (W, I_L)$ also is compatible with gray-scale morphology based on the umbra approach, under supplementary conditions on the structuring element.

The above observations are quite important and suggest that further theoretical research on fuzzy mathematical morphology should concentrate on the general framework, since that proves to be the most universal approach.

10 Bibliographical remarks

10.1 Classical morphology

The book [25] by Serra is one of the best known references to the theory of classical mathematical morphology (sections 2, 3 and 4). The books by Matheron [19], Sternberg [30], and more recently of Heijmans [16] – which treats the theory of mathematical morphology in the framework of complete lattices – are also very interesting. For detailed proofs (and counterexamples) of some of the classical properties we refer to the paper [14] of Haralick *et al.* Finally, the reader can find several theoretical and practical applications of classical morphology in the edited volumes [17], [26] and [27].

10.2 Fuzzy morphology

The general logical framework for fuzzy mathematical morphology (section 5) is extensively discussed in [10] (on the idempotence of the fuzzy closing and opening) and [11] (which focusses on a lot of other properties). In both

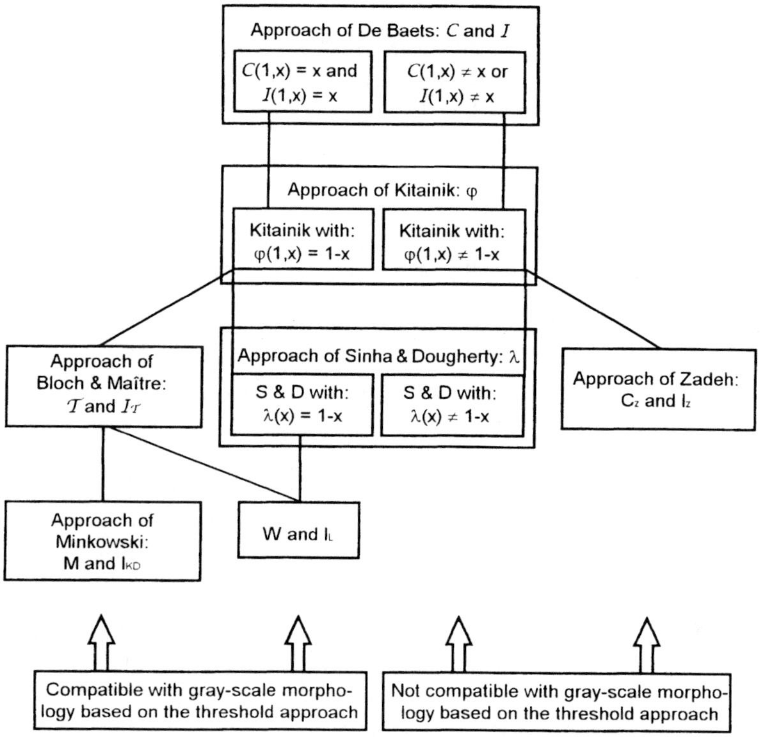

Fig. 20. Connections between the different approaches towards fuzzy mathematical morphology

papers, the reader will also find proofs of several properties mentioned in section 5.5. The decomposition properties (section 5.4) are presented and proved in [23]. In [22] these properties are investigated in a discrete framework, as encountered in practice. For an extension of the idempotence properties (section 5.5) we refer to Chapter 2 (*Generalized Idempotence in Fuzzy Mathematical Morphology*).

Besides the already mentioned papers [2] and [3] (section 6), Bloch *et al.* published several other papers in which fuzzy morphology is used to derive links with other fuzzy concepts. As examples, we mention [4] (on fuzzy relative position), [5] (on fuzzy adjacency) and [6] (on fuzzy distances). We also refer to Chapter 4 (*Fuzzy Mathematical Morphology and Derived Spatial Relationships*), in which these concepts are discussed in detail.

The approach of the Minkowski addition (section 7) has been adopted by several researchers. For a nice theoretical overview, including a lot of properties, we refer to [8] and [9].

The fuzzy set inclusion in Zadeh's sense (section 8.2) already appears in his first paper [31] on fuzzy sets. For more background on fuzzy morphology based on the fuzzified set inclusion of Sinha & Dougherty (section 8.3) we refer to [28] and [29], as well as to Chapter 3 (*Fuzzy Mathematical Morphology Based on Fuzzy Inclusion*). The fuzzified set inclusion of Kitainik (section 8.4) is discussed in [18], while the inclusion of Bandler & Kohout (section 8.5) is treated in [1].

The links between classical morphology and fuzzy morphology on the one hand (section 5.4), and the links between the different approaches towards fuzzy morphology on the other hand (sections 6, 7 and 8), are extensively discussed in [20] and [21]. The proofs can be found in [20].

References

1. Bandler W. and Kohout L., *Fuzzy Power Sets and Fuzzy Implication Operators*, Fuzzy Sets and Systems, Vol. 4, pp. 13-30, 1980
2. Bloch I. and Maître H., *Triangular Norms as a Tool for Constructing Fuzzy Mathematical Morphologies*, in: "Proceedings of the International Workshop on Mathematical Morphology and its Applications to Signal Processing" (Barcelona), pp. 157-161, 1993
3. Bloch I. and Maître H., *Fuzzy Mathematical Morphologies: a Comparative Study*, Pattern Recognition, Vol. 28, No. 9, pp. 1341-1387, 1995
4. Bloch I., *Fuzzy Relative Position between Objects in Images: a Morphological Approach*, in: "Proceedings of ICIP'96 – IEEE International Conference on Image Processing" (Lausanne), pp. 987-990, 1996
5. Bloch I., Maître H. and Anvari M., *Fuzzy Adjacency between Image Objects*, International Journal of Uncertainty, Fuzziness and Knowledge-Based Systems, Vol. 5, No. 6, pp. 615-653, 1997
6. Bloch I., *On Links Between Fuzzy Morphology and Fuzzy Distances: Euclidean and Geodesic Cases*, in: "Proceedings of IPMU'98 – Information Processing and Management of Uncertainty" (Paris), pp. 1144-1151, 1998
7. De Baets B., *Model Implicators and Their Characterization*, in: "Proceedings of ICSC'95 – International Symposium on Fuzzy Logic" (Zürich), pp. A42-A49, 1995
8. De Baets B., Kerre E. and Gupta M., *The Fundamentals of Fuzzy Mathematical Morphology Part 1: Basic Concepts*, International Journal of General Systems, Vol. 23, pp. 155-171, 1995
9. De Baets B., Kerre E. and Gupta M., *The Fundamentals of Fuzzy Mathematical Morphology Part 2: Idempotence, Convexity and Decomposition*, International Journal of General Systems, Vol. 23, pp. 307-322, 1995
10. De Baets B., *Idempotent Closing and Opening Operations in Fuzzy Mathematical Morphology*, in: "Proceedings of Joint ISUMA'95 – International Symposium on Uncertainty Modeling and Analysis – and NAFIPS'95 – North American Fuzzy Information Processing Society" (College Park, Los Alamitos), IEEE Computer Society Press, pp. 228-233, 1995
11. De Baets B., *Fuzzy Morphology: a Logical Approach*, in: "Uncertainty Analysis in Engineering and Sciences: Fuzzy Logic, Statistics, and Neural Network Approach", Kluwer Academic Publishers, Boston, 1997

12. Di Gesu V., *Mathematical Morphology Based on Fuzzy Operators*, in: "Fuzzy Logic (R. Lowen and M. Roubens, eds.)", Kluwer Academic Publishers, pp. 477-486, 1993
13. Fodor J., *Contrapositive Symmetry of Fuzzy Implications*, Fuzzy Sets and Systems, Vol. 69, pp. 141-156, 1995
14. Haralick R.M., Sternberg S.R. and Zhuang X., *Image Analysis Using Mathematical Morphology*, IEEE Transactions on Pattern Analysis and Machine Intelligence, Vol. 9, No. 4, pp. 532-550, 1987
15. Heijmans H. and Ronse C., *The Algebraic Basis of Mathematical Morphology, Part 1: Dilations and Erosions*, Computer Vision, Graphics and Image Processing, Vol. 50, pp. 245-295, 1990
16. Heijmans H., *"Morphological Image Operators"*, Academic Press, London, 1994
17. Heijmans H. and Roerdink J., *"Mathematical Morphology and Its Applications to Image and Signal Processing"*, Kluwer Academic Publishers, Dordrecht, 1998
18. Kitainik L., *"Fuzzy Decision Procedures with Binary Relations: Towards a Unified Theory"*, Kluwer Academic Publishers, 1993
19. Matheron G., *"Random Sets and Integral Geometry"*, John Wiley and Sons, New York, 1975
20. Nachtegael M. and Kerre E.E., *Connections between Binary, Gray-scale and Fuzzy Mathematical Morphology*, Fuzzy Sets and Systems, submitted
21. Nachtegael M. and Kerre E.E., *Different Approaches towards Fuzzy Mathematical Morphology*, in: "Proceedings of EUFIT'99 – European Congress on Fuzzy and Intelligent Technologies" (Aachen), 1999
22. Nachtegael M. and Kerre E.E., *Fuzzy Mathematical Morphology: General Concepts and Decomposition Properties*, in: "Proceedings of KES'99 – International Conference on Knowledge-based Intelligent Information Engineering Systems" (Adelaide, Australia), pp. 255–258,1999
23. Nachtegael M. and Kerre E.E., *On the Decomposition of Fuzzy Morphological Operations*, IEEE Transactions on Fuzzy Systems, submitted
24. Nachtegael M., Vynckier F. and Kerre E.E., *The CIQC-program: on the Choice of the Conjunctor and Implicator in Fuzzy Mathematical Morphology*, Internal Report Fuzziness and Uncertainty Modelling Research Unit, 1999
25. Serra J., *"Image Analysis and Mathematical Morphology"*, Academic Press, London, 1982
26. Serra J., *"Image Analysis and Mathematical Morphology Volume 2: Theoretical Advances"*, Academic Press, London, 1988
27. Serra J. and Soille P., *"Mathematical Morphology and Its Applications to Image Processing"*, Kluwer Academic Publishers, Dordrecht, 1994
28. Sinha D. and Dougherty R., *Fuzzification of Set Inclusion: Theory and Applications*, Fuzzy Sets and Systems, Vol. 55, pp. 15-42, 1993
29. Sinha D. and Dougherty E.R., *A General Axiomatic Theory of Intrinsically Fuzzy Mathematical Morphologies*, IEEE Transactions on Fuzzy Systems, Vol. 3, No. 4, pp. 389-403, 1995
30. Sternberg S.R., *Parallel Architectures for Image Processing*, in: "Proceedings of IEEE COMPSAC" (Chicago), 1979
31. Zadeh L., *Fuzzy Sets*, Information and Control, Vol. 8, pp. 338-353, 1965

Chapter 2

Generalized Idempotence in Fuzzy Mathematical Morphology

Bernard De Baets

Ghent University
Department of Applied Mathematics, Biometrics and Process Control
Coupure Links 653, B-9000 Gent, Belgium
email: bernard.debaets@rug.ac.be

Summary. In binary mathematical morphology, the idempotence of the binary closing and binary opening has led to the study of objects that are closed or open w.r.t. a given structuring element. For these objects, an interesting generalized idempotence law holds. In recent years, fuzzy mathematical morphology has been proposed as an alternative theory to gray-scale morphology. In this paper, we consider the most general approach, the so-called logical approach, based on fuzzy logical operators. In particular, the role of t-norms and their residual operators is stressed. It is shown that the generalized idempotence laws still hold in fuzzy mathematical morphology when choosing a continuous t-norm and its residual implicator as underlying conjunctor and implicator, and in particular when choosing a nilpotent t-norm and its residual implicator. In the latter case, the fuzzy closing and fuzzy opening are dual operations, and hence results concerning the fuzzy closing are obtained by duality from the fuzzy opening. The unique role of nilpotent t-norms, and hence of the Łukasiewicz t-norm, is demonstrated.

1 Generalized idempotence in binary morphology

An n-dimensional binary (or black-and-white) image is completely determined by its set of black pixels, or equivalently, by its set of white pixels. By the object in the image we mean the set describing the foreground region. A binary morphological operation P transforms such an object A by means of a structuring element B (another object) into a new object $P(A, B)$, where A and B are described by means of subsets of $\mathbb{R}^n$ (n-tuples of coordinates). The set A represents the structure we want to analyse, while the set B is a "small" set chosen in some restricted class, with which we probe the structure of A.

The primitive morphological operations are the (binary) dilation D and the (binary) erosion E. The dilation of an object A by a structuring element B is the set of all y for which the translation $\mathrm{T}_y(B) = \{x \mid x - y \in B\}$ of B by y has a nonempty intersection with A; the erosion is the set of all y for which the translation $\mathrm{T}_y(B)$ is contained in A. These definitions are formalized as follows [22]:

$$\mathbf{D}(A,B) = \{y \mid \mathrm{T}_y(B) \cap A \neq \emptyset\}$$
$$\mathbf{E}(A,B) = \{y \mid \mathrm{T}_y(B) \subseteq A\}.$$

The reflection $-B$ of B about the origin is defined as $-B = \{-b \mid b \in B\}$. The dilation and erosion are not inverse operations. Therefore, their compositions lead to new operations. The (binary) closing $\mathbf{C}$ and (binary) opening $\mathbf{O}$ are defined as follows [22]:

$$\mathbf{C}(A,B) = \mathbf{E}(\mathbf{D}(A,B), -B)$$
$$\mathbf{O}(A,B) = \mathbf{D}(\mathbf{E}(A,B), -B).$$

Notice that these operations are not the exact compositions of $\mathbf{D}$ and $\mathbf{E}$, since in the second operation the reflection of B is used as argument. These operations also have a very intuitive interpretation: the closing of an object A with respect to a structuring element B is the set of all y for which any translation of B that contains y has a nonempty intersection with A; the opening of A with respect to B is the union of all translations of B that are contained in A.

Morphological operations come in dual pairs: two morphological operations P and Q are called dual if for any two objects A and B it holds that $P(A,B) = \operatorname{co} Q(\operatorname{co} A, B)$. Clearly, the dilation and erosion are dual, as well as the closing and opening. An extensive overview of the properties of the above operations can be found in [20]; also refer to Chapter 1 (*Classical and Fuzzy Approaches towards Mathematical Morphology*). A very important property is the idempotence of the binary closing and opening: for any two objects A and B it holds that

$$\mathbf{C}(\mathbf{C}(A,B),B) = \mathbf{C}(A,B)$$
$$\mathbf{O}(\mathbf{O}(A,B),B) = \mathbf{O}(A,B).$$

It motivates the following definition: an object A is said to be closed (resp. open) w.r.t. a structuring element B, or shortly B-closed (resp. B-open), if $\mathbf{C}(A,B) = A$ (resp. $\mathbf{O}(A,B) = A$)). The idempotence can then be restated with this new terminology by saying that $\mathbf{C}(A,B)$ is B-closed and that $\mathbf{O}(A,B)$ is B-open. These concepts play an important role in the further development of the binary mathematical morphology. Some simple observations are recalled next.

Proposition 1. [18,22] *A is B-open if and only if $\operatorname{co} A$ is B-closed.*

Proposition 2. [18,22]

(i) *A is B-open if and only if there exists an object E such that*

$$A = \mathbf{D}(E, -B).$$

(ii) *A is B-closed if and only if there exists an object E such that*

$$A = \mathbf{E}(E, -B).$$

In view of Proposition 1 it suffices to restrict our discussion to B-open sets, for instance. The following theorem states that if A is B-open, then opening by A produces a smaller image than opening by B, and conversely for closing by A and B. Combined with the anti-extensivity of the opening and the extensivity of the closing, this leads to the following *ordering property* .

Theorem 1. [18,22] *If A is B-open, then for any object F it holds:*

$$\mathbf{O}(F, A) \subseteq \mathbf{O}(F, B) \subseteq F \subseteq \mathbf{C}(F, B) \subseteq \mathbf{C}(F, A).$$

The following theorem gives a generalization of the idempotence laws for the closing and opening. Since any object A is always A-closed, it is immediately clear why the following properties are called the *generalized idempotence* laws.

Theorem 2. [18,22] *If A is B-open, then for any object F it holds:*

$$\mathbf{O}(\mathbf{O}(F, B), A) = \mathbf{O}(\mathbf{O}(F, A), B) = \mathbf{O}(F, A)$$
$$\mathbf{C}(\mathbf{C}(F, B), A) = \mathbf{C}(\mathbf{C}(F, A), B) = \mathbf{C}(F, A).$$

Notice that in the foregoing two theorems the results concerning the closing follow by duality from the results concerning the opening.

2 Fuzzy morphology: a logical approach

2.1 Conjunctors and implicators

It is clear that intersection and inclusion play an important role in the definition of the binary dilation and binary erosion. This implies that the underlying logical operations, the Boolean conjunction and Boolean implication, bear the key to a successful fuzzification [9]. We therefore take a look at the extensions of these logical operations to the real unit interval.

Definition 1. (see e.g. [7]) A decreasing unary operator $\mathcal{N}$ on $[0, 1]$ is called:

(i) a negator if it coincides with the Boolean negation on $\{0, 1\}$;
(ii) an involutive negator if $(\forall a \in [0, 1])(\mathcal{N}(\mathcal{N}(a)) = a)$.

The prototype of an involutive negator is the standard negator $\mathcal{N}_s$ defined by $\mathcal{N}_s(a) = 1 - a$.

Definition 2. [7,17,21] An increasing binary operator $\mathcal{C}$ on $[0,1]$ is called:

(i) a conjunctor if it coincides with the Boolean conjunction on $\{0,1\}^2$;
(ii) a t-seminorm if it satisfies $(\forall a \in [0,1])(\mathcal{C}(1,a) = \mathcal{C}(a,1) = a)$;
(iii) a t-norm if it is an associative and commutative t-seminorm.

Definition 3. [7] A binary operator $\mathcal{I}$ on $[0,1]$ with decreasing first partial mappings and increasing second partial maps is called:

(i) an implicator if it coincides with the Boolean implication on $\{0,1\}^2$; any implicator induces a negator $\mathcal{N}_\mathcal{I}$ defined by $\mathcal{N}_\mathcal{I}(a) = \mathcal{I}(a,0)$;
(ii) a border implicator if it satisfies $(\forall b \in [0,1])(\mathcal{I}(0,b) = 1 \wedge \mathcal{I}(1,b) = b)$;
(iii) a model implicator if it is a contrapositive border implicator, i.e.

$$(\forall (a,b) \in [0,1]^2)(\mathcal{I}(a,b) = \mathcal{I}(\mathcal{N}_\mathcal{I}(b), \mathcal{N}_\mathcal{I}(a))),$$

that satisfies the exchange principle:

$$(\forall (a,b,c) \in [0,1]^3)(\mathcal{I}(a,\mathcal{I}(b,c)) = \mathcal{I}(b,\mathcal{I}(a,c))).$$

Example 1. [7] Consider an implicator $\mathcal{I}$ and a negator $\mathcal{N}$. The mapping $\mathcal{C}_{\mathcal{I},\mathcal{N}}$ defined by $\mathcal{C}_{\mathcal{I},\mathcal{N}}(a,b) = \mathcal{N}(\mathcal{I}(a,\mathcal{N}(b)))$ is a conjunctor.

(i) If $\mathcal{I}$ is a border implicator such that $\mathcal{N}_\mathcal{I}$ is involutive, then the conjunctor $\mathcal{C}_{\mathcal{I},\mathcal{N}_\mathcal{I}}$ is a t-seminorm.
(ii) If $\mathcal{I}$ is a model implicator, then the conjunctor $\mathcal{C}_{\mathcal{I},\mathcal{N}_\mathcal{I}}$ is a t-norm. Note that for a model implicator $\mathcal{I}$ the induced negator $\mathcal{N}_\mathcal{I}$ always is involutive.

Example 2. [7] Consider a conjunctor $\mathcal{C}$ and a negator $\mathcal{N}$. The mapping $\mathcal{I}_{\mathcal{C},\mathcal{N}}$ defined by $\mathcal{I}_{\mathcal{C},\mathcal{N}}(a,b) = \mathcal{N}(\mathcal{C}(a,\mathcal{N}(b)))$ is an implicator.

(i) If $\mathcal{C}$ is a seminorm, then the implicator $\mathcal{I}_{\mathcal{C},\mathcal{N}}$ is a border implicator.
(ii) If $\mathcal{C}$ is a t-norm and $\mathcal{N}$ is involutive, then the implicator $\mathcal{I}_{\mathcal{C},\mathcal{N}}$ is a model implicator.

2.2 Fuzzy morphological operations

In this subsection, we recall the definitions of the basic fuzzy morphological operations. Fuzzy morphological operations act on fuzzy objects, i.e. gray-scale images with the unit interval [0,1] as set of possible gray levels. Consider a conjunctor $\mathcal{C}$, an implicator $\mathcal{I}$ and two fuzzy objects A and B.

Definition 4. [8,9] The fuzzy dilation $\mathbf{D}(A,B)$ and fuzzy erosion $\mathbf{E}(A,B)$ of A by B are the fuzzy objects defined by

$$\mathbf{D}(A,B)(y) = \sup_x \mathcal{C}(B(x-y), A(x))$$
$$\mathbf{E}(A,B)(y) = \inf_x \mathcal{I}(B(x-y), A(x)).$$

If the fuzzy structuring element B has a finite support, i.e.

$$\operatorname{supp} B = \{x \mid B(x) > 0\}$$

is a finite set, then the above supremum and infimum are attained and can be replaced by maximum and minimum, tacitly assuming that these are taken over those x for which $B(x-y) > 0$. A similar observation holds when the fuzzy object A and the fuzzy structuring element B have finite ranges, i.e. the sets

$$\operatorname{rng} A = \{A(x) \mid x \in \mathbb{R}^n\}$$

and

$$\operatorname{rng} B = \{B(x) \mid x \in \mathbb{R}^n\}$$

are both finite, meaning that they only use a finite number of gray levels. The latter is trivially fulfilled when both A and B have finite supports.

Definition 5. [8,9] The fuzzy closing $\mathbf{C}(A,B)$ and fuzzy opening $\mathbf{O}(A,B)$ of A by B are the fuzzy objects defined by

$$\begin{aligned}\mathbf{C}(A,B) &= \mathbf{E}(\mathbf{D}(A,B),-B)\\ \mathbf{O}(A,B) &= \mathbf{D}(\mathbf{E}(A,B),-B).\end{aligned}$$

The explicit expressions of the fuzzy closing and fuzzy opening are given by:

$$\begin{aligned}\mathbf{C}(A,B)(y) &= \inf_x \mathcal{I}(B(y-x), \sup_z \mathcal{C}(B(z-x),A(z)))\\ \mathbf{O}(A,B)(y) &= \sup_x \mathcal{C}(B(y-x), \inf_z \mathcal{I}(B(z-x),A(z))).\end{aligned}$$

One easily verifies that for crisp objects A and B the above fuzzy morphological operations coincide with the corresponding binary operations.

2.3 Dual operations

Given an involutive negator $\mathcal{N}$, the $\mathcal{N}$-complement $\operatorname{co}_{\mathcal{N}} A$ of a fuzzy set A is defined by $\operatorname{co}_{\mathcal{N}} A(x) = \mathcal{N}(A(x))$. Two fuzzy morphological operations P and Q are called $\mathcal{N}$-dual if for any two fuzzy objects A and B it holds that $P(A,B) = \operatorname{co}_{\mathcal{N}} Q(\operatorname{co}_{\mathcal{N}} A, B)$.

Proposition 3. [9] *Consider an involutive negator $\mathcal{N}$.*

(i) *The fuzzy dilation and fuzzy erosion are $\mathcal{N}$-dual if and only if $\mathcal{I} = \mathcal{I}_{\mathcal{C},\mathcal{N}}$, or equivalently, $\mathcal{C} = \mathcal{C}_{\mathcal{I},\mathcal{N}}$.*

(ii) *If the fuzzy dilation and fuzzy erosion are $\mathcal{N}$-dual, then also the fuzzy closing and fuzzy opening are $\mathcal{N}$-dual. Conversely, if the fuzzy closing and fuzzy opening are $\mathcal{N}$-dual, $\mathcal{C}$ is a t-seminorm and $\mathcal{I}$ is a border implicator, then $\mathcal{I} = \mathcal{I}_{\mathcal{C},\mathcal{N}}$.*

3 Residual operators of triangular norms

With a t-norm $\mathcal{T}$ we associate two binary operators $\mathcal{L}_\mathcal{T}$ and $\mathcal{I}_\mathcal{T}$, called the residual operators of $\mathcal{T}$, defined by

$$\mathcal{L}_\mathcal{T}(a,b) = \inf\{c \mid c \in [0,1] \wedge \mathcal{T}(a,c) \geq b\}$$
$$\mathcal{I}_\mathcal{T}(a,b) = \sup\{c \mid c \in [0,1] \wedge \mathcal{T}(a,c) \leq b\}.$$

It is well known that the operator $\mathcal{I}_\mathcal{T}$ is a border implicator; it is called the residual implicator of $\mathcal{T}$. The operators $\mathcal{L}_\mathcal{T}$ and $\mathcal{I}_\mathcal{T}$ have shown to be extremely important in the context of fuzzy relational equation solving [5,6,10,11]. We recall two simple results.

Proposition 4. [6] *Consider a t-norm $\mathcal{T}$ and $(a,b) \in [0,1]^2$. If the partial mapping $\mathcal{T}(a,\cdot)$ is left-continuous, then the solution set of the inequality $\mathcal{T}(a,x) \leq b$ in the unknown x is given by*

$$[0, \mathcal{I}_\mathcal{T}(a,b)].$$

Proposition 5. [6] *Consider a t-norm $\mathcal{T}$ and $(a,b) \in [0,1]^2$. If the partial mapping $\mathcal{T}(a,\cdot)$ is right-continuous, then the solution set of the inequality $\mathcal{T}(a,x) \geq b$ in the unknown x is given by*

$$\begin{cases} [\mathcal{L}_\mathcal{T}(a,b), 1] \,, & \text{if } b \leq a \\ \emptyset \,, & \text{else} \,. \end{cases}$$

The above propositions indicate that left- or right-continuity of the partial mappings of a t-norm is an important property. A t-norm is called left-continuous (right-continuous) if all of its partial mappings are left-continuous (right-continuous). Left- and right-continuity can be characterized in various interesting ways, as is recalled next.

Proposition 6. [16] *Consider a t-norm $\mathcal{T}$, then the following statements are equivalent:*

(i) $\mathcal{T}$ *is left-continuous;*
(ii) $(\forall (a,b) \in [0,1]^2)(\mathcal{T}(a, \mathcal{I}_\mathcal{T}(a,b)) \leq b)$;
(iii) $(\forall (a,b,c) \in [0,1]^3)(\mathcal{T}(\mathcal{I}_\mathcal{T}(a,b), \mathcal{I}_\mathcal{T}(b,c)) \leq \mathcal{I}_\mathcal{T}(a,b))$.

The following proposition is the analogon of Proposition 6 for the operator $\mathcal{L}_\mathcal{T}$. The proof of the implications (i)$\Rightarrow$(ii) and (ii)$\Rightarrow$(iii) can be found in [5] in a lattice-theoretic setting; the proofs of the other implications are similar to those in [16].

Proposition 7. *Consider a t-norm $\mathcal{T}$, then the following statements are equivalent:*

(i) $\mathcal{T}$ *is right-continuous;*
(ii) $(\forall(a,b)\in[0,1]^2)(a\geq b\Rightarrow\mathcal{T}(a,\mathcal{L}_\mathcal{T}(a,b))\geq b)$;
(iii) $(\forall(a,b,c)\in[0,1]^3)(a\geq b\geq c\Rightarrow\mathcal{T}(\mathcal{L}_\mathcal{T}(a,b),\mathcal{L}_\mathcal{T}(b,c))\geq\mathcal{L}_\mathcal{T}(a,c))$.

We conclude this section with some advanced properties that will be applied when proving the ordering property and generalized idempotence in fuzzy mathematical morphology.

Proposition 8. *Consider a continuous t-norm $\mathcal{T}$, then it holds that*

$$\mathcal{T}(a,\mathcal{I}_\mathcal{T}(b,c))\geq d$$

$$\mathcal{T}(e,\mathcal{I}_\mathcal{T}(f,b))\geq a$$

jointly imply

$$\mathcal{T}(e,\mathcal{I}_\mathcal{T}(f,c))\geq d,$$

for any $(a,b,c,d,e,f)\in[0,1]^6$.

Proof. Consider $(a,b,c,d,e,f)\in[0,1]^6$ such that both inequalities

$$\mathcal{T}(a,\mathcal{I}_\mathcal{T}(b,c))\geq d$$

and

$$\mathcal{T}(e,\mathcal{I}_\mathcal{T}(f,b))\geq a$$

hold. Proposition 5 then implies that

$$\mathcal{L}_\mathcal{T}(a,d)\leq\mathcal{I}_\mathcal{T}(b,c)$$

and

$$\mathcal{L}_\mathcal{T}(e,a)\leq\mathcal{I}_\mathcal{T}(f,b).$$

In particular, it also follows that $e\geq a\geq d$. The monotonicity of $\mathcal{T}$ then implies that

$$\mathcal{T}(\mathcal{L}_\mathcal{T}(e,a),\mathcal{L}_\mathcal{T}(a,d))\leq\mathcal{T}(\mathcal{I}_\mathcal{T}(f,b),\mathcal{I}_\mathcal{T}(b,c)).$$

Propositions 6 and 7 then lead to

$$\mathcal{L}_\mathcal{T}(e,d)\leq\mathcal{I}_\mathcal{T}(f,c).$$

With Proposition 5 it finally follows that

$$\mathcal{T}(e,\mathcal{I}_\mathcal{T}(f,c))\geq d.\quad\square$$

Proposition 9. *Consider a continuous t-norm $\mathcal{T}$, then it holds that*

$$\mathcal{T}(a,\mathcal{I}_\mathcal{T}(b,c))\geq d$$

$$\mathcal{T}(c,\mathcal{I}_\mathcal{T}(e,f))\leq g$$

$$\mathcal{T}(d,\mathcal{I}_\mathcal{T}(e,f))\geq h$$

jointly imply

$$\mathcal{T}(a,\mathcal{I}_\mathcal{T}(b,g))\geq h,$$

for any $(a,b,c,d,e,f,g,h)\in[0,1]^8$.

Proof. Consider $(a,b,c,d,e,f,g,h) \in [0,1]^8$ such that the inequalities

$$\mathcal{T}(a, \mathcal{I}_\mathcal{T}(b,c)) \geq d,$$

$$\mathcal{T}(c, \mathcal{I}_\mathcal{T}(e,f)) \leq g$$

and

$$\mathcal{T}(d, \mathcal{I}_\mathcal{T}(e,f)) \geq h$$

all hold. Propositions 4 and 5 then imply that

$$\mathcal{L}_\mathcal{T}(a,d) \leq \mathcal{I}_\mathcal{T}(b,c),$$

$$\mathcal{I}_\mathcal{T}(e,f) \leq \mathcal{I}_\mathcal{T}(c,g)$$

and

$$\mathcal{L}_\mathcal{T}(d,h) \leq \mathcal{I}_\mathcal{T}(e,f).$$

In particular, it also follows that $a \geq d \geq h$. Combining the last two inequalities, we obtain that

$$\mathcal{L}_\mathcal{T}(d,h) \leq \mathcal{I}_\mathcal{T}(c,g).$$

Together with the first inequality, the monotonicity of $\mathcal{T}$ then implies that

$$\mathcal{T}(\mathcal{L}_\mathcal{T}(a,d), \mathcal{L}_\mathcal{T}(d,h)) \leq \mathcal{T}(\mathcal{I}_\mathcal{T}(b,c), \mathcal{I}_\mathcal{T}(c,g)).$$

Propositions 6 and 7 then lead to

$$\mathcal{L}_\mathcal{T}(a,h) \leq \mathcal{I}_\mathcal{T}(b,g).$$

With Proposition 5 it finally follows that

$$\mathcal{T}(a, \mathcal{I}_\mathcal{T}(b,g)) \geq h. \quad \square$$

To conclude this section, we list the three most important continuous t-norms and their residual operators. The residual operators of the minimum operator M are given by [5]

$$\mathcal{L}_M(a,b) = \begin{cases} 1 \ , \ \text{if } a < b \\ b \ , \ \text{else} \end{cases} \quad \text{and} \quad \mathcal{I}_M(a,b) = \begin{cases} 1 \ , \ \text{if } a \leq b \\ b \ , \ \text{else} \end{cases},$$

the residual operators of the algebraic product P are given by

$$\mathcal{L}_P(a,b) = \begin{cases} 1 \ , \ \text{if } a < b \\ \dfrac{b}{a} \ , \ \text{if } 0 < b \leq a \\ 0 \ , \ \text{else} \end{cases} \quad \text{and} \quad \mathcal{I}_P(a,b) = \begin{cases} 1 \ , \ \text{if } a \leq b \\ \dfrac{b}{a} \ , \ \text{else} \end{cases},$$

and the residual operators of the Łukasiewicz t-norm W defined by $W(a,b) = \max(a+b-1, 0)$ are given by

$$\mathcal{L}_W(a,b) = \begin{cases} 1 & , \ \text{if } a < b \\ 1 - a + b \ , & \text{if } 0 < b \leq a \\ 0 & , \ \text{else} \end{cases} \quad \text{and} \quad \mathcal{I}_W(a,b) = \min(1 - a + b, 1).$$

4 Fuzzy morphology with triangular norms and residual implicators

The fuzzy morphological model proposed in Section 2 is rather general as it requires only the choice of a conjunctor and an implicator. Due to its generality, it encompasses nearly all existing approaches to fuzzy mathematical morphology. It includes for instance the work of Bandemer and Näther [1], Bloch [2], Bloch and Maître [3,4], De Baets, Kerre and Gupta [12,13], De Baets, Kwasnikowska and Kerre [14], and Sinha and Dougherty [23]. For a detailed discussion, we refer to [8,9], as well as to Chapter 1 (*Classical and Fuzzy Approaches towards Mathematical Morphology*).

From our discussion of the duality of fuzzy morphological operations it should be clear that dependent of the desired properties of the operations in question, different logical operators will have to be chosen. In [9], we have investigated several elementary properties of the basic fuzzy morphological operations and have identified the corresponding conditions on the logical operators; see also Chapter 1 (*Classical and Fuzzy Approaches towards Mathematical Morphology*). From this study, it is clear that for our purposes left-continuous t-norms are the most appropriate conjunctors. For the implicator, we can sometimes choose between the residual implicator and a model implicator. Our preference for the residual implicator will become clear in the following sections.

We briefly recall some of these results. Consider a left-continuous t-norm $\mathcal{T}$ and three fuzzy objects A, B and C, then the following properties hold (for the definition of a continuous Archimedean t-norm, see Section 5):

(i) $\mathbf{D}(A,B) = -\mathbf{D}(B,A)$ and $\mathbf{D}(A,\mathbf{D}(B,C)) = \mathbf{D}(\mathbf{D}(A,B),-C)$;

(ii) if $\mathcal{I} = \mathcal{I}_{\mathcal{T}}$ or $\mathcal{I} = \mathcal{I}_{\mathcal{T},\mathcal{N}}$, with $\mathcal{N}$ an involutive negator:
   - (a) $\mathbf{E}(A,\mathbf{D}(B,C)) = \mathbf{E}(\mathbf{E}(A,B),-C)$
   - (b) $\mathbf{E}(\mathbf{E}(A,B),C) = \mathbf{E}(\mathbf{E}(A,C),B)$;

(iii) if $\mathcal{T}$ is a continuous Archimedean t-norm and $\mathcal{I} = \mathcal{I}_{\mathcal{T}}$, or $\mathcal{T} = M$ and $\mathcal{I} = \mathcal{I}_{M,\mathcal{N}}$, with $\mathcal{N}$ an involutive negator:
   - (a) $\mathbf{D}(A,\mathbf{E}(B,-C)) \subseteq \mathbf{E}(\mathbf{D}(A,B),C)$
   - (b) $\mathbf{D}(\mathbf{E}(A,C),B) \subseteq \mathbf{E}(\mathbf{D}(A,B),C)$
   - (c) $\mathbf{C}(A,-B) \subseteq \mathbf{O}(A,B)$;

(iv) if B contains the origin, i.e. $B(\mathbf{0}) = 1$:
   - (a) $\mathbf{E}(A,B) \subseteq A \subseteq \mathbf{D}(A,B)$
   - (b) $\mathbf{E}(A,-B) \subseteq \mathbf{C}(A,B)$
   - (c) $\mathbf{O}(A,B) \subseteq \mathbf{D}(A,-B)$.

The extensivity of the fuzzy closing, the anti-extensivity of the fuzzy opening and their idempotence are discussed in detail in the following section.

5 Idempotent fuzzy closing and fuzzy opening operations

In this section, we briefly recall the results of our study of the idempotence of the fuzzy closing and fuzzy opening. Classically, this idempotence is a consequence of the extensivity of the binary closing and the anti-extensivity of the binary opening. These properties, simple but powerful, are of paramount importance for both theoretical and practical reasons. Idempotence means that successive applications have no effect after the first application. The following propositions show that it is possible to ensure this idempotence by suitably choosing the underlying fuzzy logical operators. Consider a conjunctor $\mathcal{C}$, an implicator $\mathcal{I}$ and two fuzzy objects A and B.

Proposition 10. [8,9] *If the following property holds*

$$(\forall(a,b) \in [0,1]^2)(\mathcal{I}(a,\mathcal{C}(a,b)) \geq b),$$

then the fuzzy closing is extensive: $A \subseteq \mathbf{C}(A,B)$.

Proposition 11. [8,9] *If the following property holds*

$$(\forall(a,b) \in [0,1]^2)(\mathcal{C}(a,\mathcal{I}(a,b)) \leq b),$$

then the fuzzy opening is anti-extensive: $\mathbf{O}(A,B) \subseteq A$.

Theorem 3. [8,9] *If the following property holds*

$$(\forall(a,b) \in [0,1]^2)(\mathcal{C}(a,\mathcal{I}(a,b)) \leq b \leq \mathcal{I}(a,\mathcal{C}(a,b))),$$

then the fuzzy closing and fuzzy opening are idempotent.

In the t-norm framework, one easily verifies that the condition in Proposition 10 is fulfilled for any t-norm and its residual implicator. For the same choice of logical operators, the condition in Proposition 11 is equivalent to the left-continuity of the t-norm (see Proposition 6). Consequently, the idempotence of the fuzzy closing and fuzzy opening hold when working with a left-continuous t-norm and its residual implicator. Our earlier work was based on a particular t-norm and model implicator, namely $\mathcal{T} = M$ and $\mathcal{I} = \mathcal{I}_{M,\mathcal{N}_s}$. In that case, the extensivity of the fuzzy closing, the anti-extensivity of the fuzzy opening, and the idempotence of the fuzzy closing and fuzzy opening do not hold in general; however, they effectively hold when working with binary structuring elements. More details can be found in [12,13].

We now briefly comment on the simultaneous fulfillment of the idempotence of the fuzzy closing and fuzzy opening and of their duality. To that end, we have to recall some important characterizations of involutive negators and continuous t-norms. The following proposition recalls a well-known characterization of involutive negators in terms of transforms of the standard negator $\mathcal{N}_s$. An order-preserving permutation of the unit interval is called a $[0,1]$-automorphism. Any $[0,1]$-automorphism ϕ is continuous and satisfies the boundary conditions $\phi(0) = 0$ and $\phi(1) = 1$.

Proposition 12. [24] *A* $[0,1] \to [0,1]$*-mapping* $\mathcal{N}$ *is an involutive negator if and only if there exists a* $[0,1]$*-automorphism* ϕ *such that*

$$(\forall a \in [0,1])(\mathcal{N}(a) = \phi^{-1}(1 - \phi(a))).$$

The involutive negator determined by the $[0,1]$-automorphism ϕ is usually denoted $\mathcal{N}_\phi$. It is well known that the minimum operator and Archimedean t-norms play an important role in the class of continuous t-norms [21]. A continuous Archimedean t-norm is a continuous t-norm for which it holds that $(\forall a \in]0,1[)(\mathcal{T}(a,a) < a)$. The class of continuous Archimedean t-norms is subdivided into two disjoint subclasses: the class of strict t-norms (having strictly increasing partial mappings $\mathcal{T}(x,\cdot)$, for all $x > 0$) and the class of nilpotent t-norms, i.e. the non-strict ones. The following proposition recalls a well-known characterization of strict and nilpotent t-norms. The ϕ-transform of a t-norm $\mathcal{T}$, with ϕ a $[0,1]$-automorphism, is the t-norm $\mathcal{T}_\phi$ defined by $\mathcal{T}_\phi(a,b) = \phi^{-1}(\mathcal{T}(\phi(a),\phi(b)))$.

Proposition 13. [21]

(i) *A t-norm* $\mathcal{T}$ *is strict if and only if there exists a* $[0,1]$*-automorphism* ϕ *such that* $\mathcal{T} = P_\phi$.
(ii) *A t-norm* $\mathcal{T}$ *is nilpotent if and only if there exists a* $[0,1]$*-automorphism* ϕ *such that* $\mathcal{T} = W_\phi$.

When working with a t-norm $\mathcal{T}$, Proposition 3 tells that the fuzzy closing and fuzzy opening are $\mathcal{N}$-dual, with $\mathcal{N}$ an involutive negator, if and only if we choose as implicator the model implicator $\mathcal{I}_{\mathcal{T},\mathcal{N}}$. On the other hand, idempotence is fulfilled when choosing the residual implicator $\mathcal{I}_\mathcal{T}$. From Fodor's study of the contrapositivity of implicators [19], it immediately follows that the only *continuous* t-norms for which the model implicator $\mathcal{I}_{\mathcal{T},\mathcal{N}}$ and the residual implicator $\mathcal{I}_\mathcal{T}$ coincide are the nilpotent t-norms; moreover, the t-norm $\mathcal{T}$ and involutive negator $\mathcal{N}$ should be determined by the same $[0,1]$-automorphism ϕ, i.e. $\mathcal{T} = W_\phi$ and $\mathcal{N} = \mathcal{N}_\phi$. Hence, when both duality and idempotence are required, and a continuous t-norm is chosen as conjunctor, we are forced towards the Łukasiewicz t-norm.

6 Open and closed fuzzy objects

6.1 Introduction

As recalled in the previous section, the idempotence of the fuzzy closing and fuzzy opening can be obtained by a suitable choice of the underlying fuzzy logical operators. In this section, we will show that also the ordering property and the generalized idempotence can be safeguarded.

Consider two fuzzy objects A and B. The expressions 'A is B-open' and 'A is B-closed' will be used with the same meaning as in binary morphology.

Proposition 14. *Consider an involutive negator $\mathcal{N}$ and assume that the fuzzy closing $\mathbf{C}$ and fuzzy opening $\mathbf{O}$ are $\mathcal{N}$-dual. Then it holds that A is B-open if and only if $\mathrm{co}_{\mathcal{N}}A$ is B-closed.*

Proof. We will prove for instance the implication from left to right. Assume that A is B-open, i.e. $\mathbf{O}(A, B) = A$. Complementing both sides yields $\mathrm{co}_{\mathcal{N}}\mathbf{O}(A, B) = \mathrm{co}_{\mathcal{N}}A$. Applying duality gives

$$\mathrm{co}_{\mathcal{N}}(\mathrm{co}_{\mathcal{N}}\mathbf{C}(\mathrm{co}_{\mathcal{N}}A, B)) = \mathrm{co}_{\mathcal{N}}A.$$

Since $\mathcal{N}$ is involutive, it follows that $\mathbf{C}(\mathrm{co}_{\mathcal{N}}A, B) = \mathrm{co}_{\mathcal{N}}A$, i.e. $\mathrm{co}_{\mathcal{N}}A$ is B-closed. □

The following two propositions classically follow from the anti-extensivity of the opening and the extensivity of the closing. The proofs in the fuzzy case are identical to the classical proofs (see e.g. [18]).

Proposition 15. *Consider a conjunctor $\mathcal{C}$ and an implicator $\mathcal{I}$ such that the fuzzy opening $\mathbf{O}$ is anti-extensive and the fuzzy closing $\mathbf{C}$ is extensive. Then it holds that A is B-open if and only if there exists a fuzzy object E such that*

$$A = \mathbf{D}(E, -B).$$

Proposition 16. *Consider a conjunctor $\mathcal{C}$ and an implicator $\mathcal{I}$ such that the fuzzy opening $\mathbf{O}$ is anti-extensive and the fuzzy closing $\mathbf{C}$ is extensive. Then it holds that A is B-closed if and only if there exists a fuzzy object E such that*

$$A = \mathbf{E}(E, -B).$$

6.2 The ordering property

In this subsection, we will show that Theorem 1 can be generalized to fuzzy mathematical morphology when working with a continuous t-norm and its residual implicator.

From here on, we will have to require that the fuzzy objects have finite ranges, i.e. that they use only a finite number of gray levels. As mentioned before, this is trivially fulfilled for fuzzy objects with finite supports. From a practical point of view, when working with discretized images, this is of course not a restriction. The following theorem was announced without proof in [8], but only for the minimum operator and the Łukasiewicz t-norm, leaving the general case of a continuous t-norm as an open problem.

Theorem 4. *Consider a continuous t-norm $\mathcal{T}$ and its residual implicator $\mathcal{I}_{\mathcal{T}}$. If A is B-open and $\mathrm{rng}\,A$ and $\mathrm{rng}\,B$ are finite sets, then for any fuzzy object F it holds:*

$$\mathbf{O}(F, A) \subseteq \mathbf{O}(F; B) \subseteq F.$$

Proof. The second inclusion follows from Proposition 11. We will next show the first inclusion. Since A is B-open, it follows in particular that $\mathbf{O}(A,B) \supseteq A$. It then holds for any y that

$$\mathbf{O}(A,B)(y) = \max_x \mathcal{T}(B(y-x), \min_z \mathcal{I}_\mathcal{T}(B(z-x), A(z))) \geq A(y).$$

The increasingness of $\mathcal{T}$ then implies that

$$\mathbf{O}(A,B)(y) = \max_x \min_z \mathcal{T}(B(y-x), \mathcal{I}_\mathcal{T}(B(z-x), A(z))) \geq A(y).$$

This implies that for any y it holds that

$$(\exists x)(\forall z)(\mathcal{T}(B(y-x), \mathcal{I}_\mathcal{T}(B(z-x), A(z))) \geq A(y)) \tag{1}$$

We will now show that $\mathbf{O}(F,A) \subseteq \mathbf{O}(F,B)$. It therefore suffices to show that for any y it holds that

$$(\forall \alpha \in]0,1])(\mathbf{O}(F,A)(y) \geq \alpha \Rightarrow \mathbf{O}(F,B)(y) \geq \alpha).$$

Consider arbitrary y and $\alpha \in]0,1]$ such that $\mathbf{O}(F,A)(y) \geq \alpha$. Similarly as above, it follows that

$$(\exists x_0)(\forall z)(\mathcal{T}(A(y-x_0), \mathcal{I}_\mathcal{T}(A(z-x_0), F(z))) \geq \alpha). \tag{2}$$

Consider such x_0. Applying (1) to $y - x_0$, we obtain

$$(\exists x_1)(\forall z)(\mathcal{T}(B(y-x_0-x_1), \mathcal{I}_\mathcal{T}(B(z-x_1), A(z))) \geq A(y-x_0)). \tag{3}$$

Consider such x_1. We will now show that

$$\mathbf{O}(F,B)(y) = \max_x \mathcal{T}(B(y-x), \min_z \mathcal{I}_\mathcal{T}(B(z-x), F(z))) \geq \alpha.$$

It therefore suffices to show that

$$\mathcal{T}(B(y-x_0-x_1), \min_z \mathcal{I}_\mathcal{T}(B(z-x_0-x_1), F(z))) \geq \alpha,$$

i.e.

$$(\forall z)(\mathcal{T}(B(y-x_0-x_1), \mathcal{I}_\mathcal{T}(B(z-x_0-x_1), F(z))) \geq \alpha).$$

Consider arbitrary z, then applying (3) to $z - x_0$ yields

$$\mathcal{T}(B(y-x_0-x_1), \mathcal{I}_\mathcal{T}(B(z-x_0-x_1), A(z-x_0))) \geq A(y-x_0). \tag{4}$$

Proposition 8 applied to (2) and (4) then implies

$$\mathcal{T}(B(y-x_0-x_1), \mathcal{I}_\mathcal{T}(B(z-x_0-x_1), F(z))) \geq \alpha.$$

This concludes the proof. □

Proposition 17. *Consider an involutive negator $\mathcal{N}$ and assume that the fuzzy closing $\mathbf{C}$ and fuzzy opening $\mathbf{O}$ are $\mathcal{N}$-dual. Let A be B-open. If for any fuzzy object F it holds:*

$$\mathbf{O}(F, A) \subseteq \mathbf{O}(F, B),$$

then for any fuzzy object F it also holds:

$$\mathbf{C}(F, B) \subseteq \mathbf{C}(F, A).$$

Proof. Assume that for any fuzzy object F it holds that $\mathbf{O}(F, A) \subseteq \mathbf{O}(F, B)$. Consider $\mathrm{co}_{\mathcal{N}} F$, then also $\mathbf{O}(\mathrm{co}_{\mathcal{N}} F, A) \subseteq \mathbf{O}(\mathrm{co}_{\mathcal{N}} F, B)$. Complementing both sides yields

$$\mathrm{co}_{\mathcal{N}}(\mathbf{O}(\mathrm{co}_{\mathcal{N}} F, B)) \subseteq \mathrm{co}_{\mathcal{N}}(\mathbf{O}(\mathrm{co}_{\mathcal{N}} F, A)).$$

Applying duality gives $\mathbf{C}(F, B) \subseteq \mathbf{C}(F, A)$. □

The above results indicate that the full ordering property can be obtained in the fuzzy case when working with a continuous t-norm $\mathcal{T}$, its residual implicator $\mathcal{I}_{\mathcal{T}}$ and an involutive negator $\mathcal{N}$ such that $\mathbf{O}$ and $\mathbf{C}$ are $\mathcal{N}$-dual. From our discussion in Section 5, the following result is immediate (see also [8]).

Theorem 5. *Consider a* **nilpotent** *t-norm $\mathcal{T}$ and its residual implicator $\mathcal{I}_{\mathcal{T}}$. If A is B-open and* $\mathrm{rng}\, A$ *and* $\mathrm{rng}\, B$ *are finite sets, then for any fuzzy object F it holds:*

$$\mathbf{O}(F, A) \subseteq \mathbf{O}(F, B) \subseteq F \subseteq \mathbf{C}(F, B) \subseteq \mathbf{C}(F, A).$$

6.3 Generalized idempotence

In a similar way, we have succeeded in generalizing Theorem 2. This result was also announced without proof in [8], for the minimum operator and the Łukasiewicz t-norm, leaving the general case of a continuous t-norm as an open problem.

Theorem 6. *Consider a continuous t-norm $\mathcal{T}$ and its residual implicator $\mathcal{I}_{\mathcal{T}}$. If A is B-open and* $\mathrm{rng}\, A$ *and* $\mathrm{rng}\, B$ *are finite sets, then for any fuzzy object F it holds:*

$$\mathbf{O}(\mathbf{O}(F, B), A) = \mathbf{O}(F, A).$$

Proof. The proof of this theorem is an exact copy of that in the crisp case. We include it for the sake of clarity. Consider a fuzzy object F. The anti-extensivity of the fuzzy opening guarantees that $\mathbf{O}(F, B) \subseteq F$. The increasingness of the fuzzy opening then implies that

$$\mathbf{O}(\mathbf{O}(F, B), A) \subseteq \mathbf{O}(F, A).$$

Since A is B-open, Theorem 4 implies that $\mathbf{O}(F, A) \subseteq \mathbf{O}(F, B)$. The idempotence of the fuzzy opening then implies that

$$\mathbf{O}(F, A) = \mathbf{O}(\mathbf{O}(F, A), A) \subseteq \mathbf{O}(\mathbf{O}(F, B), A).$$

This concludes the proof. □

Theorem 7. *Consider a continuous t-norm $\mathcal{T}$ and its residual implicator $\mathcal{I}_\mathcal{T}$. If A is B-open and* $\operatorname{rng} A$ *and* $\operatorname{rng} B$ *are finite sets, then for any fuzzy object F it holds:*

$$\mathbf{O}(\mathbf{O}(F,A),B) = \mathbf{O}(F,A).$$

Proof. Since for this choice of logical connectives the fuzzy opening is anti-extensive, we only have to show that $\mathbf{O}(\mathbf{O}(F,A),B) \supseteq \mathbf{O}(F,A)$. It therefore suffices to show that for any y it holds that

$$(\forall \alpha \in]0,1])(\mathbf{O}(F,A)(y) \geq \alpha \Rightarrow \mathbf{O}(\mathbf{O}(F,A),B)(y) \geq \alpha).$$

Consider arbitrary y and $\alpha \in]0,1]$ such that $\mathbf{O}(F,A)(y) \geq \alpha$. We can of course make use of result (2) obtained in the proof of Theorem 4.

Now notice that

$$\begin{aligned}\mathbf{O}(F,A)(z) &= \max_x \mathcal{T}(A(z-x), \min_u \mathcal{I}_\mathcal{T}(A(u-x), F(u)))\\ &\geq \mathcal{T}(A(z-x_0), \min_u \mathcal{I}_\mathcal{T}(A(u-x_0), F(u))).\end{aligned}$$

Let u_0 be such that

$$\min_u \mathcal{I}_\mathcal{T}(A(u-x_0), F(u)) = \mathcal{I}_\mathcal{T}(A(u_0-x_0), F(u_0)),$$

then

$$\mathbf{O}(F,A)(z) \geq \mathcal{T}(A(z-x_0), \mathcal{I}_\mathcal{T}(A(u_0-x_0), F(u_0))). \tag{5}$$

We now have to show that $\mathbf{O}(\mathbf{O}(F,A),B)(y) \geq \alpha$, i.e.

$$\max_x \mathcal{T}(B(y-x), \min_z \mathcal{I}_\mathcal{T}(B(z-x), \mathbf{O}(F,A)(z))) \geq \alpha.$$

It therefore suffices to show that

$$(\forall z)(\mathcal{T}(B(y-x_0-x_1), \mathcal{I}_\mathcal{T}(B(z-x_0-x_1), \mathbf{O}(F,A)(z))) \geq \alpha).$$

Applying (2) to $z = u_0$ yields

$$\mathcal{T}(A(y-x_0), \mathcal{I}_\mathcal{T}(A(u_0-x_0), F(u_0))) \geq \alpha. \tag{6}$$

Consider arbitrary z, then applying Proposition 9 to (4), (5) and (6) yields

$$\mathcal{T}(B(y-x_0-x_1), \mathcal{I}_\mathcal{T}(B(z-x_0-x_1), \mathbf{O}(F,A)(z))) \geq \alpha.$$

This concludes the proof. □

Proposition 18. *Consider an involutive negator $\mathcal{N}$ and assume that the fuzzy closing* $\mathbf{C}$ *and fuzzy opening* $\mathbf{O}$ *are $\mathcal{N}$-dual. Let A be B-open. If for any fuzzy object F it holds:*

$$\mathbf{O}(\mathbf{O}(F,B),A) = \mathbf{O}(F,A),$$

then for any fuzzy object F it also holds:

$$\mathbf{C}(\mathbf{C}(F,B),A) = \mathbf{C}(F,A).$$

Proof. Assume that for any fuzzy object F it holds that $\mathbf{O}(\mathbf{O}(F,B),A) = \mathbf{O}(F,A)$. Consider $\mathrm{co}_{\mathcal{N}}F$, then also $\mathbf{O}(\mathbf{O}(\mathrm{co}_{\mathcal{N}}F,B),A) = \mathbf{O}(\mathrm{co}_{\mathcal{N}}F,A)$. Complementing both sides yields

$$\mathrm{co}_{\mathcal{N}}(\mathbf{O}(\mathbf{O}(\mathrm{co}_{\mathcal{N}}F,B),A)) = \mathrm{co}_{\mathcal{N}}(\mathbf{O}(\mathrm{co}_{\mathcal{N}}F,A)).$$

Applying duality gives $\mathbf{C}(\mathbf{C}(F,B),A) = \mathbf{C}(F,A)$. □

Similarly, the following proposition can be shown.

Proposition 19. *Consider an involutive negator $\mathcal{N}$ and assume that the fuzzy closing $\mathbf{C}$ and fuzzy opening $\mathbf{O}$ are $\mathcal{N}$-dual. Let A be B-open. If for any fuzzy object F it holds:*

$$\mathbf{O}(\mathbf{O}(F,A),B) = \mathbf{O}(F,A),$$

then for any fuzzy object F it also holds:

$$\mathbf{C}(\mathbf{C}(F,A),B) = \mathbf{C}(F,A).$$

Theorem 8. *Consider a* **nilpotent** *t-norm $\mathcal{T}$ and its residual implicator $\mathcal{I}_{\mathcal{T}}$. If A is B-open and* $\mathrm{rng}\,A$ *and* $\mathrm{rng}\,B$ *are finite sets, then for any fuzzy object F it holds:*

$$\mathbf{O}(\mathbf{O}(F,B),A) = \mathbf{O}(\mathbf{O}(F,A),B) = \mathbf{O}(F,A)$$
$$\mathbf{C}(\mathbf{C}(F,B),A) = \mathbf{C}(\mathbf{C}(F,A),B) = \mathbf{C}(F,A).$$

The non-trivial results obtained in Theorems 4–8 illustrate the richness of fuzzy mathematical morphology and establish it as a valuable alternative to gray-scale morphology.

References

1. Bandemer H. and Näther W., *"Fuzzy Data Analysis"*, Theory and Decision Library, Series B: Mathematical and statistical methods, Kluwer Academic Publishers, Dordrecht, 1992
2. Bloch I., *Normes et conormes triangulaires: un outil général pour la génération de morphologies mathématiques floues*, Télécom Paris 93D001, 1993
3. Bloch I. and Maître H., *Constructing fuzzy mathematical morphology: alternative ways*, in: "Proceedings of the Second IEEE Conference on Fuzzy Systems" (San Francisco, CA, USA), pp. 1303–1308, 1993
4. Bloch I. and Maître H., *Fuzzy mathematical morphologies: a comparative study*, Pattern Recognition, Vol. 28, pp. 1341–1387, 1995
5. De Baets B., *"Oplossen van vaagrelationele vergelijkingen: een ordetheoretische benadering"*, Ph.D. thesis, University of Gent, 1995 (in Dutch)

6. De Baets B., *An order-theoretic approach to solving sup-$\mathcal{T}$ equations*, in: "Fuzzy Set Theory and Advanced Mathematical Applications (Ruan D., ed.)", Kluwer Academic Publishers, Norwell, pp. 67–87, 1995
7. De Baets B., *Model implicators and their characterization*, in: "Proceedings of the First ICSC International Symposium on Fuzzy Logic (Steele N., ed.)" (Zürich, Switzerland), ICSC Academic Press, pp. A42–A49, 1995
8. De Baets B., *Idempotent closing and opening operations in fuzzy mathematical morphology*, in: "Proceedings of the Joint Third International Symposium on Uncertainty Modeling and Analysis and Annual Conference of the North American Fuzzy Information Processing Society (Ayyub B., ed.)" (College Park, MD, USA), Los Alamitos, IEEE Computer Society Press, pp. 228–233, 1995
9. De Baets B., *Fuzzy morphology: a logical approach*, in: "Uncertainty Analysis in Engineering and the Sciences: Fuzzy Logic, Statistics and Neural Network Approach (Ayyub B. and Gupta M., eds.)", Kluwer Academic Publishers, Norwell, pp. 53–67, 1997
10. De Baets B., *Sup-$\mathcal{T}$ equations: state of the art*, in: "Computational Intelligence: Soft Computing and Fuzzy-Neural Integration with Applications (Kaynak O., Zadeh L., Turksen B. and Rudas I., eds.)", NATO ASI Series F: Computer and Systems Sciences, Vol. 162, Springer Verlag, pp. 80–93, 1998
11. De Baets B. and Kerre E., *A primer on solving fuzzy relational equations on the unit interval*, Int. J. Uncertainty, Fuzziness and Knowledge-Based Systems, Vol. 2, pp. 205–225, 1994
12. De Baets B., Kerre E. and Gupta M., *The fundamentals of fuzzy mathematical morphology. Part 1: Basic concepts*, Int. J. General Systems, Vol. 23, pp. 155–171, 1994
13. De Baets B., Kerre E. and Gupta M., *The fundamentals of fuzzy mathematical morphology. Part 2: Idempotence, convexity and decomposition*, Int. J. General Systems, Vol. 23, pp. 307–322, 1995
14. De Baets B., Kwasnikowska N. and Kerre E., *Fuzzy morphology based on conjunctive uninorms*, in: "Proceedings of the Seventh International Fuzzy Systems Association Congress" (Prague, Czech Republic), Vol. I, pp. 215–220, 1997
15. De Baets B. and Mesiar R., *Residual implicators of continuous t-norms*, in: "Proceedings of the Fourth European Congress on Intelligent Techniques and Soft Computing (Zimmermann H.-J., ed.)" (Aachen, Germany), ELITE, Vol. 1, pp. 27–31, 1996
16. De Baets B. and Mesiar R., *Metrics and $\mathcal{T}$-equalities*, Journal of Mathematical Analysis and Applications, submitted
17. De Cooman G. and Kerre E., *Order norms on bounded partially ordered sets*, The Journal of Fuzzy Mathematics, Vol. 2, pp. 281–310, 1994
18. Dougherty E. and Giardina C., *"Image Processing - Continuous to Discrete, Volume 1"*, Prentice-Hall, 1987
19. Fodor J., *Contrapositive symmetry of fuzzy implications* Fuzzy Sets and Systems, Vol. 69, pp. 141–156, 1995
20. Haralick R., Sternberg S. and Zhuang X., *Image analysis using mathematical morphology*, IEEE Transactions on Pattern Analysis and Machine Intelligence, Vol. 9, pp. 532–550, 1987
21. Schweizer B. and Sklar A., *Associative functions and abstract semi-groups*, Publ. Math. Debrecen, Vol. 10, pp. 69–84, 1963

22. Serra J., *"Image Analysis and Mathematical Morphology"*, Academic Press, London, 1982
23. Sinha D. and Dougherty E., *Fuzzification of set inclusion: theory and applications*, Fuzzy Sets and Systems, Vol. 55, pp. 15–42, 1993
24. Trillas E., *Sobre funciones de negación en la teoriá de conjuntos diffusos*, Stochastica, Vol. 3, pp. 47–59, 1979

Chapter 3

Fuzzy Mathematical Morphology Based on Fuzzy Inclusion

Edward R. Dougherty[1] and Antony T. Popov[2]

[1] Texas A&M University, Department of Electrical Engineering
College Station, Texas 77843-3128, USA
email: edward@ee.tamu.edu

[2] St. Kliment Ohridski University of Sofia
Faculty of Mathematics and Informatics
5 J. Bourchier Blvd., BG-1164 Sofia, Bulgaria
email: atpopov@fmi.uni-sofia.bg

Summary. Fuzzy mathematical morphology has been developed to soften the classical binary morphology so as to make the operators less sensitive to image imprecision. It can also be viewed simply as an alternative gray-scale morphological theory. This chapter discusses the manner in which fuzzy morphologies result from the fuzzification of subsethood by using inclusion indicators. There are a number of axioms that an inclusion indicator should satisfy to give an operational structure that extends the basic propositions of the classical morphological algebra. Indicators that do not satisfy all of these axioms may still be useful, albeit, at the cost of invalidating basic properties typically associated with morphological operators. This chapter describes the structure of inclusion-indicator fuzzy morphology, describes various indicators that have appeared in the literature, explains the manner in which binary morphological algorithms lift to fuzzy algorithms, provides some basic representation theorems for fuzzy morphological operators, and shows how one can define approximate convexity in this context.

1 Introduction

In real vision systems, there is inherent imprecision in the spatial and intensity characterization of an image. At low levels of image representation, there are effects of noise in sensory transduction and of sampling frequency. At higher levels of image representation, there is more general imprecision related to the specifications of image quality. The use of fuzzy set theory in imaging is one way to model imprecision, and a fuzzy approach leads naturally to fuzzy generalization of the morphological operations commonly used in image processing and pattern recognition. The most primitive operation of mathematical morphology is binary erosion, ε_B, by a fixed structuring element (set) B. Applied to an input image S (subset of the d-dimensional Euclidean space $\mathbb{R}^d$), erosion yields the output $\varepsilon_B(S) = \{z | \tau_z(B) \subseteq S\}$, where $\tau_z(B)$ is the translation of B by z in $\mathbb{R}^d$. If S and B are crisp sets, then the output is crisp. Letting μ_S denote the membership function of S, $\mu_{\varepsilon_B(S)}(z) = 1$ if $\mu_{\tau_z(B)} \leq \mu_S$ (i.e. if $\mu_{\tau_z(B)}(z) \leq \mu_S(z)$ for all $z \in \mathbb{R}^d$) and $\mu_{\varepsilon_B(S)}(z) = 0$ otherwise. Extension of the definition to fuzzy sets (input image and structuring element) only requires interpreting the definition under the condition that $0 \leq \mu_{\tau_z(B)}(z), \mu_S(z) \leq 1$ rather than $\mu_{\tau_z(B)}(z), \mu_S(z) \in \{0,1\}$ ($z \in \mathbb{R}^d$). Under this extension, erosion is a binary operator on fuzzy sets. The "decision" as to whether $\tau_z(B)$ is a fuzzy subset of S is crisp: it is or is not a fuzzy subset.

Rather than making a binary statement as to whether $\tau_z(B)$ is a subset of S, suppose we wish to consider a statement of the form, "$\tau_z(B)$ is approximately a subset of S". We now have a question of fuzzy subsethood. This kind of fuzzy fitting is appropriate to image processing, in which pattern recognition often involves an approximate match, not an exact match. It is natural to consider the following sort of definition: if $\mu_{\tau_z(B)} \leq \mu_S$ then $\mu_{\varepsilon_B(S)}(z) = 1$, but if $\mu_{\tau_z(B)} \not\leq \mu_S$, then $0 \leq \mu_{\varepsilon_B(S)}(z) \leq 1$, where the closer the fit, the closer $\mu_{\varepsilon_B(S)}(z)$ is to 1. A candidate for this kind of fuzzy erosion is given by the definition

$$\mu_{\varepsilon_B(S)}(z) = \inf_{x \in \mathbb{R}^d} \min\left[1,\, 1 + \mu_S(x) - \mu_{\tau_z(B)}(x)\right]. \tag{1}$$

If $\mu_{\tau_z(B)} \leq \mu_S$ then $\mu_{\varepsilon_B(S)}(z) = 1$; however, if $\mu_{\tau_z(B)} \not\leq \mu_S$, then $\mu_{\varepsilon_B(S)}(z)$ is lowered from 1 (full fitting) by the greatest amount by which $\mu_{\tau_z(B)}$ exceeds μ_S. In Eq. (1), fuzziness has been introduced into the erosion operation itself by defining erosion via a particular inclusion indicator, namely the inclusion indicator I^* (see Section 3) [30]. More generally, it is natural to characterize fuzzy mathematical morphologies via inclusion indicators that model our intuitive notions concerning approximate subsethood. There are other approaches to fuzzifying mathematical morphology [19,4]; also refer to Chapter 1 (*Classical and Fuzzy Approaches towards Mathematical Morphology*) for an extensive overview. However, in this chapter we focus on the inclusion-indicator method [31].

2 Binary mathematical morphology and the abstract lattice theory

Mathematical morphology has been created as an approach in the field of image processing for extraction of geometric information from an image. The basic morphological operations — erosions and dilations — are introduced by Matheron [23] and Serra [27] to examine the structure of binary images which can be represented mathematically as sets. Dilations and erosions over sets are represented as Minkowski addition and subtraction by means of a fixed set, usually called a structuring element. Morphological operations have been extended to gray-scale images modeled mathematically as functions.

Serra [28] and Heijmans[17] have shown that morphological operations can be extended to any complete lattice. Another intuitive clear extension of the morphological operations to gray-scale images is by using fuzzy set theory [31]. In this work we show how the fuzzy approach matches the lattice framework.

A set $\mathcal{L}$ with a partial ordering "$\leq$" is called a *complete lattice* if every subset $\mathcal{H} \subseteq \mathcal{L}$ has a supremum (least upper bound) and infimum (greatest lower bound). The supremum and infimum operations are denoted respectively by $\bigvee \mathcal{H}$ and $\bigwedge \mathcal{H}$. The supremum of the whole lattice shall be denoted by I and infimum by O. A comprehensive discussion of the theory of morphological operations on complete lattices can be found in [17]. Let us consider the family of lattice operators $\mathcal{L}^* = \{\varphi | \varphi : \mathcal{L} \mapsto \mathcal{L}\}$. The ordering in $\mathcal{L}$ induces an ordering in $\mathcal{L}^*$, i.e. we say that $\varphi \leq \psi$ if $\varphi(X) \leq \psi(X)$ for every $X \in \mathcal{L}$. In a similar way we can define supremum and infimum operations in $\mathcal{L}^*$:

$$\left(\bigvee_i \varphi_i\right)(X) = \bigvee_i \varphi_i(X) \qquad \left(\bigwedge_i \varphi_i\right)(X) = \bigwedge_i \varphi_i(X). \tag{2}$$

Therefore the family of lattice operators has also the structure of a complete lattice.

An operator $\varphi : \mathcal{L} \mapsto \mathcal{M}$, where $\mathcal{L}$ and $\mathcal{M}$ are complete lattices, is called *dilation* if it distributes over arbitrary suprema:

$$\varphi(\textstyle\bigvee_{i\in I} X_i) = \textstyle\bigvee_{i\in I} \varphi(X_i).$$

The operator $\varphi : \mathcal{L} \mapsto \mathcal{M}$, where $\mathcal{L}$ and $\mathcal{M}$ are complete lattices, is *erosion* if it distributes over arbitrary infima:

$$\varphi(\textstyle\bigwedge_{i\in I} X_i) = \textstyle\bigwedge_{i\in I} \varphi(X_i).$$

Erosions and dilations are increasing operations, i.e. $X \leq X'$ implies $\varphi(X) \leq \varphi(X')$.

An operator $\phi \in \mathcal{L}^*$ is called a *closing* if it is increasing, idempotent ($\phi^2 = \phi$) and extensive ($\phi(X) \geq X$). An operator $\gamma \in \mathcal{L}^*$ is called an *opening* if it is increasing, idempotent and anti-extensive ($\gamma(X) \leq X$) [17].

A pair of operators (ε, δ) between two lattices, $\varepsilon : \mathcal{M} \mapsto \mathcal{L}$ and $\delta : \mathcal{L} \mapsto \mathcal{M}$ is called an *adjunction* if for every two elements $X \in \mathcal{L}$ and $Y \in \mathcal{M}$ it follows that

$$\delta(X) \leq Y \iff X \leq \varepsilon(Y).$$

In [17] it is proved that if (ε, δ) is an adjunction then ε is erosion and δ is dilation. In other hand, every dilation $\delta : \mathcal{L} \mapsto \mathcal{M}$ has a unique adjoint erosion $\varepsilon : \mathcal{M} \mapsto \mathcal{L}$, and vice-versa. If (ε, δ) is an adjunction, then the composition $\phi = \varepsilon\delta$ is a closing in $\mathcal{L}$, and the composition $\gamma = \delta\varepsilon$ is an opening in $\mathcal{M}$. The following two propositions are proved in [17] :

- If $\{(\varepsilon_i, \delta_i) | i \in I\}$ is a set of adjunctions, then $(\bigwedge_i \varepsilon_i, \bigvee_i \delta_i)$ is an adjunction.
- If $(\varepsilon_1, \delta_1)$ and $(\varepsilon_2, \delta_2)$ are adjunctions, where $\delta_1 : \mathcal{L} \mapsto \mathcal{M}$, $\delta_2 : \mathcal{M} \mapsto \mathcal{N}$, $\varepsilon_1 : \mathcal{M} \mapsto \mathcal{L}$ and $\varepsilon_2 : \mathcal{N} \mapsto \mathcal{M}$, then $(\varepsilon_1\varepsilon_2, \delta_2\delta_1)$ is an adjunction between the lattices $\mathcal{L}$ and $\mathcal{N}$.

Let us consider that $\mathcal{L} = \mathcal{M}$. Consider an abelian (i.e. commutative) group T of automorphisms of $\mathcal{L}$. Let there exist a supremum generating subset $l \subseteq \mathcal{L}$ such that every element of $\mathcal{L}$ can be represented as a supremum of elements from l, and let T act transitively over l. The transitivity means that for every two elements a and b from l there exists a (unique) transformation $\tau \in T$ such that $\tau(a) = b$. The lattice properties guarantee the uniqueness of τ (see [17]).

Let us fix an origin $o \in l$ and let $\tau_h \in T$ be the unique automorphism mapping o into h. Let B be an arbitrary element of the lattice $\mathcal{L}$, and $l(B) = \{b \in l \mid b \leq B\}$ be the supremum-generating set of B. Then the operations

$$\delta_B = \bigvee_{b \in l(B)} \tau_b \quad \text{and} \quad \varepsilon_B = \bigwedge_{b \in l(B)} \tau_b^{-1} \tag{3}$$

form an adjunction [17]. The operators δ_B and ε_B are T-invariant (which means that these operators commute with every $\tau \in T$: $\delta_B\tau = \tau\delta_B$ and $\varepsilon_B\tau = \tau\varepsilon_B$), and they are called *dilation and erosion by the structuring element* B.

As an example, let us consider the lattice $\mathcal{L}$ with elements the subsets of a linear space E (for instance the d-dimensional Euclidean vector space $\mathbb{R}^d$ or the space of integer vectors of length d, $\mathbb{Z}^d$), i.e. $\mathcal{L} = \mathcal{P}(E)$. Here and henceforth, by $\mathcal{P}(X)$ we denote the family of all subsets of the set X, referred to as the power set of X.

The supremum operation in $\mathcal{L}$ is the union, and infimum is the intersection operation. Let the group of automorphisms be the group of translations $\{\tau_b \,|\, b \in E\}$, with $\tau_b(A) = A_b = \{x \,|\, x = a + b, a \in A\}$. Then $\delta_A(B) = \delta_B(A) = A \oplus B$ and $\varepsilon_B(A) = A \ominus B$. Here $A \oplus B$ is the Minkowski addition and $A \ominus B$ is the Minkowski subtraction:

$$A \oplus B = \{a + b \mid a \in A, b \in B\} = \bigcup_{b \in B} \tau_b(A), \tag{4}$$

$$A \ominus B = \{z \,|\, \tau_z(B) \subseteq A\} = \bigcap_{b \in B} \tau_{-b}(A). \tag{5}$$

If $0 \in B$ then

$$A \ominus B \subseteq A \subseteq A \oplus B. \tag{6}$$

The closing and opening of X by the structuring element B are defined as

$$\phi_B(X) = (X \oplus B) \ominus B, \tag{7}$$

$$\gamma_B(X) = (X \ominus B) \oplus B. \tag{8}$$

Let denote by X^c the complement of the set X, i.e. $X^c = E \setminus X$. Then the following simple equalities hold [27] :

$$(A \oplus B)^c = A^c \ominus (-B), \tag{9}$$

$$\phi_B(A)^c = \gamma_{(-B)}(A^c), \tag{10}$$

where by $-B$ we denote the centrally symmetric set of B, $-B = \{-b | b \in B\}$. Therefore opening and closing operations can be represented as follows:

$$\gamma_B(X) = \bigcup \{\tau_h(B) \,|h \in E \text{ and } \tau_h(B) \subseteq X\}, \tag{11}$$

$$\phi_B(X) = \{k \in E |\, h \in \tau_k(B) \Rightarrow \tau_h(-B) \cap X \neq \emptyset\}.$$

These operations are usually referred to as *classical* or *binary morphological operations*, because they apply to binary images which could be treated mathematically as sets [27].

There are also some useful operations, which can be expressed by the operations given above. Let B be an isotropic element – for instance 3×3 square in the digital case – or any convex centrally symmetric compact set with nonempty interior in the continuous case (recall that a set B in the continuous space $\mathbb{R}^d$ is said to be convex if for each of its pair of points the line segment joining these points also belongs to B). Then we can define the *morphological gradient*

$$\nabla_B(X) = \delta_B(X) \setminus \varepsilon_B(X) \tag{12}$$

It locates the edges of the object X. Another very useful operation is the hit-or-miss transform [27]. It is determined by a pair of structuring elements with empty intersection:

$$\pi_{A,B}(X) = \{h \in E \,|\tau_h(A) \subseteq X \text{ and } \tau_h(B) \subseteq X^c\}. \tag{13}$$

This operation is very well suited for locating points inside an object with certain local geometric properties, for instance finding the place of a given letter in text. More generally, this operation forms the primary building block for translation-invariant mappings and is used extensively for pattern matching.

A key application of morphological image processing is the restoration of degraded images. Morphological operators have proved to be very useful for this purpose [17,27,7]. Sometimes the operators can be designed heuristically, whereas for complicated image-noise models satisfactory performance often requires automatic design [21,13]. Openings and closings have proven to be very useful in solving certain classes of problems, in particular, when noise components have been randomly placed into the image background to form clutter or when noise holes have been subtracted from the foreground. In particular, *alternating sequential filters,* which are sequences of openings and closings with increasing structuring elements, have provided a useful class of filters for this purpose [29], as have granulometric filters [15].

3 Fuzzy morphological operations based on inclusion indicators

3.1 Basic notions and inclusion indicators

Consider the set $\mathcal{U}$ called the universal set. A fuzzy subset A of the universal set $\mathcal{U}$ can be considered as a function $\mu_A : \mathcal{U} \mapsto [0,1]$, called the membership function of A. $\mu_A(x)$ is called the degree of membership of the point x to the set A.

An ordinary subset of $\mathcal{U}$, sometimes called a crisp set, can be considered as a particular case of a fuzzy set with membership function which maps into $\{0,1\}$. This definition leads to two possible interpretations:

- in image representation the value of the membership function $\mu_A(x)$ at a point x may be interpreted as the gray level value associated with that point of the image plane,
- in pattern recognition, the value $0 \leq \mu_A(x) \leq 1$ gives the degree that the point x is in the foreground of an image.

The usual set-theoretical relations and operations generalize naturally to fuzzy sets: $\subseteq$ becomes $\leq$, $\cup$ and $\cap$ become sup and inf, and the complement of A is the set A^c with membership function $\mu_{A^c}(x) = 1 - \mu_A(x)$ for all $x \in \mathcal{U}$. The empty fuzzy set $\emptyset$ has as its membership function the constant 0, and the universal set $\mathcal{U}$ is regarded as a fuzzy set with membership function the constant 1. But there are two possible fuzzy generalizations of set subtraction:

$$\mu_{A\setminus B}(x) = \min\left(\mu_A(x), 1 - \mu_B(x)\right),$$
$$\mu_{A-B}(x) = \max\left(0, \mu_A(x) - \mu_B(x)\right).$$

In general, the algorithms employing the first definition ('\' operation) are more robust with respect to the usage of fuzzy morphological operations [33] when the fuzzy gradient is applied to a gray-scale image. Therefore we shall use '\' as the fuzzy set difference.

Let us now suppose that the universal set $\mathcal{U}$ is $\mathbb{R}^d$ or $\mathbb{Z}^d$. Then the following definitions are suggested:

- The translate of a set X by a vector a is the set $\tau_a(X)$ such that $\mu_{\tau_a(X)}(y) = \mu_X(y-a)$.
- The symmetric set to X is the set $-X$ such that $\mu_{-X}(y) = \mu_X(-y)$.
- The homothetic (spatially scaled) kX is the set possessing membership function

$$\mu_{kX}(x) = \begin{cases} \mu_X\left(\frac{1}{k}x\right) & k \neq 0, \\ 0 & k = 0,\, x \neq 0, \\ 1 & k = 0,\, x = 0 \end{cases} \tag{14}$$

- Let $0 < \alpha \leq 1$. An α-cut of the set X (denoted by $[X]_\alpha$) is the set of points x for which $\mu_X(x) \geq \alpha$.

There is a one-to-one correspondence between a gray-scale image (a fuzzy set) and the collection of its α-cuts. It is evident that if $k \neq 0$ then $x \in [A]_\alpha$ if and only if $kx \in [kA]_\alpha$, and therefore $[kA]_\alpha = k\left([A]_\alpha\right)$. Also, for any two fuzzy sets A and B, $A \subseteq B$ in the fuzzy sense if and only if $[A]_\alpha \subseteq [B]_\alpha$ in the crisp sense for all $\alpha \in (0, 1]$.

The primitive morphological operation of erosion is based on the subset relation, and our approach to fuzzy morphology is based on fuzzification of subsethood [31]. This is accomplished by means of an *inclusion indicator* (also called an *inclusion grade operator*) that quantifies the degree of subsethood. An inclusion indicator is a $[0, 1]$-valued mapping I defined on pairs (A, B) of fuzzy sets. Axioms need to be postulated for the indicator so that the resulting fuzzy subset relation has properties that are suitable to the development of morphological algebra.

Definition 1. A morphological inclusion indicator is any two-argument function mapping a couple of fuzzy sets into the interval $[0, 1]$ satisfying the following 9 properties :

$A1$. $I(A, B) = 1$ if and only if $A \subseteq B$.
$A2$. $I(A, B) = 0$ if and only if $\{x : \mu_A(x) = 1\} \cap \{x : \mu_B(x) = 0\} \neq \emptyset$.
$A3$. From $B \subseteq C$ it follows that $I(A, B) \leq I(A, C)$.
$A4$. From $B \subseteq C$ it follows that $I(C, A) \leq I(B, A)$.
$A5$. $I(A, B) = I(\tau_x(A), \tau_x(B))$ for all x, $I(A, B) = I(-A, -B)$.
$A6$. $I(A, B) = I(B^c, A^c)$.
$A7$. $I(\bigcup_i B_i, A) = \inf_i I(B_i, A)$.
$A8$. $I(A, \bigcap_i B_i) = \inf_i I(A, B_i)$.
$A9$. $I(A, \bigcup_i B_i) \geq \sup_i I(A, B_i)$.

The first axiom sometimes is found to be too restrictive, it is not satisfied by some of the indicators in use as mentioned below, and therefore sometimes it is omitted (see for instance [25]). Axiom A2 means that for A to be classified as a fuzzy subset of B, all elements that definitely belong to A must also belong to B with non-zero uncertainty. A3 and A4 show the evident conditions that the indicator must be non-decreasing in the second argument, and non-increasing in the first argument. For crisp sets we know that inclusion is invariant under symmetry and any kind of rigid motion. Here we state in A5 the same property for the fuzzy sets. However, since we are working mainly with translation-invariant operations, only the invariance under translations and symmetry is suggested. A6 gives the evident relation between complement and set inclusion. It is clear that if the sets B_i are subsets of A (in Zadeh's sense) then so is their union $\bigcup_i B_i$; therefore we suggest A7. The reasons for introducing A8 are similar. If A is a subset of B and C, then it must be a subset of $B \cup C$. However, A can be a subset of $B \cup C$ without being a subset of either B and C. The same property holds when we have a union of more than two sets. So, this is the reason A9 to be included in the list of the indicator properties.

It is also easy to see that the upper nine axioms are not independent. For instance A5 can be deduced from A3 and A6, and A7 can be deduced from A6 and A8.

It is clear that given an inclusion indicator I then the function $[I(\cdot,\cdot)]^n$, where n is a fixed positive number, is an inclusion indicator too. If $n \geq 1$ the new indicator represents a weaker fuzzy relation. If n is less than one, then the new indicator is stronger (see [35]).

3.2 Erosion and dilation based on inclusion indicators

Following the works [31] and [32], given an indicator I and a fuzzy set A, we may define *fuzzy erosion* and *fuzzy dilation* operations $\mathcal{E}(\cdot, B)$ and $\mathcal{D}(\cdot, B)$ by

$$\mu_{\mathcal{E}(A,B)}(x) = I\left(\tau_x(B), A\right), \tag{15}$$

$$\mathcal{D}(A,B) = \mathcal{E}(A^c, -B)^c. \tag{16}$$

Note that for the fuzzy operation we write $\mathcal{D}(A,B)$ instead of $\delta_B(A)$, and $\mathcal{E}(A,B)$ instead of $\varepsilon_B(A)$ because, as we shall see later, these two operations may not form an adjunction, but anyway $\mathcal{D}(\cdot,B)$ is always a dilation and $\mathcal{E}(\cdot,B)$ an erosion. In the event that A and B are crisp sets, these fuzzy definitions reduce to the original definitions of binary morphology.

Various properties of fuzzy erosion and dilation can be derived from the axioms characterizing acceptable inclusion indicators [32]:

- (Commutativity): $\mathcal{D}(A,B) = \mathcal{D}(B,A)$.
- (Increasingness): If A is a fuzzy subset of B, then $\mathcal{E}(A,C) \subseteq \mathcal{E}(B,C)$ and $\mathcal{D}(A,C) \subseteq \mathcal{D}(B,C)$.
- (Translation invariance): $\mathcal{E}(\tau_x(A),B) = \tau_x[\mathcal{E}(A,B)]$ and $\mathcal{D}(\tau_x(A),B) = \tau_x[\mathcal{D}(A,B)]$.

For an extensive overview of the properties of fuzzy morphological operations we refer to Chapter 1 (*Classical and Fuzzy Approaches towards Mathematical Morphology*).

3.3 The indicator I_λ

Let us first consider the indicator for fuzzified set inclusion defined as

$$I_\lambda(A,B) = \inf_{x\in\mathcal{U}} \min[1, \lambda(\mu_A(x)) + \lambda(1-\mu_B(x))], \tag{17}$$

where $\lambda : [0,1] \mapsto [0,1]$. I_λ satisfies the axioms for a morphological inclusion indicator if and only if λ satisfies the following five properties [31]:

P1. λ is nonincreasing;
P2. $\lambda(0) = 1$;
P3. The equation $\lambda(x) = 0$ has a single solution;
P4. For all $\alpha \in [0.5, 1]$, the equation $\lambda(x) = \alpha$ has a single solution;
P5. For all x, $\lambda(x) + \lambda(1-x) \geq 1$.

Note that from P5 it follows immediately that, if $A \subseteq B$, then $I_\lambda(A, B) = 1$, but in general it is not true that the condition $I_\lambda(A, B) = 1$ leads to $A \subseteq B$. The most studied of the indicators is I_λ defined by $\lambda(x) = 1 - x$, which we will denote as I^*.

The following three families of functions give a variety of functions to choose from:

$$\lambda(x) = 1 - x^n \,, \; n \geq 1 \tag{18}$$

$$\lambda(x) = \frac{1-x}{1+nx} \,, \; 0 \geq n > -1 \tag{19}$$

$$\lambda(x) = \frac{1}{1+x^n} - \frac{x}{2} \,, \; n > \frac{\ln 3}{\ln 2} = 1.5849\ldots . \tag{20}$$

Using 15) and (16), we find that the respective erosion and dilation are:

$$\mu_{\mathcal{E}(A,B)}(x) = \inf_{z \in \mathcal{U}} \min[1, \lambda(\mu_B(z-x)) + \lambda(1 - \mu_A(z))], \tag{21}$$

$$\mu_{\mathcal{D}(A,B)}(x) = \sup_{z \in \mathcal{U}} \max[0, 1 - \lambda(\mu_B(x-z)) - \lambda(\mu_A(z))]. \tag{22}$$

Owing to their definition in terms of an indicator function, this erosion and dilation satisfy certain properties that are not derivable from the axioms alone. In particular, they possess fitting characterizations that extend the classical fitting characterizations of classical binary morphology [30–32,4].

A fundamental problem concerns the construction of λ functions satisfying P1 through P5. Let us first consider functions $\lambda : [0,1] \mapsto [0,1]$ of the form

$$\lambda(x) = \int_0^{1-x} f(t)dt \,, \tag{23}$$

where f is a nonnegative integrable function on $[0,1]$ possessing L_1-norm $\|f\|_1 = 1$. λ, which is absolutely continuous, satisfies properties P1 through P5 if and only if

(1) f is non-zero a.e. in neighborhoods of $x = 1$ and $x = 0$;
(2) for all $p \in [0,1)$,

$$\int_0^p f(t)dt \geq \int_{1-p}^1 f(t)dt; \tag{24}$$

and (3) if $f(t) = 0$ a.e. on $[p,q]$ with $p < q$, then

$$\int_0^p f(t)dt < \int_q^1 f(t)dt; \tag{25}$$

[31]. Note that (24) holds for all strictly decreasing f. A more general family of λ functions can be constructed by considering a positive Borel measure ν on $[0,1)$ for which $\nu([0,1)) = 1$ and defining $\lambda(x) = \nu([0, 1-x))$. Define the

inverse set $K_\nu = \{x \mid \nu([x,1)) \leq 0.5\}$. Then λ satisfies conditions P1 through P5 if and only if

(1) there does not exist a relatively compact subset $K \subset [0,1)$ such that $0 \notin K$ and ν is concentrated on K;

(2) there does not exist a nonempty open subset $U \subset K_\nu$ such that ν is concentrated on $[0,1) \setminus U$; and

(3) $\nu([0,x)) \geq \nu([1-x,1))$ [31]. If the three conditions are satisfied, then we will say that ν is *I_λ-inducing.*

We now state a theorem that provides a complete characterization of λ functions that are continuous from the right by employing the Lebesgue decomposition (see [31]):

Theorem 1. A function λ that is continuous from the right satisfies properties P1 through P5 if and only if it is of the form

$$\lambda(x) = \lambda_s(x) + \int_0^{1-x} f(t)dt$$

where

1. f is a nonnegative integrable funciton on $[0,1]$ such that $\|f\|_1 \leq 1$.
2. λ_s, the singular part of λ, is nonincreasing, possesses zero derivative a.e., and vanishes identically if and only if λ is absolutely continuous.
3. $\lambda_s(1) = 0$, $\lambda_s(0) = 1 - \|f\|_1$.
4. The Borel measure ν generated by $\nu([x,y)) = \lambda(1-y) - \lambda(1-x)$ is I_λ-inducing.

3.4 The indicator I_*

Let us consider the function

$$I_*(A,B) = \inf_{x \in \mathcal{U}} \max[\mu_B(x), 1 - \mu_A(x)], \tag{26}$$

It satisfies axioms A2 through A9. As for axiom A1, if $I_*(A,B) = 1$, then $A \subseteq B$. But it may happen that $A \subset B$ while $I_*(A,B) < 1$.

For the indicator I_* it is easy to show that dilation and erosion with respect to I_* have the form of the operations originally proposed by Werman and Peleg [34]:

$$\mu_{\mathcal{D}(B,A)}(x) = \sup_b \min(\mu_A(b), \mu_B(x-b)), \tag{27}$$

$$\mu_{\mathcal{E}(B,A)}(x) = \inf_b \max(\mu_B(b), 1 - \mu_A(b-x)), \tag{28}$$

Hence, we can derive a simple representation of the dilation of Werman and Peleg:

$$\mu_{\mathcal{D}(B,A)}(x) = \sup\{\alpha \mid x \in [A]_\alpha \oplus [B]_\alpha\}, \tag{29}$$

where $\oplus$ is the standard Minkowski addition in the crisp d-dimensional continuous or discrete space discussed in Section 2. Henceforth we shall write $A \oplus B$ instead of $\mathcal{D}(A, B)$ or $\mathcal{D}(B, A)$ when the dilation is taken with respect to I_*. Note that a similar property for the fuzzy erosion and crisp Minkowski subtraction operation does not exist.

Definition 2. A function $F : \mathbb{R}^d \mapsto \mathbb{R}$ is called *upper semicontinuous (u.s.c.)* in $x \in \mathbb{R}^d$ if for any $t \in \mathbb{R}$ such that $t > F(x)$ there exists a neighborhood $B_r(x)$ such that $t > F(y)$ for every point $y \in B_r(x)$.

It is a well known result from mathematical analysis that if $f_i : \mathbb{R}^d \mapsto [0, 1]$ are u.s.c. functions for $i \in I$, then $\inf_i f_i$ is also upper semicontinuous. Here and henceforth the domain $\{x \in \mathcal{U} : f(x) \neq 0\}$ will be referred to as support of the function f. In image processing it is common to use a model of gray-scale images based on fuzzy subsets of $\mathbb{R}^d$, whose membership functions are upper semicontinuous with bounded support [5]. From the upper semicontinuity it follows immediately that the α-cuts for $\alpha \in (0, 1]$ are compact.

The upper semicontinuity condition is not restrictive. Even Aubin has included it in the definition of a fuzzy subset of Euclidean space [1]. This condition does not affect the discretization process: every pixel can be considered as a part of the image, such that all of its points have the same brightness value and therefore the closed disk $B_r(x)$ of radius r centered at x can be limited to the pixel itself. Also, given two adjacent pixels, without loss of generality we may suppose that their common boundary segment belongs to the pixel with greater intensity or brightness value. Therefore every real gray-scale image can be regarded as a fuzzy set whose membership function is upper semicontinuous and has bounded support.

Let $\{A_i\}$ be a given family of fuzzy subsets of $\mathbb{R}^d$ whose membership functions are u.s.c. with bounded support. Then from the reasons listed above, it follows that the membership function of their intersection $\inf_i (\mu_{A_i})$ is also u.s.c. with bounded support, and for any $\alpha > 0$, $\bigcap_i [A_i]_\alpha = [\bigcap_i A_i]_\alpha$. It is proved in [25] that if A and B are fuzzy sets whose membership functions are upper semicontinuous with bounded support, then the same is true for $A \oplus B$, and

$$[A \oplus B]_\alpha = [A]_\alpha \oplus [B]_\alpha. \tag{30}$$

Equation (30) has been used by Kaufmann as a definition for fuzzy Minkowski addition [19].

If A is a fuzzy set whose membership function is upper semicontinuous with bounded support, then $0.5A \oplus 0.5A \subseteq A$. The fact will be used in Section 6.

It is clear that, when applied to crisp sets, the indicators I_λ and I_* take only values 0 and 1. This is however not the case for the indicator I^K, which is discussed in the following subsection.

3.5 The indicator I^K

In the case of fuzzy subsets of a finite space $\mathcal{S} \subset \mathbb{Z}^d$, which is the most natural situation in image processing tasks, the indicator considered by Kosko can be considered (see [4]):

$$I^K(A,B) = 1 - \frac{\sum_{x \in \mathcal{S}} \max(0, \mu_A(x) - \mu_B(x))}{\sum_{x \in \mathcal{S}} \mu_A(x)}.$$

It does not satisfy A7 and A8, thereby making it problematic for the design of morphological operations. But, as shown in Section 6, the indicator of Kosko is found to be useful in the construction of measures of approximate convexity because it is easy to compute and is not sensitive to noise [25]. In the case of a continuous universe $\mathcal{U} \subset \mathbb{R}^d$ it takes the form

$$I^K(A,B) = 1 - \frac{\int_{\mathcal{U}} \max(0, \mu_A(x) - \mu_B(x))\,dx}{\int_{\mathcal{U}} \mu_A(x)\,dx}.$$

Therefore, when A and B are crisp compact sets in the Euclidean plane, it takes the form

$$I^K(A,B) = 1 - \frac{\sigma(A \setminus B)}{\sigma(A)},$$

where σ means the area.

3.6 Adjoint fuzzy morphological operations

Let us now consider again the dilation and erosion of Werman and Peleg (27), obtained from the inclusion indicator I_*. It is easy to find an example showing that they do not form an adjunction [24]. So, let us now consider only the Werman-Peleg dilation $\delta_B(A) = A \oplus B$, $\mu_{\delta_B(A)}(x) = \sup_{y \in \mathcal{U}} \min(\mu_A(y), \mu_B(x-y))$. Here the universe $\mathcal{U}$ may be either the continuous d-dimensional Euclidean space $\mathbb{R}^d$, or the discrete space $\mathbb{Z}^d$. It can be checked directly that the adjoint erosion of δ_B, denoted by ε_B, takes the form

$$\mu_{\varepsilon_B(A)}(x) = \inf_{y \in \mathcal{U}} \left(h\left(\mu_A(y) - \mu_B(y-x)\right)(1 - \mu_A(y)) + \mu_A(y)\right),$$

where $h(x) = 1$ when $x \geq 0$ and is zero otherwise. Therefore, we see that the usual case when using inclusion indicators is to obtain non-adjoint erosion-dilation pairs.

By chance, the erosion and dilation obtained by the inclusion indicator I^*, which is I_λ for $\lambda(x) = 1 - x$, are adjoint. Using (21), we find the following expression for them:

$$\mu_{\varepsilon_B(A)}(x) = \inf_{z \in \mathcal{U}} \min[1, 1 + \mu_A(z) - \mu_B(z-x)], \tag{31}$$

$$\mu_{\delta_B(A}(x) = \sup_{z \in \mathcal{U}} \max[0, \mu_A(z) + \mu_B(x-z) - 1]. \tag{32}$$

3.7 Openings and closings

In [32], given a fuzzy dilation operation $\mathcal{D}(\cdot, B)$ and a fuzzy erosion $\mathcal{E}(\cdot, B)$, an opening operation is defined iteratively by

$$\mathcal{O}(\cdot, B) = \mathcal{D}(\mathcal{E}(\cdot, B), B).$$

Conversely, we may define closing by

$$\mathcal{C}(\cdot, B) = \mathcal{E}(\mathcal{D}(\cdot, B), B).$$

Opening and closing are translation-invariant and increasing operations. If the dilation and erosion are adjoint, then they are also idempotent. Furthermore, the opening will be anti-extensive, and the closing will be extensive. This means that in this case the opening is a true (lattice) opening (i.e. increasing, anti-extensive and idempotent) and the closing is a true (lattice) closing (i.e. increasing, extensive and idempotent) in the sense of [17].

In [33] the authors have observed that when using operations derived from the inclusion indicator I_λ for $\lambda(x) = 1 - x^n$, the best noise cleaning results are obtained when n is close to one, i.e. when the erosion and the dilation are nearly adjoint.

4 Algorithms

4.1 Introduction

Binary morphological algorithms often operate on binary images that have been derived from gray-scale realizations by some binarization procedure, such as thresholding. From a modeling perspective, we can view the binary image as ideal and the gray-scale image as a degraded observation of the underlying ideal binary image. This paradigm is quite general.

To motivate this viewpoint, consider finding the edge of a binary shape (say, a text character) $\underline{A}$ from an observed gray-scale image $f_{\underline{A}}$. One way to proceed is to apply a threshold operator β to $f_{\underline{A}}$ to obtain a binary image $\beta(f_{\underline{A}})$ and then apply a binary morphological edge operator $\underline{\Psi}$ to obtain an estimate $\underline{\Psi}[\beta(f_{\underline{A}})]$ of $\underline{A}$. An alternative approach is to apply some operation ζ to normalize the gray-scale image over the valuation interval $[0,1]$ in such a way that $\zeta(f_{\underline{A}})$ can be interpreted as giving a degree-of-certainty map. For instance, if $\underline{C}$ is the binary shape whose ideal edge is $\underline{A}$, then we can view the value of pixel v in $\zeta(f_{\underline{A}})$ as giving our degree of certainty that $v \in \underline{C}$. ζ can simply be some sort of contrast stretching so that $\zeta(f_{\underline{A}})$ better fits the degree-of-certainty model, or, if the original image capture produces an illumination gradient, then ζ might involve a correction to the illumination gradient followed by contrast stretching. Indeed, we might operate directly on $f_{\underline{A}}$ by letting ζ be the identity. A gray-scale morphological edge operator (say, the morphological gradient) Ψ can now be applied to $\zeta(f_{\underline{A}})$ to produce a gray-scale edge image, $\Psi[\zeta(f_{\underline{A}})]$, that corresponds to $\underline{\Psi}[\beta(f_{\underline{A}})]$. One could threshold $\Psi[\zeta(f_{\underline{A}})]$ to obtain a binary counterpart to $\underline{\Psi}[\beta(f_{\underline{A}})]$ but this is not necessary. The end goal of this procedure might be to make a decision as to what geometric shape is being observed. In this case, there is a decision procedure applied to the final output, say $\underline{\delta}$ to $\underline{\Psi}[\beta(f_{\underline{A}})]$ or δ to $\Psi[\zeta(f_{\underline{A}})]$, where binarization may or may not be part of δ. The better algorithm is the one that produces the better decision. *Ipso facto,* $\underline{\delta}$ employs features from a binary image, whereas δ can employ gray-scale features, as well as binary features.

An immediate paradigm for defining fuzzy morphological operators is to *lift* each binary operator $\underline{\Psi}$ to a gray-scale operator Ψ by fuzzifying the primitive operations composing $\underline{\Psi}$. If an algorithm $\underline{\Psi}$ is composed of operations in the binary morphological algebra, say union, intersection, complement, spatial translation, reflection, erosion, and dilation, then $\underline{\Psi}$ lifts to Ψ by replacing each operation by a fuzzy operation. This is not to say that there cannot be other candidates for Ψ, but certainly direct lifting of the binary operations is a natural choice. Moreover, depending on the inclusion indicator, there can be many liftings. One might even choose to use erosions and dilations that are not adjoint, or are obtained by a different inclusion indicator.

4.2 The morphological gradient

Let us first consider the *morphological gradient,* which is defined in classical binary morphology by Eq. (12). In the event that B is a symmetric structuring element and $0 \in B$, then by (6) we obtain that $\varepsilon_B(X) \subseteq X$. Therefore we can rewrite the binary gradient operator as

$$\nabla_B(X) = \delta_B(X) \setminus (X \cap \varepsilon_B(X)).$$

In the fuzzy case, $\mathcal{E}(A, B) \subseteq A$ only under rather stringent conditions. Then we can define a fuzzy morphological gradient operator as follows:

$$\tilde{\nabla}_B(X) = \mathcal{D}(X, B) \setminus (X \cap \mathcal{E}(X, B)). \qquad (33)$$

In [33] the problem of noise sensitivity of the fuzzy edge detection operation, based on fuzzy gradient defined by the indicator I_λ, is analysed. The structuring element B used is a 3×3 square, $\mu_B(x) = 1$ for all nine points, and a uniform random noise in the interval $J = [-10\%, 10\%]$ is added to each pixel. In the case $\lambda(x) = 1 - x^n$, the smallest and the average certainty of the pixels that should belong to an edge are shown to decrease almost linearly with n. Also, the gradient based on the λ function defined via (19) is the least suspectible to both the perturbations in the value of n and the noise level (the width of J). An image example of applying fuzzy morphological gradient can be found in [9].

4.3 The hit-or-miss transform

From Eq. (13) it is clear that the classical binary morphological *hit-or-miss transform* can be rewritten as

$$\pi_{A,B}(X) = \varepsilon_A(X) \cap \varepsilon_B(X^c) \qquad (34)$$

where A and B make a pair of disjoint structuring elements. It naturally lifts to the fuzzy morphological operator

$$\tilde{\pi}_{A,B}(X) = \mathcal{E}(X, A) \cap \mathcal{E}(X^c, B).$$

A key difference is that, since A and B are fuzzy sets, we do not assume that $A \cap B = \emptyset$. The experiments described in [33] indicate that, in the case of noisy images, it is preferable for the structuring elements to be slightly fuzzy, which means that the values of their membership functions have to be close to one. Also, for the indicators I_λ, $\lambda(x) = 1 - x$ appears to work the best.

The next example illustrates the use of the fuzzy hit-or-miss transform to recognize noisy realizations of the word "cat" among 14 words that make up a dictionary. The dictionary consists of the possible three letter English words that can be constructed from the alphabet $\mathbf{A} = \{$a, b, c, o, r, t$\}$. The dictionary is the word set $\mathbf{D} = \{$cat, tab, rat, rot, tar, rob, bat, tao, boa, car art, act, bar, cab$\}$.

All six realizations of the word "cat" are illustrated in Fig. 1. These include the original (word 1), a seriously deformed version of the original (word 4), two warped versions of the original (word 2 and word 3) and carved and blurred versions of these (word 5 and word 6). Needless to say that all "noisy" versions of the object (the word "cat") are gray-scale in nature.

Sparse fuzzy hit and miss templates are manually constructed for each of the letters in the alphabet from their original versions (Fig. 2). Figures 2(a) and 2(d) show the "miss" patterns for "t" and "c", while figures 2(b) and 2(c) show the "hit" patterns for these characters. All realizations are probed by each of the 6 fuzzy hit and miss templates for the letters "c", "a" and "t". Then the modes, extracted automatically, are stored for the recognition module. Remark that the traditional hit-or-miss operation with these templates would only mark the letters in the original word but would not in the noisy realizations. Unlike its classical counterpart, the fuzzy hit-or-miss operation always marked the desired letters. However, the markings spread over many pixels and other letters than the probing template started, thus showing some fuzzy likelihood of being marked. The modes for templates "c", "a" and "t" are automatically extracted by a 9×9 moving Max filter [33]. In this manner the fuzzy likelihood of each character in all six realizations of the word "cat" to be one of the six letters in the alphabet is calculated. These numbers are then used to assign fuzzy likelihoods to each realization of "cat" to be one of the 14 possible three letter words in the dictionary. The corresponding fuzzy rule is multiplication: the likelihood of a given realization

Fig. 1. Observations of the word "cat"

to be the word "cat" is calculated by multiplying the fuzzy likelihood of having a "c" as the first letter with the fuzzy likelihood of having an "a" as the second letter and a "t" as the last one. For each of the six realizations, the likelihood for the word "cat" was the highest (see Fig. 3).

5 Morphological representation

Historically, there has been much interest in operator representation via primitive morphological operators – in particular, the representation of translation-invariant operators, increasing translation-invariant operators, and openings. Since our perspective is that fuzzy morphology represents an extension of binary morphology based on fuzzification of the erosion operation via an inclusion grade operator, we briefly review the binary morphological representation theory for increasing translation-invariant crisp-set operators and for binary openings, and then discuss fuzzy extensions of these representations. We refer to [14] for a more complete discussion of the binary representation

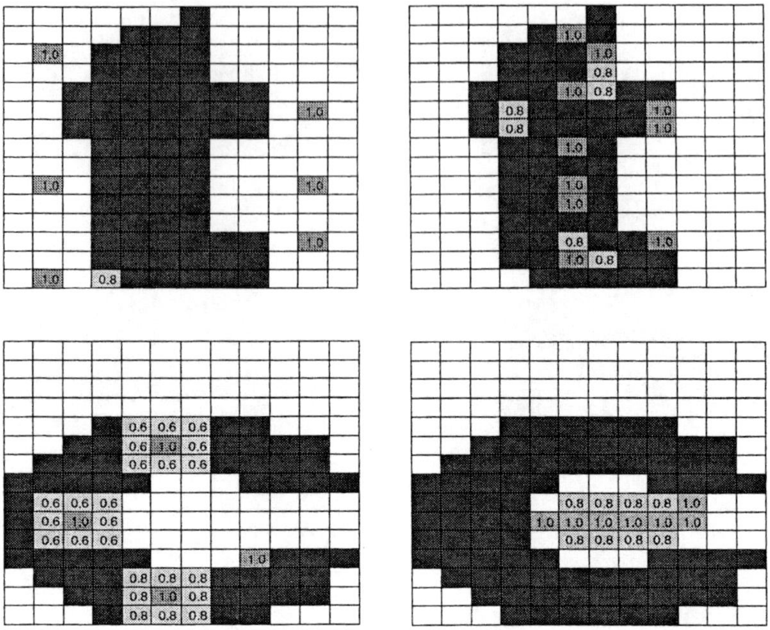

Fig. 2. Fuzzy hit-or-miss structuring pairs for letters "t" and "c"

theory, including proofs. We will close the section with the morphological computational representation for fuzzy erosion.

5.1 Representation for increasing, translation-invariant operators

Denoting $\mathcal{P} = \mathcal{P}(\mathbb{R}^d)$, a set operator $\Psi : \mathcal{P} \mapsto \mathcal{P}$ is called a τ-mapping if it is translation-invariant, which means that for every vector z, $\Psi(S_z) = \Psi(S)_z$. Here and henceforth we denote by X_z the translate of X, i.e. $X_z = \tau_z(X)$.

The *kernel* of Ψ is defined by $\mathtt{K}[\Psi] = \{S \in \mathcal{P} \,|\, 0 \in \Psi(S)\}$. The basic representation theorem for increasing translation-invariant set operators is that Ψ is such an operator if and only if it possesses the representation:

$$\Psi(S) = \bigcup_{B \in \mathtt{K}[\Psi]} \varepsilon_B(S). \tag{35}$$

where ε_B denotes erosion by the set B [23]. A subset $\mathtt{B}[\Psi] \subseteq \mathtt{K}[\Psi]$ is called a *(increasing) basis* for Ψ if: (1) no set in $\mathtt{B}[\Psi]$ is a proper subset of a distinct set in $\mathtt{B}[\Psi]$; and (2) for any $A \in \mathtt{K}[\Psi]$, there exists $B \in \mathtt{B}[\Psi]$ such that $B \subseteq A$. The notation "$\mathtt{B}[\Psi]$" is permitted since there can be at most one basis. If Ψ commutes with intersection, then it possesses a basis. If Ψ is increasing,

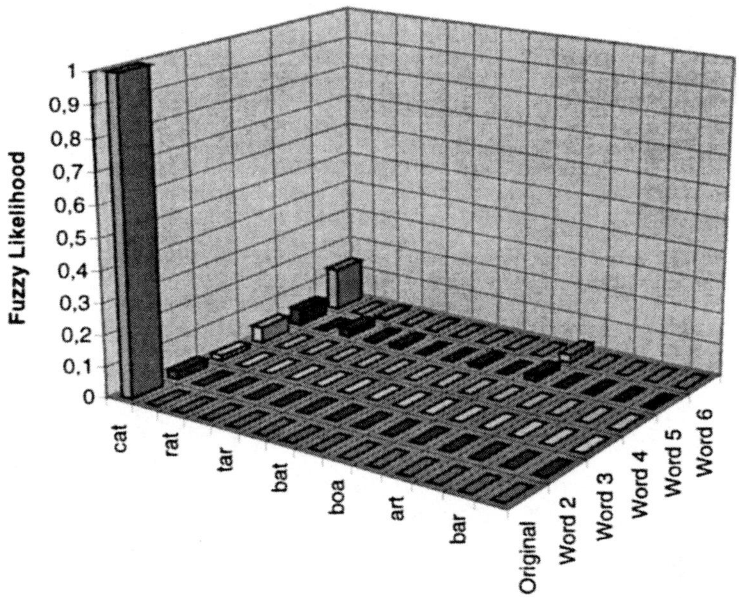

Fig. 3. Fuzzy hit-or-miss likelihoods of observed words with respect to the words in the dictionary

translation-invariant, and possesses a basis, then the union operation in (35) can be taken over $\mathtt{B}[\Psi]$ instead of $\mathtt{K}[\Psi]$, and the basis expansion is minimal since no basis set can be excluded from the union over $\mathtt{K}[\Psi]$ [16,22]. Note that there exist more general kernels and reduced representations for operators that are translation-invariant, but not necessarily increasing [2].

Now let $\mathcal{F}$ denote the class of fuzzy sets relative to the Euclidean plane. A fuzzy-set operator $\Psi : \mathcal{F} \mapsto \mathcal{F}$ is called an H-mapping if it is translation-invariant. The change in terminology is necessitated by the isomorphism between fuzzy sets and their membership functions; that is, we view Ψ as a membership-function mapping, $\Psi : \mathcal{M} \mapsto \mathcal{M}$, where $\mathcal{M}$ is the space of membership functions, and translation invariance means that Ψ is domain (horizontally) translation-invariant The *kernel* of an H-mapping Ψ on fuzzy sets is the family of sets, $\mathtt{K}[\Psi] = \{\mathtt{K}_t[\Psi] \,|\, 0 \leq t \leq 1\}$, where

$$\mathtt{K}_t[\Psi] = \{S \in \mathcal{F} \,|\, \mu_{\Psi(S)}(0) \geq t\}. \tag{36}$$

It is straightforward to show from the definition of fuzzy union that the kernel commutes with fuzzy union. For fuzzy erosion by B we have $\mathtt{K}_t[\mathcal{E}(\cdot, B)] = \{S \,|\, I(B, S) \geq t\}$. Thus, for any increasing H-mapping Ψ and for any $t, r \in (0,1]$:

$$\mathrm{K}_t\left[\bigcup_{B\in \mathrm{K}_r[\Psi]} \mathcal{E}(\cdot,B)\right] = \bigcup_{B\in \mathrm{K}_r[\Psi]} \mathrm{K}_t[\mathcal{E}(\cdot,B)] = \bigcup_{B\in \mathrm{K}_r[\Psi]} \{S \mid I(B,S) \geq t\}. \quad (37)$$

In particular, for $r = t = 1$,

$$\mathrm{K}_t\left[\bigcup_{B\in \mathrm{K}_1[\Psi]} \mathcal{E}(\cdot,B)\right] = \bigcup_{B\in \mathrm{K}_1[\Psi]} \{S \mid B \subseteq S\} = \mathrm{K}_1[\Psi], \quad (38)$$

the first equality following from axiom 1 and the second from the assumption that Ψ is increasing. Now, the kernel formulation of the classical Matheron result for crisp sets (35) is

$$\mathrm{K}\left[\bigcup_{B\in \mathrm{K}[\Psi]} \varepsilon_B\right] = \mathrm{K}[\Psi] \quad (39)$$

Since $K = K_1$ for crisp-set operators, we see that (37) is the fuzzy generalization of the classical representation. The generalization cannot be strengthened, not even for I^*.

5.2 Representation for openings

As discussed in Section 2, a set mapping operator $\Psi : \mathcal{P} \mapsto \mathcal{P}$ is called an *(algebraic) opening* if it is increasing, anti-extensive, and idempotent. It is called a τ-opening if it is translation-invariant. The *invariant class,* $\mathrm{Inv}\,[\Psi]$, of Ψ is the collection of all sets S for which $\Psi(S) = S$. An opening Ψ is a τ-opening if and only if $\mathrm{Inv}\,[\Psi]$ is closed under translation. A class $\mathcal{B}$ is called a *base* for a τ-opening Ψ if $\mathrm{Inv}\,[\Psi]$ is the class generated by $\mathcal{B}$ under translations and unions. Openings by structuring elements are primary for representation of τ-openings [23]: a set mapping Ψ is a τ-opening if and only if there exists a base $\mathcal{B}$ for Ψ such that

$$\Psi(S) = \bigcup_{B\in\mathcal{B}} \gamma_B(S), \quad (40)$$

where γ_B denotes opening by B.

Since fuzzy sets are defined by their membership functions, it is natural for their representation to be framed in terms of their membership functions. Hence, we are really talking about gray-scale morphological representation. If we let $\mathcal{G}$ denote the lattice of extended real-valued functions, then a gray-scale opening $\Psi : \mathcal{G} \mapsto \mathcal{G}$ is called a τ-opening (or T-opening) if it is translation-invariant in both the domain and the range, which means $\Psi(f_x + y) = \Psi(f)_x + y$. $\mathcal{B} \subseteq \mathcal{G}$ is a base for Ψ if $\mathrm{Inv}\,[\Psi]$ is the closure of

$\mathcal{B}$ under domain translations, range translations and suprema. A structural T-opening is defined via a function $g \in \mathcal{G}$ by $\gamma_g(f) = \bigvee\{g_x + y | g_x + y \leq f\}$. A mapping $\Psi : \mathcal{G} \mapsto \mathcal{G}$ is a T-opening if and only if there exists a base $\mathcal{B}$ for Ψ such that

$$\Psi(f) = \bigvee_{g \in \mathcal{B}} \gamma_g(f) \tag{41}$$

(see [16,28]) . If an opening $\Psi : \mathcal{G} \mapsto \mathcal{G}$ is only domain translation-invariant, then it is called an H-opening. If Ψ is an H-opening, then $\mathcal{B}$ is a base for Ψ if Inv $[\Psi]$ is the closure of $\mathcal{B}$ under domain translations and suprema. A structural H-opening is defined via a function $g \in \mathcal{G}$ by $\eta_g(f) = \bigvee\{g_x \mid g_x \leq f\}$. There is the following representation for H-openings [17,20]: a mapping $\Psi : \mathcal{G} \mapsto \mathcal{G}$ is an H-opening if and only if there exists a base $\mathcal{B}$ for Ψ such that

$$\Psi(f) = \bigvee_{g \in \mathcal{B}} \eta_g(f) \tag{42}$$

For fuzzy morphology, $\mathcal{M} \subseteq \mathcal{G}$, and $\mathcal{F}$ and $\mathcal{M}$ are isomorphic via $S \leftrightarrow \mu_S$.

An operator $\Psi : \mathcal{F} \mapsto \mathcal{F}$ is a *fuzzy (algebraic) opening* if it is anti-extensive, idempotent, and increasing in the fuzzy sense, which means that, as an operator on the function space $\mathcal{M}$, it is an opening. It is called an F-opening if it is domain translation-invariant. $\mathcal{B}$ is a base for an F-opening Ψ if Inv $[\Psi]$ is the closure of $\mathcal{B}$ under domain translation and fuzzy union. Since $\mathcal{M} \subseteq \mathcal{G}$, if $\mu_B \in \mathcal{M}$, where B is a fuzzy set, then η_{μ_B} defines a structural H-opening on $\mathcal{G}$. Again since $\mathcal{M} \subseteq \mathcal{G}$, this structural H-opening is an operator on $\mathcal{M}$ when restricted thereto. *Ipso facto,* B defines a structural opening $\tilde{\gamma}_B$ on $\mathcal{F}$, where the membership function of $\tilde{\gamma}_B(S)$ is $\eta_{\mu_B}(\mu_S)$. There is the following fuzzy-union representation [32]: Ψ is an F -opening if and only if there exists a base $\mathcal{B}$ such that

$$\Psi(S) = \bigcup_{B \in \mathcal{B}} \tilde{\gamma}_B(S) \tag{43}$$

The representation of an F-opening is not in terms of structural F-openings, but is in terms of (isomorphic copies of) structural H-openings. In fact, an example of an F-opening that cannot be represented as a fuzzy union of structural F-openings is given in [32] for the inclusion operator I_λ with $\lambda(x) = 1 - x$. This counterexample is particularly interesting because, for this I_λ, fuzzy openings are F-openings, so it means that F-openings with respect to I_λ cannot be represented as fuzzy unions of fuzzy openings.

5.3 Computational morphological representation of fuzzy erosion

Computational mathematical morphology was developed to provide a formal structure for both the morphological representation and optimization of windowed digital image operators [8]. It treats a digital image as an $\mathcal{L}$-valued function defined on the Cartesian grid, where $\mathcal{L}$ is a complete lattice. We denote the image space by $\mathrm{F}_{\mathcal{L}}$. Given complete lattices $\mathcal{L}$ and $\mathcal{N}$, an operator $\Psi : \mathrm{F}_{\mathcal{L}} \mapsto \mathrm{F}_{\mathcal{N}}$ is *windowed* if there exists a finite window $W = \{w_1, w_2, \dots, w_N\}$ and product-lattice operator $\psi : \mathcal{L}^N \mapsto \mathcal{N}$ such that $\Psi(f)(x) = \psi(f(x + w_1), \dots, f(x + w_N)) \in \mathcal{N}$. From the definition, Ψ is domain translation-invariant. The *kernel* of Ψ is defined by $\mathrm{K}[\Psi] = \{\mathrm{K}_y[\Psi] \,|\, y \in \mathcal{N}\}$, where $\mathrm{K}_y[\Psi] = \{f \in \mathrm{F}_{\mathcal{L}} \,|\, \Psi(f)(0) \geq y\}$. The *basis* of Ψ is defined by $\mathrm{B}[\Psi] = \{\mathrm{B}_y[\Psi] \,|\, y \in \mathcal{N}\}$, where $\mathrm{B}_y[\Psi]$ is the set of minimal elements in $\mathrm{K}_y[\Psi]$. Ψ is said to be *inf-complete* if, for all $y \in \mathcal{N}$, $\mathrm{K}_y[\Psi]|_W$ has the following property (where the notation $\mathcal{F}|_W$ denotes that the supports of the images from the family $\mathcal{F}$ have been restricted to W) : for any $f \in \mathrm{K}_y[\Psi]|_W$ there exists $g \in \mathrm{B}_y[\Psi]|_W$ such that $g \leq f$. If Ψ is windowed, then there exist representation theorems for both the nonincreasing and increasing cases [10]. Here we only consider the increasing case.

Fixing W, a structuring element is a function $g \in \mathrm{F}_{\mathcal{L}}$ whose support lies in W (i.e. is 0 outside of W). Letting $\mathcal{T} = \{0, 1\}$, the binary lattice, we define the gray-to-binary erosion $\varepsilon_g : \mathrm{F}_{\mathcal{L}} \mapsto \mathrm{F}_{\mathcal{T}}$ by $\varepsilon_g(f)(x) = 1$ if $g_x \leq f$ and $\varepsilon_g(f)(x) = 0$ otherwise. ε_g distributes over infimum and is a true erosion. If $\Psi : \mathrm{F}_{\mathcal{L}} \mapsto \mathrm{F}_{\mathcal{N}}$ is windowed and inf-complete, then it is increasing if and only if it possesses the representation

$$\Psi(f)(x) = \bigvee \left\{ y \in \mathcal{M} \mid \left(\bigvee_{g \in \mathrm{B}_y[\Psi]|_W} \varepsilon_g(f) \right)(x) = 1 \right\}. \tag{44}$$

In the typical case in which the gray range is quantized, so that $\mathcal{N} = \{0, 1, \dots, c\}$, the finiteness of the range guarantees that Ψ is inf-complete and the representation becomes

$$\Psi(f)(x) = \sum_{y=1}^{c} \left(\bigvee_{g \in \mathrm{B}_y[\Psi]|_W} \varepsilon_g(f) \right)(x) \tag{45}$$

Note that $g \in \mathrm{B}_y[\Psi]|_W$ guarantees that the support of g lies in W, so that g can be treated as a vector of length N defined over W. The representations of computational mathematical morphology are special cases of the general lattice-representation theory [3], and an account of the computational theory as it applies to the range $\{0, 1, \dots, c\}$ is given in [12].

For representation of fuzzy erosion, we consider only the inclusion operator I_λ, where $\lambda(x) = 1 - x$. Representation follows from Eq. (45) by recognizing two points. First, quantization of the interval $[0, 1]$ results in the lattice $\mathcal{N}_c = \{0, 1/c, 2/c, \dots, 1\}$, so that, relative to membership functions, fuzzy erosion by a fuzzy set B is an increasing mapping of the form $\mathcal{E}(., B) : \mathcal{F}_{\mathcal{N}_c} \mapsto \mathcal{F}_{\mathcal{N}_c}$. Second $\mathrm{B}_y[\mathcal{E}(., B)]|_W$ consists of the single N-vector

$$\mathbf{b}_y = (0 \vee (b_1 + y/c - 1), \dots, 0 \vee (b_N + y/c - 1)) \tag{46}$$

where $(b_1, b_2, \ldots, b_N) = \mu_B|_W$. Hence, for any fuzzy set S,

$$\mu_{\mathcal{E}(S,B)}(x) = \frac{1}{c}\sum_{y=1}^{c}\bigwedge_{y=1}^{N}\zeta\left(0 \vee (b_i + y/c - 1), \mu_S(x+w_i)\right) \tag{47}$$

where ζ is defined by $\zeta(a,b) = 1$ if $a \leq b$ and $\zeta(a,b) = 0$ otherwise [11]. The sum provides computational representation in terms of the comparator ζ.

6 Indicators of approximate convexity

In computer vision systems, true convexity is rarely encountered. Moreover, it is difficult to define whether a discrete set of pixels is convex or not. One can easily say whether an object looks convex or not. So, one can use fuzzy set theory to try to measure the perception of convexity. It is well known from convex analysis that a crisp compact set X in $\mathbb{R}^d$ is convex if and only if $X = 0.5X \oplus 0.5X$.

Having in mind this result, in [25] the notion of a convexity indicator, or precisely, indicator of approximate convexity is proposed.

Definition 3. The convexity indicator of the fuzzy set A with respect to the inclusion indicator I and the dilation operation $\mathcal{D}(.,.)$ is defined as

$$C(A) = I(\mathcal{D}(0.5A, 0.5A), A).$$

The indicator I may not satisfy all of the inclusion indicator axioms. So, for instance, we may consider convexity indicators for which $I = I^K$.

As defined in [26], a fuzzy subset A in $\mathbb{R}^d$ is called *convex* if

$$\mu_A(\lambda x_1 + (1-\lambda)x_2) \geq \min(\mu_A(x_1), \mu_A(x_2))$$

for all $x_1, x_2 \in \mathbb{R}^d$ and every $\lambda \in [0,1]$. There is a well known result saying that a fuzzy set is convex if and only if its α−cuts for $\alpha \in (0,1]$ are convex crisp sets in $\mathbb{R}^d$.

Let us consider two examples of convexity indicators. In both, the dilation operation is the dilation of Werman and Peleg, denoted in Section 3 by $\oplus$. For the first convexity indicator, denoted by C_*, we take as inclusion indicator I^*. For the second, denoted by C_K, the square of the indicator of Kosko I^K is suggested.

The main results proved in [25] for these indicators are:

- If A is a fuzzy subset of $\mathbb{R}^d$ whose membership function is upper semicontinuous with bounded support, then $C_*(A) = 1$ if and only if A is fuzzy convex.
- For any fuzzy convex subset A of $\mathbb{R}^d$ whose membership function is upper semicontinuous with bounded support, it follows that $C_K(A) = 1$. On the contrary, if $C_K(A) = 1$, then there exists a fuzzy set X whose support has Lebesgue measure 0 such that $A \cup X$ is fuzzy convex.

These properties show that the proposed definition of an approximate convexity measure by means of an inclusion indicator and fuzzy dilation is reasonable. In practical image processing we usually deal with objects represented as finite collections of pixels. Even for objects in binary images it is not easy to express formally the meaning of convexity. The task is more difficult in the case of gray-scale images when the objects do not have well defined boundaries. So, if A is a binary or gray-tone image and C is a convexity indicator, we say that A *is convex of degree* α *with respect to the indicator* C if $C(A) = \alpha$.

Experiments have shown that the indicator C_* is very sensitive to noise, in contrast to C_K. Also, C_K can be applied both to binary and gray-scale images, while the use of C_* makes sense only in the gray-scale case [25].

Using psychophysical experiments with humans, it has been shown that the measure C_K yields results near to typical human perception [25]. Fifteen people were asked to order the three shapes in Fig. 4 according to their intuitive perception of convexity. The most convex shape in any answer gained 3 points, the medium 2 points, and the least convex 1 point. The overall result was: shape A (left): 31 points; shape B (middle): 20 points; shape C (right): 39 points. The results of applying the indicator C_K to these shapes were the following: for shape A: 0.79; for shape B: 0.72; for shape C: 0.83, which shows that the ratios of the gained points are nearly the same as the ratios of the C_K values.

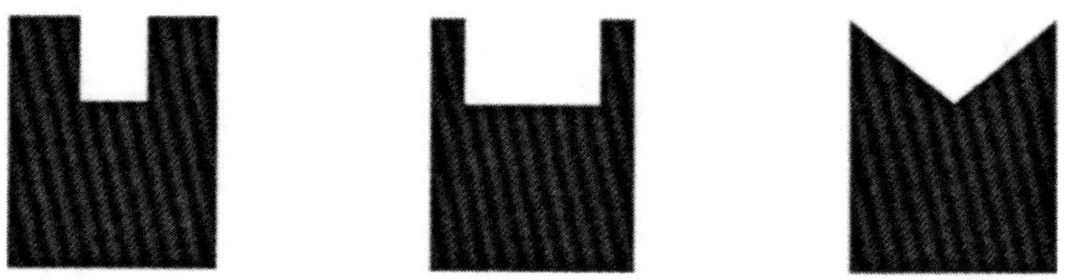

Fig. 4. Shapes used in the psychophysical experiment

References

1. Aubin J.-P., *"Mutational and morphological analysis : Tools for shape regulation and optimization"*, manuscript, Paris, 1997
2. Banon G.J.F. and Barrera J., *Minimal representation of translation-invariant set mappings by mathematical morphology*, SIAM Journal on Applied Mathematics, Vol. 51, No. 6, pp. 1782–1798, 1991

3. Banon G.J.F. and Barrera J., *Decomposition of mappings between complete lattices by mathematical morphology, Part I: General lattices*, Signal Processing, Vol. 30, pp. 299 - 327, 1993
4. Bloch I. and Maître H., *Fuzzy mathematical morphologies: A comparative study*, Pattern Recognition, Vol. 28, No. 9, pp. 1341–1387, 1995
5. Cabrelli C.A., Forte B., Molter U.M. and Vrscay E.R., *Iterated fuzzy set systems: A new approach to the inverse problem for fractals and other sets*, Journal of Mathematical Analysis and Applications, Vol. 171, pp. 79–99, 1992
6. De Baets B., *Fuzzy morphology: a logical approach*, in: "Uncertainty Analysis in Engineering and the Sciences (B. Ayyub and M.M. Gupta, eds.)", Kluwer Academic Publishers, Norwell, 1997
7. Dougherty E.R., *"An introduction to morphological image processing"*, SPIE Press, Bellingham WA, 1992
8. Dougherty E.R. and Sinha D., *Computational mathematical morphology*, Signal Processing, Vol. 38, pp. 21 - 29, 1994
9. Dougherty E.R., Sinha D. and Sinha. P, *Fuzzy morphological algorithms*, in: "Mental and Fuzzy Systems (S. Mitra, M.M. Gupta and W.F. Kraske, eds.)", SPIE Press, Bellingham WA, 1994
10. Dougherty E.R. and Sinha D., *Computational gray-scale morphology on lattices (A comparator-based image algebra) Part I: Architecture*, Real-Time Imaging, Vol. 1, No. 1, pp. 69–85, 1995
11. Dougherty E.R. and Sinha D., *Computational gray-scale morphology on lattices (A comparator-based image algebra) Part II: Image operators*, Real-Time Imaging, Vol. 1 , No. 4, pp. 283–295, 1995
12. Dougherty E.R. and Barrera J., *Computational gray-scale image operators*, in: "Nonlinear Filters for Image Processing (E.R. Dougherty and J. Astola, eds.)", SPIE and IEEE Presses, Bellingham WA, 1999
13. Dougherty E.R. and Barrera J., *Logical image operators*, in: "Nonlinear Filters for Image Processing (E.R. Dougherty and J. Astola, eds.)", SPIE and IEEE Presses, Bellingham WA, 1999
14. Dougherty E.R., *Translation-invariant set operators*, in: "Nonlinear Filters for Image Processing (E.R. Dougherty and J. Astola, eds.)", SPIE and IEEE Presses, Bellingham WA, 1999
15. Dougherty E.R. and Chen Y., *Granulometric filters*, in: "Nonlinear Filters for Image Processing (E.R. Dougherty and J. Astola, eds.)", SPIE and IEEE Presses, Bellingham WA, 1999
16. Giardina C.R. and Dougherty E.R., *"Morphological methods in image processing"*, Prentice Hall, Englewood Cliffs, 1988
17. Heijmans H.J.A.M., *"Morphological image operators"*, Academic Press, Boston MA, 1994
18. Held A. and Abe K., *On approximate convexity*, Pattern Recognition Letters, Vol. 15, pp. 611–618, 1994
19. Kaufmann A. and Gupta M., *"Fuzzy mathematical models in engineering and management science"*, North-Holland, Amsterdam, 1988
20. Kraus E., Heijmans H.J.A.M. and Dougherty E.R., *Gray-scale morphological granulometries compatible with spatial scaling*, Signal Processing, Vol. 34, pp. 1–17, 1993
21. Loce R.P. and Dougherty E.R., *Enhancement and restoration of digital documents: Statistical design of nonlinear algorithms*, SPIE Press, Bellingham WA, 1997

22. Maragos P. and Schafer R., *Morphological filters – Part I: Their set- theoretic analysis and relations to linear shift- invariant filters*, IEEE Trans. on Acoustics, Speech, and Signal Processing, Vol 35, pp. 1153 – 1169, 1987
23. Matheron G., *"Random sets and integral geometry"*, Wiley, New York, 1975
24. Popov A.T., *Morphological operations on fuzzy sets*, in: "Proceedings of the 5th Int. Conf. on Image Processing and its Applications" (Edinburgh), pp. 837 – 840, 1995
25. Popov A.T., *Convexity indicators based on fuzzy morphology*, Pattern Recognition Letters, Vol. 18, No. 3, 259 -267, 1997
26. Rosenfeld A., *The fuzzy geometry of image subsets*, Pattern Recognition Letters, Vol. 2, pp. 311–317, 1984
27. Serra J., *"Image analysis and mathematical morphology"*, Academic Press, London, 1982
28. Serra J., *Mathematical morphology for complete lattices*, in: "Image analysis and mathematical morphology, Vol. 2 (J. Serra, ed.)", Academic Press, London, 1988
29. Serra J., *Alternating Sequential Filters*, in: "Image analysis and mathematical morphology, Vol. 2 (J. Serra, ed.)", Academic Press, London, 1988
30. Sinha D. and Dougherty E.R., *Fuzzy mathematical morphology*, Visual Communication and Image Representation, Vol. 3, No. 3, pp. 286–302, 1992
31. Sinha D. and Dougherty E.R., *Fuzzification of Set Inclusion, Theory and Applications*, Fuzzy Sets and Systems, Vol. 55, pp. 15–42, 1993
32. Sinha D. and Dougherty E.R., *A general axiomatic theory for intrinsically fuzzy mathematical morphologies*, IEEE Transactions on Fuzzy Systems, Vol. 3, No. 4, pp. 389–403, 1995
33. Sinha D., Sinha P., Dougherty E.R. and Batman S., *Design and analysis of fuzzy morphological algorithms for image processing*, IEEE Transactions on Fuzzy Systems, Vol. 5, No. 4, pp. 570 – 584, 1997
34. Werman M. and Peleg S., *Min - max operators in texture analysis*, IEEE Trans. on Pattern Analysis and Machine Intelligence, Vol. 7, No. 2, pp. 730–733, 1985
35. Zadeh L., *"Fuzzy sets and their applications to cognitive processes"*, Academic Press, London, 1975

Chapter 4

Fuzzy Mathematical Morphology and Derived Spatial Relationships

Isabelle Bloch

Ecole Nationale Supérieure des Télécommunications, département TSI
CNRS URA 820 - 46 rue Barrault, 75013 Paris, France
email: bloch@ima.enst.fr

Summary. The joint importance of mathematical morphology in image processing and of fuzzy sets for representing imprecisely defined image objects has led to an increased interest in fuzzy mathematical morphology. In this chapter, we first review the main definitions of fuzzy mathematical morphology operators and show that the most important properties of classical mathematical morphology are kept. Then we use these operators, mainly fuzzy dilation, for defining some spatial relationships between fuzzy objects: distances, adjacency and boundary, directional relative position. Such spatial fuzzy relationships are important in pattern recognition (for instance model-based structural pattern recognition). Indeed, objects can be recognized in a scene using their own characteristics, but also using their relationships to other objects of the scene. Therefore the proposed operations and relationships between fuzzy objects lead to applications in structural pattern recognition under imprecision.

1 Introduction

Among the different possible uses of fuzzy techniques in image processing, some of them address the problem of dealing with spatial imprecision in the images. In this framework, objects or regions in the image are defined as fuzzy objects. We denote by $\mathcal{S}$ the image space, typically $\mathbb{Z}^2$ or $\mathbb{Z}^3$ for digital 2D or 3D images, or, in the continuous case, $\mathbb{R}^2$ or $\mathbb{R}^3$. We are interested in the objects of the image that we may describe as fuzzy sets. Thus we often call them fuzzy image objects. A fuzzy image object is a fuzzy set defined on $\mathcal{S}$, i.e. a spatial fuzzy set. Its membership function μ represents the imprecision in the spatial extent of the object. For any point x of $\mathcal{S}$ (pixel or voxel), $\mu(x)$ is the degree to which x belongs to the fuzzy object. We denote by $\mathcal{F}$ the set of fuzzy sets on $\mathcal{S}$.

As an illustrative example, a slice of a brain image is shown in Figure 1. It is obtained using a T1 weighted acquisition in magnetic resonance imaging (MRI). A few internal structures are represented in Figure 2 as spatial fuzzy sets, where membership degrees are represented using grey levels. The use of fuzzy sets may represent different types of imprecision, either on the boundary of the objects (due for instance to partial volume effect, or to the spatial resolution), or on the individual variability of these structures, etc.

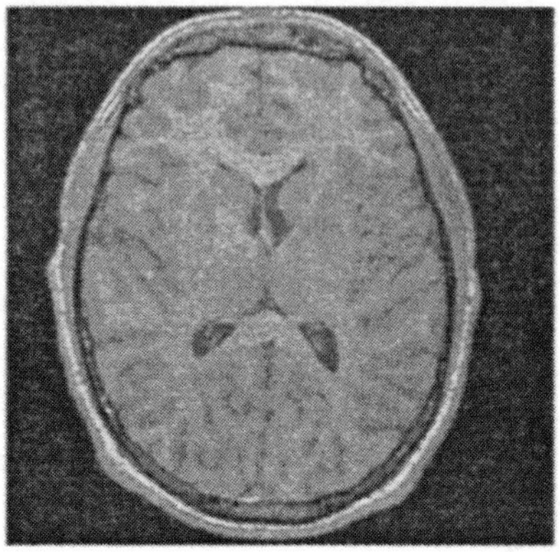

Fig. 1. MR image of a brain (one slice of a 3D volume).

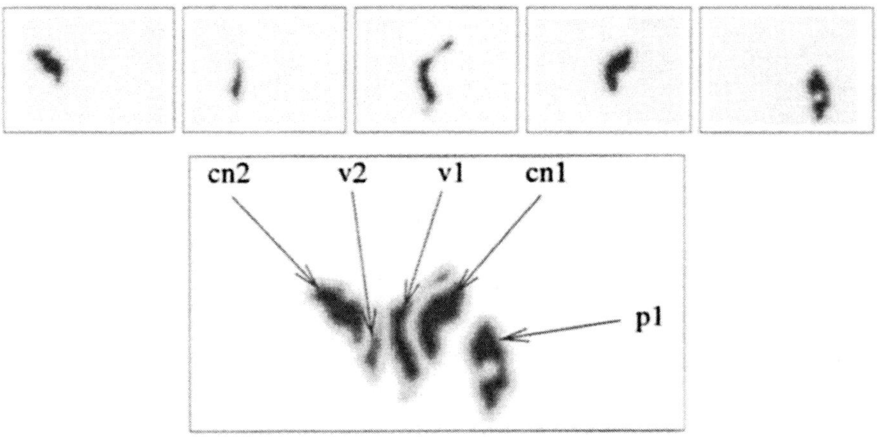

Fig. 2. Top: 5 fuzzy objects representing internal brain structures (top part of the ventricular system and surrounding objects) of the image shown in Figure 1 (membership values rank between 0 and 1, from white to black). From left to right: right caudate nucleus (cn2), right lateral ventricle (v2), left lateral ventricle (v1), left caudate nucleus (cn1), left putamen (p1) (using the standard "left is right" convention, e.g. cn1 is on the right in this figure). Bottom: superposition of these fuzzy objects (the maximum membership value is displayed at each point).

Several operations have already been defined on these types of fuzzy sets. Among the operations often used in classical image processing, mathematical morphology operators gained a large importance. Therefore its extension to fuzzy sets is interesting. Moreover, mathematical morphology serves as a basis for defining several spatial relationships between objects. Objects can be recognized in a scene using their own characteristics, but also, and this is very important, using their relationships to other objects of the scene. Extending mathematical morphology to fuzzy sets also leads to extensions of such relationships between fuzzy objects, and to applications in structural pattern recognition under imprecision.

In this chapter, we first review the main definitions of fuzzy mathematical morphology operators in Section 2. Then we use these operators, mainly fuzzy dilation, for defining some spatial relationships between fuzzy objects: distances in Section 3, adjacency in Section 4, directional relative position in Section 5.

2 Definition of basic fuzzy mathematical morphology operators

Fuzzy mathematical morphology appears as a logical consequence of the research efforts that have been made to process imprecise spatial information. Indeed, since the introduction of fuzzy sets in 1965 by Zadeh [54], elementary set operations have been defined (intersection, union, complementation, inclusion, etc.) [54,30,53,8], followed by several concepts useful in image processing such as topological [46] or geometrical [47] operations, etc. These developments motivated further extensions of image processing operators to fuzzy sets, in particular mathematical morphology operators. Several definitions have been proposed since a few years. Some of them just consider grey level as membership functions [36,35,40,25,26,41], or only use binary structuring elements [47]. Here we restrict the presentation to really fuzzy approaches, where fuzzy sets have to be transformed according to fuzzy structuring elements. Initial developments can be found in the definition of fuzzy Minkowski addition [29,37]. Then this problem has been addressed by several authors independently [17,19,20,50,2,1,3,45,52]

Attention will be paid here only to the 4 basic operations of mathematical morphology (erosion, dilation, opening, closing), but it should be clear for the reader that for every definition, a complete set of morphological operations could be derived.

For the sake of clarity, we call binary mathematical morphology (denoted by BMM) the morphology which uses binary sets and binary structuring elements; grey level mathematical morphology (GMM) will stand for classical morphology with a function (or a grey level image) and a binary structuring element, whereas functional mathematical morphology (FMM) will represent classical mathematical morphology on functions with a functional structuring element. Links between FMM and BMM are obtained by considering the umbra or subgraph of the functions. Links between GMM and BMM come from the fact that the binary dilations (for instance) of the thresholds of a function by a binary structuring element are equal to the thresholds of the dilation using GMM[1]. We are interested in developing a fuzzy morphology (ΦMM). As mentioned before, considering a fuzzy set as a grey level function does not allow to use FMM as a ΦMM (see Table 1) since, for instance, the dilation of a set defined in $[0, 1]$ by a set defined in $[0, 1]$ provides a new set defined in $[0, 2]$.

Set	Structuring element	Classical MM	ΦMM
Binary	Binary	BMM	possibly compatible
Fuzzy	Binary	GMM	possibly compatible
Fuzzy	Fuzzy	FMM	*not compatible*

Table 1. As binary sets are special fuzzy sets, we may expect ΦMM to be compatible with classical mathematical morphology, when at least one of the two sets is binary. On the contrary, FMM cannot guarantee this internal property (except in very particular cases).

2.1 General methods for extending an operation to fuzzy sets

We present some common and generic methods that can be used for defining a fuzzy operator or fuzzy relationship from the corresponding binary ones. These methods can be categorized in three main classes. The first type relies on the "extension principle", as introduced by Zadeh [55]. The second class relies on computation on α-cuts. These two classes of definitions explicitly involve the operations or relations on crisp sets. The third class of methods consists in providing directly fuzzy definitions of the operations or of the relationships, by substituting all crisp expressions by their fuzzy equivalents.

Extension principle Originally, the first generic method for extending binary operators to fuzzy ones is due to Zadeh [55] and known as the extension principle.

Let us first consider a function f from $\mathcal{S}$ to a space $\mathcal{V}$. Let μ be a fuzzy set defined on $\mathcal{S}$. The image of the fuzzy set μ by the extension of f is a fuzzy set μ' defined on $\mathcal{V}$. It is constructed as follows:

$$\forall y \in \mathcal{V},\ \mu'(y) = \begin{cases} 0 \text{ if } f^{-1}(y) = \emptyset \\ \sup_{x \in \mathcal{S} | y = f(x)} \mu(x) \text{ else.} \end{cases} \tag{1}$$

[1] An extensive overview of BMM, GMM and FMM is presented in Chapter 1 (*Classical and Fuzzy Approaches towards Mathematical Morphology*). In that chapter, GMM is referred to as gray-scale morphology based on the threshold approach, while FMM is referred to as gray-scale morphology based on the umbra approach.

For an injective function, this equation reduces to:

$$\forall y \in \mathcal{V},\ \mu'(y) = \begin{cases} 0 & \text{if } f^{-1}(y) = \emptyset, \\ \mu[f^{-1}(y)] & \text{else.} \end{cases} \tag{2}$$

Next, let us consider the more general case where f is defined on a product space $\mathcal{S}_1 \times \mathcal{S}_2 \times \cdots \times \mathcal{S}_n$. Let $\mu_1, \ldots, \mu_n$ be n fuzzy sets defined respectively on $\mathcal{S}_1, \ldots, \mathcal{S}_n$. The image of $(\mu_1, \ldots, \mu_n)$ by the extension of f is a fuzzy set μ' in $\mathcal{V}$ defined by, for all $y \in \mathcal{V}$:

$$\mu'(y) = \begin{cases} 0 \ \text{ if } f^{-1}(y) = \emptyset \\ \sup_{(x_1,\ldots,x_n) \in \mathcal{S}_1 \times \cdots \times \mathcal{S}_n \mid y = f(x_1,\ldots,x_n)} \min[\mu_1(x_1), \ldots, \mu_n(x_n)] \ \text{ else.} \end{cases} \tag{3}$$

If the supremum is attained, i.e. if:

$$\forall y \in \mathcal{V}, \exists (x_1, ...x_n) \in \mathcal{S}_1 \times ... \times \mathcal{S}_n \mid \mu'(y) = \min[\mu_1(x_1), ...\mu_n(x_n)], \tag{4}$$

then the fuzzy extension of a function commutes with the α-cuts. i.e.:

$$\forall \alpha \in [0,1], [f(\mu_1, ...\mu_n)]_\alpha = f[(\mu_1)_\alpha, ...(\mu_n)_\alpha]. \tag{5}$$

Other extension principles can be defined, using for instance the product instead of the minimum [28].

Combination of results on α-cuts One way to define crisp sets from a fuzzy set consists in taking the α-cuts of this set. Conversely, a fuzzy set can be reconstructed from its α-cuts. Therefore, a class of methods for defining fuzzy operations from crisp ones relies on the application of the crisp operation on each α-cut, and then combining the results to construct a fuzzy operation by stacking up the α-cuts.

Let us denote by μ the membership function of a fuzzy set defined on the space $\mathcal{S}$. Let us consider a crisp set function R_B (or operation on sets) taking values in a space $\mathcal{V}$. The fuzzy equivalent R of R_B is then defined as a function from $\mathcal{F}$ in $\mathcal{V}$ (see e.g. [27,39,20]):

$$R(\mu) = \int_0^1 R_B(\mu_\alpha) d\alpha, \tag{6}$$

where $\mu_\alpha = \{x \in \mathcal{S} \mid \mu(x) \geq \alpha\} = \{x \in \mathcal{S} \mid \mu_\alpha(x) = 1\}$, in order to simplify the notations.

Other fuzzification equations are possible, like:

$$R(\mu) = \sup_{\alpha \in [0,1]} \min(\alpha, R_B(\mu_\alpha)), \tag{7}$$

if the relation takes values in $[0,1]$, or:

$$R(\mu) = \sup_{\alpha \in [0,1]} (\alpha R_B(\mu_\alpha)). \tag{8}$$

These equations may provide different results. But there also exist some links between them. For instance if R_B is two-valued (0/1 or true/false), and decreasing (respectively increasing) with respect to α (i.e. to inclusion), then Equations 6, 7 and 8 provide exactly the same value.

Let us now consider a crisp operation R_B having two arguments (typically a relation between sets). The fuzzy equivalent R of R_B, applied to two fuzzy sets μ and ν of $\mathcal{S}$, is defined as a generalization of the previous equations:

$$R(\mu, \nu) = \int_0^1 R_B(\mu_\alpha, \nu_\alpha) d\alpha, \tag{9}$$

or, using a double integration, as:

$$R(\mu, \nu) = \int_0^1 \int_0^1 R_B(\mu_\alpha, \nu_\beta) d\alpha d\beta. \tag{10}$$

The other fuzzification equations (7 and 8) can also be directly extended to operations on more than one fuzzy set. The extension to n-ary operators is straightforward.

Another method for combining the results on α-cuts is similar to the extension principle [55]. In general, it leads to a fuzzy set on $\mathcal{V}$. For instance if $\mathcal{V} = \mathbb{R}$, the crisp relation provides real values, and then the corresponding fuzzy relation defined by the previous equations provides also numbers, while the following one provides fuzzy numbers. For a binary relation, we have:

$$\forall n \in \mathcal{V}, R(\mu, \nu)(n) = \sup_{R_B(\mu_\alpha, \nu_\alpha) = n} \alpha. \tag{11}$$

We have similar equations for unary or n-ary relations.

If the relationship to be extended only takes binary values (0/1 or true/false), then this equation reduces to:

$$R(\mu, \nu) = \sup_{R_B(\mu_\alpha, \nu_\alpha) = 1} \alpha. \tag{12}$$

The extension principle based on the α-cuts can be interpreted as follows: taking an α-cut of the sets corresponds to taking a binary decision on the boundaries of the objects. Then we look at the obtained value of the crisp relationship for this decision. If the same value of the relation can be obtained from different values of α, then the highest value of α is retained.

Translating binary terms into functional ones A last class of methods consists in translating binary equations into their fuzzy equivalent. This approach completely differs from the two previous ones in the sense that it does not use explicitly the crisp relation or operation. Indeed, in the approaches based on the extension principle as well as on α-cuts, the definition of a fuzzy operation is a function of the corresponding crisp operation. Here, a fuzzy operation is given directly by an equation involving fuzzy terms, that just mimics the corresponding crisp equation.

This translation is generally done term by term. For instance, intersection is replaced by a t-norm, union by a t-conorm, sets by fuzzy set membership functions, etc. This translation is particularly straightforward if the binary relationship can be expressed in set theoretical and logical terms. Table 2 summarizes these main crisp concepts involved in set equations, and their fuzzy equivalents.

crisp concept	**equivalent fuzzy concept**
set X	fuzzy set / membership function μ
complement of a set	fuzzy complementation c
intersection $\cap$	t-norm t
union $\cup$	t-conorm T
existence $\exists$	supremum
universal symbol $\forall$	infimum

Table 2. Translation of crisp concepts in their fuzzy equivalents.

The many possibilities to translate for instance set union using a t-conorm induce many definitions issued from this method, depending on the choice of the fuzzy operators used for translating the crisp corresponding ones.

Let us take a simple example to illustrate this method. A fuzzy set μ is said to be included in another fuzzy set ν if:

$$\forall x \in \mathcal{S}, \ \mu(x) \leq \nu(x).$$

This is a crisp definition of inclusion of fuzzy sets. We may also consider that if two sets are imprecisely defined, their inclusion relationship may be imprecise too. Therefore inclusion of fuzzy sets becomes a matter of degree. This degree of inclusion can be obtained using the translation principle.

In the crisp case, the set equation expressing inclusion of a set X in a set Y can be written as follows:

$$X \subset Y \Leftrightarrow X^C \cup Y = \mathcal{S} \quad (13)$$

$$\Leftrightarrow \forall x \in \mathcal{S}, \ x \in X^C \cup Y. \quad (14)$$

Using the equivalence of Table 2 for each term, we have:

$$\forall x \in \mathcal{S} \leftrightarrow \inf_{x \in \mathcal{S}}, \tag{15}$$

$$x \in X^C \leftrightarrow c[\mu(x)], \tag{16}$$

$$x \in Y \leftrightarrow \nu(x), \tag{17}$$

$$X^C \cup Y \leftrightarrow T[c(\mu), \nu]. \tag{18}$$

Finally, the degree of inclusion of μ in ν is defined as:

$$\mathcal{I}(\mu, \nu) = \inf_{x \in \mathcal{S}} T[c(\mu(x)), \nu(x)], \tag{19}$$

where T is a t-conorm and c a fuzzy complementation.

The question of which extension should be used does not have a definite answer until now. Our point of view is that the extension principle is well adapted for translating analytical expressions, while the formal translation is well adapted if the operators to be extended can be expressed using set theoretical and logical terms. The properties of the obtained extended operators have to play an important role in the choice of a method, since they may vary depending on the method. Here we will mainly use the formal translation principle.

2.2 Fuzzy morphology using the α-cuts

Let us first consider the fuzzification method based on the integration of the equivalent crisp operation over all α-cuts [19,18].

For two fuzzy sets μ and ν, the dilation $D_\nu(\mu)$ of μ by ν is obtained by fuzzification over μ followed by fuzzification over ν, or equivalently by the converse (see Equation 10):

$$D_\nu(\mu)(x) = \int_0^1 D_\nu(\mu_\beta)(x) d\beta = \int_0^1 \int_0^1 D_{\nu_\alpha}(\mu_\beta)(x) d\alpha d\beta \tag{20}$$

$$= \int_0^1 D_{\nu_\alpha}(\mu)(x) d\alpha = \int_0^1 \int_0^1 D_{\nu_\alpha}(\mu_\beta)(x) d\beta d\alpha. \tag{21}$$

A straightforward derivation provides:

$$\forall x \in \mathcal{S},\ D_\nu(\mu)(x) = \int_0^1 \sup_{y \in (\nu_\alpha)_x} \mu(y) d\alpha. \tag{22}$$

In the same way, the erosion $E_\nu(\mu)$ of μ by ν is obtained by:

$$\forall x \in \mathcal{S},\ E_\nu(\mu)(x) = \int_0^1 \inf_{y \in (\nu_\alpha)_x} \mu(y) d\alpha, \tag{23}$$

where $(\nu_\alpha)_x$ denotes the translation of ν_α at x.

These definitions guarantee that $D_\nu(\mu)$ and $E_\nu(\mu)$ are the membership functions of fuzzy sets (i.e. taking values in $[0, 1]$). By construction, if ν is crisp, the definitions coincide with the classical ones (in the GMM framework).

Using the other fuzzification principles (Equations 7 and 8), we obtain respectively:

$$\forall x \in \mathcal{S},\ D_\nu(\mu)(x) = \sup_{y \in \mathcal{S}} \min[\mu(y), \nu(y - x)], \tag{24}$$

$$\forall x \in \mathcal{S},\ E_\nu(\mu)(x) = \inf_{y \in \mathcal{S}} \max[\mu(y), 1 - \nu(y - x)]. \tag{25}$$

and:

$$\forall x \in \mathcal{S},\ D_\nu(\mu)(x) = \sup_{y \in \mathcal{S}} [\mu(y)\nu(y - x)], \tag{26}$$

$$\forall x \in \mathcal{S},\ E_\nu(\mu)(x) = \inf_{y \in \mathcal{S}} [\mu(y)\nu(y - x) + 1 - \nu(y - x)]. \tag{27}$$

The proofs of these derivations can be found in [4].

The extension principle applied to the α-cuts (Equation 12) also leads to:

$$\forall x \in \mathcal{S},\ D_\nu(\mu)(x) = \sup_{y \in \mathcal{S}} \min[\mu(y), \nu(y - x)], \tag{28}$$

$$\forall x \in \mathcal{S},\ E_\nu(\mu)(x) = \inf_{y \in \mathcal{S}} \max[\mu(y), 1 - \nu(y - x)]. \tag{29}$$

These equations happen to be particular cases of the definitions obtained by formal translation, as will be seen in the next section.

2.3 Fuzzy morphology by formal translation based on t-norms and t-conorms

Another way to build ΦMM is to base the initial definitions on the translation of set operations (inclusion, intersection, union) into functional terms, i.e. to exhibit, for each operation, functions from $[0, 1] \times [0, 1]$ to $[0, 1]$ which satisfy some given limit conditions expressing the compatibility with binary set operations. Several definitions exist, that may receive a unified presentation by means of t-norms (and associated t-conorms) as they can be interpreted respectively as fuzzy intersection and fuzzy union (from which a fuzzy inclusion can be derived). This follows exactly the formal translation principle described above. The corresponding definitions have been proposed in [5,20], and coincide with the definitions independently developed in [3].

The construction calls for formal translation of intersection and inclusion. From the following set equivalence (where $E_B(X)$ denotes the erosion of the set X by B):

$$x \in E_B(X) \Leftrightarrow B_x \subseteq X \Leftrightarrow X \cup B_x^C = \mathcal{S} \Leftrightarrow \forall y \in \mathcal{S},\ y \in X \cup B_x^C, \tag{30}$$

a natural way to define the erosion of a fuzzy set μ by a fuzzy structuring element ν is:

$$\forall x \in \mathcal{S},\ E_\nu(\mu)(x) = \inf_{y \in \mathcal{S}} T[c(\nu(y-x)), \mu(y)]. \tag{31}$$

In this equation, the union $\cup$ has been translated in terms of a t-conorm T and the universal symbol $\forall$ by an infimum. This corresponds to the extension of inclusion described before.

By duality with respect to the complementation c, fuzzy dilation is then defined by:

$$\forall x \in \mathcal{S},\ D_\nu(\mu)(x) = \sup_{y \in \mathcal{S}} t[\nu(y-x), \mu(y)], \tag{32}$$

where t is the t-norm associated to the t-conorm T with respect to the complementation c, i.e. $t(a,b) = c(T(c(a), c(b))$ for all $a, b \in [0,1]$.

This definition of dilation corresponds to the following set equivalence:

$$x \in D_B(X) \Leftrightarrow B_x \cap X \neq \emptyset \Leftrightarrow \exists y \in \mathcal{S},\ y \in B_x \cap X. \tag{33}$$

Here, intersection $\cap$ has been translated in terms of a t-norm t and the existential symbol by a supremum.

This form of fuzzy dilation and fuzzy erosion are very general, and several definitions found in the literature appear as particular cases. For instance, the definitions proposed in [17,5,3,2], correspond to Equations 31 and 32, for $t = \min$ and $T = \max$:

$$\forall x \in \mathcal{S},\ D_\nu(\mu)(x) = \sup_{y \in \mathcal{S}} \min[\mu(y), \nu(y-x)], \tag{34}$$

$$\forall x \in \mathcal{S},\ E_\nu(\mu)(x) = \inf_{y \in \mathcal{S}} \max[\mu(y), 1 - \nu(y-x)]. \tag{35}$$

The definitions introduced in [17] correspond to Equations 31 and 32, for the product as t-norm and the algebraic sum as t-conorm:

$$\forall x \in \mathcal{S},\ D_\nu(\mu)(x) = \sup_{y \in \mathcal{S}} [\mu(y)\nu(y-x)], \tag{36}$$

$$\forall x \in \mathcal{S},\ E_\nu(\mu)(x) = \inf_{y \in \mathcal{S}} [\mu(y)\nu(y-x) + 1 - \nu(y-x)]. \tag{37}$$

The definitions introduced in [50] correspond to Equations 31 and 32, for the Lukasiewicz t-norm and t-conorm:

$$\forall x \in \mathcal{S},\ D_\nu(\mu)(x) = \sup_{y \in \mathcal{S}} \max[0, \mu(y) + \nu(y-x) - 1], \tag{38}$$

$$\forall x \in \mathcal{S},\ E_\nu(\mu)(x) = \inf_{y \in \mathcal{S}} \min[1, 1 + \mu(y) - \nu(y-x)]. \tag{39}$$

It is straightforward to see that the definitions proposed in previous works for particular cases [47,37,36] fall within the general definitions using t-norms and t-conorms.

Finally, fuzzy opening (respectively fuzzy closing) is simply defined as the combination of a fuzzy erosion followed by a fuzzy dilation (respectively a fuzzy dilation followed by a fuzzy erosion), by using dual t-norms and t-conorms.

2.4 Using weak t-norms and t-conorms

If we replace, in the previous construction, the t-norm by a weak t-norm, and the t-conorm by a weak t-conorm (which are not associative and do not admit 1 (respectively 0) as unit element, in general), Equations 31 and 32 appear as a generalization of the definitions proposed in [51]:

$$\forall x \in \mathcal{S},\ D_\nu(\mu)(x) = \sup_{y \in \mathcal{S}} \max[0, 1 - \lambda(\mu(y)) - \lambda(\nu(y-x))], \tag{40}$$

$$\forall x \in \mathcal{S},\ E_\nu(\mu)(x) = \inf_{y \in \mathcal{S}} \min[1, \lambda(1 - \mu(y)) + \lambda(\nu(y-x))], \tag{41}$$

with λ a function from $[0,1]$ to $[0,1]$ satisfying the 6 following conditions:

1. $\lambda(z)$ is a non-increasing function of z,
2. $\lambda(0) = 1$,
3. $\lambda(1) = 0$,
4. the equation $\lambda(z) = 0$ has a unique solution,
5. $\forall \alpha \in [0.5, 1]$, the equation $\lambda(z) = \alpha$ has a unique solution,
6. $\forall z \in [0,1], \lambda(z) + \lambda(1-z) \geq 1$.

The weak t-norm and t-conorm involved in these definitions are:

$$\forall (a,b) \in [0,1]^2, t(a,b) = \max[0, 1 - \lambda(a) - \lambda(b)], \tag{42}$$

$$\forall (a,b) \in [0,1]^2, T(a,b) = \min[1, \lambda(1-a) + \lambda(1-b)]. \tag{43}$$

Note that the case where $\lambda(z) = 1 - z = \lambda_0(z)$ leads to a true t-norm and t-conorm. The corresponding definitions for fuzzy dilation and erosion exactly correspond to Equations 32 and 31 for the Lukasiewicz operators (i.e. Equations 38 and 39).

We will see in Section 2.6 that the definitions using a weak t-norm and t-conorm have weaker properties than the ones using a true t-norm and t-conorm. We also refer to Chapter 1 (*Classical and Fuzzy Approaches towards Mathematical Morphology*) for an extensive discussion regarding this approach.

2.5 Fuzzy morphology using residual implications

Fuzzy implication is often defined as [32]:

$$Imp(a, b) = T[c(a), b)]. \tag{44}$$

Fuzzy inclusion is related to implication by the following equation:

$$\mathcal{I}(\nu, \mu) = \inf_{x \in \mathcal{S}} Imp[\nu(x), \mu(x)], \tag{45}$$

which allows to relate directly fuzzy erosion to fuzzy implication, leading to the general definition using t-conorm, and by duality also fuzzy dilation.

This suggests another way to define fuzzy erosion (and dilation), by using other forms of fuzzy implication. One interesting approach is to use residual implications:

$$Imp(a, b) = \sup\{\varepsilon \in [0, 1] | t(a, \varepsilon) \leq b\}. \tag{46}$$

This provides the following expression for the degree of inclusion:

$$\mathcal{I}(\nu, \mu) = \inf_{x \in \mathcal{S}} \sup\{\varepsilon \in [0, 1] | t(\nu(x), \varepsilon) \leq \mu(x)\}. \tag{47}$$

This definition coincides with the previous one if t is an Archimedian t-norm with nilpotent elements, typically Lukasiewicz t-norm: $t(a, b) = \max(0, a + b - 1)$ (the corresponding t-conorm being $T(a, b) = \min(1, a + b)$).

The derivation of fuzzy morphological operators from residual implication has been proposed in [1]. One of its main advantages is that it leads to idempotent fuzzy closing and opening; also refer to Chapter 2 (*Generalized Idempotence in Fuzzy Mathematical Morphology*).

2.6 Properties of basic fuzzy morphological operations

The detail of properties for various definitions can be found in [20], with the main proofs in [4]. We summarize here the main properties; also refer to Chapter 1 (*Classical and Fuzzy Approaches towards Mathematical Morphology*). The general definition using t-norms and t-conorms satisfies most properties:

- erosion and dilation (respectively opening and closing) are dual with respect to the complementation c;
- if the structuring element is binary, the same definitions as in GMM are obtained;
- compatibility with translations;
- local knowledge property;
- continuity if the t-norm is continuous (which is most often the case);
- increasingness of all operations with respect to inclusion;
- extensivity of dilation and anti-extensivity of erosion iff $\nu(0) = 1$ (this corresponds to the condition that the origin should belong to the structuring element in the crisp case);
- extensivity of closing, anti-extensivity of opening and idempotence of these two operations iff $t[b, u(c(b), a)] \leq a$, which is for example satisfied for Lukasiewicz t-norm and t-conorm;
- commutation with union of dilation (with intersection for erosion);
- iteration property of dilation.

For the definitions obtained by integration over the α-cuts, extensivity of closing, anti-extensivity of opening, idempotence of opening and closing, commutation with union of dilation (with intersection for erosion), and iteration property of dilation are lost. The other properties are kept.

For the definitions derived from weak t-norm and t-conorm, several properties hold only for the case where $\lambda = \lambda_0$.

For the definitions derived from a residual implication, opening and closing are idempotent and anti-extensive, respectively extensive.

3 Fuzzy distances derived from fuzzy dilation

The importance of distances in image processing is well established. Their extensions to fuzzy sets can be useful in several parts of image processing under imprecision. Let us mention a few possible applications of these distances for image processing problems where imprecision has to be taken into account. Distance from a point to a fuzzy set can be used for classification purposes, where a point has to be attributed to the nearest fuzzy class. When considering distance from a point to the complement of a fuzzy set μ, we obtain the basic information for computing a fuzzy skeleton of μ. Mean distance is useful for registration: if we want to register a fuzzy set with respect to another one, we may use this distance as a minimization criterion, that can be optimized over all possible positions (typically translation and rotation) of one fuzzy set with respect to the other. Hausdorff distance has an interest in terms of properties, since it has the best ones. Also in the crisp case it is related to hit-or-miss topology restricted to compact sets, which is the basic topological tool for mathematical morphology. Therefore, fuzzy mathematical morphology inherits also topological support through the definition of fuzzy Hausdorff distance. All these applications deserve a deeper study and analysis. They justify the interest of defining fuzzy distances.

Several definitions can be found in the literature for distances between fuzzy sets (which is the main addressed problem). They can be roughly divided in two classes: distances that only take membership functions into account and that compare them pointwise, and distances that additionally include spatial distances. The definitions which combine spatial distance and fuzzy membership comparison allow for a more general analysis of structures in images, and for applications where topological and spatial arrangement of the structures of interest is important (such as segmentation, classification, scene interpretation). This is permitted by the fact that these distances combine membership values at different points in the space, and take into account their proximity or farness in $\mathcal{S}$. The price to pay is an increased complexity, generally quadratic in the cardinality of $\mathcal{S}$.

In [6,15], we proposed original approaches for defining fuzzy distances taking into account spatial information, which are based on fuzzy mathematical morphology. They are summarized below. The idea is that in the binary case, there exist strong links between mathematical morphology (in particular dilation) and distances (from a point to a set, and between two sets), and this can also be exploited in the fuzzy case. The advantage is that distances are expressed in set theoretical terms, and are therefore easier to translate (with nice properties) than usual analytical expressions.

3.1 Distances from a point to a fuzzy set

Distances from a point to a fuzzy set can be defined using a weighting approach or using a fuzzification from α-cuts (see e.g. [6]). In this way, they are defined as numbers.

We propose an original approach for defining the distance $d(x, \mu)$ from a point x of $\mathcal{S}$ to a fuzzy object μ as a fuzzy number, by translating crisp equations into their fuzzy equivalent. A formalism where distances are expressed in set theoretical terms is provided by mathematical morphology, since the distance from a point to a set can be expressed in terms of morphological dilation.

In the crisp case, and in a finite discrete space (which is the most interesting case in image processing), we have respectively for $n = 0$ and for $n > 0$:

$$d_B(x, X) = 0 \Leftrightarrow x \in X \tag{48}$$

$$d_B(x, X) = n \Leftrightarrow x \in D^n(X) \text{ and } x \notin D^{n-1}(X) \tag{49}$$

where D^n denotes the dilation by a ball of radius n centered at the origin of $\mathcal{S}$ (with $D^0(X) = X$) (see e.g. [23] for a study of discrete balls and discrete distances in the crisp case). In this case, the extensivity property of the dilation holds [49], and $x \notin D^{n-1}(X)$ is equivalent to $\forall n' < n, x \notin D^{n'}(X)$. Equation 49 is equivalent to:

$$x \in D^n(X) \cap [D^{n-1}(X)]^C, \tag{50}$$

where A^C denotes the complement set of A in $\mathcal{S}$. This is a pure set theoretical expression, that we can now translate into fuzzy terms. This leads to the following definition of the degree to which $d(x, \mu)$ is equal to n:

$$\delta_{(x,\mu)}(0) = \mu(x), \tag{51}$$

$$\delta_{(x,\mu)}(n) = t[D_\nu^n(\mu)(x), c[D_\nu^{n-1}(\mu)(x)]], \tag{52}$$

where t is a t-norm (fuzzy intersection), c a fuzzy complementation (typically $c(a) = 1 - a$ for $a \in [0, 1]$), and ν a fuzzy structuring element used for performing the dilation. Several choices for ν are possible. It can be the unit ball, or a fuzzy set representing for instance the smallest sensitive unit in the image, along with the imprecision attached to it. In this case, ν has to be equal to 1 at the origin of $\mathcal{S}$, such that the extensivity of the dilation still holds [20].

The properties of this definition are the following [6]: If $\mu(x) = 1$, then $\delta_{(x,\mu)}(0) = 1$ and $\forall n > 0, \delta_{(x,\mu)}(n) = 0$, i.e. the distance is a crisp number in this case. If μ and ν are binary, the proposed definition coincides with the binary one. The fuzzy set $\delta_{(x,\mu)}$ can be interpreted as a density distance, from which a distance distribution can be deduced by integration. Finally, $\delta_{(x,\mu)}$ is a non normalized fuzzy number (in the discrete finite case).

Figure 3 presents an example of fuzzy numbers $\delta_{(x,\mu)}$ obtained for different points.

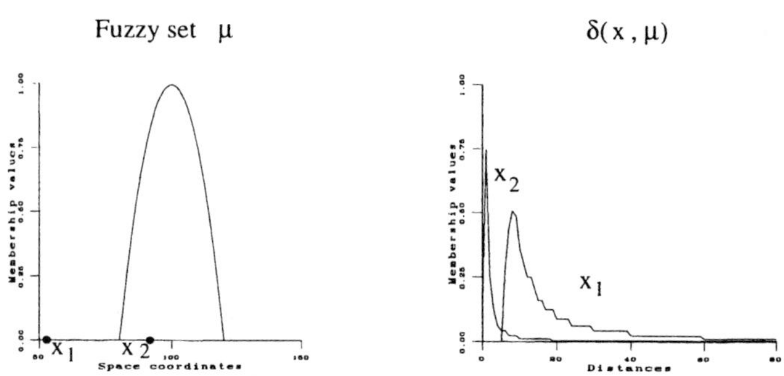

Fig. 3. Fuzzy numbers representing $\delta_{(x,\mu)}$ for two different x (μ being shown on the left in a 1D space).

From this definition, distances between two fuzzy sets can be derived using supremum or infimum computation of fuzzy numbers using the extension principle [28]. The details are given in [6]. The maximum of p fuzzy numbers representing the fuzzy distance from x_i to μ is obtained by:

$$\forall n \geq 0, \max(\delta_{(x_1,\mu)}, \delta_{(x_2,\mu)}, ..., \delta_{(x_p,\mu)})(n) = \sup_{\substack{(n_1,\dots,n_p) \\ n=\max(n_1,\dots,n_p)}} \min[\delta_{(x_1,\mu)}(n_1), ...\delta_{(x_p,\mu)}(n_p)]. \tag{53}$$

In a similar way, the fuzzy minimum is defined as:

$$\forall n \geq 0, \min(\delta_{(x_1,\mu)}, \delta_{(x_2,\mu)}, ..., \delta_{(x_p,\mu)})(n) = \sup_{\substack{(n_1,\dots,n_p) \\ n=\min(n_1,\dots,n_p)}} \min[\delta_{(x_1,\mu)}(n_1), ...\delta_{(x_p,\mu)}(n_p)]. \tag{54}$$

Now if we consider points in another fuzzy set ν defined on $\mathcal{S}$, i.e. if we want to compute a function of $\delta_{(x_i,\mu)}$ over a set of x_i having non binary membership degrees to ν, we have to introduce the values of $\nu(x_i)$ in equations 53 and 54, for instance as:

$$\forall n \geq 0, \max(\delta_{(x_1,\mu)}, \delta_{(x_2,\mu)}, ..., \delta_{(x_p,\mu)})(n) = \sup_{\substack{(n_1,\dots,n_p) \\ n=\max(n_1,\dots,n_p)}} \min_{i=1\dots p}[\min[\delta_{(x_i,\mu)}(n_i), \nu(x_i)]]. \tag{55}$$

Similarly we may define the minimum of fuzzy numbers as:

$$\forall n \geq 0, \min(\delta_{(x_1,\mu)}, \delta_{(x_2,\mu)}, ..., \delta_{(x_p,\mu)})(n) = \sup_{\substack{(n_1,\dots,n_p) \\ n=\min(n_1,\dots,n_p)}} \min_{i=1\dots p}[\min[\delta_{(x_i,\mu)}(n_i), \nu(x_i)]]. \tag{56}$$

3.2 Distances between two fuzzy sets

We defined distances between two fuzzy objects using a morphological approach in [6,15], in an original way. They are obtained again by direct translation of crisp equations expressing distances in terms of mathematical morphology into fuzzy ones. We just give the examples of nearest point distance and Hausdorff distance.

Fuzzy nearest point distance The minimum or nearest point distance between X and Y is defined (in the discrete finite case) as:

$$\begin{aligned} d_N(X,Y) &= \min_{(x,y)\in X\times Y} d_E(x,y) \\ &= \min_{x\in X} d_E(x,Y) = \min_{y\in Y} d_E(y,X), \end{aligned} \tag{57}$$

where d_E denotes the Euclidean distance in $\mathcal{S}$. This has an equivalent morphological expression:

$$\begin{aligned} d_N(X,Y) &= \inf\{n \in \mathbb{N} \,|\, X \cap D^n(Y) \neq \emptyset\} \\ &= \inf\{n \in \mathbb{N} \,|\, Y \cap D^n(X) \neq \emptyset\}. \end{aligned} \tag{58}$$

By translating equation 58, we define a distance distribution $\Delta_N(\mu,\mu')(n)$ that expresses the degree to which the distance between μ and μ' is less than n by:

$$\begin{aligned} \Delta_N(\mu,\mu')(n) = f[&\sup_{x\in\mathcal{S}} t[\mu(x), D^n_\nu(\mu')(x)], \\ &\sup_{x\in\mathcal{S}} t[\mu'(x), D^n_\nu(\mu)(x)]], \end{aligned} \tag{59}$$

where f is a symmetrical function.

A distance density, i.e. a fuzzy number $\delta_N(\mu,\mu')(n)$ representing the degree to which the distance between μ and μ' is equal to n, can be obtained implicitly by:

$$\Delta_N(\mu,\mu')(n) = \int_0^n \delta_N(\mu,\mu')(n')dn'. \tag{60}$$

Clearly, this expression is not very attractable and does not lead to a simple explicit expression for $\delta_N(\mu,\mu')(n)$. Therefore, we suggest to use an explicit method, exploiting the fact that, for $n > 0$, the nearest point distance can be expressed in morphological terms by:

$$d_N(X,Y) = n \Leftrightarrow D^n(X) \cap Y \neq \emptyset \text{ and } D^{n-1}(X) \cap Y = \emptyset \tag{61}$$

or equivalently by the symmetrical expression. For $n = 0$ we have:

$$d_N(X,Y) = 0 \Leftrightarrow X \cap Y \neq \emptyset. \tag{62}$$

The translation of these equivalences provides, for $n > 0$, the following distance density:

$$\delta_N(\mu,\mu')(n) = t[\sup_{x\in\mathcal{S}} t[\mu'(x), D^n_\nu(\mu)(x)], c[\sup_{x\in\mathcal{S}} t[\mu'(x), D^{n-1}_\nu(\mu)(x)]]] \tag{63}$$

or a symmetrical expression derived from this one, and:

$$\delta_N(\mu,\mu')(0) = \sup_{x\in\mathcal{S}} t[\mu(x),\mu'(x)]. \tag{64}$$

Fuzzy Hausdorff distance Like for the nearest point distance, we can extend the Hausdorff distance by translating directly the binary equation defining the Hausdorff distance:

$$d_H(X,Y) = \max[\sup_{x\in X} d_B(x,Y), \sup_{y\in Y} d_B(y,X)]. \tag{65}$$

This distance can be expressed in morphological terms as:

$$d_H(X,Y) = \inf\{n \mid X \subseteq D^n(Y) \text{ and } Y \subseteq D^n(X)\}. \tag{66}$$

From equation 66, a distance distribution can be defined using fuzzy dilation:

$$\Delta_H(\mu,\mu')(n) = t[\inf_{x\in\mathcal{S}} T[D^n_\nu(\mu)(x), c(\mu'(x))], \inf_{x\in\mathcal{S}} T[D^n_\nu(\mu')(x), c(\mu(x))]], \tag{67}$$

where c is a complementation, t a t-norm and T a t-conorm. A distance density can be derived implicitly from this distance distribution.

A direct definition of a distance density can be obtained from:

$$d_H(X,Y) = 0 \Leftrightarrow X = Y, \tag{68}$$

and for $n > 0$:

$$\begin{aligned} d_H(X,Y) = n \Leftrightarrow X \subseteq D^n(Y) \text{ and } Y \subseteq D^n(X) \\ \text{and } \left(X \not\subseteq D^{n-1}(Y) \text{ or } Y \not\subseteq D^{n-1}(X)\right). \end{aligned} \tag{69}$$

Translating these equations leads to a definition of the Hausdorff distance between two fuzzy sets μ and μ' as a fuzzy number:

$$\delta_H(\mu,\mu')(0) = t[\inf_{x\in\mathcal{S}} T[\mu(x), c(\mu'(x))], \inf_{x\in\mathcal{S}} T[\mu'(x), c(\mu(x))]], \tag{70}$$

$$\begin{aligned} &\delta_H(\mu,\mu')(n) \\ = \; &t[\inf_{x\in\mathcal{S}} T[D^n_\nu(\mu)(x), c(\mu'(x))], \inf_{x\in\mathcal{S}} T[D^n_\nu(\mu')(x), c(\mu(x))], \\ &T(\sup_{x\in\mathcal{S}} t[\mu(x), c(D^{n-1}_\nu(\mu')(x))], \sup_{x\in\mathcal{S}} t[\mu'(x), c(D^{n-1}_\nu(\mu)(x))])]. \end{aligned} \tag{71}$$

Properties The above definitions of fuzzy nearest point and Hausdorff distances (defined as fuzzy numbers) between two fuzzy sets do not necessarily share the same properties as their crisp equivalent. In particular, this is due to the fact that, depending on the choice of the involved t-norms and t-conorms, excluded-middle and non-contradiction laws may not be satisfied. All distances are positive, in the sense that the defined fuzzy numbers have always a support included in $\mathbb{R}^+$. By construction, all defined distances are symmetrical with respect to μ and μ'. The separability property (i.e. $d(\mu,\nu) = 0 \Leftrightarrow \mu = \nu$) is not always satisfied. However, if μ is normalized, we have for the nearest point distance $\delta_N(\mu,\mu)(0) = 1$ and $\delta_N(\mu,\mu)(n) = 0$ for $n > 1$. For the Hausdorff distance, $\delta_H(\mu,\mu')(0) = 1$ implies $\mu = \mu'$ for T being the bounded sum ($T(a,b) = \min(1, a+b)$), while it implies μ and μ' crisp and equal for $T = \max$. Also the triangular inequality is not satisfied in general.

3.3 Example

We illustrate these definitions on an example taken from brain imaging. We use the five fuzzy structures shown in Figure 2. These structures may be recognized using an anatomical atlas for instance, by comparing relationships between atlas structures and relationships between image structures.

Examples of distances between brain structures are shown in Table 3, as fuzzy numbers issued from the morphological definition of Hausdorff distance. The results are in agreement with what is expected: the model of v2 provided by an anatomical atlas is near from cn2 and v1, quite far from cn1 and very far from p1. We do not obtain a null value for v2, since it does not perfectly match the model of v2, but we obtain values that are still much lower than those obtained for the other structures. This shows that distances can be used both for identifying a structure among several possible ones, by using distance as a dissimilarity measure, and for describing the spatial arrangement of objects in terms of nearness or farness.

Distance between a model of v2 and:		
cn2	v2	v1
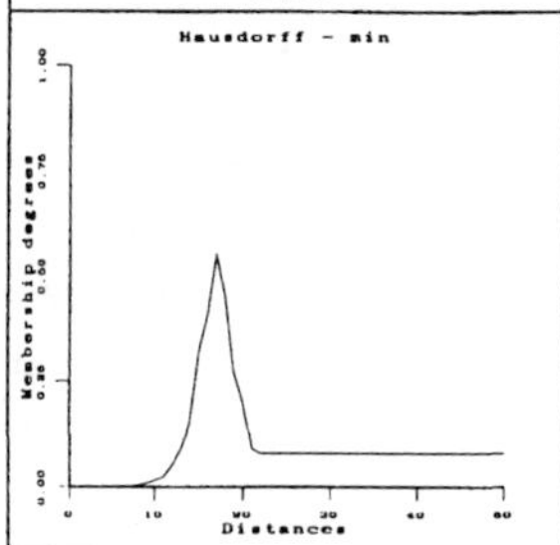	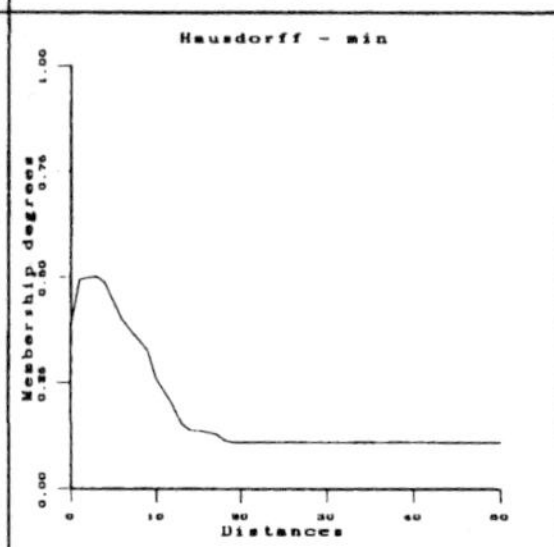	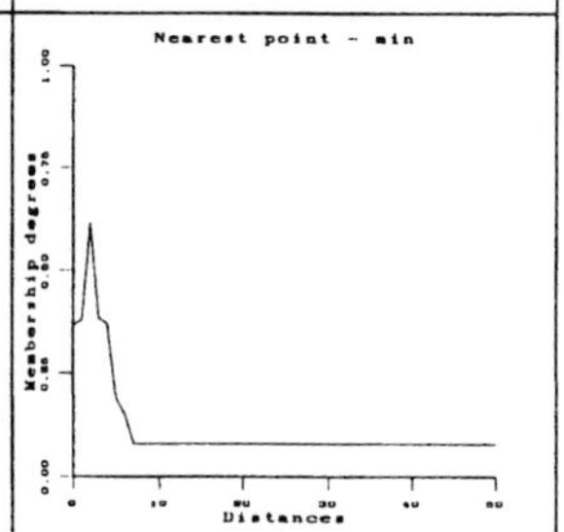
cn1	p1	
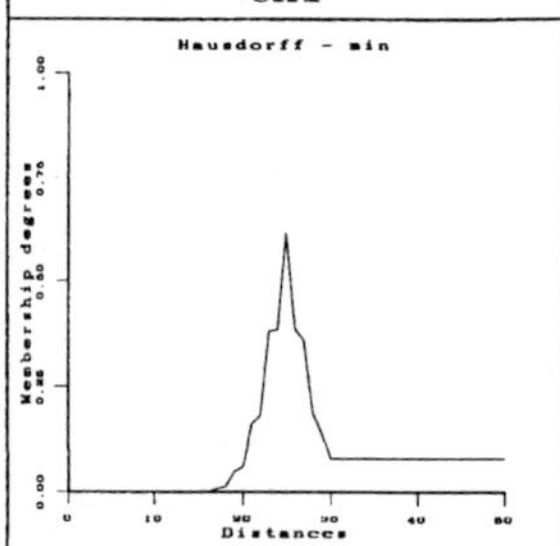	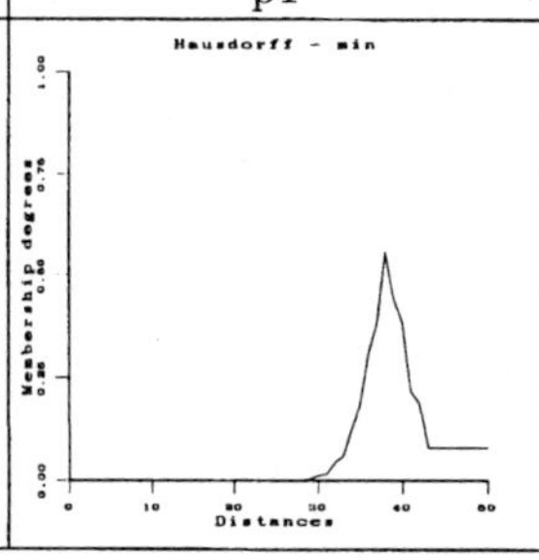	

Table 3. Distances between fuzzy sets using the morphological approach, for the Hausdorff distance, using minimum as t-norm. The distance is computed between each of the 5 structures and a model of v2 given by an anatomical atlas.

4 Fuzzy adjacency from fuzzy dilation and set operations

Adjacency has a large interest in image processing and pattern recognition, since it denotes an important relationship between image objects or regions [48], widely used as a feature in model-based pattern recognition.

A crisp definition of adjacency between crisp objects often leads to a low robustness in case of noise or segmentation errors. Let us consider for instance a problem of model-based pattern recognition, where spatial relationships are an important part of the recognition process. If two model objects are adjacent, we expect the corresponding image objects to be adjacent too, otherwise they will be difficult to recognize. However, if classical crisp adjacency is used, the fact that two objects are adjacent or not may depend on one point only. Figure 4 illustrates the sensitivity of the binary adjacency concept to errors in segmentation or definition of the objects.

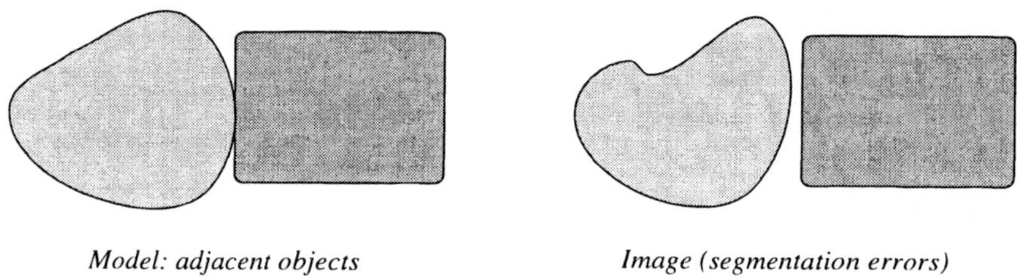

Fig. 4. Sensitivity of crisp adjacency: small modifications in the shapes may completely change the adjacency relation, and thus prevent a correct recognition based on this relationship.

In order to include possible errors or imprecision in the processing and in the recognition, the framework of fuzzy sets is very useful. Two completely different ways for representing imprecision can be considered. In the first one, the satisfaction of the adjacency property between two objects is considered to be a matter of degree; this can be more appropriate than a binary index [46,47]. The second one consists in introducing imprecision in the objects themselves, and to deal with fuzzy objects. For instance, spatial imprecision due to the limited quality of image information can be represented in an adequate way by considering fuzzy objects. Then obviously adjacency is also a matter of degree. Only the second way is addressed in this chapter. More details can be found in [21].

4.1 Crisp discrete case

Here, we restrict ourselves to the discrete case, and use discrete topology as derived from discrete connectivity for defining adjacency between two image regions X and Y, subsets of the discrete space. Let us consider an n-dimensional discrete space (typically $\mathbb{Z}^n$), and any discrete connectivity defined on this space, denoted c-connectivity (for instance, for $n = 3$, we may consider 6-, 18- or 26-connectivity on a cubic grid). Since we would like to distinguish between connectedness and adjacency relationships, we use the following definition of crisp adjacency, where we denote by $n_c(x, y)$ the Boolean variable stating that x and y are neighbors in the sense of the discrete c-connectivity: for any two subsets X and Y in $\mathbb{Z}^n$, X and Y are adjacent according to the c-connectivity if: $X \cap Y = \emptyset \ and \ \exists x \in X, \exists y \in Y : n_c(x, y)$.

For the discrete boundary of a set X, we consider its interior boundary defined as: $\partial X = X - E(X, B_c)$ where $E(X, B_c)$ denotes the morphological erosion of X by the structuring element B_c of size 1 defined according to the c-connectivity [49] (i.e. B_c contains the center point and its c neighbors). Using this definition, the discrete adjacency can be related to the boundary in the following way: if X and Y are adjacent, then any $x \in X$ and $y \in Y$ that satisfy $n_c(x, y)$ belong to the boundary of X and Y respectively.

Therefore, the fuzzy extension of this definition can be obtained either by considering only the constraint on the neighborhood, or by also considering the constraint on the boundary.

This definition can also be expressed equivalently in terms of morphological dilation, namely as: $X \cap Y = \emptyset \ and \ D(X, B_c) \cap Y \neq \emptyset, \ \ D(Y, B_c) \cap X \neq \emptyset$, where $D(X, B_c)$ denotes the dilation of X by the structuring element B_c.

This property provides a third way to extend the definition to fuzzy sets, either directly from fuzzy dilation, or by means of distance computation, which is closely related to dilation. This is the definition we will use here.

4.2 Extending adjacency to fuzzy objects using morphological operators

We consider fuzzy objects and define fuzzy adjacency between such objects. As mentioned before, in the discrete case, a fuzzy object is simply defined by its membership function, defined on $\mathbb{Z}^n$ and taking values in $[0, 1]$.

The properties we require for fuzzy adjacency are the following:

- symmetry, i.e. the degree of adjacency between μ and ν has to be the same as between ν and μ;
- consistency with binary definitions, i.e. if μ and ν are crisp sets (note that this corresponds to the case where no imprecision has to be taken into account), their degree of adjacency should be equal to 1 or 0, depending on whether they are adjacent or not, according to the definitions in the crisp case. This consistency will be automatically satisfied if we use one of the above methods;
- decreasingness with respect to the distance between both sets: this will be taken into account in the notion of fuzzy neighborhood;
- a last property, often desirable although not mandatory, is invariance with respect to geometrical transformations.

Adjacency from fuzzy dilation We define adjacency from fuzzy dilation by translating the property involving dilation in the crisp case into fuzzy terms. A direct translation of this property leads to the following definition: the degree of adjacency between μ and ν involving fuzzy dilation is defined as:

$$\mu_{adj}(\mu, \nu) = t[\mu_{\neg int}(\mu, \nu), \mu_{int}[D(\mu, B_c), \nu], \mu_{int}[D(\nu, B_c), \mu]]. \tag{72}$$

This definition represents a conjunctive combination of a degree of non-intersection $\mu_{\neg int}$ between μ and ν and a degree of intersection μ_{int} between one fuzzy set and the dilation of the other. The degree of intersection can be defined using a supremum of a t-norm (as for fuzzy dilation):

$$\mu_{int}(\mu, \nu) = \sup_{x \in \mathcal{S}} t[\mu(x), \nu(x)], \tag{73}$$

or using the fuzzy volume of the t-norm in order to take more spatial information into account:

$$\mu_{int}(\mu, \nu) = \frac{V_n[t(\mu, \nu)]}{\min[V_n(\mu), V_n(\nu)]}, \tag{74}$$

where

$$V_n(\mu) = \sum_{x \in \mathcal{S}} \mu(x). \tag{75}$$

The degree of non-intersection is simply defined by $\mu_{\neg int} = 1 - \mu_{int}$. B_c can be taken as the elementary structuring element related to the considered connectivity, or as a fuzzy structuring element, representing for instance spatial imprecision (i.e. the possibility distribution of the location of each point).

We proved that this definition is symmetrical, consistent with the binary definition if μ, ν and B_c are binary, and decreases if the distance between μ and ν increases.

Adjacency involving boundary constraints Fuzzy dilation can also serve for defining the fuzzy boundary of a fuzzy set, as follows: the fuzzy boundary b_μ of a fuzzy set μ is defined from fuzzy dilation as:

$$b_\mu(x) = t[\mu(x), D(c(\mu), B_c)(x)]. \tag{76}$$

The translation of the crisp expression of adjacency along with the property on boundary leads now to the following definition: the degree of adjacency between μ and ν involving boundary constraints is defined by:

$$\mu_{adj}(\mu, \nu) = t\left[\mu_{\neg int}(\mu, \nu), \sup_x \sup_y t[b_\mu(x), b_\nu(y), n_{xy}]\right], \tag{77}$$

where the supremum is taken over $\mathcal{S}$. In this equation n_{xy} represents the degree to which x and y are neighbors (it can been defined as in the crisp case, using a discrete connectivity, or as a decreasing function of the distance between x and y as in [24,21]).

The degree of adjacency obtained from this boundary definition (with any structuring element) is still symmetrical, consistent with the binary case and decreasing when the distance between both fuzzy sets increases.

Adjacency from fuzzy nearest point distance Finally, since in the discrete binary case the equation using dilation means that the minimum (nearest point) distance between X and Y is equal to 1, we can also exploit this fact in the fuzzy case by using the fuzzy nearest point distance, defined from fuzzy dilation. It leads to similar definitions, sharing the same properties as the previous ones:

$$\mu_{adj}(\mu, \nu) = \delta_N(\mu, \nu)(1), \tag{78}$$

where $\delta_N(\mu, \nu)(1)$ is obtained as in Equation 63, by taking $n = 1$.

4.3 Example

We again use the five fuzzy structures shown in Figure 2 to illustrate the above definitions. The adjacency degrees between some of the obtained fuzzy objects are given in Table 4. The results are in agreement with what can be expected from the model (crisp adjacency between atlas objects). In this case, crisp adjacency would provide completely different results in the model and in the image, preventing its use for recognition. This suggests that fuzzy adjacency degree can indeed be used for pattern recognition purposes, of course combined with other spatial relationships.

Fuzzy object 1	Fuzzy object 2	degree of adjacency	adjacency in the model (crisp)
v1	v2	0.368	1
v1	cn1	0.463	1
v1	p1	0.000	0
v1	cn2	0.035	0
v2	cn2	0.427	1
cn1	p1	0.035	0

Table 4. Results obtained for fuzzy adjacency. Labels of structures are given in Figure 2. High degrees are obtained between structures where adjacency is expected, while very low degrees are obtained in the opposite case.

5 Fuzzy directional relative position from conditional fuzzy dilation

The spatial arrangement of objects in images provides important information for recognition and interpretation tasks, in particular when the objects are embedded in a complex environment like in medical or remote sensing images. Relationships between objects can be partly described in terms of relative position, like "to the left of". It should be noted that such concepts are rather ambiguous, they defy precise definitions, but human beings have a rather intuitive and common way of understanding and interpreting them. From our every day experience, it is clear that any "all-or-nothing" definition leads to unsatisfactory results in several situations, even of moderate complexity (see examples of Fig. 5).

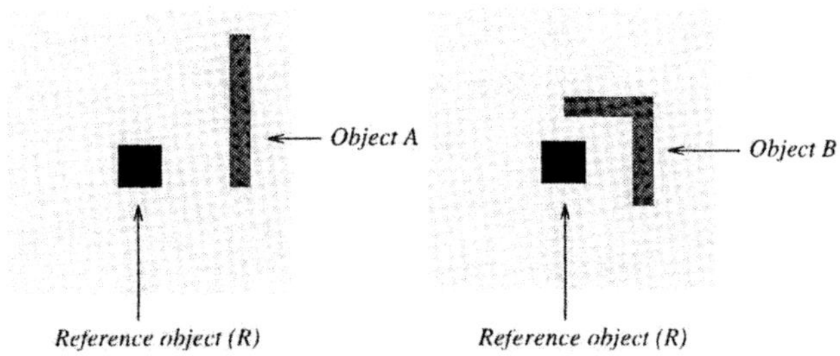

Fig. 5. Two examples where the relative position of objects with respect to the reference object is difficult to define in a "all-or-nothing" manner: the object A is to the right of R but it can also be considered to be to some extent above it; object B is strongly to the right of R and above it.

Therefore, relative position concepts may find a better understanding in the framework of fuzzy sets, as fuzzy relationships. This framework makes it possible to propose flexible definitions which fit the intuition and may include subjective aspects, depending on the application and on the requirements of the user. The interest of fuzzy approaches for representing spatial constraints has been emphasized e.g. in [33]. In structural pattern recognition we are not just interested in the dominating relationships between objects: an object may satisfy several relationships with respect to the other components of the image (see e.g. the right of Figure 5) and it is clear that the shape of the considered objects has to play an important role in assessing its relative position.

5.1 Overview: morphological fuzzy pattern matching approach

Our motivation for proposing a definition for relative position between objects is to provide a definition that should: (i) work directly in the image space; (ii) be generic enough in order to apply to relative positions defined by any direction (not only four or six basic ones); (iii) introduce morphological information on the considered objects themselves, with the aim of pattern recognition applications; (iv) be applicable to 3D objects (for applications to medical imaging for instance) and to fuzzy objects (in order to take into account spatial imprecision in the objects); (v) verify algebraic and geometrical properties and (vi) behave according to the intuition in a large variety of situations.

Let us consider a reference object R and an object A for which the relative position with respect to R has to be evaluated. In order to evaluate the degree to which A is in some direction with respect to R, we propose the following approach [12,13]:

1. We first define a fuzzy "landscape" around the reference object R as a fuzzy set such that the membership value of each point corresponds to the degree of satisfaction of the spatial relation under examination. Therefore the fuzzy landscape is directly defined in the same space as the considered objects, in contrast to the solution proposed in [38].
2. We then compare the object A to the fuzzy landscape attached to R, in order to evaluate how well the object matches with the areas having high membership values (i.e. areas that are in the desired direction). This is done using a fuzzy pattern matching approach, which provides an evaluation as an interval instead of one number only. This makes a major difference with respect to all the previous approaches, and, to our opinion, it provides a richer information about the considered relationship.

5.2 Relative position from fuzzy pattern matching

We denote by $\mathcal{S}$ the Euclidean space where the objects are defined. $\mathcal{S}$ is typically a 2D or 3D discrete space (as in image processing). In the 3D Euclidean space, a direction is defined by two angles α_1 and α_2 (see Figure 6), where $\alpha_1 \in [0, 2\pi]$ and $\alpha_2 \in [-\frac{\pi}{2}, \frac{\pi}{2}]$ ($\alpha_2 = 0$ in the 2D case). The direction in which the relative position of an object with respect to another one is evaluated is given by: $\boldsymbol{u}_{\alpha_1,\alpha_2} = (\cos\alpha_2 \cos\alpha_1, \cos\alpha_2 \sin\alpha_1, \sin\alpha_2)^t$, and we note $\alpha = (\alpha_1, \alpha_2)$.

We consider two (possibly fuzzy) objects, R and A, and define the degree to which A is in direction $\boldsymbol{u}_{\alpha_1,\alpha_2}$ with respect to R. Let us denote by $\mu_\alpha(R)$ the fuzzy set defined in the image in such a way that points of areas which satisfy to a high degree the relation "to be in the direction $\boldsymbol{u}_{\alpha_1,\alpha_2}$ with respect to reference object R" have high membership values. In other terms, the membership function $\mu_\alpha(R)$ has to be an increasing function of the degree of satisfaction of the relation. It is a spatial fuzzy set (i.e. a function of the image space $\mathcal{S}$ into [0,1]) and directly related to the shape of R. The precise definition of $\mu_\alpha(R)$ is given in the next subsection.

Let us denote by μ_A the membership function of the object A, which is a function of $\mathcal{S}$ into [0,1]. The evaluation of the relative position of A with

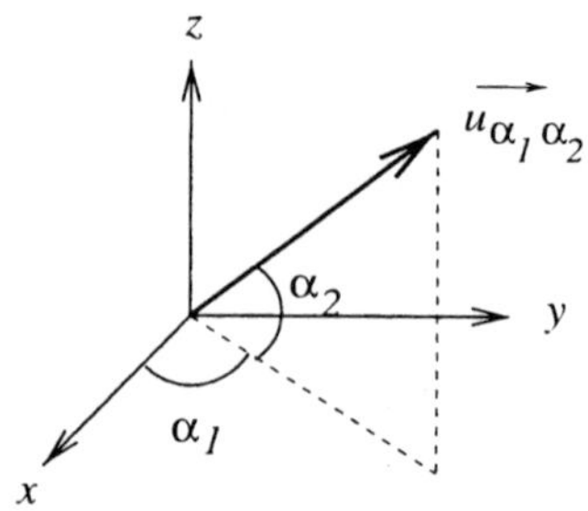

Fig. 6. Definition of a direction in 3D by two angles.

respect to R is given by a function of $\mu_\alpha(R)(x)$ and $\mu_A(x)$ for all x in $\mathcal{S}$. An appropriate tool for defining this function is the fuzzy pattern matching approach [31]. Following this approach, the evaluation of the matching between two possibility distributions consists of two numbers, a necessity degree N (a pessimistic evaluation) and a possibility degree Π (an optimistic evaluation), as often used in the fuzzy set community. In our application, they take the following forms:

$$\Pi^R_{\alpha_1,\alpha_2}(A) = \sup_{x\in\mathcal{S}} t[\mu_\alpha(R)(x), \mu_A(x)], \tag{79}$$

$$N^R_{\alpha_1,\alpha_2}(A) = \inf_{x\in\mathcal{S}} T[\mu_\alpha(R)(x), 1 - \mu_A(x)], \tag{80}$$

where t is a t-norm (fuzzy intersection) and T a t-conorm (fuzzy union) [30]. In the crisp case (i.e. if A is crisp), these equations reduce to:

$$\Pi^R_{\alpha_1,\alpha_2}(A) = \sup_{x\in A} \mu_\alpha(R)(x),$$
$$N^R_{\alpha_1,\alpha_2}(A) = \inf_{x\in A} \mu_\alpha(R)(x).$$

The possibility corresponds to a degree of intersection between the fuzzy sets A and $\mu_\alpha(R)$, while the necessity corresponds to a degree of inclusion of A in $\mu_\alpha(R)$. They can also be interpreted in terms of fuzzy mathematical morphology, since the possibility $\Pi^R_{\alpha_1,\alpha_2}(A)$ is equal to the dilation of μ_A by $\mu_\alpha(R)$ at the origin, while the necessity $N^R_{\alpha_1,\alpha_2}(A)$ is equal to the erosion, as shown in [20]. These two interpretations, in terms of set theoretic operations and in terms of morphological ones, explain how the shape of the objects is taken into account.

Several other functions combining $\mu_\alpha(R)$ and $\mu_A(x)$ can be constructed. The extreme values provided by the fuzzy pattern matching are interesting because of their morphological interpretation, and because they provide an interval and not only a single value and may represent in this way the ambiguity of the relation, if any. An average measure can also be useful from a practical point of view, and is defined as:

$$M^R_{\alpha_1,\alpha_2}(A) = \frac{1}{|A|} \sum_{x\in\mathcal{S}} \mu_A(x)\mu_\alpha(R)(x), \tag{81}$$

where $|A|$ denotes the fuzzy cardinality of A: $|A| = \sum_{x \in \mathcal{S}} \mu_A(x)$.

5.3 Definition of μ_α

The key point in the previous definition relies in the definition of $\mu_\alpha(R)$. The requirements stated above for this fuzzy set are not strong and leave room for a large spectrum of possibilities. This flexibility allows the user to define any membership function according to the application at hand and the context requirements. We propose here a definition that looks precisely at the domains of space that are visible from a reference object point in the direction $\boldsymbol{u}_{\alpha_1,\alpha_2}$. This applies to objects of any kind, in particular having strong concavities, and therefore differs from solutions proposed in [7].

Let us denote by P any point in $\mathcal{S}$, and by Q any point in R. Let $\beta(P,Q)$ be the angle between the vector $\boldsymbol{QP}$ and the direction $\boldsymbol{u}_{\alpha_1,\alpha_2}$, computed in $[0, \pi]$:

$$\beta(P,Q) = \arccos \left[\frac{\boldsymbol{QP} \cdot \boldsymbol{u}_{\alpha_1,\alpha_2}}{||\boldsymbol{QP}||} \right], \quad and \;\; \beta(P,P) = 0. \tag{82}$$

We then determine for each point P the point Q of R leading to the smallest angle β, denoted by $\beta_{\min}$. In the crisp case, this point Q is the reference object point from which P is visible in the direction the closest to $\boldsymbol{u}_{\alpha_1,\alpha_2}$ (see Figure 7): $\beta_{\min}(P) = \min_{Q \in R} \beta(P,Q)$. The fuzzy landscape $\mu_\alpha(R)$ at point P is then defined as: $\mu_\alpha(R)(P) = f(\beta_{\min}(P))$, where f is a decreasing function of $[0, \pi]$ into $[0, 1]$. In our experiments, we have chosen a simple linear function (Figure 7 right): $\mu_\alpha(R)(P) = \max(0, 1 - \frac{2\beta_{\min}(P)}{\pi})$.

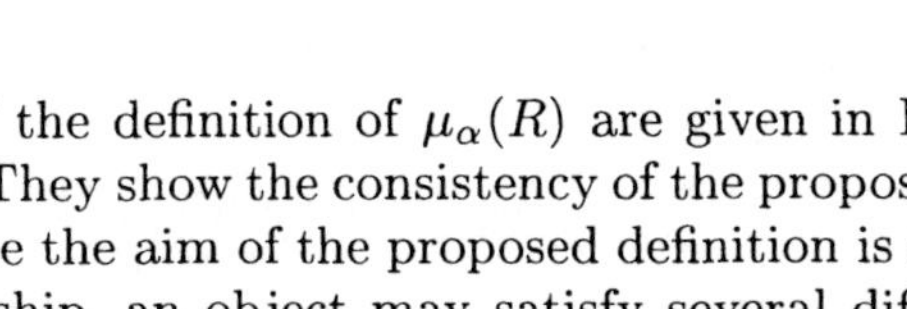

Fig. 7. Definition of $\beta_{\min}$ (left) and of $f(\beta_{\min})$ (right).

Illustrations of the definition of $\mu_\alpha(R)$ are given in Figure 8 for several reference objects. They show the consistency of the proposed approach in case of concavities: since the aim of the proposed definition is not to find only the dominant relationship, an object may satisfy several different relationships with high degrees. Therefore, "to be to the right of R" does not mean that the object should be completely to the right of the reference object, but only that it is at least to the right of some part of it. This is the case for instance in Figure 8, where we obtain high values for being right" inside the concavities (note that we obtain high values for any direction inside the hole, which is

Fig. 8. A few examples of $\mu_\alpha(R)$ for $\alpha_1 = \alpha_2 = 0$ corresponding to the relative position "right" (high grey values correspond to high membership values) using the angle of visibility method, for different types of reference objects (reference objects are black).

actually a way to model the fact that an object is in the hole using directional relationships).

In the fuzzy case, we propose a method which combines membership values, one describing the membership to R, and the other to the fuzzy landscape. This corresponds to translating binary equations and propositions into fuzzy ones: in the binary case, we express that: $Q \in R$ and $f(\beta_{\min}) = \max_{Q \in R} f(\beta(P,Q))$ (since f is decreasing), which translates in fuzzy terms as:

$$\mu_\alpha(R)(P) = \max_{Q \in Supp(R)} t[\mu_R(Q), f(\beta(P,Q))], \tag{83}$$

where t is a t-norm, and $Supp(R)$ denotes the support of μ_R. Figure 9 illustrates the obtained result on a fuzzy object.

Fig. 9. Left: a fuzzy reference object. Right: fuzzy landscape representing the relationship "to the left of" for the proposed combination method (equation 83).

An advantage of this approach is its interpretation in terms of morphological operations. It can be shown that $\mu_\alpha(R)$ is exactly the fuzzy dilation of μ_R by ν, where ν is a fuzzy structuring element defined on $\mathcal{S}$ as:

$$\forall P \in \mathcal{S},\ \nu(P) = \max[0, 1 - \frac{2}{\pi} \arccos \frac{\boldsymbol{OP} \cdot \boldsymbol{u}_\alpha}{||\boldsymbol{OP}||}],\ \text{and}\ \nu(O) = 1, \tag{84}$$

where O is the center of the structuring element. This structuring element is illustrated in 2D in Figure 10. The following definition is used for the fuzzy dilation:

$$\forall P \in \mathcal{S},\ D_\nu(\mu)(P) = \max_{Q \in \mathcal{S}} t[\mu(Q), \nu(P - Q)], \tag{85}$$

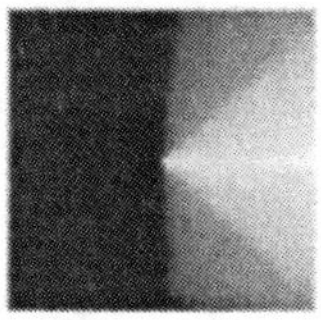

Fig. 10. Structuring element ν for $\alpha_1 = 0$, and $\alpha_2 = 0$ in this 2D case (high grey values correspond to high membership values).

where t is a t-norm. This equivalence provides an additional morphological interpretation of our definition.

Moreover, defining the fuzzy landscape as a fuzzy dilation and using fuzzy pattern matching for assessing the relative position correspond to a conditional dilation of the reference object with respect to the other object.

The direct computation of the proposed formula for $\beta_{\min}$, with an exhaustive method (search over all points Q), can be computationally very expensive in the 3D case. The computation can be made faster by storing the list of points in R (which are often much less numerous than all image points), and by tabulating angles (since $\boldsymbol{QP}$ takes a finite number of integer values in discrete images). The interpretation of the proposed definition as a fuzzy dilation may suggest a further way to reduce the computation time by reducing the precision of $\mu_\alpha(R)$: it consists in performing the fuzzy dilation with a limited support for the structuring element. This amounts to have a rough quantification of angles, and therefore an approximate result is obtained. We also proposed a fast algorithm for computing $\mu_\alpha(R)$ [12], that still provides an approximation of $\mu_\alpha(R)$, based on a propagation technique inspired by chamfer methods used for instance for discrete distance computation [23]. This idea comes from the observation that membership values in the fuzzy set μ_α are constant along lines issued from contour points of the reference object.

Concerning the properties of the proposed definitions, we proved [13] that the possibility has a symmetry property (i.e. the possibility for A to be in some direction from B is equal to the possibility of B to be in the opposite direction with respect to A). Also, the proposed definition is invariant with respect to translation, rotation and scaling, for 2D and 3D objects (crisp and fuzzy). We have also studied the influence of the distance between objects on their relative position. We proved that when the distance between the objects increases, the objects are seen as points. The value of their relative position can be predicted only from the direction of interest and the direction in which one object goes far away from the reference object. Therefore the shape of the objects does no longer play any role in the assessment of their relative position. Finally, we looked at the behavior of the proposed definition in cases where the reference object has strong concavities, and showed that the behavior corresponds to what can be intuitively expected.

5.4 Example

We illustrate these definitions again on the fuzzy structures shown in Figure 2.

The fuzzy landscapes representing the degree of satisfaction of the relations "left to", "right to", " below" and "above" object v1 are shown in Figure 11. The relative position degrees between some of the obtained fuzzy objects are given in Figure 12. The interpretation of these results is straightforward with respect to the intuitive expected relative positions. Object cn1 is mainly to the right of v1 (and only with very low degree to its left), and quite above and below. This expresses that it is "in the right concavity of v1", an example of a more complex relationship derived from the basic relative positions. Object cn2 is to the left of v1, with no ambiguity at all concerning the right relationship (i.e. no point of cn2 is to the right of v1). It is quite above v1, and less below it than cn1. Similar interpretations can be given for p1 and v2 with respect to v1.

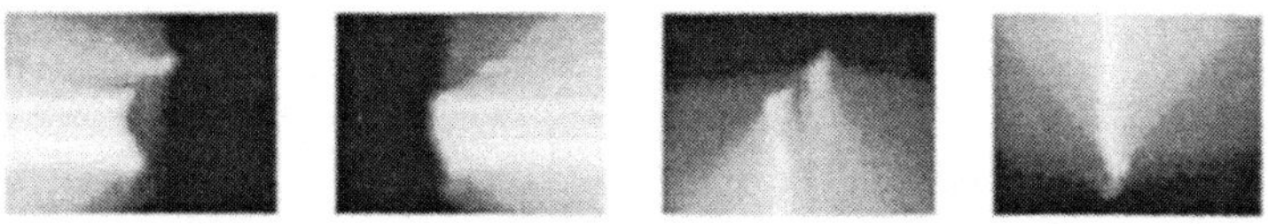

Fig. 11. Fuzzy areas corresponding to four relationships of Figure 12 for the object v1 of Figure 2.

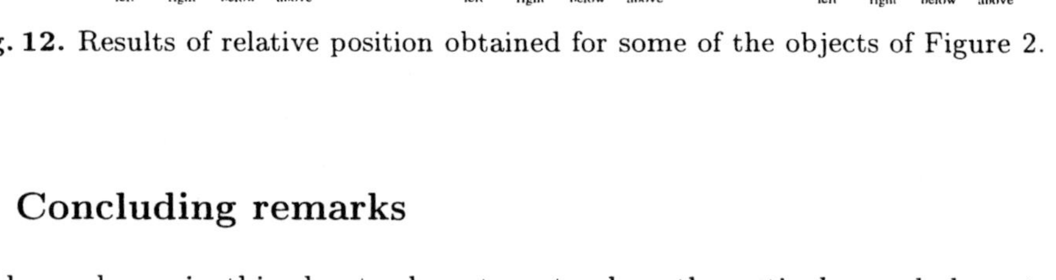

Fig. 12. Results of relative position obtained for some of the objects of Figure 2.

6 Concluding remarks

We have shown in this chapter how to extend mathematical morphology to fuzzy sets, and how to derive some spatial relationships between objects. This leads to a consistent and rigorous framework, having nice formal properties and good behaviors, in order to deal with spatial imprecision in image processing, shape recognition and scene interpretation.

Other relations can also be obtained from fuzzy dilation, like convexity indicators [44] (by extending the theorem stating that a compact set X is convex iff $2X = D_X(X)$; also refer to Chapter 3 (*Fuzzy Mathematical Morphology based on Fuzzy Inclusion*)), or "between" relationships, etc., and certainly deserve to be further investigated.

Extensions of mathematical morphology have been proposed for defining more complex operations (like filtering) [20,52], and geodesic operations [10,14].

Several interesting links can be further investigated. For instance, the t-norms and t-conorms used in the definitions of basic morphological operators are also used in information fusion [30,8]. Merging both interpretations can lead to interesting developments in image fusion taking spatial imprecision into account. This has been exploited for instance in [22]. Again in the domain of information fusion under uncertainty, links with Dempster-Shafer theory have been established in [9]. Links with fuzzy pattern matching, as already exploited for defining relative directional position, can be used for recognizing a particular object in an image, based on a model of it. Fuzzy distances can also been used for this. Links with fuzzy implication [20] and with rough sets, as established in [16], might lead to interesting investigation in spatial reasoning under imprecision.

Interesting applications concern spatial reasoning and structural pattern recognition [11]. The proposed method for assessing spatial relationships provides a useful tool for spatial reasoning. We are currently developing two ways of using fuzzy spatial relationships derived from fuzzy morphology for recognizing 3D objects in a scene (typically in a brain image) using a model (typically an anatomical atlas). The first approach consists in first recognizing simple structures, and then progressively more and more difficult structures, based on relationships between these structures and previously recognized structures [34]. In this approach, each relationship is translated into a spatial fuzzy set representing the area satisfying this relation, to some degrees. The fuzzy sets representing all relationships involved in the recognition processed are fused using a numerical fusion operator leading to segmentation and recognition. The second approach is a global one: structures and their relationships are represented as a fuzzy attributed graph. The recognition of the structures amounts then to find a matching (modeled as a fuzzy morphism) between a graph representing the atlas, and a graph obtained from an over-segmentation of the MR image [42,43].

References

1. De Baets B., *Idempotent Closing and Opening Operations in Fuzzy Mathematical Morphology*, in: "Proceedings of ISUMA-NAFIPS'95" (College Park, MD), pp. 228–233, 1995
2. De Baets B. and Kerre E., *An Introduction to Fuzzy Mathematical Morphology*, in: "Proceedings of NAFIPS'93" (Allentown, Pennsylvania), pp. 129–133, 1993

3. Bandemer H. and Näther W., *"Fuzzy Data Analysis"*, Theory and Decision Library, Serie B: Mathematical and Statistical Methods, Kluwer Academic Publisher, Dordrecht, 1992
4. Bloch I., *"About Properties of Fuzzy Mathematical Morphologies: Proofs of Main Results"*, Technical report, Télécom Paris 93D023, December 1993
5. Bloch I., *Triangular Norms as a Tool for Constructing Fuzzy Mathematical Morphologies*, in: "Proceedings of the Int. Workshop on Mathematical Morphology and its Applications to Signal Processing" (Barcelona, Spain), pp. 157–161, 1993
6. Bloch I., *Distances in Fuzzy Sets for Image Processing derived from Fuzzy Mathematical Morphology*, in: "Proceedings of IPMU'96 – Information Processing and Management of Uncertainty in Knowledge-Based Systems" (Granada, Spain), pp. 1307–1312, 1996
7. Bloch I., *Fuzzy Relative Position between Objects in Images: a Morphological Approach*, in: "Proceedings of ICIP'96 – IEEE Int. Conf. on Image Processing" (Lausanne), Vol. 2, pp. 987–990, 1996
8. Bloch I., *Information Combination Operators for Data Fusion: A Comparative Review with Classification*, IEEE Trans. on Systems, Man, and Cybernetics, Vol. 26, No. 1, pp. 52–67, 1996
9. Bloch I., *Using Fuzzy Mathematical Morphology in the Dempster-Shafer Framework for Image Fusion under Imprecision*, in: "Proceedings of IFSA'97" (Prague), pp. 209–214, 1997
10. Bloch I., *Fuzzy Morphology and Fuzzy Distances: New Definitions and Links in both Euclidean and Geodesic Cases*, in: "Lecture Notes in Artificial Intelligence: Fuzzy Logic in Artificial Intelligence, towards Intelligent Systems (A. Ralescu, ed.)", Springer Verlag, 1998
11. Bloch I., *Fusion of Numerical and Structural Image Information in Medical Imaging in the Framework of Fuzzy Sets*, in: "Fuzzy Systems in Medicine (P. Szczepaniak, ed.)", Springer Verlag, 1999
12. Bloch I., *Fuzzy Relative Position between Objects in Image Processing: a Morphological Approach*, IEEE Trans. on Pattern Analysis and Machine Intelligence, Vol. 21, No. 7, pp. 657–664, 1999
13. Bloch I., *Fuzzy Relative Position between Objects in Image Processing: New Definition and Properties based on a Morphological Approach*, International Journal of Uncertainty, Fuzziness and Knowledge-Based Systems, Vol. 7, No. 2, pp. 99–133, 1999
14. Bloch I., *Geodesic Balls in a Fuzzy Set and Fuzzy Geodesic Mathematical Morphology*, Pattern Recognition, to appear
15. Bloch I., *On Fuzzy Distances and their Use in Image Processing under Imprecision*, Pattern Recognition, Vol. 32, No. 11, pp. 1873–1895, 1999
16. Bloch I., *On Links between Mathematical Morphology and Rough Sets*, Pattern Recognition, 1999
17. Bloch I. and Maître H., *Constructing a Fuzzy Mathematical Morphology: Alternative Ways*, in: "Proceedings of FUZZ-IEEE'93 – Second IEEE International Conference on Fuzzy Systems" (San Fransisco, California), pp. 1303–1308, 1993
18. Bloch I. and Maître H., *Mathematical Morphology on Fuzzy Sets*, in: "Proceedings of the Int. Workshop on Mathematical Morphology and its Applications to Signal Processing" (Barcelona, Spain), pp. 151–156, 1993
19. Bloch I. and Maître H., *Fuzzy Mathematical Morphology*, Annals of Mathematics and Artificial Intelligence, Vol. 10, pp. 55–84, 1994

20. Bloch I. and Maître H., *Fuzzy Mathematical Morphologies: A Comparative Study*, Pattern Recognition, Vol. 28, No. 9, pp. 1341–1387, 1995
21. Bloch I., Maître H. and Anvari M., *Fuzzy Adjacency between Image Objects*, International Journal of Uncertainty, Fuzziness and Knowledge-Based Systems, Vol. 5, No. 6, pp. 615–653, 1997
22. Bloch I., Pellot C., Sureda F. and Herment A., *Fuzzy Modelling and Fuzzy Mathematical Morphology applied to 3D Reconstruction of Blood Vessels by Multi-Modality Data Fusion*, in: "Fuzzy Set Methods in Information Engineering: A Guided Tour of Applications (D. Dubois, R. Yager and H. Prade, eds.)", John Wiley & Sons, New York, pp. 93–110, 1996
23. Borgefors G., *Distance Transforms in the Square Grid*, in: "Progress in Picture Processing, Les Houches, Session LVIII, 1992 (H. Maître, ed.)", North-Holland, Amsterdam, pp. 46–80, 1996
24. Demko C. and Zahzah E.H., *Image Understanding using Fuzzy Isomorphism of Fuzzy Structures*, in: "Proceedings of the IEEE Int. Conf. on Fuzzy Systems" (Yokohama, Japan), pp. 1665–1672, 1995
25. di Gesu V., *Mathematical Morphology and Image Analysis: A Fuzzy Approach*, in: "Proceedings of the Workshop on Knowledge-Based Systems and Models of Logical Reasoning", 1988
26. di Gesu V., Maccarone M.C. and Tripiciano M., *Mathematical Morphology based on Fuzzy Operators*, in: "Fuzzy Logic (R. Lowen and M. Roubens, eds.)", Kluwer Academic, pp. 477–486, 1993
27. Dubois D. and Jaulent M.-C., *A General Approach to Parameter Evaluation in Fuzzy Digital Pictures*, Pattern Recognition Letters, Vol. 6, pp. 251–259, 1987
28. Dubois D. and Prade H., *"Fuzzy Sets and Systems: Theory and Applications"*, Academic Press, New York, 1980
29. Dubois D. and Prade H., *Invers Operations for Fuzzy Numbers*, in: "Fuzzy Information, Knowledge Representation and Decision Analysis (E. Sanchez and M. Gupta, eds.)", IFAC Symposium (Marseille, France), pp. 391–396, 1983
30. Dubois D. and Prade H., *A Review of Fuzzy Set Aggregation Connectives*, Information Sciences, Vol. 36, pp. 85–121, 1985
31. Dubois D. and Prade H., *Weighted Fuzzy Pattern Matching*, Fuzzy Sets and Systems, Vol. 28, pp. 313–331, 1988
32. Dubois D. and Prade H., *Fuzzy Sets in Approximate Reasoning, Part I: Inference with Possibility Distributions*, Fuzzy Sets and Systems, Vol. 40, pp. 143–202, 1991
33. Dutta S., *Approximate Spatial Reasoning: Integrating Qualitative and Quantitative Constraints*, International Journal of Approximate Reasoning, Vol. 5, pp. 307–331, 1991
34. Géraud T., Bloch I. and Maître H., *Atlas-guided Recognition of Cerebral Structures in MRI using Fusion of Fuzzy Structural Information*, in: "Proceedings of CIMAF'99 Symposium on Artificial Intelligence" (La Havana, Cuba), pp. 99–106, 1999
35. Giardina C.R. and Sinha D., *Image Processing using Pointed Fuzzy Sets*, in: SPIE Intelligent Robots and Computer Vision VIII: Algorithms and Techniques, Vol. 1192, pp. 659–668, 1989
36. Goetcherian V., *From Binary to Grey Tone Image Processing using Fuzzy Logic Concepts*, Pattern Recognition, Vol. 12, pp. 7–15, 1980
37. Kaufmann A. and Gupta M.M., *"Fuzzy Mathematical Models in Engineering and Management Science"*, North-Holland, Amsterdam, 1988

38. Koczy L.T., *On the Description of Relative Position of Fuzzy Patterns*, Pattern Recognition Letters, Vol. 8, pp. 21–28, 1988
39. Krishnapuram R., Keller J.M. and Ma Y., *Quantitative Analysis of Properties and Spatial Relations of Fuzzy Image Regions*, IEEE Transactions on Fuzzy Systems, Vol. 1, No. 3, pp. 222–233, 1993
40. Laplante P.A. and Giardina C.R., *Fast Dilation and Erosion of Time Varying Grey Valued Images with Uncertainty*, in: SPIE Image Algebra and Morphological Image Processing II, Vol. 1568, pp. 295–302, 1991
41. Nakatsuyama M., *Fuzzy Mathematical Morphology for Image Processing*, in: "Proceedings of ANZIIS-93" (Perth, Western Australia), pp. 75–79, 1993
42. Perchant A. and Bloch I., *A New Definition for Fuzzy Attributed Graph Homomorphism with Application to Structural Shape Recognition in Brain Imaging*, in: "Proceedings of IMTC'99 – 16th IEEE Instrumentation and Measurement Technology Conference" (Venice, Italy), pp. 1801–1806, 1999
43. Perchant A., Boeres C., Bloch I., Roux M. and Ribeiro C., *Model-based Scene Recognition Using Graph Fuzzy Homomorphism Solved by Genetic Algorithm*, in: "Proceedings of GbR'99 – 2nd International Workshop on Graph-Based Representations in Pattern Recognition" (Castle of Haindorf, Austria), 1999
44. Popov A.T., *Convexity Indicators based on Fuzzy Morphology*, Pattern Recognition Letters, Vol. 18, pp. 259–267, 1997
45. Popov A.T., *Morphological Operations on Fuzzy Sets*, in: IEE Image Processing and its Applications, Edinburgh, UK, pp. 837–840, 1995
46. Rosenfeld A., *Fuzzy Digital Topology*, Information and Control, Vol. 40, pp. 76–87, 1979
47. Rosenfeld A., *The Fuzzy Geometry of Image Subsets*, Pattern Recognition Letters, Vol. 2, pp. 311–317, 1984
48. Rosenfeld A. and Kak A.C., *"Digital Picture Processing"*, Academic Press, New York, 1976
49. Serra J., *"Image Analysis and Mathematical Morphology"*, Academic Press, London, 1982
50. Sinha D. and Dougherty E., *Fuzzy Mathematical Morphology*, Journal of Visual Communication and Image Representation, Vol. 3, No. 3, pp. 286–302, 1992
51. Sinha D. and Dougherty E.R., *Fuzzification of Set Inclusion: Theory and Applications*, Fuzzy Sets and Systems, Vol. 55, pp. 15–42, 1993
52. Sinha D., Sinha P., Dougherty E.R. and Batman S., *Design and Analysis of Fuzzy Morphological Algorithms for Image Processing*, IEEE Trans. on Fuzzy Systems, Vol. 5, No. 4, pp. 570–584, 1997
53. Yager R.R., *Connectives and Quantifiers in Fuzzy Sets*, Fuzzy Sets and Systems, Vol. 40, pp. 39–75, 1991
54. Zadeh L.A., *Fuzzy Sets*, Information and Control, Vol. 8, pp. 338–353, 1965
55. Zadeh L.A., *The Concept of a Linguistic Variable and its Application to Approximate Reasoning*, Information Sciences, Vol. 8, pp. 199–249, 1975

Part II

Fuzzy Image Filtering

Chapter 5

Fuzzy Image Enhancement: An Overview

Hamid R. Tizhoosh

University of Magdeburg, Department for Technical Computer Science
P.O.Box 4120, D-39016 Magdeburg, Germany
email: tizhoosh@ipe.et.uni-magdeburg.de

Summary. Image enhancement is one of the fundamental tasks in image processing. Fuzzy techniques offer a suitable framework for the development of new methods because they are nonlinear and knowledge-based. In this work, we give an overview of existing fuzzy image enhancement techniques, where contrast adaptation methods and filtering techniques are considered.

1 Introduction

Due to the physical properties of imaging devices and due to the image transmission, images have sometimes poor contrast, are corrupted with different kinds of noise, or are blurred. Image enhancement encompasses different classes of point and spatial operations to increase the contrast, smooth the regions of interest and sharpen the edges and fine structures. In the literature on image processing, there already exists a large number of techniques for improvement of image quality: gray-level modification, histogram operations, filters based on order statistics, adaptive filters, filters using Fourier/wavelet transform, anisotropic diffusion, morphological filters, genetic algorithms etc. [14,15,55,25].

Fuzzy set theory [56] has obtained great popularity in the image processing community in the last decades. Fuzzy techniques are nonlinear and knowledge-based. They can process imperfect data if this imperfection originates from vagueness and ambiguity rather than randomness. In this chapter, a brief overview of fuzzy image enhancement techniques will be given. In section 2, some basic definitions are discussed to outline the general framework of fuzzy image processing. In section 3, some fuzzy algorithms for adjustment of image contrast/brightness are described. Section 4 gives a brief overview of fuzzy filtering techniques. In section 5, an observer-dependent system for contrast adaptation will be presented. Finally, a future view concludes the chapter. Although many techniques are explained, it should be noted that due to the numerous publications in this area during recent years, this chapter does not claim to be complete.

2 Framework of fuzzy image processing

An image X of size $M \times N$ with L gray levels $g = 0, 1, 2, \cdots, L-1$ can be defined as an array of fuzzy singletons (fuzzy sets with only one supporting point) indicating the membership value of each pixel regarding to a predefined image property (e.g. brightness, smoothness, edginess etc.) [29,46,47]:

$$X = \bigcup_{m=1}^{M} \bigcup_{n=1}^{N} \frac{\mu_{mn}}{g_{mn}} \quad \text{with } \mu_{mn} \in [0,1], \tag{1}$$

where μ_{mn}/g_{mn} denotes in the notation of fuzzy sets the membership of the mn-th pixel. The definition of the membership values depends on the specific requirements of the particular application and on the corresponding expert knowledge.

Fuzzy image processing consists (as all other fuzzy approaches) of three stages: fuzzification Φ, suitable operation Γ on membership values and, if necessary, defuzzification Ψ(Fig. 1). The output Y of the system for an input X is given by the processing chain

$$Y = \Psi(\Gamma(\Phi(X))). \tag{2}$$

The main difference to other methodologies in image processing is that input data X (histograms, gray levels, features, ...) will be processed in the so-called *membership plane* where one can use the great diversity of fuzzy logic, fuzzy set theory and fuzzy measure theory to modify/aggregate the membership values, classify data, or make decisions using fuzzy inference. The new membership values are re-transformed in the gray-level plane to generate new histograms, modified gray-levels, image segments, or classes of objects.

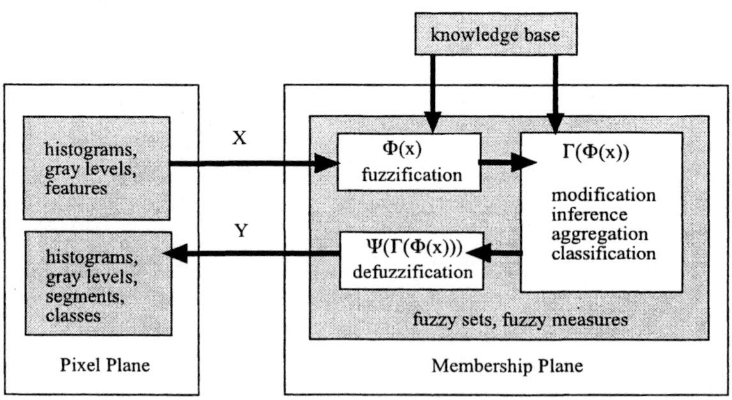

Fig. 1. The general structure of fuzzy image processing [47]

Regarding images as digital fuzzy sets, one may need some information theoretical measures. Here, different measures of fuzziness are presented. They should find a quantitative answer to the question "*how fuzzy is an image?*".

Kaufmann [16] introduced the index of fuzziness γ of a fuzzy set $A \subseteq X$:

$$\gamma(A) = \frac{2}{n^k} \times d(A, A^{near}), \tag{3}$$

where d is a suitable metric on the power set of X, k a positive real number and n the number of supporting points of A. A^{near} is the nearest crisp (dual) set to A. Using the Minkowski q-norm as a metric, and putting $k = \frac{1}{q}$, the index of fuzziness can be defined as follows:

$$\gamma(A) = \frac{2}{n^{\frac{1}{q}}} \left\{ \sum_i \mid \mu_A(x_i) - \mu_{A^{near}}(x_i) \mid^q \right\}^{\frac{1}{q}}. \tag{4}$$

Using the minimum operator as a T-norm, the (linear) index of fuzziness γ_{linear} for an image A with gray levels g and the histogram $h(g)$ can be given by [10,16]:

$$\gamma_{linear}(A) = \frac{2}{MN} \sum_{g=0}^{L-1} h(g) \cdot min[\mu_A(g), \bar{\mu}_A(g)], \tag{5}$$

where $\bar{\mu}_A(g) = 1 - \mu_A(g)$. Considering the spatial image information, the index of fuzziness can be rewritten as follows:

$$\gamma_{linear}(A) = \frac{2}{MN} \sum_{i=1}^{N} \sum_{j=1}^{M} min[\mu_A(g_{ij}), \bar{\mu}_A(g_{ij})]. \tag{6}$$

Other measures of fuzziness are the quadratic index of fuzziness $\gamma_{quadratic}$, the fuzzy entropy H_S and exponential fuzzy entropy H_{exp} [10,16,30,46]:

$$\gamma_{quadratic}(A) = \frac{2}{\sqrt{MN}} \sqrt{\sum_{g=0}^{L-1} [h(g) \times min[\mu_A(g), \bar{\mu}_A(g)]]^2}, \tag{7}$$

$$H_S(A) = \frac{1}{MN \log 2} \sum_{g=1}^{L-2} h(g)[-\mu_A(g) \log(\mu_A(g)) - \bar{\mu}_A(g) \log(\bar{\mu}_A(g)], \tag{8}$$

$$H_{exp}(A) = \frac{1}{MN(\sqrt{e} - 1)} \sum_{g=0}^{L-1} h(g)[\mu_A(g) e^{\bar{\mu}_A(g)} + \bar{\mu}_A(g) e^{\mu_A(g)} - 1]. \tag{9}$$

These measures are usually used during image enhancement, thresholding and classification.

3 Fuzzy contrast/brightness adaptation

Contrast and brightness are image qualities that are specially important if the preprocessing should be done for human perception (e.g. in medical applications). There are mainly two different ways to adapt the image contrast/brightness: gray-level modification with a suitable function f:

$$g' = f(g), \tag{10}$$

or histogram operations. The performance of the first approach depends on the shape of the selected function. Some automatic ways are introduced to choose an appropriate function [2,28]. The second approach modifies the image histogram. The histogram equalization is one of the best known histogram techniques. The modified gray levels g' are computed by

$$g' = f_h(g) = (L-1)\sum_{i=0}^{g} \frac{h(i)}{MN}, \tag{11}$$

where the right side should be round off in order to achieve integer values for g'.

Fuzzy techniques use different tools of fuzzy set theory to adjust the image contrast:

- Minimization of fuzziness: reduction of amount of fuzziness
- Equalization using fuzzy expected value: application of the most typical gray level
- Hyperbolization: nonlinear modification of membership values
- λ-enhancement: optimization of fuzziness using involutive membership functions
- Rule-based approach: integration of expert knowledge into the enhancement task
- Enhancement using fuzzy relations

In the following, each of these techniques is described briefly. An approach to locally-adaptive implementation of fuzzy contrast enhancement is also described.

3.1 Minimization of fuzziness

This method is probably the first fuzzy approach to image enhancement and is also known in the literature as contrast intensification operator [26,27,29,46]. The main idea is to reduce the amount of image fuzziness. The general algorithm can be formulated as follows:

- Gray-level fuzzification ($\mu(g)$ denotes the degree of *brightness*)

$$\mu(g) = \left[1 + \frac{g_{max} - g}{F_d}\right]^{-F_e} \tag{12}$$

- Membership modification using successive application of Zadeh's intensification operator

$$\mu'(g) = \begin{cases} 2[\mu(g)]^2 & \text{if} \quad 0 \le \mu(g) \le 0.5 \\ 1 - 2[1-\mu(g)]^2 & \text{if} \quad 0.5 < \mu(g) \le 1 \end{cases} \tag{13}$$

- New gray-levels by defuzzification

$$g' = g_{max} - F_d\left((\mu'(g))^{\frac{-1}{F_e}} - 1\right), \quad (1 + \frac{g_{max}}{F_d})^{-F_e} \le \mu'(g) \le 1 \tag{14}$$

F_e and F_d are the exponential and denominational fuzzifiers that control the amount of grayness ambiguity in the membership plane. Suitable values for F_e are 1 and 2. F_d can then be computed with respect to the crossover point g_c of the membership function ($\mu(g_c) = 0.5$). Fig. 2 shows an example of this approach.

Fig. 2. Enhancement by minimization of image fuzziness. From left to right: Original image ($\gamma_{linear} = 0.8$), after one iteration ($\gamma_{linear} = 0.63$), after two iterations ($\gamma_{linear} = 0.36$)

De and Chatterji [9] have modified this approach and introduced a new intensification operator. They also used another membership function. The main idea of their modification is to consider the subjectivity of the human observer during the enhancement procedure. The modified algorithm for minimization of fuzziness can be given as follows:

- Gray-level fuzzification

$$\mu(g) = \begin{cases} 0.5\left(1 - \dfrac{m-g}{m-g_{min}}\right) & g_{min} \le g \le m \\ 0.5\left(1 + \dfrac{g-m}{g_{max}-m}\right) & m \le g \le g_{max} \end{cases} \tag{15}$$

- Modification with (modified) intensification operator:

$$\mu'_{ij} = \begin{cases} \frac{1}{2}\left[1 - \left\{\frac{\sin(\theta_1)(1-2\mu_{ij})}{\sin(\theta_1)}\right\}^{p_1}\right] & \text{for} \quad 0 \leq \mu_{ij} \leq 0.5 \\ \frac{1}{2}\left[1 + \left\{\frac{\sin(\theta_2)(2\mu_{ij}-1)}{\sin(\theta_2)}\right\}^{p_2}\right] & \text{for} \quad 0.5 \leq \mu_{ij} \leq 1.0 \end{cases} \tag{16}$$

- Defuzzification

$$g' = \begin{cases} n - (n - g_{min,new})(1 - 2\mu'(g)) & 0 \leq \mu' \leq 0.5, \\ n + (g_{max,new} - n)(2\mu'(g) - 1) & 0.5 \leq \mu' \leq 1 \end{cases} \tag{17}$$

m and n are subjective thresholds determined by the user. p_1 and p_2 are exponential powers for the regions under and above the crossover point respectively. θ_1 and θ_2 are the angular equivalences of the dark and white band. In contrast to the original version, a successive application of the intensification operator is not necessary since the *crispening behavior* of the operator can be controlled by various choice of p's and θ's. Fang and Cheng [11] proposed an automatic technique to select the crossover point if the interactive selection of parameters is not desired. A suitable objective function is used to find the crossover point.

The fuzzy relaxation [21] is also an approach that minimizes the amount of image fuzziness. However, no intensification operator is applied. Instead, an iterative scheme for reduction of fuzziness is proposed:

1. Divide the image into subimages
2. In each subimage, choose the parameters a, b and c (proper rank statistics such as min, max, mean, median etc.)
3. Gray-level fuzzification with membership function $S(g; a, b, c)$
4. New gray-levels via defuzzification
5. Go to step 2 and repeat until the image is sufficiently enhanced

The membership function S is given by

$$S(g;a,b,c) = \begin{cases} 0 & \text{if} \quad g \leq a \\ S_1 & \text{if} \quad a < g \leq b \\ S_2 & \text{if} \quad b < g \leq c \\ 1 & \text{if} \quad g > c \end{cases} \tag{18}$$

S_1 and S_2 can be of second or third order:

$$S_{1,second}(g;a,b,c) = \frac{(g-a)^2}{(b-a)(c-a)}, \tag{19}$$

$$S_{2,second}(g;a,b,c) = 1 - \frac{(g-c)^2}{(c-b)(c-a)}, \tag{20}$$

$$S_{1,third}(g;a,b,c) = \frac{(g-a)^3}{(b-a)^2(c-a)}, \tag{21}$$

$$S_{2,third}(g;a,b,c) = 1 - \frac{(g-c)^3}{(c-b)^2(c-a)}. \tag{22}$$

3.2 Equalization using fuzzy expected value

In this approach [38], the fuzzy expected value (FEV) or its weighted version (WFEV) [13] is calculated to improve the image quality with respect to the distance of all gray-levels from FEV.

A fuzzy relation over the universe X yields a fuzzy set F with the membership function χ_F with $0 \leq \chi_F(x) \leq 1, x \in X$. Let $\xi_T = \{x \mid \chi_F(x) \geq T, T \in [0,1]\}$ be a subset and let μ a fuzzy measure defined over subsets of F:

$$\mu(\xi_T) = \frac{N_{x:\chi_F(x)\geq T}}{N}, \tag{23}$$

where N is the total number of elements. The fuzzy expected value of χ_F over F is defined by:

$$\text{FEV} = \sup_{0\leq T\leq 1} \{min[T, \mu(\xi_T)]\}. \tag{24}$$

The weighted fuzzy expected s value can be calculated by

$$s = \frac{\sum\limits_{i=0}^{L-1} \chi_i e^{-\beta(|\chi_i - s|)} n_i^{\lambda}}{\sum\limits_{i=0}^{L-1} e^{-\beta(|\chi_i - s|)} n_i^{\lambda}}. \tag{25}$$

β and λ are constants (e.g. $\beta = 0.1$, $\lambda = 2$), n_i is the frequency of i-th gray level (histogram), and χ_i is the membership value of the i-th gray level (e.g. normalized intensities in [0,1]). Equation (25) has the general form $x = F(x)$ and can be solved iteratively by $x_{n+1} = F(x_n)$ where $x_0 = FEV$ [13]. The algorithm can be formulated as follows:

1. Calculation of the image histogram
2. Calculation of the most typical value K (K = FEV or WFEV)

3. Calculation of the distance D of each gray level from the most typical value K:

$$D = \sqrt{\mid K^2 - g^2 \mid} \tag{26}$$

4. Generation of the new gray levels g':

$$g' = \begin{cases} \max(0, K - D) & \text{if} \quad g < M \\ \min(L - 1, K + D) & \text{if} \quad g > M \\ K & \text{otherwise} \end{cases} \tag{27}$$

Fig.3 shows an example of this technique.

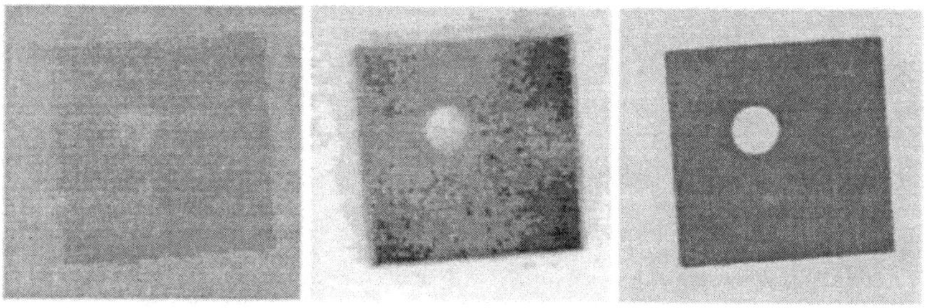

Fig. 3. Equalization using fuzzy expected value. From left to right: Original image, histogram equalized, equalized using WFEV.

3.3 Fuzzy histogram hyperbolization

The histogram equalization maximizes the image information using the entropy as an information measure. The human's brightness perception, however, is nonlinear. The histogram hyperbolization modifies therefore the image histogram in a logarithmic way instead of flattening it [1,12,46]:

$$g' = c\left(\exp\left(log(1 + \frac{1}{c}) \int_0^g p(g)dg\right) - 1\right) \quad \text{with } p(g) = \frac{h(g)}{MN}. \tag{28}$$

To extend the idea of histogram hyperbolization, suitable membership values $\mu(g)$ should be used instead of relative frequencies $p(g)$. Considering the conditions

$$g' = 0 \mid_{\mu(g)=0} \quad \text{and} \quad g' = (L - 1) \mid_{\mu(g)=1} \tag{29}$$

the fuzzy extension can be given by [46,48]:

$$g' = \left(\frac{(L - 1)(e^{-\mu(g)^\beta} - 1)}{e^{-1} - 1}\right). \tag{30}$$

β is a linguistic hedge for additional modification of membership values where $\beta \to 0$ produces very bright images, and $\beta \to \infty$ produces very dark images. The algorithm is as follows:

- Select a suitable membership function, e.g. a S-function or

$$\mu(g) = \frac{g - g_{min}}{g_{max} - g_{min}} \tag{31}$$

- Set the value of fuzzifier β
- Compute the membership values for each gray level
- Generate new gray levels using equation (30)

Fig. 4 shows an example of this approach. The *goodness* of the result depends on the selected membership function and the value of β, respectively.

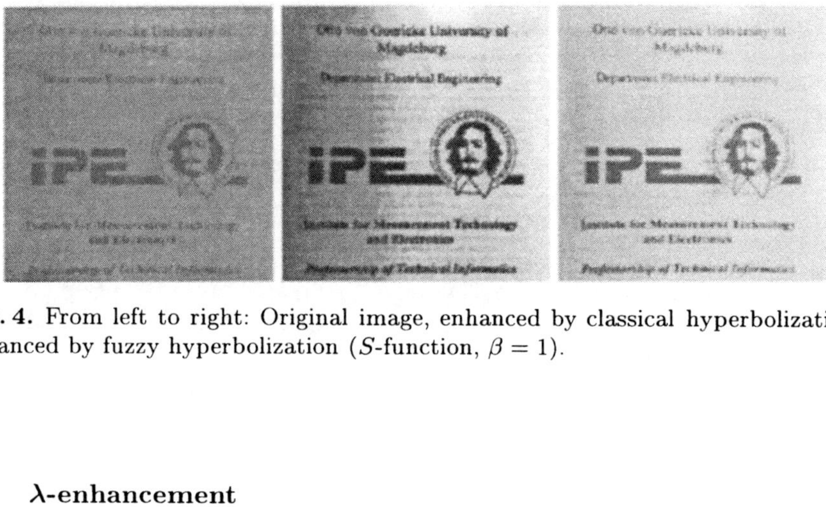

Fig. 4. From left to right: Original image, enhanced by classical hyperbolization, enhanced by fuzzy hyperbolization (S-function, $\beta = 1$).

3.4 λ-enhancement

Assuming an image X of size $M \times N$, gray levels $g = 0, ..., L-1$ (L = number of gray levels), and the membership values $\mu(g)$, the complement $\bar{\mu}$ of a membership function μ was defined by Zadeh [56] as:

$$\bar{\mu}(g) = 1 - \mu(g). \tag{32}$$

Sugeno introduced a class of involutive fuzzy complements:

$$\bar{\mu}_\lambda = \frac{1-\mu}{1+\lambda\mu}, \tag{33}$$

where λ belongs to the interval $(-1, \infty)$. Based on Sugeno's definition, we intuitively define the following class of involutive membership functions [45]:

$$\begin{aligned} \mu^*_\lambda(g) &= 1 - \bar{\mu}_\lambda(g) \\ &= \frac{(1+\lambda)\mu(g)}{1+\lambda\mu(g)} \quad \cdot g = 1, 2, \ldots, L-1 \end{aligned} \tag{34}$$

where $\mu(g)$ is the initial membership value (by the attribute *involutive* we mean that the membership function is based on *involutive complements*, i.e. $\bar{\bar{\mu}}_\lambda^*(g) = \mu_\lambda^*(g)$; in general $\mu_\lambda^*(\mu_\lambda^*(g)) \neq g$).

If we understand the image as a *bright image* and define a monotone membership function μ, then we can generate images with different levels of brightness if we vary λ. For $\lambda \to -1$ the result image will be absolutely black and for $\lambda \to \infty$ the result image will be absolutely white. It is clear that for the extreme values of λ the amount of grayness ambiguity is very low because in both cases there exist a lot of pixels with very low and very high membership values, respectively. It is also obvious that the images in the middle of the sequence are more suitable for human perception. One could (should) expect that one of these images (which are more fuzzy than the extreme cases) is the best one. Since the grayness fuzziness of the middle images is higher, we can apply the involutive membership functions to detect the image with maximal fuzziness. The grayness ambiguity (or fuzziness) of an image can be used as a quality measure for the enhancement procedure. The index of fuzziness (equation (5)) can be modified using the product operator instead of the minimum operator:

$$\gamma(\lambda) = \frac{4}{MN} \sum_{g=0}^{L-1} h(g)\mu_\lambda^*(g)(1 - \mu_\lambda^*(g)), \tag{35}$$

where the normalization factor is changed from $2/(MN)$ to $4/(MN)$. The advantage of this definition is that one can calculate the derivative w.r.t λ to find maximums/minimums of $\gamma(\lambda)$:

$$\frac{d}{d\lambda}\gamma(\lambda) = \frac{4}{MN} \sum_{g=0}^{L-1} \frac{h(g)(\mu(g) - \mu^2(g)(3+\lambda) + \mu^3(g)(2+\lambda))}{(1+\lambda\mu(g))^3}. \tag{36}$$

If $\gamma(\lambda_{optimal})$ becomes maximum, then the value $\lambda_{optimal}$ is a characteristic point and can be used to define new membership values:

$$\mu_{new}^*(g) = \frac{(1+\lambda_{optimal})\mu(g)}{1+\lambda_{optimal}\mu(g)}. \tag{37}$$

The algorithm for λ-enhancement can be formulated as follows:

1. Calculate the image histogram
2. Initialize the membership values $\mu(g)$
3. Calculate the amount of fuzziness $\gamma(\lambda)$
4. Solve the equation $\frac{d}{d\lambda}\gamma(\lambda_{optimal}) = 0$
5. Calculate new membership values with equation (37)
6. Generate new gray levels g', e.g. with

$$g' = (L-1)\mu_{new}^*(g) \tag{38}$$

Fig. 5. From left to right: Original image, histogram equalized, λ-enhanced.

In Fig. 5 a result of λ-enhancement is illustrated.

In fuzzy systems we generally endeavor to reduce the amount of fuzziness because it produces uncertainties and makes decisions more difficult. But in image processing, and especially for human brightness perception, it can be sometimes useful to increase the grayness ambiguity by increasing the number of gray levels. The initialization of membership values plays an important role in the achievement of satisfactory results. Any kind of membership function can be applied regarding to the specific requirements of the application. One can also interpret the cumulative histogram (normalized in $[0, 1]$) as a membership function representing the fuzziness of a bright image:

$$\mu(g) = \begin{cases} \dfrac{h(g)}{\max_g h(g)} & \text{if} \quad g = 0, \\[2ex] \dfrac{h(g) + h(g-1)}{\max_g h(g)} & \text{otherwise.} \end{cases} \tag{39}$$

In this case, the results of λ-enhancement are similar to those of histogram equalization.

3.5 Rule-based contrast enhancement

The fuzzy rule-based approach is a powerful and universal method for many tasks in the image processing. In [44] a simple inference system is proposed to increase the contrast of medical image data (see also [53,22,6,7]). The algorithm can be given as follows:

- Initialization of the parameters of the inference system (number of input and output membership functions, their shapes and locations with respect to first order statistics etc.)
- Fuzzification of gray levels (e.g. membership values to the *dark*, *gray* and *bright* sets of gray levels (Fig. 6))
- Inference procedure evaluating appropriate rules (e.g. if *dark* then *black*, if *gray* then *gray*, if *bright* then *white*)

- Defuzzification of the output using three singletons (e.g. $S_1 = g_{min}, S_2 = g_{mid}, S_3 = g_{max}$):

$$g' = \frac{\mu_{dark}(g) \times S_1 + \mu_{gray}(g) \times S_2 + \mu_{bright}(g) \times S_3}{\mu_{dark}(g) + \mu_{gray}(g) + \mu_{bright}(g)}. \tag{40}$$

Fig. 7 shows an example of rule-based enhancement.

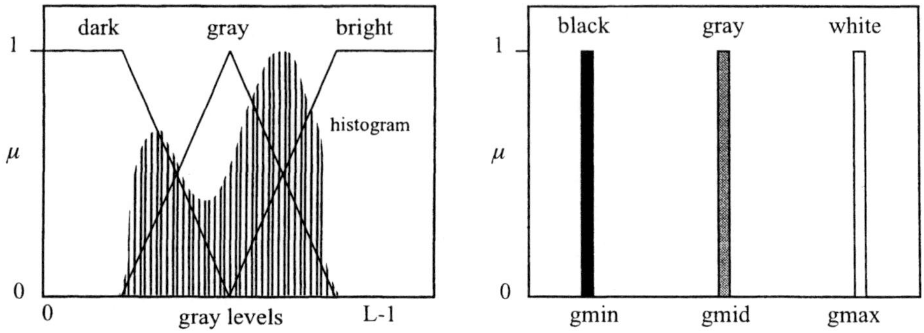

Fig. 6. Rule-based contrast enhancement. Left: input membership functions for gray-level fuzzification; right: output singletons for generation of modified gray-levels

Fig. 7. Left to right: Original image, histogram equalized, rule-based enhanced

3.6 Enhancement based on fuzzy relations

Bhutani and Battou [3] used fuzzy relations to develop a new enhancement technique. Considering an image with M rows and N columns, one can view the image as a weighted relation from a set X with M elements into a set Y

with N elements where g_{ij} represents the weight at the location (i,j). The image can be defined as a fuzzy relation μ from X into Y with membership values μ_{ij} at each location (i,j):

$$\mu_{ij} = \begin{cases} 0 & \text{if} \quad g_{ij} < T_1, \\ 0.5(\frac{g_{ij} - T_1}{T - T_1}) & \text{if} \quad T_1 \leq g_{ij} \leq T, \\ 0.5(\frac{T_2 - g_{ij}}{T_2 - T}) + (\frac{g_{ij} - T}{T_2 - T}) & \text{if} \quad T < g_{ij} \leq T_2, \\ 1 & \text{if} \quad g_{ij} > T_2 \end{cases} \tag{41}$$

where the thresholds T (average gray-level of segment), $T_1 < T$ (average gray-level of pixels with gray-value less than T) and $T_2 > T$ (average gray-level of pixels with gray-value greater than T) can be defined by the user. For each image segment (e.g. objects, background), the following fuzzy sets are defined:

$$\sigma_{minX}(a) = \min_{y \in Y} \mu_{ay}, \quad \sigma_{minY}(b) = \min_{x \in X} \mu_{xb}, \tag{42}$$

$$\sigma_{maxX}(a) = \max_{y \in Y} \mu_{ay}, \quad \sigma_{maxY}(b) = \max_{x \in X} \mu_{xb}, \tag{43}$$

where the minimums and maximums are computed over the fuzzy values $(0 < \mu_{ij} < 1)$. The dual complement μ^{cc} of the membership values is given by:

$$\mu_{ij}^{cc} = \begin{cases} 0 & \text{for} \quad \mu_{ij} = 0, \\ \sigma_{minX}(i) \wedge \sigma_{minY}(j) & \text{for} \quad 0 < \mu_{ij} < 0.5, \\ 0.5[\sigma_{minX}(i) \wedge \sigma_{minY}(j)] & \\ +0.5[\sigma_{maxX}(i) \wedge \sigma_{maxY}(j)] & \text{for} \quad \mu_{ij} = 0.5, \\ \sigma_{maxX}(i) \wedge \sigma_{maxY}(j) & \text{for} \quad 0.5 < \mu_{ij} < 1, \\ 1 & \text{otherwise.} \end{cases} \tag{44}$$

The new gray-levels are calculated by:

$$g_{ij}^{cc} = \begin{cases} g_{ij} & \text{for} \quad \mu_{ij}^{cc} \in \{0, 1\}, \\ 2\mu_{ij}^{cc}(T - T_1) + T_1 & \text{for} \quad \mu_{ij}^{cc} < 0.5, \\ 2\mu_{ij}^{cc}(T_2 - T) + (2T - T_2) & \text{for} \quad \mu_{ij}^{cc} > 0.5, \\ T & \text{otherwise.} \end{cases} \tag{45}$$

Fig. 8 shows an example of this approach.

Fig. 8. From left to right: Original image, enhanced by fuzzy relations (Source of images Bhutani and Battou [3])

3.7 Locally adaptive contrast improvement

It is a well-known problem that global histogram operations (also called point operations) are very fast but have a limited performance because they do not use the spatial image information. A locally adaptive implementation is therefore often necessary. The classical approach to locally adaptive image enhancement, e.g. for histogram equalization, defines an $N \times N$ neighborhood and moves the center of this area from pixel to pixel. At each location, the histogram of the subimage is calculated to obtain a histogram equalization function. This function is finally used to map the level of the pixel centered in the neighborhood [33].

In the case of fuzzy techniques, however, we need some parameters in each neighborhood for adjustment of the membership function (e.g. minimum and maximum gray-levels g_{min} and g_{max}). Therefore, we can find the parameters of the membership function for some subimages and interpolate these values to obtain corresponding values for each pixel (Fig. 9). These will not be the precise parameters really existing for each region if we move the local window pixel by pixel, but since we are using the concept of fuzziness we do not need exact input data [43]. This kind of local enhancement is very fast compared to the classical approach.

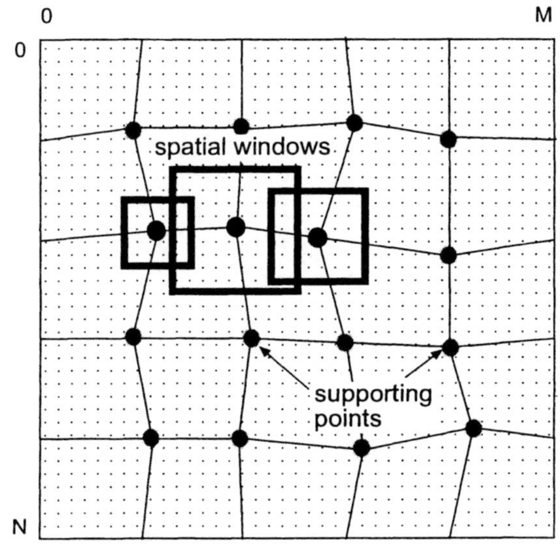

Fig. 9. Principle of locally adaptive contrast adaptation. The parameters of the membership functions are first computed in some spatial windows surrounding supporting points. By interpolation, membership values can be achieved for every image pixel

To increase the performance of the approach, variable window sizes can be used. Here, simple if-then rules can be used to determine the suitable size of the window with respect to the characteristics of the current neighborhood:

If the neighborhood is *homogenous*,
then choose a *large* window,
else choose a *small* window.

The degree of homogenity μ_H can be calculated as follows:

$$\mu_H = \frac{g_{max}^{local} - g_{min}^{local}}{g_{max}^{global} - g_{min}^{global}}. \tag{46}$$

The suitable window size W for each supporting point is calculated as follows:

$$W = \mu_H W_{max} + (1 - \mu_H) W_{min}. \tag{47}$$

W_{max} and W_{min} are the appropriate maximum and minimum window sizes. To make sure that outliers do not affect the spatial operations, one may define a relevance matrix R with elements r_{ij}:

$$r_{ij} = \begin{cases} 1 & \text{if } \frac{|g_{ij}-g_{mn}|}{T} \leq 2.5, \\ 0 & \text{otherwise.} \end{cases} \tag{48}$$

where the g_{ij}'s are the gray levels of the neighborhood, and g_{mn} the center pixel of the spatial window. The threshold T is calculated as follows [37]:

$$T = 1.4926 \times (1 + \frac{5}{N^2 - 1}) \times \underset{i,j}{median}(| g_{ij} - g_{mn} |). \tag{49}$$

The degree of homogenity can be redefined in a more robust way:

$$\mu_H = \frac{\max\limits_{i,j,r_{ij}\neq 0}(g_{ij}) - \min\limits_{i,j,r_{ij}\neq 0}(g_{ij})}{g_{max}^{global} - g_{min}^{global}}. \tag{50}$$

Fig. 10 shows examples for the locally adaptive implementation of fuzzy rule-based approach (FRB), its adaptive version (AFRB), fuzzy histogram hyperbolization (FHH) and its adaptive version (AFHH). As test image, a portal image is used. Portal images are online images in radiation therapy (cancer treatment) and have a very poor quality due to the imaging physics.

4 Fuzzy filtering

Image filtering is necessary to enhance edges and/or suppress noise. Various *classical* techniques already exist in the literature. The main problem of filtering is the dilemma of concurring image properties, such as sharpness and smoothness, respectively. Removing noise in an image, the fine details are usually also filtered out. Enhancing the edges and fine structures, on the other side, the noise will also be amplified. To solve this conflict, many approaches have already been developed. A widespread approach is the *adaptive filtering* where the image pixels g_{mn} in each $N \times N$ neighborhood (N an odd number) are assigned with suitable weights w_{ij}. The result of the filtering can be achieved by:

$$g'_{mn} = \frac{\sum\limits_{i}\sum\limits_{j} w_{m+i,n+j} \cdot g_{m+i,n+j}}{\sum\limits_{i}\sum\limits_{j} w_{m+i,n+j}}, \tag{51}$$

where $i, j \in [-(N-1)/2, (N-1)/2]$. The weights are computed regarding to the desired filtering effect. Of course, the performance of this technique depends on the reliable and correct computation of the weights.

In recent years, many fuzzy approaches to image filtering have been proposed. One can distinguish between the following approaches:

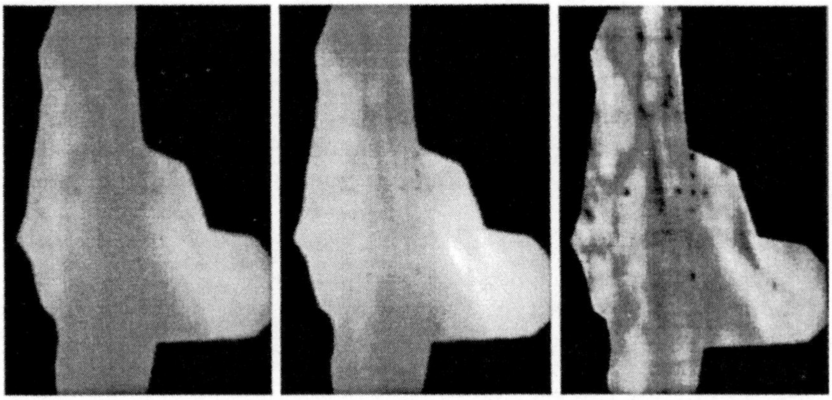

(a) Original image (b) result of FRB (c) result of AFRB

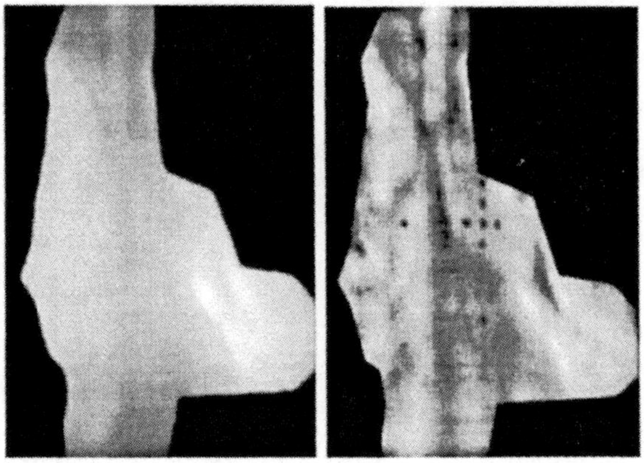

(d) result of FHH (e) result of AFHH

Fig. 10. Globally versus locally-adaptive fuzzy image enhancement of medical images ($W_{min} = 10$ and $W_{max} = 30$)

- Pure fuzzy filtering: uses only fuzzy if-then rules,
- Fuzzy extension of existing algorithms: uses membership functions or fuzzy rules to extend the classical filters to fuzzy sets, and
- Fuzzy fusion techniques: aggregates the results of different filters to combine their advantages.

In the following, examples are presented for each of these approaches.

4.1 Pure fuzzy filtering

Pure fuzzy filters are mainly based on fuzzy if-then rules, where the desired filtering effect can be achieved using a suitable set of linguistic rules. Russo *et al.* [34–36] proposed the class of FIRE operators (fuzzy inference ruled by else-action) that can be applied for image filtering. A fuzzy smoother, for instance, can be designed using luminance differences between the center pixel of a neighborhood and its surrounding pixels. Fuzzy rules for smoothing are of the following (general) form:

If a pixel is *darker* than its neighboring pixels,
then make it *brighter*;
If a pixel is *brighter* than its neighboring pixels,
then make it *darker*;
else leave it unchanged.

The input variables x_{ij} of the fuzzy smoother are the luminance differences:

$$x_{ij} = g_{ij} - g_{mn}. \tag{52}$$

where g_{mn} marks the center of the neighborhood that should be filtered. The output y_{mn} of the inference system will be then used to produce the new gray level:

$$g'_{mn} = g_{mn} + y_{mn}. \tag{53}$$

Recall that triangular fuzzy sets in $[-L+1, L-1]$ are defined by:

$$\mu(x_{ij}) = \begin{cases} 0 & -L+1 \leq x_{ij} \leq c-w, \\ \dfrac{w- \mid x_{ij} - c \mid}{w} & c-w < x_{ij} < c+w, \\ 0 & c+w \leq x_{ij} \leq L-1, \end{cases} \tag{54}$$

where c is the center position and w the half-width of the triangular membership function. Using this class of membership functions, the fuzzy sets *medium positive* (MP) and *medium negative* (MN) are defined for the input variables x_{ij}. The output y_{ij} can be represented using three fuzzy sets *small positive* (SP), *zero* (ZE) and *small negative* (SN) (Fig. 11).

The aforesaid fuzzy rules can be rewritten as:

If $x_{m-1,n-1}$ is MP **and** $\cdots$ **and** $x_{m+1,n+1}$ is MP, **then** y_{mn} is SP,
If $x_{m-1,n-1}$ is MN **and** $\cdots$ **and** $x_{m+1,n+1}$ is MN, **then** y_{mn} is SN,
else y_{mn} is ZE.

Fig. 12 shows two examples of the enhancement effect of this approach using different spatial window sizes.

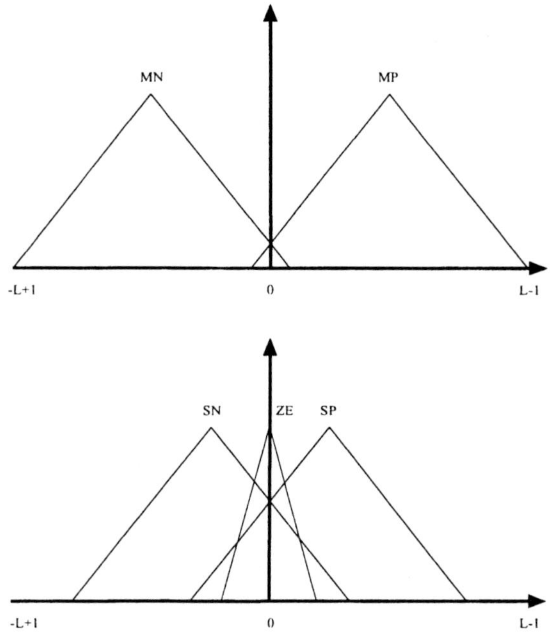

Fig. 11. Membership functions based on luminance difference to the center point for the inputs (top) and outputs (bottom) [34]

(a) (b) (c)

Fig. 12. Example of pure fuzzy filtering [34]: (a) noisy image, (b) 5×5-filtered, (c) 7×7-filtered

4.2 Fuzzy extension of existing filters

Another possibility to apply the concept of fuzziness to image filtering is the extension of existing filters. The extension is sometimes the use of a simple membership function that substitutes a threshold function (especially for weighting [31]), or the application of fuzzy rules to adapt the parameters of the corresponding filter. In the following, some possible ways for extension of Gaussian, median and mean filters are briefly described. It should be noted that the following approaches are not the one and only way to extend the filters to fuzzy sets. One may use other components of fuzzy set/measure theory to carry out the desired extension.

Fuzzy Gaussian filtering Law *et al.* [17] proposed a rule-based extension of the Gaussian filter. Generally, Gaussian filtering can be regarded as the convolution of the original image I with a Gaussian kernel K:

$$I' = I * K, \tag{55}$$

where the convolution kernel has the form

$$K(i,j) = \frac{1}{2\pi\sigma^2} \exp\left[-\frac{i^2+j^2}{2\sigma^2}\right]. \tag{56}$$

Rotating the kernel K to the angle of the gradient, a new coordinate system (u,v) can be defined:

$$K(u,v) = \frac{1}{2\pi}\left(\frac{1}{\sigma_u}\exp\left[-\frac{u^2}{2\sigma_u^2}\right]\right)\left(\frac{1}{\sigma_v}\exp\left[-\frac{v^2}{2\sigma_v^2}\right]\right). \tag{57}$$

The degree of smoothing can be determined by controlling the value of σ. Defining fuzzy sets *Gradient* and *Straightness*, fuzzy if-then rules can be formulated to control σ_u and σ_v (the straightness is determined by comparing pixels translated along the direction of the edge):

If Gradient is small AND Straightness is low,
then σ_u is large AND σ_v is large;
If Gradient is small AND Straightness is high,
then σ_u is large AND σ_v is large;
If Gradient is large AND Straightness is low,
then σ_u is small AND σ_v is small;
If Gradient is large AND Straightness is high,
then σ_u is small AND σ_v is large;

Fig. 13 shows an example of the enhancement effect of this approach.

Fuzzy median filtering Taguchi extended the weighted median filter (WM) to fuzzy sets [41,42]. The weighted median filter is a stack filter that can be defined as follows: Considering a $(2N+1)$ window, the output of WM filter is given by

$$y(i) = [W_{-N} \diamond x(i-N), \cdots, W_0 \diamond x(i), \cdots, W_N \diamond x(i+N)], \tag{58}$$

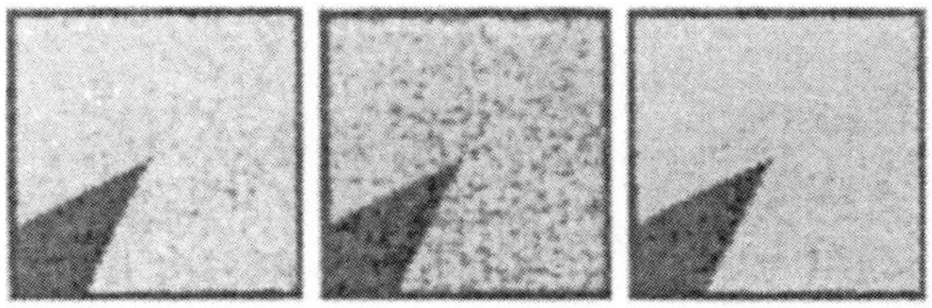

(a) (b) (c)

Fig. 13. Example for fuzzy Gaussian filtering [17]: (a) noisy image, (b) Gaussian smoothing, (c) fuzzy extension

where $x(i)$ is the M-valued input and the operator $\diamond$ denotes the duplication. Let $r^{(m)}(i)$ be defined by

$$r^{(m)}(i) = \frac{\sum_{j=-N}^{N} W_j x^{(m)}(i+j)}{\sum_{j=-N}^{N} W_j}, \tag{59}$$

where

$$x^{(m)}(i) = \begin{cases} 1 & \text{if } \; x(i) \geq m \\ 0 & \text{otherwise.} \end{cases} \tag{60}$$

The Boolean function of WM filter is given by

$$f_{WM}(r^{(m)}(i)) = \begin{cases} 1 & \text{if } \; r^{(m)}(i) \geq 0.5 \\ 0 & \text{otherwise.} \end{cases} \tag{61}$$

The output of WM filter is given by

$$y(i) = \sum_{m=1}^{M-1} f_{WM}(r^{(m)}(i)). \tag{62}$$

A fuzzy weighted median filter (FWM)can be defined using a membership function

$$f_{FWM}(r^{(m)}(i)) = \begin{cases} \dfrac{1}{1 + exp(-\alpha_1(r^{(m)}(i) - \beta))} & \text{if } \; r^{(m)}(i) > \beta \\[2ex] \dfrac{1}{1 + exp(-\alpha_2(r^{(m)}(i) - \beta))} & \text{otherwise.} \end{cases} \tag{63}$$

The weights of the filter are defined by

$$W_j = \begin{cases} 1 - 2j^2/\gamma^2 & \text{if} \quad 0 \leq \mid j \mid \leq \gamma/2 \\ 2(\mid j \mid - \gamma)^2/\gamma^2 & \text{if} \quad \gamma/2 < \mid j \mid < \gamma \\ 0 & \text{if} \quad \gamma \leq \mid j \mid . \end{cases} \tag{64}$$

To determine the parameters α_1, α_2 and β of the membership function, and the weights W_j, the LMS algorithm can be used [41,42]. Of course, this extension of median filtering is expensive in computing.

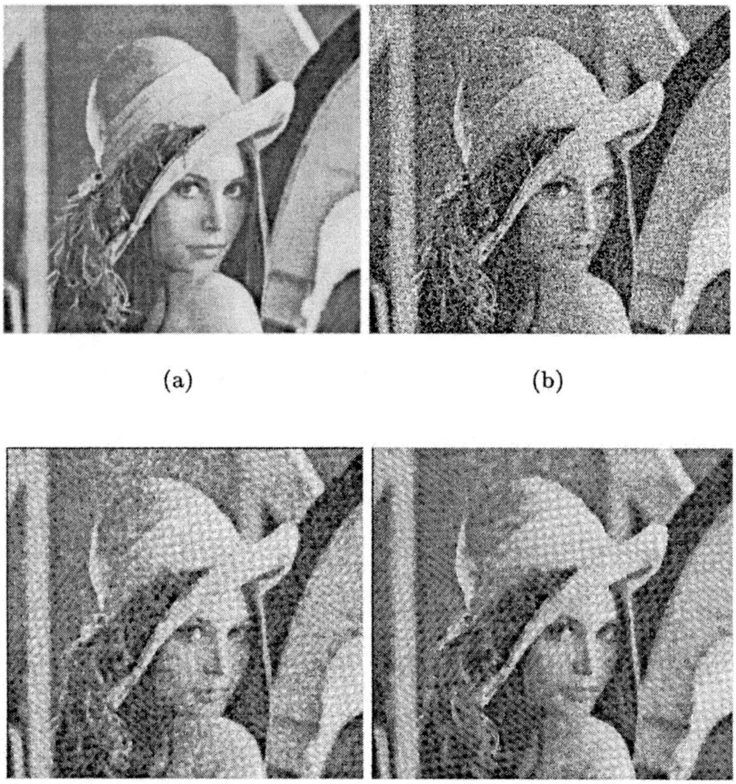

(a) (b) (c) (d)

Fig. 14. Fuzzy weighted median filtering [41,42]: (a) original image, (b) corrupted with Gaussian noise $\sigma = 900$, (c) result of WM, (d) result of FWM

Fuzzy mean filtering The mean filter and its variations are used in image processing to smooth noisy images [32], but they fail to deliver good results for heavy-tailed additive noise. Lee *et al.* [18–20] introduced the weighted fuzzy mean filter, that is a mean filter operating with three fuzzy numbers *dark* (DK), *median* (MD) and *bright* (BR) of the LR-type:

$$f(x) = \begin{cases} L\left(\dfrac{m-x}{\alpha}\right) & \text{for} \quad x \leq m, \\ \\ R\left(\dfrac{x-m}{\beta}\right) & \text{for} \quad x > m. \end{cases} \tag{65}$$

Three fuzzy rules in 3×3 neighborhoods are processed where three subresults $\bar{y}_1(i,j)$, $\bar{y}_2(i,j)$ and $\bar{y}_3(i,j)$ are produced by each rule. The final result is

$$y(i,j) = \frac{\sum\limits_{k=1}^{3} w_r \times \bar{y}_k(i,j)}{\sum\limits_{k=1}^{3} w_r}. \tag{66}$$

Some considerations are made to compute the crisp weights w_r [18].

The fuzzy rule for *dark* is as follows:

If
$x(i-1,j-1)$ is DK **and** $x(i-1,j)$ is DK **and** $x(i-1,j+1)$ is DK **and**
$x(i,j-1)$ is DK **and** $x(i,j)$ is DK **and** $x(i,j+1)$ is DK **and**
$x(i+1,j-1)$ is DK **and** $x(i+1,j)$ is DK **and** $x(i+1,j+1)$ is DK,
then

$$\bar{y}_1(i,j) = \frac{\sum\limits_{k=-1}^{1} \sum\limits_{l=-1}^{1} f_{DK}(x(i+k,j+l)) \times x(i+k,j+l)}{\sum\limits_{k=-1}^{1} \sum\limits_{l=-1}^{1} f_{DK}(x(i+k,j+l))}. \tag{67}$$

Rules for *median*(MD) and *bright*(BR) can be defined in an analogue way. Fig. 15 shows an example of the enhancement effect of this approach.

For an extensive discussion regarding the weighted fuzzy mean filter, its extensions and their performances, we refer to Chapter 6 (*Adaptive Fuzzy Filter and its Application to Image Enhancement*) of this volume.

4.3 Soft fusion of existing filters

In many situations, the filtering procedure has to fulfil different requirements. For instance, the image should be smoothed without loss of fine details. In

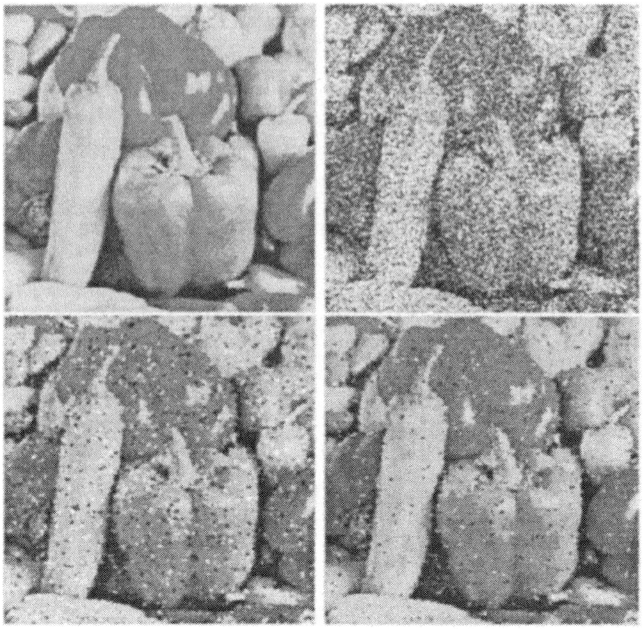

Fig. 15. Fuzzy mean filtering. From top left to bottom right: Noise-free image Peppers, noisy image with Gaussian impulse noise 100%, result of median, and result of fuzzy mean filtering (source: Lee *et al.* [20])

spite of all approaches to image filtering, it is not possible to develop a *super filter* that solves all conflicts in all possible situations (each filter has its strengths and disadvantages). Therefore, it is often more appropriate to combine existing filters using their advantages, and simultaneously, excluding their shortcomings. Fuzzy techniques enable us to implement the fusion in a robust way because they make soft decisions possible. This property is fundamental since in real images it is nearly impossible to find a crisp answer to the question whether a neighborhood is edgy, noisy or smooth. Choi and Krishnapuram [8] proposed a fusion scheme with fuzzy if-then rules using a degree of compatibility of the center pixel to its neighbors:

If the compatibility is *small* (outlier), **then** use the filter F_1,
If the compatibility is *medium* (edge), **then** use the filter F_2,
If the compatibility is *large* (smooth), **then** use the filter F_3,

The filters F_1 (outlier filter), F_2 (edge sharpening) and F_3 (smoothing) can be selected regarding to the specific requirements of the actual application. Let $g_1, \cdots, g_N$ be the gray levels in a given window, then the amount of total compatibility TC can be represented by three fuzzy subsets *small*, *medium* and *large* (Fig. 16) and is given by:

$$TC = \frac{\sum\limits_{j=1,j\neq i}^{N} \mu_{ji}}{\sum\limits_{j=1,j\neq i}^{N} w_{ji}}. \tag{68}$$

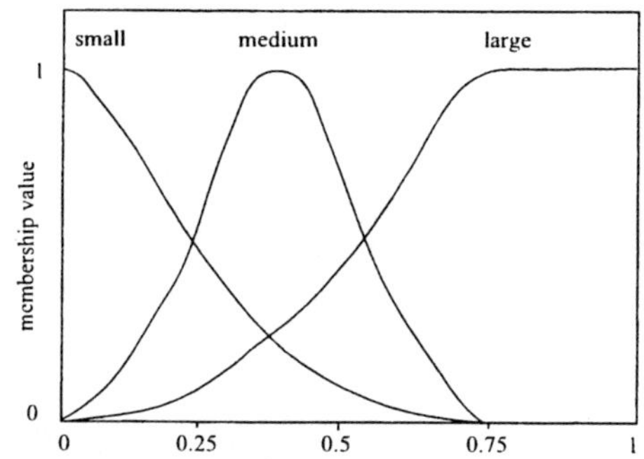

Fig. 16. Fuzzification of total compatibility TC using three fuzzy subsets [8]

The membership function is given by

$$\mu_{ij} = w_{ij} \exp(\frac{-d_{ij}^2}{\beta_i}), \tag{69}$$

where

$$d_{ij}^2 = [g_i - g_j]^2 \quad \text{and} \quad w_{ij} = \exp(\frac{-\|g_i - g_j\|_2^2}{\alpha}). \tag{70}$$

The scale estimate β_i is a measure of the dispersion of the gray-level differences between the center point and its neighbors. Some ways are proposed to determine the scale estimate [8]. The parameter w_{ij} can be ignored for small window sizes. The final filter respond is given by:

$$g' = \frac{\mu_{ij,small} \times g_1' + \mu_{ij,medium} \times g_2' + \mu_{ij,large} \times g_3'}{\mu_{ij,small} + \mu_{ij,medium} + \mu_{ij,large}}. \tag{71}$$

where g_k' is the answer of filter F_k. Tizhoosh [49] proposed a similar technique where an OWA-operator is used for determining the scale estimate (see also [23]). In this approach fuzzy rules are applied to combine the results of median and Wiener filter, respectively:

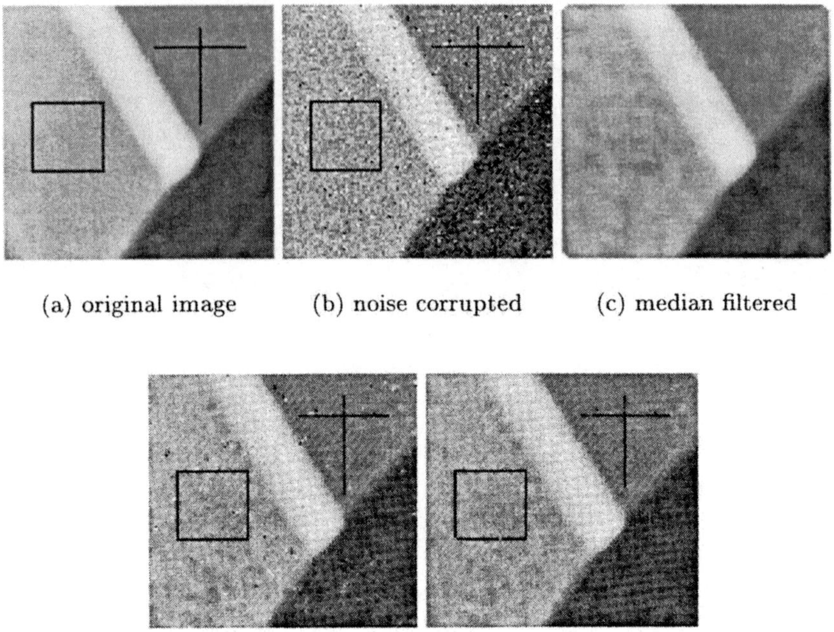

(a) original image (b) noise corrupted (c) median filtered

(d) Wiener filtered (e) result of fusion

Fig. 17. Filter fusion by fuzzy rules. The original image is corrupted with 50% mixed noise (Source: Tizhoosh [49])

If the pixel is an outlier, **then** apply the median filter,
else apply Wiener filter.

Other fuzzy rules can be used to enhance real scene images:

If the center pixel is an outlier, **then** apply the median filter,
If the neighborhood is an edge, **then** apply the unsharp masking,
else apply the Wiener filter.

Fig. 17 and 18 show the results of rule-based fusion for a test and real scene image. The individual advantages of both filters are obviously combined.

5 Subjectivity and image enhancement

Once the images are enhanced, the question of their quality arises. Generally, some measures of quality such as SNR, RMS and PSNR are used in

(a) original image (b) median filtered

(c) unsharp masking (d) result of fusion

Fig. 18. Filter fusion by fuzzy rules. Three filters are combined to achieve better result. The result of Wiener is not presented since it is very similar to the result of the median filter (Source: Tizhoosh [49])

image processing to ensure good quality. However, if the observer's demands should play a central role, these measures are not suitable for judgement of the image quality. The main reason is that there is no direct and logical relationship between such objective measures on the one hand, and the subjective impression of the human observer on the other hand. Another reason to avoid such quality measures is that they generally calculate the distance between the original image and the enhanced image. However, in practical cases we are not provided with noiseless and good original images. Therefore, one can use subjective tests to ensure the quality of the results. Thus, the recommendations of ITU (*International Telecommunication Union*) can be applied to compare the performance of different enhancement algorithms[1]. The observer judges the image quality using a scale from 1 to 5 where 1 is

[1] ITU BT.500-9 (11/98): Methodology for the subjective assessment of the quality of television pictures 43pp ITU-R Recommendations, 1997 - BT Series - Supplement 2 to Volume 1997.

excellent, 2 *good*, 3 *fair*, 4 *poor* and 5 *bad*. Finally, the MOS (*Mean Opinion Score*) is calculated as the total quality measurement.

In [44,50], some different contrast adaptation techniques are compared where the index of fuzziness is used as quality measure. In regards to human subjectivity, it is more appropriate to use MOS instead of an amount of image fuzziness (Table 1). In two test series, 16 observers judged the contrast of 80 noisy and noiseless images in a randomised order. As is shown in Table 1, the rule-based approach achieved the best MOS. In a case where subjectivity plays the central role, as a reason to choose a certain method, this approach may be used as the best method.

Table 1. Evaluation of contrast adaptation techniques after ITU-BT 500 for noiseless and noisy images (σ =standard deviation)

	Histogram Equalisation	Fuzzy Hyperbolization	Rule-Based Enhancement	Minimisation of fuzziness
MOS	2.440	2.220	1.740	2.560
σ	±0.645	±0.651	±0.751	±0.826
MOS_{noisy}	4.220	2.870	2.660	3.450
σ	±0.728	±0.680	±0.782	±1.481

However, every observer has a different characteristic brightness perception. Therefore, it is necessary to come up with some solutions to develop an observer-dependent system for image enhancement.

Tizhoosh *et al.* [50–52] introduced an observer-dependent system which consists of five phases (top image in Fig. 19). These phases are as follows: Image enhancement by different algorithms, extraction of objective quality criteria for image contrast, learning the fuzzy measure (subjective quality evaluation), aggregation (concerning different images and different observers), and finally, inference (final quality measurement for each image). The result of the offline system is an aggregation matrix Υ, which determines the relevance of each algorithm for each observer. After parameter determination, the algorithms of the preprocessing phase, and the aggregation matrix Υ are used for on-line image enhancement (bottom image in Fig. 19). The expert identification is also used as an additional information. In the forthcoming paragraphs, we will give a brief description for each system phase.

Phase 1 (Enhancement): the first phase of the system is the enhancement of the original image. Of course, the enhancement algorithms are selected in accordance with the quality criterion (or criteria) in which we are interested. This quality criterion can be contrast, sharpness, smoothness, and etc., or a combination of them. Here, we use the aforesaid techniques: Minimization of image fuzziness, fuzzy histogram hyperbolization and rule-based

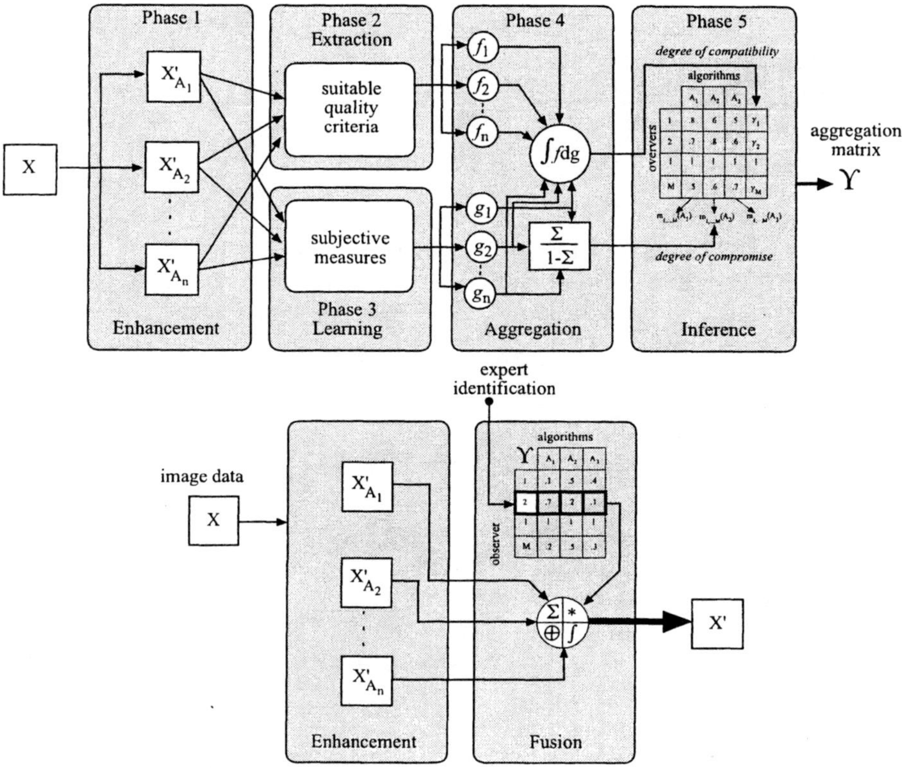

Fig. 19. Observer-dependent system for improvement of image quality: (top) offline system structure for fusion or parameter adaptation, (bottom) online system structure

approach. The algorithms were implemented in a locally adaptive environment.

Phase 2 (Extraction): a suitable measure of image contrast should be extracted in this phase. These criteria serve as an objective quality measurement and will be aggregated with subjective measurements in the forth phase via a fuzzy integral.

Phase 3 (Learning of fuzzy measure): fuzzy integration is already successfully applied in some image processing applications [46,47,54]. The Sugeno measure g_λ (also called λ-fuzzy measure [40,46,54]) is a suitable way for representation of the subjective evaluation of image quality by the human observer. This is due to the fact that the problem is non-additive in nature (generally super-additive and sometimes sub-additive). On the other hand, the construction of the Sugeno measure in our case is very simple since the subjective evaluations can be regarded as fuzzy density values g^i:

$$g_\lambda(A_1 \cup A_2) = g^1 + g^2 + \lambda g^1 g^2, \tag{72}$$

where A_1, A_2 are the alternative enhancement techniques. The parameter λ can be computed from the condition $g_\lambda(X) = 1$:

$$\lambda + 1 = \prod_{i=1}^{n}(1 + \lambda g^i). \tag{73}$$

By mapping the acquired MOS values into the interval [0, 1], they can be regarded as fuzzy density values to construct the fuzzy measure.

Phase 4 (Aggregation of criteria/judgements): the aggregation phase consists of two parts. In the first part, we calculate the degree of compatibility γ between the objective criterion (in our case contrast values $C(A_i)$) and the subjective measure ($g_\lambda(\{A_i\})$) with fuzzy integrals:

$$\gamma_i = \int C(A) \circ g_\lambda = \bigvee_{i=1}^{n} [C(A_i) \wedge g_\lambda(\{A_1, \cdots, A_i\})]. \tag{74}$$

In the second part, the fuzzy densities are normalised and interpreted as basic probabilities so that the degree of compromise m^* among all M observers (experts) can be recursively calculated with the Dempster rule of aggregation [4,39,54]:

$$m^*(A_i) = (m_1 \oplus m_2)(A_i) = \frac{\sum_{A_p \cap A_q = A_i} m_1(A_p) \cdot m_2(A_q)}{1 - \sum_{A_p \cap A_q = \emptyset} m_1(A_p) \cdot m_2(A_q)}. \tag{75}$$

Also, the aggregation phase generates two vectors $\Gamma = (\gamma_1, \gamma_2, \ldots, \gamma_M)$ and $\Phi = (m^*(A_1), m^*(A_2), \ldots, m^*(A_N))$. These vectors will be used as inputs for the inference phase.

Phase 5 (Inference): the elements of vectors Γ (degree of compatibility) and Φ (degree of compromise) are fuzzified with three symmetric membership functions. The output of the inference system is an aggregation matrix Υ which quantifies the image quality and is represented by five non-symmetric membership functions. The if-then rules are formulated heuristically as listed in Table 2. One can also use simple fuzzy connectives (e.g. minimum or algebraic product) to aggregate the degrees of compatibility and compromise. Since the Dempster rule aggregates basic probabilities that have to be absolutely reliable, and since we know that the normalised fuzzy densities (scores of the observers) are not exact values, then in this case the use of an inference system is the appropriate way to overcome the inherent uncertainties.

The simplest way to generate images using the aggregation matrix Υ is to build a convex combination. For an observer b the output image can be generated as follows:

$$X' \mid_b = \sum_{i=1}^{n} \Upsilon(b, A_i) \cdot X'_{A_i}. \tag{76}$$

Table 2. Fuzzy if-then rules for generation of aggregation matrix

	if	and	then
rule	γ	m^*	$\Upsilon(b, A_i)$
R_1	*LOW*	*LOW*	*LOW*
R_2	*LOW*	*MEDIUM*	*LOW*
R_3	*LOW*	*HIGH*	*LOW*
R_4	*MEDIUM*	*LOW*	*LOW*
R_5	*MEDIUM*	*MEDIUM*	*MEDIUM*
R_6	*MEDIUM*	*HIGH*	*MEDIUM*
R_7	*HIGH*	*LOW*	*MEDIUM*
R_8	*HIGH*	*MEDIUM*	*HIGH*
R_9	*HIGH*	*HIGH*	*HIGH*

X'_{A_i} denotes the result of the $i-$th algorithm. This simple kind of final aggregation is selected because, as an interesting quality criterion, the contrast of individual results allows such additive fusion. However, For more complex quality criteria, we need other approaches to carry out the final aggregation (e.g. if we consider the sharpness as quality criteria, a global fusion can not be used!).

To test the performance of the system 30 images were used according to the contrast as an interesting quality. Each of the images was enhanced using the described algorithms and the observer-dependent system (i.e. each observer judged 120 randomly ordered images). 20 of the images were used as training data to learn subjectivity. These images were evaluated by five observers using the ITU recommendations. The scores were mapped into the interval $[0, 1]$ and interpreted as fuzzy density values. The other 10 images were used to verify whether the system could meet the subjective expectations of the same observers. The result of the system was presented among four other alternatives. The observers judged the new results using the same quality scale (Table 3).

6 Future view

Fuzzy techniques offer a new and flexible framework for the development of image enhancement algorithms. They are nonlinear, knowledge-based and robust. The potentials of fuzzy set theory with respect to image enhancement are still not investigated as well as other established methodologies. Therefore, one of the main goals of the research in this area will be a thorough investigation of each fuzzy approach. Information-theoretical approaches that use the amount of image fuzziness are very fast, whereas the fuzzy rule-based techniques are very expensive in computing if they use the spatial image information. Some hardware solutions are already proposed to increase the practicability of fuzzy inference in image processing [5,24].

Table 3. Subjective evaluation of the results. In an optimal case, i.e. MOS= 1, the observers should perceive all outputs of the system as the best one among other alternatives that are presented to him in a randomised order

observer	best	good	medium	poor	bad
1	60%	30%	10%	0%	0%
2	50%	30%	20%	0%	0%
3	70%	10%	20%	0%	0%
4	70%	20%	10%	0%	0%
5	60%	10%	30%	0%	0%
total	62%	20%	18%	0%	0%
MOS			1.56		
σ			± 0.25		

Acknowledgement

The author would like to thank the following colleagues for their support: Dr. C.-S. Lee (National Cheng Kung University, Taiwan), Dr. Bhutani (Catholic University of America, Washington, USA) and Dr. A. Taguchi (Musashi Institute of Technology, Tokyo, Japan).

References

1. Banks S., *"Signal Processing, Image Processing and Pattern Recognition"*, Prentice Hall, Great Britain, 1990
2. Bhandari D., Pal S.K. and Kundu M.K., *Image enhancement incorporating fuzzy fitness function in genetic algorithms*, in: "Proceedings of FUZZ-IEEE'93", Vol. 2, pp. 1408–1413, 1993
3. Bhutani K.R. and Battou A., *An application of fuzzy relations to image enhancement*, Pattern Recognition Letters, Vol. 16, pp. 901–909, 1995
4. Bouchon-Meunier B., *"Aggregation and Fusion of Imperfect Information"*, Physica-Verlag, Heidelberg, New York, 1998
5. Cardarilli G.C., Marco Re, Lojacono R., D'Lena M. and Scrimaglio R., *A VLSI Architecture for High-Speed Fuzzy Image Processing*, in: "Proceedings of EUFIT'98", pp. 1350–13554, 1998
6. Chen B.-T., Chen Y.-S. and Hsu W.-H., *Automatic histogram specification based on fuzzy set operations for image enhancement*, IEEE Signal Processing Letters, Vol. 2, No. 2, pp. 37–40, 1995
7. Chen B.-T., Chen Y.-S. and Hsu W.-H., *Image processing & understanding based on fuzzy inference approach*, in: "Proceedings of FUZZ-IEEE'94", Vol. 1, pp. 254–259, 1994
8. Choi Y.S. and Krishnapuram R., *A robust Approach to Image Enhancement Based on Fuzzy Logic*, IEEE Trans. Image Processing, Vol. 6, No. 6, pp. 808–825, 1997
9. De T.K. and Chatterji B.N., *An approach to a generalized technique for image contrast enhancement using the concept of fuzzy set*, Fuzzy Sets and Systems, Vol. 25, pp.145–158, 1998

10. De Luca A. and Termini S., *A definition of a nonprobabilistic entropy in the setting of fuzzy set theory*, Information and Control, Vol. 20, pp. 301-312, 1972
11. Fang N. and Cheng M.-C, *An automatic crossover point selection technique for image enhancement using fuzzy sets*, Pattern Recognition Letters, Vol. 14, pp. 397–406, 1993
12. Frei W., *Image Enhancement by Histogram Hyperbolization*, CGIP, Vol. 6, No. 3, pp. 286–294, 1977
13. Friedman M., Schneider M. and Kandel A., *The use of weighted fuzzy expected value (WFEV) in fuzzy expert systems*, Fuzzy Sets and Systems, Vol. 31, pp. 37–45, 1989
14. Haralick R.M. and Shapiro L.G., *"Computer and Robot Vision, Volume 1"*, Addison Wesley, 1992
15. Jähne B., *"Digital Image Processing"*, Springer, Heidelberg, 1995
16. Kaufmann A., *"Introduction to the Theory of Fuzzy Subsets - Fundamental Theoretical Elements"*, Vol. 1, Academic Press, New York, 1975
17. Law T., Itoh H. and Seki H., *Image Filtering, Edge Detection, and Edge Tracing Using Fuzzy Reasoning*, IEEE Trans. Pattern Analysis and Machine Intelligence, Vol. 18, No. 5, pp. 481–491, 1996
18. Lee C.-S., Kuo Y.-H. and Yu P.-T., *Weighted fuzzy mean filters for image processing*, Fuzzy Sets and Systems, Vol. 89, pp.157–180, 1997
19. Lee C.-S. and Kuo Y.-H., *Adaptive weighted fuzzy mean filter*, in: "Proceedings of FUZZ-IEEE'96", USA, pp. 2110 – 2116, 1996
20. Lee C.-S. and Kuo Y.-H., *The Important Properties and Applications of the Adaptive Weighted Fuzzy Mean Filter*, Int. Journal of Intelligent Systems, Vol. 14, pp. 253–274, 1999
21. Li H. and Yang H.S., *Fast and reliable image enhancement using fuzzy relaxation technique*, IEEE Trans. Syst. Man and Cybern., Vol. 19, No. 5, pp. 1276–1281, 1989
22. Mancuso M., Poluzzi R. and Rizzotto G.G., *A fuzzy filter for dynamic range reduction and contrast enhancement*, in: "Proceedings of FUZZ-IEEE'94", Vol. 1, pp. 264–267, 1994
23. Mari M. and Dellepiane S., *A non-linear image processing approach through fuzzy measures*, Pattern Recognition Letters, Vol. 18, pp. 1109–1115, 1997
24. Ooki S. and Shono K., *Image processing employing fuzzy inference*, in: "Proceedings of the 3rd Int. Conf. Fuzzy Logic and Soft Computing" (Iizuka), pp. 395–397, 1994
25. Pal S.K., Bhandari D. and Kundu M.K., *Genetic algorithms for optimal image enhancement*, Pattern Recognition Letters, Vol. 15, pp. 261–271, 1994
26. Pal S.K. and King R.A., *Image enhancement using smoothing with fuzzy sets*, IEEE Trans. Syst. Man and Cybern., Vol. 11, No. 7, pp. 494-501, 1981
27. Pal S.K. and Rosenfeld A., *Image enhancement and thresholding by optimization of fuzzy compactness*, Pattern Recognition Letters, Vol. 7, pp. 77–86, 1988
28. Pal S.K. and Kundu M.K., *Automatic selection of object enhancement operator with quantitative justification based on fuzzy set theoretic measures*, Pattern Recognition Letters, Vol. 11, pp. 811–829, 1990
29. Pal S.K. and Dutta Majumder D., *"Fuzzy Mathematical Approach to Pattern Recognition"*, John Wiley & Sons, New York, 1986
30. Pal N.R. and Bezdek J.C., *Measures of Fuzziness: A Review and several New Classes*, in: "Fuzzy Sets, Neural Networks, and Soft Computing (Yager R.R. and Zadeh L.A., eds.)", Van Nostrand Reinhold, New York, pp. 194-212, 1994

31. Peng S. and Lucke L., *Fuzzy Filtering for Mixed Noise Removal During Image Processing*, in: "Proceedings of FUZZ-IEEE'94", Vol. 1, pp. 89–93, 1994
32. Pitas I. and Venetsanopoulos A.N., *Nonlinear mean filters in image processing*, IEEE Trans. ASSP, Vol. 34, No. 3, pp. 573–584, 1986
33. Pizer S., Amburn E.P., Austin J.D., Cromartie R., Geselowitz A., Greer T., Romeny B.H., Zimmerman B. and Zuiderveld K., *Adaptive histogram equalization and its variations*, Computer Vision, Graphics and Image Processing, Vol. 39, pp. 355–368, 1987
34. Russo F. and Ramponi G., *Combined FIRE Filter for Image Enhancement*, in: "Proceedings of FUZZ-IEEE'94", Vol. 1, pp. 260–264, 1994
35. Russo F., *FIRE operators for image processing*, Fuzzy Sets and Systems, Vol. 103, pp. 265–275, 1999
36. Russo F. and Ramponi G., *A fuzzy filter for images corrupted by impulse noise*, IEEE Signal Processing Letters, Vol. 3, No. 6, pp. 168–170, 1996
37. Rousseeuw P.J. and Leroy A.M., *"Robust Regression and Outlier Detection"*, Wiley, New York, 1987
38. Schneider M. and Craig M., *On the use of fuzzy sets in histogram equalization*, Fuzzy Sets and Systems, Vol. 45, pp. 271-278, 1992
39. Shafer G., *"A Mathematical Theory of Evidence"*, Princeton University Press, New Jersey, 1976
40. Sugeno M., *"Theory of Fuzzy Integrals and Its Applications"*, Dissertation, Tokyo Institute of Technology, Japan, 1974
41. Taguchi A., *A design method of fuzzy weighted median filters*, in: "Proceedings of ICIP'96", pp.423–426, 1996
42. Taguchi A. and Takaku S., *Fuzzy weighted median filters*, in: "Proceedings of IEEE Workshop on Nonlinear Signal and Image Processing" (Michigan, USA), 1997
43. Tizhoosh H.R., Krell G. and Michaelis B., *Locally Adaptive Fuzzy Image Enhancement*, in: "Computational Intelligence, Theory and Applications; Proceedings of 5th Fuzzy Days'97 (B. Reusch, ed.)" (Dortmund, Germany), Springer, pp. 272–276, 1997
44. Tizhoosh H.R., Krell G. and Michaelis B., *On Fuzzy Image Enhancement of Megavoltage Images in Radiation Therapy*, in: "Proceedings of FUZZ-IEEE'97" (Barcelona), pp. 1399–1404, 1997
45. Tizhoosh H.R., Krell G. and Michaelis B., *λ-Enhancement: Contrast adaptation based on Optimization of Image Fuzziness*, in: "Proceedings of FUZZ-IEEE'98", pp. 1548–1553, 1998
46. Tizhoosh H. R., *"Fuzzy Image Processing"* (in German), Springer, Heidelberg, 1997
47. Tizhoosh H.R. and Haußecker H., *Fuzzy Image Processing: An Overview*, in: "Handbook on Computer Vision and Applications, Vol. 2 (Jähne B., Haußecker H. and Geißler P., eds.)", Academic Press, Boston, pp. 683–727, 1999
48. Tizhoosh H.R., Krell G., Lilienblum T., Moore C.J. and Michaelis B., *Enhancement and Associative Restoration of Electronic Portal Images in Radiotherapy*, International Journal of Medical Informatics, Vol. 49/2, Elsevier Science Ireland, pp. 157–171, 1998
49. Tizhoosh H.R., *An Universal Filter Based on Soft Computing Techniques*, in: "Proceedings of NN'99 – 4th Int. Workshop Neural Networks in Applications" (Magdeburg, Germany), pp. 219–224, 1999

50. Tizhoosh H.R., Krell G., Michaelis B., *Enhancement of Megavoltage Images in Radiation Therapy Using Fuzzy and Neural Image Processing Techniques*, in: "Fuzzy Systems in Medicine (P.S. Szczepaniak, P.J.G. Lisboa and S. Tsumoto, eds.)", Studies in Fuzziness and Soft Computing, Physica-Verlag, 1999
51. Tizhoosh H.R., Michaelis B., *Improvement of Image Quality Based on Subjective Evaluation and Fuzzy Aggregation techniques*, in: "Proceedings of EUFIT'98" (Aachen, Germany), Vol. 2, pp. 1325–1329, 1998
52. Tizhoosh H.R., Michaelis B., *Image Enhancement Based on Fuzzy Aggregation Techniques*, in: "Proceedings of IMTC'99" (Venice, Italy), Vol. 3, pp. 1813–1817, 1999
53. Tyan C.-Y. and Wang P.P., *Image Processing – Enhancement, Filtering and Edge Detection Using Fuzzy Logic Approach*, in: "Proceedings of FUZZ-IEEE'93", pp. 600–605, 1993
54. Wang Z., Klir G.J., *"Fuzzy Measure Theory"*, Plenum Press, New York, 1992
55. Weeks A.R., *"Fundamentals of Electronic Image Processing"*, SPIE Optical Engineering Press, IEEE Press, USA, 1996
56. Zadeh L.A., *Fuzzy sets*, Information and Control, Vol. 8, pp. 338–353, 1965

Chapter 6

Adaptive Fuzzy Filter and Its Application to Image Enhancement

Chang-Shing Lee and Yau-Hwang Kuo

National Cheng Kung University
Department of Computer Science and Information Engineering
Intelligent System and Media Processing Lab
No. 1, University Road, Tainan, Taiwan
email: {leecs,kuoyh}@cad.csie.ncku.edu.tw

Summary. This chapter describes the design and evaluation of a novel adaptive fuzzy filter, and discusses its application to image enhancement. Most traditional edge detectors can perform well for uncorrupted images but are highly sensitive to impulse noise, so they can not work efficiently for blurred images. The proposed adaptive fuzzy filter consists of two major mechanisms: Adaptive Weighted Fuzzy Mean (AWFM) filter and Fuzzy Normed Inference System (FNIS) to realize the function of edge detection for smeared images. The membership functions of all fuzzy sets used in this filter can be adaptively determined for different images. Moreover, the adaptive fuzzy filter is capable of converting blurred edges to clear ones and suppressing noise at the same time. According to the experimental results, it works well in full range of random impulse noise probability and performs efficiently in the environment of mixed Gaussian impulse noise. This chapter also analytically evaluates the important properties of the filter to show its high performance in general cases.

1 Introduction

The principal goal of enhancement techniques is to process an image so that the result is more suitable than the original image for a specific application. The problems of image enhancement can be stated as those of removing impulse noise, smoothing nonimpulse noise and enhancing edges in the input image. Noise smoothing and edge enhancement are inherently conflicting processes, since smoothing a region might destroy edges and sharpening an edge might lead to unnecessary noise [3]. Recently, the fuzzy logic approach is being widely used to combine heuristic rules with traditional methods, which leads to a more flexible design paradigm of image enhancement [2], [1]. For example, Yang and Toh [16] used heuristic rules in order to improve the performance of the traditional multilevel median filter. Russo and Ramponi [14] applied heuristic knowledge to build fuzzy rule based operators for smoothing, sharpening and edge detection. Since the fuzzy rules in these methods were constructed based on region contours, they can perform smoothing efficiently and preserve edges well. The common drawback of these methods is that they are sensitive to impulse noise when the noise rate becomes high.

Another task of fundamental importance in image enhancement is edge detection. The most common and historically earliest edge detection algorithms are those based on the gradient, such as Robert, Prewitt and Sobel operators [4]. The axiom of gradient operator depends on the differential theory and the assumption that the magnitude of a gradient at an edge is obviously larger than at its neighborhoods. Using gradient operators, we can detect edges of uncorrupted image well, but they will fail in a noisy environment because noise and edges both have great gradient magnitudes. Smoothing filters are commonly used as prefilters when images are corrupted by high-level noise. For example, a median filter can be used to remove impulses. Hardie and Boncelet [5], [7] proposed a gradient-based edge detection method, called lower-upper-middle (LUM) filter, which can work efficiently in low impulse noise probability but fails in the condition of high noise probability. Choi and Krishnapuram [3] used a powerful robust approach to image enhancement based on fuzzy logic, which can remove impulse noise, smooth out nonimpulse noise, and preserve edges efficiently. In [10], we proposed an efficient Weighted Fuzzy Mean (WFM) filter that can overcome the drawbacks of conventional filters such as Rank Conditioned Rank Selection (RCRS), Weighted Order Statistic (WOS), Center Weighted Median (CWM), stack and median filters in the environment with high impulse noise probability (the RCRS, WOS, CWM and stack filters are discussed in [5,8,17]). However, it tends to reduce edge gradients as the conventional filters. For this reason, an enhanced WFM model, the Adaptive WFM (AWFM) filter [11], was further developed, which preserves edges better than the other filters, especially in high noise conditions.

In this chapter, a Fuzzy Normed Inference System (FNIS) is developed and embedded into the AWFM model so that we can detect image edges well from noise-free to noise-full conditions. Such a novel model is called Extended AWFM (EAWFM) filter. FNIS consists of Sobel operator and fuzzy normed operators which adopt fuzzy logic methodology to extract features from an image and Sugeno-typed fuzzy reasoning strategy for edge enhancement. The analysis of EAWFM properties proves its high stability for impulse noise.

In the next section, the AWFM filter is presented. Then, the EAWFM filter to perform the task of edge enhancement is proposed in Section 3. In Section 4, the important properties of EAWFM are analyzed to show the high stability for impulse noise. In Section 5, some experiments are presented and discussed. The experimental results show that EAWFM has the highest stability compared with the other filters. Finally, in Section 6, the conclusion is given.

2 Adaptive weighted fuzzy mean filter

In [11], we proposed a high-stability filter, called Adaptive Weighted Fuzzy Mean (AWFM) filter, for mixed mode noise such as Gaussian impulse noise and random additive impulse noise on full range of noise occurrence probability. The kernel of AWFM is the WFM filter which is supported by a simple knowledge base. WFM can remove heavy additive impulse noise well, which is better than conventional mean filters and median filter. But when the noise probability is lower than 0.1, it can not do well. Therefore, AWFM contains two extra mechanisms, fuzzy detectors and a dynamic selector, to overcome the drawbacks of WFM filter. The fuzzy detectors can detect the amplitude of impulse noise well. The dynamic selector determines the final output for each filtered pixel based on four decision rules according to the outputs of WFM and the fuzzy detectors. Now we introduce the WFM filter briefly.

2.1 Weighted fuzzy mean (WFM) filter

Consider a noise-free image S sized $N_1 \times N_2$ pixels with L gray levels. For convenience, we denote it as $S = [s(i,j)]_{N_1 \times N_2}$ where $s(i,j) \in \{0, 1, \ldots, L-1\}$ is a pixel of the noise-free source image, for $0 \leq i \leq N_1 - 1$ and $0 \leq j \leq N_2 - 1$. Then, some fuzzy subsets defined on the universe of discourse $\{0, \ldots, L-1\}$ can be built. Each of the fuzzy subsets represents an abstract concept for the gray level (that is, the intensity feature) of image pixels. For example, the "very dark" (VDK), "dark" (DK), "median" (MD), "bright" (BR) or "very bright" (VBR), and its corresponding membership function specifies the membership grade of which a certain pixel belongs to this abstract concept. For instance, according to Fig. 1, we know that the pixel with the gray level 160 has the intensity property: "*not* dark", "*quite* median" and "*poorly* bright".

The fuzzy sets of the intensity features of an image can be derived from the histogram of this image [10], and they together constitute the knowledge base of WFM. The fuzzy sets to describe the intensity features of an image in WFM are of the LR type fuzzy number [18], formulated by the following equation:

$$f(x) = \begin{cases} L(\frac{m_{LR}-x}{\alpha_{LR}}) & for\ x \leq m_{LR} \\ R(\frac{x-m_{LR}}{\beta_{LR}}) & for\ x \geq m_{LR} \end{cases} \tag{1}$$

where $\alpha_{LR} > 0$, $\beta_{LR} > 0$ and $L(y) = R(y) = \max(0, 1-y)$, i.e. L and R have the same shape function. In the following, $f(x)$ will be represented as a triplet $[m_{LR}, \alpha_{LR}, \beta_{LR}]$. An example of a LR type fuzzy number is given in Fig. 2.

In this chapter, the number of fuzzy sets will be set to three (DK, MD and BR), while the number can be increased if necessary. Besides, the knowledge base of WFM also contains a fuzzy interval for the global estimation of image.

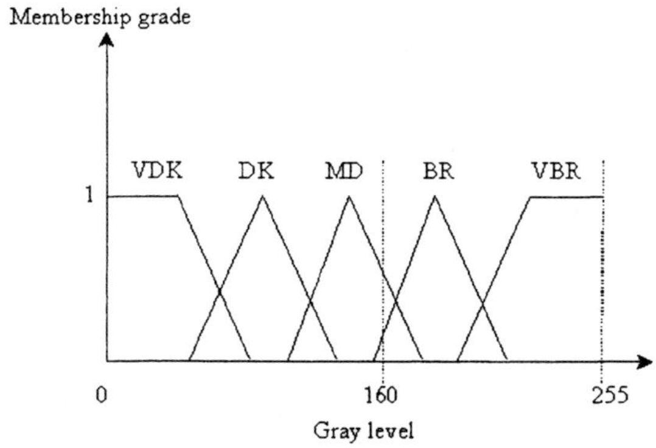

Fig. 1. Example of membership functions for the fuzzy sets VKD, DK, MD, BR and VBR.

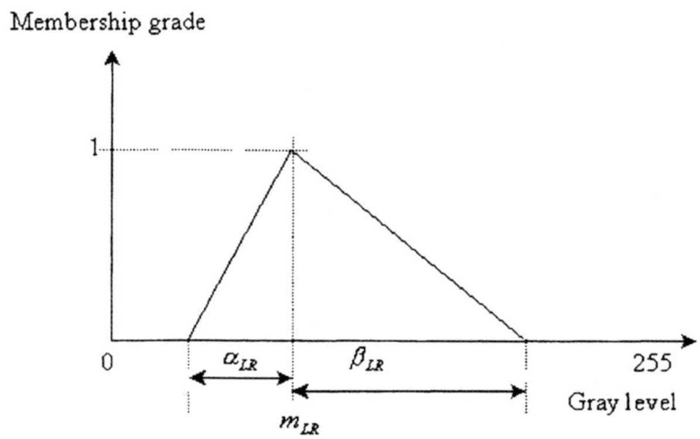

Fig. 2. Example of a *LR* type fuzzy number.

A fuzzy interval I [18] is of the LR-type if there exist two shape functions L and R and four parameters $(m_l, m_r) \in \mathbb{R}^2, \alpha_I > 0, \beta_I > 0$ to constitute the membership function of I:

$$f_{LR_I}(x) = \begin{cases} L(\frac{m_l - x}{\alpha_I}) & for\ x \leq m_l \\ 1 & for\ m_l \leq x \leq m_r \\ R(\frac{x - m_r}{\beta_I}) & for\ x \geq m_r \end{cases} \tag{2}$$

The fuzzy interval is then denoted by $I = [m_l, m_r, \alpha_I, \beta_I]$; an example is given in Fig. 3.

Assume I is the fuzzy interval stored in the knowledge base of WFM, and

$$\sum_{k=\frac{-(n_1-1)}{2}}^{\frac{n_1-1}{2}} \sum_{l=\frac{-(n_2-1)}{2}}^{\frac{n_2-1}{2}} f_{LR_I}(x(i+k, j+l)) \neq 0,$$

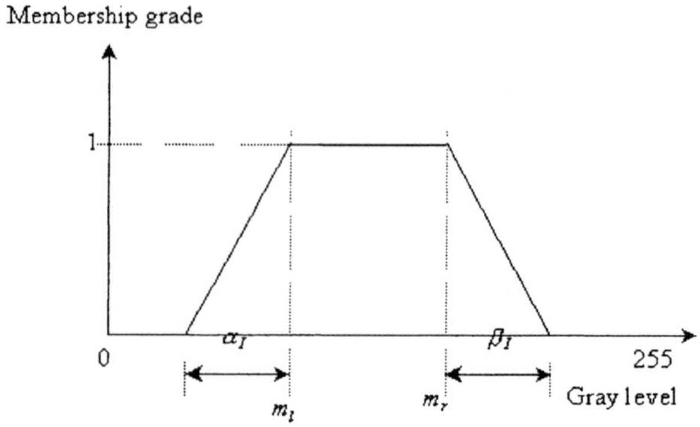

Fig. 3. Example of an LR type fuzzy interval.

then a fuzzy estimator $f_{LR_E}(\cdot)$ can be produced by the following formula:

$$f_{LR_E}(X_{n_1\times n_2}(i,j)) = \frac{\sum_{k=\frac{-(n_1-1)}{2}}^{\frac{n_1-1}{2}} \sum_{l=\frac{-(n_2-1)}{2}}^{\frac{n_2-1}{2}} f_{LR_I}(x(i+k,j+l)) \cdot x(i+k,j+l)}{\sum_{k=\frac{-(n_1-1)}{2}}^{\frac{n_1-1}{2}} \sum_{l=\frac{-(n_2-1)}{2}}^{\frac{n_2-1}{2}} f_{LR_I}(x(i+k,j+l))} \tag{3}$$

Otherwise $f_{LR_E}(\cdot) = 0$, where $X_{n_1\times n_2}(i,j)$ is a $n_1 \times n_2$ sample matrix centered at the input pixel $x(i,j)$, for $1 \leq n_1 \leq N_1$ and $1 \leq n_2 \leq N_2$, both n_1 and n_2 are odd. Note that f_{LR_E} is in fact a weighted maximum-likelihood estimator based on the fuzzy interval I.

Basically, WFM filter is a mean filter operating with the fuzzy numbers stored in the knowledge base. For executing the filtering task, WFM adopts a $n_1 \times n_2$ sample window to determine the gray level value of each filtered signal, where this signal is located on the central cell of the sample window. Let $X = [x(i,j)]_{N_1\times N_2}$ and $Y = [y(i,j)]_{N_1\times N_2}$ be the input image and filtered output image of WFM, respectively. In the X, each entry $x(i,j)$ may be corrupted by a noise $n(i,j)$ so that it has the gray level

$$x(i,j) = s(i,j) \oplus n(i,j). \tag{4}$$

Now, let $WFM(\cdot)$ denote the function of the WFM filter. Then, the (i,j)th pixel of the filtered image Y can be formulated as:

$$y(i,j) = WMF(X_{n_1\times n_2}(i,j)). \tag{5}$$

Usually we set $n_1 = 3$ and $n_2 = 3$.

$WMF(\cdot)$ is realized by three fuzzy mean processes based on the Sugeno-typed inference approach and one decision process. For filtering a pixel, the following rules are fired first:

- **Rule 1**: if

$$\{x(i-1,j-1)\ is\ DK, x(i-1,j)\ is\ DK, x(i-1,j+1)\ is\ DK,$$
$$x(i,j-1)\ is\ DK, x(i,j)\ is\ DK, x(i,j+1)\ is\ DK,$$
$$x(i+1,j-1)\ is\ DK, x(i+1,j)\ is\ DK, x(i+1,j+1)\ is\ DK\}$$

and

$$\sum_{k=-1}^{1}\sum_{l=-1}^{1} f_{DK}(x(i+k,j+l)) \neq 0,$$

then $\bar{y}_1(i,j) = \frac{\sum_{k=-1}^{1}\sum_{l=-1}^{1} f_{DK}(x(i+k,j+l))\cdot x(i+k,j+l)}{\sum_{k=-1}^{1}\sum_{l=-1}^{1} f_{DK}(x(i+k,j+l))}$

else $\bar{y}_1(i,j) = 0$;

- **Rule 2**: if

$$\{x(i-1,j-1)\ is\ MD, x(i-1,j)\ is\ MD, x(i-1,j+1)\ is\ MD,$$
$$x(i,j-1)\ is\ MD, x(i,j)\ is\ MD, x(i,j+1)\ is\ MD,$$
$$x(i+1,j-1)\ is\ MD, x(i+1,j)\ is\ MD, x(i+1,j+1)\ is\ MD\}$$

and

$$\sum_{k=-1}^{1}\sum_{l=-1}^{1} f_{MD}(x(i+k,j+l)) \neq 0,$$

then $\bar{y}_2(i,j) = \frac{\sum_{k=-1}^{1}\sum_{l=-1}^{1} f_{MD}(x(i+k,j+l))\cdot x(i+k,j+l)}{\sum_{k=-1}^{1}\sum_{l=-1}^{1} f_{MD}(x(i+k,j+l))}$

else $\bar{y}_2(i,j) = 0$;

- **Rule 3**: if

$$\{x(i-1,j-1)\ is\ BR, x(i-1,j)\ is\ BR, x(i-1,j+1)\ is\ BR,$$
$$x(i,j-1)\ is\ BR, x(i,j)\ is\ BR, x(i,j+1)\ is\ BR,$$
$$x(i+1,j-1)\ is\ BR, x(i+1,j)\ is\ BR, x(i+1,j+1)\ is\ BR\}$$

and

$$\sum_{k=-1}^{1}\sum_{l=-1}^{1} f_{BR}(x(i+k,j+l)) \neq 0$$

then $\bar{y}_3(i,j) = \dfrac{\sum_{k=-1}^{1}\sum_{l=-1}^{1} f_{BR}(x(i+k,j+l)) \cdot x(i+k,j+l)}{\sum_{k=-1}^{1}\sum_{l=-1}^{1} f_{BR}(x(i+k,j+l))}$

else $\bar{y}_3(i,j) = 0$.

Finally, the decision process is realized by a weighted average approach for the three intermediate fuzzy inference results, that is,

$$y(i,j) = \frac{\sum_{r=1}^{3} w_r \cdot \bar{y}_r(i,j)}{\sum_{r=1}^{3} w_r}, \tag{6}$$

where each weight w_r is 1 if the 2-norm of the associated intermediate inference result $\bar{y}_r(i,j)$ and the fuzzy estimator $f_{LR_E}(X(i,j))$ is minimum; otherwise it is zero. Formula (6) can also be expressed as follows: $y(i,j)$ equals the fuzzy inference result $\bar{y}_r(i,j)$ $(r = 1,2,3)$ for which the absolute value $\mid \bar{y}_r(i,j) - f_{LR_E}(X(i,j)) \mid$ is smallest.

2.2 Fuzzy detectors and dynamic selector

After describing the WFM, we propose the operations of fuzzy detectors and dynamic selector in this subsection. In summary, the mechanisms in AWFM work in a fuzzy signal space. Before discussing the fuzzy signal space, we first roughly classify impulse noise into three kinds based on the 2-norm value between the noise-free signal and its corrupted signal.

(1) For a n-bits/pixel image (that is, $L = 2^n$), if the 2-norm of a noise-free signal $s(i,j)$ and its corrupted signal $x(i,j)$ is between 0 to 2^{n-3}, we say that $x(i,j)$ is a signal corrupted by a short-tailed impulse noise such as the uniform noise.
(2) If the 2-norm is between 2^{n-3} to 2^{n-1}, then $x(i,j)$ is a signal corrupted by a median-tailed impulse noise; for example, Gaussian impulse noise or random additive impulse noise can be viewed as of this type.
(3) Finally, if the 2-norm is between 2^{n-1} to $2^n - 1$, the $x(i,j)$ is a signal corrupted by a long-tailed impulse noise; for example the positive impulse or negative impulse noise can be considered as of this type.

In this chapter, we restrict our goal to design a filter for processing both the median-tailed impulse noise and long-tailed impulse noise, that is, the Gaussian impulse noise and random impulse noise, from noise-free condition to noise-full condition. Let:

$$x(i,j) - y(i,j) = \delta(i,j), \tag{7}$$

where $y(i,j)$ is the WFM-filtered output of $x(i,j)$ determined by (5). Then we define the fuzzy detectors for evaluating the amplitudes of positive impulse noise and negative impulse noise as follows. The fuzzy detectors $f_{LR_{D\_pos}}(\cdot)$ and $f_{LR_{D\_neg}}(\cdot)$ are the mechanisms to detect the amplitudes of positive impulse noise ξ_{pos} and negative impulse noise ξ_{neg} of the whole smeared image, respectively. If $\sum_{i=1}^{N_1}\sum_{j=1}^{N_2} f_{LR_{D\_pos}}(\delta(i,j)) \neq 0$ and $\sum_{i=1}^{N_1}\sum_{j=1}^{N_2} f_{LR_{D\_neg}}(\delta(i,j)) \neq 0$, then they are realized by invoking the following formulas:

$$f_{LR_{D\_pos}}(X) = \frac{\sum_{i=1}^{N_1}\sum_{j=1}^{N_2} |\delta(i,j)| \cdot f_{LR_{I\_D\_pos}}(\delta(i,j))}{\sum_{i=1}^{N_1}\sum_{j=1}^{N_2} f_{LR_{I\_D\_pos}}(\delta(i,j))} \tag{8}$$

$$f_{LR_{D\_neg}}(X) = \frac{\sum_{i=1}^{N_1}\sum_{j=1}^{N_2} |\delta(i,j)| \cdot f_{LR_{I\_D\_neg}}(\delta(i,j))}{\sum_{i=1}^{N_1}\sum_{j=1}^{N_2} f_{LR_{I\_D\_neg}}(\delta(i,j))}, \tag{9}$$

where $I\_D\_pos = [2^{n-1}, 2^n - 2, 2^{n-1} - 2^{n-2}, 1]_{LR}$ is the fuzzy interval for detecting positive impulse noise, $I\_D\_neg = [-(2^n-2), -2^{n-1}, 2^{n-1}-2^{n-2}, 1]_{LR}$ is the fuzzy interval for detecting negative impulse noise, and where $X = [x(i,j)]_{N_1 \times N_2}$ is the received image. Otherwise, $\xi_{pos} = 0$ and $\xi_{neg} = 0$.

Next, we give the definition of fuzzy signal space for the usage of the dynamic selector. Traditionally, the signal space of AWFM can be partitioned into an uncorrupted subspace, a positive subspace, a negative subspace, and an undecided subspace by the following rules:

(1) if $-2^{n-3} < \delta(i,j) < 2^{n-3}$, then $x(i,j)$ may be a signal corrupted by short-tailed impulse noise or a noise-free signal, so that it is assigned to the uncorrupted subspace because WFM distorts the fine structure of this signal;
(2) if $\delta(i,j) > \xi_{pos}$, then $x(i,j)$ is viewed as a signal corrupted by positive Gaussian impulse noise or random impulse noise since $x(i,j)$ is much larger than $y(i,j)$, so it belongs to the positive subspace;
(3) if $\delta(i,j) < -\xi_{neg}$, then $x(i,j)$ is corrupted by negative Gaussian impulse noise or random impulse noise, and belongs to the negative subspace by similar reason;
(4) if $2^{n-3} < \delta(i,j) < \xi_{pos}$ or $-\xi_{neg} < \delta(i,j) < -2^{n-3}$, then $x(i,j)$ can not be determined whether it is corrupted or not, so it will be assigned to the undecided subspace.

In fact, it is difficult to judge which subspace the corrupted signal exactly belongs to from the above partition because of the high uncertainty for the decision of the noise type. Therefore, we propose a more reasonable partition for the signal space based on fuzzy intervals as follows. A fuzzy signal space is a signal space whose partitions are decided by fuzzy intervals. The partitions include fuzzy uncorrupted subspace, fuzzy positive subspace, fuzzy negative subspace and fuzzy undecided subspace by the following four fuzzy intervals:

(1) the fuzzy interval I_unc of fuzzy uncorrupted subspace is defined as follows:

$$I\_unc = [-2^{n-3}, 2^{n-3}, 2^{\lfloor \frac{n}{2} \rfloor}, 2^{\lfloor \frac{n}{2} \rfloor}]_{LR}; \tag{10}$$

(2) the fuzzy interval I_pos of fuzzy positive subspace is defined as follows:

$$I\_pos = [\xi_{pos}, 2^n - 1, 2^{\lfloor \frac{n}{2} \rfloor}, 1]_{LR}; \tag{11}$$

(3) the fuzzy interval I_neg of fuzzy negative subspace is defined as follows:

$$I\_neg = [-(2^n - 1), -\xi_{neg}, 1, 2^{\lfloor \frac{n}{2} \rfloor}]_{LR}; \tag{12}$$

(4) the fuzzy interval I_und of fuzzy undecided subspace is defined as follows:

$$I\_und = [2^{n-3} + 1, \xi_{pos} - 1, 2^{\lfloor \frac{n}{2} \rfloor}, 2^{\lfloor \frac{n}{2} \rfloor}]_{LR}; \tag{13}$$

$$\cup[-\xi_{neg} + 1, -2^{n-3} - 1, 2^{\lfloor \frac{n}{2} \rfloor}, 2^{\lfloor \frac{n}{2} \rfloor}]_{LR}. \tag{14}$$

Then, the dynamic selector decides the final filtering result $z(i,j)$ according to the following rules:

- **Rule 4**: if

$$\begin{aligned}\max \quad & (f_{LR_{I\_unc}}(\delta(i,j)), f_{LR_{I\_und}}(\delta(i,j)), \\ & f_{LR_{I\_pos}}(\delta(i,j)), f_{LR_{I\_neg}}(\delta(i,j))) = f_{LR_{I\_unc}}(\delta(i,j)),\end{aligned}$$

  then the final output $z(i,j) = x(i,j)$.

- **Rule 5**: if

$$\begin{aligned}\max \quad & (f_{LR_{I\_unc}}(\delta(i,j)), f_{LR_{I\_und}}(\delta(i,j)), \\ & f_{LR_{I\_pos}}(\delta(i,j)), f_{LR_{I\_neg}}(\delta(i,j))) = f_{LR_{I\_und}}(\delta(i,j)),\end{aligned}$$

  then the final output $z(i,j) = y(i,j)$.

- **Rule 6**: if

$$\begin{aligned}\max \quad & (f_{LR_{I\_unc}}(\delta(i,j)), f_{LR_{I\_und}}(\delta(i,j)), \\ & f_{LR_{I\_pos}}(\delta(i,j)), f_{LR_{I\_neg}}(\delta(i,j))) = f_{LR_{I\_pos}}(\delta(i,j)),\end{aligned}$$

  then the final output $z(i,j) = x(i,j) - \xi_{pos}$.

- **Rule 7**: if

$$\begin{aligned}\max \quad & (f_{LR_{I\_unc}}(\delta(i,j)), f_{LR_{I\_und}}(\delta(i,j)), \\ & f_{LR_{I\_pos}}(\delta(i,j)), f_{LR_{I\_neg}}(\delta(i,j))) = f_{LR_{I\_neg}}(\delta(i,j)),\end{aligned}$$

  then the final output $z(i,j) = x(i,j) + \xi_{neg}$.

3 Extended AWFM filter for edge enhancement

An edge denotes the area between two neighboring regions with obviously different gray level characteristics. Therefore, if we find a pixel that is obviously different from its neighboring pixels in gray level, the probability that the pixel is on an edge would be high. In [9] we proposed a fuzzy Sobel method to improve the performance of the Sobel operator. The fuzzy Sobel method calculates the gradient value and invokes two fuzzy rules to determine whether the pixel is on an edge or not. It can work well in noise-free images but will fail in a noisy environment. To overcome this drawback, we combine the high-stability AWFM filter and the Fuzzy Normed Inference System (FNIS) to perform image edge enhancement, and call it the Extended AWFM (EAWFM) filter.

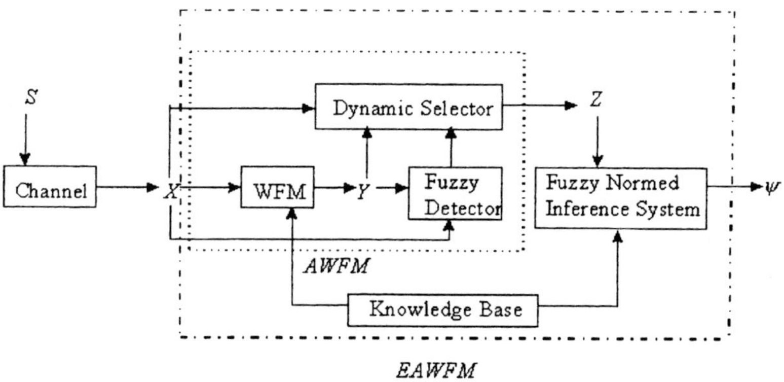

Fig. 4. Block diagram of EAWFM for detecting images transmitted by a noise channel.

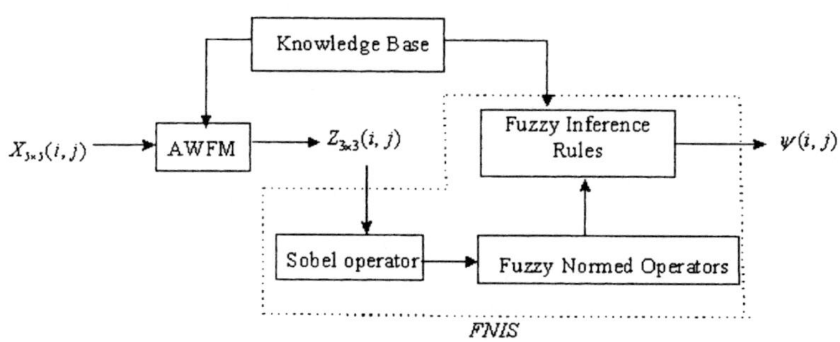

Fig. 5. The detail process of the FNIS.

Fig. 4 shows the block diagram of EAWFM, where Z is the output of AWFM and ψ is the final result of EAWFM. The detail process of FNIS is shown in Fig. 5, where $X_{5\times5}(i,j)$ is a 5×5 matrix centered at the pixel $x(i,j)$, $Z_{3\times3}(i,j)$ is a 3×3 output matrix of AWFM centered at the pixel $z(i,j)$, and $\psi(i,j)$ is the final result of EAWFM for $x(i,j)$. The proposed FNIS is constituted by the Sobel operator, fuzzy normed operators and fuzzy inference rules. The Sobel operator [4] is adopted to calculate the gradient values of the pixel $z(i,j)$, namely $G_x(i,j)$ and $G_y(i,j)$, which are formulated as follows:

$$G_x(i,j) = \sum_{p=-1}^{1} \sum_{q=-1}^{1} z(i+p,j+q) \cdot w_x(i+p,j+q), \tag{15}$$

$$G_y(i,j) = \sum_{p=-1}^{1} \sum_{q=-1}^{1} z(i+p,j+q) \cdot w_y(i+p,j+q), \tag{16}$$

where $w_x(i,j)$ and $w_y(i,j)$ are the weighted values of Sobel operators for x-direction and y-direction, respectively. The fuzzy normed operators are defined as follows.

Definition 1 *For a vector of signals $\boldsymbol{x} = [x_1, x_2, \ldots, x_p]_{1\times p}$, the fuzzy normed operators: fuzzy 1-norm, fuzzy 2-norm and fuzzy ∞-norm of FNIS are denoted as $\|\cdot\|_{f1}$, $\|\cdot\|_{f2}$ and $\|\cdot\|_{f\infty}$ respectively and defined as follows:*

1. $\|\boldsymbol{x}\|_{f1} = |x_1| \oplus |x_2| \oplus \cdots \oplus |x_p|$,
2. $\|\boldsymbol{x}\|_{f2} = \min(\sqrt{|x_1|^2 + |x_2|^2 + \cdots + |x_p|^2}, 2^n - 1)$,
3. $\|\boldsymbol{x}\|_{f\infty} = \max(|x_1|, |x_2|, \ldots, |x_p|)$.

To explain the detail operation of FNIS, we must consider the knowledge base of EAWFM first. This knowledge base is an extended version of the one of WFM, since it must contain some additional fuzzy intervals that will be used in edge detection. For image edge detection, we can roughly divide an image into two fuzzy regions: Fuzzy Smooth Region (FSR) and Fuzzy Edge Region (FER), by two fuzzy intervals

$$I\_FSR = [m_{l\_FSR}, m_{r\_FSR}, \alpha_{I\_FSR}, \beta_{I\_FSR}]_{LR}$$

and

$$I\_FER = [m_{l\_FER}, m_{r\_FER}, \alpha_{I\_FER}, \beta_{I\_FER}]_{LR},$$

respectively. For a pixel, if the gray-level characteristic of its neighboring pixels is similar to itself, it would have a high probability as an element in FSR. Otherwise, the pixel more likely belongs to FER. Before describing the construction algorithm of the knowledge base, the concept of histogram [4] and a new concept of Fuzzy Infinite Norm Histogram (FINH) should be presented. The histogram of a digital image with gray levels in the range $[0, L-1]$ is a discrete function:

$$p(s_k) = \frac{n_k}{n}, \tag{17}$$

where s_k is the k-th gray level of image S, n_k is the number of pixels with the k-th gray level in S, n is the total number of pixels in S, and $k = 0, 1, 2, \ldots, L-1$. In other words, $p(s_k)$ gives an estimate of the occurrence probability of gray level s_k. Then we propose the Fuzzy Infinite Norm Histogram (FINH) as follows.

The Fuzzy Infinite Norm Histogram (FINH) of EAWFM is built by calculating the fuzzy ∞-norm of the difference vector $\boldsymbol{d}_{3\times3}(i,j) = [d_1, d_2, \ldots, d_8]_{1\times8}$ of every pixel $x(i,j)$, with respect to the eight pixels around it, by the following formula:

$$||\boldsymbol{d}_{3\times3}(i,j)||_{f\infty} = \max(|d_1|, |d_2|, \ldots, |d_8|), \tag{18}$$

where

$$\begin{aligned}[d_1, \ldots, d_8]_{1\times8} = \quad & [x(i,j) - x(i-1,j-1), x(i,j) - x(i-1,j), \\ & x(i,j) - x(i-1,j+1), x(i,j) - x(i,j-1), \\ & x(i,j) - x(i,j+1), x(i,j) - x(i+1,j-1), \\ & x(i,j) - x(i+1,j), x(i,j) - x(i+1,j+1)]_{1\times8}.\end{aligned}$$

Therefore, the value of the fuzzy ∞-norm is in the range $[0, L-1]$. The FINH of a digital image X with gray levels in the range $[0, L-1]$ is a discrete function:

$$p_{FINH}(k) = \frac{N_k}{T}, \tag{19}$$

where $k = 0, 1, 2, \ldots, L-1$, which denotes one resultant value of fuzzy ∞-norm, N_k is the number of pixels in X whose fuzzy ∞-norm is k, and T is the total number of pixels in X.

Now we develop a new construction algorithm for the knowledge base of EAWFM.

Construction Algorithm for the Knowledge Base of EAWFM

1. Decide the intervals $[DK_{begin}, DK_{end}]$, $[MD_{begin}, MD_{end}]$ and $[BR_{begin}, BR_{end}]$ of the fuzzy sets DK, MD and BR, respectively.
   1.1 Set $DK_{end} = \lfloor\frac{L-1}{N_f}\rfloor$, $BR_{begin} = (N_f - 1) \cdot \lfloor\frac{L-1}{N_f}\rfloor$, $MD_{begin} = DK_{end} - l_{over}$ and $MD_{end} = BR_{begin} + r_{over}$, where N_f is the number of fuzzy sets, and l_{over} and r_{over} denote the overlapping range of the fuzzy sets.
   1.2 Set DK_{begin} the first s_k such that $n_k > t$ from 0 to DK_{end}, where t is a threshold.

1.3 Set BR_{end} the last s_k such that $n_k > t$ from BR_{begin} to $L-1$.

2. Find a point s_k with the maximum value of $p(s_k)$ in the interval $[DK_{begin}, DK_{end}]$, then generate the membership function f_{DK} of the fuzzy set DK by the following substeps:
   2.1 $m_{LR_{DK}} \leftarrow s_k$.
   2.2 $\alpha_{LR_{DK}} \leftarrow m_{LR_{DK}} - DK_{begin}$.
   2.3 $\beta_{LR_{DK}} \leftarrow DK_{end} - m_{LR_{DK}}$.

3. Find a point s_k with the maximum value of $p(s_k)$ in the interval $[MD_{begin}, MD_{end}]$, then generate the membership function f_{MD} of the fuzzy set MD by the following substeps:
   3.1 $m_{LR_{MD}} \leftarrow s_k$.
   3.2 $\alpha_{LR_{MD}} \leftarrow m_{LR_{MD}} - MD_{begin}$.
   3.3 $\beta_{LR_{MD}} \leftarrow MD_{end} - m_{LR_{MD}}$.

4. Find a point s_k with the maximum value of $p(s_k)$ in the interval $[BR_{begin}, BR_{end}]$, then generate the membership function f_{BR} of the fuzzy set BR by the following substeps:
   4.1 $m_{LR_{BR}} \leftarrow s_k$.
   4.2 $\alpha_{LR_{BR}} \leftarrow m_{LR_{BR}} - BR_{begin}$.
   4.3 $\beta_{LR_{BR}} \leftarrow BR_{end} - m_{LR_{BR}}$.

5. Find the expected values e_{FSR} and e_{FER} in the intervals of FINH, $[0, \frac{L-1}{2}]$ and $[\frac{L-1}{2}, L-1]$ respectively, by the following substeps:
   5.1 $e_{FSR} \leftarrow \sum_{k=0}^{\frac{L-1}{2}} k \cdot p_{FINH}(k)$.
   5.2 $e_{FER} \leftarrow \sum_{k=\frac{L-1}{2}}^{L-1} k \cdot p_{FINH}(k)$.

6. Generate the membership function $f_{LR_{I\_FSR}}$ of the fuzzy interval I_FSR by the following substeps:
   6.1 $m_{l\_FSR} \leftarrow 0$.
   6.2 $m_{r\_FSR} \leftarrow e_{FSR}$.
   6.3 $\alpha_{I\_FSR} \leftarrow 1$.
   6.4 $\beta_{I\_FSR} \leftarrow \lfloor \frac{L-1}{2} - e_{FSR} \rfloor$.

7. Generate the membership function $f_{LR_{I\_FER}}$ of the fuzzy interval I_FER by the following substeps:
   7.1 $m_{l\_FER} \leftarrow e_{FER}$.
   7.2 $m_{r\_FER} \leftarrow L-1$.
   7.3 $\alpha_{I\_FER} \leftarrow e_{FER} - e_{FSR}$.
   7.4 $\beta_{I\_FER} \leftarrow 1$.

8. Stop.

Totally, the knowledge base contains three fuzzy numbers represented by the triplet $[m_{LR}, \alpha_{LR}, \beta_{LR}]$ as the concepts of DK, MD, and BR, and three fuzzy intervals represented by

$$[m_{l\_FSR}, m_{r\_FSR}, \alpha_{I\_FSR}, \beta_{I\_FSR}],$$
$$[m_{l\_FER}, m_{r\_FER}, \alpha_{I\_FER}, \beta_{I\_FER}],$$
$$[m_l, m_r, \alpha_I, \beta_I]$$

as the base concepts of FSR, FER and fuzzy estimator respectively. Obviously, the knowledge base is very simple, since it is only composed of twenty-one parameters.

Now the operations of FNIS can be formulated as two Sugeno-type fuzzy rules [15]:

- **Rule 8.** if $z(i,j)$ is FSR, then $z_{FSR}(i,j) = e_{FSR} \cdot f_{LR\_I\_FSR}(\|\boldsymbol{G}(i,j)\|_{f1})$,
- **Rule 9.** if $z(i,j)$ is FER, then $z_{FER}(i,j) = e_{FER} \cdot f_{LR\_I\_FER}(\|\boldsymbol{G}(i,j)\|_{f1})$,

where $\boldsymbol{G}(i,j) = [G_x(i,j), G_y(i,j)]_{1\times 2}$.

Let $\boldsymbol{EAWFM}(i,j) = [z_{FSR}(i,j), z_{FER}(i,j)]_{1\times 2}$, then the final result $\psi(i,j)$ of EAWFM is the ∞-norm of $\boldsymbol{EAWFM}(i,j)$, that is,

$$\psi(i,j) = \|\boldsymbol{EAWFM}(i,j)\|_{f\infty}. \tag{20}$$

4 Properties of EAWFM filter

In this section, some deterministic and statistical properties of EAWFM filter are developed. By Fig. 4, we know that the main functions of EAWFM are WFM, fuzzy detectors, dynamic selector, and FNIS. Hence we consider the properties of WFM first.

Property 1 *The output range of the fuzzy estimator $f_{LR_E}(\cdot)$ of WFM is $[m_l - \alpha_I + 1, m_r + \beta_I - 1]$ or 0, i.e., for any $n_1 \times n_2$ sample matrix $X_{n_1\times n_2}(i,j)$, $f_{LR_E}(X_{n_1\times n_2}(i,j)) = 0$ or $m_l - \alpha_I + 1 \le f_{LR_E}(X_{n_1\times n_2}(i,j)) \le m_r + \beta_I - 1$, where $m_l, m_r, \alpha_I, \beta_I \in I$.*

Then we analyze the output range of WFM which is influenced by the output of the fuzzy estimator, and show that WFM can remove positive impulse noise completely when the membership functions are well defined.

Property 2 *The output of WFM is 0 or ranged in the interval $[\lfloor\frac{L-1}{N_f}\rfloor - \alpha_{LR_{DK}} - \beta_{LR_{DK}} + 1, (N_f - 1)\cdot\lfloor\frac{L-1}{N_f}\rfloor + \alpha_{LR_{DK}} + \beta_{LR_{DK}} - 1]$, i.e. $y(i,j) = 0$ or $\lfloor\frac{L-1}{N_f}\rfloor - \alpha_{LR_{DK}} - \beta_{LR_{DK}} + 1 \le y(i,j) \le (N_f - 1)\cdot\lfloor\frac{L-1}{N_f}\rfloor + \alpha_{LR_{DK}} + \beta_{LR_{DK}} - 1$, $\forall X_{3\times 3}(i,j)$, $y(i,j) = WFM(X_{3\times 3}(i,j))$, where $N_f \ge 1$ is the number of fuzzy sets.*

Now, we consider the statistical property of WFM, called the impulse noise breakdown probability [6]. Consider the case of an identical independent distribution (i.i.d.) signal corrupted by independent impulse noise where a signal sample is replaced by $\pm\infty$ with probability p; otherwise it is unaltered. Let the probability of negative impulse noise be $\frac{p}{2}$ and the probability of a positive impulse be $\frac{p}{2}$, then the breakdown probability of the WFM filter is defined in the following properties.

Property 3 *If* $(N_f-1)\cdot\lfloor\frac{L-1}{N_f}\rfloor+\alpha_{LR_{DK}}+\beta_{LR_{DK}} < L-1$, *then the breakdown probability for positive impulse noise* $+\infty$ *of WFM is 0.*

Property 4 *The breakdown probability for negative impulse noise* $-\infty$ *of WFM is* $[p+(1-p)\cdot(1-\frac{B-A-1}{L-2})]^{n_1\times n_2}$, *for any* $n_1 \times n_2$ *sample matrix* $X_{n_1\times n_2}(i,j)$, *where* $0 < A = \lfloor\frac{L-1}{N_f}\rfloor - \alpha_{LR_{DK}} - \beta_{LR_{DK}} < L-1$ *and* $0 < B = (N_f-1)\cdot\lfloor\frac{L-1}{N_f}\rfloor + \alpha_{LR_{DK}} + \beta_{LR_{DK}} < L-1$.

By property 3 and property 4, we conclude that WFM can remove positive impulse noise completely, and still preserve some negative impulse noise in the filtered image. Next, we discuss the property of the fuzzy detectors. The fuzzy detector is an important function for AWFM to decide the amplitude of impulse noise, so deciding its bound is necessary.

Property 5 *The output range of the fuzzy detector* $f_{LR_{D\_pos}}(\cdot)$ *for the amplitude* ξ_{pos} *of positive impulse noise is 0 or bounded in* $[2^{n-2}+1, 2^n-1]$.

By the same deduction of property 5, we can easily conclude that the output range of ξ_{neg} is the same as the output of ξ_{pos}. Hence we know that the fuzzy detectors are efficient for median and long tailed impulse noise that we defined in the previous section. Now we focus attention on root signal analysis. A root signal of a filter is one which is left unchanged by the filtering operation. Root signal analysis has proven to be a useful tool for evaluating nonlinear filters [12].

Property 6 *If the difference between an input signal* $x(i,j)$ *and its WFM-output signal* $y(i,j)$ *is ranged in* $[-2^{n-3}, 2^{n-3}]$, *then* $x(i,j)$ *is the root signal of AWFM filter, i.e.,* $AWFM(X_{n_1\times n_2}(i,j)) = x(i,j)$, $\forall\delta(i,j) \in [-2^{n-3}, 2^{n-3}]$.

Finally, we discuss the property of fuzzy normed operators as follows.

Property 7 *The bounds of fuzzy 1-norm, fuzzy 2-norm, and fuzzy* ∞*-norm of EAWFM are all ranged in* $[0, 2^n-1]$, *i.e., they all satisfy the closed property.*

Proof. The ranges of fuzzy 2-norm and fuzzy ∞-norm are trivial because of Definition 1. Now we prove the range of fuzzy 1-norm by mathematical induction.

(a) Basic step: $k = 1$. $\|\boldsymbol{x}_k\|_{f1} = \|\boldsymbol{x}_1\|_{f1} = |x_1|$. Since x_1 is ranged in $[0, 2^n - 1]$, hence $|x_1|$ is also in the same range. Therefore, $\|\boldsymbol{x}_k\|_{f1}$ is in the range of $[0, 2^n - 1]$.

(b) Inductive hypothesis: $k = p$. Assume that $\|\boldsymbol{x}_k\|_{f1} = \|\boldsymbol{x}_p\|_{f1} = |x_1| \oplus |x_2| \oplus \cdots \oplus |x_p|$ ranged in $[0, 2^n - 1]$ holds.

(c) Inductive step: $k = p + 1$. Since

$$0 \le \|\boldsymbol{x}_p\|_{f1} = |x_1| \oplus |x_2| \oplus \cdots \oplus |x_p| \le 2^n - 1,$$
$$0 \le |x_{p+1}| \le 2^n - 1,$$

we obtain:

$$\begin{aligned} 0 \le \|\boldsymbol{x}_{p+1}\|_{f1} &= |x_1| \oplus |x_2| \oplus \cdots \oplus |x_p| \oplus |x_{p+1}| \\ &= \|\boldsymbol{x}_p\|_{f1} \oplus |x_p| \\ &= \min(\|\boldsymbol{x}_p\|_{f1} + |x_{p+1}|, 2^n - 1) \\ &\le 2^n - 1. \end{aligned}$$

Therefore, $\|\boldsymbol{x}_{p+1}\|_{f1}$ is ranged in $[0, 2^n - 1]$. $\diamondsuit$

With the above discussion, we know that the fuzzy normed operators are all closed in the signal space.

5 Experimental results

In this section, some experiments are made to verify the performance of the AWFM filter on different noise types such as random additive impulse noise with different impulse amplitudes and mixed Gaussian impulse noise, and the effectiveness of EAWFM on edge detection for the images corrupted by different noise conditions. The images corrupted by impulse noise are considered here because most edge detectors are highly sensitive to impulse noise. LUM filter combines the function of edge enhancement and noise suppression and performs well in an impulse noise environment [5], [7]. But when the noise probability is high, LUM can not work effectively. Median filter is one of the most popular filters for impulse noise, and arithmetic mean (AM) filter [13] is efficient for Gaussian noise, so we compare them with our approach in this section.

To perform the experiments, some parameters must be determined first. The gray level value of the experiments is ranged in $[0, 255]$. The parameters for LUM used in this chapter are the same as those used by Hardie and Boncelet [7]. The window size for median, arithmetic mean, WFM and AWFM filters are 3×3. For the noise model used in the experiments, the source image is corrupted by additive impulse noise randomly or Gaussian impulse noise with occurrence probability p, and the impulses take on positive and negative values with an equal probability $\frac{p}{2}$. The impulse amplitude used in this chapter is ± 100 or ± 200. The image with mixed noise is constructed by adding zero-mean Gaussian noise with variances 5 and random impulse noise with different percentages to the original image. To construct the knowledge base, we set $N_f = 3$, $t = 10$ and $l_{over} = r_{over} = 1$, from which we can get the values of the parameters to be stored in the knowledge base. Furthermore, we use two popular images with different characteristics to test our approach. Fig. 6 shows the noise-free images "Boat" and "Chessboard" respectively.

Fig. 6. Noise-free Boat (left) and noise-fee Chessboard (right).

The first experiment shows the actual image corrupted by random additive impulse noise and its filtered results. Fig. 7 shows the noisy image "Boat" with noise probability 50%, together with the filtered results of LUM, median and AWFM filters. Fig. 8 shows the edge detection results of the noisy image "Boat". In this experiment, the LUM and median filters are combined with Sobel operator which is the most famous and simplest technique for edge detection. By these results, we notice that the lines in the Boat image can be preserved well when the EAWFM is adopted.

The second experiment is to test the edge detection capability on the Chessboard image corrupted by mixed Gaussian impulse noise. In this experiment, we compare EAWFM with the popular filters such as LUM, median and AM filters. Since the AM filter is effective for removing Gaussian noise with small variance, we use it in this experiment. For EAWFM, we adopt WFM and AWFM as the prefilters because they both have high stability for heavily impulsive noise images. Fig. 9 shows the noisy image corrupted by Gaussian impulse noise with probability 20%, together with the filtered results of LUM, AM, median, and EAWFM filters respectively. Fig. 10 shows the same experimental results on Gaussian impulse noise with noise probability 100%. From the simulation results, we find that when noise probabil-

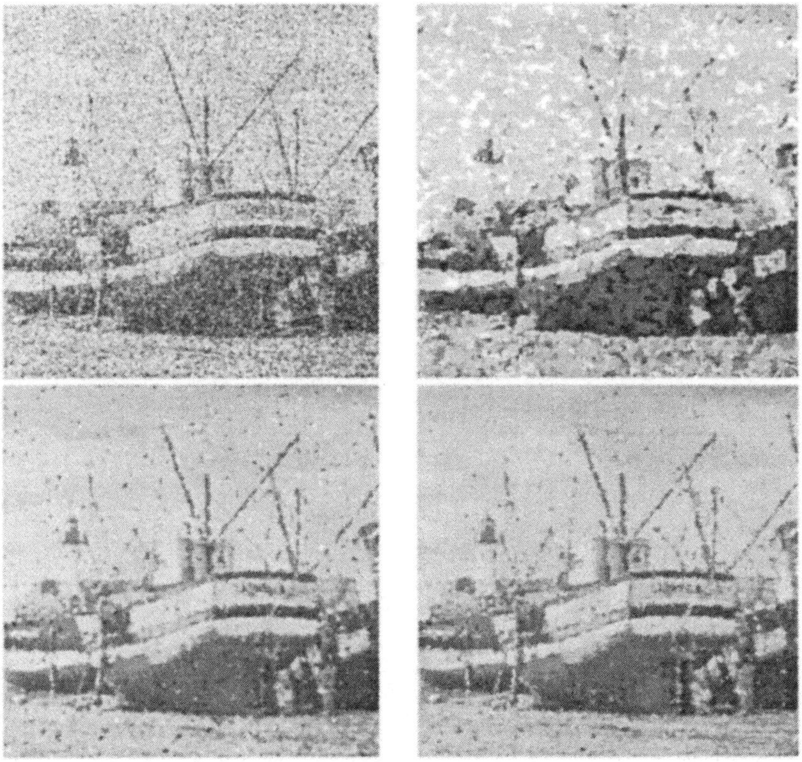

Fig. 7. "Boat" with random impulse noise 50% (upper left); Result of LUM (upper right); Result of median filter (lower left); Result of AWFM filter (lower right).

ity is low, for instance 20%, most filters including EAWFM detect the lines well. But when "Chessboard" is corrupted by heavy noise, for example 100% Gaussian impulse noise, EAWFM exhibits much better performance than the others. As a result, we declare that EAWFM has the best performance.

6 Conclusion

A series of novel adaptive fuzzy filters such as WFM, AWFM, and EAWFM filters have been developed for image enhancement. The EAWFM filter combines AWFM and FNIS to perform edge enhancement with high stability. It can improve the drawbacks of conventional edge detectors for images corrupted by random additive impulse noise or mixed Gaussian impulse noise. In summary, there are nine fuzzy inference rules in EAWFM to efficiently remove random additive impulse noise, smooth out mixed Gaussian impulse noise, and enhance edges for images corrupted by various kinds of noise. They exhibit better performance than the other filters, especially when the noise

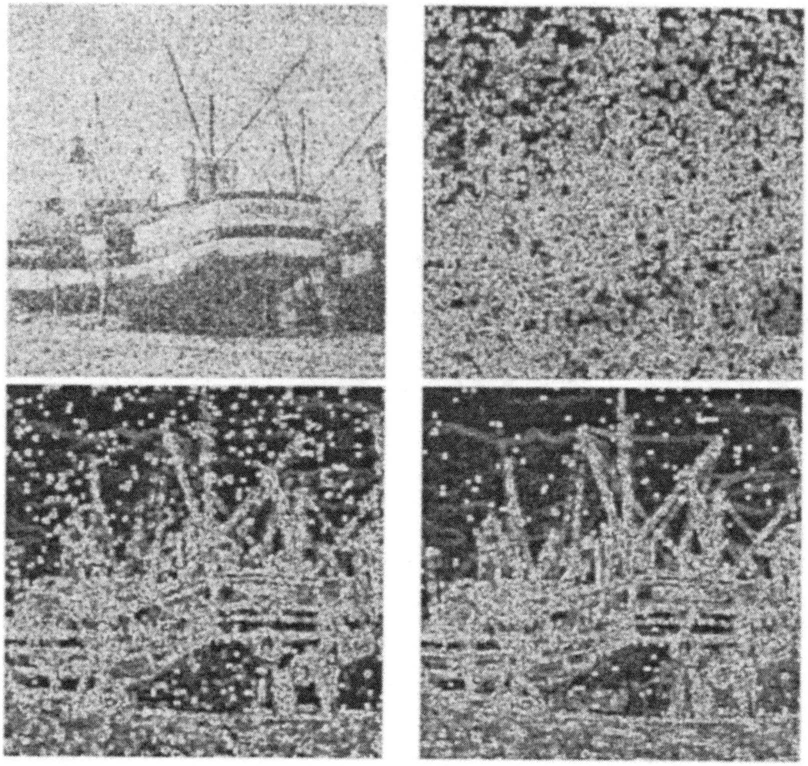

Fig. 8. "Boat" with random impulse noise 50% (upper left); Result of LUM (upper right); Result of median filter (lower left); Result of AWFM filter (lower right).

rate is over 50%. Furthermore, several important properties of these filters have also been analyzed in this chapter.

The analysis of deterministic and statistical properties of EAWFM also proves that EAWFM can suppress impulse noise and detect image edges simultaneously. By the experimental results, we declare that EAWFM filter has the best performance and highest stability among the compared filters. In the future, we will extend EAWFM to be able to work in short-tailed impulse noise such as uniform noise, and Gaussian noise with different means and variances, and investigate its hardware realization.

References

1. Arakawa K., *Median filter based on fuzzy rules and its application to image restoration*, Fuzzy sets and systems, Vol. 77, pp. 3–13, 1996
2. Bezdek J.C. and Pal S.K., *"Fuzzy models for pattern recognition"*, IEEE Press, New York, 1992

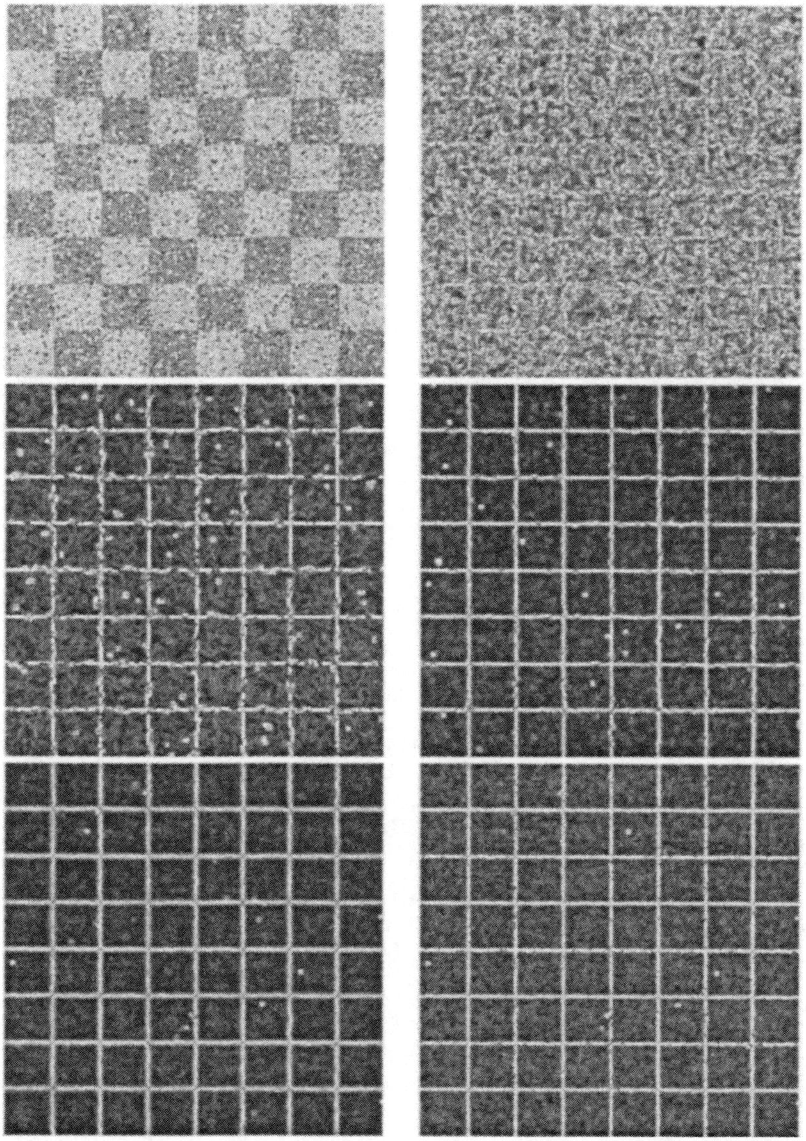

Fig. 9. "Chessboard" with Gaussian impulse noise 20% (upper left); Result of AM filter (upper right); Result of LUM filter (middle left); Result of median filter (middle right); Result of EAWFM with WFM; (lower left); Result of EAWFM with AWFM (lower right).

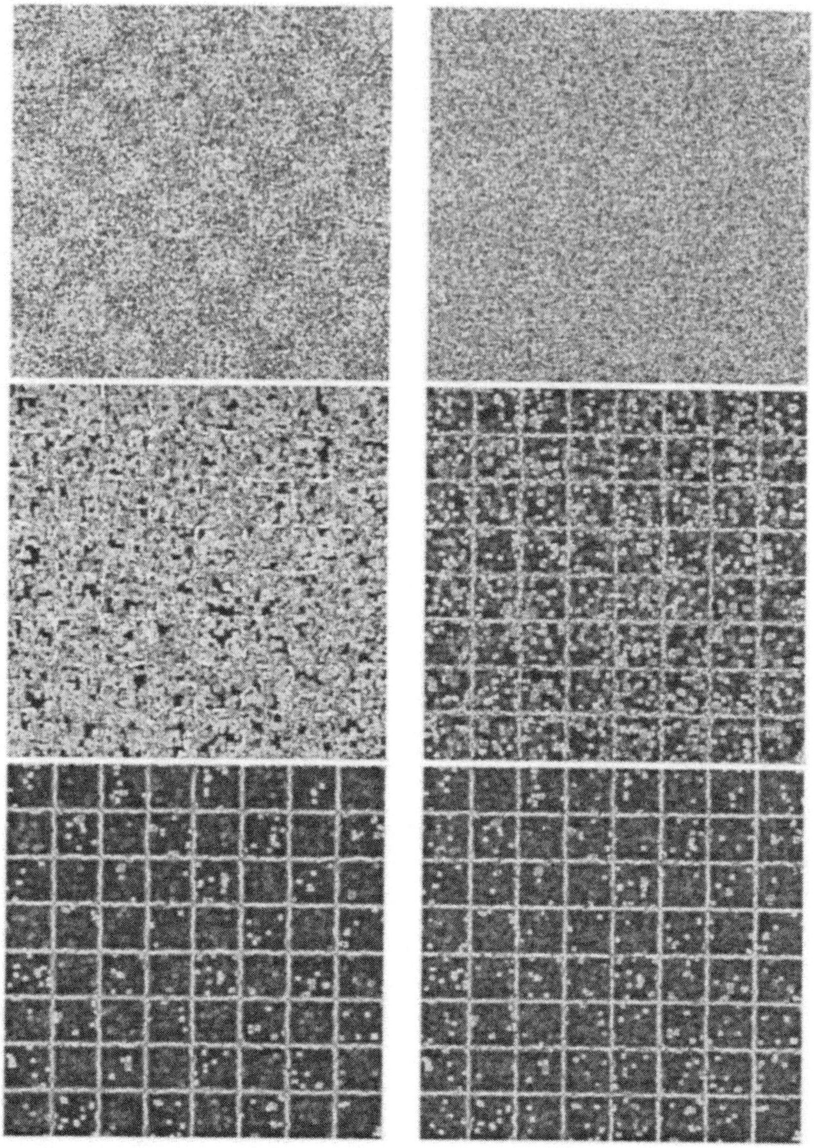

Fig. 10. "Chessboard" with Gaussian impulse noise 100% (upper left); Result of AM filter (upper right); Result of LUM filter (middle left); Result of median filter (middle right); Result of EAWFM with WFM; (lower left); Result of EAWFM with AWFM (lower right).

3. Choi Y.S. and Krishnapuram R., *A robust approach to image enhancement based on fuzzy logic*, IEEE Trans. on image processing, Vol. 6, No. 6, pp. 808–825, 1997
4. Gonzalez R.C. and Woods R.E., *"Digital image processing"*, Addison-Wesley publishing Company Inc., New York, 1992
5. Hardie R.C. and Boncelet C.G., *LUM filters: A class of rank-order-based filters for smoothing and sharpening*, IEEE Trans. on signal processing, Vol. 41, No. 3, pp. 1061–1076, 1993
6. Hardie R.C. and Barner K.E., *Rank conditioned rank selection filters for signal restoration*, IEEE Trans. on Image Processing, Vol. 3, No. 2, pp. 192–206, 1994
7. Hardie R.C. and Boncelet C.G., *Gradient-based edge detection using nonlinear edge enhancing prefilters*, IEEE Trans. on Image Processing, Vol.4, No. 11, pp. 1572–1577, 1995
8. Jeong B. and Lee Y.H., *Design of weighted order statistic filters using the perceptron algorithm*, IEEE Trans. on Signal Processing, Vol. 42, No. 11, pp. 3264–3268, 1994
9. Kuo Y.-H., Lee C.-S. and Liu C.-C., *A new fuzzy edge detection method for image enhancement*, in: "Proceedings of the IEEE International Conf. on Fuzzy Systems" (Barcelona, Spain), pp. 1069–1074, 1997
10. Lee C.-S., Kuo Y.-H. and Yu P.-T., *Weighted fuzzy mean filter for image processing*, Journal of Fuzzy Sets and Systems, Vol. 89, No. 2, pp. 157–180, 1997
11. Lee C.-S. and Kuo Y.-H., *The important properties and applications of the adaptive weighted fuzzy mean filter*, International Journal of Intelligent System, Vol. 14, pp. 253–274, 1999
12. Node T.A. and Gallagher N.C. Jr., *Median filters: Some modifications and their properties*, IEEE Trans. on ASSP, Vol. ASSP-30, No. 5, pp. 739–746, 1982
13. Pitas I. and Venetsanopoulos A.N., *Nonlinear mean filters in image processing*, IEEE Trans. on ASSP, Vol. ASSP-34, No. 3, pp. 573–584, 1986
14. Russo F. and Ramponi G., *A fuzzy operator for the enhancement of blurred and noisy images*, IEEE Trans. on Image Processing, Vol. 4, No. 8, pp. 1169–1174, 1995
15. Terano T., Asai K. and Sugeno M., *"Fuzzy systems theory and its applications"*, Academic Press Inc., Boston, 1992
16. Yang X. and Toh P.-S., *Adaptive fuzzy multilevel median filter*, IEEE Trans. on Image Processing, Vol. 4, No. 5, pp. 680–682, 1995
17. Zeng B. and Neuvo Y., *Optimal parallel stack filtering under the mean absolute error criterion*, IEEE Trans. on Image Processing, Vol. 3, No. 3, pp. 324–327, 1994
18. Zimmermann H.J., *"Fuzzy set theory and its applications"*, Kluwer Academic Publishers, Boston, 1991

Chapter 7

A Fuzzy Logic Control Based Approach for Image Filtering

Farzam Farbiz and Mohammad Bagher Menhaj

Amirkabir University of Technology, Electrical Engineering Department
No. 424 Hafez Ave, Tehran 15914, Iran
email: {farbiz,menhaj}@cic.aku.ac.ir

Summary. This chapter is devoted to introduce a new filtering approach based on fuzzy-logic control concepts with the properties of removing impulsive noise and smoothing out Gaussian noise while, simultaneously, preserving edges and image details efficiently. The main idea behind the proposed filtering approach is that each pixel is not allowed to be uniformly fired by each of the fuzzy rules. In this chapter, different modifications of this filtering approach (Iterative Fuzzy Control based Filter - IFCF) named by MIFCF, EIFCF, SFCF, SSFCF, FFCF, AFCF and ACFCF are presented along with some test experiments highlighting the merit of each filter. From the experimental results we may list the concluding remarks of the proposed filtering approach: high quality of edge preserving ability, high filtering quality especially for complex images, multiplicative noise removing property for IFCF based filters, floating point free calculations and very fast performance for FFCF based filters.

1 Introduction

Knowing that 1) any digitized image transmitted over a noisy channel is degraded and consequently 2) removal of such degradation while preserving the integrity of the original image plays an important role in image processing, image filtering is an important step in most of image processing applications. The problem of image filtering can be stated as removing impulsive noise, smoothing non-impulsive noise, and enhancing edges or certain salient structures in the input image.

Noise filtering can be viewed as replacing the gray-level value of every pixel in the image with a new value depending on the local context. Ideally, the filtering algorithm should vary from pixel to pixel based on the local context. For example, if the local region is relatively smooth, then the new value of the pixel is worth being determined by averaging neighboring pixels values. On the other hand, if the local region contains edge or impulse noise pixels, a different type of filtering should be used. However, it is extremely hard, if not impossible, to set the conditions under which a certain filter should be selected, since the local conditions can be evaluated only vaguely in some portions of an image. Therefore, a filtering system needs to be capable of performing reasoning with vague and uncertain information; this is a clear justification of fuzzy logic common usage.

Noise smoothing and edge enhancement are inherently conflicting processes, since smoothing a region might destroy an edge while sharpening edges might lead to unnecessary noise. A plethora of techniques for this problem have been proposed in the literature [19,8,15,17,12,2]. In this chapter, we propose a new filter, based on fuzzy logic control [11], that removes impulsive noise and, furthermore, smoothes Gaussian noise while edges and image details are efficiently preserved. This filter is based on the idea of not letting each pixel to be uniformly fired by each fuzzy rule, and it performs properly all the three tasks of image filtering mentioned above.

1.1 Fuzzy based previous work

Because fuzzy set theory has the potential capability to efficiently represent input/output relationships of dynamic systems, this theory has gained popularity, especially in pattern recognition and computer vision applications [2,17,12,10]. In this area there have been many efforts to develop fuzzy filters for signal/image processing with promising results [20,21,14,1]. In the well known rule-based approach for image processing [3], one may use human intuitive knowledge expressed heuristically in linguistic terms. This is highly nonlinear in nature and cannot be easily characterized by traditional mathematical modeling. In addition, this approach allows us to incorporate heuristic fuzzy rules into conventional methods, leading to a more flexible design technique. For instance, in reference [33] Yang and Tou applied heuristic fuzzy rules to improve the performance of the traditional multi-level median filter.

Russo proposed fuzzy rule-based operators for smoothing, sharpening, and edge detection [20–28], and he also employed heuristic knowledge to build the rules for each of the underlying operations. Reference [20] proposed the use of operators with different windowing sizes (i.e. 5×5 or 7×7), where the window size is dependent on the uniformity of the local region. The degree of the region's uniformity is determined by employing a certain set of fuzzy rules [23]. Based on the output given by the uniformity detection rule, the two outputs from the 5×5 and 7×7 windowing operators are linearly combined. Since the fuzzy rules in this approach are constructed based on region contours, this approach is in fact performing smoothing while preserving image edges. Reference [26] proposed the use of fuzzy if-then rules to sharpen edges in a noisy image. Furthermore, Russo in references [27,28] presented a dual-step fuzzy-rule-based filter to detect and remove a large variety of patterns of noise pulses with a detailed preservation of the original image.

In reference [5] a fuzzy rule-based approach to image enhancement is presented that addresses its seemingly conflicting goals: (a) removing impulsive noise, (b) smoothing out non-impulsive noise, and (c) enhancing edges or other salient features. Three different filters for each task are derived using the weighted least mean squares method. Criteria for selecting each filter are defined. The criteria are based on the local context as well as the particular situation. They constitute the antecedent clauses of the fuzzy rules, and the corresponding filters constitute the consequent clauses of the fuzzy rules. The overall result of the fuzzy-rule-based system is computed as the combination of the results of the individual filters, where each result contributes to the degree that the corresponding antecedent clause is satisfied. This approach gives us a powerful and flexible image enhancement paradigm.

In [30] a class of stack filters is enlarged by defining the output of a Boolean function, continuously from 0 to 1 (i.e., the stack filter is defined by a Boolean function). This filter is called the Fuzzy Weighted Median Filter (FWM). In [34] fuzzy stack filters were proposed to extend the filtering capability of conventional stack filters, and it was shown how capable such filters are in removing impulsive noise.

In [16], Muneyasu *et al.* proposed a novel type of edge-preserving smoothing filter applicable to images corrupted with impulsive and white Gaussian noise. This kind of filter is based on weighted mean filters, whose coefficients could be varied adaptively using local features in the window. The fuzzy control laws are used for the implementation of this filter, and a standard optimization technique is employed for estimation of the membership function parameters.

In [29,6,7] applications of fuzzy clustering for removal of impulsive noise were fully described. Other fuzzy filters for removing impulsive noise have also been proposed in [32,4,13].

Reference [18] presented a new hybrid filter design methodology containing a nonlinear filter for removing impulsive noise and a fuzzy weighted linear filter. This hybrid filter can efficiently remove large amounts of mixed Gaussian and impulsive noise while preserving the image details.

1.2 Chapter organization

The remainder of this chapter is organized as follows: In section 2 the FLC based filtering approach is proposed. This filter is called Iterative Fuzzy Control based Filter- IFCF. Different modifications of IFCF such as MIFCF and EIFCF will be also introduced in this section. The MIFCF makes the IFCF performance more enhanced especially for low noise images while the EIFCF makes the IFCF more efficient for image noise removal by tuning the fuzzy rules term sets membership functions. In section 3 we present a Smoothing Fuzzy Control based Filter- SFCF. This filter, which is a variation of IFCF, does not apply iteratively. In this section we further introduce a criterion to measure quantitatively the quality behavior of filters in edge preserving. In addition by adding two extra rules to the rule base of the SFCF, we will present a new image enhancement approach which can make image edges sharper without noise magnification. Section 4 presents a fixed-point version of the proposed SFCF, called FFCF, along with its adaptive forms such as AFCF and ACFCF. These filters do not require any floating-point calculations and perform very fast compared with the SFCF filter. Finally, section 5 concludes the chapter.

2 The iterative fuzzy control based filter - IFCF

This section presents the architecture of our proposed rule-based image processing system. In this system, we adopt the general structure of fuzzy if-then-else rule mechanism. Our approach is mainly based on the idea of not letting each point in the area of concern being uniformly fired by each of the basic fuzzy rules. This idea is widely used in fuzzy control applications. To furnish this goal, the following fuzzy rules and membership functions given in figure 1 are proposed for image filtering:

R1: IF (**more** of x_i are NB) THEN y is NB
R2: IF (**more** of x_i are NM) THEN y is NM
R3: IF (**more** of x_i are NS) THEN y is NS
R4: IF (**more** of x_i are PS) THEN y is PS
R5: IF (**more** of x_i are PM) THEN y is PM
R6: IF (**more** of x_i are PB) THEN y is PB
R0: ELSE y is Z (1)

In the above, the x_i's are the luminance differences between neighboring pixels I_i (located in a window of size $N \times N$), and the central pixel I, i.e. $x_i = I_i - I$. The output variable y is the quantity which is added to I to yield the resulting pixel luminance I'. The term sets NB (Negative Big), NM (Negative Medium), NS (Negative Small), PS (Positive Small), PM (Positive Medium), PB (Positive Big) are the fuzzy sets which represent the proper yet finer fuzzy partitioning of input and output spaces, whose proper choice of membership functions with the general triangular shape are given in figure 1. These values are the linguistic values of the linguistic variables x_i and y in the universe of discourse [-256, 256]. The term **more** represents a S-type fuzzy function and may be described by the following formula:

$$\mu_{more}(t) = \begin{cases} 0 & t < a \\ 0.5\left\{1 - \cos\left[\frac{\pi(t-a)}{b-a}\right]\right\} & a < t < b \\ 1 & t > b \end{cases} \tag{2}$$

The values used in the experiments are $a = 0.2$ and $b = 0.8$.

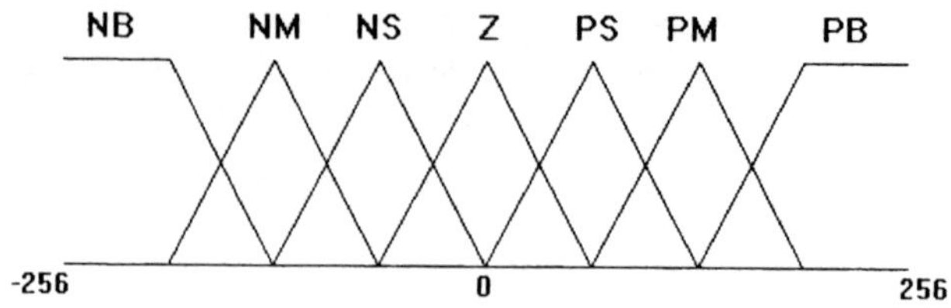

Fig. 1. Membership functions of NB, NM, NS, PS, PM and PB.

2.1 Degree of activity of the if-then rules

The activity degree of R1 is computed by the following relationship (the other if-then rules' degree of activities are computed similarly).

$$\lambda_1 = \min[\mu_{NB}(x_i) \ : \ x_i \in support(NB)] \times \\ \mu_{more}\left[\frac{number \ of \ x_i \in support(NB)}{Total \ number \ of \ x_i}\right] \tag{3}$$

For the ELSE rule, R0, we may apply the following formula to evaluate the degree of activity:

$$\lambda_0 = \max\left\{0, 1 - \sum_{i=1}^{6} \lambda_i\right\} \tag{4}$$

To infer the output numerically from the fuzzy rules given in equation 1, we employ the correlation-product inference mechanism [12] as:

$$y = \frac{\sum_{i=0}^{6} C_i w_i \lambda_i}{\sum_{i=0}^{6} w_i \lambda_i} \tag{5}$$

where C_i and w_i are respectively the center point and width of the membership function used in the i-th fuzzy rule in equation 1. Since all w_i's are equal and $C_0 = 0$, equation 5 can be simplified to:

$$y = \sum_{i=1}^{6} C_i \lambda_i \tag{6}$$

2.2 Experimental results

Experiment 1 In order to demonstrate the performance of the filter in a Gaussian noise environment, we consider the Lena image as a case study. This image is first contaminated by Gaussian noise with $\mu = 0, \sigma^2 = 400$. Then, the proposed filter is applied. The result of filtering process is depicted in figure 2, labeled (a). We can easily observe from this figure that as the number of iterations increases, we will have better image restoration in the sense of MSE (which for the noisy image it was 384.3). To show the performance of the filter in the mixed noise case, we take the image considered in this experiment added by [%2.5, %2.5] impulsive noise (the notation [%p,%q] for impulsive noise means that p% of the image pixels were corrupted by positive (white) and q% of the image pixels were corrupted by negative (black) impulsive noise). The result is also shown in figure 2; in this case the plot is labeled by (b). From these two results, cases of Gaussian noise and mixed noise, we may conclude that the proposed filter has good ability in image restoration as the number of iteration increases.

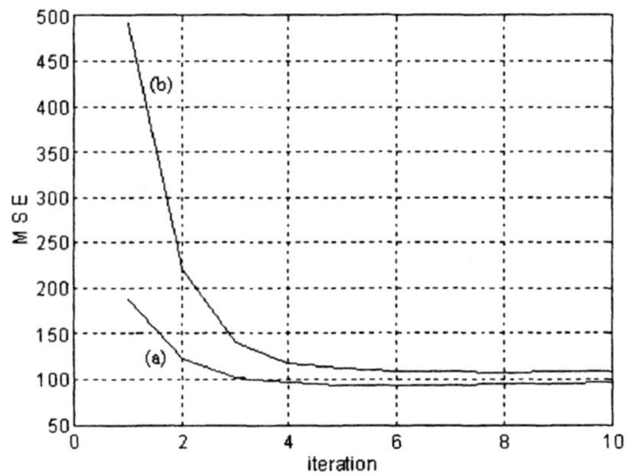

Fig. 2. Performance of the proposed filter on 256 × 256 Lena image contaminated by Gaussian noise with $\mu = 0$, $\sigma^2 = 400$ and a) without impulsive noise; b) with [%2.5, %2.5] impulsive noise . The MSE of the noisy image was 384.3 for (a) and 1272 for (b).

Experiment 2 In this experiment we aim to show how the noise variance affects performance of the IFCF filter. Here again we use the Lena image corrupted by zero mean Gaussian noise with different variances (σ^2 =0, 100, 200, 300, 400). Figure 3, which shows the MSE of the restored images as a function of the variance of Gaussian noise, compares the performance of the IFCF filter with that of the FWM (proposed in [30]) and EPS (proposed in

[16]) with two window size 5×5 and 7×7 filters. These results are encouraging and indicate the satisfactory performance of the IFCF filter.

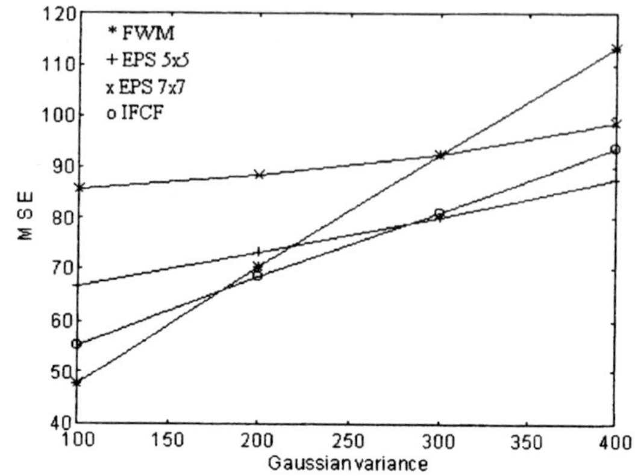

Fig. 3. MSE as a function of variance of Gaussian noise, computed for the Lena image.

Experiment 3 This experiment aims to show how the IFCF filter would behave as the variance of Gaussian noise changes in a mixed noisy environment. The image in experiment 2 is mixed by [%2.5, %2.5] impulsive noise and used as an input to the filter. The results in image restoration shown in figure 4 demonstrate that the IFCF filter in mixed noise has the best performance among the other filters.

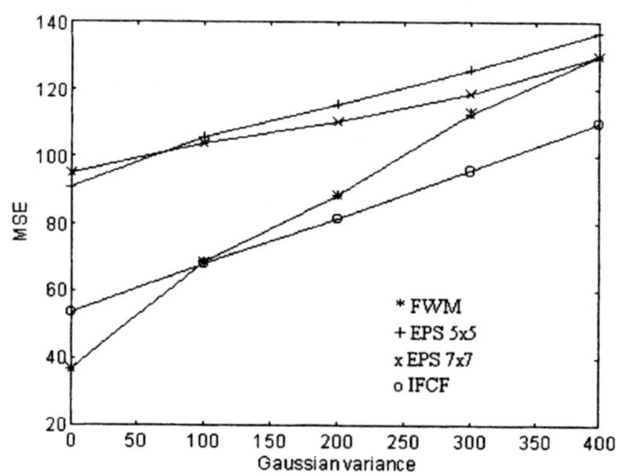

Fig. 4. MSE of restored images of different filters for the Lena image corrupted by mixed noise (Gaussian and [%2.5, %2.5] impulsive noise).

2.3 Modified IFCF - MIFCF

Unfortunately, as observed from several test experiments, in each iteration the output image edges get a little blurred. Therefore, increasing the iteration numbers makes the image more unsharp. Especially for low noise cases, this makes the image, after a few iterations, become more degraded instead of getting enhanced. To resolve this problem, in each step we tune the **more** function in a way that it becomes sharper at the boundaries as shown in figure 5. The reason behind this is that we enforce the filter to become more active when it is needed. At the other hand, the filter becomes less active on those parts of the image that do not need to change more.

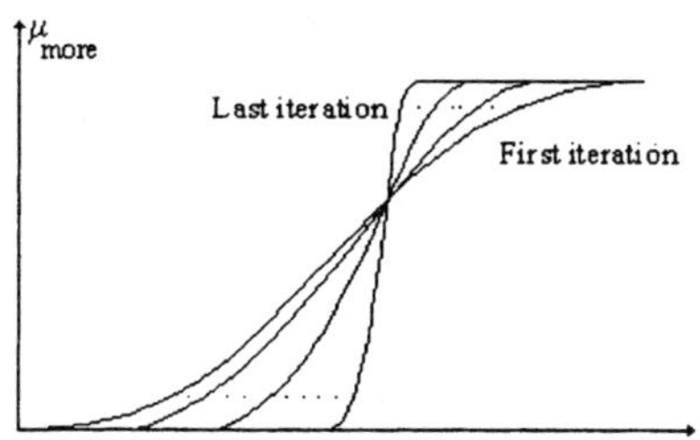

Fig. 5. The changes of the shape of the **more** function in iterations.

By sharpening the shape of the **more** function in each iteration, its range of activity becomes less; this makes that the rules R1-R6 will only be fired in those regions in which they have higher possibility of firing. Thus, after a few iterations the rules are not activated for most image pixels. This feature allows us to rise the number of iterations without having any edge blurring problem. By referring to the previous section, we may enhance the filtering property of the IFCF filter by increasing the number of iterations without loosing edge information.

This modification can also be employed as a stopping criterion for our algorithm which is explained as follows. When the number of pixels, for which at least one of the rules R1-R6 is activated, becomes less than a certain threshold value (which can be set to a low percent of the total pixels in the image), there is no use in running more iterations to have better image enhancement. Consequently, it is worth terminating the algorithm at that moment.

Experiment 4 In this experiment we aim to show the better performance of MIFCF compared to IFCF, especially for low noise cases. In this case we consider the Lena image contaminated by additive Gaussian noise with different variances (σ^2 =100, 200, 300, 400, 500, 600). The MSE of the restored image obtained by these two filters are drawn in figure 6. For mixed noise case, we added the [%2.5, %2.5] impulsive noise to the previous image and the results are depicted in figure7. These two figures show the MIFCF outperforms the IFCF especially in low noise cases.

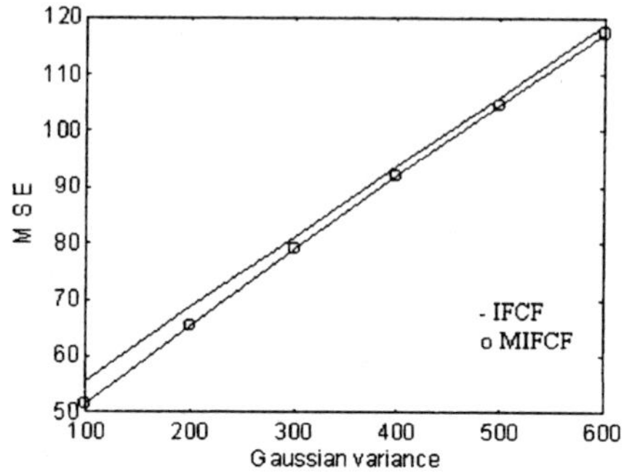

Fig. 6. MSE as a function of variance of Gaussian noise, computed for the Lena image for IFCF and MIFCF filters with 3x3 window size.

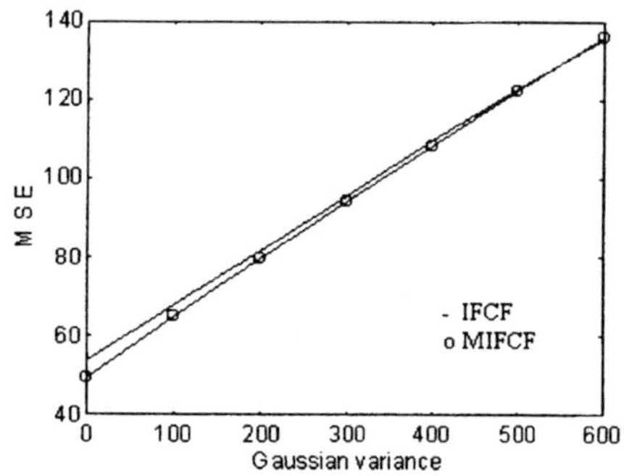

Fig. 7. MSE of restored images of IFCF and MIFCF filters with 3x3 window size for the Lena image corrupted by mixed noise (Gaussian and [%2.5, %2.5] impulsive noise

Experiment 5 In order to demonstrate the performance of the MIFCF in a Gaussian noise environment, we again consider the Lena image. This image is first contaminated by multiplicative Gaussian noise with $\mu = 0$, $\sigma^2 = 0.4$. Then, the MIFCF filter is applied. The result of the filtering process is depicted in figure 8(a). In figure 8(b) we did the same experiment with $\sigma^2 = 0.7$. We can easily observe from this figure that as the number of iterations increases, we will have better image restoration in the sense of MSE.

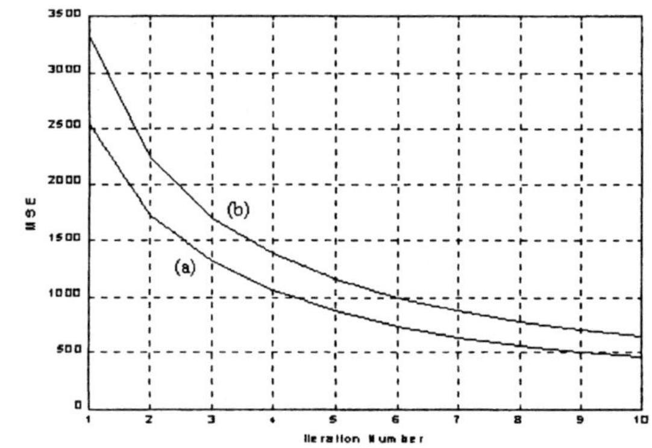

Fig. 8. The MSE of the MIFCF filter for the Lena image contaminated by multiplicative Gaussian noise with a) $\sigma^2 = 0.4$, and b) $\sigma^2 = 0.7$ versus the iteration number.

Experiment 6 In this experiment we aim to show how the noise variance affects performance of the MIFCF filter. Here again we use the Lena image corrupted by multiplicative zero mean Gaussian noise with different variances (σ^2 =0.1, 0.4, 0.7, 1.0). Figure 9, which shows the MSE of the restored images as a function of the variance of Gaussian noise, compares the performance of the MIFCF filter with that of the ENHANCE [5], FWM [30] and EPS [16] filters. Again, these results are encouraging and indicate the satisfactory performance of the MIFCF filter.

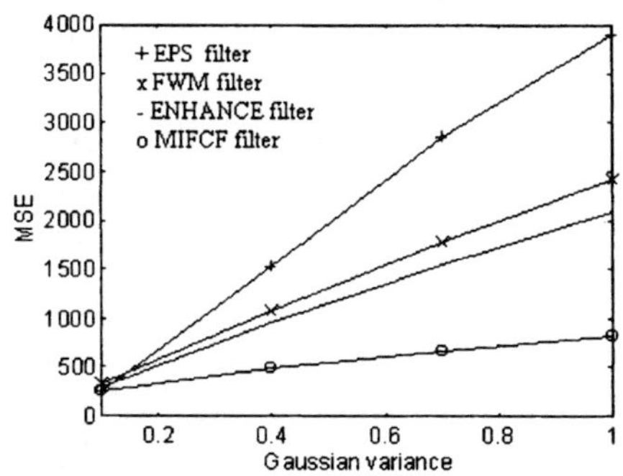

Fig. 9. The MSE of different filters for the Lena image contaminated by different multiplicative Gaussian noise.

2.4 Extended IFCF - EIFCF

This section presents the architecture of the proposed EIFCF filter. In this filter, in contrast to the IFCF, the approach is mainly based on the idea that in each iteration the domain of the fuzzy linguistic terms gets more shrunk, as shown in figure 10. This makes the filter preserve its filtering performance during iterations. The intuition behind this idea is that in each iteration the image gets more filtered. Therefore, the amount of noise in the sense of average and peak values will have decreased. Hence, by shrinking the domains of the fuzzy linguistics, i.e. by compressing their membership functions, we may force the number of fired fuzzy rules to keep unchanged in order to preserve the filtering ability of the filter.

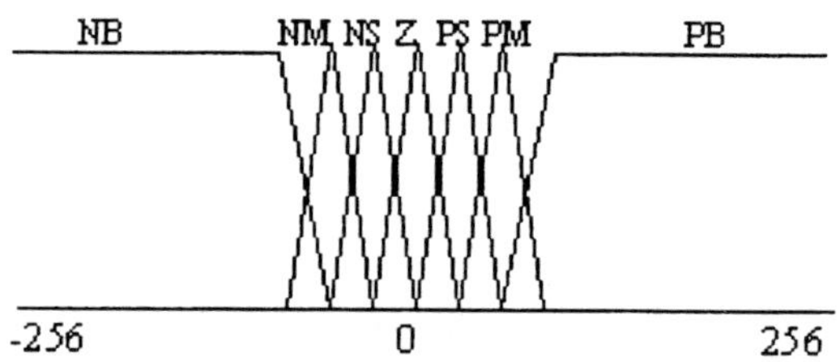

Fig. 10. Membership functions after some iterations.

Experiment 7 In this experiment, we compare the performance of EIFCF with that of IFCF as the number of iterations increases. In this case, we applied both filters to the Lena image contaminated by Gaussian noise with $\sigma^2 = 400$ and [%2.5, %2.5] impulsive noise as a test image and computed the MSE of both filters in each iteration. Figure 11 shows the experimental results. As can easily be seen from this figure, initially both filters respond uniquely, but after some iterations the EIFCF filter preserves its capability of filtering. From this figure we further observe that it is useless to run the filtering algorithm more than 6 iterations because no extra image enhancement will be obtained.

Experiment 8 In this experiment we aim to show how the noise variance affects performance of the EIFCF filter. Here we use the Lena image corrupted by zero mean Gaussian noise with different variances (σ^2 = 100, 200, 300, 400, 500, 600). Figure 12, which shows the MSE of the restored images as a function of the variance of Gaussian noise, compares the performance of the EIFCF filter with that of the FWM, EPS, ENHANCE [5], and IFCF filters. These results are encouraging and indicate the satisfactory performance of the EIFCF filter.

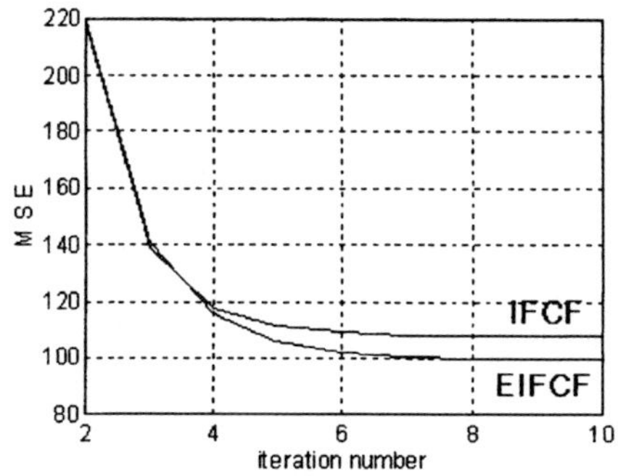

Fig. 11. Comparison of IFCF and EIFCF filters on the degraded Lena image for different iteration numbers.

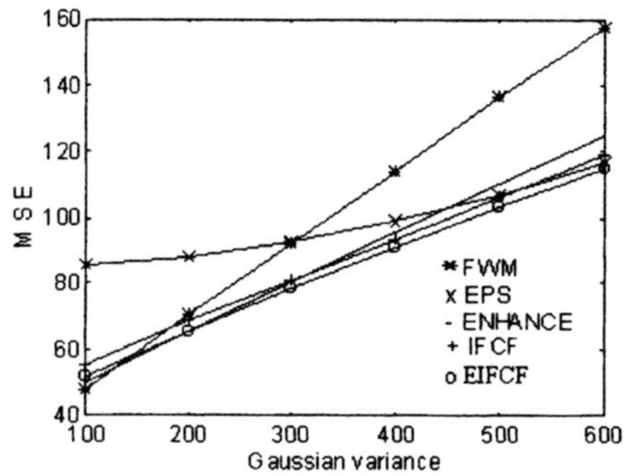

Fig. 12. MSE of restored images of different filters for the Lena image corrupted by Gaussian noise.

Experiment 9 This experiment aims to show how the EIFCF filter would behave as the variance of Gaussian noise changes in a mixed noisy environment. The image in experiment 8 is mixed by [%2.5, %2.5] impulsive noise and used as an input to the filter. The results in image restoration shown in figure 13 demonstrate that the EIFCF filter in mixed noise has the best performance among the other filters mentioned above.

3 Smoothing fuzzy control based filter - SFCF

In the previous section we introduced the IFCF filter and presented its performances. In this section we aim to increase the run-time of the filter by presenting a non-iterative filter based on the IFCF acronymed by SFCF (Smoothing Fuzzy Control based Filter). To make the IFCF non-iterative, we made the following modifications on the IFCF:

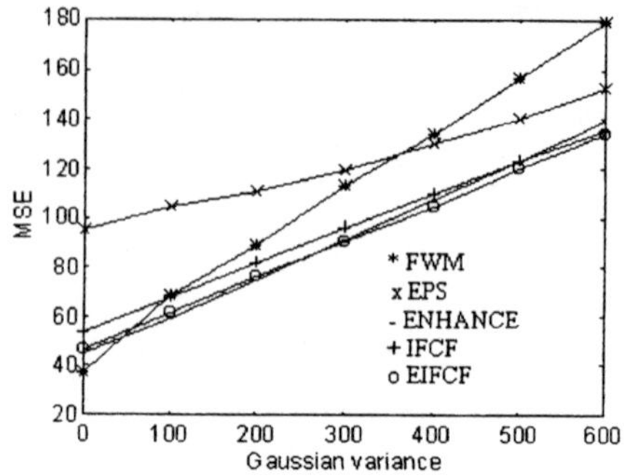

Fig. 13. MSE of restored images of different filters for the Lena image corrupted by mixed noise (Gaussian and [%2.5, %2.5] impulsive noise).

- The ELSE rule in (1) is replaced by the following rule to make the filter more insensitive to Gaussian noise:

  R'0: ELSE IF (**fairly more** of x_i are **Z**) THEN y is $ave(x_i)$ (7)

  where,

  $$ave(x_i) = average(x_i : x_i \in Support(Z)). \tag{8}$$

  The term **fairly more** is a fuzzy linguistic value like **more**, but with a smoother slope modeled by:

  $$\mu_{fairly\,more}(t) = \frac{1}{1 + e^{-at+b}} \tag{9}$$

  Typical values for a and b are $a = 6$ and $b = 3$.
- The **min** function in equation 3 is replaced by the **Median** function.

The output y of the rules given in 1 is computed by:

$$y = k.ave(x_i) + (1 - k)\sum_{i=1}^{6} C_i\lambda_i, \tag{10}$$

where

$$k = \mu_{fairly\,more}\left[\frac{number\ of\ x_i \in support(Z)}{Total\ number\ of\ x_i}\right] \tag{11}$$

3.1 A new quantitative criterion for edge preserving ability of image filters

Since the SFCF filter represents a non-iterative filter, we expect to have high ability of image edge preservation. To compare quantitatively this feature of the filter with other filters, we compute the Mean Square Error (MSE) between edges of the original test image and those of the image after filtering (note that the image edges are extracted by the Sobel operator). We use the acronym MSEE to indicate this criterion. We consider the image given in figure 14 as a test image for this criterion since it is a complex image with irregular edges.

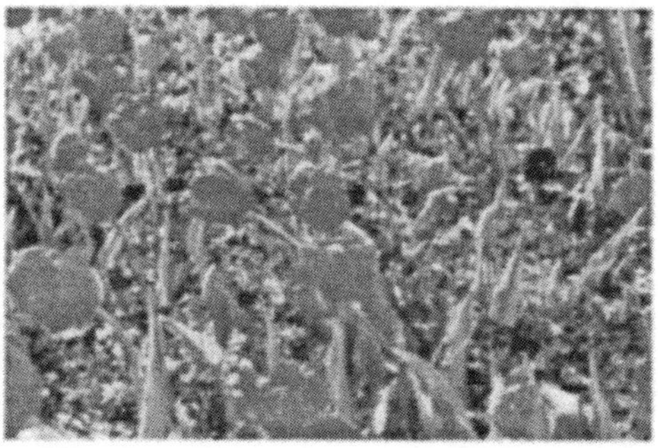

Fig. 14. A complex test image used for computing the MSEE of filters.

3.2 Experimental results for the SFCF filter

Experiment 1 To compare the edge preserving ability of filters, the MSEE of the proposed SFCF filter, the median and the FWM, EPS and ENHANCE filters are summarized in table 3. By looking at column 5 of table 3, we can easily observe that the SFCF filter has the best image edge preservation compared to the already mentioned filters. To show how good the SFCF filter works in a noisy environment, we further perform the following experiments.

Experiment 2 In this experiment we aim to show how the noise variance affects performance of the SFCF filter. Here, we use the Lena image corrupted by zero mean Gaussian noise with different variances (σ^2 =0, 100, 200, 300, 400). Figure 15, which shows the MSE of the restored images as a function of Gaussian noise variance, compares the performance of the SFCF filter with those of the FWM, EPS and ENHANCE filters. These results are encouraging and indicate the high performance of the SFCF.

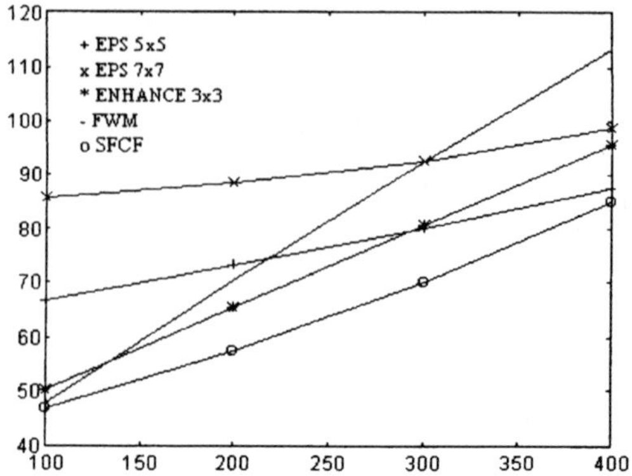

Fig. 15. MSE as a function of variance of Gaussian noise, computed for the Lena image.

Experiment 3 The goal of this experiment is to show how the SFCF filter would behave as the variance of Gaussian noise changes in a mixed noisy environment. The image in experiment 2 is mixed by [%2.5, %2.5] impulsive noise and used as an input to our filter. The results in image restoration shown in figure 16 demonstrate that the SFCF filter in mixed noise environments also keeps its high performance compared to most of the filters listed in table 3, such as FWM and EPS.

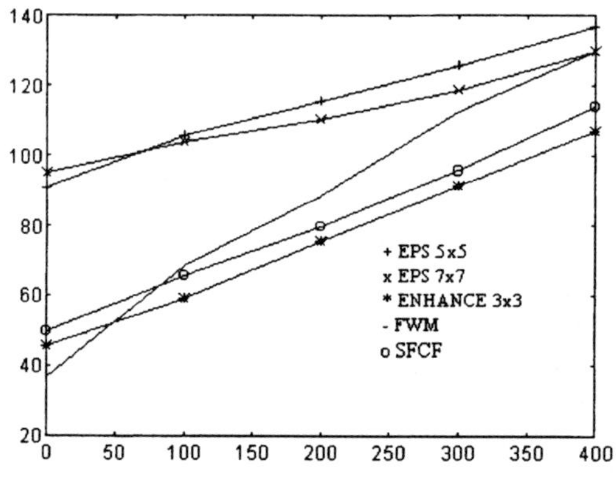

Fig. 16. MSE of restored images of different filters for the Lena image corrupted by mixed noise (Gaussian and [%2.5, %2.5] impulsive noise).

Experiment 4 In this experiment we wish to show how the SFCF filter works for complex noisy images. Here we consider the image given in figure 14 corrupted by zero mean Gaussian noise with different variances (σ^2 =0,

100, 200, 300, 400). The performance of the SFCF filter is shown in figure 17. By comparing these results with those observed in experiment 2 we may conclude that, in case of complex noisy images, the SFCF filter among the filters such as FWM, ENHANCE, etc., has better image restoration.

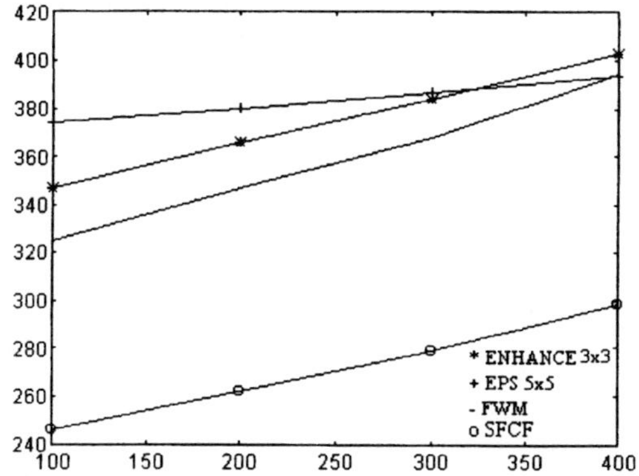

Fig. 17. MSE as a function of variance of Gaussian noise computed, for figure 14.

Experiment 5 The purpose of performing this experiment is to illustrate how the filter behaves for complex mixed noisy images. The image in experiment 4 mixed by [%2.5, %2.5] impulsive noise is considered. Figure 18 demonstrates the results in image restoration. From these results, we may observe that, in case of complex mixed noisy images, the SFCF filter performance still becomes more highlighted compared to the other filters mentioned above.

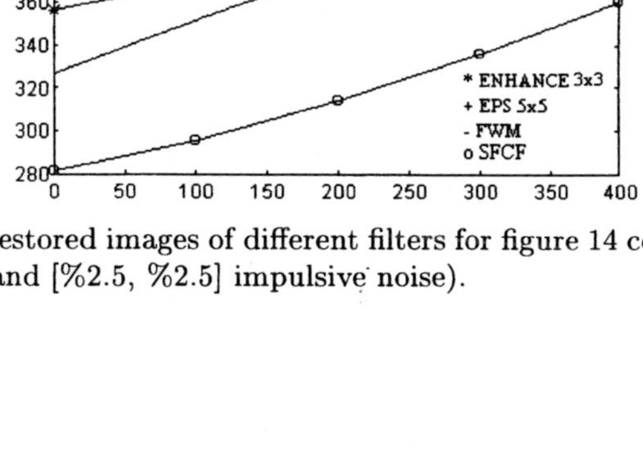

Fig. 18. MSE of restored images of different filters for figure 14 corrupted by mixed noise (Gaussian and [%2.5, %2.5] impulsive noise).

Experiment 6 In this experiment we computed the run-time of the SFCF filter and compared it with the run-time of other filters. In this case we consider a 256×256 test image with 256 gray levels and simulated all filters on a Pentium-166 PC-AT by BorlandC 4.5 for windows. The results of this experiment are depicted in the table 3. It can be seen from this table that the SFCF filter has faster performance with respect to other recently proposed filters.

3.3 The sharpening & smoothing filter - SSFCF

By adding two extra rules to the fuzzy rules of the SFCF filter, we may have a filter which can smooth noise while at the same time sharpen the image edges. This is important because sharpening and smoothing are two conflicting processes (image smoothing makes images get blurred while sharpening amplifies image noises).

These rules are as follows:

R7: IF (**more** of x_i are **Z**) & (**not few** of x_i are **A1**)) THEN y is B1
R8: IF (**more** of x_i are **Z**) & (**not few** of x_i are **A2**)) THEN y is B2

where the term **not few** is a S-Type fuzzy function and may be defined by the sigmoid function given in equation 9 with different parameters. The membership functions of **A1**, **A2**, **B1** and **B2** are depicted in figure 19.

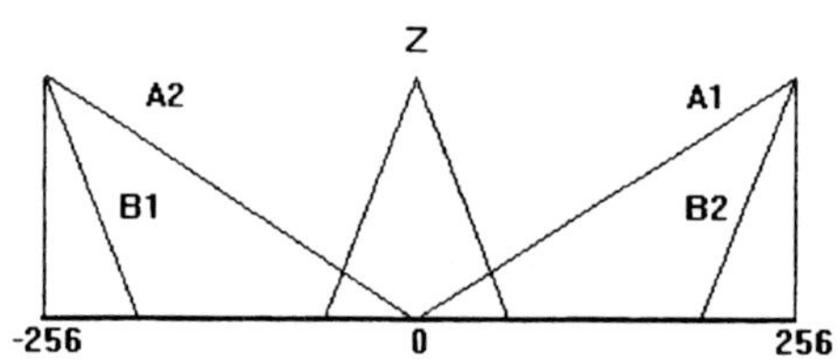

Fig. 19. The membership functions of **A1**, **A2**, **B1**, **B2**.

The activity degree of the rule R7, λ_7 is computed by equation 12. The activity degree of the rule R8 is computed similarly.

$$\lambda_7 = \min\left[\mu_{A1}(x_i) : \mu_{A1}(x_i) > \mu_Z(x_i)\right] \times \\ \mu_{more}\left[\frac{number\ of\ x_i : \mu_Z(x_i) > \mu_{A1}(x_i)}{Total\ number\ of\ x_i}\right] \times \\ \mu_{notfew}\left[\frac{number\ of\ x_i : \mu_{A1}(x_i) > \mu_Z(x_i)}{Total\ number\ of\ x_i}\right] \tag{12}$$

The output y is calculated by:

$$y = k.ave(x_i) + (1 - k)\left[\sum_{i=1}^{6} C_i\lambda_i + SC.\sum_{i=1}^{2} C_{B_i}\lambda_{i+6}\right] \tag{13}$$

In equation 13, *SC* is the *Sharpening Coefficient* and by this factor we can change the sharpening rate of the image.

The reason why the rules R7 and R8 have been established is so that the rules are fired only in edge regions (the regions consisting of two or more different areas). This makes only the edges become sharper. We will identify this modified filter as the Sharpening and Smoothing Fuzzy Control Filter (SSFCF).

In order to show the achievable performances of the SSFCF from a quantitative point of view, we computed the local variances in background (BV) and in detailed (DV) areas of the image as defined in [31]. These values for the Lena image contaminated by Gaussian noise with $\sigma^2 = 100$ are listed in Table 1. Noting that smaller values for BV indicate less noise amplification while bigger values for DV imply higher sharpening, we may observe in Table 1 that our filter performance is remarkably high. For example, our method with SC=1, gives small noise magnification (a BV value of 42, which is smaller than that of the original noisy image) and has a much more remarkable sharpening in the detailed areas (with a DV of 2332). This table also lists the BV and DV values of the SSFCF and the methods taken from [26] and [9]. In short, in the case of noisy data (corrupted images), the SSFCF performs much better than the methods given in [26] and [9], with less noise amplification and significant sharpening of details.

Table 1. Comparison results for Lena image.

Image	BV	DV
Noisy image	99	1002
FIRE [26]	129	2075
FIRE II [26]	146	2515
unsharp masking [9]	504	2484
SSFCF with SC=2	53	3171
SSFCF with SC=1	42	2332

4 The fixed point fuzzy control based filter - FFCF

To increase the run-time speed of the SFCF filter and to make it easier for hardware implementation, we made the following modifications on the SFCF filter to have a new, yet powerful filter named by FFCF (Fixed-point Fuzzy Control based Filter) which does not need any floating point calculations. Consequently, it can be easily implemented by hardware with very fast performance.

The modifications are:

- Based on experimental results we consider two 5 bits Look Up Tables (LUT) for the functions **more** and **fairly more**.
- To reduce the quantization error, we changed the sequence of algorithm computations, i.e. we first perform multiplications, then additions and at last divisions. For example, consider the following formula:

$$\frac{a}{b} \times \left(\frac{c}{d} + \frac{e}{f}\right)$$

  This can be evaluated as:

$$\frac{\{[(c \times f) + (d \times e)] \times a\}}{(b \times d \times f)}$$

- In order to increase the filter speed more, we tried to make the multiplicant and divisor parameters become powers of 2, because in this case we can change these operators by a left and right shift, respectively.

By these modifications the activity degree of rules and the output of the SFCF filter are computed with the following formulas:

$$\begin{aligned}\lambda_1 = & \, median\,(\mu_{NB}(x_i) : x_i \in support(NB)) \times \\ & LUT_{more}\,[number\ of\ x_i \in support(NB)]\end{aligned} \tag{14}$$

$$t = k.ave(x_i) + (32 - k) \sum_{i=1}^{6} C_i \lambda_i \tag{15}$$

$$y = right\_shifted(t) \tag{16}$$

where,

$$k = LUT_{fairly\,more}\,[number\ of\ x_i \in support(Z)] \tag{17}$$

The comparison results of the FFCF and SFCF filters are demonstrated in table 3. By looking at this table we can see that these two filters have the same filtering and edge preserving property for complex and non-complex images but the FFCF filter has 2.1 second run-time while the run-time of the SFCF was 15 seconds. This obviously approves the claim mentioned above.

5 Adaptive fixed point fuzzy control based filter - AFCF

Computations in the previous section have shown that to evaluate the equation 15, we at least need 19 bits. Therefore, we should use 32 bits registers and microprocessors for computations of the FFCF filter (while we indeed require only 19 bits). To resolve this problem and pay a cheaper hardware implementation cost, we modified the FFCF filter by tuning the membership functions of NB, NM, NS, PS, PM and PB in each pixel in order to make the $C_i\lambda_i$ terms in equation 15 be a multiplicand of 8. Consequently, the lower 3 bits of the summation in equation 15 will be zero and we do not need to consider them.

In this case, the equation 15 is changed as follows:

$$t = \alpha.k.ave(x_i) + (32 - k)\sum_{i=1}^{6} \gamma_i m_i \tag{18}$$

where,

$$\gamma_i = 8 \times \text{integer\_value}\left[\frac{\theta_i}{8} + 1 - \epsilon\right] \tag{19}$$

$$\theta_i = C_i\lambda_i \tag{20}$$

$$\lambda_1 = median\{\mu_{NB}(x_i) : x_i \in support(NB)\} \tag{21}$$

We acronym this modified FFCF filter by Adaptive FFCF, AFCF, filter. The role of ϵ in (19) is to make the boundary more vivid and clear. It plays an effective role only at jump discontinuities (for example, for $\frac{\theta_i}{8} = 8.1$ the output equals $8 \cdot 9$, while for $\frac{\theta_i}{8} = 8$ the output becomes $8 \cdot 8$).

The experimental results listed in table 3 comparing the two filters FFCF and AFCF show that the AFCF filter preserves almost all performances of the FFCF filter, with a cheaper hardware implementation cost.

6 The adaptive C-average fuzzy control based filter - ACFCF

6.1 Construction of the ACFCF filter

We can rewrite the activity degree of R1 in general form by the following relationship:

$$\lambda_1 = Function[\mu_{NB}(x_i) \ : \ x_i \in support(NB)] \times \mu_{more}\left[\frac{number\ of\ x_i \in support(NB)}{Total\ number\ of\ x_i}\right] \tag{22}$$

The *Function* term in equation 22 is responsible for selecting the membership degree of one of the most proper x_i's belonging to support(NB). To do so, we may take one of the following different choices. Each choice has its own advantages and disadvantages explained below:

- $Function(.) = \frac{\sum_{x_i \in support(NB)} \mu_{NB}(x_i)}{Total\ number\ of\ x_i \in support(NB)}$.
  This equation computes the average of membership degrees of x_i's which are in support(NB).
- $Function(.) = \min[\mu_{NB}(x_i) : x_i \in support(NB)]$.
- $Function(.) = median[\mu_{NB}(x_i) : x_i \in support(NB)]$.

Note that the above three formulas, which compute the first term in equation 3, have the following advantages and disadvantages:

- Although method 1, compared to the other two methods, performs fast, it makes the output image get some blurred.
- Method 2, like method 1, performs fast but it shows poor filtering performance. To remedy this problem, we have to apply method 2 to the input image iteratively, which in turn weakens its fast computing property.
- The third method is very slow, but it performs well.

To remedy the above disadvantages while keeping the fast computation property of the algorithm, we came up with the following formula named as C-average:

$$Function(.) = \mu_{NB}(x_c) \tag{23}$$

where,

$$x_c = \arg[\min_{x_i}(|\gamma - \mu_{NB}(x_i)|)] \tag{24}$$

and

$$\gamma = \frac{\sum_{x_i \in support(NB)} \mu_{NB}(x_i)}{Total\ number\ of\ x_i \in support(NB)} \tag{25}$$

Table 2 summarizes the performance of the four methods explained above. As easily seen in column 3, the C-average takes 1.5 microsecond to evaluate a string with 9 integer elements on a PC Pentium-166, and at the same time it shows good performance of the C-Averaging method for the image restoration problem.

Table 3 lists the comparison results of the ACFCF filters with the other filters given in this table. By looking at table3, we may conclude that the filtering ability of the AFCF and ACFCF filters are the same but the former has faster performance. Reader may also see the comparison results of ACFCF, SFCF and IFCF filters on noise removal for the Lena image corrupted by Gaussian noise with different variances and [%2.5 , %2.5] impulsive noise in figures 20 and 21.

Table 2. Comparison of different methods for the *Function*.

Method	Filtering Ability[a]	Run Time (in microseconds[b])
Average	blur	0.425
Minimum	poor	0.575
Median	good	5.25
C-Average	good	1.5

[a]Here the Lena image is considered as a test case for a comparison study.
[b]The run times are computed for a string with 9 integer elements. Programs are written on a PC AT Pentium-166 with the software of BorlandC 4.5 for windows.

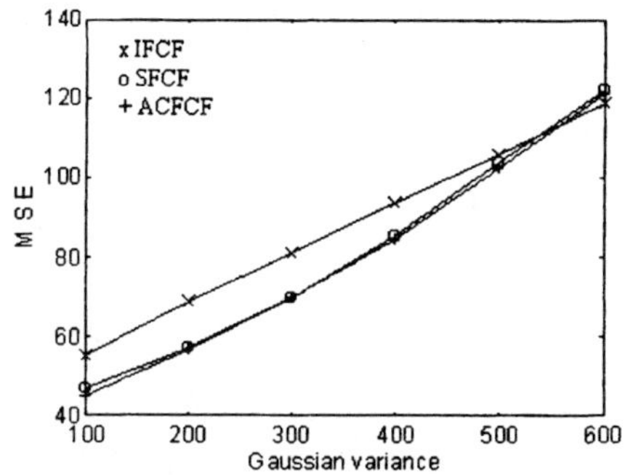

Fig. 20. MSE as a function of variance of Gaussian noise, computed for the Lena image.

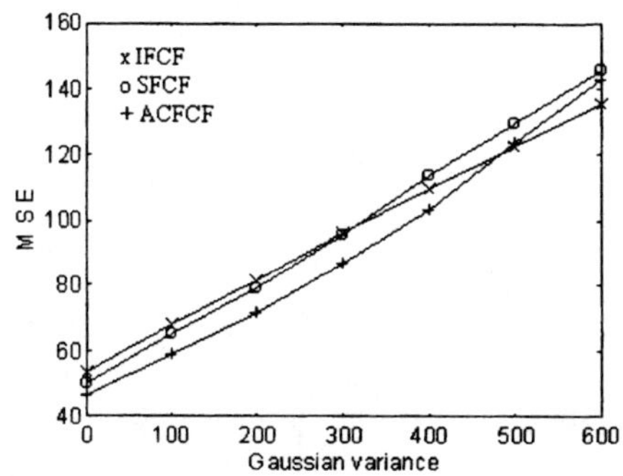

Fig. 21. MSE of restored images of different filters for the Lena image corrupted by mixed noise (Gaussian and [%2.5, %2.5] impulsive noise).

Table 3. MSE, MSEE and Run-Time of filters.

Filter	image 1[a]	image 2[b]	image 3[c]	MSEE	Run Time (second)[d]
noisy image	384.3	1272	1356	-	-
median 3x3	111.1	127.9	529.1	610	1
median 5x5	127.1	134	907.6	1682	4
FWM	113.4	130.2	427.8	506	440
EPS 5x5	87.61	136.9	460.3	847	78
EPS 7x7	98.67	129.7	488.5	1053	151
ENHANCE 3x3	96.12	107.6	430.9	577	30
ENHANCE 5x5	102.4	110.8	588	1102	110
SFCF	85.11	113.8	359.6	421	15
FFCF	86.45	110	342.8	389	2.1
AFCF	87.02	105.9	365	411	2
ACFCF	85.33	103.9	373	433	1.5

[a] The Lena image contaminated by Gaussian noise with $\sigma^2 = 400$.
[b] The Lena image contaminated by Gaussian noise with $\sigma^2 = 400$ and [%2.5 %2.5] impulsive noise.
[c] The image given in figure 14 contaminated by Gaussian noise with $\sigma^2 = 400$ and [%2.5 %2.5] impulsive noise.
[d] The run times are computed for a 256x256 test image with 256 gray-levels. Programs are written on a PC AT Pentium-166 with the software of BorlandC 4.5 for windows.

6.2 Application of the ACFCF filter in template matching

Experiment 1 Since the ACFCF filter has good capability in edge preserving along with noise removing, it can be used for template matching. In this experiment we consider figure 22 as a test image and the character '2', which has been circled in the figure, represents the template. The image is then corrupted by zero mean Gaussian noise with σ^2=400 and [%2.5, %2.5] impulsive noise. Different filtering algorithms listed in table 4 are applied to the image and we then find the position of the template in the resulting images. The results are shown in table 4. We can easily observe that only two methods (ENHANCE and ACFCF filters) succeeded to find correctly the right position of the template.

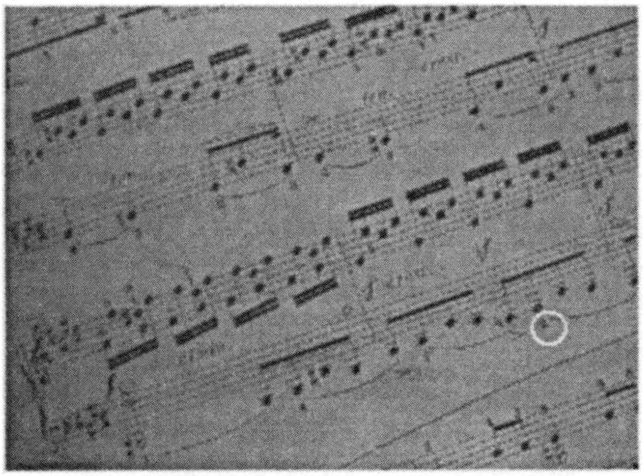

Fig. 22. Test image for experiment 1.

Table 4. Template matching results for experiment 1

Image	x	y	MINSE	SE
Main Image	255	153	0	0
Noisy Image	103	95	948.1	1821
Median 3 × 3	285	116	1031	1326
FWM	268	42	1066	1100
EPS 5 × 5	152	80	899.4	1038
EPS 7 × 7	152	80	876.2	1033
ENHANCE	255	153	977.4	977.4
ACFCF Filter	255	153	641.4	641.4

x,y : The coordinates of the point in the image on which it is most likely the original template is being located.
MINSE: The MINimum Square Error between the original template and the different pixels in the image
SE: Square error between the original template and the process template.

Experiment 2 This experiment is the same as experiment 1, but in this case we consider figure 23 as a test image with the eye of the alligator chosen as the desired template. The results are depicted in table 5.

Fig. 23. Test image for experiment 2.

Table 5. Template matching results for experiment 2

Image	x	y	MINSE	SE
Main Image	178	141	0	0
Noisy Image	171	71	545.1	2283
Median 3×3	141	134	314.9	556.3
FWM	178	141	316.1	316.1
EPS 5×5	244	9	333.4	349.3
EPS 7×7	178	141	285.9	285.9
ENHANCE	142	134	277.1	311.9
ACFCF Filter	178	141	337.1	337.1

Experiment 3 This experiment is the same as experiment 1 but in this case we consider figure 24 as a test image and the target has been indicated by black rectangle. The results are depicted in table 6. As it can be seen from tables 4, 5, 6 our method performs well while the other methods could perform satisfactorily only for some cases.

Fig. 24. Test image for experiment 3.

Table 6. Template matching results for experiment 3

Image	x	y	MINSE	SE
Main Image	235	91	0	0
Noisy Image	185	25	301.4	388
Median 3 × 3	156	8	65.38	68.67
FWM	156	8	66.15	86.6
EPS 5 × 5	235	91	35.98	35.98
EPS 7 × 7	235	91	35.98	35.98
ENHANCE	12	47	48.78	68.5
ACFCF Filter	235	91	64.25	64.25

7 Conclusion

This chapter introduced a new fuzzy logic control based filtering approach with the properties of removing impulsive noise and smoothing out Gaussian noise while, simultaneously, preserving edges and image details efficiently. Different modifications of this filtering approach named by IFCF, MIFCF, EIFCF, SFCF, SSFCF, FFCF, AFCF and ACFCF, are presented along with some test experiments highlighting the merit of the proposed filters.

As future work, we are applying the proposed filtering ideas for other image processing tasks such as segmentation. We are also working on the rules optimization using some other aspects of computational intelligence.

8 Acknowledgments

This chapter is a collection of several papers presented at different international conferences such as ICASSP'98, ICIP'98, EUFIT'98 and KES'99. Parts of this chapter have also been accepted for publication in IEEE Trans. SMC.

The authors are grateful to thank Dr. S. A. Motamedi for his kind support and advise. We delight in thanking Prof. Martin Hagan for his kind remarks on some parts of the chapter.

References

1. Arakawa K., *Digital signal processing based on fuzzy rules*, in: "Proceedings of the Fifth IFSA World Congress", pp. 1305–1308, 1994
2. Bezdek J.C. and Pal S.K., *"Fuzzy Models for Pattern Recognition"*, IEEE Press, New York, 1992
3. Chen B.T., Chen Y. and Hsu W., *Image processing and understanding based on the fuzzy inference approach*, in: "Proceedings of FUZZ-IEEE'94 – 3rd IEEE Int. Conf. Fuzzy Systems", pp. 279–83, 1994
4. Chen C.L., Lee C.S. and Kuo Y.H., *Design of high speed weighted fuzzy mean filters with generic LR fuzzy cells*, in: "Proceedings of ICIP'96 – 3rd IEEE Int. Conf. Image Processing", Vol. 2, pp. 1027–1030, 1996
5. Choi Y. and Krishnapuram R., *A robust approach to image enhancement based on fuzzy logic*, IEEE Trans. Image Processing, Vol. 6, No. 6, pp. 808–825, 1997
6. Doroodchi M. and Reza A.M., *Fuzzy cluster filter*, in: "Proceedings of ICIP'96 – 3rd IEEE Int. Conf. Image Processing", Vol. 2, pp. 939–942, 1996
7. Doroodchi M. and Reza A.M., *Implementation of fuzzy cluster filter for non-linear signal and image processing*, in: "Proceedings of ICIP'96 – 3rd IEEE Int. Conf. Image Processing", Vol. 3, pp. 2117–2122, 1996
8. Haralick R.M. and Shapiro L.G., *"Computer and Robot Vision, Volume 1"*, Addison Weseley, 1992
9. Jain A.K., *"Fundamentals of digital image processing"*, Prentice-Hall, 1989
10. Kim J.S. and Cho H.S., *A fuzzy logic and neural network approach to boundary detection for noisy imagery*, Fuzzy Sets and Systems, Vol. 65, No. 2/3, pp. 141–159, 1994
11. Kosko B., *"Neural Networks and Fuzzy Systems"*, Prentice-Hall, 1992
12. Krishnapuram R. and Keller M., *Fuzzy sets theoretic approach to computer vision: an overview*, in: "Proceedings of FUZZ-IEEE'92 – First IEEE Int. Conf. Fuzzy Systems", pp. 135–142, 1992
13. Lee C.S., Kuo Y.H. and Yu P.T., *Weighted fuzzy mean filters for heavy-tailed noise removal*, in: "Proceedings of the Joint Third Int. Symp. Uncertainty Modeling and Analysis and Annual Conference of the North American Fuzzy Information Processing Society", pp. 601–606, 1995
14. Mancuso M., Poluzzi R. and Rizzotto G., *A fuzzy filter for dynamic range reduction and contrast enhancement*, in: "Proceedings of FUZZ-IEEE'94 – 3rd IEEE Int. Conf. Fuzzy Systems", pp. 264–267, 1994
15. Mastin G.A., *Adaptive filters for digital image noise smoothing: an evaluation*, Computer Vision, Graphics, Image Processing, Vol. 31, pp. 103–121, 1985

16. Muneyasu M., Wada Y. and Hinamoto T., *Edge-preserving smoothing by adaptive nonlinear filters based on fuzzy control laws*, in: "Proceedings of ICIP'96 – 3rd IEEE Int. Conf. Image Processing", Vol. 1, pp. 785–788, 1996
17. Pal S.K., *Fuzzy sets in image processing and recognition*, in: "Proceedings of FUZZ-IEEE'92 – First IEEE Int. Conf. Fuzzy Systems", pp. 119–126, 1992
18. Peng S. and Lucke L., *A hybrid filter for image enhancement*, in: "Proceedings of ICIP'95 – 2nd IEEE Int. Conf. Image Processing", Vol. 1, pp. 163–166, 1995
19. Pitas I. and Venetsanopoulos A.N., *"Nonlinear Digital Filters: Principles and Applications"*, Kluwer Academic Publishers, 1990
20. Russo F. and Ramponi G., *Edge detection by FIRE operators*, in: "Proceedings of FUZZ-IEEE'94 – 3rd IEEE Int. Conf. Fuzzy Systems", pp. 249–253, 1994
21. Russo F. and Ramponi G., *Combined FIRE filters for image enhancement*, in: "Proceedings of FUZZ-IEEE'94 – 3rd IEEE Int. Conf. Fuzzy Systems", pp. 261–264, 1994
22. Russo F. and Ramponi G., *Fuzzy operator for sharpening of noisy images*, IEEE Electron Lett., Vol. 28, pp. 1715–1717, 1992
23. Russo F., *A user-friendly research tool for image processing with fuzzy rules*, in: "Proceedings of FUZZ-IEEE'92 – First IEEE Int. Conf. Fuzzy Systems", pp. 561–568, 1992
24. Russo F. and Ramponi G., *Nonlinear fuzzy operators for image processing*, Signal Processing, Vol. 38, pp. 429–440, 1994
25. Russo F. and Ramponi G., *A noise smoother using cascaded FIRE filters*, in: "Proceedings of FUZZ-IEEE'95 – 4th IEEE Int. Conf. Fuzzy Systems", Vol. 1, pp. 351–358, 1995
26. Russo F. and Ramponi G., *An image enhancement technique based on the FIRE operator*, in: "Proceedings of ICIP'95 – 2nd IEEE Int. Conf. Image Processing", Vol. 1, pp. 155–158, 1995
27. Russo F. and Ramponi G., *Removal of impulsive noise using a FIRE filter*, in: "Proceedings of ICIP'96 – 3rd IEEE Int. Conf. Image Processing", Vol. 2, pp. 975–978, 1996
28. Russo F. and Ramponi G., *A fuzzy filter for images corrupted by impulse noise*, IEEE Signal Processing Letters, Vol. 3, No. 6, pp. 168–170, 1996
29. Sucher R., *A self-organizing nonlinear filter based on fuzzy clustering*, in: "Proceedings of IEEE-ISCAS'96 – IEEE International Symposium on Circuits and Systems", Vol. 2, pp. 101–103, 1996
30. Taguchi A., *A design method of fuzzy weighted median filters*, in: "Proceedings of ICIP'96 – 3rd IEEE Int. Conf. Image Processing", Vol. 1, pp. 423–426, 1996
31. Vanzo A., Ramponi G. and Sicuranza G.L., *An image enhancement technique using polynomial filters*, in: "Proceedings of ICIP'94 – First IEEE Int. Conf. Image Processing", pp. 477–481, 1994
32. Wang J.H. and Yu M.D., *Image restoration by adaptive fuzzy optimal filter*, in: "Proceedings of the IEEE Int. Conf. Systems, Man and Cybernetics, Intelligent Systems for the 21st Century", Vol. 1, pp. 845–848, 1995
33. Yang X. and Toh P.S., *Adaptive fuzzy multilevel median filter*, IEEE Trans. Image Processing, Vol. 4, pp. 680–682, 1995
34. Yu P.T. and Chen R.C., *Fuzzy stack filters- Their definitions, fundamental properties, and application in image processing*, IEEE Trans. Image Processing, Vol. 5, No. 6, pp. 838–854, 1996

Chapter 8

Fuzzy Rule-Based Image Processing with Optimization

Kaoru Arakawa

Meji University, Department of Computer Science
1-1-1, Higashimita, Tama-ku, Kawasaki, 214-8571, Japan
email: arakawa@cs.meiji.ac.jp

Summary. Fuzzy rule-based image processing technologies for noise reduction and edge extraction are described. Here, two types of noises are considered in noise reduction, namely white Gaussian noise and impulsive noise. Fuzzy rules are applied in order to consider the nonstationarity and uncertainty of signals. Moreover, the fuzzy reasoning part is designed optimally by expressing the system as a nonlinear function of multiple local characteristics of signals, and by setting the nonlinear function so that the mean square error of the output is the minimum for some training image data. Accordingly, the membership function and the rules are automatically designed from this optimization. Computer simulations verify the effective performance of this image processing technology.

1 Introduction

An image is a typical nonstationary signal. In order to process it, the nonstationarity must be taken into consideration. One of the powerful methods for this, is to control the system parameters depending on the local characteristics of the image [1,7,11,12]. For instance, when an image is contaminated with additive random noise, usual filtering techniques cannot be applied for the noise removal, since they smooth out the edges as well. Thus, the system must distinguish flat regional parts of the image from abruptly changing ones, such as edges, and then set the system parameters for each part independently. However, such control cannot be performed definitely, since the definition of the signal characteristics and the rules to describe how to control the system parameters are usually expressed in an ambiguous form. For example, we can say that if the signal difference between two adjacent pixels is small they are included in the same flat region. However, it is difficult to find a definite threshold to distinguish small signal differences from large differences. That is to say, in some part of the edges, the signal difference may be relatively small and in some part of the flat region the signal difference may be relatively large because of noises. Moreover, we can say that the window size of the noise-removal filter must be large enough in the flat region, while it must be small enough in the part of edges. However, it is difficult to define the large window size and the small window size definitely.

In this way, ambiguity must be considered in image processing. In this chapter, fuzzy rule-based image processing, especially for noise removal and edge extraction, is introduced taking this ambiguity into consideration. This image processing system is realized as a time-variant system in which the system parameters change continuously depending on the local characteristics of the images. This system also corresponds to a nonlinear system, in which the system parameters are expressed as continuous nonlinear functions of the local image characteristics. Here, the system is optimally designed for training image data by optimizing the nonlinear functions.

The chapter is organized as follows. In Section 2, the fundamental ideas of the fuzzy rule-based image processing system are presented. It is shown how the system parameters are estimated by fuzzy rules. By applying fuzzy rules, the system parameters are expressed as continuous nonlinear functions of some local characteristics of the input image. These functions are shown to be estimated optimally by minimizing the mean square error of the system output for training image data. Usually in fuzzy systems, membership functions must be known beforehand to design the system. However, this is not required here. The only thing needed is what kind of local characteristics should be used to create the rules.

In Section 3, the application of this methodology to noise removal is presented. First, white Gaussian noise is considered. The system is realized as a weighted-averaging type filter in which the weights are controlled by fuzzy rules. Next, impulsive noise is considered. In this case, the system is realized as a conditional median filter in which the output is controlled depending on the signal characteristics. Some examples of computer simulations are presented to verify their high performance.

In Section 4, the application to edge extraction is presented, with some results of computer simulations. Finally Section 5 gives concluding remarks.

2 Principles of fuzzy rule-based image processing

2.1 Fundamental ideas of the fuzzy rule-based system

Suppose that the input image signal at the pixel (i,j) is denoted as $x(i,j)$. The output of the image processing system $y(i,j)$ is generally expressed as a function of $X(i,j)$, a set of input image signals $x(i-k,j-m)$ around $x(i,j)$ (with $-N \le k \le N$ and $-N \le m \le N$), and some system parameters. For example, the output of the weighted averaging filter is expressed as follows:

$$y(i,j) = \frac{\sum\limits_{k=-N}^{N} \sum\limits_{m=-N}^{N} w(k,m) \cdot x(i-k,j-m)}{\sum\limits_{k=-N}^{N} \sum\limits_{m=-N}^{N} w(k,m)}, \tag{1}$$

where the $w(k,m)$ denote the weights, which corresponds to the system parameters.

If the image signal is flat or contains just smooth changes, this weighted averaging filter is powerful to reduce additive random noise if the $w(k,m)$'s take the following values:

$$w(k,m) = 1, \qquad \forall k, \ \forall m. \tag{2}$$

However, since an image signal usually contains large-amplitude abrupt-changes, such as edges, this filter using $w(k,m)$ as in (2) makes the image blurred when it is used for noise reduction. In order to keep the edges sharp, the weights must take values as follows:

$$w(k,m) = \begin{cases} 1 \text{ for } k = m = 0 \\ 0 \text{ else} \end{cases} \tag{3}$$

In this case, the noise cannot be smoothed at all. Thus, the value of the weight $w(k,m)$ should be controlled depending on the local characteristics of the image signal, so that the image signals are averaged inside the edges. If the pixel $(i-k, j-m)$ belongs to the same flat area as the pixel (i,j), the weight $w(k,m)$ should take a value one, but if an edge exists between these two pixels, the weight $w(k,m)$ should be equal to zero because such a pixel should not be used in the averaging. Here, the amplitude of the signal difference $|x(i,j) - x(i-k, j-m)|$ can be used to separate the two states. We can say that if $|x(i,j) - x(i-k, j-m)|$ is small, $x(i-k, j-m)$ and $x(i,j)$ are supposed to be in the same flat area, but if not, they are supposed to be in different areas. Now the problem is how to define the smallness and the largeness of $|x(i,j) - x(i-k, j-m)|$. If the edges of the image are clear, that is to say,

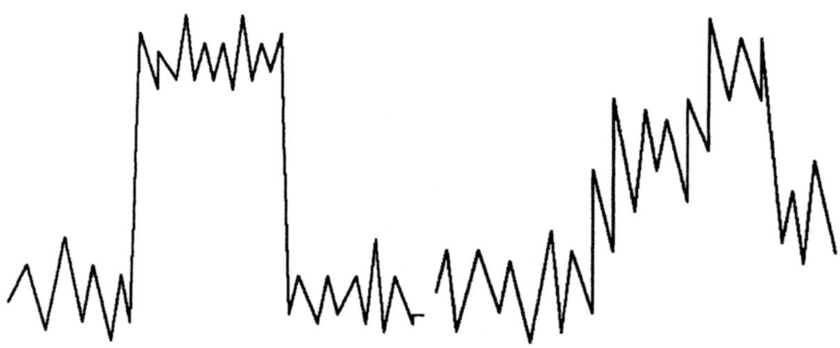

(a) (b)

Fig. 1. Examples of signals: (a) = clear edge; (b) = unclear edge.

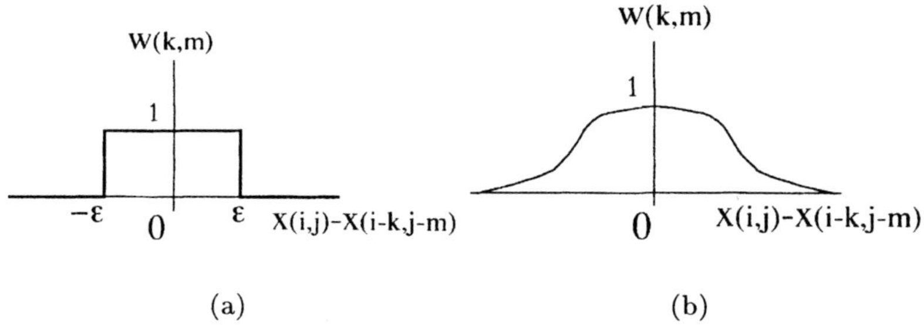

Fig. 2. The value $w(k,m)$ versus the signal difference $x(i,j) - x(i-k,j-m)$: (a) = the crisp case; (b) = the fuzzy case.

if the signal jump at the edge is clear as shown in Fig. 1(a), the threshold to classify the small signal difference and the large one is easy to obtain. The weight $w(k,m)$ can be a function of $x(i,j) - x(i-k,j-m)$, as shown in Fig. 2(a). However, since natural images usually contain ambiguous edges, the sectional waveform of which is as shown in Fig. 1(b), it is difficult to set a definite threshold for $|x(i,j) - x(i-k,j-m)|$ to separate the two states, and accordingly the weight $w(k,m)$ becomes a function of $x(i,j) - x(i-k,j-m)$ as depicted in Fig. 2(b). The form of this function $w(k,m)$ in this ambiguous case can be designed by fuzzy approximate reasoning. That is to say, the rule to control the value $w(k,m)$ is described in a fuzzy style as follows:

Rule 1: if $|x(i,j) - x(i-k,j-m)|$ is small
then $w(k,m)$ is large (about a value one)
else $w(k,m)$ is close to zero.

In fuzzy theory, the value $w(k,m)$ is estimated from the membership function concerning $|x(i,j) - x(i-k,j-m)|$ and $w(k,m)$. The membership function for the smallness and the largeness of $|x(i,j)-x(i-k,j-m)|$ can be expressed as shown in Fig. 3(a), while that representing the states of $w(k,m)$ can be as shown in Fig. 3(b). By applying Mamdani's approximate reasoning [10] – as illustrated in Fig. 3(c), where the center of gravity of the shaded part is taken for all the value $|x(i,j) - x(i-k,j-m)|$ – $w(k,m)$ is obtained as a continuous nonlinear function of $|x(i,j) - x(i-k,j-m)|$ as shown in Fig. 4(a), which represents the feature of the function form in Fig. 2(b).

Moreover, other rules can be added to this system. For example, since an image signal has some correlation in adjacent pixels, the input $x(i-k,j-m)$ with small spatial distance from $x(i,j)$ should be largely used in averaging, while that with large distance should not. A measure for this distance is given by k^2+m^2. When this rule is taken into consideration, Rule 1 can be modified as follows:

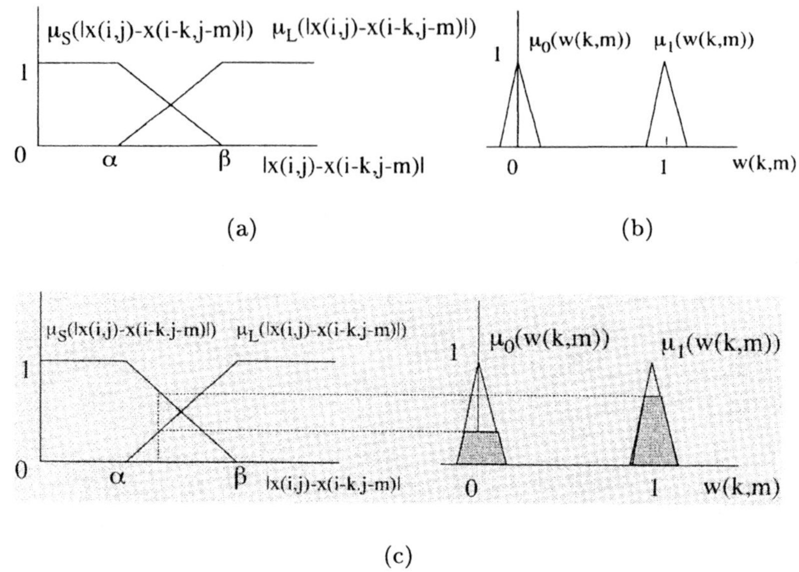

Fig. 3. (a): membership functions for the smallness μ_S and largeness μ_L of $|x(i,j)-x(i-k,j-m)|$; (b): membership functions μ_0 (about 0") and μ_1 (about 1") for $w(k,m)$; (c): application of Mamdani's approximate reasoning.

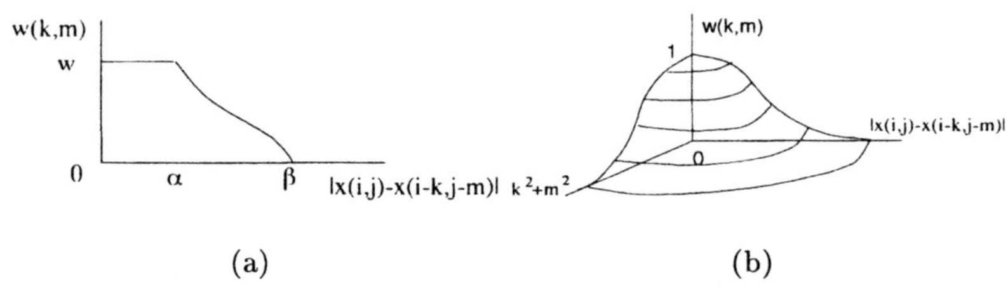

Fig. 4. Examples of the system parameter $w(k,m)$ obtained from fuzzy rules: (a) = obtained from Rule 1; (b) = obtained from Rule 2.

Rule 2: if $|x(i,j)-x(i-k,j-m)|$ is small and k^2+m^2 is small then $w(k,m)$ is very large;
if $|x(i,j)-x(i-k,j-m)|$ is small and k^2+m^2 is large then $w(k,m)$ is not so large;
if $|x(i,j)-x(i-k,j-m)|$ is large and k^2+m^2 is small then $w(k,m)$ is relatively small;
if $|x(i,j)-x(i-k,j-m)|$ is large and k^2+m^2 is large then $w(k,m)$ is very small.

In this case, $w(k, m)$ is represented as a two-dimensional nonlinear function of $|x(i, j) - x(i - k, j - m)|$ and $k^2 + m^2$ as shown in Fig. 4(b). If more rules are added, $w(k, m)$ is represented as a multi-dimensional continuous nonlinear function of the parameters appearing in the rules.

In this way, a fuzzy rule-based image processing is realized as a system in which the system parameters $w(k, m)$ are expressed as continuous nonlinear functions of some local characteristics of the input.

2.2 How to design the fuzzy rule-based image processing system

The nonlinear function $w(k, m)$ representing the fuzzy rule-based image processing system depends on the rules concerning the local characteristics of the input and $w(k, m)$, on the membership functions, and on the used defuzzification method. Accordingly, the performance of the image processing system depends upon these factors. In order to make the system performance as high as possible, these factors must be determined to be the most appropriate ones. Some methods are proposed for such optimization of fuzzy systems, using training methods such as genetic algorithms [9]. In the fuzzy rule-based image processing system presented here, since these factors are reflected in the nonlinear function $w(k, m)$, the total optimization of them can be more simply realized by optimizing the nonlinear function $w(k, m)$. In this section, a method for designing the optimum nonlinear function directly from the local characteristics of training data is presented. Here, the rules, the membership functions, and the way of defuzzification are not necessary to be known. The design of these factors are involved in the design of the nonlinear function $w(k, m)$, thus obtaining the optimum nonlinear function is enough for designing the image processing system. The only thing needed is what kind of local characteristics of the image should be used for the rule-based system.

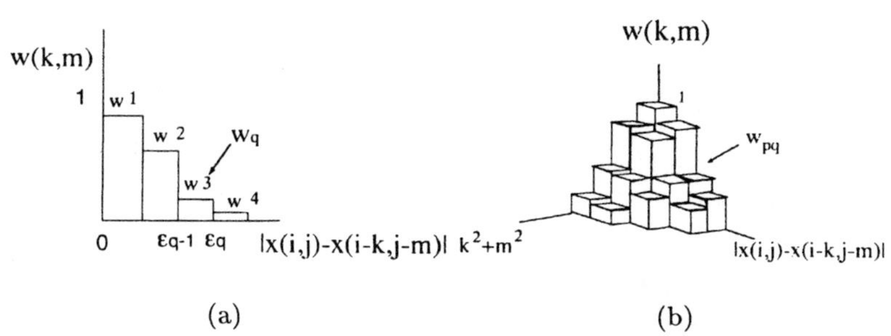

Fig. 5. Approximation of the system parameter $w(k, m)$ as a steplike function: (a) = one-dimensional case; (b) = two-dimensional case.

As is shown in the example of Fig. 4(a), the nonlinear function can be approximated as a step-like function shown in Fig. 5(a) (here, the case where only $|x(i,j)-x(i-k,j-m)|$ is considered is treated). Then, the height of each step can be set, so that the mean square error between the system output and the desired output for some known training image data be the minimum. In order to perform this training, a gradient method can be used. The gradient method gives the optimum value for a parameter, which minimizes a certain cost function by iteration. If the current value of the parameter is larger than the optimum one, the gradient of the cost function at this current parameter takes a positive value, while it takes a negative one if the current parameter is smaller. In the gradient method, the parameter is updated by subtracting a value which is proportional to the gradient of the cost function [8].

Supposed that the height of the q-th step of the step-like function is denoted as w_q, the output signal $y(i,j)$ is expressed as:

$$y(i,j) = \frac{\sum_{q=1}^{Q} \sum_{k=-N}^{N} \sum_{m=-N}^{N} c_{kmq} w_q x(i-k, j-m)}{\sum_{q=1}^{Q} \sum_{k=-N}^{N} \sum_{m=-N}^{N} c_{kmq} w_q}, \tag{4}$$

where

$$c_{kmq} = \begin{cases} 1 & \text{if } |x(i,j) - x(i-k, j-m)| \text{ is included in the } q\text{-th region} \\ 0 & \text{else} \end{cases} \tag{5}$$

The value w_q is obtained from the following iteration:

$$w_q[n+1] = w_q[n] - \alpha \frac{\partial E}{\partial w_q}[n]. \tag{6}$$

Here, $w_q[n]$ denotes the value w_q at time point n, α a small positive coefficient, and E the mean square error. Recall that, if $d(i,j)$ denotes the desired output signal for the pixel (i,j), the mean square error is given by the mean of $(y(i,j) - d(i,j))^2$, also denoted by $\mathtt{E}[(y(i,j) - d(i,j))^2]$, for all (i,j). When α is small enough, E can be replaced by the square error $E' = [y(i,j) - d(i,j)]^2$ at time point n as the LMS-algorithm [14]. For example, in the case of the weighted averaging type filter (1) when the weight $w(k,m)$ is represented as a nonlinear function of $|x(i,j) - x(i-k, j-m)|$, we obtain:

$$E' = \left(\frac{\sum_{q=1}^{Q} \sum_{k=-N}^{N} \sum_{m=-N}^{N} c_{kmq} w_q x(i-k, j-m)}{\sum_{q=1}^{Q} \sum_{k=-N}^{N} \sum_{m=-N}^{N} c_{kmq} w_q} - d(i,j) \right)^2. \tag{7}$$

Accordingly, $\frac{\partial E'}{\partial w_q}$ is obtained as:

$$\frac{\partial E'}{\partial w_q} = 2\left(\sum_{(k,m)\in Q(q)} x(i-k,j-m)D \right.$$
$$\left. -N(q)\cdot\sum_{q=1}^{Q}\sum_{k=-N}^{N}\sum_{m=-N}^{N} c_{kmq}w_q x(i-k,j-m)\right)\cdot\frac{y(i,j)-d(i,j)}{D^2}$$
$$= 2\left(\sum_{(k,m)\in Q(q)} x(i-k,j-m) - N(q)y(i,j)\right)\cdot\frac{y(i,j)-d(i,j)}{D}, \tag{8}$$

where

$$D = \sum_{q=1}^{Q}\sum_{k=-N}^{N}\sum_{m=-N}^{N} c_{kmq}w_q, \tag{9}$$

$Q(q)$ is the set of (k,m) for which $|x(i,j)-x(i-k,j-m)|$ is included in the q-th region of the step-like function, $N(q)$ is the number of the members of $Q(q)$, and the parameter c_{kmq} takes a value 1 if $|x(i,j)-x(i-k,j-m)|$ is included in the q-th region and a value 0 if it is not. Finally, w_q can be obtained by:

$$w_q[n+1] = w_q[n] +$$
$$\beta\left(\sum_{(k,m)\in Q(q)} x(i-k,j-m) - N(q)y(i,j)\right)\cdot\frac{d(i,j)-y(i,j)}{D}. \tag{10}$$

Here, β is equal to 2α. The training is performed till the value w_q converges for all q [3][4].

As to the value β, if this value is too large, the system becomes unstable, while if too small, the convergence speed becomes very small. Thus, the value β should be as large as possible under the condition that the system is kept stable. Such value of β is obtained for some simple cases. For example, for a transversal filter with window size M, β is to be smaller than $1/MP$, where P is the power of the input signal [8]. In general however, it is difficult to obtain the appropriate value for β theoretically, thus the value β should be found experimentally.

As to the convergence, w_q converges to a unique optimum solution if the cost function E is a continuous function of w_q with a unique minimum. However, if E has multiple local minima, w_q may converge to an undesirable value. In this case, methods for avoiding local minima used in the training of neural networks may be useful. One of the simple methods for this is setting the initial values for w_q at appropriate ones which can converge to the desirable optimum solution by making a rough estimation for w_q. Especially, in the case of the filter (4), since w_q is used as w_q/D in eq. (4), w_q may converge to an infinity along with the increase of D. In order to avoid this, w_q for $k = m = 0$ should be set at a certain value such as one.

Especially when the output $y(i,j)$ is simply expressed as a linear combination of the system parameters, the optimum value for the steplike system parameters is obtained directly by setting $\frac{\partial E}{\partial w_q} = 0$; no iterative training is required. The following is a simple case using a single system parameter w. Suppose that the output signal $y(i,j)$ is expressed as:

$$y(i,j) = w \cdot g(X(i,j)) + h(X(i,j)), \tag{11}$$

where $g(\cdot)$ and $h(\cdot)$ are some functions of the set of input signals $X(i,j)$ (here, $g(X(i,j))$ is supposed not to be equal to zero constantly), and w is controlled depending on a feature value of $X(i,j)$, denoted as $p(X(i,j))$ (for example, in Rule 2 the signal difference $|x(i,j) - x(i-k, j-m)|$ and the spatial distance $k^2 + m^2$ are adopted as this $p(X(i,j))$). The value w is also approximated as a steplike function w_q for the q-th region in $p(X(i,j))$. In this case, the optimum value w_q is obtained from $\frac{\partial E}{\partial w_q} = 0$, with:

$$E = \mathrm{E}[(y(i,j) - d(i,j))^2] = \mathrm{E}[(w \cdot g(X(i,j)) + h(X(i,j)) - d(i,j))^2] \tag{12}$$

Since:

$$\begin{aligned}\frac{\partial E}{\partial w_q} &= 2 \cdot E_q[g(X(i,j))(w \cdot g(X(i,j)) + h(X(i,j)) - d(i,j))] \\ &= 2 \cdot \left(w \cdot E_q[g(X(i,j))^2] + E_q[(h(X(i,j)) - d(i,j)) \cdot g(X(i,j))]\right),\end{aligned}$$

w_q is obtained as:

$$w_q = \frac{E_q[(d(i,j) - h(X(i,j))) \cdot g(X(i,j))]}{E_q[g(X(i,j))^2]}. \tag{13}$$

Here, $E_q[Z(i,j)]$ denotes the average of $Z(i,j)$ under the condition that the feature value $p(X(i,j))$ is included in the q-th region. Since E is a polynomial of degree two for each w_q, and the coefficient multiplied with w_q^2 is positive as $E_q[g(X(i,j))^2]$, the value w_q obtained in (13) makes E minimal. Here, we suppose that $E_q[g(X(i,j))^2] \neq 0$; if $E_q[g(X(i,j))^2] = 0$ for a certain region q, w_q for such a region is set by interpolating other w_q's around that region.

In designing the system parameter w, any other approximation than the steplike one can be considered. However, by applying the steplike approximation, the optimization can be realized simply as (13), without any trouble of local minima.

The above explanation is for the one-dimensional case, but this method can easily be extended to the multi-dimensional case. Fig. 5(b) shows the step-like approximation of the two-dimensional nonlinear function as Fig. 4(b). The height of each step w_{pq}, for the p-th region on the first axis and the q-th region on the second axis, is optimized in the same way as in the one-dimensional case. For example, in the case of the weighted averaging type filter (1), w_{pq} is obtained from the iteration as:

$$w_{pq}[n+1] = w_{pq}[n] + \beta \left(\sum_{(k,m)\in Q(p,q)} x(i-k, j-m) - N(p,q)y(i,j) \right) \cdot \frac{d(i,j)-y(i,j)}{D}, \quad (14)$$

where $Q(p,q)$ is the set of (k,m) where k^2+m^2 is in the p-th region and $|x(i,j) - x(i-k, j-m)|$ is in the q-th region, and where the denominator D is given by:

$$D = \sum_{p=1}^{P} \sum_{q=1}^{Q} \sum_{k=-N}^{N} \sum_{m=-N}^{N} c_{kmpq} w_{pq}, \quad (15)$$

with $c_{kmpq} = 1$ if k^2+m^2 is in the p-th region and $|x(i,j) - x(i-k, j-m)|$ is in the q-th region; otherwise $c_{kmpq} = 0$. As for the case of (11), w_{pq} is obtained as:

$$w_{pq} = \frac{E_{pq}[(d(i,j) - h(X(i,j))) \cdot g(X(i,j))]}{E_{pq}[g(X(i,j))^2]}, \quad (16)$$

where $E_{pq}[Z(i,j)]$ denotes the average of $Z(i,j)$ under the condition that the first feature value $p_1(X(i,j))$ is in the p-th region and the second feature value $p_2(X(i,j))$ is in the q-th region.

In this step-like approximation, how to determine the width of the step seems to be a problem. However, it was shown that the performance is not so much influenced by the value of this width; the performance is robust to this width and the width can be set roughly [3]. For example, it is usually effective enough to set the width at about a tenth of the 99% range of each feature value representing the local characteristics [3][6].

3 Fuzzy rule-based systems for noise removal

In this section we will discuss fuzzy rule-based systems for the removal of white Gaussian noise (also see [3] and [4]), and for the removal of impulsive noise (also see [2] and [5]).

3.1 Removal of white Gaussian noise

The weighted averaging filter (1) is suitable for reducing white Gaussian noise. As is mentioned in section 2, the signal difference $|x(i,j) - x(i-k, j-m)|$ and the spatial distance are considered to be used to control the weight. Moreover, local variance of the input image can be considered to create the rule. That is, if the local variance is small around the pixel (i,j), the image area in the filter window corresponds to a flat signal part, thus $w(k,m)$ should take a large value for large spatial distances k^2+m^2 in order to smooth the signal adequately. On the other hand, if the local variance is large, the image area corresponds to a changing signal part such as edges and textures, thus $w(k,m)$ should be concentrated around $k=m=0$, taking a large value just around the pixel (i,j) in order to keep the signal waveform unchanged. In this case, the weight $w(k,m)$ becomes a three-dimensional function $w(s_{ijkm}, t_{km}, \sigma_{ij})$, where $s_{ijkm} = |x(i,j) - x(i-k, j-m)|$, $t_{km} = k^2+m^2$, and σ_{ij} the local variance around the pixel (i,j). In approximating this weight as a steplike function, $w(s_{ijkm}, t_{km}, \sigma_{ij})$ is expressed as w_{pqr} when the value s_{ijkm} is in the p-th region, t_{km} in the q-th region, and σ_{ij} in the r-th region. The value w_{pqr} is obtained by the gradient method as follows [4]:

$$w_{pqr}(n+1) = w_{pqr}(n) + \beta\left(\sum_{(k,m)\in K(p,q,r)} x(i-k, j-m) - N(p,q,r)y(i,j)\right) \cdot \frac{d(i,j)-y(i,j)}{D}. \quad (17)$$

Here, $K(p,q,r)$ is the set of k and m which satisfy that s_{ijkm} is in the p-th region, t_{km} is in the q-th region, and σ_{ij} is in the r-th region. $N(p,q,r)$ is the number of the elements in $K(p,q,r)$. Finally, the denominator D is given by:

$$D = \sum_{p=1}^{P}\sum_{q=1}^{Q}\sum_{r=1}^{R}\sum_{k=-N}^{N}\sum_{m=-N}^{N} c_{kmpqr} w_{pqr}. \quad (18)$$

The parameter c_{kmpqr} takes a value 1 if s_{ijkm} is in the p-th region, t_{km} is in the q-th region, and σ_{ij} is in the r-th region; else c_{kmpqr} takes a value 0. The procedure (17) is repeated till $w_{pqr}(n)$ converges.

Fig. 6 shows some computer simulations of this fuzzy rule-based weighted averaging-type filter. Fig. 6(a) is the original input signal and (b) the original training image signal to set the system parameters; the image signal takes a value from 0 to 255. White Gaussian noise with zero mean and standard deviation 15 is added to these images. Fig. 6(c) is the noisy input image to be processed, (d) is the output of a usual averaging filter, (e) is when two rules concerning the spatial distance and the signal difference are used, and (f) is when the rule concerning the local variance is added to the case of (e). We can see the advantage of using rules, especially all three rules, as illustrated in Fig. 6(f).

3.2 Removal of impulsive noise

Median filtering is a powerful method for removing impulsive noise while keeping step-like edges sharp. However, this filter removes fine structures of

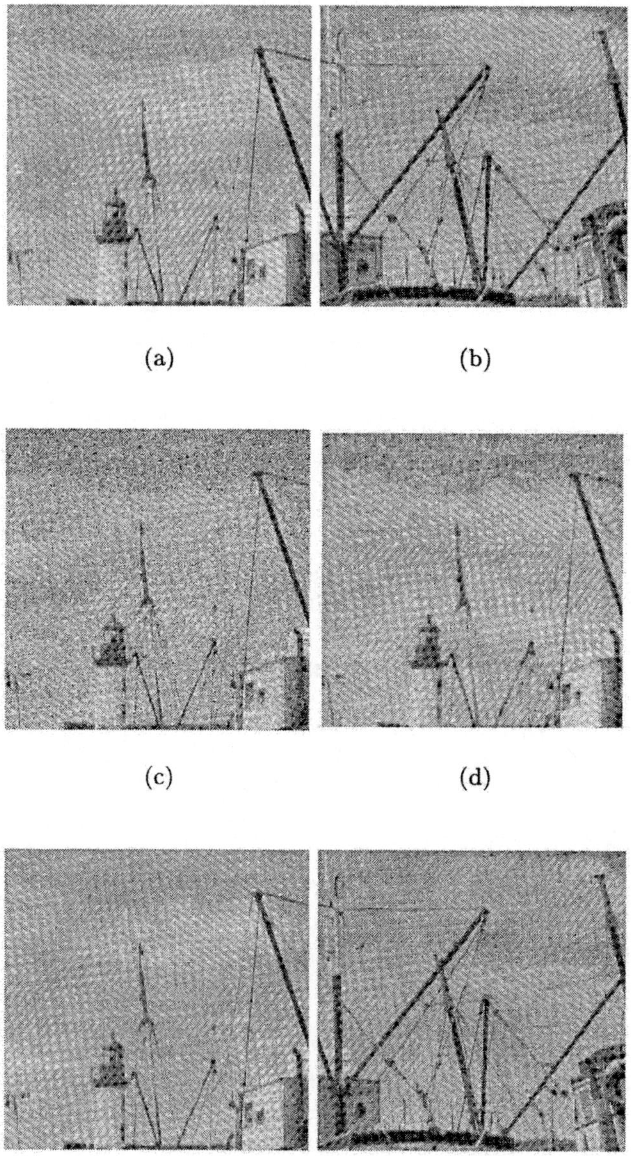

(a) (b)

(c) (d)

(e) (f)

Fig. 6. Results of reducing additive white Gaussian noise by the fuzzy rule-based filters: (a) = original input image; (b) = original training image; (c) = noisy input image; (d) = output of the optimum linear filter (MSE = 59); (e) = output of the fuzzy rule-based filter using 2 rules (MSE = 34); (f) = output of the fuzzy rule-based filter using 3 rules (MSE = 27).

the image signals as well. Therefore, the output of the system $y(i,j)$ should be modified as follows:

$$y(i,j) = m(i,j) + w[X(i,j)] \cdot [x(i,j) - m(i,j)]. \tag{19}$$

Here, $m(i,j)$ denotes the output of the median filter for the pixel (i,j), and $w[X(i,j)]$ is a system parameter which is a function of the set of $x(i-k, j-m)$ around the pixel (i,j). The schematic diagram of this system is shown in Fig. 7. When $w[X(i,j)]$ is equal to 0, this system corresponds to a median filter,

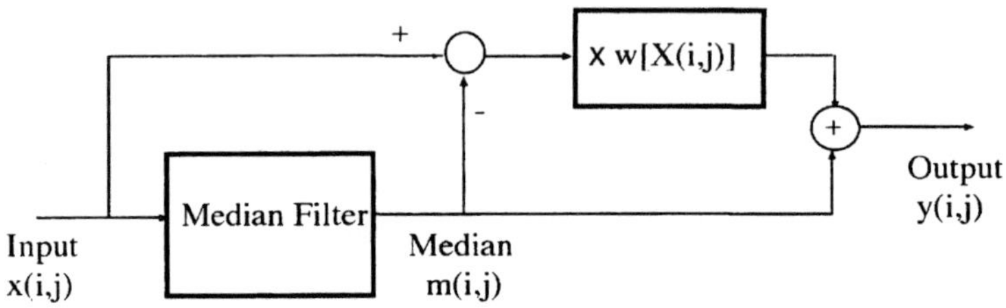

Fig. 7. Schematic diagram of the median filter with control.

but when $w[X(i,j)]$ is 1, this filter just puts out the input as it is. We can see that if an impulsive noise exists at the pixel (i,j), the output should be equal to that of a median filter and $w[X(i,j)]$ should be equal to 0. On the other hand, if an impulsive noise does not exist, the input should be put out as it is, so $w[X(i,j)]$ should be equal to 1. However, it is difficult to classify the two cases definitely for given noisy images. The amplitude of the difference between the input $x(i,j)$ and the output of the median filter $m(i,j)$ can be used to classify them, since the amplitude of the impulsive noises are supposed to be high compared with that of the signal variation:

Rule 3: if $|x(i,j) - m(i,j)|$ is large
then an impulse noise is assumed to exist at the pixel (i,j)
else no impulse noise is assumed to exist.

Since the threshold for this classification is ambiguous, a fuzzy rule-based system as mentioned in Section 2 is applied. The parameter $w[X(i,j)]$ corresponds to a continuous nonlinear function of $x(i,j) - m(i,j)$ as shown in Fig. 8.

Rule 3 is simple and can remove prominent impulsive noises. However, this rule cannot remove impulsive noises the amplitude of which is not so large compared with the signal variation. In order to remove such not-so-large impulsive noises, another rule should be considered as well. Suppose that two input signals $s_1(i,j)$ and $s_2(i,j)$, the values of which are the closest to that of $x(i,j)$, are selected among the 8 pixels surrounding $x(i,j)$ as shown in Fig. 9, then the absolute difference between $x(i,j)$ and these two inputs

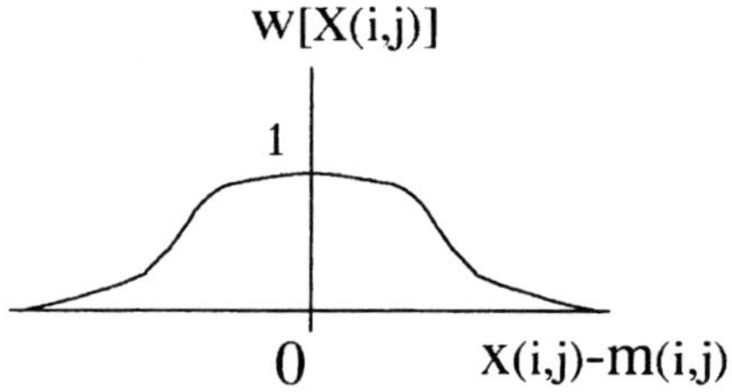

Fig. 8. The value of $w[X(i,j)]$ as a function of $x(i,j) - m(i,j)$.

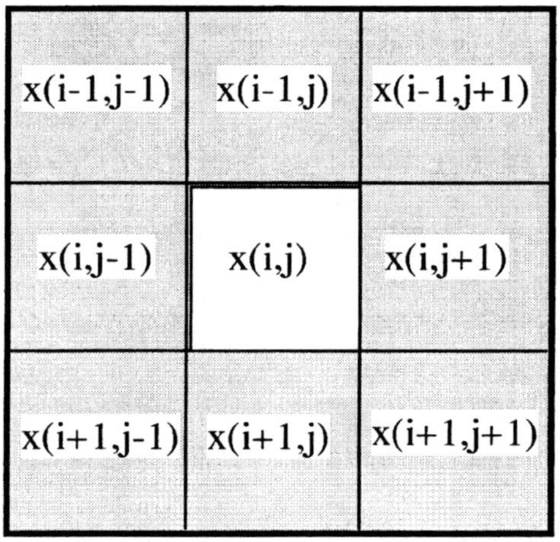

Fig. 9. The shaded pixels are the surrounding 8 pixels of $x(i,j)$.

are obtained as a and b respectively, i.e.:

$$a = |x(i,j) - s_1(i,j)|,$$
$$b = |x(i,j) - s_2(i,j)|.$$

Further, let $v(i,j)$ denote the average of a and b, i.e. $v(i,j) = \frac{a+b}{2}$.

Rule 4: if $v(i,j)$ is large
then an impulse noise is assumed to exist at the pixel (i,j)
else no impulse noise is assumed to exist.

Rule 4 takes the isolation of impulsive noises into consideration, in order to separate the impulsive noise from the fine components in images. For example, suppose that an image contains very fine components such as thin but strong line components, the width of which is just one pixel but the amplitude is large compared with the background. When $x(i,j)$ is located on the line with no impulsive noise, the output of the median filter $m(i,j)$ takes a value equal to one of the pixels in the background, thus the signal difference between $x(i,j)$, which takes a value of the line component, and $m(i,j)$ becomes large. Here, if only Rule 3 is applied, an impulsive noise is assumed to exist on the pixel because $|x(i,j) - m(i,j)|$ is large. However, by adding Rule 4, no impulsive noise is assumed to exist, since the value $v(i,j)$ is small in this case. Using both Rule 3 and Rule 4, a system that can judge that there is no impulsive noise at the pixel can be realized.

Taking both Rule 3 and 4 into consideration, $w[X(i,j)]$ becomes a two-dimensional nonlinear function of $|x(i,j) - m(i,j)|$ and $v(i,j)$, as shown in Fig. 10. Here, we do not have to know how the rule should be, but just have to know what kind of local characteristics of the image should be considered to realize the rule. The rule is automatically designed by training as described in Section 2.2.

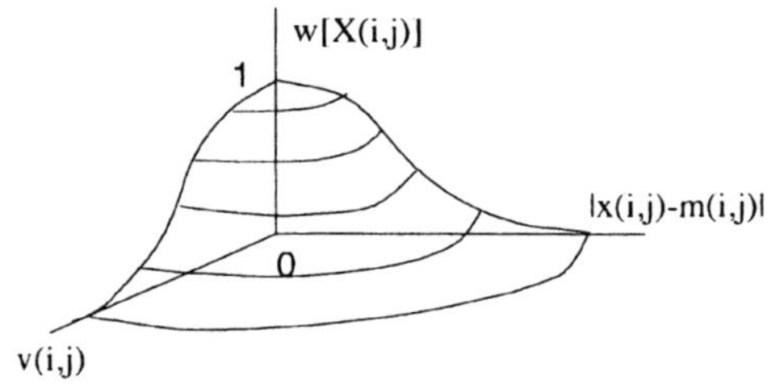

Fig. 10. The value of $w[X(i,j)]$ on the basis of Rule 3 and 4.

The input-output relationship (19) corresponds to a linear case as (11), because $g(X(i,j))$ can be replaced by $x(i,j) - m(i,j)$ and $h(X(i,j))$ by $m(i,j)$. Thus, the value $w[X(i,j)]$ is directly obtained from (13) as:

$$w_{pq} = \frac{\sum_{(i,j)\in K_{pq}} (x(i,j) - m(i,j)) \cdot (d(i,j) - m(i,j))}{\sum_{(i,j)\in K_{pq}} (x(i,j) - m(i,j))^2}, \tag{20}$$

where K_{pq} denotes the set of pixels (i,j) which satisfy the condition that $|x(i,j) - m(i,j)|$ is involved in the p-th region and $v(i,j)$ is in the q-th region in step-like approximation. The summation is taken only for the pixels which satisfy the condition for every combination of p and q.

Fig. 11 shows examples of processing an image with impulsive noises by the fuzzy rule-based system. The original image to be processed and the training image are the same as Fig. 6(a) and (b), respectively. Fig. 11(a) is the input image, the sum of the original image and impulsive noises, the occurrence rate of which is 11% and the value of which takes Gaussian distribution with zero mean and standard deviation 200. Fig. 11(b) is the output of a median filter; (c) is the output of (19) when the value $w[X(i,j)]$ is controlled

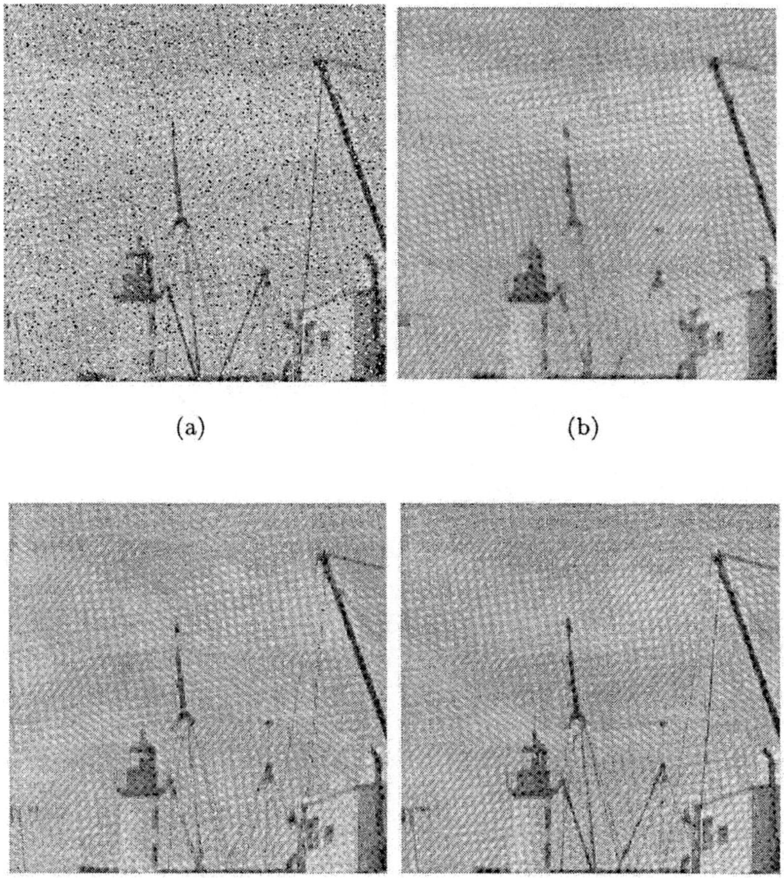

(a) (b)

(c) (d)

Fig. 11. Results of removing additive impulsive noise by the fuzzy rule-based filter and other filters: (a) = noisy input image; (b) = output a median filter (MSE = 64); (c) = output of a crisply controlled median filter (MSE = 40); (d) = output of the fuzzy rule-based filter (MSE = 12).

crisply to take a value zero or one by a certain threshold for $|m(i,j) - x(i,j)|$ (in the experiments this threshold is 40); (d) is the output of the fuzzy rule based system in which $w[X(i,j)]$ is expressed as a two-dimensional nonlinear function of $|m(i,j) - x(i,j)|$ and $v(i,j)$. We can see that the fuzzy rule-based system can remove the noise adequately while keeping the fine structures of the image unchanged. Fig. 12 shows the weight function w_{pq} obtained by training. We can see that the form of this function represents the Rules 3 and 4, since it looks like Fig. 10.

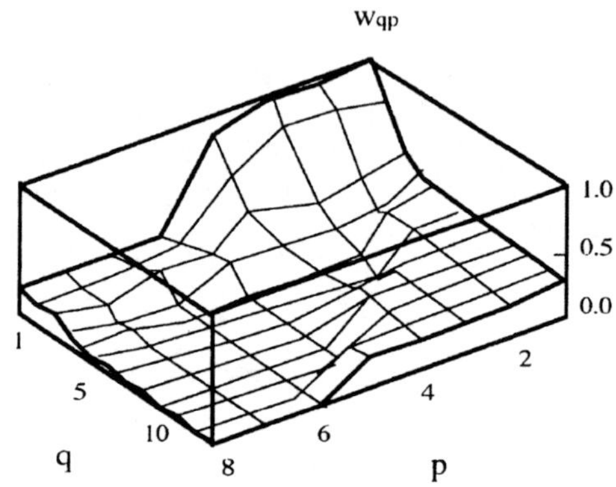

Fig. 12. The weight function w_{pq} obtained by training in the fuzzy median filter.

4 Fuzzy rule-based processing for edge extraction

4.1 Fundamental idea

Edges can usually be obtained by extracting large-amplitude parts of signal changes in adjacent pixels; if the signal change is large at the pixel (i,j) an edge is supposed to exist there, but if small, an edge is not. Here, the problem is how to distinguish large signal differences from small ones. Because of the ambiguity of image characteristics, the threshold to distinguish it is hard to obtain. Moreover, the threshold should be changed depending on some local characteristics of the image. For instance, when a weak edge exists in a smooth area, the threshold should be small. However, in processing a rough area, the threshold should be large. Therefore, a fuzzy rule-based system should be used.

Suppose that the value of the signal change at the pixel (i,j) is represented as $u(i,j)$, the output of the edge extracting system $y(i,j)$ can be expressed as:

$$y(i,j) = F[u(i,j), X(i,j)], \tag{21}$$

where F is a binary function taking a value either 0 or 1 ($F[\cdot,\cdot] = 1$ means an edge exists at pixel (i,j); $F[\cdot,\cdot] = 0$ means an edge does not exist), $X(i,j)$ represents a set of input image signals around the pixel (i,j), and $y(i,j)$ is determined from the values of $u(i,j)$ and the $X(i,j)$. If edges can be definitely determined from the value $u(i,j)$, $y(i,j)$ can be a function of only $u(i,j)$ as illustrated in Fig. 13. However, since image signals are nonstation-

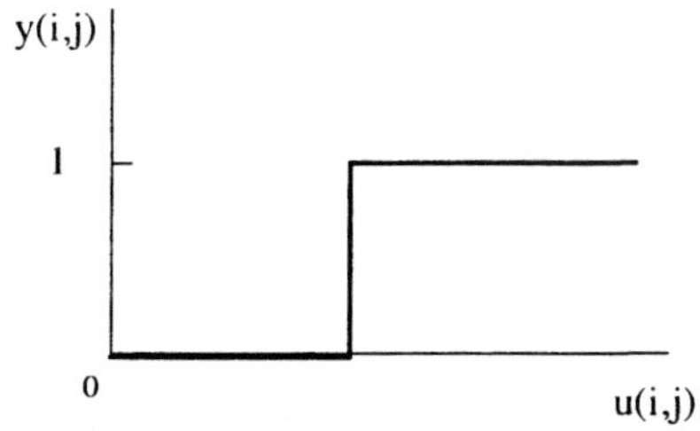

Fig. 13. The signal value $y(i,j)$ of the edge image as a function of the signal change $u(i,j)$ when the edges are definite.

ary, the threshold in Fig. 13 changes depending on other local characteristics in $X(i,j)$. Here, a parameter $w(i,j)$ is introduced indicating to what extent the pixel (i,j) is considered to be an edge point. The value $w(i,j)$ takes a continuous value from 0 to 1; the pixel is considered to be an edge point if the value $w(i,j)$ is large. By cutting the value $w(i,j)$ with a threshold, binary edge images as $y(i,j)$ are obtained. As will be shown in Section 4.2, the parameter $w(i,j)$ is obtained from fuzzy approximate reasoning from various local characteristics around the pixel (i,j) including $u(i,j)$, and accordingly, the $w(i,j)$ is expressed as a nonlinear function of these local characteristics.

4.2 Fuzzy rule-based edge extraction using multiscale edge images

In order to overcome the problem of nonstationarity, multi-scaled analysis attracted attention in edge detection recently. In this analysis, an image is processed by multiple differential operators with different window sizes to obtain multiscale edges. When the window size is large, coarse edges are obtained, which represent large structures of the image objects but cannot represent fine structures. On the other hand, when the window size is small, fine edges which contain both the fine structures and noisy components are obtained. By combining these multiscale edges, we can make a more precise judgement on the edges than using monoscale edges. Therefore, such multiscale edge images, i.e. the outputs of multiscale differential operators, can be the local characteristics which are effective to determine the value $w(i,j)$ for precise edge extraction [6].

The value $w(i,j)$ can be determined from the multiscale edge images by fuzzy rules such as the following:

Rule 5: if small-scale edge is weak and large-scale edge is weak
then $w(i,j)$ is small;
if small-scale edge is strong and large-scale edge is strong
then $w(i,j)$ is large;
else $w(i,j)$ is medium.

Here, we do not have to know the exact form of the rules as mentioned in section 2.2. The parameter $w(i,j)$ is expressed as a continuous nonlinear function of the small and large scale edge images. The signal difference $u(i,j)$ corresponds to the small-scale edge image here. Since it is not clear how small or how large the window size should be for the small-scale and the large-scale edge images, a filter bank of several differential operators with different window sizes, such as 3×3, 5×5 and 7×7, is prepared. The schematic diagram of this system is shown in Fig. 14.

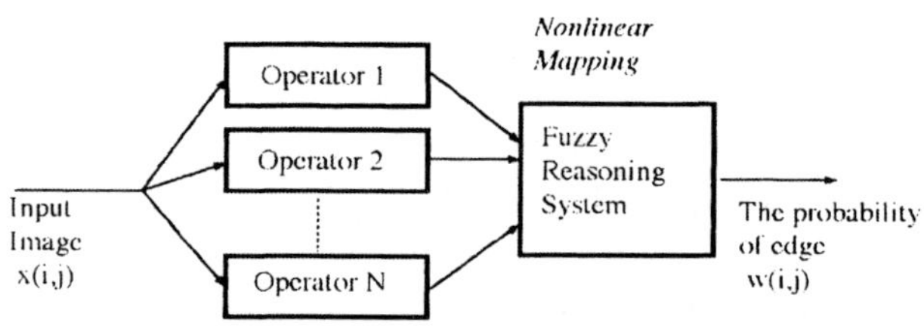

Fig. 14. Schematic diagram of the fuzzy edge-extracting system using multi-scale edge images.

The function $w(i,j)$ is approximated by a step-like function which is optimized, so that the mean square error between the system output $w(i,j)$ and the desired edge image $d(i,j)$ for some training image $x(i,j)$ be the minimum. Here, the desired edge image is composed of binary signals 0 and 1; if the pixel (i,j) is an edge point, $d(i,j)$ takes a value 1, but if the pixel is not, $d(i,j)$ takes a value 0.

Suppose that $w(i,j)$ is denoted as w_{pq} when $o_1(i,j)$ – the output of Operator 1 – is in the p-th divided region and $o_2(i,j)$ – the output of Operator 2 – is in the q-th divided region. The system output $w(i,j)$ is expressed as:

$$w(i,j) = \sum_{p=1}^{P} \sum_{q=1}^{Q} c_{ijpq} w_{pq}, \tag{22}$$

where

$$c_{ijpq} = \begin{cases} 1 & \text{if } o_1(i,j) \text{ is in the } p\text{-th region} \\ & \text{and } o_2(i,j) \text{ is in the } q\text{-th region}\,. \\ 0 & \text{else} \end{cases}$$

The mean square error between $w(i,j)$ and $d(i,j)$ is expressed as:

$$E = \mathrm{E}[(w(i,j) - d(i,j))^2] = \mathrm{E}[(\sum_p \sum_q c_{ijpq} w_{pq} - d(i,j))^2]. \quad (23)$$

Finally w_{pq}, which minimizes E, is obtained from $\frac{\partial E}{\partial w_{pq}} = 0$ as follows:

$$w_{pq} = E_{pq}[(d(i,j)]. \quad (24)$$

Here, $E_{pq}[d(i,j)]$ denotes the average of $d(i,j)$ only on the condition that $o_1(i,j)$ and $o_2(i,j)$ are in the (p,q)-th region. This explanation is only done for the Operators 1 and 2, but this method can easily be extended to more dimensions with more differential operators.

4.3 How to get a binary edge image

The parameter $w(i,j)$ takes continuous values from 0 to 1. The definite binary edge image $y(i,j)$ can be obtained by reducing this $w(i,j)$ to 0 and 1 by a threshold. For instance, if $w(i,j)$ is expressed as Fig. 15(a), the final edge image can be obtained by separating the feature space nonlinearly as illustrated in Fig. 15(b) (the right side of the solid curve is judged as the edge part and the left side is as the non-edge part). For reference, the separation of the space when only the output of the small-scale differential operator $o_1(i,j)$ is considered is shown by a dotted straight line (here, the right side of the dotted line is judged as the edge part and the left part is as the non-edge part). We can see that the fuzzy rule-based multiscale system can realize an appropriate control of the threshold for separating the small-scale output $o_1(i,j)$ depending on the value of the large-scale output $o_2(i,j)$, because the value of $o_1(i,j)$, which makes judgement about edginess, is changed depending on the value of $o_2(i,j)$.

Moreover, using the fact that the edges usually connect to each other, edge tracking can be performed in order to get edges more precisely as follows.

First, divide the amplitude of the output into three parts using two thresholds T_1 and T_2 ($T_1 > T_2$). Then make a decision by the following algorithm:

Rule 6: if $w(i,j) > T_1$
then decide the pixel (i,j) as an edge point;
if $w(i,j) \leq T_2$
then decide the pixel (i,j) as a non-edge point;
if $T_1 \geq w(i,j) > T_2$ and the pixel (i,j) is connected to an edge point
then decide the pixel (i,j) as an edge point.

4.4 Computer simulations

Computer simulations are performed using Robinson's operator [13] as the differential operator, since it takes the direction of the edge into consideration.

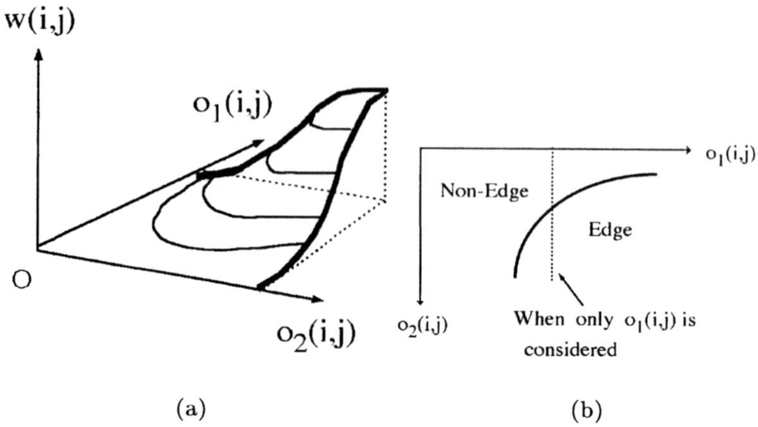

Fig. 15. How to get a binary edge image: (a) = example of the value $w(i,j)$ as a function of two feature parameters $o_1(i,j)$ and $o_2(i,j)$; (b) = nonlinear separation of the feature space.

The Robinson's operator gives the gradient in four directions, a horizontal one, a vertical one and two slanting ones in 45° and 135°, using the following eight 3×3 matrices:

$$\begin{pmatrix} 1 & 2 & 1 \\ 0 & 0 & 0 \\ -1 & -2 & -1 \end{pmatrix} \quad \begin{pmatrix} -1 & 0 & 1 \\ -2 & 0 & 2 \\ -1 & 0 & 1 \end{pmatrix} \quad \begin{pmatrix} 0 & 1 & 2 \\ -1 & 0 & 1 \\ -2 & -1 & 0 \end{pmatrix} \quad \begin{pmatrix} 2 & 1 & 0 \\ 1 & 0 & -1 \\ 0 & -1 & -2 \end{pmatrix}$$
$$\begin{pmatrix} -1 & -2 & -1 \\ 0 & 0 & 0 \\ 1 & 2 & 1 \end{pmatrix} \quad \begin{pmatrix} 1 & 0 & -1 \\ 2 & 0 & -2 \\ 1 & 0 & -1 \end{pmatrix} \quad \begin{pmatrix} 0 & -1 & -2 \\ 1 & 0 & -1 \\ 2 & 1 & 0 \end{pmatrix} \quad \begin{pmatrix} -2 & -1 & 0 \\ -1 & 0 & 1 \\ 0 & 1 & 2 \end{pmatrix}.$$

Each of these matrices is multiplied to the 3×3 input image signal around each pixel (i,j), i.e. if:

$$G = \begin{pmatrix} g_{-1,-1} & g_{-1,0} & g_{-1,1} \\ g_{0,-1} & g_{0,0} & g_{0,1} \\ g_{1,-1} & g_{1,0} & g_{1,1} \end{pmatrix},$$

denotes such a matrix, we obtain:

$$Z_{ij} = \sum_{k=-1}^{1} \sum_{m=-1}^{1} g_{k,m} \cdot x(i-k, j-m). \tag{25}$$

The maximum amplitude (i.e. the maximum absolute value) in these Z_{ij}'s for the 8 matrices is taken as the output of the operator. Here, since the amplitude is taken, only the upper 4 matrices are used.

Three differential operators are used in the filter bank. The first one is sized 3×3, and corresponds to the conventional Robinson's operator (see above). The second is sized 7×7, which corresponds to an extension of the Robinson's operator to a 7×7 window, as follows:

$$\begin{pmatrix} 1 & 1 & 1 & 1 & 1 & 1 & 1 \\ 1 & 1 & 1 & 1 & 1 & 1 & 1 \\ 1 & 1 & 1 & 2 & 1 & 1 & 1 \\ 0 & 0 & 0 & 0 & 0 & 0 & 0 \\ -1 & -1 & -1 & -2 & -1 & -1 & -1 \\ -1 & -1 & -1 & -1 & -1 & -1 & -1 \\ -1 & -1 & -1 & -1 & -1 & -1 & -1 \end{pmatrix} \begin{pmatrix} 1 & 1 & 1 & 0 & -1 & -1 & -1 \\ 1 & 1 & 1 & 0 & -1 & -1 & -1 \\ 1 & 1 & 1 & 0 & -1 & -1 & -1 \\ 1 & 1 & 2 & 0 & -2 & -1 & -1 \\ 1 & 1 & 1 & 0 & -1 & -1 & -1 \\ 1 & 1 & 1 & 0 & -1 & -1 & -1 \\ 1 & 1 & 1 & 0 & -1 & -1 & -1 \end{pmatrix}$$

$$\begin{pmatrix} 0 & 1 & 1 & 1 & 1 & 1 & 1 \\ -1 & 0 & 1 & 1 & 1 & 1 & 1 \\ -1 & -1 & 0 & 1 & 2 & 1 & 1 \\ -1 & -1 & -1 & 0 & 1 & 1 & 1 \\ -1 & -1 & -2 & -1 & 0 & 1 & 1 \\ -1 & -1 & -1 & -1 & -1 & 0 & 1 \\ -1 & -1 & -1 & -1 & -1 & -1 & 0 \end{pmatrix} \begin{pmatrix} 1 & 1 & 1 & 1 & 1 & 1 & 0 \\ 1 & 1 & 1 & 1 & 1 & 0 & -1 \\ 1 & 1 & 2 & 1 & 0 & -1 & -1 \\ 1 & 1 & 1 & 0 & -1 & -1 & -1 \\ 1 & 1 & 0 & -1 & -2 & -1 & -1 \\ 1 & 0 & -1 & -1 & -1 & -1 & -1 \\ 0 & -1 & -1 & -1 & -1 & -1 & -1 \end{pmatrix}.$$

The third differential operator is again a larger one. Since the window larger than 7×7 consumes a lot of computation time, a one-dimensional derivative operator sized 11 is used as the third one for simplicity. The output of this operator is expressed as follows:

$$o_3(i,j) = |\sum_{k=1}^{5} z(k) - \sum_{k=1}^{5} z(-k)|. \tag{26}$$

Here, $z(k)$ and $z(-k)$ are the values of the input image $x(i,j)$ which are aligned perpendicular to the direction of the edge detected by the 3×3 operator as shown in Fig. 16. In this case, the number of the pixels considered in smoothing is reduced, but wider regions perpendicular to the edge can be considered.

Fig. 17 shows computer simulations of the edge detecting system for a test image. Fig. 17(a) is the input image. Here two types of images are used for training: Fig. 17(b) is the training image No.1 with (c) as the desired edge image (the desired edge image is made by processing an image like Fig. 17(b) without the noisy component by the 3×3 Robinson's operator, and selecting the pixels where the output exceeds a threshold as the edge part), and (d) is the training image No.2 with (e) as the desired edge image (this image is made by processing Fig. 17(d) itself by the 3×3 Robinson's operator, and selecting the pixels with large-amplitude output). Fig. 17(f),(g),(h) are the results of edge extraction by differential operators with window sized 3×3, window sized 7×7, and the one-dimensional window sized 11 respectively. We can see that if the window size is small, the noisy components are also extracted

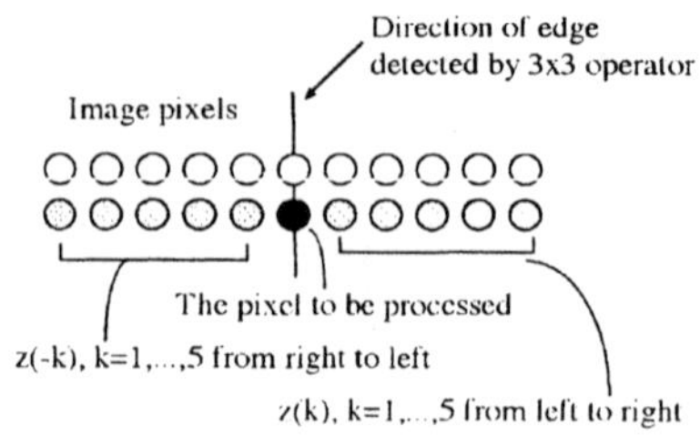

Fig. 16. Pixels used in the one-dimensional operator. The shaded pixels are used as $z(k)$ and $z(-k)$.

as edges, but if the window size is large, the edges around fine structures such as thin lines are missed. Fig. 17(i) is the output of the proposed fuzzy rule-based system for multiscale edges. We can see that the edges around fine structure can be extracted, while suppressing noisy components. Here two-level thresholding is used to get the binary edge image.

Fig. 18 shows the output for a natural image: (a) is the input image, (b) and (c) are the results of edge extraction using a single derivative operator, sized 3×3 and 7×7 respectively, and (d) is the result of the proposed system. Fig. 18(e) is the training image, and the desired edge image for (e) is depicted in Fig. 18(f) (this image is made by first processing (e) by the 3×3 Robinson's operator, cutting the output with a threshold, and then modifying the output with a graphic tool in order to erase some undesirable components and to add some necessary edge lines). Edge tracking is performed to get the binary edge image in (b),(c) and (d). We can see the background waves are much more suppressed in (d), while keeping the edge lines clear.

5 Concluding remarks

An image processing technique based on fuzzy rules is introduced. This system is created using our knowledge about image processing which is represented as fuzzy rules and is automatically designed by training. Training image data, the characteristics of which are supposed to be close to the image to be processed, are used here. In this chapter, the application of this system to noise removal and edge extraction is presented. The methodology to represent fuzzy rules as a nonlinear function for optimization can be applied to other signal processing and control problems as well. In optimizing the nonlinear function, any other optimizing method can be applied. However, here step-like approximation is adopted for its simplicity and for avoiding local minima.

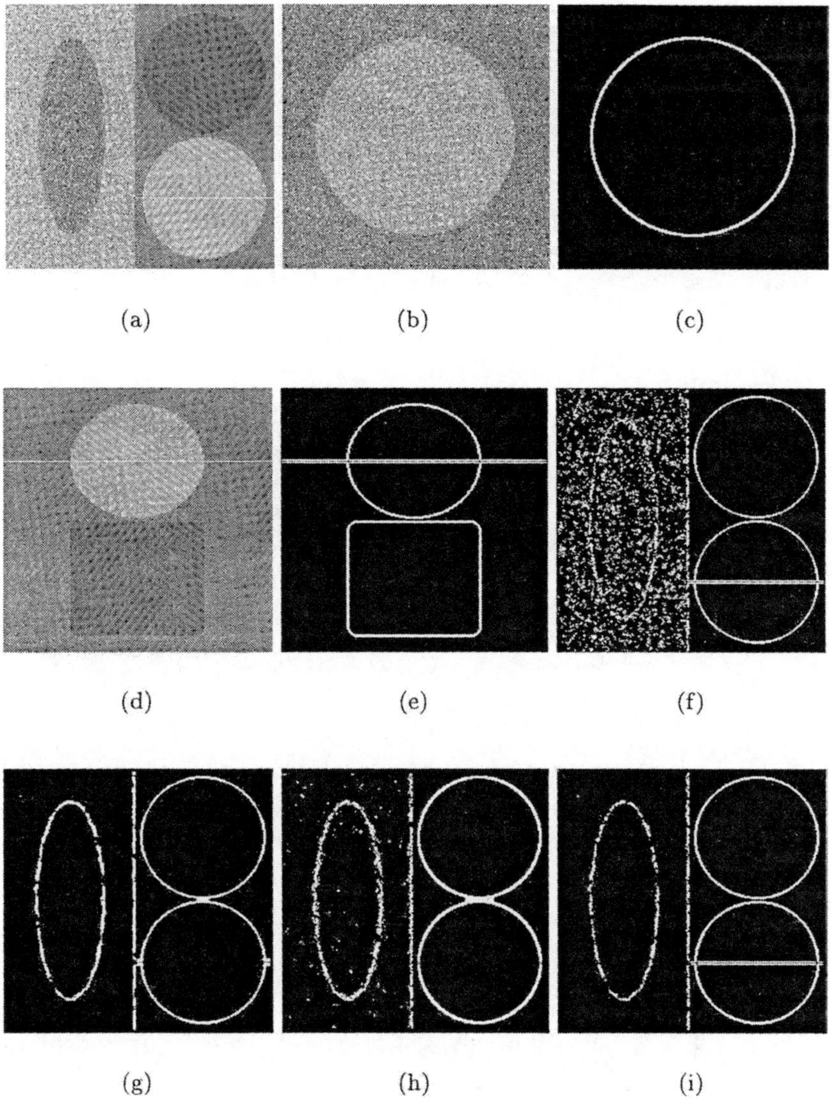

Fig. 17. Results of edge detection for a test image; see Subsection 4.4 for details.

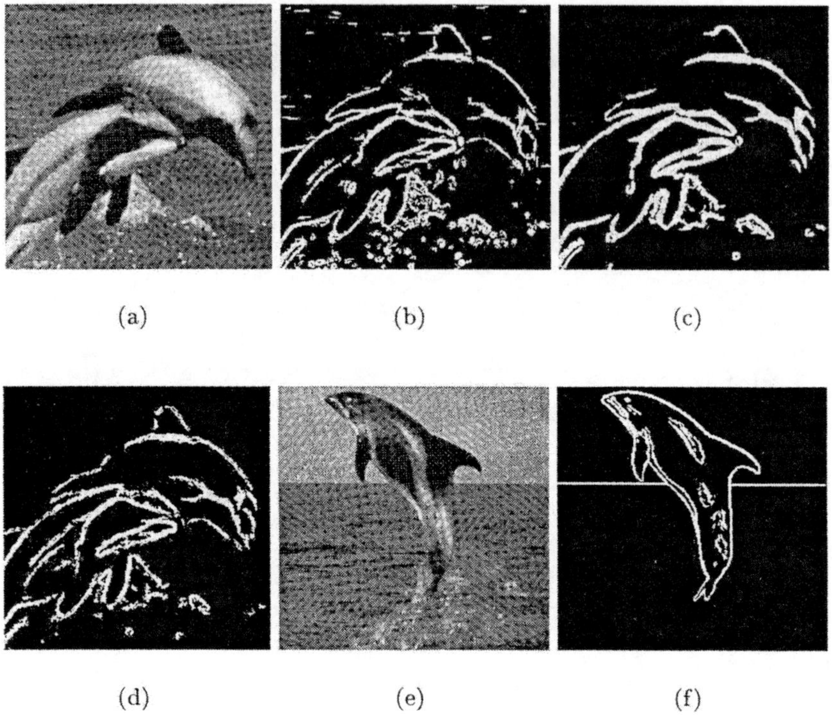

Fig. 18. Results of edge detection for a natural image (images for processing are from Kujira Iruka Daizukan", Heibonsha); see Subsection 4.4 for details.

References

1. Abramatic J.F. and Netravali A.N., *Nonlinear restoration of noisy images*, IEEE Trans. Pattern Anal. & Mach. Intell., Vol. 4, No. 2, pp. 141–149, 1982
2. Abreu E., Lightstone M., Mitra S.K. and Arakawa K., *A new efficient approach for the removal of impulsive noise from highly corrupted images*, IEEE Trans Image Processing, Vol. 5, No.6, pp. 1012–1025, 1996
3. Arakawa K. and Arakawa Y., *A nonlinear digital filter using fuzzy clustering*, in: "Proceedings of IEEE-ICASSP'92", Vol. IV, pp. 309–312, 1992
4. Arakawa K., *Fuzzy rule-based signal processing and its application to image restoration*, IEEE, Journal on Select. Areas in Comm., Vol. 12, No. 9, 1994
5. Arakawa K., *Median filter based on fuzzy rules and its application to image restoration*, Fuzzy Sets and Systems, Vol. 77, pp. 3–13, 1996
6. Arakawa K., *Fuzzy rule-based edge detection using multiscale edge images*, in: "Proceedings of IEEE-ISPACS'98", pp. 204–208, 1998
7. Harashima H., Odajima K., Shishikui Y and Miyakawa H., *e-separating nonlinear digital filter and its application*, Trans. IEICE Japan, Vol. J65-A, No. 4, pp. 297–304, 1982

8. Haykin S., *"Introduction to adaptive filters"*, Macmillan, 1984
9. Homaifar H. and McCormick E., *Simultaneous design of membership functions and rule sets for fuzzy controllers using genetic algorithms*, IEEE Trans. Fuzzy Systems, Vol. 3, No. 2, pp. 129–139, 1995
10. Mizumoto M. and Zimmermann H.-J., *Comparison of fuzzy reasoning methods*, Fuzzy Sets and Systems, Vol. 8, pp. 253–283, 1982
11. Pomalaza-Raez C.A. and McGillem C.D., *An adaptive, nonlinear edge-preserving filter*, IEEE Trans. Acoust. Speech Signal Processing, Vol. 32, No. 3, pp. 571–576, 1984
12. Rajala S.A. and DeFigueiredo R.J., *Adaptive nonlinear image restoration by a modified Kalman filtering approach*, IEEE Trans. Acoust. Speech Signal Processing, Vol. 29, No. 5, pp. 1033–1041, 1981
13. Robinson G.S., *Edge detection by compass gradient masks*, CGIP, Vol. 6, pp. 492–501, 1977
14. Widrow B., McCool J.M., Larimore M.G. and Johnson C.R. Jr., *Adaptive noise canceling: Principles and applications*, Proc. IEEE, Vol. 63, No. 12, pp. 1692–1716, 1975

Chapter 9

Fuzzy Nonlinear Filtering of Color Images: A Survey

Constantin Vertan[1] and Vasile Buzuloiu[2]

[1] Universitatea Politehnica Bucureşti
Image Processing and Analysis Laboratory (LAPI)
P.O. Box 35-57, Bucharest 35, Romania
email: vertan@alpha.imag.pub.ro

[2] Universitatea Politehnica Bucureşti
Image Processing and Analysis Laboratory (LAPI)
P.O. Box 61-73, Bucharest 61, Romania
email: buzuloiu@alpha.imag.pub.ro

Summary. This contribution is intended as a survey of the existing fuzzy (or fuzzy related) filtering techniques for multichannel (and color in particular) images. We propose a classification of all these approaches to color image processing into four categories, based on the importance that fuzzy theory receives during the filter design: *crude fuzzy*, *fuzzy paradigm based*, *fuzzy aggregative* and *fuzzy inferential*. These categories are not necessarily mutually exclusive, and their boundaries can also be fuzzy. We will show how the perceptual notion of JND (Just Noticeable Difference) can provide a fuzzy-like approach to color correctness evaluation.

1 Introduction

The term "multichannel (vector valued, multivariate) image" means that every sample of the image signal is characterized by a vector (set); each item of this set is called a component of the sample (or observation). The multichannel signal and image processing has recently arisen as a must, following the observation that the simple "stack-of-scalars" model of the multichannel sample is not appropriate. In particular, the independent component processing suggested by the mentioned approach fails to consider the existing correlation between the signal components and can produce artifacts (false colors, in the case of color images [2])[1].

Since the inter-component correlation seemed to be responsible for producing artifacts through independent component processing, an idea that

[1] We can argue that the example from [2] is produced for an artificial, highly saturated color image. The test image consists of two vertical, green and red strips; after a median marginal filtering a yellow line appears at the separation of the color regions. Generally, this is not the case for natural images.

appeared very soon was to remove this dependency using classical decorrelation techniques, such as the Karhunen-Loève transform [20]. This approach is not extensively used, due to some problems associated with the computational complexity of the decorrelation transform and its strong dependencies on images from a certain class. Furthermore, the re-correlation procedure that concludes the processing is done according to the inverse of the initial decorrelation, which implies the assumption that the statistical properties of the image are the same, before and after filtering. For such reasons, a growing attention has been devoted to vector processing.

1.1 Filtering color images

The common definition accepted for the filtering operation is the removal (or reduction) of noise artifacts superimposed onto the image, while preserving the contrast and contours of its objects.

The most common filtering method for both scalar and multichannel images is the sliding (or moving) window technique. A planar shape (subsequently called filtering mask) scans the entire bidimensional structure; in each position it selects some pixel values which will be combined to yield the new value of the same spatial location in the filtered image. One of the most general processing paradigms is the weighted linear combination of either the selected values, or of their order statistics. The use of the linear combination of pixel values is equivalent to a frequency domain filtering [28]; this approach is proven to be effective only if the weights are modified at each spatial location according to the specific (local) vector values. Thus, the filtering structure is adaptive; but such a filter is no longer linear.

The use of the order statistics produces a class of nonlinear, ordering based filters, known as L-filters [20]; they proved to be very effective and versatile in the processing of scalar images. Their extension to the case of multichannel images is limited by the difficulty of introducing a simple, topology-preserving ordering relation for vectors [3]. However, the median statistics has been widely used and there are several multichannel extensions, based on sub-ordering principles [24], which all start from the seminal paper that introduced the Vector Median Filtering (VMF) [2].

Either way, it is clear that the filters we are dealing with are nonlinear (intrinsic, as a result of their definition, or as a result of the adaptation procedure); the simple, linear filters, cannot achieve reasonable performances in the presence of noise other than additive and Gaussian distributed (such as the "long tailed" distributed noise or the impulsive "salt and pepper" noise).

In the case of the multichannel (or color) images, the use of ordering is less immediate, so it is reasonable to focus on the adaptive (locally linear) filtering. Assuming that each pixel value is characterized by a p-dimensional vector, $\boldsymbol{x}_i = (x_{i1}, x_{i2}, ..., x_{ip})$ and that the filtering mask selects n vectors, $\boldsymbol{x}_1, \boldsymbol{x}_2, ..., \boldsymbol{x}_n$, associated to the pixels within the mask, then the local operation which produces the outcome $\boldsymbol{y}$ is characterized (at every spatial location within the image) by:

$$\boldsymbol{y} = \sum_{j=1}^{n} w_j \boldsymbol{x}_j \tag{1}$$

The weighting factors w_j in (1) are usually positive scalars which have to sum to 1 (in order to perform a smoothing, uniformity enhancing filtering operation [8], [24]):

$$\sum_{j=1}^{n} w_j = 1 \tag{2}$$

The choice of the weighting factors is done according to the distribution in the sample space of the selected vectors $\boldsymbol{x}_i$; the basic idea is to assign weights that are decreasing with respect to the distance from each noise affected vector to the desired correct value. We will emphasize in this contribution several methods of weight determination, more or less influenced by fuzzy logic theory.

1.2 Fuzzy logic

Fuzzy logic was introduced in the late '60 [38] as an attempt to deal with uncertainty and indetermination inherent in the descriptions of the real world. Some classical examples concern the interpretation of the concepts of a person's height or weight and the difficulty of the adaptation of the classical binary logic to a gradual reality [38], [25].

A fuzzy set is just a function that maps each element of the problem's universe into a positive, subunitary number.

It is worthy to add to this definition a remark from [5]. According to the definition, each real function that maps the universe into the $[0, 1]$ interval is a fuzzy set. Although correct from a formal point of view, there are functions that satisfy this constraint and cannot be interpreted as a realization of a conceptual fuzzy set, i.e. these functions can be fuzzy sets, but they actually become fuzzy sets if and only if they fit a semantically plausible description for the properties of the objects within the universe.

Digital images are mappings of natural scenes (sampled and quantized slices of the 3-dimensional reality) and thus they embed an important amount of uncertainty, in both value and location (spatial support). This uncertainty is due to the imprecise nature of pixel values[2] and to the indetermination existing along the border regions of the image.

We propose a classification of the fuzzy approaches to color image processing into four categories that are differentiated according to the importance of the fuzzy logic principles used during the filter design: *crude fuzzy*, *fuzzy*

[2] In a complex, natural scene, most likely there is no perceivable difference between the gray levels 99 and 100, or the colors – expressed as RGB triples – (200,175,150) and (200,175,151).

paradigm based, *fuzzy aggregative* and *fuzzy inferential* (see Fig. 1). Each of these classes will be described, and we will show how existing nonlinear color filters fit into the proposed categories.

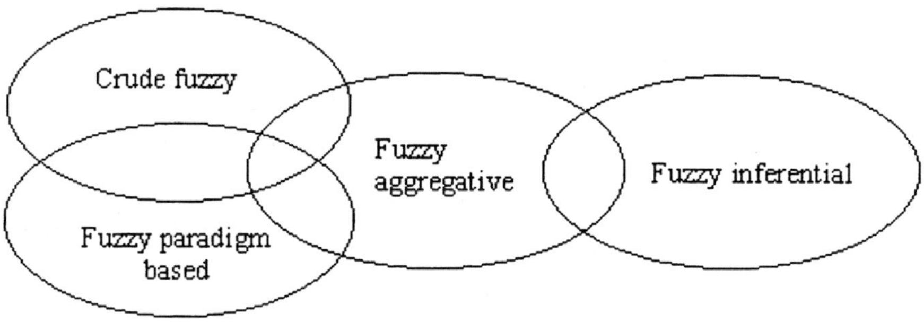

Fig. 1. The proposed 4-classes classification of the fuzzy approach to nonlinear color image filtering

2 Crude or pseudo–fuzzy approaches

The crude or pseudo–fuzzy approach consists simply of determining some weights w_i that satisfy (2) and are "fuzzy numbers", that is $w_i \in [0,1]$. This normalization is achieved in two steps: for each selected vector $\boldsymbol{x}_i$ some positive scalar a_i is computed (according to some rules reflecting the spatial distribution of the $\boldsymbol{x}_i$ vectors in the $\mathbb{R}^p$ samples space), and then each a_i coefficient is normalized to their sum:

$$w_i = \frac{a_i}{\sum_{j=1}^{n} a_j} \tag{3}$$

It is clear that the weights w_i computed according to (3) satisfy (2) and are within $[0,1]$. This type of filtering uses no fuzzy rules and the actual weights are computed based on a "membership function strenghts" approach [24]. This approach is extensively used for several classes of filters, their particular nature being given by the choice of a specific function ("membership function") that maps some statistical measure of the vectors (colors) within the filtering window.

Two main statistical measures are used in order to characterize the position of a color vector with respect to a set of color vectors, namely magnitude-based measures and angular-based measures. The use of magnitude-based measures yields various filter classes: the so-called Multichannel Distance Filters (MDF) [12], Adaptive Nonlinear Filters (ANL) [6] or Distance Dependent Multichannel Filters (DDMF) [13]. If the angular measures are used (arguing that angle is specific to the vectors), the filter names embed the directional attribute, such as the Basic Vector Directional Filter (BVDF) [31].

The functions according to which the weight is determined have to be monotonic decreasing, i.e. assigning more important weights to the vectors that are closer to the center of the vector cluster. The polynomial and exponential approaches are the most popular ones. The polynomial approach [12], [13] is based on the a_i coefficients computed according to (4):

$$a_i = d_i^{-r} \tag{4}$$

where d_i is the statistical measure associated to the color vector $\boldsymbol{x}_i$. The d_i measure used is the aggregate Euclidean distance (the sum of Euclidean distances from the current sample $\boldsymbol{x}_i$ to all the other samples within the filtering window, given by (5)), or the distance to some fixed point (marginal median, as in the example presented in Fig. 2(c)) [12], or the sum of distances to some fixed points (marginal median, average, current vector) [13].

$$d_i = \sum_{j=1}^{n} (\boldsymbol{x}_i - \boldsymbol{x}_j)(\boldsymbol{x}_i - \boldsymbol{x}_j)^T \tag{5}$$

The exponential approach mainly proposes a negative exponential (6) or sigmoidal (7) function:

$$a_i = \exp\left(-\frac{d_i \ln \alpha}{\beta d_{\max}}\right) \tag{6}$$

$$a_i = (1 + \exp(-d_i))^{-r} \tag{7}$$

The DDMF4 [13] uses an aggregate Euclidean distance, and the function given in (6) (a DDMF4 filtered image is presented in Fig. 2(d)). The FVDF (Fuzzy Vector Directional Filter) [21] uses the sum of angles between vectors (given in (8)) as a measure of spatial distribution, and the sigmoidal function 7) (a FVDF filtered image is presented in Fig. 3(a)):

$$d_i = \sum_{j=1}^{n} \widehat{\boldsymbol{x}_i \boldsymbol{x}_j} \tag{8}$$

The trimming factors (the power r, the constants α, β and $d_{\max}$) are computed according to experience, empiric deduction and extensive testing ($\alpha = 2$, $\beta = 0.05$ in [13]), specific data constraints ($d_{\max}$, which equals the maximum inter-color distance, in [13]) or by adaptation. The power r is connected to the underlying distribution of the noise superimposed on the image; tests showed that the best results are obtained with $r = 1$ for uniform distributed noise, $r = 0$ for Gaussian noise and $r = -2$ for any "long tailed" distributed noise.

Of course, we can finally accept that the filters labeled as *crude fuzzy* measure, in some way, the membership of each color vector into the set "correct filter output"; otherwise these filters cannot be considered more fuzzy than any other adaptive filter.

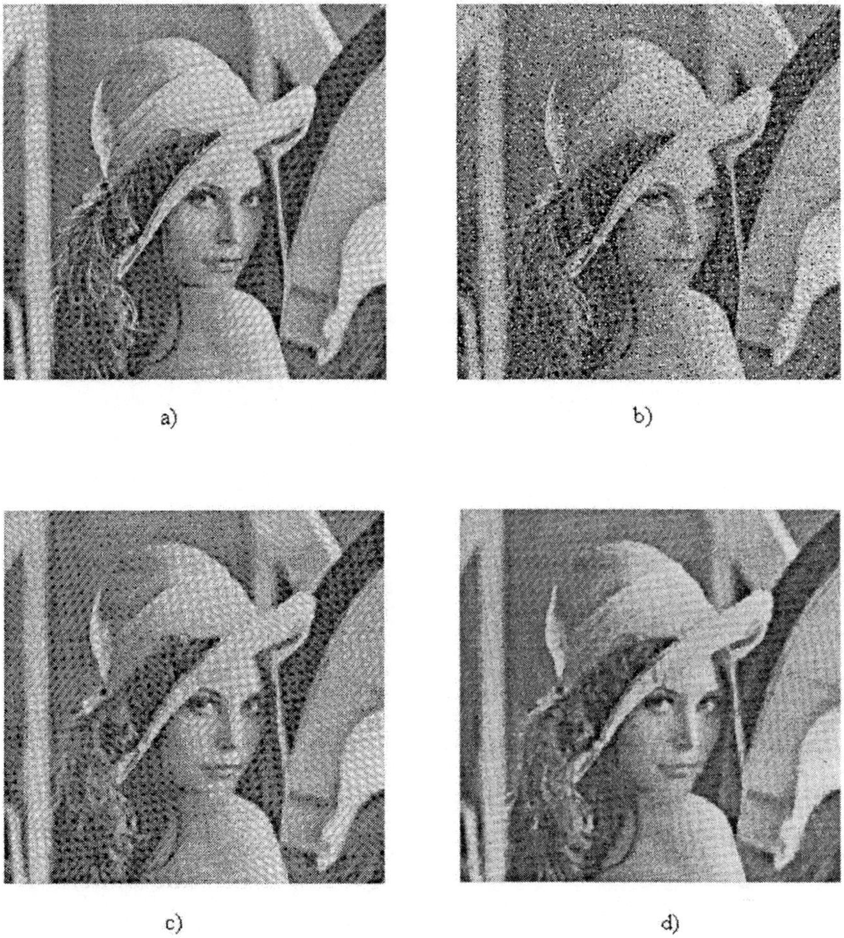

Fig. 2. (a) Original true color (8 bits per color component) test image "Lena". (b) Impulsive noise degraded image from figure (a); 10 % of the pixels in each color component are replaced by extreme values; the noise channels are not correlated (SNR=20.36 dB). (c) MDF filtered image from figure (b); the filter coefficients are computed according to (4) with $r = 2$ (SNR=48.27 dB). (d) DDMF filtered image from figure (b); the filter coefficients are computed according to (6) with $\alpha = 2$, $\beta = 0.05$ and $d_{max} = 255\sqrt{3}$ (SNR=47.94 dB).

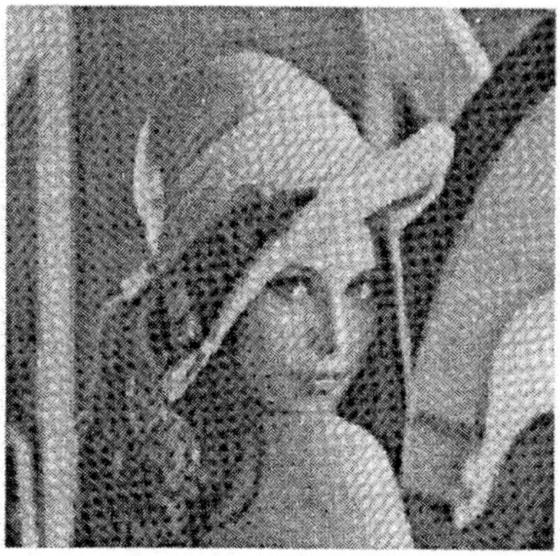

a)

b)

c)

d)

Fig. 3. (a) FVDF filtered image from Fig. 2(b) (SNR=45.05 dB). (b) Median-like cluster filtering of the image from Fig. 2(b); the clustering is performed according to the possibilistic model (described by (12) (SNR=47.36 dB). (c) Aggregative median filtering of the image from Fig. 2 (b); the filter aggregates the influences of both directional and magnitude oriented processing by (15) with $\gamma = 0.75$ (SNR=45.39 dB); (d) Median-like filtering of the image from Fig. 2(b) by the use of perceptual information; the color are represented in the HSI color space and fuzzy rules are used for a soft decision regarding the relative importance of the color components (SNR=45.58 dB).

3 Fuzzy paradigm based filters

The aforementioned methods of composing the crude fuzzy weights based on distances or angles (i.e. relative positions of the vectors) are supposed to follow a linguistic description of an outlier with respect to a given vector set. The linear combination of vectors is an estimate of the undegraded (correct) vector at the given location and thus, the farther a vector lies from this correct value, the smaller its weighting factor should be.

Regardless of the specific expression of the weighting coefficients attached to the color vectors currently selected by the filtering window, a certain pattern of behavior can be easily noticed: the weights are smaller when the color vectors are more marginal with respect to the general cluster of colors. This association hides, at the limit, the sifting of the selected color vectors, which rejects the outliers (and this description also matches the partial ordering method [3], also known in statistics as the "potato peeling"). This idea is the starting point of the nearest-neighbor and adaptive-neighborhood filtering. The nearest-neighbor filters [10], [22] select color vectors according to some locally computed distance maps. The adaptive-neighborhood filtering [9] aims at determining a filtering window for each pixel of the image, by a process which is very similar to the region growing. Two main goals are simultaneously achieved: an improved boundary contrast preservation and an increased region smoothing performance.

The two mentioned approaches are crisp: a color vector belongs or not to the region of interest. The obvious alternative is to introduce more freedom degrees for this partitioning process, considering more partitioning classes and fuzzy degrees of membership associated to the color vectors.

Such a model is the clustering filter, introduced in [32], [33]. This approach assumes the partitioning of the selected color vectors into three classes. These three classes correspond to the central region of the signal sample space (containing the undegraded image samples) and two extreme regions. Each region will be characterized by its prototype (some sort of weighted mean of the color vectors). If we denote by u_{ij} the membership of color vector $\boldsymbol{x}_i$ into class j, the protoype $\boldsymbol{\mu}_j$ of class j is given by (9):

$$\boldsymbol{\mu}_j = \frac{\sum_{i=1}^{n} u_{ij}^m \boldsymbol{x}_i}{\sum_{i=1}^{n} u_{ij}^m}. \tag{9}$$

The fuzziness degree m controls the overall separation between the $C = 3$ classes (classically, $m = 2$; an increased fuzziness degree allows a more vague partitioning). The membership degrees u_{ij} are obtained as functions of the distances from the vector to all the prototypes; for instance, the fuzzy k-means algorithm [4], [15] uses membership degrees computed according to

(10):

$$u_{ij} = \left(\sum_{k=1}^{C} \left(\frac{\|\boldsymbol{x}_i - \boldsymbol{\mu}_j\|}{\|\boldsymbol{x}_i - \boldsymbol{\mu}_k\|} \right)^{\frac{1}{m-1}} \right)^{-1} . \tag{10}$$

The prototype of the central class is an estimate of the correct pixel value, equivalent to the vector median [32] (see Fig. 4). The filtering effect is very simple and intuitive to explain: the central class of the partition is made of vectors lying far from the extremes, and thus the outliers will have very little influence on the filter output; the mean-type formula for the class prototype ensures a rejection of normal, additive noise, superimposed on the correct colors. In Fig. 3(b) the result of a median-like clustering based filtering operation is presented. The prototypes of the extreme classes are equivalent to expressions of the local extremes (minimum and maximum) and thus, can approximate the output of mathematical morphology operators (erosion, dilation) [33].

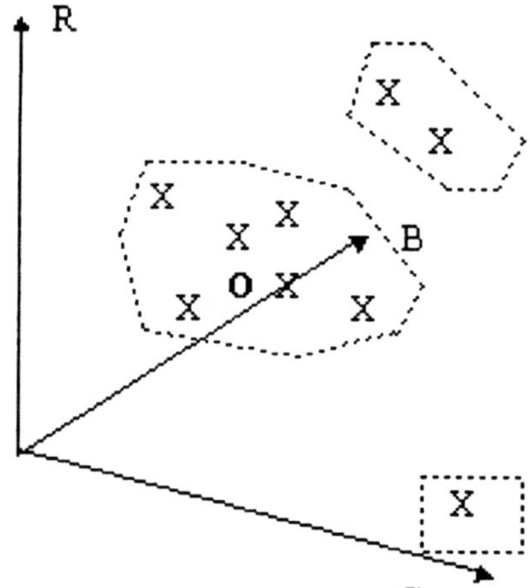

Fig. 4. Nine color vectors forming a three-classes crisp partition; the prototype of the central class is a robust vector median

The implementation of the fuzzy clustering algorithm is usually done by a fuzzy k-means procedure which implies an *iterative* pass through the set of selected color vectors. Usually the centroids $\boldsymbol{\mu}_j$ are initialized first by taking some appropriate values (e.g. the marginal median and extremes in the case of colors); then (10) and (9) are solved recursively until a convergence of $\boldsymbol{\mu}_j$ and u_{ij} values is reached [4], [15]. The number of passes through the data set until convergence is highly dependent on the intrinsic structure of the vector set and increases with the fuzziness degree m. Thus, the main problem of these filters is their relative high computational requirements, in terms of multiplications and involutions, even for small vector populations selected by the filtering window (typically 9 to 25).

Since any clustering algorithm may be used for the partitioning [16] (and the fuzzy variants are providing an increased quality of the filtered image), two main paradigms are at hand: the classical (probabilistic) model and the possibilistic model [18]. Both approaches can deal with images degraded by mixture noise (impulsive and Gaussian) [35], [36]. The difference between the models is the interpretation of the membership degree of a vector to a class of the partition: as a sharing between all classes in the probabilistic model (with memberships that sums up to 1 (11)), or as a typicality [18] with respect to each single class (12) in the possibilistic model (for any i within $[1, n]$):

$$\sum_{j=1}^{C} u_{ij} = 1 \tag{11}$$

$$0 \leq \sum_{j=1}^{C} u_{ij} \leq C \tag{12}$$

An efficient alternative is to replace the iterative clustering algorithm to a *hierarchical approach*. Apart from the obvious difference of the approach (the number of classes in the partition varies during the algorithmic flow) these algorithms are driven by conditions that measure the class compactness and the inter-vector distances [19] rather than the quality of the approximation of the vectors within a class by its prototype. The hierarchical algorithms are mainly used in statistical multivariate data analysis; as for the iterative clustering algorithms, they emerged from the pattern recognition and vector quantization approaches [14]. The strong crisp-set background of the hierarchical class construction does not seem very appealing (or appropriate) for fuzzy implementations, although such an approach was developed in [34] for a simplified hierarchical algorithm, the MPNN - Modified PNN [11].

4 Fuzzy aggregative filters

The nonlinear multichannel filters (fuzzy or not) have various performances and behaviors, in terms of both noise types successfully reduced and original color and contour preservation. Under these circumstances, the idea of combining various filters naturally appeared as a way to improve the filtering results. The initial combinations where convex linear (13) or switches (14) of the outputs $\boldsymbol{y}_1$ and $\boldsymbol{y}_2$ of two classical (usually marginal) filters (mean, median, all-pass, etc.):

$$\boldsymbol{y} = \alpha \boldsymbol{y}_1 + (1 - \alpha) \boldsymbol{y}_2 \tag{13}$$

$$y = \begin{cases} y_1 \text{ if some condition holds} \\ y_2 \text{ otherwise} \end{cases} \tag{14}$$

The decision in (14) can be further refined as a soft decision (as, for instance, the adaptive recursive median proposed in [1]).

As the vector processing evolved and the reduced ordering (based on distances to reference points) was imposed as the best-suited sub-ordering principle, the same structures were used, but combining filters derived from different distances. The filter proposed in [30] (Adaptive Hybrid Median Filters) uses a combination as in (13) for trimming its behavior in mixture noise environments (impulsive and Gaussian).

Another approach is to use a single filter, driven by a composite criterion. Since both the magnitude based and the angle based methods of outlier determination are correct and provide sometimes complementary behaviors, it is natural to combine the two approaches into a more effective and flexible structure [17], [13]. The cited papers proposed to construct a reduced ordering using the scalars s_i from (15), i.e. a convex product-type combination of aggregate directional and Euclidean distances:

$$s_i = \left(\sum_{j=1}^{n} \widehat{\boldsymbol{x}_i \boldsymbol{x}_j}\right)^{\gamma} \left(\sum_{j=1}^{n} \|\boldsymbol{x}_i - \boldsymbol{x}_j\|\right)^{1-\gamma} \tag{15}$$

In (15) the γ factor controls the relative importance of each type of behavior; γ is set to 0.5 for equal importance of the two filtering criteria (orientation and magnitude). In [17] the value $\gamma = 0.75$ is recommended as a suitable choice in the case of any noise distribution. The output of the filter is the vector which minimizes (15); a typical filtering result is presented in Fig. 3(c).

The approach suggested in [23] is to combine filters (sets of weights) instead of distances into a single set of weights. The combination of the different filters into a single operator is performed by a *fuzzy aggregator*. Such aggregators are, for instance, the compensative operators [39], defined as weighted averages of some logical OR ($\cup$) and AND ($\cap$) operators applied to the sets of weights:

$$A \odot_{\gamma} B = (A \cap B)^{1-\gamma} (A \cup B)^{\gamma} \tag{16}$$

Using various logical operations (OR is a t-conorm, AND is a t-norm) and the standard Lukasiewicz negation, various aggregators can be obtained. In [23] the aggregation (16) is based on the Zadeh (min) t-norm and the probabilistic (product type) t-norm, obtaining:

$$w_j = \left(\min_{i=1,k} w_{ji}\right)^{1-\gamma} \left(\max_{i=1,k} w_{ji}\right)^{\gamma} \tag{17}$$

$$w_j = \prod_{i=1}^{k} w_{ji}^{1-\gamma} \left(1 - \prod_{i=1}^{k}(1 - w_{ji})\right)^{\gamma} \tag{18}$$

In (17) and (18), k is the number of individual filters to be combined, w_{ji} is the j-th order weight for the i-th filter.

The applications in [23] are based on the equally weighted combination ($\gamma = 0.5$) of two filters ($k = 2$): a magnitude based vector median (such as the already mentioned DDMF or MDF) and an angle (directional) based vector median FVDF [21].

The filters within the fuzzy aggregative class are characterized by the synthesis of their coefficients through a fusion procedure. The fusion aims to balance the behaviors of the filters used as primary data into the composite resulted structure.

5 Fuzzy inferential filters

A fuzzy inferential (or rule-based) filter combines several fuzzy associations concerning the relational definitions of the objects of the universe with respect to some given linguistic notions:

R_i : **if** (v_1 **is** A_{1i}) **and** (v_2 **is** A_{2i}) **and** ... (v_n **is** A_{ni}) **then** (o **is** B_i).

Each association represents a linguistic rule (R_i), where A_{ji} and B_i are fuzzy sets which map linguistic concepts (e.g. important, irelevant, big, small) to each input and to the output variable in the i-th rule respectively. The information contained in the set of fuzzy rules (rule base) is numerically processed by the inference mechanism, which evaluates, for a given set of input data (or variables) v_i, the activation of each fuzzy rule and then their superposition. The output of the system (o) is obtained by defuzzification.

5.1 Direct extensions of gray-level approaches

The overview from [27] enumerates several fuzzy inferential filtering approaches for the processing of gray scale images. The enumerated filters are scalar, for gray-scale images (with the exception of the FVDF [21]) and fit in the crude fuzzy or fuzzy inferential categories. The fuzzy inferential filters are those from the FIRE (Fuzzy Inference Ruled by Else-action) family [26]. Basically, all of them rely on the use of luminance difference between various pixel pairs within the filtering window as input variables v_i. In [26] these differences are computed between each pixel of the filtering window and its center (the pixel being processed); in [37] the differences are computed within linear subsets of the filtering window with respect to the median. The differences are usually expressed by linguistic descriptions of Positive, Zero and Negative (or their absolute values are labeled as Small, Medium, Big). However, more detailed descriptions have also been occasionally used (Positive Small, Positive Medium, Positive Big, Zero, Negative Small, Negative Medium, Negative Big).

As a typical example of this approach, in [37] the rules that describe the credibility (how appropriate a value is as a filter output) are applied for the values within linear-shaped sub-windows W_i (horizontal, vertical and diagonal) centered in the currently processed location.

1. **if** (the absolute difference between the median value z_i and the other points from W_i **is** very big) **then** (the credibility of z_i **is** low).
2. **if** (the absolute difference between the median value z_i and the other points from W_i **is** very small) **then** (the credibility of z_i **is** low).
3. **if** (the absolute difference between the median value z_i and the other points from W_i **is** medium) **then** (the credibility of z_i **is** high).

Finally, the median values with the highest credibilities are selected as candidates for the output and a further median is performed upon this set. The membership function that measures the credibility has the classical trapezoidal, triangular or parabolic shape.

As shown in [35], a simple and direct way of extending such scalar filters to the multichannel case is to replace the linguistic sintagm *luminance difference* to *inter-vector distance.* Any fuzzy, rule-based, scalar filter can be thus directly translated for multichannel (not necessarily color) images. Yet, such an extension does not take into account the specific characteristics of the colors.

5.2 Exploiting the intrinsic color space fuzziness

Another way of dealing with fuzzy rules in the color environment is to consider the particular properties of the colors, and mainly, their characterization in a more suited space than the primary RGB (Red, Green, Blue) space: the HSI (Hue, Saturation, Intensity) space. The Hue is a description of the color type (if the color is blue, or orange, or green etc.) and the Saturation measures how pure the color is (the degree of mixing with uniform white). A very low saturation (0, at the limit) means that the color is a shade of gray and the RGB components are all the same. The Intensity is a measure of the perceived color luminance and is associated to a vertical axis of rotational symmetry of the new color space; the Hue is interpreted as an angle that divides the hull of the space in areas that correspond to pure colors. The HSI color space is obtained from the RGB color space by a rotation (19) and a nonlinear transform (20) (similar to the Cartesian to polar coordinates change) [8], [7].

$$\begin{pmatrix} I \\ C_1 \\ C_2 \end{pmatrix} = \begin{pmatrix} \frac{1}{3} & \frac{1}{3} & \frac{1}{3} \\ 1 & -\frac{1}{2} & -\frac{1}{2} \\ 0 & -\frac{\sqrt{3}}{2} & \frac{\sqrt{3}}{2} \end{pmatrix} \begin{pmatrix} R \\ G \\ B \end{pmatrix} \tag{19}$$

$$\begin{cases} S = \sqrt{C_1^2 + C_2^2} \\ H = \arctan \frac{C_2}{C_1} \end{cases} \tag{20}$$

Several important properties of the HSI color representation have been noticed and exploited: in natural images the Saturation is relatively low and is proportional to the degree of significance of the Hue; the (independent) noise components acquired on the R, G, B channels is reduced in the Intensity component (a linear combination of the three original channels). Thus, in [7] fuzzy rules are introduced for measuring the relevance of each of the three HSI components:

1. **if** (Saturation **is** low) **then** (the Hue **is** irrelevant).
2. **if** (Saturation **is** medium) **then** (the Hue **is** weakly relevant).
3. **if** (Saturation **is** high) **then** (the Hue **is** very relevant).

This primary set of rules highlights a specific characteristic of Hue, which can be used for the further processing (color image segmentation, in the particular case of [7]) by a cooperation between Hue and Intensity, depending on the Saturation. This new set of fuzzy rules establishes a soft decision for the relative importance of the three color components and their further use for segmentation (or filtering):

1. **if** (Saturation **is** low) **then** (the Intensity **is** used for further processing).
2. **if** (Saturation **is** medium) **then** (Hue and Intensity **are** jointly used for further processing).
3. **if** (Saturation **is** high) **then** (the Hue **is** used for further processing).

A typical result of a median filtering based on such a fuzzy rule set is shown in Fig. 3(d). This approach opens a very interesting perspective on the use of specific inter-color relations for filtering purposes. It is obvious that using the RGB color space, although appealing for some reasons (most of the color sensors are RGB, all components are equally important in perception), proves its limitation in terms of measuring the inter-color distances. Perception experiments have shown that the human eye cannot properly differentiate certain colors, which are just noticeable different and are placed sufficiently close in the color space, below the *Just Noticeable Difference* - JND [29]. The JND is equivalent to the Euclidean distance between colors expressed as CIELAB triples, provided that it is smaller than 2.3. Thus, the JND offers a natural way for the integration of visual uncertainty.

We expect interesting developments in the field of color image filtering through the use of the JND: it embeds the possibility of defining color multi-sets – all colors that are just noticeable different with respect to some given colors – hence allowing the construction of larger sample populations (and thus providing more robust estimates) without increasing the size of the filtering window. The JND can act as a threshold for the perceived error measurement, which can be incorporated in some quality measures of the type of Normalized Color Difference - NCD (a mean squared error computed in the CIELAB color space) and thus gaining some perceptual support for the objective quality measures.

6 Conclusions and comments

The fuzzy inferential (rule-based) filters are a very particular category of filters. Still based on expert experience and test-and-trial for the rule generation and requiring fuzzy inference, these filters are the only "true" fuzzy filters (or gradually adaptive).

The filters from the other categories are primarily influenced by statistical methods that combine measurements of the vectors in order to characterize correct and incorrect values (with respect to the given vector set). The fuzzy aggregative approach melts influences from two different combinations of vectors; the weighting associated to each of them ensures a fuzzy balance of the influences. Obviously, any single filter can be assigned a weighting factor of 1, and thus resulting in the original filter (that can be crude fuzzy or fuzzy paradigm based). It is difficult to trace a clear boundary between the crude fuzzy and the fuzzy paradigm based approaches. Finally we can accept that both of them measure in some way the membership of each color vector into the set "correct filter output" by either an analytical expression or an iterative calculation.

From a practitioner's point of view, the fuzzy inferential filters are more time-consuming, in both the design and the actual running time. Their performance, determined by classical objective quality measures, offers some improvement compared to the normal implementations (as the crude fuzzy filters).

From an academic point of view, the literature survey shows that the applications of fuzzy logic in the area of multichannel and color imaging are rather sparse and they are concentrated in the field of image segmentation (due to the direct application of the fuzzy clustering algorithms).

References

1. Abbas J. and Domanski M., *Vector Nonlinear Recursive Filters for Color Images*, in: "Proceedings of IWSSIP'99 – 6th International Workshop on Systems, Signals and Image Processing" (Bratislava, Slovakia), pp. 30–33, 1999
2. Astola J., Haavisto P. and Neuvo Y., *Vector Median Filters*, Proc. IEEE, Vol. 78, No. 4, pp. 678–689, 1990
3. Barnett V., *The Ordering of Multivariate Data*, Journal of Royal Stat. Soc. A, Vol. 139, No. 3, pp. 318–354, 1976
4. Bezdek J.C., *"Pattern Recognition with Fuzzy Objective Function Algorithms"*, Plenum Press, New York, 1981
5. Bezdek J.C., *Fuzzy Models – What Are They and Why ?*, IEEE Trans. on Fuzzy Systems, Vol. 1, No. 1, pp. 1–5, 1993

6. Buchowicz A. and Pitas I., *Multichannel Distance Filters*, in: "Proceedings of ICIP'94 – IEEE Conference on Image Processing" (Austin, TX), pp. 575–578, 1994
7. Carron T. and Lambert P., *Symbolic Fusion of Hue-Chroma-Intensity Features for Region Segmentation*, in: "Proceedings of ICIP'96 – IEEE Conference on Image Processing" (Lausanne, Switzerland), pp. 971–974, 1996
8. Castleman K.R., *"Digital Image Processing (2nd edition)"*, Prentice Hall, Englewood Cliffs NJ, 1996
9. Ciuc M., Rangayyan R.M., Zaharia T. and Buzuloiu V., *Adaptive Neighbourhood Filters for Color Image Filtering*, in: "Proceedings of the 9th SPIE Nonlinear Image Processing Conference" (San Jose, California, USA), SPIE 3304, pp. 277–286, 1998
10. Cohen H.A., *Image Restoration via N-Nearest Neighbor Classification*, in: "Proceedings of ICIP'96 – IEEE Conference on Image Processing" (Lausanne, Switzerland), Vol. 1, pp. 1005–1008, 1996
11. Comaniciu D., *An Efficient Clustering Algorithm for Vector Quantization*, in: "Proceedings of the 9th Scandinavian Conference on Image Analysis" (Uppsala, Sweden), pp. 423–430, 1995
12. Economou G. and Fotopoulos S., *A Family of Adaptive Nonlinear Lox Complexity Filters*, in: "Proceedings of ECCTD'93 – European Conference on Circuit Theory and Design" (Davos, Switzerland), pp. 521–524, 1993
13. Fotopoulos S. and Economou G., *Multichannel Filters Using Composite Distance Metrics*, in: "Proceedings of the IEEE Workshop on Nonlinear Signal and Image Processing" (Neos Marmara, Halkidiki, Greece), Vol. 2, pp. 503–506, 1995
14. Gersho A. and Gray R.M., *"Vector Quantization and Signal Compression"*, Kluwer Academic Publ., Boston MA, 1992
15. Hathaway R.J. and Bezdek J.C., *Optimization of Clustering Criteria by Reformulation*, IEEE Trans. on Fuzzy Systems, Vol. 3, No. 2, pp. 241–245, 1995
16. Jain A.K. and Dubes R.C., *"Algorithms for Clustering Data"*, Prentice Hall, Englewood Cliffs NJ, 1988
17. Karakos D.G. and Trahanias P.E., *Generalized Multichannel Image Filtering Structures*, IEEE Trans. on Image Processing, Vol. 6, No. 7, pp. 1038–1045, 1997
18. Krishnapuram R. and Keller J.M., *A Possibilistic Approach to Clustering*, IEEE Trans. on Fuzzy Systems, Vol. 1, No. 2, pp. 98–110, 1993
19. Krzanowski W.J., *"Principles of Multivariate Analysis: A User's Perspective"*, Clarendon Press, Oxford, 1993
20. Pitas I. and Venetsanopoulos A.N., *"Nonlinear Digital Filters – Principles and Applications"*, Kluwer Academic Publ., Norwell MA, 1990
21. Plataniotis K.N., Androutsos D. and Venetsanopoulos A.N., *Color Image Processing using Fuzzy Vector Directional Filters*, in: "Proceedings of the IEEE Workshop on Nonlinear Signal and Image Processing" (Neos Marmara, Halkidiki, Greece), Vol. 2, pp. 535–538, 1995
22. Plataniotis K.N., Androutsos D. and Venetsanopoulos A.N., *Nearest Neighbour Multichannel Filters for Image Processing*, in: "Proceedings of EUSIPCO'96 – 8th European Signal Processing Conference" (Trieste, Italy), Vol. 1, pp. 157–160, 1996

23. Plataniotis K.N., Androutsos D. and Venetsanopoulos A.N., *Multichannel Filters for Image Processing*, Signal Processing: Image Communications, Vol. 9, No. 2, pp. 143–158, 1997
24. Plataniotis K.N. and Venetsanopoulos A.N., *Vector Filtering*, in: "The Colour Image Processing Handbook (Sangwine J.S. and Horne R.E.N., eds.)", Chapman & Hall, pp. 188–209, 1998
25. Reusch B., *Mathematics of Fuzzy Logic*, in: "Real World Applications of Intelligent Technologies (Dascalu D., Negoita M.G. and Zimmermann H.J., eds.)", Romanian Academy Publ. House, pp. 15–52, 1996
26. Russo F. and Ramponi G., *A Fuzzy Operator for the Enhancement of Blurred and Noisy Images*, IEEE Trans. on Image Processing, Vol. 4, No. 8, pp. 1169–1174, 1995
27. Russo F., *Nonlinear Fuzzy Filters: An Overview*, in: "Proceedings of EUSIPCO'96 – 8th European Signal Processing Conference" (Trieste, Italy), Vol. 1, pp. 257–260, 1996
28. Sangwine J.S. and Thornton A. L., *Frequency Domain Methods*, in: "The Colour Image Processing Handbook (Sangwine J.S. and Horne R.E.N., eds.)", Chapman & Hall, pp. 228–241, 1998
29. Sharma G. and Trusell H.G., *Digital Color Imaging*, IEEE Trans. on Image Processing, Vol. 6, No. 7, pp. 901–932, 1997
30. Tang K., Astola J. and Neuvo Y., *Nonlinear Multivariate Image Filtering Techniques*, IEEE Trans. on Image Processing, Vol. 4, No. 6, pp. 788–798, 1995
31. Trahanias P.E. and Venetsanopoulos A.N., *Vector Directional Filters – A New Class of Multichannel Image Processing Filters*, IEEE Trans. on Image Processing, Vol. 2, No. 4, pp. 528–534, 1993
32. Vertan C. and Geangălă C.I., *Fuzzy Unsupervised Clustering for Color Image Filtering*, in: "Proceedings of EUFIT'96 – 4th European Congress on Intelligent Techniques and Soft Computing" (Aachen, Germany), Vol. 3, pp. 1751–1753, 1996
33. Vertan C., Malciu M., Zaharia T. and Buzuloiu V., *A Clustering Approach to Vector Mathematical Morphology*, in: "Proceedings of ICECS'96 – IEEE International Conference on Electronics, Circuits and Systems" (Rodos, Greece), Vol. 1, pp. 187–190, 1996
34. Vertan C. and Geangălă C.I., *FMPNN - A New Fuzzy Unsupervised Clustering Algorithm*, in: "Proceedings of EUFIT'96 – 4th European Congress on Intelligent Techniques and Soft Computing" (Aachen, Germany), Vol. 3, pp. 1812–1815, 1996
35. Vertan C., Vertan C.I. and Buzuloiu V., *Fuzzy Developments of Multichannel Filters*, in: "Proceedings of KES'97 – First International Conference on Conventional and Knowledge-Based Intelligent Electronic Systems" (Adelaide, Australia), 1997
36. Vertan C., Grava C. and Buzuloiu V., *Cluster Filtering Revisited: Probabilistic and Possibilistic Approaches to Multichannel Signal Processing*, in: "Proceedings of EMES'97 – 4th International Conference on Engineering of Modern Electrical Systems" (Oradea, Romania), pp. 276–281, 1997
37. Yang X. and Toh P.S., *Adaptive Fuzzy Multilevel Median Filter*, IEEE Trans. on Image Processing, Vol. 4, No. 8, pp. 680–682, 1995
38. Zadeh L., *Fuzzy Sets*, Information and Control, Vol. 8, pp. 338–353, 1965
39. Zimmermann H.J., *"Fuzzy Sets, Decision Making and Expert Systems"*, Kluwer Academic Publ., Boston MA, 1987

Part III

Applications of Fuzzy Techniques in Image Processing

Chapter 10

Fuzzy Color Processing

Lars Hildebrand and Bernd Reusch

University of Dortmund, Department of Computer Science
Otto-Hahn-Strasse 16, 44221 Dortmund, Germany
email: hildebra@ls1.informatik.uni-dortmund.de, reusch@ls1.cs.uni-dortmund.de

Summary. Fuzzy logic has proven its applicability in solving many control problems mainly in engineering and financial applications. If fuzzy control is extended towards fuzzy rule-based reasoning, the number of successful applications is smaller and some topics have only rarely been examined. The processing of color is one of these. Reasons for this are given in this chapter, as well as a new approach for linguistic color processing based on fuzzy logic. The methods developed and presented here for fuzzy color processing can be directly embedded in existing fuzzy rulebased systems.

1 The human vision system

Color is an experience in human perception, created by light of a specific wavelength falling on the different cones in the eye´s retina. As a result, color is created in our brain, when we see a distribution of lights of different wavelengths. The human brain distinguishes color by comparison and not by an absolute scale. To justify the use of fuzzy logic for the improvement of image processing, a closer look at colors and the human ability to see colors is needed [2,10].

The human organ, that enables us to see is the eye. The eye consists of different parts, each of them performing special tasks (see Fig. 1).

- Pupil
  The pupil is an aperture of the eye, that appears to be dark. All light that reaches the light sensitive parts of the eye has to pass through the pupil.
- Iris
  The iris is a circular muscle, that controls the size of the pupil. Different sizes allow that more or less light can enter the eye. By contracting and relaxing the iris, the eye can adapt to different light conditions, like day or night.
- Cornea, inner lens
  The cornea covers both the pupil and the iris. It is the first lens of the human vision system and allows, in conjunction with the inner lens, the

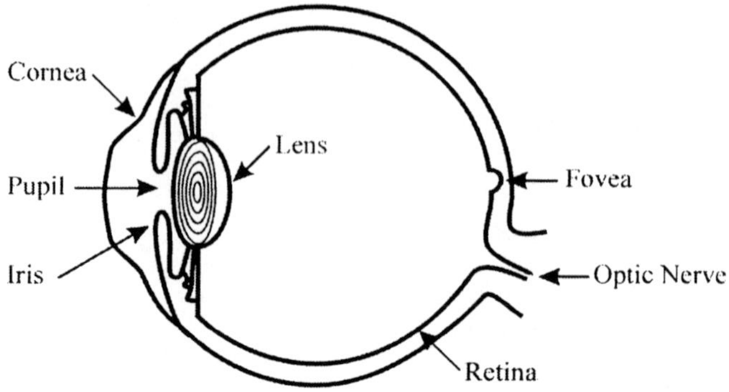

Fig. 1. Schematic diagram of the human eye

production of images at the light sensitive part (the retina). The inner lens is a transparent body that is able to contract and relax. This contraction and relaxation changes the shape of the lens, and allows the eye to adapt to a large range of distances.

- Retina
  The light that is focused through the cornea and the inner lens falls on the retina. The retina covers a large part inside the eye, and is structured in seven layers. Each layer serves a different purpose, from receiving the light to the complex processing of electrical signals [8].
- Fovea
  The fovea is the center of the retina and is the region of the highest visual sensitivity. The fovea is also the part of the retina with the highest sensitivity to color perception.

The retina contains two different kinds of light receptors: cones and rods. The rods are most sensitive to light and dark changes and therefore not suited for the detection of different colors. The cones are not as sensitive to light as the rods. Their main characteristic is that they are sensitive to one of three colors (red, green, or blue). Color itself is a electromagnetic radiation and can be measured by its wavelength. Humans are only able to see a small range of the electromagnetic spectrum (see Fig. 2). However, only pure colors can be characterized using their wavelength. All other colors are a mix of pure colors in different intensities.

It is almost impossible to characterize human color perception in exact mathematical terms, wavelength intervals, or spectral distributions. Another, more fuzzy, way of describing colors has to be found [19,20].

2 Color models

Depending on the way colors are used and processed, many different methods for the specification and visualization of colors have been developed [11,13].

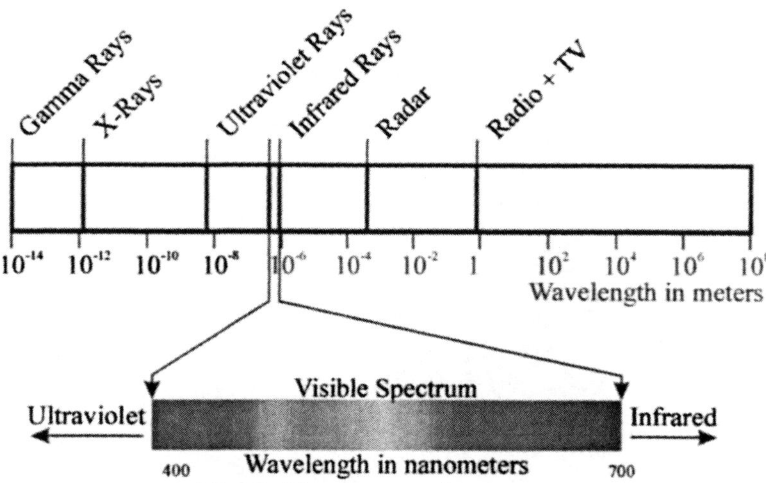

Fig. 2. Electromagnetic spectrum

Color models are used to describe colors, so that the description is clear and colors can be reproduced. Many color models with different purposes and different areas of application are used. The next two paragraphs focus on two of the most frequently used classes of color models: the technical and the artistic color models.

2.1 Technical color models

Two of the most common technical color models are the RGB model (used for television) and the CMY model (used for printed media).

The RGB model is an additive color system based on the trichromatic theory where the colors are produced by mixing the base colors red, green and blue [7]. The best-known application of this color model is the cathode ray tube used in color televisions. Here the colors are produced by red-, green- and blue-emitting phosphor. All colors defined in the RGB model can be visualized using the RGB cube (see Fig. 3). The CMY model is a subtractive color system and uses the inverse base colors of the RGB model cyan, magenta and yellow. It is mainly used in the printing industry and in photography. Figure 4 shows a diagram of the CMY model [4].

These models have a technical origin and therefore some disadvantages for their use in more linguistic-oriented color processing. Areas of similar colors are 3-dimensional subspaces, and hence are not easy to visualize. The boundaries of these color ranges are not straight lines, so the definition of the subspaces is complex and not intuitive. Another problem is that pure colors and grey colors cannot be distinguished by considering one color channel. An example for this is that a red color, made by the RGB values (0.5, 0.0, 0.0) has the same value for the R channel as 50% grey color, made by the

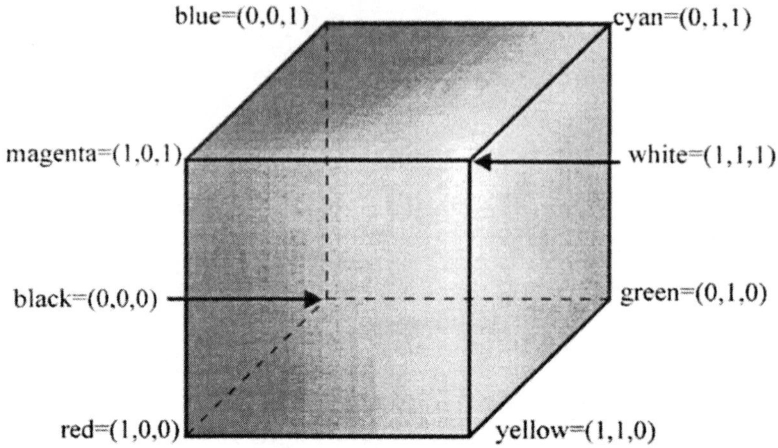

Fig. 3. The RGB color space

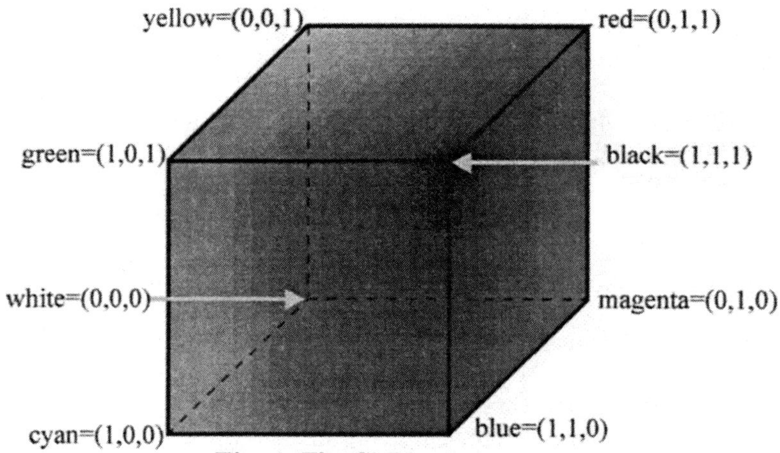

Fig. 4. The CMY color space

RGB values (0.5, 0.5, 0.5). If linguistic descriptions of colors are defined, an additional dimension is needed to contain information as to what degree a certain color belongs to a color name. This information extends the RGB and CMY color models to 4-dimensional real-valued spaces, that cannot be visualized. But visualization is important for the design of ergonomic user interfaces. It is not possible to reduce this space to a 3-dimensional subspace without significant loss of colors.

2.2 Artistic color models

The disadvantages of technical-oriented color models stated above are well-known and more artistic-oriented models have been developed. These models use information like hue (the quality, by which colors can be distinguished from another), saturation, and lightness. Modelling colors in this way is more like an artist's view of mixing colors: Starting from a pure color (hue), white pigments are used to lighten the color (decrease of saturation), and black pigments are used to darken it (decrease of lightness). One of the earliest of these color models was the one originated by A. H. Munsell in 1915 [12,14]. He used the parameters hue, chroma and value, that correspond to the basic parameters dominant wavelength, purity and reflection. He divided the hue (dominant wavelength) into ten basic colors, the chroma (purity) into five, and the value (reflection) into ten steps. Small rectangular slips of paper were painted with watercolor of sufficient permanence to represent the 500 different colors. The interesting fact in this color model is that he arranged the hues in a 360° polar coordinate system. The same arrangement of colors is used in the HSI color model, which is very close to Munsells color model [21,22]. It uses the parameters hue (H), saturation (S), and intensity (I). The HSI model is well-suited for the linguistic processing of color, because colors which are similar for humans are grouped close together and there is a clear distinction of colors and greys. The 3-dimensional model can be easily reduced to a 2-dimensional one, by simply dropping the intensity coordinate when the pure and light colors are important (HS color space), or by dropping the saturation coordinate when pure and dark colors are important (HI color space). The definition of colors on these reduced color spaces is covered in the next section [5].

2.3 Color model conversion

The previous paragraph explained why the HSI color model is suitable for linguistic color processing. Most camera systems that are available on the market output the video signal as a composite signal or as a RGB signal. The RGB channels can be converted into HSI channels, as specified in the this paragraph. If the camera system outputs a composite signal, it has to be converted into the RGB channels first. The conversion from the RGB color model to the HSI color model can be done using the following set of constants and equations [22]. The operations $\|\boldsymbol{v}\|$, $\boldsymbol{u} \cdot \boldsymbol{v}$, and $\boldsymbol{u} \times \boldsymbol{v}$ stand for vector normalization, vector dot, and vector cross product, and are defined as follows, assuming that the dimension of the vectors is 3:

$$\|\boldsymbol{v}\| = \frac{v}{|v|} = \begin{pmatrix} v_1/\sqrt{v_1^2+v_2^2+v_3^2} \\ v_2/\sqrt{v_1^2+v_2^2+v_3^2} \\ v_3/\sqrt{v_1^2+v_2^2+v_3^2} \end{pmatrix} \tag{1}$$

$$\boldsymbol{u} \cdot \boldsymbol{v} = \begin{pmatrix} u_1 \\ u_2 \\ u_3 \end{pmatrix} \cdot \begin{pmatrix} v_1 \\ v_2 \\ v_3 \end{pmatrix} = u_1v_1 + u_2v_2 + u_3v_3 \tag{2}$$

$$\boldsymbol{u} \times \boldsymbol{v} = \begin{pmatrix} u_1 \\ u_2 \\ u_3 \end{pmatrix} \times \begin{pmatrix} v_1 \\ v_2 \\ v_3 \end{pmatrix} = \begin{pmatrix} u_2 v_3 - u_3 v_2 \\ u_3 v_1 - u_1 v_3 \\ u_1 v_2 - u_2 v_1 \end{pmatrix} \tag{3}$$

Using this notation, the conversion from RGB to HSI is:

$$\boldsymbol{I}_u = \left\| \begin{pmatrix} 1 \\ 1 \\ 1 \end{pmatrix} \right\| = \left\| \begin{pmatrix} 1/\sqrt{3} \\ 1/\sqrt{3} \\ 1/\sqrt{3} \end{pmatrix} \right\| \tag{4}$$

$$\boldsymbol{R} = \begin{pmatrix} 2 \\ -1 \\ -1 \end{pmatrix} \tag{5}$$

$$\boldsymbol{G}_u = \|\boldsymbol{I}_u \times \boldsymbol{R}\| = \begin{pmatrix} 0 \\ \frac{1}{\sqrt{2}} \\ -\frac{1}{\sqrt{2}} \end{pmatrix} \tag{6}$$

$$\boldsymbol{R}_u = \|\boldsymbol{R}\| = \begin{pmatrix} \frac{\sqrt{6}}{3} \\ -\frac{\sqrt{6}}{6} \\ -\frac{\sqrt{6}}{6} \end{pmatrix} \tag{7}$$

A color $\boldsymbol{C}_{RGB}$ of the RGB color model given as

$$\boldsymbol{C}_{RGB} = \begin{pmatrix} R \\ G \\ B \end{pmatrix} \tag{8}$$

where R, G, and B denote the red, green, and blue part of the color can be converted into a color $\boldsymbol{C}_{HSI}$ of the HSI color model

$$\boldsymbol{C}_{HSI} = \begin{pmatrix} H \\ S \\ I \end{pmatrix} \tag{9}$$

where H, S, and I denote the values for hue, saturation, and intensity, by the following formulas:

$$H(\boldsymbol{C}_{RGB}) = \text{atant}(\boldsymbol{C}_{RGB} \cdot \boldsymbol{G}_u, \boldsymbol{C}_{RGB} \cdot \boldsymbol{R}_u) \tag{10}$$

$$S\left(\boldsymbol{C}_{RGB}\right) = 1 - \frac{\min\left(\boldsymbol{C}_{RGB}\right)}{I\left(\boldsymbol{C}_{RGB}\right)} \tag{11}$$

$$I\left(\boldsymbol{C}_{RGB}\right) = \frac{1}{\sqrt{3}}\boldsymbol{C}_{RGB} \cdot \boldsymbol{I}_u \tag{12}$$

The function atant in formula (10) is defined as:

$$\operatorname{atant}(x,y) = \begin{cases} \operatorname{atanx}(x,y) & \text{, if } \operatorname{atanx}(x,y) \geq 0 \\ \operatorname{atanx}(x,y) + 2\pi & \text{, else} \end{cases}, \tag{13}$$

with

$$\operatorname{atanx}(x,y) = \begin{cases} \arctan\left(\frac{y}{x}\right) & \text{, if } x > 0 \\ \arctan\left(\frac{y}{x}\right) + \pi & \text{, if } x < 0,\ y > 0 \\ \arctan\left(\frac{y}{x}\right) - \pi & \text{, if } x < 0,\ y < 0 \end{cases} \tag{14}$$

The not defined value of atanx for $x = 0$ is set to:

$$\operatorname{atanx}(0,y) = \begin{cases} 0 & \text{, if } y = 0 \\ \frac{\pi}{2} & \text{, if } y > 0 \\ -\frac{\pi}{2} & \text{, else} \end{cases} \tag{15}$$

Note that the result of the function atant is in the interval $[0, 2\pi]$.

2.4 Notation

For further clarification of the equations used, some terms and symbols should be defined:

Definition 1. (HS color space)
The HS color space is a 2-dimensional subspace of the HSI color space, generated by the HSI color model. The I value is constantly set to 1.0.

The HS color space can be represented as the unity circle, where the pure colors are on the circumference. The colors toward the centre of the unity circle have gradually decreasing saturation resulting in the color `white` at the centre.

Definition 2. (HI color space)
The HI color space is a 2-dimensional subspace of the HSI color space, generated by the HSI color model. The S value is constantly set to 1.0.

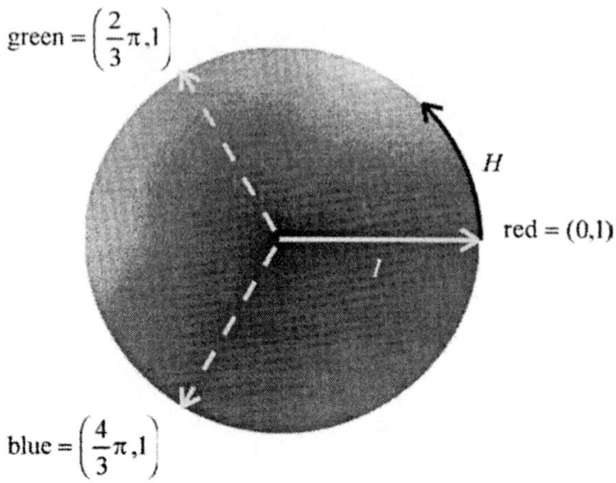

Fig. 5. HS color space, depicted as unity circle

The HI color space can be represented as the unity circle, similar to the HS color space. The only difference is that the gradually decreasing intensity results in the color `black` at the centre of the unity circle. The HS as well as the HI color space have the advantage that an important set of the visible colors can be represented in a two dimensional way (see Figs. 6 and 5). This characteristic allows the definition of fuzzy sets in a straightforward way and leads to a simple and reasonable description of the fuzzy sets.

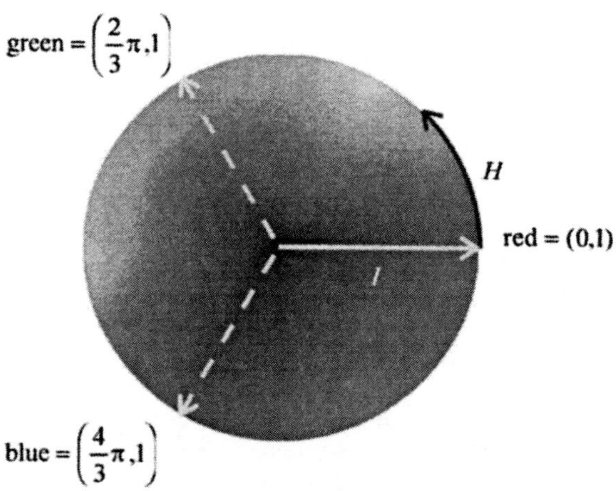

Fig. 6. HI color space, depicted as unity circle

In order to define fuzzy sets over the HI and HS color space the terms HI point and HS point have to be defined.

Definition 3. (HI point)

A HI point is defined within the HI color space. Each HI point P consists of two real numbers $P = (\measuredangle_P, r_P)$, with $\measuredangle_P \in [0, 2\pi[$ and $r_P \in [0,1]$. $\measuredangle_P$ represents the hue value and r_P represents the intensity value of the color at the HI point P.

Using the polar coordinate system on the unity circle, the hue is represented by the angle, while the intensity is represented by the radius. Each HI point corresponds directly to the color found at the position P of the HI color space. A HS point is defined in a similar way:

Definition 4. (HS point)

A HS point is defined within the HS color space. Each HS point P consists of two real numbers $P = (\measuredangle_P, r_P)$, with $\measuredangle_P \in [0, 2\pi[$ and $r_P \in [0,1]$. $\measuredangle_P$ represents the hue value and r_P represents the saturation value of the color at the HS point P.

All following definitions and equations are based on the HS color space. By exchanging the saturation value with the intensity value, they are valid for the HI color space, too.

During the calculations, different HS points have to be compared. To simplify the equations, the following short forms are used:

Definition 5. ($=_\measuredangle$and $=_r$)

Two HS points $P = (\measuredangle_P, r_P)$ and $Q = (\measuredangle_Q, r_Q)$ are equal with respect to the hue, if the hue of P is equal to the hue of Q:

$$P =_\measuredangle Q \Leftrightarrow \measuredangle_P = \measuredangle_Q.$$

Two HS points $P = (\measuredangle_P, r_P)$ and $Q = (\measuredangle_Q, r_Q)$ are equal with respect to the saturation, if the saturation of P is equal to the saturation of Q:

$$P =_r Q \Leftrightarrow r_P = r_Q.$$

The definition 5 can be extended to simplify the notation of other relations like $\leq$, $<$, $>$, and $\geq$. These definitions are similar to definition 5 and result in the following set of new relations (Table 1):

To determine the membership value of a certain color, some basic calculations have to be done. These calculations can also be written in a clear and efficient way if some abbreviations are used:

Definition 6. (basic operations)

The sum of the hues $\measuredangle_P + \measuredangle_Q$of two colors $P = (\measuredangle_P, r_P)$ and $Q = (\measuredangle_Q, r_Q)$, given as HS points can be abbreviated as:

$$P +_\measuredangle Q.$$

The sum of the saturation $r_P + r_Q$of two colors $P = (\measuredangle_P, r_P)$ and $Q = (\measuredangle_Q, r_Q)$, given as HS points can be abbreviated as:

$$P +_r Q.$$

The definition of the other basic operations $-$, $\cdot$, and $\div$ is straightforward. Table 2 shows a summary.

Table 1. Basic relations

relation	remark
$P <_\measuredangle Q$	hue of P is less than hue of Q
$P \leq_\measuredangle Q$	hue of P is less than or equal to hue of Q
$P \geq_\measuredangle Q$	hue of P is greater than or equal to hue of Q
$P >_\measuredangle Q$	hue of P is greater than hue of Q
$P <_r Q$	saturation of P is less than saturation of Q
$P \leq_r Q$	saturation of P is less than or equal to saturation of Q
$P \geq_r Q$	saturation of P is greater than or equal to saturation of Q
$P >_r Q$	saturation of P is greater than saturation of Q

Table 2. Basic operations

operation	definition	remark
$P -_\measuredangle Q$	$\measuredangle_P - \measuredangle_Q$	difference of hues
$P \cdot_\measuredangle Q$	$\measuredangle_P \cdot \measuredangle_Q$	product of hues
$P \div_\measuredangle Q$	$\measuredangle_P \div \measuredangle_Q$	quotient of hues
$P -_r Q$	$r_P - r_Q$	difference of saturations
$P \cdot_r Q$	$r_P \cdot r_Q$	product of saturations
$P \div_r Q$	$r_P \div r_Q$	quotient of saturations

3 Fuzzy color processing

Fuzzy sets are an extension of classical sets. In contrast to the classical sets, where an element e is either in the set or not, a fuzzy set allows an element e to be member of the set to a certain degree $\mu(e) \in [0,1]$. More information concerning fuzzy logic can be found in Zadehs excellent summary of his ideas [3]. An introduction to fuzzy logic is also given in [15,23]. An application of fuzzy logic and evolutionary algorithms in mechanical engineering applications can be found in [4]. The next definition gives the representation of the fuzzy sets, defined over the HS color space.

3.1 Definition and calculus

Definition 7. (fuzzy set over HS color space)

A fuzzy set over the HS color space is defined by eight HS points S_{ia}, S_{ib}, S_{oa}, S_{ob}, C_{ia}, C_{ib}, C_{oa} and C_{ob}. Each point represents one corner of the fuzzy set, the letters S and C stand for the terms support and core, the letters i and o for the terms inner and outer, respectively. The eight points must fulfil the following conditions:

1. $S_{oa} =_\measuredangle S_{ia}$, $C_{oa} =_\measuredangle C_{ia}$
2. $S_{ob} =_\measuredangle S_{ib}$, $C_{ob} =_\measuredangle C_{ib}$
3. $S_{ia} =_r S_{ib}$, $C_{ia} =_r C_{ib}$
4. $S_{oa} =_r S_{ob}$, $C_{oa} =_r C_{ob}$

This definition results in an extension of the polar coordinate system of the HS color space towards a cylindrical coordinate system, as shown in Fig. 7.

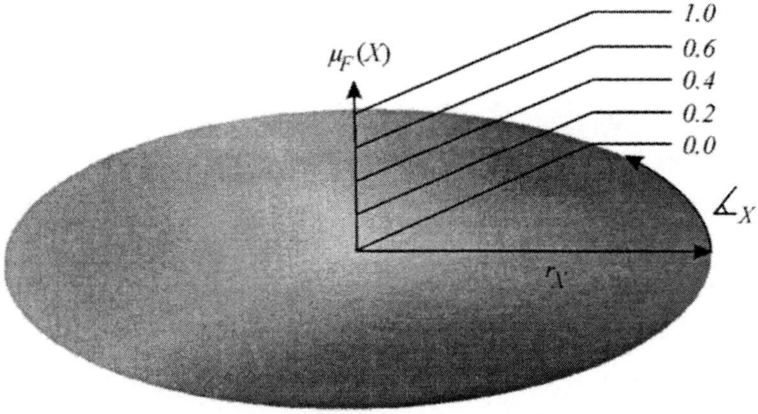

Fig. 7. Cylindrical coordinate system

An example of a fuzzy set defining a color according to definition 7 is shown in figure 8 where the term `blue` is modelled.

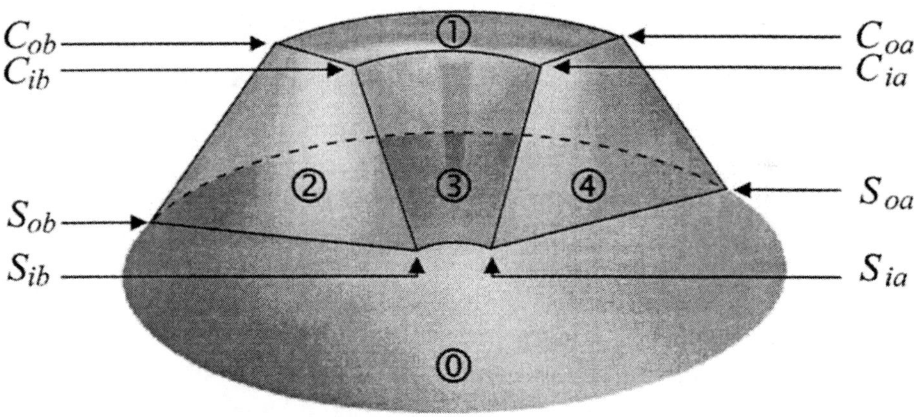

Fig. 8. Fuzzy set, defined over the HS color space

If fuzzy logic is applied, a method for determining the membership value of an element of the universe related to a fuzzy set has to be found. Due to the fairly simple structure of the allowed fuzzy sets, this calculation is not complex. To calculate the membership value $\mu_F(X)$ of a given color X, with respect to the fuzzy color F, two steps are necessary. In the first step, the region code of the color $X = (\measuredangle_X, r_X)$ has to be determined. The second step calculates the membership value, depending on the region code. We can distinguish the following six cases:

1. The color X has a membership value $\mu_F(X) = 0$, if X is outside of the support of F (region code 0):

$$X \leq_{\measuredangle} S_{ia}, \text{ or } X >_{\measuredangle} S_{ib}, \text{ or } X \leq_r S_{ia}, \text{ or } X >_r S_{oa}.$$

2. The color X has a membership value $\mu_F(X) = 1$, if X is inside the core of F (region code 1):

$$X \leq_{\measuredangle} C_{ib}, \text{ and } X >_{\measuredangle} C_{ia}, \text{ and } X \leq_r C_{oa}, \text{ and } X >_r C_{ia}.$$

If X is neither in region 0, nor in region 1, the determination of the region code is more complex.

3. The color X has a membership value $\mu_F(X) = 1 - \frac{1}{C_{ia} -_{\measuredangle} S_{ia}} (S_{ia} -_{\measuredangle} X)$, if the following conditions are true (region code 2)

$$\begin{gathered} X \leq_{\measuredangle} C_{ia}, \text{ and } X >_{\measuredangle} S_{ia}, \text{ and} \\ X \leq_r \frac{S_{oa} -_r C_{oa}}{S_{oa} -_{\measuredangle} C_{oa}} (X -_{\measuredangle} S_{oa}) +_r S_{oa}, \text{ and} \\ X >_r \frac{S_{ia} -_r C_{ia}}{S_{ia} -_{\measuredangle} C_{ia}} (X -_{\measuredangle} S_{ia}) +_r S_{ia}. \end{gathered}$$

4. The color X has a membership value $\mu_F(X) = 1 - \frac{1}{C_{ia} -_r S_{ia}} (S_{ia} -_r X)$, if the following conditions are true (region code 3)

$$\begin{gathered} X \leq_r C_{ia}, \text{ and } X >_r S_{ia}, \text{ and} \\ X \leq_{\measuredangle} \frac{C_{ib} -_{\measuredangle} S_{ib}}{C_{ib} -_R S_{ib}} (X -_r C_{ib}) +_{\measuredangle} C_{ib}, \text{ and} \\ X >_{\measuredangle} \frac{S_{ia} -_{\measuredangle} C_{ia}}{S_{ia} -_r C_{ia}} (X -_r S_{ia}) +_{\measuredangle} S_{ia}. \end{gathered}$$

5. The color X has a membership value $\mu_F(X) = \frac{1}{S_{ib} -_{\measuredangle} C_{ib}} (C_{ib} -_{\measuredangle} X)$, if the following conditions are true (region code4)

$$\begin{gathered} X \leq_{\measuredangle} S_{ob}, \text{ and } X >_{\measuredangle} C_{ob}, \text{ and} \\ X \leq_r \frac{S_{ob} -_r C_{ob}}{S_{ob} -_{\measuredangle} C_{ob}} (X -_{\measuredangle} C_{ob}) +_r C_{ob}, \text{ and} \\ X >_r \frac{S_{ib} -_r C_{ib}}{S_{ib} -_{\measuredangle} C_{ib}} (X -_{\measuredangle} C_{ib}) +_r C_{ib}. \end{gathered}$$

6. The color X has a membership value $\mu_F(X) = \frac{1}{S_{ob} -_r C_{ob}} (S_{ob} -_r X)$, if the following conditions are true (region code 5, reverse of region 3)

$$\begin{gathered} X \leq_r S_{oa}, \text{ and } X >_r C_{oa}, \text{ and} \\ X \leq_{\measuredangle} \frac{S_{ob} -_{\measuredangle} C_{ob}}{S_{ob} -_R C_{ob}} (X -_r S_{ob}) +_{\measuredangle} S_{ob}, \text{ and} \\ X >_{\measuredangle} \frac{S_{oa} -_{\measuredangle} C_{oa}}{S_{oa} -_r C_{oa}} (X -_r S_{oa}) +_{\measuredangle} S_{oa}. \end{gathered}$$

If the fuzzy set, that defines a certain color contains the hue-value 0 it is convenient to transform the hue interval from $[0, 2\pi]$ to $[2\pi, 4\pi]$ to avoid negative values.

3.2 Generation of the fuzzy sets

An important aspect in the fuzzy color processing is the proper definition of the fuzzy sets. Depending on the number of color samples, the application, and the source of information the following methods for the generation of fuzzy sets can be taken into consideration [6]:

- Manual generation
  If the practical expert in the field is able to characterize the colors using the HS and HI color space, the fuzzy sets can be generated directly. An example of this method is the fuzzy set `blue` in Fig. 8.
- Generation by sample
  If a sufficient number of color samples is available, the fuzzy sets can be generated by analyzing the frequency distribution of the sample colors. An average of all frequency distributions can be calculated to remove disturbances. The fitting fuzzy set can be calculated by balancing the edge points using methods like least square calculation.
- Using frequency distributions
  If the shape of the fuzzy set need not fulfil the definition 7 above, the frequency distribution of some samples can be used. The membership value of a color corresponds to its normalized frequency in the distribution. Examples of this method are the Figs. 11 - 14. This method differs from the previous one, due to the fact that the resulting fuzzy sets don't have to be regularly shaped.
- Generation by modifiers
  The idea of modifying fuzzy sets by regular expressions can be used to generate a large set of related color definitions. Examples are the generation of color definitions like `light_blue` or `dark_blue`, if the definition of `blue` is known. See [1] for more information on modifiers.

4 Example: analysis of welding points

The following example illustrates the use of fuzzy color processing in rule based systems. It is chosen because of its simplicity, as well as its remarkable reduction of the necessary rules [16].

4.1 Resistance spot welding

Resistance spot welding is a welding process that uses the inherent resistance of metal workpieces to join two sheets of metal by the flow of electrical current. This current is passed through the metal sheets and generates the welding heat. The same electrodes that supply the current, apply simultaneously a force and the two metal parts are joined. This welding process is economical, fast, and robust, and no secondary materials are needed. Resistance spot welding is mainly used to join metal sheets up to 5 mm in thickness. Typical areas are automotive, aerospace and engineering industry. Resistance spot welding can easily be automated and in most cases only assistants or robots are needed to supply the material. This fact has led to the economical success of resistant spot welding as well as to the need for quality-testing systems.

Most of the quality-testing systems have to destroy the welding joint in order to obtain quality measures like longitudinal and transverse tensile strength, bend strength, or hardness. Microscopic and macroscopic examination of the joint also requires destructive operations. Non-destructive tests often need large and expensive equipment, like gamma or X-ray tubes, or are too sensitive to be used directly at the welding machine, like most ultrasonic sensors.

The quality criteria of a single welding spot can be divided into two major ranges: physical and optical criteria. Physical criteria, like tensile or bend strength describe the physical properties of a welding joint and are not covered in this chapter. We will concentrate on optical properties, like the color of the spot or the surrounding metal, and on properties that can be measured using optical methods, like the diameter or the shape of the spot.

Knowledge acquisition with welders and welding engineers resulted in the following list of significant criteria, that are suitable for advanced knowledge-based reasoning (see Fig. 9).

- size, color and shape of the inner spot
- size, color and shape of the outer spot
- size, color and shape of the impact zone

The next figure (10) shows a welding spot with good quality (on the left) as well as a welding spot with bad quality (on the right). It can be clearly seen, that the shape, the size, and above all the color, is different.

The specific properties of the different quality criteria are given in Table 3. The size of the spots depend on the thickness of the sheets as well as on the diameter of the electrodes. The thickness in this example is 3 mm, and the diameter of the electrodes is 8 mm.

Table 3. Quality criteria for good and poor welding spots

quality criteria	good quality	poor quality
size of inner spot	8 mm	7.5 mm
size of outer spot	13.8 mm	9.9 mm
size of impact zone	18.7 mm	10.7 mm
shape of inner spot	circular	elliptical
shape of outer spot	circular	elliptical
shape of impact zone	circular	circular
color of inner spot	blue - dark blue	light grey - light red
color of outer spot	light blue	blue - red
color of impact zone	red - dark red	red - light red

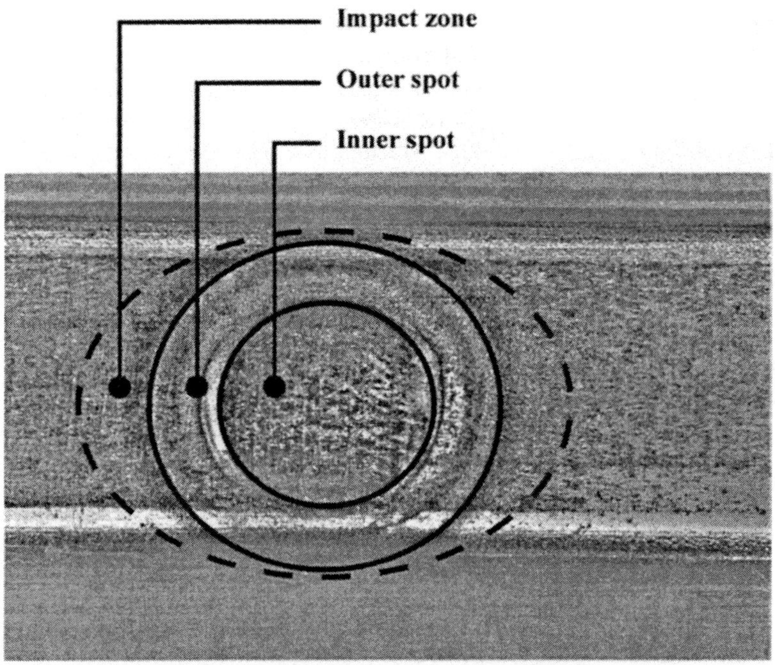

Fig. 9. Features of a resistance spot welding point

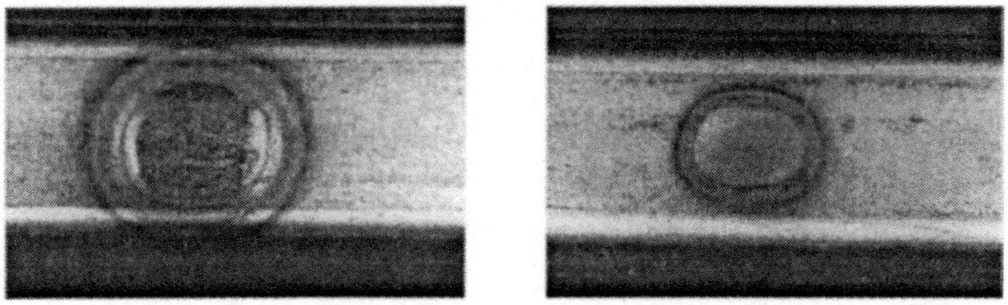

Fig. 10. Welding points of different quality (left one is good, right one is poor)

4.2 Knowledge based quality assessment

In the past few years, a knowledge based system has been developed at the university of Dortmund that is able to tell wether a welding point is of good or of poor quality [16]. The system is also able to give advice, about how the basic parameters of welding current, welding time, and electrode force should be adjusted to improve the quality. The knowledge-based system is based on rule-based reasoning and uses fuzzy logic to allow the user to enter optical and physical properties of a welding spot as numbers as well as linguistic descriptions. The user has to assess the properties, therefore a sound knowledge of the welding process is important. The system consists of more than 200 rules, with 80 rules for the quality assessment and all other rules for the improvement of the quality.

To automate the optical analysis a camera system was installed. Using standard techniques of image processing, the shape and size of the welding points could be measured [17,18]. Other features like splashes of metal or burned electrodes could also be detected using image processing. A closer look at the colors of the different zones, showed a distinct correlation of color and quality. A processing of the characteristic colors using the wavelength of dominant colors or the technical-oriented color models did not result in reliable quality assessments. For this reason fuzzy color processing, based on the HSI color model was developed. The next four figures show typical color distributions at the inner point of spot welding points. The color distribution for a welding point with good quality (Figs. 11, 12) and the distributions for a welding point with poor quality (Figs. 13, 14) are shown.

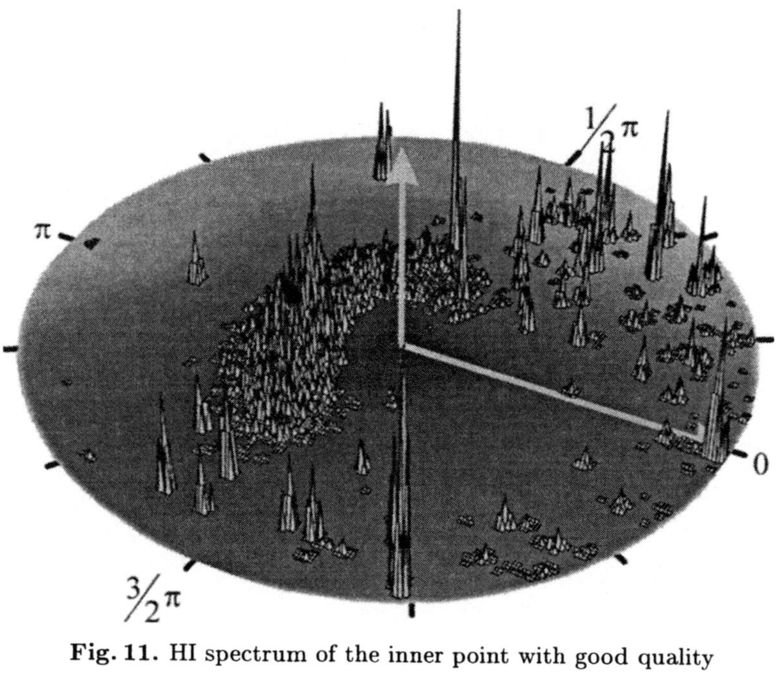

Fig. 11. HI spectrum of the inner point with good quality

These frequency distributions of the colors can be used to generate the related fuzzy sets representing the characteristic colors. All four methods, described in paragraph 3.2 are applicable. Whatever the method used to generate the fuzzy sets, the set of rules shown in Table 4 can be extracted.

These rules are extended by another set of rules, that are based on classical fuzzy sets. These fuzzy sets describe the properties (size and shape) of the

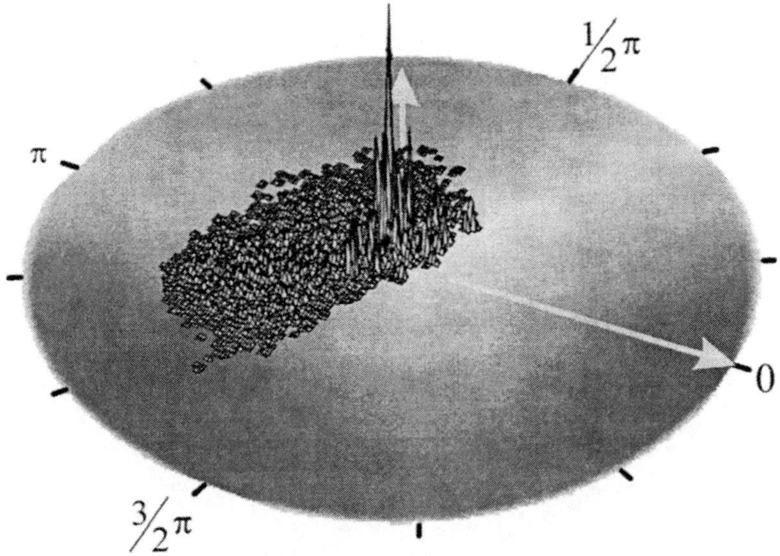

Fig. 12. HS spectrum of the inner point with good quality

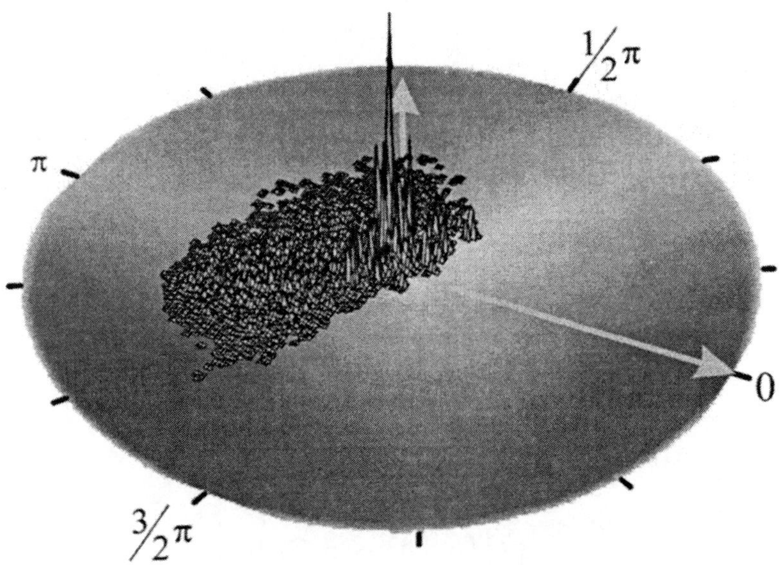

Fig. 13. HI spectrum of the inner point with poor quality

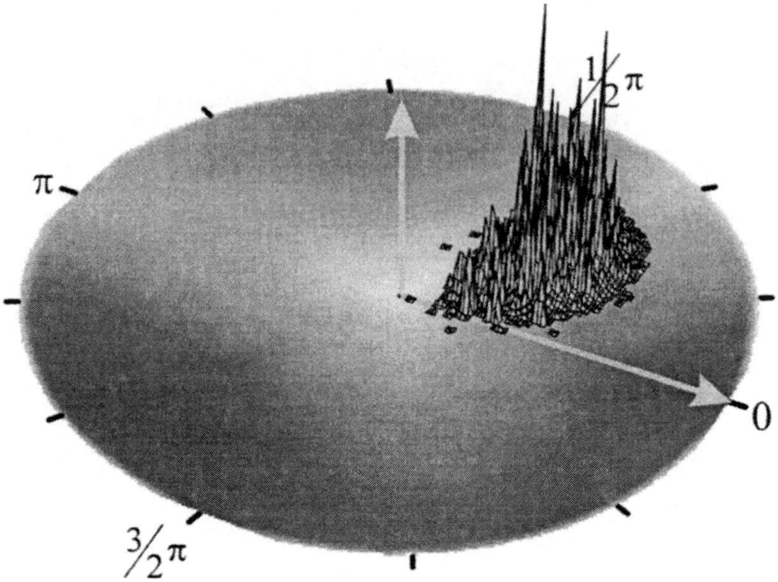

Fig. 14. HS spectrum of the inner point with poor quality

1. IF	color_of_inner_spot	IS	`blue`
THEN	quality	IS	good
2. IF	color_of_outer_spot	IS	`light_blue`
THEN	quality	IS	good
3. IF	color_of_impact_zone	IS	`dark_red`
THEN	quality	IS	good
4. IF	color_of_inner_spot	IS	`light_red`
THEN	quality	IS	poor
5. IF	color_of_outer_spot	IS	`blue`
THEN	quality	IS	poor
6. IF	color_of_outer_spot	IS	`red`
THEN	quality	IS	poor
7. IF	color_of_impact_zone	IS	`light_red`
THEN	quality	IS	poor

Table 4. Rule base for color criteria

different zones of a spot welding point. An extract from these rules is given in Table 5.

The complete rule base consists of the following parts:

- color of inner spot criteria for good and poor quality
- color of outer spot criteria for good and poor quality
- color of impact zone criteria for good and poor quality
- size of inner spot criteria for good and poor quality
- size of outer spot criteria for good and poor quality

1. IF	size_of_inner_spot	IS large
THEN	quality	IS good
2. IF	size_of_inner_spot	IS small
THEN	quality	IS poor
3. IF	size_of_inner_spot	IS very_large
THEN	quality	IS poor
4. IF	shape_of_inner_spot	IS circular
THEN	quality	IS good
5. IF	shape_of_inner_spot	IS elliptical
THEN	quality	IS poor

Table 5. Partial rule base for size and shape criteria

- size of impact zone criteria for good and poor quality
- shape of inner spot criteria for good and poor quality
- shape of outer spot criteria for good and poor quality

Applying the complete set of rules for the analysis of the optical criteria to welding points is a reliable method of determining the quality of welding spots. All the criteria that are used can be inspected by an automated system. For the example a camera system positioned at the assembly line was sufficient.

5 Summary

Fuzzy color processing is a powerful approach to extend existing quality testing systems. Using more sophisticated color model like HSI, HS or HI models, it is possible to describe colors in a natural, linguistic way. Only a few rules are needed to solve complex problems. In our example, the evaluation of a total of seven rules is enough to distinguish between welding points with a good and those with a bad quality. The computational demand is low, so simple microcontrollers can be used to solve this task. The ideas of linguistic hedges can be integrated, which means that from the definition of the term `red` other definitions like `light_red`, `dark_red` or `more_or_less_red` can be generated automatically. This will reduce the development time for new applications.

References

1. Bouchon-Meunier B., *Fuzzy Logic and Knowledge Representation Using Linguistic Modifiers*, in: "Fuzzy Logic for the Management of Uncertainty (Zadeh L.A. and Kacprzyk J., eds.)", John-Wiley, New York, pp. 399–414, 1992
2. Curcio C.A. and Hendrickson A.E., *Organization and Development of the Primate Photoreceptor Mosaic*, Prog Ret. Ret., Vol. 10, pp. 89–120, 1991
3. Dubois D., Prade H. and Yager R.Y., *"Fuzzy Sets for Intelligent Systems"*, Morgan Kaufmann Publishers, San Mateo, 1993

4. Fathi M. and Hildebrand L., *Model-free Optimization of Fuzzy Rulebased Systems Using Evolutionstrategies*, IEEE Transactions on System, Man, and Cybernetics, Part B: Cybernetics, Vol. 27, No. 2, pp. 270–277, 1997
5. Foley J. et al., *"Computer Graphics: Principles and Practice (second edition)"*, Addison-Wesley, Reading, 1990
6. Hildebrand L. and Fathi M., *Soft Computing as a Methodology for Color Processing*, in: "Proceedings of the EUSFLAT–ESTYLF Joint Conference" (Palma de Mallorca, Spain), 1999
7. Hunt R.W.G., *"The Production of Color (third edition)"*, John Wiley, New York, 1975
8. Kolb H., *The Neural Organization of the Human Retina*, in: "Principles and Practises of Clinical Elektropysiologie of Vision (Heckenlively J.R. and Arden G.B., eds.)", Mosby Year Book Inc, St. Louis, pp. 25–52, 1991
9. Laycock J. and Chorley R.A., *Human Factors Consideration for the Interface Between an Electro-Optical Display and the Human Vision System*, Displays, Vol. 4, pp. 304–314, 1981
10. Mann I., *"The development of the Human Eye"*, Grune and Stralton, New York, 1964
11. Meyer G.W. and Greenberg D.P., *Perceptual Color Spaces for Computer Graphics*, in: "Color and the Computer (Durret H.J., ed.)", Academic Press, San Diego, pp. 83–100, 1986
12. Munsell A.H., *"A Color Notation"*, Munsell Color Company, Baltimore, 1946
13. Murch G., *Color Display and Color Science*, in: "Color and the Computer (Durret H.J., ed.)", Academic Press, San Diego, pp. 1–26, 1986
14. Nickerson D., *"History of the Munsell Color System, Company, and Foundation – Part 1 Color Research and Application"*, pp. 7–10, 1976
15. Novák V., *Fuzzy Logic as a Base for Approximate Reasoning*, in: "Fuzzy Logic for the Management of Uncertainty (Zadeh L.A. and Kacprzyk J., eds.)", John-Wiley, New York, pp. 247–264, 1992
16. Reusch B., Fathi M. and Hildebrand L., *Fuzzy Color Processing for Quality Improvement*, in: "Soft Computing, Multimedia, and Image Processing – Proceedings of the World Automation Congress (Jamshidi M., Bien Z. and Fathi M., eds.)" (U.S.A.), TSI Press, Albuquerque, pp. 841–848, 1998
17. Rosenfeld A. and Kak A.C., *"Digital Picture Processing – Volume 1 (second edition)"*, Academic Press, San Diego, 1982
18. Rosenfeld A. and Kak A.C., *Digital Picture Processing – Volume 2 (second edition)"*, Academic Press, San Diego, 1982
19. Silverstein L.D., *Human Factors for Color CRT Displays*, Society for Information Displays, pp. 1–41, 1982
20. Teichner W.H., *Color and Information Coding*, in: "Proceedings of the Society for Information Displays", Vol. 20, pp. 3–9, 1979
21. Watt A.H., *"Fundamentals of Three-dimensional Computer Graphics"*, Addison-Wesley, Wokingham, 1989
22. Wyszecki G. and Siles W.S., *"Color Science (second edition)"*, John Wiley, New York, 1982
23. Yager R.R. and Filev D.P., *"Essentials of Fuzzy Modelling and Control"*, John Wiley, New York, 1994

Chapter 11

Ranking Segmentation Paths Using Fuzzified Decision Rules

Zhongkang Lu[1], Zheru Chi[2], Pengfei Shi[3], and Eam Khwang Teoh[1]

[1] Nan Yang Technological University
School of Electrical and Electronic Engineering
Intelligent Machines Research Laboratory
Nan Yang Avenue, Singapore 639798
email: {ezklu,eekteoh}@ntu.edu.sg

[2] The Hong Kong Polytechnic University
Department of Electronic and Information Engineering
Hung Hom, Kowloon, Hong Kong
email: enzheru@polyu.edu.hk

[3] Shanghai Jiaotong University
Institute of Pattern Recognition and Image Processing
Shanghai 200052, P.R. of China
email: pfshic@online.sh.cn

Summary. Connected characters are usually recognized using a segmentation-based approach in which individual characters are segmented first by segmentation paths before they are fed to a character classifier. Good ranking of segmentation paths can significantly shorten the processing time in evaluating segmentation paths and improve the recognition rate by avoiding misinterpretation. In this chapter, we present a method of using fuzzified decision rules to rank segmentation paths. The fuzzified decision rules are obtained by fuzzifying the decision rules extracted from a decision tree learned from examples. Nine measures of the properties of a segmentation path are extracted as the input and the centroid defuzzification method is adopted to defuzzify the output. Our method of ranking segmentation paths has been tested on the NIST Special Database 3 with good results.

1 Introduction

High recognition rate and high processing speed are two important but usually conflicting requirements for a character recognition system. Research of more than three decades all over the world in printed and handwritten character recognition has led to deliveries of many commercial products. However, the recognition performance of off-line connected characters and on-line cursive words is still far from satisfactory for practical uses. The main difficulty lies in the segmentation of individual characters from character strings. Active research has been carried out in this field [1,16,21]. A survey of various techniques for recognizing connected characters was given by Lu et. al. [12]. Most of the available techniques require intensive computation.

In recognizing connected handwritten characters, human beings can perform far better than machines. We believe that the superiority of human recognition is partially because we have sufficient knowledge on the problem and adopt a very robust recognition scheme, in particular, in dealing with noisy and fuzzy patterns. As a fuzzy logic approach is a way to achieve this robustness, we apply fuzzified decision rules to rank the segmentation paths obtained by a background-thinning-based algorithm presented in [14]. In our approach, the "goodness" degree to which a candidate is a good segmentation path is determined by fuzzified decision rules with nine properties associated with the path and the separated parts segmented by the path.

Since Zadeh introduced the fuzzy set theory in 1965 [27], the fuzzy logic approach has been an increasing interest of many scientists and researchers. In the recent years, we have seen the booming of applications of fuzzy algorithms in pattern recognition. Increasing popularity of fuzzy algorithms are because:

1. fuzzy rules are found to be naturally effective for any human-like cognition systems such as image understanding and pattern recognition; and
2. fuzzy sets provides a good platform for dealing with noisy and imprecise information that is often encountered in our daily life [3].

In our algorithm, fuzzified decision rules, which are derived from the C4.5 algorithm presented by Quinlan [20], are used to rank the segmentation paths.

The flowchart of our segmentation and recognition system for connected 2-digit strings is shown in Fig. 1. The system includes three steps: (1) identification of segmentation paths using a background-thinning-based algorithm; (2) ranking of the segmentation paths by fuzzified decision rules; (3) selection of a good enough path based on the ranking and recognition results. If no satisfactory segmentation path is found, the input digit string is rejected.

Fig. 2 shows examples of connected 2-digit strings extracted from the NIST Special Database 3 and their pre-processed forms [13].

This chapter is organized as follows. Relevant techniques (the background-thinning-based segmentation algorithm, the ID3 decision tree and the C4.5 algorithm) are introduced in Section 2. Feature extraction of a segmentation path and generation of fuzzified decision rules are presented in Section 3 and Section 4, respectively. Centroid defuzzification is discussed in Section 5. Experimental results and discussions are presented in Section 6. Finally, concluding remarks are drawn in Section 7.

2 Relevant techniques

2.1 Background-thinning-based segmentation algorithm

There are normally two categories of segmentation algorithms for separating connected digits: algorithms based on contour features [2,22,23,26,28] and

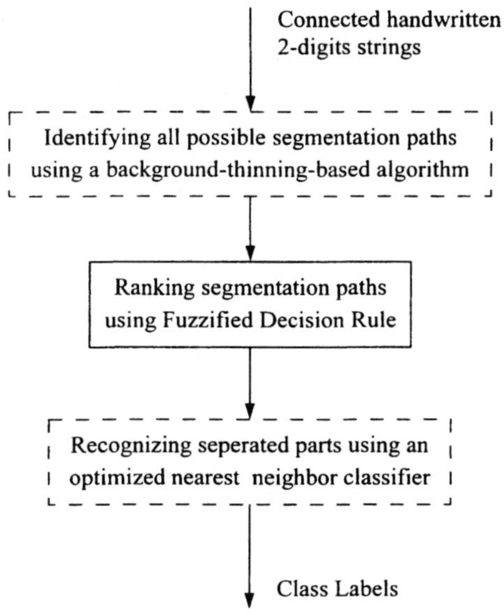

Fig. 1. Flowchart of our segmentation and recognition system for connected 2-digit strings

algorithms based on stroke information [21]. One weakness of the former approach is that too many segmentation candidates are often generated. For the latter approach, the extraction of strokes is usually difficult and prune to error. In this section, a segmentation algorithm based on the analysis of the background (regions excluding the characters) skeleton of a digit string image is briefly introduced.

In order to get a complete background skeleton, each digit image should be placed on a rectangle window with a small space to each of the four frames. The background regions of a digit string image are thinned using a skeletonization algorithm adapted from Hilditch's thinning algorithm [7]. In order to avoid the connection of upper and bottom background skeletons, segments generated between the foreground and the left or right image frame are not considered in the subsequent matching processing.

A segmentation path is constructed by connecting several feature points (fork points, end points and curve points) on the background skeleton with possible extension(s) to the top and/or bottom of an image. A fork point is a point that has more than two connected branches and an end point is a point that has only one neighbor. A curve point is a point at which the direction of the line changes sharply. Segmentation paths are formed by matching feature points. Obviously, only considering these feature points on background skeletons makes the matching and analysis procedure simple and fast.

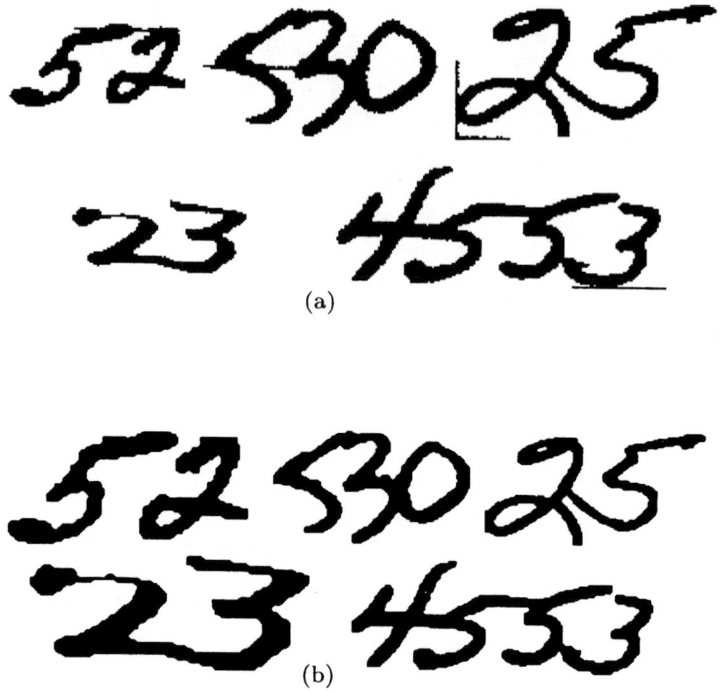

Fig. 2. Examples of connected 2-digit strings from the NIST Special Database 3 and the results after pre-processing: top = original character strings; bottom = pre-processed character strings

A three-step feature points matching scheme is applied, as shown in Fig. 3. The first step is to search the feature points from top to bottom (the top-down searching), as shown in Fig. 4. We can see that it is a recursive procedure. The black thick lines in Fig. 6(a) show the partial paths traced. If there exist unmatched feature points on lower segments, a bottom-up searching is conducted from these points at the second step (see Fig. 6(b)). This step is similar to the first step except the direction is from bottom to top. If there still exist unmatched feature points on hole segments (mainly are those feature points on the skeletons generated by hole of the image), another search is conducted at the third step in which searching is conducted upward and downward separately (double-way searching) and the two traced segments are then integrated into a segmentation path, as shown in Fig. 5. The black thick lines shown in Fig. 6(c) are the paths generated by this step. As a result, all possible segmentation paths can be identified by this three-step searching scheme.

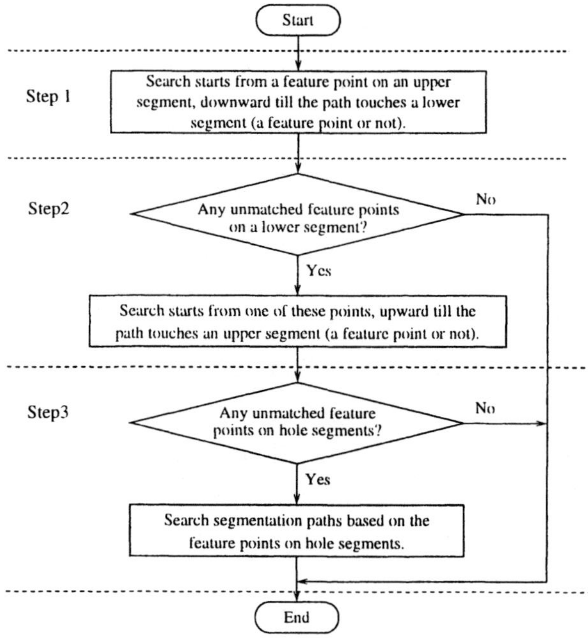

Fig. 3. The flowchart of the three-step searching

2.2 ID3 decision tree and C4.5 algorithm

ID3 (Interactive dichotomizing 3) decision tree and C4.5 algorithms are introduced by Quinlan [18–20] for inducing classification models from data. Given a set of records, each record has the same structure, consisting of a number of attributes or values. One of these attributes represents the category of the record. The problem is to determine a decision tree that on the basis of answers to questions about the non-category attributes predicts correctly the value of the category attribute. Usually the category attribute takes only the values {true, false}, or {success, failure}, or something equivalent. In any case, one of its values will mean failure. Fig. 7 is an example of a decision tree from [20] that deals with records reporting on weather conditions for playing golf.

The basic ideas behind ID3 are the following:

1. In the decision tree each node corresponds to a non-categorical attribute and each arc to a possible value of that attribute. A leaf of the tree specifies the expected value of the categorical attribute for the records described by the path from the root to that leaf.

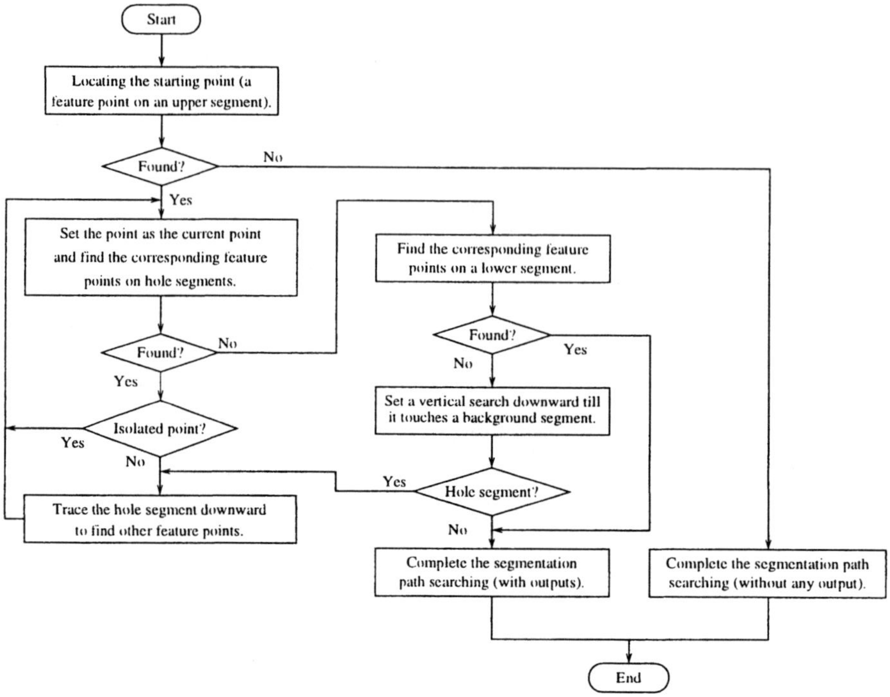

Fig. 4. The flowchart of the top-down searching

2. In the decision tree, each node should be associated with the non-categorical attribute which is most informative among the attributes not yet considered in the path from the root.
3. Entropy is used to measure how informative is a node.

C4.5 is an extension of ID3 that accounts for unavailable values, continuous attribute value ranges, pruning of decision trees, rule derivation, and so on.

If a set T of records is partitioned into disjoint exhaustive classes $C_1, C_2, \ldots, C_k$ on the basis of the value of the categorical attribute, and P is the probability distribution of the partition $(C_1, C_2, \cdots, C_k)$, then the information $Info(T)$ needed to identify the class of an element of T is equal to the entropy of P, $I(P)$.

$$Info(T) = I(P) \tag{1}$$

If we first partition T on the basis of the value of a non-categorical attribute X into sets $T_1, T_2, \cdots, T_n$ then the information needed to identify

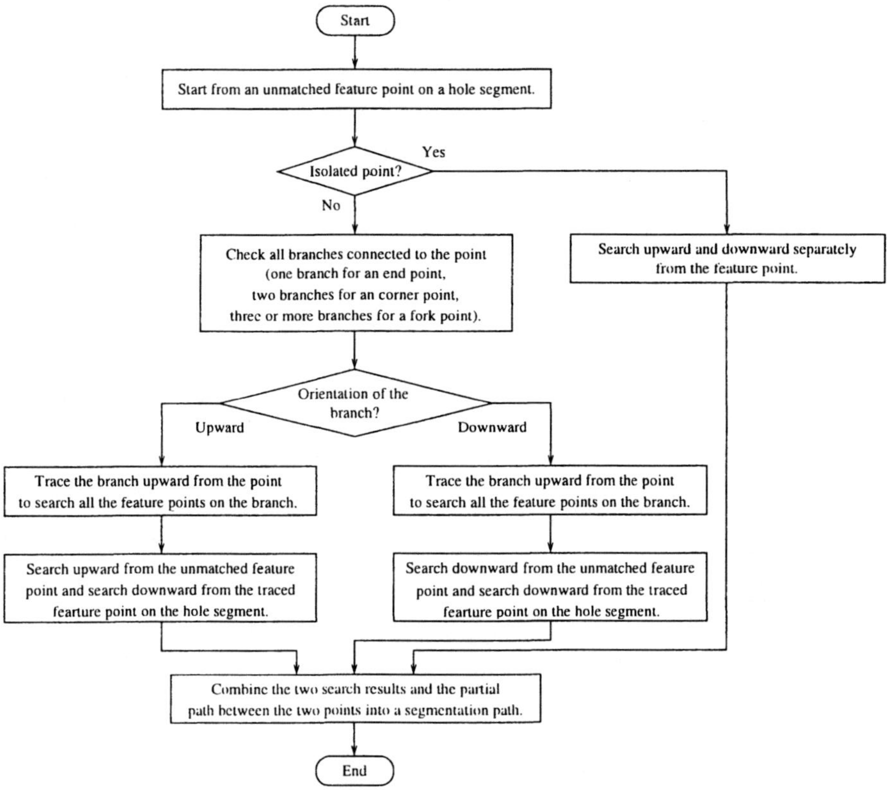

Fig. 5. The flowchart of double-way searching

the class of an element of T becomes the weighted average of the information needed to identify the class of an element of T_i, i.e. the weighted average of $Info(T_i)$:

$$Info(X,T) = \sum_{i=1}^{n} \frac{|T_i|}{|T|} Info(T_i) \tag{2}$$

Consider the quantity $Gain(X,T)$ defined as

$$Gain(X,T) = Info(T) - Info(X,T) \tag{3}$$

This represents the difference between the information needed to identify an element of T and the information needed to identify an element of T

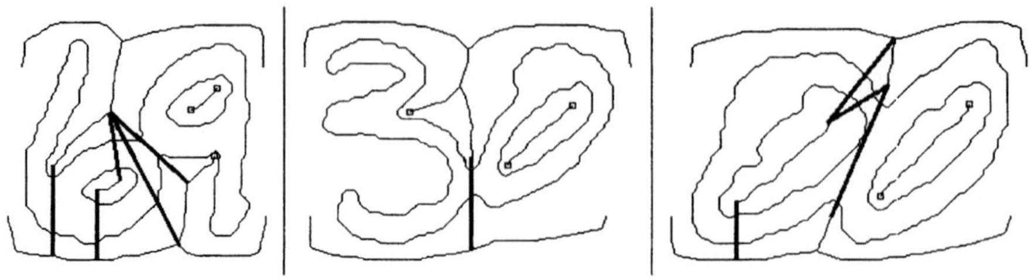

(a)

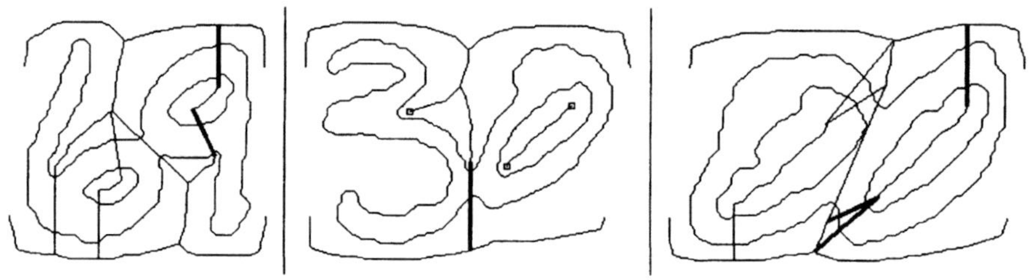

(b)

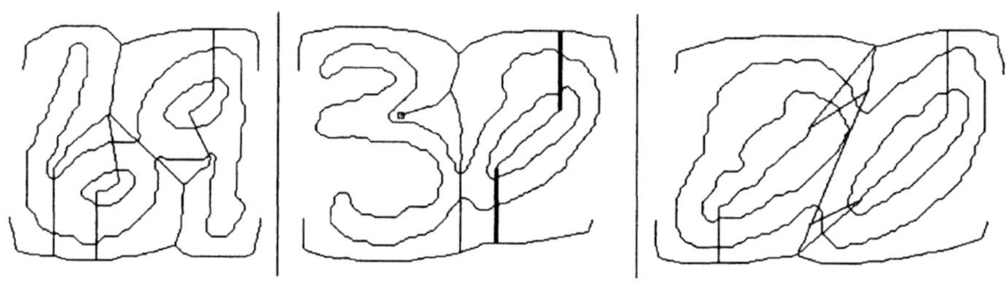

(c)

Fig. 6. Examples of segmentation paths identified by three-step feature point matching (marked feature points are unmatched points): (a) segmentation paths found (thick black lines) by the top-down searching; (b) segmentation paths found by the bottom-up searching; and (c) segmentation paths found by searching from hole segments

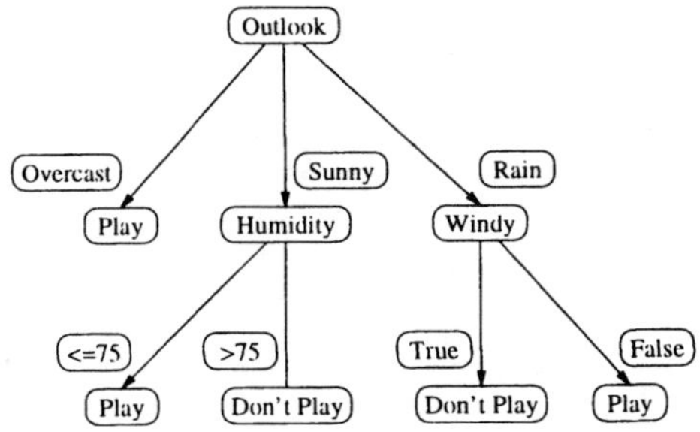

Fig. 7. An example of a decision tree dealing with records reporting on weather conditions for playing golf

after the value of attribute X has been obtained, that is, this is the gain in information due to attribute X.

$Gain(X, T)$ is used to rank attributes and to build decision trees where each node is associated with the attribute with the greatest gain among the attributes not yet considered in the path from the root.

The ID3 algorithm for building a decision tree can be presented as a recursive procedure [20]:

Initialize: R, *a set of non-categorical attributes;*
C, *the categorical attribute;*
S, *a training set*

Function ID3 (R,C,S) returns a decision tree;

begin
If S is empty, return a single node with value Failure;
If S consists of records all with the same value for the categorical attribute, return a single node with that value;
If R is empty, then return a single node with the most frequent categorical attribute value that is found in records of S;
Let D be the attribute with largest $Gain(D, S)$ among attributes in R; Let $\{d_j | j = 1, 2, \ldots, m\}$ be the values of attribute D; Let $\{S_j | j = 1, 2, .., m\}$ be the subsets of S consisting respectively of records with value d_j for attribute D; Return a tree with root labeled D and arcs labeled $d_1, d_2, \cdots, d_m$ going respectively to the trees:

$$ID3(R - D, C, S_1), ID3(R - D, C, S_2), .., ID3(R - D, C, S_m) \tag{4}$$

end;

Because of the way a decision tree is built, it can response correctly with most of the records in the training set. In fact, in order to do so, it may become quite complex, with long and very uneven paths. This is very similar to the 'over training' problem of artificial neural networks.

Pruning of a decision tree is done by replacing a whole subtree by a leaf node. The replacement takes place if a decision rule establishes that the expected error rate in the subtree is greater than in the single leaf.

Winston [24] shows how to use Fisher's exact test to determine if the category attribute is truly dependent on a non-categorical attribute. If it is not, then the non-categorical attribute need not appear in the current path of the decision tree.

Deriving a rule set from a decision tree is straightforward. Each path in the pruned decision tree from the root to a leaf is equivalent to a rule. The resulting rule can be simplified based on the following principles:

Let LHS be the left hand side of a rule in a decision tree. Let LHS' be obtained from LHS by eliminating some of its conditions. We can certainly replace LHS by LHS' in this rule if the subsets of the training set that satisfy respectively LHS and LHS' are equal.

3 Properties of a segmentation path

A connected 2-digit string is split into the left and right parts by a segmentation path. Some parameters associated with this segmentation are given in the following:

- L = length of a segmentation path in the number of pixels;
- L_f = number of pixels on a segmentation path which are in the foreground of the image;
- N_1 = number of pixels in the left part;
- N_2 = Number of pixels in the right part;
- $x_L^{(1)}, x_L^{(2)}$ = horizontal coordinates of the leftmost pixel of each part;
- $x_R^{(1)}, x_R^{(2)}$ = horizontal coordinates of the rightmost pixel of each part;
- $y_H^{(1)}, y_H^{(2)}$ = vertical coordinates of the highest pixel of each part; and
- $y_L^{(1)}, y_L^{(2)}$ = vertical coordinates of the lowest pixel of each part.

Segmentation paths are ranked based on the nine properties associated with each path and the separated parts by the path. The nine properties are adapted from [2], which were successfully used to rank segmenting paths for recognizing handwritten single- and double-touching digit strings. The nine properties (F_0, F_1, ..., F_8) associated with each segmentation path are given below:

- F_0 = ratio between the sizes of left and right parts:

$$F_0 = \begin{cases} N_1/N_2 & : \text{ if } \quad N_1 \le N2, \\ N_2/N_1 & : \text{ otherwise.} \end{cases} \tag{5}$$

$F_0 \in [0.0, 1.0]$.

- F_1 = ratio between the value of L_f and the height of the image:

$$F_1 = \frac{L_f}{\max(y_L^{(1)}, y_L^{(2)}) - \min(y_H^{(1)}, y_H^{(2)})} \tag{6}$$

  F_1 is set to 1.0 when its value is greater than 1.0.
- F_2 = ratio between the horizontal length of any overlap of the two parts, and the smaller of the widths of the two parts:

$$F_2 = \frac{x_R^{(1)} - x_L^{(2)}}{\min[x_R^{(1)} - x_L^{(1)}, x_R^{(2)} - x_L^{(2)}]} \tag{7}$$

  F_2 is set to 1.0 when its value is greater than 1.0.
- F_3 = ratio between the heights of the two parts:

$$F_3 = \begin{cases} (y_L^{(1)} - y_H^{(1)})/(y_L^{(2)} - y_H^{(2)}) & : \text{ if } \quad (y_L^{(1)} - y_H^{(1)}) \leq (y_L^{(2)} - y_H^{(2)}) \\ (y_L^{(2)} - y_H^{(2)})/(y_L^{(1)} - y_H^{(1)}) & : \text{ otherwise.} \end{cases} \tag{8}$$

  $F_3 \in [0.0, 1.0]$.
- F_4 = ratio between the widths of the two parts:

$$F_4 = \begin{cases} (x_R^{(1)} - x_L^{(1)})/(x_R^{(2)} - x_L^{(2)}) & : \text{ if } \quad (x_R^{(1)} - x_L^{(1)}) \leq (x_R^{(2)} - x_L^{(2)}) \\ (x_R^{(2)} - x_L^{(2)})/(x_R^{(1)} - x_L^{(1)}) & : \text{ otherwise.} \end{cases} \tag{9}$$

  $F_4 \in [0.0, 1.0]$.
- F_5 = average angle, with the horizontal axis, of the segments of a path which are in the foreground of an image. $F_5 \in [-\pi/2, \pi/2]$.
- F_6 = normalized distance of the center of segmentation path (x_{lc}) to the center of the image on the horizontal axis (x_C):

$$F_6 = \frac{2|x_{lc} - x_C|}{x_R^{(2)} - x_L^{(1)}} \tag{10}$$

  where x_{lc} is obtained by

$$x_{lc} = \frac{\sum_{i=0}^{L} x_i^s}{L} \tag{11}$$

  where x_i^s $(i = 0, 1, ..., L)$ are the horizontal coordinates of pixels on the segmentation path.
- F_7, F_8 = ratios of the width to the height of the left part and right part, respectively.

4 Fuzzified decision rules

Fuzzy rules can be generated from examples using various techniques. Kasabov presented a neural network approach for generating fuzzy rules [11]. Fuzzy rules can also be generated by a clustering technique [10] and statistical measures [17]. Malaviya *et al.* [15] presented a hybrid approach, which combined fuzzy statistical measures, neural networks and expert's knowledge, to generate fuzzy rules. On the other hand, Ishibuchi *et al.* used genetic algorithms to select fuzzy rules for pattern classification [8,9].

We believe the fuzzy rules extracted by genetic algorithms can achieve the best performance. However, the computational cost of using a genetic algorithm is very high if there is a large number of training patterns.

A rule extracted from a Quinlan's ID3 decision tree and C4.5 algorithm has the following form:

$$F_1(f_{1j}) \wedge F_2(f_{2j}) \wedge \cdots \wedge F_n(f_{nj}) \Longrightarrow C(L_j) \tag{12}$$

$F_i(f_{ij})$ is true when feature F_i takes a value in the region f_{ij}. For a discrete feature, f_{ij} is a single value. $C(L_j)$ denotes the class label associated with leaf L_j.

Decision rules work well when input data is noise-free. However, its performance degrades quite a bit when input data is uncertain or noisy. Chi *et al.* proposed to use fuzzified decision rules to deal with the uncertain problems in handwritten digit recognition [4].

There are five definitions of value regions used for a feature (F_i) with continuous values in decision rules. They are determined by:

1. $F_i > f_{ij}$;
2. $F_i \leq f_{ij}$;
3. $F_i > f_{ij1} \wedge F_i \leq f_{ij2}$, $f_{ij1} < f_{ij2}$;
4. $F_i \leq f_{ij1} \vee F_i > f_{ij2}$, $f_{ij1} < f_{ij2} \wedge (1+\alpha)f_{ij1} < (1-\alpha)f_{ij2}$; and
5. $F_i \leq f_{ij1} \vee F_i > f_{ij2}$, $f_{ij1} < f_{ij2} \wedge (1+\alpha)f_{ij1} \geq (1-\alpha)f_{ij2}$,

where α is an extension factor. In this algorithm, the value of α represents the degree of fuzziness of the rules. The fuzziness increases with the increase of the value of α. When $\alpha = 0$, the fuzzified decision rules are just equal to the decision rules.

For value region 1, we define a membership function as:

$$m(F_i) = \begin{cases} 1.0 & : \text{ if } \quad F_i \leq f_{ij} \\ 0.0 & : \text{ if } \quad F_i > (1+\alpha)f_{ij} \\ \frac{(1+\alpha)f_{ij} - F_i}{\alpha f_{ij}} & : \text{ if } \quad f_{ij} < F_i \leq (1+\alpha)f_{ij} \end{cases} \tag{13}$$

where α reflects the fuzziness of the data. The greater α is, the more fuzzy the data are. The membership function is shown in Fig. 8(a).

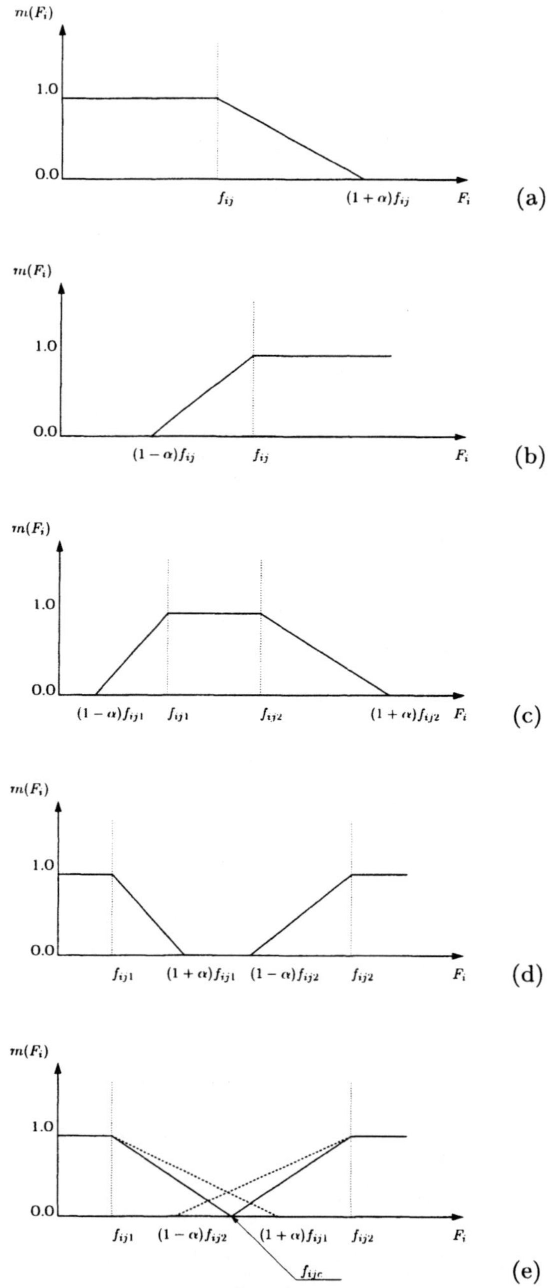

Fig. 8. Membership functions for five definitions of value regions: (a) $F_i > f_{ij}$; (b) $F_i \leq f_{ij}$; (c) $F_i > f_{ij1} \wedge F_i \leq f_{ij2}$, $f_{ij1} < f_{ij2}$; (d) $F_i \leq f_{ij1} \vee F_i > f_{ij2}$, $f_{ij1} < f_{ij2} \wedge (1+\alpha)f_{ij1} < (1-\alpha)f_{ij2}$; and (e) $F_i \leq f_{ij1} \vee F_i > f_{ij2}$, $f_{ij1} < f_{ij2} \wedge (1+\alpha)f_{ij1} \geq (1-\alpha)f_{ij2}$

For value region 2, we have (see Fig. 8(b)):

$$m(F_i) = \begin{cases} 1.0 & : \text{ if } \quad F_i \geq f_{ij} \\ 0.0 & : \text{ if } \quad F_i < (1-\alpha) f_{ij} \\ \frac{F_i - (1-\alpha) f_{ij}}{\alpha f_{ij}} & : \text{ if } \quad (1-\alpha) f_{ij} < F_i \leq f_{ij} \end{cases} \tag{14}$$

For value region 3, we have (see Fig. 8(c)):

$$m(F_i) = \begin{cases} 1.0 & : \text{ if } \quad F_i \geq f_{ij1} \wedge F_i \leq f_{ij2} \\ 0.0 & : \text{ if } \quad F_i > (1+\alpha) f_{ij2} \vee F_i < (1-\alpha) f_{ij1} \\ \frac{(1+\alpha) f_{ij2} - F_i}{\alpha f_{ij2}} & : \text{ if } \quad f_{ij2} < F_i \leq (1+\alpha) f_{ij2} \\ \frac{F_i - (1-\alpha) f_{ij1}}{\alpha f_{ij1}} & : \text{ if } \quad (1-\alpha) f_{ij1} < F_i \leq f_{ij1} \end{cases} \tag{15}$$

For value region 4, we have (see Fig. 8(d)):

$$m(F_i) = \begin{cases} 1.0 & : \text{ if } \quad F_i \leq f_{ij1} \vee F_i \geq f_{ij2} \\ 0.0 & : \text{ if } \quad F_i > (1+\alpha) f_{ij1} \wedge F_i < (1-\alpha) f_{ij2} \\ \frac{(1+\alpha) f_{ij1} - F_i}{\alpha f_{ij1}} & : \text{ if } \quad f_{ij1} < F_i \leq (1+\alpha) f_{ij1} \\ \frac{F_i - (1-\alpha) f_{ij2}}{\alpha f_{ij2}} & : \text{ if } \quad (1-\alpha) f_{ij2} < F_i \leq f_{ij2} \end{cases} \tag{16}$$

For value region 5, we define a membership function as

$$m(F_i) = \begin{cases} 1.0 & : \text{ if } \quad F_i \leq f_{ij1} \vee F_i \geq f_{ij2} \\ 0.0 & : \text{ if } \quad F_i > (1+\alpha) f_{ij1} \wedge F_i < (1-\alpha) f_{ij2} \\ \frac{f_{ijc} - F_i}{f_{ijc} - f_{ij1}} & : \text{ if } \quad f_{ij1} < F_i \leq f_{ijc} \\ \frac{F_i - f_{ijc}}{f_{ij2} - f_{ij2}} & : \text{ if } \quad f_{ijc} < F_i \leq f_{ij2} \end{cases} \tag{17}$$

where $f_{ijc} = \frac{f_{ij1} + f_{ij2}}{2}$. The membership function is shown in Fig. 8(e).

Using the membership grades instead of binary values 0 and 1 for the degree to which a rule is triggered, the decision rules become a set of fuzzy rules.

Nine properties, $F_0, F_1, ..., F_8$, discussed in Section 3 are used for ranking segmentation paths. A rule outputs one of two classes: a good segmentation path or a bad segmentation path. Some of the rules we used for classifying a segmentation path are given below:

1. Rule 1: IF $F_0 \leq 0.70$ AND $F_1 > 0.10$ AND $F_5 > -0.73$ AND $F_5 \leq 0.84$ AND $F_8 > 0.89$, THEN the path is a bad segmentation path.
2. Rule 2: IF $F_1 > 0.70$ AND $F_2 \leq 0.24$ AND $F_3 > -0.40$ AND $F_4 > 0.52$ AND $-0.21 < F_7 \leq 0.30$, THEN the path is a good segmentation path.
3. Rule 3: IF $F_2 \leq 0.09$ AND $F_4 > 0.64$ AND $-0.30 < F_7 \leq 0.57$, THEN the path is a good segmentation path.

5 Defuzzification

Centroid defuzzification is defined as

$$O_p = \frac{\sum_{i=1}^{N} w_i D_p^i O^i}{\sum_{i=1}^{N} w_i D_p^i} \tag{18}$$

where N is the number of fuzzy rules and w_i weighs the confidence of rule i with $\sum_{i=1}^{N} w_i = 1$. O_p represents the defuzzified output of pattern p. In this application, we have two classes, good or bad segmentation path. The value of O^i is assigned as 1 if the output of rule i is "good segmentation path", otherwise it is assigned as -1. If the output O_p is greater than 0, the segmentation path p is regarded as a "good segmentation path", otherwise, it is a "bad segmentation path". D_p^i measures how the pth pattern matches the antecedent conditions (IF-part) of the ith rule. D_p^i is given by the product of the matching degrees of the pattern in the fuzzy subsets that the ith rule holds, that is,

$$D_p^i = \prod_{k=1}^{N_f} m_{ki} \tag{19}$$

where N_f is the number of features used in that rule (called the size of the rule) and m_{ki} is the membership grade of the k-th feature in the fuzzy subset that the ith rule holds. We use $P = \frac{1+O_p}{2}$, which reflects the degree to which a candidate is a good segmentation path, to rank all of possible segmentation paths.

6 Experimental results and discussion

All the parameters used in the construction of segmentation paths should be set according to the size of an image. In our experiments, the height of the normalized image is 160 pixels. Decision rules were generated and tested using 6697 manually classified segmentation paths, which were extracted from 823 connected two-digit strings from NIST special database 3. With 4000 as training samples, 28 decision rules were generated. Among them, 17 rules were fuzzified and the others were discarded because they have little impact on training samples. Experimental results show that the correct path classification rate is 81.1% on the 4000 training paths and 79.9% on the remaining 2697 test paths.

A comparison of the correct path classification rates among the fuzzified decision rules (with different α values), straightforward decision trees (unpruned and pruned) [18], decision rules, and multi-layer perceptron (MLP) classifier are shown in Table 1. The inputs of these classifiers are the nine properties of a path given in Section 3 and the outputs are two classes, good

Table 1. A comparison of the correct path classification rates among fuzzified decision rules (with different α values), decision rules, straightforward decision trees (unpruned and pruned) and multi-layer perceptron classifier

Techniques	Training set (%)	testing set (%)
Fuzzified decision rules ($\alpha = 0.1$)	81.1	79.9
Fuzzified decision rules ($\alpha = 0.5$)	79.8	77.6
Decision rules	92.5	77.3
Decision tree (unpruned)	98.1	73.9
Decision tree (pruned)	93.5	76.2
Multi-layer perceptron (9-11-2)	85.0	81.6

segmentation path and bad segmentation path. We set "good" as 1 and "bad" as 0. The output values of the classifiers are used for testing in the comparison. As to the decision rules and decision trees, the outputs are discrete values, 0 or 1, which is easy for testing; and as to the fuzzified decision rules and Multi-layer perceptron, the outputs are values between 0 and 1, a threshold was set for each technique. If the output is higher than the threshold, the segmentation path was labelled as "good", or set to "bad".

The size of the MLP classifier is 9-11-2, and it was trained using the backpropagation algorithm with the conjugate-gradient optimization technique. Here, the value of α is chosen manually, compare with $\alpha = 0.5$, and $\alpha = 0$ (decision rules), when $\alpha = 0.1$, the fuzzified decision rules can achieve a best performance. Evaluated on the test set, the correct path classification rate of fuzzified decision rules is better than those of the straightforward decision trees (unpruned or pruned), but slightly lower than that of the MLP classifier. However, our approach of path ranking based on the fuzzified decision rules has the following advantages:

1. The defuzzified output of fuzzified decision rules naturally reflects a degree to which a candidate path is a good segmentation path, which is more suitable for the ranking problem.
2. Using only 17 rules is computationally efficient.
3. Rules extracted from human recognition experience can be easily incorporated into our system.

The separated digits were recognized using an optimized nearest-neighbor classifier proposed by Yan [25]. Sixty-four intensities on the 8×8 image, rescaled from an original 160×160 normalized binary image, were used as features. The classifier returns both the assigned class and the Euclidean distance of the image from the closest class prototype. The distance is termed as the "recognition measure" and used as an estimation of the reliability of a classification [2].

The classifier was trained using isolated digits extracted from NIST special database 3. In total, 53449 isolated digits were extracted and classified for training the classifier, and other 53185 samples for the testing. The correct rate is 98.9% for training samples and 97.8% for test samples, without rejection. The mean values M_i ($i = 0, 1, \ldots, 9$) of the recognition measures for the correctly classified digits in the training samples were obtained and used to decide whether a classification was accepted or not. On the other hand, 3355 connected two-digit strings, which were also extracted from NIST special database 3, were used as the test data for the whole system. Note that the digits from these 4178 connected two-digit strings (3355 for testing the whole system and the 823 for generating and testing fuzzy decision rules) were not included in training the optimized nearest-neighbor classifier. For the 3355 two-digit strings, in average 8.1 segmentation paths were constructed from each digit string.

Table 2. A performance comparison of our approach with other digit separation algorithms, for our algorithm, high rejection rate means $\beta = 1.2$, and low rejection means $\beta = 2.0$

Techniques	High rejection rate (%)		Low rejection rate (%)	
	Rejection	Wrong	Rejection	Wrong
Our algorithm (with ranking)	28.6	3.0	4.7	7.5
Our algorithm (without ranking)	28.6	3.7	4.7	9.2
MCM of Chi [2]	32.7	4.9	3.7	10.8
Fenrich algorithm [5]	53.3	5.8	5.3	27.1
Fujisawa algorithm [6]	33.5	7.7	0.7	21.9
Zhao *et al.* algorithm [28]	38.3	4.4	3.4	13.3

Suppose that the tolerance radius is β. If the recognition measure is smaller than βM_i, then the classification is accepted. For a comparison, we also applied several other algorithms to separate the same two-digit strings used in our experiments. These algorithms include the MCM (Modified Curvature Method) of Chi *et al.* [2], and those of Fenrich [5], Fujisawa *et al.* [6] and Zhao *et al.* [28].

Chi's Modified Curvature Method [2] is a three-step algorithm for separating and recognizing single- and double-touching digit strings, which is given below:

- The cutting points are found by curvature of contour; the separation paths are constructed by linking pairs of these cutting points; and a two-cut-link technique is used to deal with the double-touching problem.
- Use weighted geometric property measures to rank both one- and two-cut links.

- A rejection scheme is used to reject poor links at both ranking and recognition stages.

Results of the other three algorithms were all obtained in two steps. In Fenrich's method [5], the algorithm was implemented as described in the original publication to produce one or more link candidates. the algorithm sequentially tests for suitable links using four separate features of the image, stopping if an acceptable link is identified. The rejection criteria are not explicitly described in the original publication, so we rejected a link if it extended outside the external contour of the image, or if it was too close to either the left or right side of the image. In the algorithm of Fujisawa *et al.* [6], the segmentations are located by identifying the vertical width graph below some threshold. In our implementation, we slowly increased the threshold from zero until an acceptable link was found, while retaining the rejection criteria used for the Fenrich method. These rejection criteria, among others, are built into Zhao *et al.*'s algorithm.

The second step involved recognizing the separated digits. The methods of Fenrich and Zhao *et al.* resulted in at most one link candidate, while that of Fujisawa *et al.* generally produced at least two. Provided at least one link was found, the digits were separated and the recognition measure criteria (for either high or low rejection rates) used to select the most likely link, or to reject candidates.

Table 2 summarizes the experimental results of these algorithms together with ours algorithm with and without ranking of segmentation paths. We can see that the performance of our algorithm is better than those of others. Moreover, our algorithm can achieve a slightly better recognition rate when segmentation paths are ranked. Experimental results also show that when ranking is performed, the average number of segmentation paths to be evaluated is 1.95, which is less than 8.1, the average number of segmentation paths to be evaluated when ranking is not carried out. This suggests that our ranking approach based on fuzzy decision rules is quite reliable.

Fig. 9 shows some correctly segmented and recognized digit strings. The think black lines are winning segmentation paths. Some arbitrarily selected failure segmentation paths are shown in Fig. 10. We can see that the segmentation path in the last sample can also be classified as 'success' segmentation path. But it is rejected because there exists a better segmentation path, as the last sample of Fig. 9.

7 Conclusion

In this chapter, a method of using fuzzified decision rules for ranking segmentation paths of connected 2-digit strings is presented to reduce the number of paths to be evaluated by a classifier and to improve the recognition rate. A background-thinning-based algorithm is applied to identify all potential

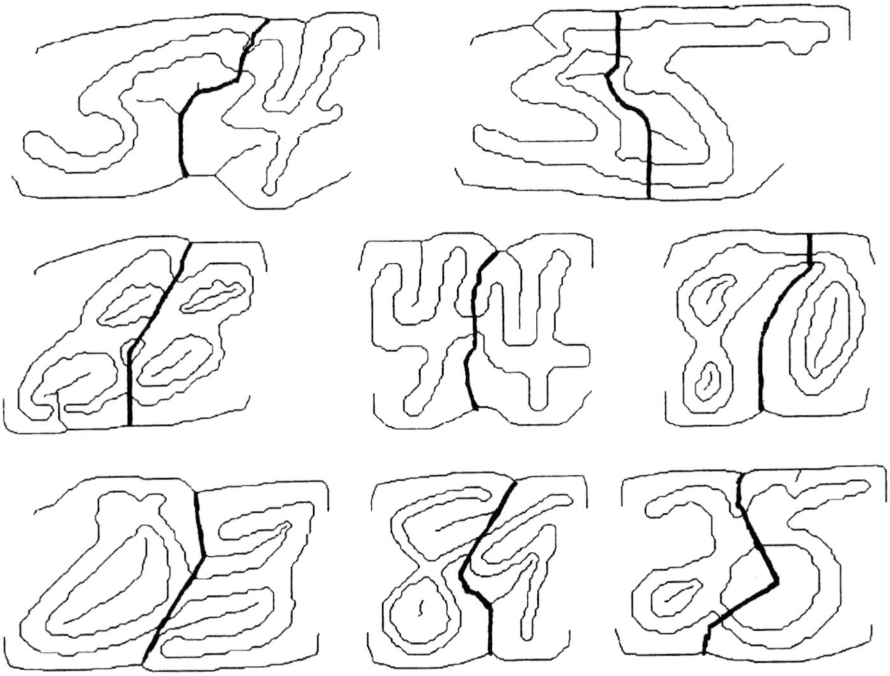

Fig. 9. Some correctly segmented and recognized digit strings

segmentation paths. Decision rules extracted from a decision tree are fuzzified by applying membership functions. Nine features, which measure the properties of a segmentation path, are used as the input of the fuzzy system, and centroid defuzzification method is adopted for defuzzifying the output. Experimental results on NIST Special Database 3 show that our approach is compared favorably with several techniques tested in terms of the recognition rate and processing time.

References

1. Casey R.G. and Nagy G., *Recursive Segmentation and Classification of Composite Character Patterns*, in: "Proceedings of the 6th International Conference on Pattern Recognition" (Munich, Germany), pp. 1023–1026, 1982
2. Chi Z., Suters M. and Yan H., *Separation of Single- and Double-touching Handwritten Numeral Strings*, Optical Engineering, Vol. 34, No. 4, pp. 1159–1165, 1995
3. Chi Z., Yang H. and Pham T., *"Fuzzy Algorithms: with Applications to Image Processing and Pattern Recognition"*, World Scientific, Singapore, 1996

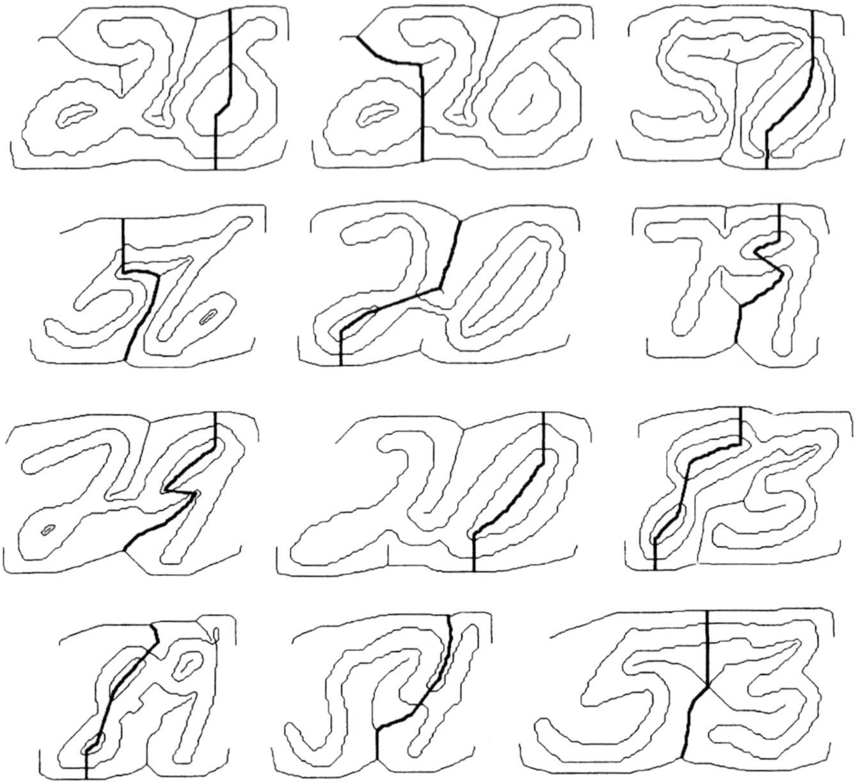

Fig. 10. Some failure segmentation paths rejected by the ranking process

4. Chi Z., Suter M. and Yan H., *Handwritten Digit Recognition using Combined ID3-Derived Fuzzy Rules and Markov Chains*, Pattern Recognition, Vol. 29, No. 11, pp. 1821–1833, 1996
5. Fenrich R., *Segmentation of automatically located Handwritten Numeric Strings*, in: "From Pixels to Features III: Frontiers in Handwriting Recognition (S. Impedovo and J.C. Simon, eds.)", Elsever Science, pp. 47–59, 1992
6. Fujisawa H., Yasuaki N. and Kurino K., *Segmentation Methods for Character Recognition: from Segmentation to Document Structure Analysis*, Proc. IEEE, Vol. 80, No. 7, pp. 1079–1092, 1992
7. Gonzalez R.C. and Woods R.E., *Digital Image Processing*, Addison-wesley Publishing Company, Boston, 1992
8. Ishibuchi H., Nozaki K. and Tanaka H., *Distributed Representation of Fuzzy Rules and its Application to Pattern Classification*, Fuzzy Sets and Systems, Vol. 52, pp. 21–32, 1992
9. Ishibuchi H., Nozaki K. and Yanamoti N., *Selecting Fuzzy Rules by Genetic Algorithms for Classification Problems*, in: "Proceedings of FUZZ-IEEE'93 – 2nd IEEE Int. Conf. on Fuzzy Systems", Vol. 2, pp. 1119–1124, 1993

10. Ivancic F., Malaviya A. and Peters L., *An Automatic Rule Base Generation Method for Fuzzy Pattern Recognition*, in: "Proceedings of KES'98" (Adelaide, Australia), 1998
11. Kasabov N.K., *Learning Fuzzy Rules through Neural Networks*, in: "Proceedings of the First New Zealand Int. Conf. on Artificial Neural Networks and Expert Systems", pp 137–139, 1993
12. Lu Y. and Shridhar M., *Character Segmentation in Handwritten Words - An Overview*, Pattern Recognition, Vol. 29, No. 1, pp. 77–96, 1996
13. Lu Z., Chi Z. and Siu W.C., *Length Estimation of Digit Strings Using a Neural Network with Structure Based Features*, Journal of Electronic Imaging, Vol. 7, No. 1, pp. 79–85, 1998
14. Lu Z., Chi Z., Siu W.C. and Shi P., *A Background-thinning-based Approach for Separating and Recognizing connected Handwritten Digit Strings*, Pattern Recognition, Vol. 32, No. 6, pp. 921–933, 1999
15. Malaviya A., Leja C. and Peters L., *A Hybrid Approach of Automatic Fuzzy Rule Generation for Handwriting Recognition Progress*, in: "Handwriting Recognition (Downtown and Impedevo, eds.)", World Scientific, Singapore, 1997
16. Pervez A. and Suen C.Y., *Segmentation of Unconstrained Handwritten Numeric Postal Zip Codes*, in: "Proceedings of the 6th International Conference on Pattern Recognition", pp. 545–547, 1992
17. Peters L., Leja C. and Malaviya A., *A fuzzy Statistical Rule Generation Method for Handwriting Recognition*, Expert Systems, Vol. 15, No. 1, 1998
18. Quinlan J.R., *Introduction of Decision Trees*, Machine Learning, Vol. 1, No. 1, pp. 81–106, 1986
19. Quinlan J.R., *Simplifying Decision Trees*, International Journal of Man-Machine Studies, Vol. 27, pp. 221–234, 1987
20. Quinlan J.R., *"C4.5: Programs for Machine Learning"*, Morgan Kauffman, 1993
21. Shi Z. and Govindaraju V., *Segmentation and Recognition of Connected Handwritten Numeral Strings*, Pattern Recognition, Vol. 30, No. 9, pp. 1501–1504, 1997
22. Strathy N.W., Suen C.Y. and Krzyzak A., *Segmentation of Handwritten Digits using Contour*, in: "Proceedings of ICDAR'93", pp. 577–580, 1993
23. Westall J.M. and Narasimha M.S., *Vertex Directed Segmentation of Handwritten Numerals*, Pattern Recognition, Vol. 26, No. 10, pp. 1473–1486, 1993
24. Winston P.H., *"Artificial Intelligence (third edition)"*, Addison-Wesley, 1992
25. Yan H., *Handwritten Digit Recognition using Optimized Prototypes*, Pattern Recognition Letters, Vol. 15, pp. 207–211, 1994
26. Yu D. and Yan H., *Separation of Touching Handwritten Numeral Strings based on Structural Analysis*, in: "Proceedings of Real World Computing Symposium", pp. 238–245, 1997
27. Zadeh L.A., *Fuzzy Sets*, Information and Control, Vol. 8, pp. 338–353, 1965
28. Zhao Z., Suters M. and Yan H., *Connected Handwritten digit Separation by Optimal Contour Partition*, in: "Proceedings of DICTA'93 – Conference on Digital Image Computing: Techniques and Applications", pp. 786–793, 1993

Chapter 12

Fuzzy Techniques in Mammographic Image Processing

Andreas Rick[12], Sylvie Bothorel[2], Bernadette Bouchon-Meunier[1], Serge Muller[2], and Maria Rifqi[1]

[1] Université Pierre et Marie Curie, LIP6, Case 169
4 place Jussieu, 75252 Paris CEDEX 05, France
email: {bernadette.bouchon-meunier,maria.rifqi}@lip6.fr

[2] General Electric Medical Systems
283 rue de la Minière, 78533 Buc, France
email: {rickand,bothosy,mullese}@gemse.fr

Summary. In this chapter we discuss fuzzy techniques for the detection and analysis of potential breast cancer lesions on mammograms. We show how fuzzy measurements can be performed on the images and how this information can be used in the different stages of the processing.

1 Introduction

Medical decision problems are typical examples of multi-criteria decision problems in which no single criterium is sufficient to arrive at a decision with a comfortable level of certainty. In many cases only the combination of many information sources, like patient interview, patient history and examinations allow the doctor to pronounce his diagnosis. As different pieces of information acquired and fused for the final decision have different degrees of certainty and precision, the fusion process should be able to reflect these uncertainties. Until recently, all information in mammography was acquired, fused and evaluated by the doctor. Today however, with the increasing performance of image processing techniques, we are at a point where doctors using a computer aided detection (CAD) system perform better in some aspects than the doctors alone. The strong points of CAD systems are their precision and repeatability. Logically, efforts are being made to combine the expert knowledge of the doctor with the precision and repeatability of the CAD system. Fuzzy logic is a powerful tool for the formulation of expert knowledge and the combination of imprecise information from different sources. To achieve meaningful results the imprecision in all information used to come to a conclusion should be taken into account.

In this chapter we discuss fuzzy techniques for the detection of cancer on mammograms. We show how fuzzy measurements can be performed on the images and how this information can be used in the different stages of the processing.

We show that the use of a fuzzy representation allows the decisions to be taken whenever sufficient information is available in the processing stage and to propagate the information including its uncertainty level to the next processing stage if the decision cannot be performed with sufficient confidence.

In the first part we discuss techniques for mammographic image processing and in the second part we show some applications of these methods on clinical problems.

Part 1: Techniques

The signs of cancer visible on mammograms can be separated in two groups: microcalcifications and fibrous lesions. Figure 1 shows zoomed views of two examples.

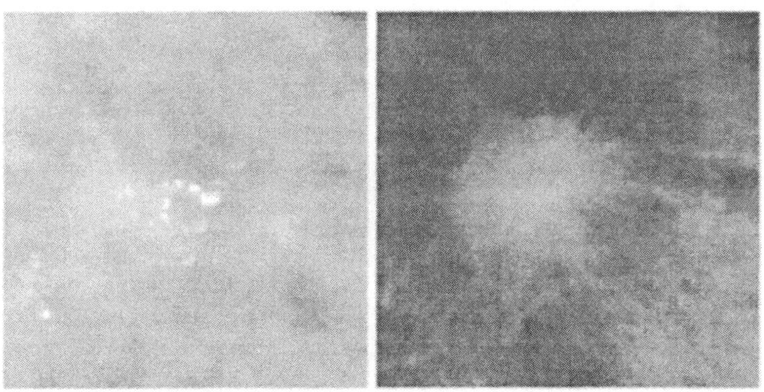

Fig. 1. Examples of microcalcifications (left) and fibrous lesions (right)

The microcalcifications are small depositions of radiologically very opaque materials like $Ca_3(PO_4)_2$, $CaCO_3$, $Mg_3(PO_4)_2$ [17] which can be seen on mammography exams as small bright spots. In section 2 we will discuss how fuzzy contours and measurements of fuzzy attributes can be used for the characterization of microcalcifications. In section 2 we describe an adaptive method to determine membership functions for classification with attributes that present significant variability from one image to the other. This technique can be applied to microcalcifications as well as to fibrous lesions. In section 3 we will discuss techniques for comparison of fuzzy measurements which are needed in many parts of mammographic image processing.

2 Fuzzy contours and fuzzy measurements

The first stage of a CAD system is the detection of the microcalcifications on the mammographic images. A number of methods have been proposed in the literature for this purpose. We will not go into details here, interested readers may refer to [16]. The detection stage gives a number of markers for potential microcalcifications. For the distinction between real microcalcifications and other structures the marked signs have to be analyzed. The attributes that can be calculated on the microcalcifications can be separated into those which are calculated without segmentation and those using a segmentation of the calcification. Information captured by attributes without segmentation tend to be somewhat deluded by the fact that some background is being taken into account for their calculation. On the other hand, attributes that use a segmentation have to rely on the segmentation. Segmentation of microcalcification is a difficult task because of their small size, their not always well defined contour and the possibility of overlapping due to the projection. Due to the image acquisition by projection for X-rays, the 3D-structures may superimpose and more than one microcalcification may be projected at the same position on the image. Therefore for some microcalcifications a unique contour can easily be found, but for other microcalcifications more than one contour can potentially be chosen.

We propose to use a fuzzy approach to catch the uncertainty of the segmentation, and to transmit it to the other processing stages.

2.1 Segmentation of microcalcification and fuzzy contours

A set of contour candidates is calculated for each microcalcification by region growing [3]. This ordered set of contours is considered the universe of all possible contours describing the given microcalcification. An example of a zoomed part of a mammogram including the set of possible contours is given in figure 2.

The prior knowledge about the contours of microcalcifications, which can be resumed by "*microcalcifications are small and have a high contrast*", is translated into a fuzzy set description using two attributes namely the *area* and the *gradient* shown in figure 3.

The two functions express the degree of membership to the class *contour of a microcalcification* as a function of the size (*size is small*) and the image gradient under the contour (*the gradient is high*). Using these membership functions the membership value for each contour is calculated by the conjunction of the membership values for *small* and *high gradient.* Figure 4 shows the application of this method for one particular microcalcification: the two graphs at the left show the area and the gradient for each contour obtained by the region growing process. The right graph shows the resulting membership function of the class *contour of the microcalcification* for each contour in the universe.

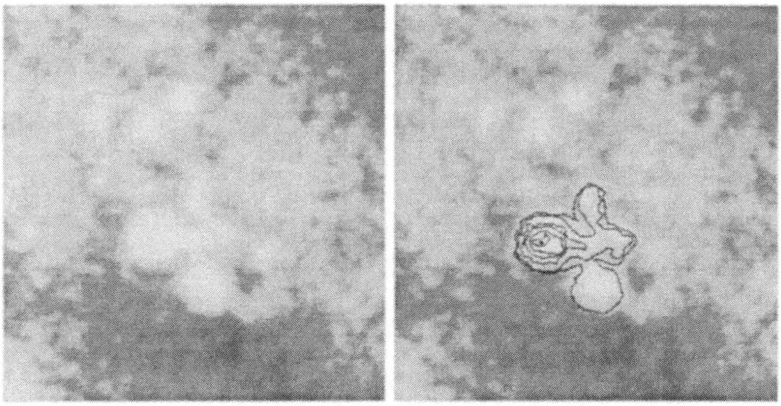

Fig. 2. The set of possible contours for a microcalcification

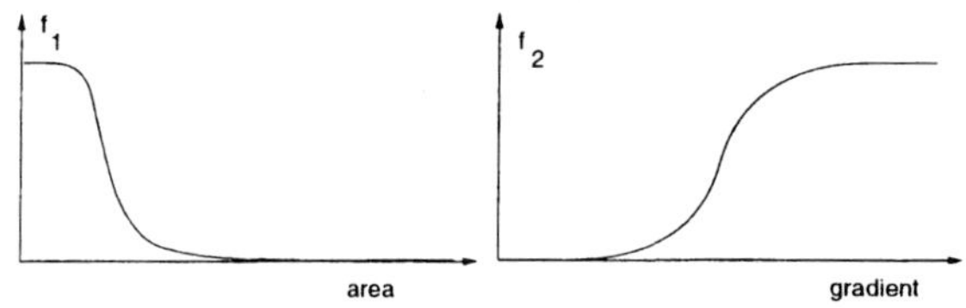

Fig. 3. Translation into fuzzy rules of the a priori information: *microcalcifications are small and have a high contrast*

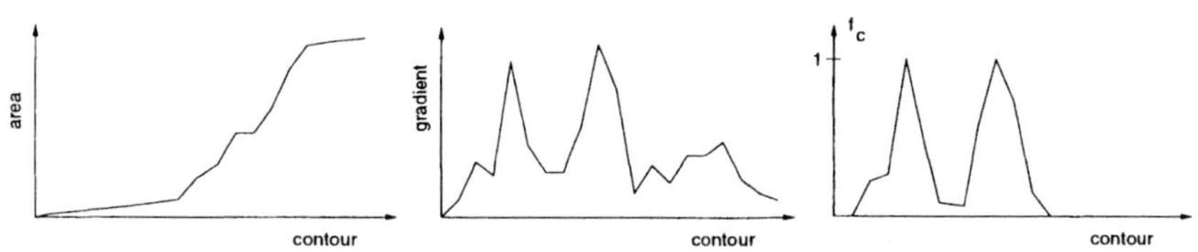

Fig. 4. Measured area and gradient values for all contours of a microcalcification

In this example the bi-lobed membership function can be interpreted in the following way: there are two possibilities for the segmentation, one that corresponds to a small microcalcification and another that corresponds to a bigger one. Each of the two contours with very high membership values are surrounded by some contours with slightly lower degrees of membership which translate the imprecision of the contour position.

Once the membership function for *contour of a microcalcification* on the universe of all contours has been calculated, the attributes of this fuzzy contour can be evaluated.

2.2 Measurements of fuzzy attributes

Several attributes are calculated for each of the contours with a non-zero membership value. To transform the attribute measurements performed on all the contours of the universe to a fuzzy measure which characterizes the microcalcification we can use the extension principle.

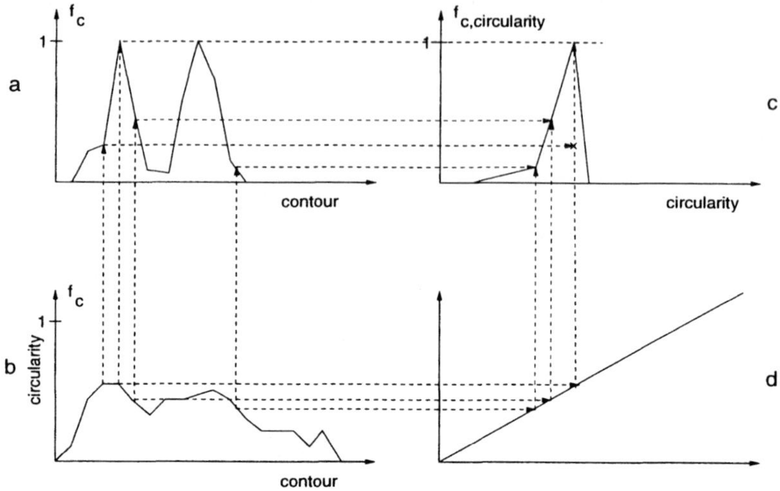

Fig. 5. Fuzzy measurements on contours using the extension principle

Figure 5 shows the application of the extension principle to calculate the degree of circularity of a microcalcification. Figure 5(a) shows the degree of membership to the class *contour of a microcalcification* for each contour obtained by the fuzzy segmentation and figure 5(b) shows a crisp circularity measure for each contour. By combining the two graphs we obtain the membership function for the *circularity* of a fuzzy contour which describes a microcalcification. While using the extension principle as shown in figure 5, it is possible to obtain more than one degree of membership for a given attribute value whenever the original membership functions are not monotonous. As we interpret the membership function as a degree of possibility for the microcalcification to have a certain attribute value, we use the maximum operator to obtain a unique degree of membership for each value of the attribute.

In the example shown in figure 5(c), we have computed the membership function for the circularity measurement using the example shown in figure 4, which can be interpreted in the following way: the ambiguity about the contours has disappeared in the circularity measure as all possible contours for the microcalcification exhibit a high circularity. Therefore the circularity measurement does not show any ambiguity, but some imprecision remains.

2.3 Conclusion

The fuzzy contours allow to capture the uncertainty and imprecision of the contours. The extension principle makes it possible to forward these uncertainties to any attribute that can be measured on a single contour to obtain fuzzy measurements for any attribute. The fuzzy measurements can be used in many applications like semiological classification of lesion or matching of microcalcifications (see section about applications).

3 Adaptive membership functions

A priori, the fuzzy segmentation and measurement methods presented in the previous section should be applicable to fibrous lesions as well as to microcalcifications.

Unfortunately the attributes calculated on mammographic images for the detection or classification of fibrous lesions show a significant variability from one image to the other which are due to the large variability of the breast tissue.

This big variability of the normal structures in mammograms between patients makes it extremely difficult to distinguish between normal and abnormal findings using rules with predefined membership functions applied to the fuzzy measurements.

We propose the construction of adaptive prototypes for the membership functions. The prototypes are adapted to the current image to obtain a more discriminative representation of the class memberships and thereby extract the maximum of information from each attribute. With this approach we can use a single set of rules for the identification of lesions.

3.1 Adaptive membership functions for classification

In the following we consider the fuzzy decision problem that consists in classifying each pixel of the image into one of two classes *normal* or *suspect*. A simple way of creating probabilistic membership functions for the classes is to use attribute histograms as illustrated in figure 6:

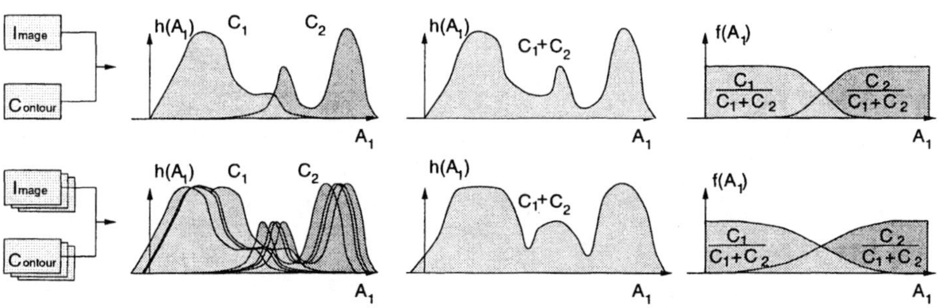

Fig. 6. Classification using varying attributes

The histogram of the attributes over all pixels of each class in the learning database is calculated. The histogram is normalized by the joint histogram of all classes together. If the attribute under consideration exhibits variation coming from other factors than the class membership of the pixels (like exposition parameter setup for the image acquisition) the histogram may be shifted in the universe. The variations will be modeled in the membership functions by an increase in uncertainty. If the variability between images is much bigger than the variations between classes, the membership functions have a very small discrimination power.

A way to reduce this uncertainty is to extract some information about the current case from the joint histogram of all classes. A simple method to do this, would be to adapt the average of the different membership functions to the average of the current image. Nevertheless this will not allow to take advantage of regularities which cannot be described by a simple shift of the histogram.

In order to find more complicated relationships we have to find some parameters to describe the form of the histogram and then find the relationships between these parameters.

3.2 Parametrization of the histogram

The parametrization of the histogram must satisfy a certain number of conditions in order to be useful for expressing the relationships between the joint histogram of all classes and the histogram of one class.

- Robustness: The parametrization must change little if the histogram changes little
- Completeness: All histograms which may be encountered for the problem under consideration must be supported by the selected parameters.
- Compactness: The number of parameters must be as low as possible.

The parametrization we propose to use is a weighted sum of parametric functions f_k.

$$f(x|p_k, \Theta_k) = \sum_{k=1}^{K} p_k \cdot f_k(x|\Theta_k) \tag{1}$$

for example a weighted sum of Gaussian:

$$f(x|\boldsymbol{\Phi}) = \sum_{k=1}^{K} p_k \cdot g_k(x, \mu_k, \sigma_k) \tag{2}$$

with :

$$g_k(x, \mu_k, \sigma_k) = \frac{1}{\sqrt{2\pi}\sigma_k} e^{-\frac{1}{2}\left(\frac{x-\mu_k}{\sigma_k}\right)^2} \tag{3}$$

and :

$\boldsymbol{\Phi} = (\boldsymbol{p}, \boldsymbol{\mu}, \boldsymbol{\sigma})$
$\boldsymbol{p} = (p_1, \cdots, p_k)$, with p_k = weight of Gaussian k
$\boldsymbol{\mu} = (\mu_1, \cdots, \mu_k)$, with μ_k = average of Gaussian k
$\boldsymbol{\sigma} = (\sigma_1, \cdots, \sigma_k)$, with σ_k = variance of Gaussian k

3.3 Parameter estimation with the EM-algorithm

There exists a variety of algorithms for the parameter estimation of a Gaussian mixture model. Most of them are iteration methods based on the *EM-algorithm* proposed by Demster [8]. The idea of the EM-algorithm is to start with an initial estimate $(\boldsymbol{p}_0, \boldsymbol{\mu}_0, \boldsymbol{\sigma}_0)$ for the parameters of the component functions and estimate a membership value λ_{ki} for each example i to each component k. During the iterations two steps are performed alternately:

- E-step: Update the λ_{ki} based on the last set of parameters $(p^{(m-1)}, \mu^{(m-1)}, \sigma^{(m-1)})$:

$$\lambda_{ki}^{(m)} = \frac{p_k^{(m-1)} \cdot g(x_i, \mu_k^{(m-1)}, \sigma_k^{(m-1)})}{\sum_{j=1}^{K} p_k^{(m-1)} \cdot g(x_i, \mu_j^{(m-1)}, \sigma_j^{(m-1)})} \tag{4}$$

- M-step: Optimize the parameters of the Gaussian with the examples weighted by the λ_{ki}:

$$p_k^{(m)} = \sum_{i=1}^{N} \lambda_{ki}^{(m)} \qquad \mu_k^{(m)} = \frac{\sum_{i=1}^{N} \lambda_{ki}^{(m)} x_i}{p_k^{(m)}} \tag{5}$$

$$\sigma_k^{(m)} = \sqrt{\frac{\sum_{i=1}^{N} \lambda_{ki}^{(m)} (x_i - \mu_k^{(m)})^2}{p_k^{(m)}}} \tag{6}$$

The problem of the standard EM-algorithms is the necessity of an initialization close to the optimal state. Based on the initialization, the obtained result corresponds to a local minimum close to the starting position which in general is not the global minimum. As an illustration we present a histogram approximated by 8 or 12 Gaussian which were initially equally spaced in the universe (figure 7).

The main lobe in the histogram is approximated with one or two components, depending on the initialization. This method of parameter estimation is not well adapted for variance modeling, as the parameters depend not only on the histogram itself but also on the initialization.

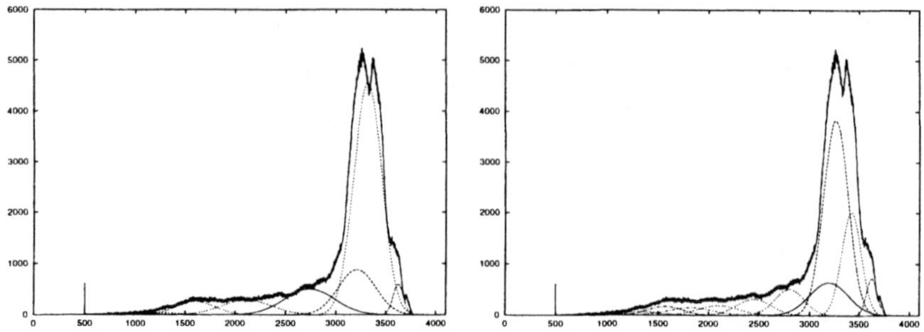

Fig. 7. Approximation of a distribution by 8 or 12 components

3.4 Parameter estimation with the hierarchical EM-algorithm

A modified version of the EM-algorithm is proposed by Huang *et al.* [31]. This approach adds the components one by one to the model and estimates their parameters under the assumption of uniform noise. Uniform noise is used as a simplification for all components which are to be identified later. This hierarchical decomposition is much more stable. In figure 8 the same histogram is used to identify 2 or 12 components.

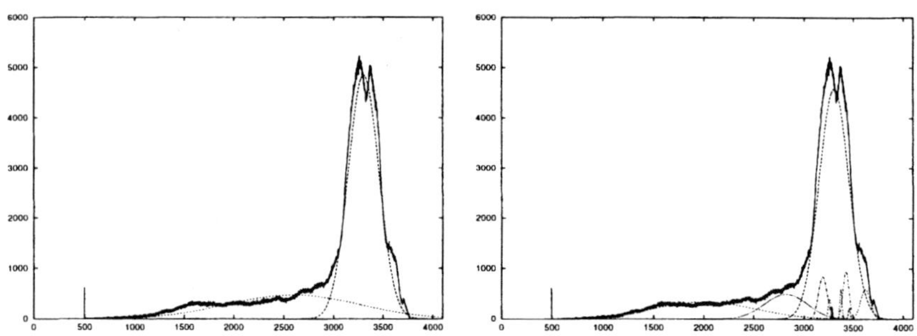

Fig. 8. Hierarchical approximation by 2 or 12 components

The principal components are always identified in the same way, and are independent of the number of total components that are used. In the following we will call this algorithm *H-EM*.

3.5 Modeling of variability

Once the histogram has been parametrized the links between the joint histogram of all classes and the membership functions for each class must be established. Figure 9 summarizes the learning phase in which the parameter models for two classes are identified.

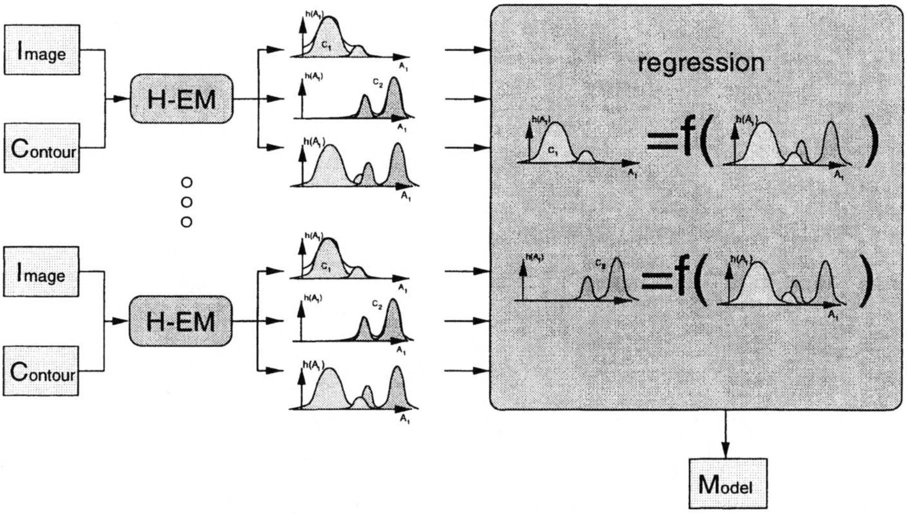

Fig. 9. Regression of membership function parameters

The regression fits some function to the parameters of the joint histogram to predict the membership functions for each class. In some practical applications the estimated parameters by means of the hierarchical EM algorithm are not sufficiently stable for a regression (e.g. with a linear model). One of the reasons for this can easily be understood for a histogram with two equally high and well separated components. The H-EM algorithm will detect the two components, but the order of the components is undetermined.

3.6 Generation of a prototype

In order to further stabilize the parameters we propose to calculate a prototype for the components and use the prototype during the histogram approximation phase. A simple static prototype can be described with an average value for all parameters of the mixture and a variance around this value. It can be shown that this approach is equivalent to specify a prior probability distribution of the parameters of the Gaussian components which are themselves Gaussian.

To use the prototype during the estimation of the mixture components, the EM algorithm must be modified. We will call the modified algorithm P-EM (prototype-EM).

- E-step: Update the λ_{ki} based on the last set of parameters ($p^{(m-1)}$,$\mu^{(m-1)}$, $\sigma^{(m-1)}$).
- M-step: The optimization of the parameters of the Gaussians with the examples weighted by the λ_{ki}.

- P-step: Update the parameters of the Gaussians to take into account the prototype:

$$p_i^{(m+1)} = \alpha_{i_p} p_{i_c} + (1 - \alpha_{i_p}) p_i^{(m)} \tag{7}$$
$$\mu_i^{(m+1)} = \alpha_{i_\mu} \mu_{i_c} + (1 - \alpha_{i_\mu}) \mu_i^{(m)} \tag{8}$$
$$\sigma_i^{(m+1)} = \alpha_{i_\sigma} \sigma_{i_c} + (1 - \alpha_{i_\sigma}) \sigma_i^{(m)} \tag{9}$$
$$\tag{10}$$

For the static prototype, the P-step consists in taking a weighted average between the prototype center values $(p_{i_c}, \mu_{i_c}, \sigma_{i_c})$ and the current parameters $(p_i^{(m)}, \mu_i^{(m)}, \sigma_i^{(m)})$ calculated in the M-step. The weights $(\alpha_{i_p}, \alpha_{i_\mu}, \alpha_{i_\sigma})$ determine the importance of the protoype versus the importance of the histogram.

3.7 Prototype with parameter interactions

The P-EM algorithm is able to avoid instabilities in the parametrization of the histogram like exchanged components. On the other hand, there is no direct link between the components during the approximation. In case of a histogram which contains a pattern that has not the form of a single component (like a triangular area when using Gaussian components) the pattern can be approximated by a number of components. To find these patterns in a histogram, a link between the parameters of the components used to describe the pattern is necessary, otherwise each component will be updated independently of the others during iteration.

An efficient way to incorporate parameter interactions into the model is to change the P-step in the P-EM algorithm with an update which includes interactions. One example of interaction is a linear relationship between parameters. We can define a matrix A that describes a linear relationship between the components of the parameter vector $\boldsymbol{\Phi}$.

$$\mathbf{A} \cdot \boldsymbol{\Phi} = 0 \tag{11}$$

In the general case the parameters of the model do not show a perfectly linear relation so that the equation 11 becomes:

$$\mathbf{A} \cdot \boldsymbol{\Phi} = \boldsymbol{\epsilon} \tag{12}$$

The error of the linear model $\boldsymbol{\epsilon}$ can be used to define the internal energy of the mixture components:

$$E_{int} = [\mathbf{A}\boldsymbol{\Phi}]^T \mathbf{R}_i^{-1} [\mathbf{A}\boldsymbol{\Phi}] \tag{13}$$

where $\mathbf{R}_i$ is the diagonal matrix of the standard deviation of the linear model. With this notation the algorithm P-EM minimizes an energy function which is the sum of the external energy E_{ext} which describes the correspondence between the mixture model and the histogram, and the internal energy E_{int} which describes the distance of the adapted mixture model to the prototype model. E_{ext} is minimized by the E- and M- steps of the algorithm P-EM, and E_{int} is minimized in the P-step.

3.8 Prototype model learning from a database

The parameters for the adaptive membership functions are the center of the prototype $\boldsymbol{\Phi}_0$, the distance matrix $\mathbf{A}$ and its standard deviation matrices $\mathbf{R}_i$ (standard deviation of the linear prototype) and $\mathbf{R}_e$ (standard deviation of the static prototype). To learn these parameters from a learning data base, we first apply the hierarchical-EM algorithm on all histograms. This will give a first estimation of the components that are encountered, but they are not necessarily ordered. The next step is to find histogram components that are present in most of the images, in other words to apply a clustering algorithm to the components estimated by the H-EM. The clustering of the components establishes the order which is needed for a successful estimation of the interaction between components

After the clustering, a matrix $\bar{\Phi}$ containing all the ordered parameters $\boldsymbol{\Phi}_i$ for all images can be constructed and the matrix $\mathbf{A}$ can be calculated by a least square approach minimizing $\mathbf{A} \cdot \bar{\Phi}$. Using $\mathbf{A}$, $\mathbf{R}_e$ and $\mathbf{R}_i$ the P-step can now be formulated as:

$$\tilde{\boldsymbol{\Phi}} = \left(\mathbf{R}_e^{-1} + \mathbf{A}^T\mathbf{R}_i^{-1}\mathbf{A}\right)\boldsymbol{\Phi} \tag{14}$$

3.9 Conclusion

For applications such as detection of fibrous lesions on mammograms, fuzzy rule based reasoning can be applied, but the amount of uncertainty introduced by different sources of variability seriously reduces the classification performance. The use of adaptive membership functions can help to reduce the uncertainty by extracting a model for at least some part of the variability and thereby increase the classification performance.

4 Comparison measures and prototypes for image processing

Comparison of objects is a widespread operation necessary in many frameworks. It is based on the idea that if two objects are sufficiently similar then a transfer of knowledge is possible from one to the other. This comparison is frequently achieved through a measure intended to determine to which extent the descriptions have common points or differ from each other.

Many measures of comparison have been proposed and studied. We have proposed a general form for measures of comparison, enabling us to classify the main existing ones with respect to their properties. Thus, the framework we have obtained provides a means to choose a measure of comparison relevant and appropriate for a given problem. We use the formalization and the framework introduced in [4] to deal with measures of comparison. We show the interest of this framework in two kinds of problems: classification and construction of a fuzzy prototype.

4.1 A framework to compare fuzzy subsets

We propose the construction of a general framework enabling to include the majority of all the measures, indices and relations of comparison. For this purpose, different classes of measures are defined according to their properties: comparison, similitude, dissimilarity, satisfiability, inclusion, resemblance... This framework, described in detail in [4], is a tool for a classification of the existing measures as well as for a creation of new quantities.

For any set Ω of elements, let $F(\Omega)$ denote the set of fuzzy subsets of Ω, and f_A the membership function of any description A in $F(\Omega)$. We use the classical definition of intersection: $f_{A \cap B}(x) = \min(f_A(x), f_B(x))$ to describe the elements belonging to A and B. The definition used for the difference between two fuzzy subsets is the following:

An operation on $F(\Omega)$ is called a **difference** and denoted by $-$, if it satisfies for every A and B in $F(\Omega)$:

- if $A \subseteq B$, then $A - B = \emptyset$.
- $B - A$ is monotonous with regard to $B : B \subseteq B'$ entails $B - A \subseteq B' - A$

We suppose that we have a way of evaluating the weight of the elements of the universe characterized by a fuzzy set through a **fuzzy set measure** M. This fuzzy set measure M is a mapping $F(\Omega) \rightarrow I\!R^+$ such that, for every A and B in $F(\Omega)$:

- $M(\emptyset) = 0$
- if $B \subseteq A$, then $M(B) \leq M(A)$.

A **measure of comparison** between A and B, in the most general sense, takes into account common features $(A \cap B)$, and distinctive features $(B - A$ and $A - B)$. Therefore a M-measure of comparison on Ω is a mapping $S : F(\Omega) \times F(\Omega) \rightarrow [0,1]$ such that $S(A, B) = F_S(M(A \cap B), M(B - A), M(A - B))$, for a given mapping $F_S : I\!R^+ \times I\!R^+ \times I\!R^+ \rightarrow [0,1]$ and a fuzzy set measure M on $F(\Omega)$.

One example of a M-measure of comparison is Zadeh's inclusion:

$$S(A,B) = \frac{1}{|\Omega|} \Sigma_x \min(1, 1 - f_A(x) + f_B(x)) = 1 - \frac{1}{|\Omega|} M(A -_1 B),$$

with $f_{A -_1 B}(x) = \max(0, f_A(x) - f_B(x))$ and M the sigma-count [7].

A M-measure of comparison can either evaluate the likeliness of two descriptions (it is called a M-measure of similitude), or their differences (it is then called a M-measure of dissimilarity). We consider the following properties for F_S:

- symmetry: $F_S(u,v,w) = F_S(u,w,v)$
- minimality: $F_S(u,0,0) = 0$
- reflexivity: $F_S(u,0,0) = 1$
- containment: $F_S(u,0,w) = 1$ whatever u and w may be.
- exclusiveness: $F_S(0,v,w) = 0$ whatever $(v,w) \neq (0,0)$ may be.

Obviously, symmetry of F_S implies that S satisfies $S(A,B) = S(B,A)$. Minimality of F_S entails that $S(A,A) = 0$ while reflexivity corresponds to $S(A,A) = 1$. The containment property yields $S(A,B) = 1$ if $B \subseteq A$. The exclusiveness property implies that $S(A,B) = 0$ as soon as $A \cap B = \emptyset$.

A M-**measure of similitude** S on Ω is a M-measure of comparison S such that $F_S(u,v,w)$ is non decreasing in u, non increasing in v and w.

An example of a f-measure of similitude is the relation given by Tversky [28], generalized to fuzzy sets [26], [4]:

$$S(A,B) = f(A \cap B)/(f(A \cap B) + \alpha f(A - B) + \beta f(B - A)),$$

with $\alpha, \beta \geq 0$ and f a fuzzy set measure.

The **measure of dissimilarity** is not defined as the dual of a measure of similitude, but it has specific properties. A M-measure of dissimilarity S on Ω is a M-measure of comparison satisfying the minimality property and such that $F_S(u,v,w)$ is independent of u and non decreasing in v and w.

A definite symmetrical M-measure of dissimilarity (i.e. $S(A,B) = S(B,A)$, $\forall A$ and B) satisfying the triangular inequality (i.e. $S(A,B) \leq S(A,C) + S(C,B)$, $\forall A, B$ and C) is a distance.

In order to classify the existing measures more subtle, we distinguish three types of M-measures of similitude: satisfiability, inclusion and resemblance.

A **measure of resemblance** is used for a comparison between the descriptions of two objects, of the same level of generality, to decide if they have many common characteristics. A M-measure of resemblance on Ω is a M-measure of similitude S which satisfies the reflexivity and the symmetry properties.

In the case where T is the minimum, we obtain extensions of measures of similarity. Examples of M-measures of resemblance are the following:

- $S(A,B) = exp(-\beta |d_r(A,B)|)$[19]
  where $\beta > 0$ and $d_r(A,B) = (\sum_x |f_A(x) - f_B(x)|^r)^{1/r}$, for $r \geq 1$. This quantity is a product-transitive indistinguishability relation.
- $S(A,B) = M(A \cap B)/M(A \cup B)$ [10] for M such that: $M(A \cup B) = M(A \cap B) + M(A - B) + M(B - A)$.

- $S(A,B) = 1 - \frac{1}{|\Omega|}\sum_x |f_A(x) - f_B(x)| = 1 - \frac{1}{|\Omega|}(M(A-B) + M(B-A))$ [10] with the sigma-count $M(A) = \sum_x f_A(x)$ as a fuzzy set measure.

A **measure of satisfiability** corresponds to a situation in which we consider a reference object or class and we decide if a new object is compatible with it or satisfies the reference. A M-measure of satisfiability S on Ω is a M-measure of similitude S satisfying the containment and the exclusiveness properties and such that $F_S(u, v, w)$ is independent of w.

Analogy relations [5]:

$$S(A,B) = \inf_x \min(1 - f_B(x) + f_A(x), 1),$$

and fuzzy similitude [6]:

$$S(A,B) = 1 - \sup_{f_A(x)=0} f_B(x)$$

are particular M-measures of satisfiability. Measures of satisfiability have proven [4] to be compatible with the contrast model introduced by Tversky, satisfying major properties such as matching, monotonicity, independence, solvability [28].

A **measure of inclusion** also concerns a situation with a reference object and measures if the points common to A and B are important with regard to A. A M-measure of inclusion S on Ω is a M-measure of similitude satisfying the reflexivity and the exclusiveness properties such that $F_S(u, v, w)$ is independent of v.

As an example of M-measure of inclusion, we can find the degree introduced by Sanchez [25]:

$$S(A,B) = |A \cap B|/|A| = M(A \cap B)/(M(A \cap B) + M(A - B)),$$

with the sigma-count as M.

A classification of all the measures of comparison discussed above is shown in figure 10. We point out that there exist measures of comparison which are neither similitudes nor dissimilarities. The same holds for measures of similitude: they can be different from satisfiability, inclusion or resemblance. In the rest of this section, we show the use of this framework for two kinds of problems in mammographic image processing: classification and construction of fuzzy prototypes.

4.2 Measures of comparison for classification process

A similarity based-classification method has to solve the problem of the choice of a measure of similarity or, more generally, a family of measures of comparison. A new object we do not know the class is often classified thanks to a comparison with a rule. Indeed, a prototype can be considered as a rule describing a class. For example, the prototype of the class "round" might be:

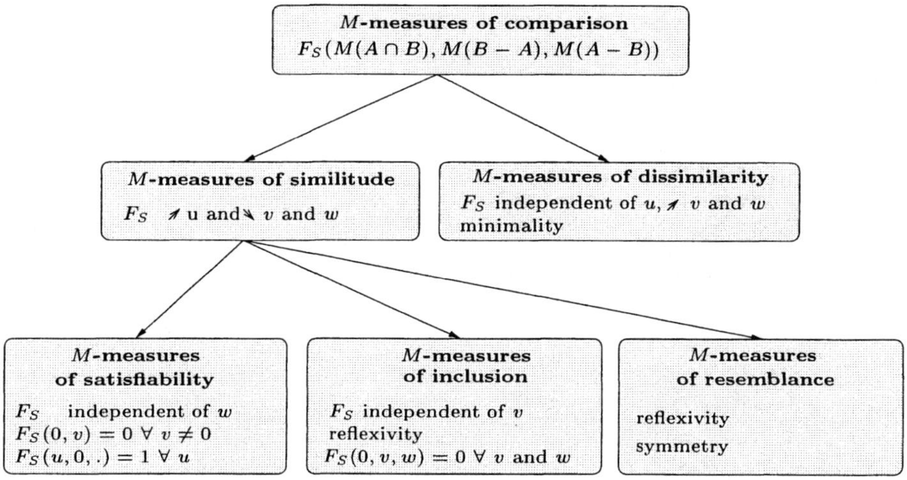

Fig. 10. Classification of M-measures of comparison

`around 15 pixels` for surface, `between 5 and 6` for compacity. In other words, `if` surface = `around 15 pixels`, and compacity = `between 5 and 6` then class = `round`. A decision tree is also equivalent to a set of IF...THEN rules. Each path in the tree is associated with a rule, where premises are composed by the tests of the encountered nodes, and the conclusion of the rule is composed by the class associated with the leaf of the path.

The classification process is based on the question: *does the new object satisfy the rule?* This question entails the use of a measure which is *maximal when the object is included in the prototype* (exclusiveness property) and can be considered as a particular case of the prototype, and *minimal when no common features are shared by the two objects* (minimality property). In the proposed framework, these properties are shared by *measures of satisfiability.*

4.3 Construction of a fuzzy prototype

The prototype is intrinsically interesting because of its power of description. This power can be used for a classification process, for example the semiological classification of microcalcifications in mammography.

According to E. Rosch [23], all objects do not represent the category they belong to in the same manner, but they are spread along a scale of typicality. According to Rosch and Mervis [24] :

> *[..] categories tend to become defined in terms of prototypes or prototypical instances that contain the attributes most representative of items inside and least representative of items outside the category.*(p.30)

Therefore the notion of prototype is linked to the notion of typicality. Zadeh [30] has emphasized this aspect: the typicality is a matter of degree and it implies that the concept of prototype is a fuzzy concept. A prototype, as L. A. Zadeh said, is not a unique object or a group of objects. It is more a fuzzy schema enabling us to generate a set of objects because of the synthesized information it contains.

In the approach we describe here, we retain Rosch's idea that an object is all the more typical as it resembles the members of its class and it is distinct with regard to the members of others classes and Zadeh's idea that a prototype is not a particular example but a fuzzy schema. The difference with the standard methods for determining prototypes lies on the fact that values of attributes rather than objects themselves are compared pair by pair.

We need to determine the typicality of *each value appearing* in a learning database in order to construct a fuzzy prototype.

This situation of comparison is based on the assumption that the values of attributes are considered to have the same level of generality, and no value can be taken as a reference. This situation needs a *symmetrical* measure because all values have the same level of generality, and a *reflexive* measure because there does not exist any pair of distinctive objects which perfectly look like each other. In the proposed framework, these properties are shared by *measures of resemblance.*

Let X be a set of objects. We suppose that there exists a partition on X, composed by crisp classes C_j. For an object O of the class C_i, the typicality of the value v of an attribute A is computed as follows:

Step 1. Compute the resemblance $r(v, v_j)$ between v and the value v_j of the attribute A for any example of the same class C_i. The global resemblance $R(v)$ relative to the set of values of A present in the examples, is obtained by aggregating the degrees $r(v, v_j)$.

Step 2. Compute the dissimilarity $d(v, v_j)$ between v and the value v_j of the attribute A for any example of class C_k different from C_i. The total dissimilarity $D(v)$ relative to the set of values of A present in the examples, is obtained by aggregating the degrees $d(v, v_j)$.

Step 3. The aggregation of these two values (for example with a t-norm), $R(v)$ and $D(v)$, gives the typicality $T(v)$ of v, according to the attribute A, for the class C_i.

Degrees of typicality participate in the construction of a fuzzy prototype of a given class. For an attribute A, the degree of typicality of each value of A is computed for each class. Then, the fuzzy prototype of any given class is characterized by the most typical value(s) of each attribute. This means that a fuzzy prototype is a virtual object described by means of the same attributes as the objects in the learning database. The values taken by the fuzzy prototype are the most typical.

One of the intermediate steps of the semiological classification is the classification of the microcalcifications according to their form: *round* or *not round*. Figure 11 shows the prototypes obtained for the classes *round* and *not round* by the method described above, applied to a learning database of annotated mammograms. More specifically, these prototypes have been obtained by using :

- $M(A) = \int_{\Omega} f_A(x)dx$ for the fuzzy set measure,
- $S(A, B) = \frac{2}{\pi}\arctan(\frac{2M(A\cap B)\sup_x f_{A\cap B}(x)}{M(A\cup B))})$ for the measure of resemblance,
- $S(A, B) = \frac{1}{\Omega}(\sum_{x/f_A>f_B} f_{A-B}(x) + \sum_{x/f_B>f_A} f_{B-A}(x))$ for the measure of dissimilarity,
- the median for the aggregation of resemblance and for the aggregation dissimilarity in the steps 1 and 2 of the method.
- the probabilistic t-conorm (i.e. $\perp(x, y) = x + y - xy$) for the aggregation operator in the third step of the method.

The prototypes can be provided to the radiologist as a help to formalize his reasoning, and to better understand the structure of microcalcifications and its link to the semiological classes. For example the first row in figure 11 shows that the microcalcifications in the class *round* have a surface of about 15 pixels and at the same time that the surface of microcalcifications in the class *not round* is less specific (between 16 and 44 pixels).

4.4 Conclusion

The proposed formal framework of comparison measures can help to choose the right fuzzy measures for different tasks which require comparisons between fuzzy objects. The two applications in mammography to which we have applied it (the classification of microcalcifications, and the matching of microcalcifications) have confirmed its efficiency. Furthermore, degrees of typicality based on measures of comparison can be used for the construction of fuzzy prototypes which are effective for a classification problem [22].

Part 2: Applications

In this part we will discuss two applications of the fuzzy methods described above. First, we will describe a system for the semiological classification of microcalcification clusters. In the second section we will show some results of the application of fuzzy comparisons to the matching of microcalcifications seen on different views of a stereotactic exam. The matching is used for the reconstruction of a 3D representation of a microcalcification cluster.

5 Computer-aided diagnosis for mammography

Systems for computer-aided diagnosis for breast cancer are in most cases multi-level decision processes. The knowledge of uncertainty in each part of

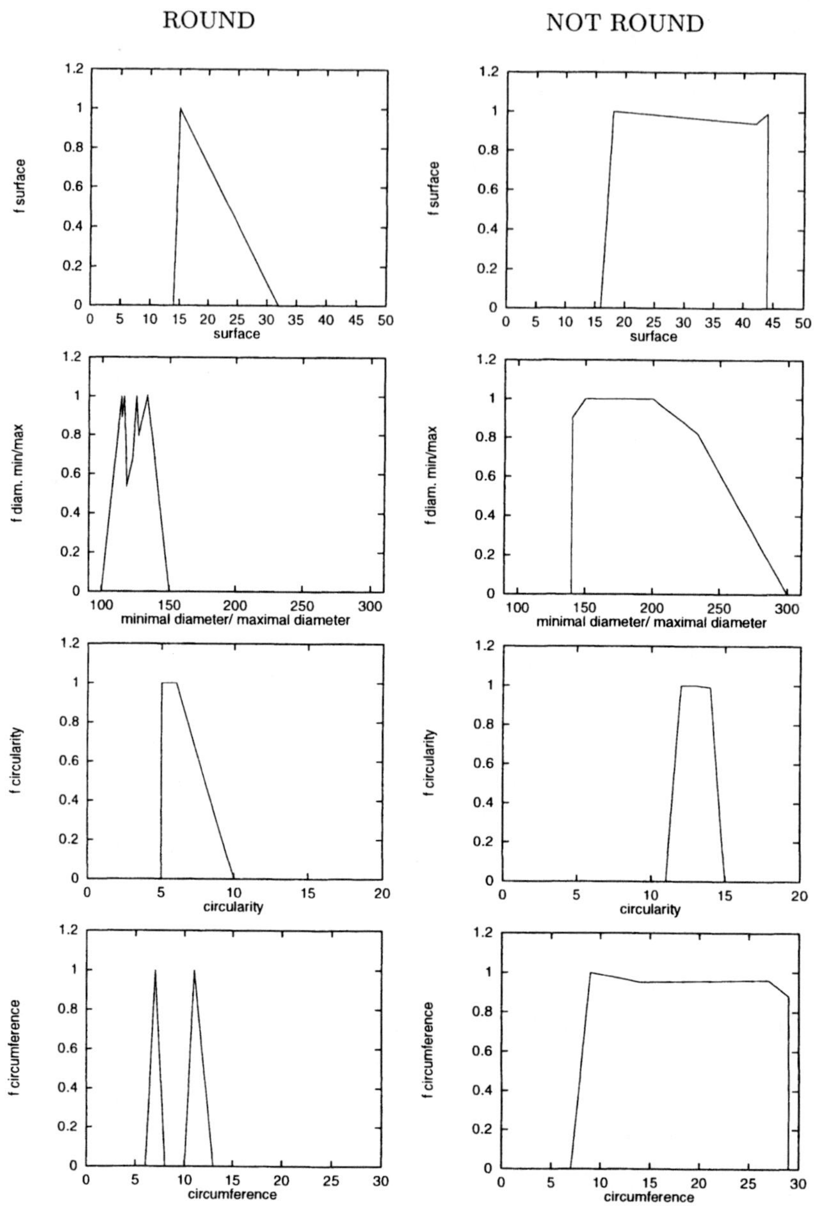

Fig. 11. Prototypes of the classes "round" and "not round"

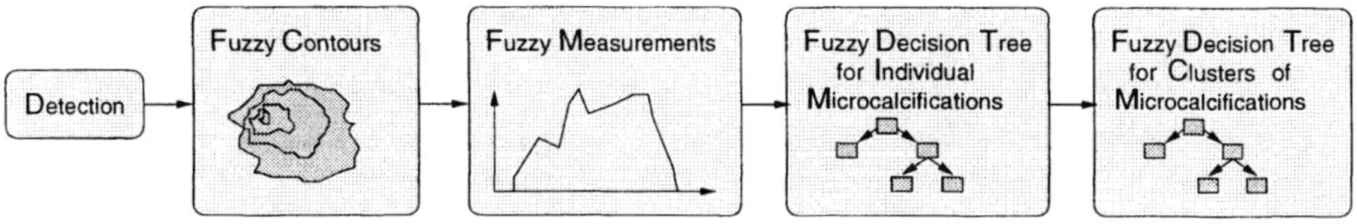

Fig. 12. Overview of the CAD system

the processing is important for a decision process, if the uncertainty can be transmitted from step to step. In the computer-aided detection and characterization system we describe here (fig. 12), this principle has been realized using a fuzzy representation. The steps of the algorithm are:

- detection of the microcalcifications
- fuzzy segmentation of the microcalcifications
- fuzzy measurements on each calcification
- fuzzy decision tree for the classification of individual microcalcifications
- fuzzy decision tree for the classification of microcalcification clusters.

5.1 Automated construction a fuzzy decision tree for the classification of lesions from a learning database

The image database is transformed into an attribute database by using the fuzzy measurements described in section 2. Each case is characterized by 73 attributes. We have to classify them to give a diagnosis. Radiologists provide us some indications about the way they examine the mammographic images. But they only study the films, and only have qualitative information. On the contrary, we have digital images, with measurable qualitative information. Images can also be filtered, and they provide a kind of data ignored by the radiologists (gradient, ...). Among all these attributes, a few are relevant and should be identified by a learning system.

We choose the decision tree as a learning and classification system for the following reasons:

- It can learn from a small database (our database, which is noisy, has 118 examples for 73 attributes),
- It is able to handle a large number of attributes, choosing only the most relevant among them,
- The rules provided by the radiologists can easily be translated into nodes in the tree,
- It is possible to track the path followed by an example through the tree and to compare this path to the radiologist's reasoning.

5.2 Decision tree

Learning step: The tree looks for a partition of the database according to an attribute, which is well suited for the ideal partition realized by the class.

The values of attributes we use are numerical, and the partition corresponds to a threshold. The error between the two partitions is evaluated with an entropy (as in the method ID3 proposed by Quinlan [20]), or other measures (contrast, ...). We use the following contrast measure:

$$C = \frac{\int \min(f_{A_1}(x), f_{A_2}(x))dx}{\int \max(f_{A_1}(x), f_{A_2}(x))dx} \tag{15}$$

If f_{A_1} is the membership function for the attribute *compacity* for all malignant calcifications and f_{A_2} the membership function for the same attribute for all benign calcifications, C gives the contrast for the attribute *compacity.* The attribute which minimizes this contrast is chosen to constitute a test associated with the node. Each element of the partition follows the branches of the tree, and the operation is repeated, until a predefined stopping criterion is reached (e.g. the homogeneity of the classes of the elements in the leaf is sufficiently high). An example for a decision tree, constructed in this way from a training set of different shaped microcalcifications, is shown in figure 13

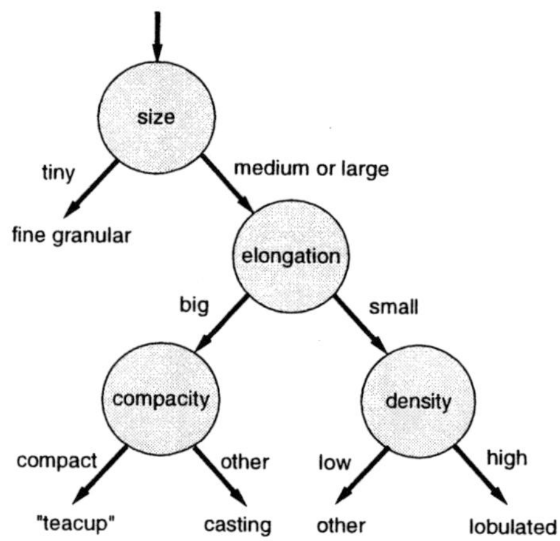

Fig. 13. Decision tree

Classification step: A new example is introduced at the root of the tree. At each node a fuzzy measure of satisfiability is calculated to estimate to which degree the example satisfies the test on the attribute. According to the outcome of this measure, the example is propagated to one or several branches with its corresponding degree of satisfiability. At the end, the example falls into one or several leaves with different degrees which are aggregated to determine the final class of the example.

In our implementation, we have used the following satisfiability:

$$S(A,B) = \frac{\int f_{A \cap B}(x)dx}{\int f_B(x)dx} \tag{16}$$

and the Zadeh t-norm (i.e. the minimum) for the aggregation operator.

5.3 Classification results

We compared the performance of our approach with several other approaches for the classification of microcalcifications into small, round and elongated classes, which are the usual categories used by the doctors to determine the risk of cancer (table 1). It is not easy to compare an optimized fuzzy logic approach with crisp methods that are not necessarily optimized. Nevertheless, it is interesting to have some comparative figures. We tested our database with the MLC (Inducer) software. The techniques provided by this software handle only crisp data, therefore the database has been defuzzified with the max operator for those methods.

Table 1. Comparison of fuzzy tree performance with other classification methods

Method	KNN	Naive Bayes	ID3	Fuzzy tree
Success for "small" class	91.8 %	93.7%	93.1%	96.4 %
Success for "round" class	79.6 %	74.1%	84.2%	84.4 %
Success for "elongated" class	73.5 %	72.8%	80.1%	83.1 %

These results represent the characterization of individual microcalcifications. We added a second decision tree to take into account the global cluster attributes. For difficult cases, especially those with many superimpositions, we observed that even if a high level of uncertainty remains in the classification of some of the individual microcalcifications, the system can make use of the more certain measurements of the majority of microcalcifications in the cluster to give a valid result. We think this behavior is similar to that of radiologists.

6 3D reconstruction of microcalcification clusters

When breast lesions containing ambiguous microcalcifications are detected, a biopsy using stereotactic guidance can be used to confirm the diagnostic. The stereotactic exam consists in taking two views of the breast from two different directions. If the object to be punctured - typically a microcalcification - can be detected on both views and the geometry of the acquisition is known, the 3D position of the object can be calculated. A positioning device can

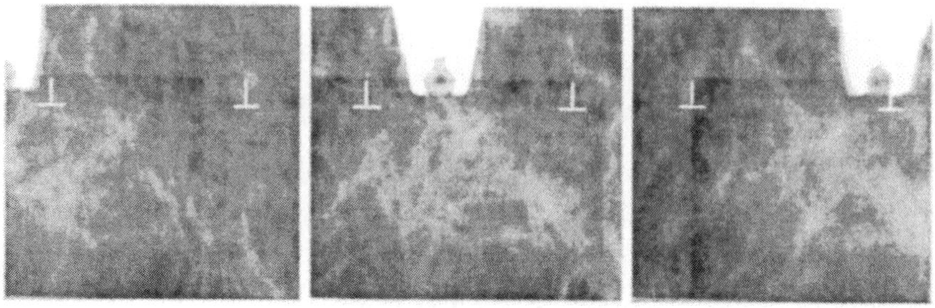

Fig. 14. Stereotactic exam

then be used to introduce a needle at the exact position of the object, to obtain a tissue sample. Figure 14 shows images obtained for the two angles and the *scout view*, which is a centered view that is taken to verify the correct positioning. Generally, the radiologist has to identify the object to be analyzed on both images from the two images only.

The application we show in this chapter is the 3D reconstruction of the microcalcification cluster from these two views.

6.1 Microcalcifications matching

The 3D reconstruction of a microcalcification cluster from two or more views requires that the microcalcifications can be matched between the views.

An overview of the matching process we propose is shown in figure 15. The first step is the detection of all microcalcifications on all views. We construct a correspondence matrix which has one row for every candidate in the left image and one column for every candidate in the right image. This correspondence matrix is initialized to 1.0 for each element to indicate that all matches between any pair of candidates is possible. The geometrical constraints from the known acquisition geometry (epipolar line) are used to eliminate all candidates combinations which are not possible by setting to zero the corresponding matrix component. If a scout view was taken (a third view with a centered tube angle) it can be used to eliminate further candidate combination which do not project at the right place on the third view.

6.2 Using measures of similarity and dissimilarity for comparing microcalcifications

The remaining candidates are compared by using fuzzy attributes calculated on the fuzzy contours of the calcifications. All candidates from one view are compared to all remaining candidates in the second view by calculating

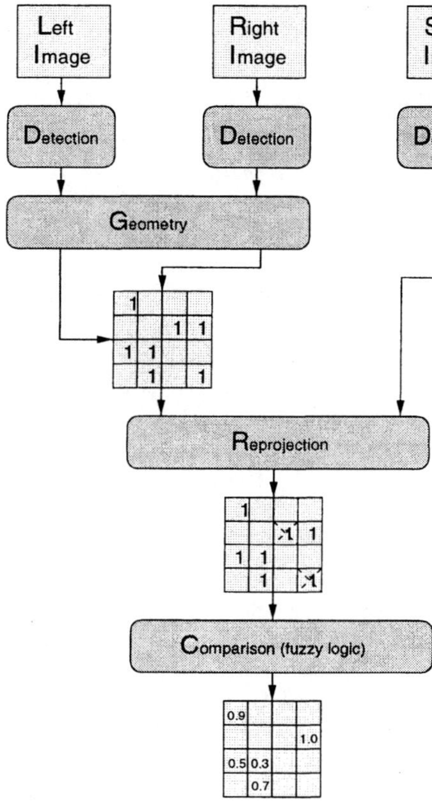

Fig. 15. Matching process for microcalcifications

similarity measures based on the fuzzy attribute. We use the same approach as for the construction of a fuzzy prototype of a class of objects (see 4.3). For a given microcalcification m in the first view we need to find in the second view the microcalcification m' which *resembles the most* m, and which is the *most dissimilar* to the other microcalcifications in the first view. For the same reasons given for the construction of a fuzzy prototype, the similarity is determined thanks to the computation of a resemblance measure.

Comparisons of microcalcifications are made attribute by attribute. A step of aggregation is needed to give a single index of similarity or dissimilarity.

We denote the value of attribute j of the microcalcification l for the view i by $m^i_{l,j}$. The method is decomposed as follows: for a given microcalcification on the first view (described by $m^1_{l,1\cdots J}$ or in short m^1_l),

Step 1. For each non-zero cell in the corresponding column (i.e. a matched microcalcification m^2_k in the second view), compute the resemblance

$r(m^1_{l,j}, m^2_{k,j})$ for all j. The global resemblance $R(m^1_l, m^2_k)$ is obtained by aggregating the degrees $r(m^1_{l,j}, m^2_{k,j})$.

Step 2. For each non-zero cell in the row of m^2_k (i.e. a matched microcalcification m^1_h in the first view), compute the dissimilarity $d(m^2_{k,j}, m^1_{h,j})$ for all j. The dissimilarity $D(m^2_k, m^1_h)$ is obtained by aggregating the degrees $d(m^2_{k,j}, m^1_{h,j})$. The global dissimilarity $D(m^2_k)$ of m^2_k relative to all matched m^1_h is given by aggregating the degrees $D(m^2_k, m^1_h)$.

The result is a matrix obtained from the correspondence matrix where, in each non-zero cell, two indices are computed: the resemblance index and the dissimilarity index.

Several approaches can be imagined to use the correspondence matrix. The most obvious possibility is to aggregate the resemblance index and the dissimilarity index into a single similarity value A by taking the value obtained by:

$$A(m^1_l, m^2_k) = \top(R(m^1_l, m^2_k), n(D(m^2_k))) \quad (17)$$

where $\top$ is a triangular norm and n is a strict negation.

If the remaining uncertainty about the matching is to be transmitted to the user, the remaining candidates may be visualized in 3D using a color indication for the similarity measure which can be interpreted as a confidence level in the reconstruction position. An example of this approach is shown in the following section.

In most cases the visualization of results after defuzzification is preferable. In other words, only the reconstructions with the highest confidence levels are shown. In this case we have to define a defuzzification method for the similarity matrix.

Several defuzzification methods can be considered:

1. take the maximal similarity value in the matrix and display it, remove the example from both images (take out the row and column of the similarity matrix) and continue with the next maximum
2. find the combination of candidates that maximizes the total sum of similarity values without using a candidate in two combinations
3. maximize the number of possible combinations and the sum of similarity values without using a candidate in two combinations
4. maximize the contrast (similarity between the chosen candidates versus similarity with regard to the other candidates)

From a complexity point of view, the first method is by far the most favorable, but its tendency to emphasize the maximal similarity values, even if this choice prevents many other matches with a slightly lower similarity, is problematic. The choice of a defuzzification method for this type of application with constraints between the fuzzy values needs further investigation.

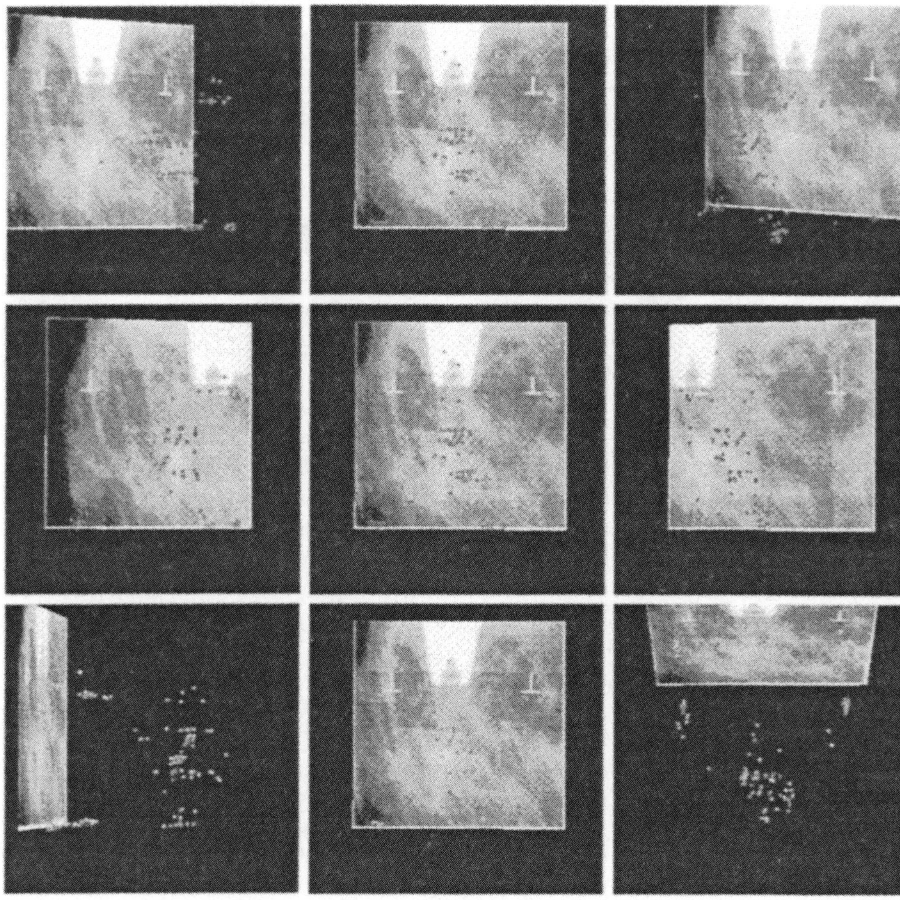

Fig. 16. Visualization of the reconstructed clusters

6.3 3D visualization

In figure 16 the reconstructed 3D-positions corresponding to the result of the matching process are shown. Each candidate is represented by a small point in 3D in front of one of the images acquired during the stereotactic exam. The image is positioned exactly where the detector was during the exam. In the top row all combinations of candidates are shown from three different positions, the underlying image is the scout view. In the middle row the candidates are shown as if the eye position were at the X-ray tube position to show the exact projection onto the acquired images. In the last row, the similarity measure of the remaining candidates after projection on the scout view is shown using different shades of grey. The most similar correspondences are shown in dark grey, the most different in light grey.

7 Conclusion

Fuzzy techniques can effectively be used in mammographic image processing to represent and treat the uncertainty present in the different steps of the processing. The use of fuzzy techniques during the segmentation allows to capture the ambiguity of the segmentation without taking a decision about the true contour too early. Fuzzy rules (as a part of a fuzzy decision tree or any other framework) can be useful to represent expert knowledge or knowledge acquired by learning from a database. Adaptive membership functions can be used to represent class memberships even with varying attributes so that fuzzy rules remain valid across large variations.

Using these fuzzy techniques, many applications in mammographic image processing can be realized. In the second part of this chapter we presented two of them: the classification of breast lesions and the 3D reconstruction of microcalcifications clusters from a stereotactic exam.

References

1. Aylward S.R., Hemminger B.M. and Pisano E.D., *Mixture Modeling for Digital Mammogram Display and Analysis*, in: "Digital Mammography (Karssemeijer N., Thijssen M., Hendriks J. and van Erning L., eds.)", Kluwer Academic Publishers, Nijmegen, pp. 305–312, 1998
2. Bothorel S., *"Analyse d'image par arbre de décision floue – Application à la classification sémiologique des amas de microcalcifications en mammographie numérique"*, Thèse de l'université Paris 6, 1996
3. Bothorel S., Bouchon B. and Muller S., *A Fuzzy Logic-based Approach for Semiological Analysis of Microcalcification in Mammographic Images*, International Journal of Intelligent Systems, Vol. 12, pp. 819–843, 1997
4. Bouchon-Meunier B., Rifqi M. and Bothorel S., *Towards general measures of comparison of objects*, Fuzzy Sets and Systems, Vol. 84, No. 2, pp. 143–153, 1996
5. Bouchon-Meunier B. and Valverde L., *Analogy relations and inference*, in: "Proceedings of FUZZ-IEEE'93 – IEEE International Conference on Fuzzy Systems" (San Fransisco), pp. 1140–1144, 1993
6. Bouchon-Meunier B., *Fuzzy similitude and approximate reasoning*, in: "Advances in Fuzzy Theory and Technology (P.P. Wang, ed.)", Bookwrights Press, pp. 161–166, 1993
7. De Luca A. and Termini S., *A definition of a non-probability entropy in the setting of fuzzy sets theory*, Information and Control, Vol. 20, pp. 301–312, 1972
8. Demster M., Laird N.M. and Jain D.B., *Maximum likelihood for incomplete data via the EM algorithm*, J. Royal Statistics Society, Series B, Vol. 39, pp 1–38, 1977
9. Dhawan A.P., Chitre Y., Kaiser-Bonasso C. and Moskowitz M., *Analysis of mammographic Microcalcifications Using Gray-Level Image Structure Features*, IEEE Transactions on Medical Imaging, Vol. 15, No. 3, pp. 246–259, 1996

10. Dubois D. and Prade H., *"Fuzzy Sets and Systems, Theory and Applications"*, Academic Press, New York, 1980
11. Ema T., Doi K., Nichikawa R.M., Jiang Y. and Papaioannou J., *Image feature analysis and computer-aided diagnosis in mammography: Reduction of false-positive clustered microcalcifications using local-gradient analysis*, Medical Physics, Vol. 22, No. 2, pp. 161–169, 1995
12. Grimaud M., *"La géodesie numérique en morphologie mathématique - Application a la détection automatique de microcalcifications en mammographie numérique"*, Thèse de doctorat à l'Ecole Nationale Supérieure des Mines de Paris, 1991
13. Gupta R. and Undrill P.E., *The use of texture analysis to delineate suspicious masses in mammography*, Phys. Med. Biol., Vol. 40, pp. 835–855, 1995
14. Highnam R., Brady M. and Shepstone B., *A representation for mammographic image processing*, Medical Image Analysis, Vol. 1, No. 1, pp. 1–18, 1996
15. Karssmeijer N. and te Brake G.M., *Detection of Stellate Distortions in Mammograms*, IEEE Transactions on Medical Imaging, Vol. 15, No. 5, pp. 611–619, 1996
16. Karssemeijer N., Thijssen M., Hendriks J. and van Erning L., *"Digital Mammography"*, Kluwer Academic Publishers, Nijmegen, 1998
17. Lanyi M., *"Diagnosis and Differential Diagnosis of Breast Calcifications"*, Springer Verlag, 1986
18. Marsala C., *"Apprentissage inductif en présence de données imprécises: construction et utilisation d'abres de décision flous"*, Thèse de l'informatique, Université Paris 6, 1998
19. Ovchinnikov S.V., *Representations of transitive fuzzy relations*, in: "Aspects of Vagueness (Skala H.J., Termini S. and Trillas E., eds.)", D. Reidel Publishing Company, pp. 105–118, 1984
20. Quinlan, *Induction of decision trees*, Machine Learning, Vol. 1 No. 1, pp. 86–106, 1986
21. Rifqi M., *"Mesures de comparaison, typicalité et classification d'objets flous: théorie et pratique"*, Thèse de doctorat de l'informatique, Université Paris 6, 1996
22. Rifqi M., Bothorel S., Bouchon-Meunier B. and Muller S., *Similarity and prototype based approach for classification of microcalcifications*, in: "Proceedings of the 7th IFSA World Congress" (Prague), pp. 123–128, 1997
23. Rosch E., *"Principles of categorization, Cognition and categorization"*, Hillsdale, N. J.: Laurence Erlbaum Associates, 1978
24. Rosch E. and Mervis C.B., *Family resemblances: Studies in the internal structure of categories*, Cognitive Psychology, Vol. 7, pp. 573–605, 1975
25. Sanchez E., *Inverses of fuzzy relations - Applications to possibility distributions and medical diagnosis*, Fuzzy Sets and Systems, Vol. 2, pp. 75–86, 1979
26. Shiina K., *A fuzzy-set-theoretic feature model and its application to asymmetric data analysis*, Japanese psychological research, Vol. 30, pp. 95–104, 1988
27. Trillas E. and Valverde L., *On implication and indistinguishability in the setting of fuzzy logic*, in: "Management Decision Support Systems Using Fuzzy Sets and Possibility Theory (Kacprzyk J. and Yager R.R., eds.)", Verlag TUV, Rheinland, 1984
28. Tversky A., *Features of similarity*, Psychological Review, Vol. 84, pp. 327–352, 1977

29. Valverde L., *On the structure of t-indistinguishability operators*, Fuzzy Sets and Systems, Vol. 17, pp. 313–328, 1985
30. Zadeh L.A., *A note on prototype theory and fuzzy sets*, Cognition, Vol. 12, pp. 291–297, 1982
31. Zhuang X., Huang Y., Palaniappan K. and Zhao Y., *Gaussian Mixture Density Modeling, Decomposition, and Applications*, IEEE Transactions on Image Processing, Vol. 5, No. 9, pp. 1293–1302, 1996

Chapter 13

Fuzzy-Based Motion Detection and Its Application to De-Interlacing

Dimitri Van De Ville[1], Wilfried Philips[2], and Ignace Lemahieu[1]

[1] Ghent University
Department of Electronics and Information Systems (ELIS)
Sint-Pietersnieuwstraat 41, B-9000 Gent, Belgium
email: dvdevill@lama.elis.rug.ac.be, ignace.lemahieu@rug.ac.be

[2] Ghent University
Department for Telecommunication and Information Processing (TELIN)
Sint-Pietersnieuwstraat 41, B-9000 Gent, Belgium
email: philips@telin.rug.ac.be

Summary. This chapter presents a motion detector for interlaced video based on the principles of fuzzy logic control. Interlaced video exhibits several possible artifacts such as line flicker and line crawling. De-interlacing algorithms convert interlaced to progressive scan video formats by interpolating the missing lines. These algorithms can be used to improve picture quality but are also necessary to display interlaced video on progressive output devices. A good de-interlacing technique should adapt to the presence of motion. This chapter presents a motion adaptive de-interlacing technique incorporating a fuzzy motion detector and investigate how the quality of the results depends on the parameters of the technique. We also compare the technique numerically to other de-interlacing methods on several test-sequences.

1 Introduction

Video formats can be classified into two categories, the progressive scan format and the interlaced scan format. The progressive scan format is the most direct approach and scans all lines of each frame. The interlaced scan format consists of fields of even and odd "polarity". Even fields only contain the even-numbered lines while odd fields contain the odd-numbered lines. Even and odd fields of the video signal alternate in time. Although progressive scanning is more straightforward, the television industry is still committed to the interlaced scan format [20]. Also the future digital television (DTV) standards will contain interlaced formats [2].

When the interlaced video scan format was introduced in the early years of television, there were some good reasons for this [3].
First of all, interlacing allows cathode ray tubes (CRTs), for a given bandwidth, to display more frames per second and hence increase the frame rate

and give better motion rendition. Secondly, the apparent vertical resolution is increased compared to a progressive scan format using the same frame rate and bandwidth. Interlacing allows to maintain the apparent frame rate and resolution relieving the bandwidth requirements. On the other hand, interlacing introduces well known artifacts like flicker, twitter and line crawling. Flicker artifacts are produced, e.g., in static scenes containing evenly spaced black and white lines. After interlacing, this kind of texture appears as alternating black and white fields. Twitter is a specific kind of flicker when fine horizontal lines appear to "twitter" up and down. Line crawling occurs when diagonal edges slowly move in the vertical direction. The display's line structure becomes very visible and seems to 'crawl' across the edge that is being tracked [29].
Furthermore, interlaced video is unsuitable for devices which prefer or require the progressive scan format, e.g., video printers [23], computers [18], and plasma and LCD displays [1,26].
Finally, interlaced video complicates image-processing tasks like video coding, scan-format conversion, i.e., the conversion between different TV broadcast standards, between normal-definition TV and HDTV, or between different devices for video phone applications [6].

De-interlacing techniques produce a progressively scanned video signal from an interlaced version with a frame rate equal to the original field rate. De-interlaced video is supposed to have improved image quality by reduction of the aforementioned artifacts. De-interlacing comes down to interpolation: calculate the values for the pixels of the missing lines, using available data from the same field (intra-field) or from adjacent fields (inter-field). Several simple intra-field methods like line-replication, line-averaging or directional spatial interpolation are not capable of removing flicker artifacts. Inter-field methods are better in this respect. Simple inter-field methods like field insertion, which replaces missing lines with the corresponding lines from the previous field, work very well for static scenes and restore fine spatial details. However, they are not satisfactory because they cause "ghosting" artifacts when there is motion present in the video sequence.[1]

Many techniques have been proposed to make the interpolation dependent on motion. Mainly, two categories of techniques can be distinguished:

- Motion adaptive techniques rely on a motion detector which produces a signal indicating the presence of motion. Such a signal can be binary (motion or no motion) or preferably multi-level (e.g., probability of motion). Motion detection can be implicit, as in median-based techniques [7,8,12], or explicit, using a motion detector [21]. Typically, the former compute the difference between two fields of the same polarity and compare it to

[1] When the interlaced signal originates from a telecine (motion picture), both odd and even field come from the same image, so no motion artifacts will be obtained from such processing. This is not the case when the interlaced signal comes from an interlaced camera source.

a single threshold, several thresholds, or a soft threshold. The choice of the threshold values for a classical motion detector has a critical effect on the operation of the algorithm.

- Motion compensating methods are another class of techniques and try to make use of an estimate of the displacement or velocity vector for each pixel or block of pixels [24]. This detailed information about motion can be used to applications such as interpolation and coding. Unfortunately, motion estimation requires a lot of computation time and complex processing.

In this chapter we propose a motion adaptive de-interlacing scheme using a fuzzy motion detector [28] inspired by the model of a fuzzy logic controller. The motion detector contains several rules which combine the information available in the neighbourhood of a pixel to generate a multi-level estimate (in the interval $[0, 1]$) of the probability of motion. This signal steers an adaptive linear interpolation filter. A future goal is to implement this scheme in hardware for real-time de-interlacing applications.

Fuzzy logic has successful applications in process control where binary decisions do not yield good results. Other examples of applications of fuzzy controllers in low-level image processing are a fuzzy edge detector by Michaud [19], fuzzy rate control for MPEG video [27] and fuzzy operators for filtering and edge detection [22].

The chapter is organized as follows. The fuzzy controller is explained in Sect. 2. Next, Sect. 3 applies this motion detector in a motion adaptive de-interlacing algorithm. Finally, we examine the results using numerical measurements and compare the fuzzy technique with other de-interlacing methods.

2 Fuzzy motion detection

Fuzzy logic allows reasoning with levels of truth instead of binary values. A fuzzy logic controller (FLC) implements these principles in a "controller device". An FLC typically follows three processing steps [5,15]: fuzzification of inputs, rule inference, and defuzzification to produce an output. Before we describe these stages in detail, we introduce some notions from fuzzy logic.

2.1 Some notions from fuzzy set theory

Definition 1. (Fuzzy set) A fuzzy set F in a universe of discourse U is characterized by a membership function μ_F which takes values in $[0, 1]$,

$$F : U \mapsto [0, 1], \; u \rightarrow \mu_F(u). \tag{1}$$

The support of a fuzzy set F is the crisp set of all points u in U such that $\mu_F(u) > 0$. A fuzzy set whose support is a single point u_0 in U with $\mu_F(u_0) = 1$ is referred to as a fuzzy singleton.

Definition 2. (Fuzzy intersection) The fuzzy intersection of two fuzzy sets A and B in a universe U is defined as

$$A \cap B : U \mapsto [0,1],\ u \to \mu_A(u) \wedge \mu_B(u), \tag{2}$$

where the $\wedge$ operator (fuzzy conjunction) represents a triangular norm [15] such as minimum, algebraic product, bounded product, or drastic product (see Table 2).

Definition 3. (Fuzzy union) The fuzzy union of two fuzzy sets A and B in a universe U is defined as

$$A \cup B : U \mapsto [0,1],\ u \to \mu_A(u) \vee \mu_B(u), \tag{3}$$

where the $\vee$ operator (fuzzy disjunction) represents a triangular co-norm [15] such as maximum, algebraic sum, bounded sum, or drastic sum (see Table 3).

Definition 4. (Fuzzy relation) A fuzzy relation R from U to V is a fuzzy set in $U \times V$, expressed as

$$R : U \times V \mapsto [0,1],\ (u,v) \to \mu_R(u,v). \tag{4}$$

In general, a fuzzy control rule "IF antecedent THEN consequent" can be considered as a conditional statement. The antecedent formulates the necessary condition for the consequent (or control action) to become true. A fuzzy control rule R, such as "IF x is F THEN y is G," is represented by a fuzzy relation from U to V, using a fuzzy implication function $\mathcal{I}$:

$$\begin{aligned} R : U \times V \mapsto [0,1],\ (u,v) \to \mu_R(u,v) &= \mu_{F\to G}(u,v) \\ &= \mu_F(u) \to \mu_G(v) \\ &= \mathcal{I}(\mu_F(u), \mu_G(v)). \end{aligned} \tag{5}$$

The fuzzy implication function $\mathcal{I}$ can be defined in many different ways, each of which leads to a different type of fuzzy reasoning. An FLC typically makes use of Mamdani's minimum operation rule [17] or Larsen's product operation rule [14] which are both listed in Table 1 [15][2].

Rules are activated or fired by an inference mechanism. The inference mechanisms employed in an FLC are generally much simpler than those used in a typical expert system. In particular, in an FLC we do not employ the chaining inference mechanism in which the consequent of a rule can be applied to the antecedent of another rule. The control actions in an FLC are based

[2] Note that both the minimum and the product operation are no extensions of the binary implication. Therefore, they are not "real" implicators (cf. Chapter 1 (*Classical and Fuzzy Approaches towards Mathematical Morphology*) for the definition of the notion of implicator and some examples)

on a so-called one-level forward data-driven inference. This comes down to the application of the generalized modus ponens (GMP):

$$\begin{array}{ll} \text{premise 1:} & x \text{ is } F' \\ \text{premise 2:} & \text{IF } x \text{ is } F \text{ THEN } y \text{ is } G \\ \hline \text{consequence:} & y \text{ is } G' \end{array} \tag{6}$$

In fact, the rule of the second premise is evaluated given the first premise. The result is obtained by the "sup-star composition".

Definition 5. (Sup-star composition) If R is a fuzzy rule in $U \times V$, and F' is a fuzzy set in U, the "sup-star compositional rule of inference" asserts that the fuzzy set G' in V induced by F' is given by

$$G' = F' \circ R : V \mapsto [0,1], \; v \to \mu_{G'}(v) = \sup_u (\mu_R(u,v) \star \mu_{F'}(u)), \tag{7}$$

where $F' \circ R$ is the sup-star composition of F' and R. The star operator can be any fuzzy conjunction operator such as those of Table 2.

Until now we have only handled simple antecedents. A compound antecedent such as "x_1 is F_1 and x_2 is F_2" can be implemented by a fuzzy conjunction:

$$\mu_{F_1 \wedge F_2}(u_1, u_2) = \mu_{F_1}(u_1) \wedge \mu_{F_2}(u_2). \tag{8}$$

Definition 6. (Rule base) An FLC typically has state evaluation fuzzy control rules. In the case of a multiple-input-single-output (MISO) system, the rule base is a collection of rules of the form

$$\begin{aligned} R_1 &: \text{IF } x \text{ is } A_1 \wedge \ldots \wedge y \text{ is } B_1 \text{ THEN } z \text{ is } C_1 \\ R_2 &: \text{IF } x \text{ is } A_2 \wedge \ldots \wedge y \text{ is } B_2 \text{ THEN } z \text{ is } C_2 \\ &\ldots \\ R_n &: \text{IF } x \text{ is } A_n \wedge \ldots \wedge y \text{ is } B_n \text{ THEN } z \text{ is } C_n \end{aligned} \tag{9}$$

In its canonical form, these rules may contain compound antecedents which use the fuzzy conjunction operator. If several rules imply the same consequent, these results are unified using an "also-sentence connective", which is typically a fuzzy disjunction operator.

Figure 1 depicts the graphical representations of several fuzzy conjunction and disjunction implementations.

2.2 The interlaced video signal

The inputs of the FLC are derived from the interlaced video signal. Therefore, we need a mathematical description of an interlaced video signal.

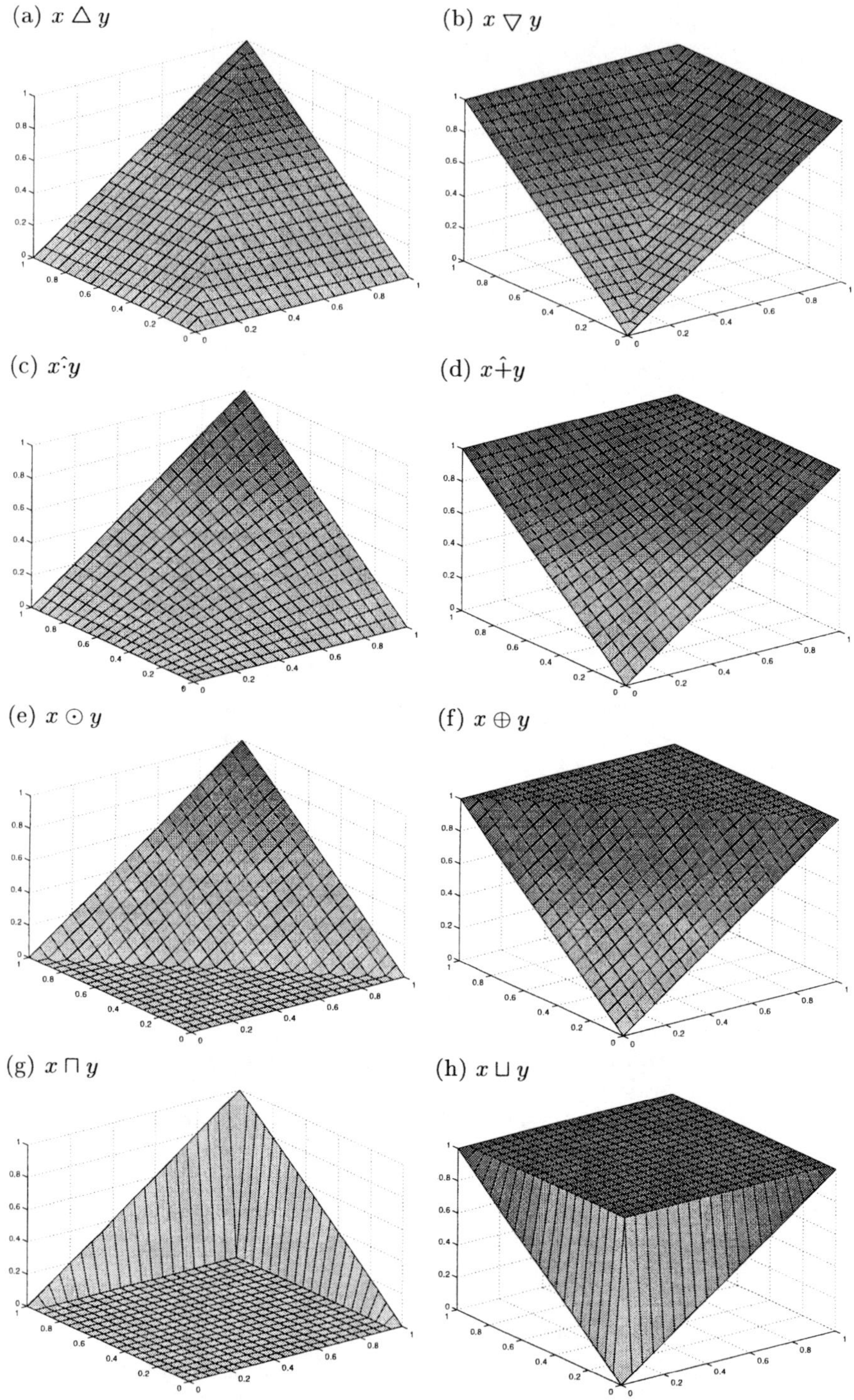

Fig. 1. Graphical representation of several implementations of fuzzy conjunction and disjunction operators

Table 1. Fuzzy "implication" operators frequently used in FLCs

Fuzzy implication function	
Mamdani	$\mathcal{I}(x, y) = \min(x, y)$
Larsen	$\mathcal{I}(x, y) = xy$

Table 2. Fuzzy conjunction operators

Fuzzy conjunction $x \wedge y$	
minimum	$x \bigtriangleup y = \min(x, y)$
algebraic product	$x \hat{\cdot} y = xy$
bounded product	$x \odot y = \max(0, x + y - 1)$
drastic product	$x \sqcap y = \begin{cases} x, & y = 1 \\ y, & x = 1 \\ 0, & x, y < 1 \end{cases}$

Table 3. Fuzzy disjunction operators

Fuzzy disjunction $x \vee y$	
maximum	$x \bigtriangledown y = \max(x, y)$
algebraic sum	$x \hat{+} y = x + y - xy$
bounded sum	$x \oplus y = \min(1, x + y)$
drastic sum	$x \sqcup y = \begin{cases} x, & y = 0 \\ y, & x = 0 \\ 1, & x, y > 0 \end{cases}$

Video can be represented as a two-dimensional time-varying image. The scene captured by the camera is a function of three variables, namely a temporal, horizontal and vertical variable. Converting this function into a one-dimensional signal requires sampling two of these variables (analogue devices) or three of them (digital devices). Furtheron, we assume the signal is sampled for the three variables. Sampling requires to choose the number of pixels per line (X) and number of lines per picture (Y) which determine the spatial resolution, while the number of pictures per time unit (T) determines the time resolution and is governed by requirements of adequate motion rendition and absence of flicker. Smooth motion rendition takes approximately 25 pictures per second, at least 50 pictures per second are necessary to eliminate flicker.

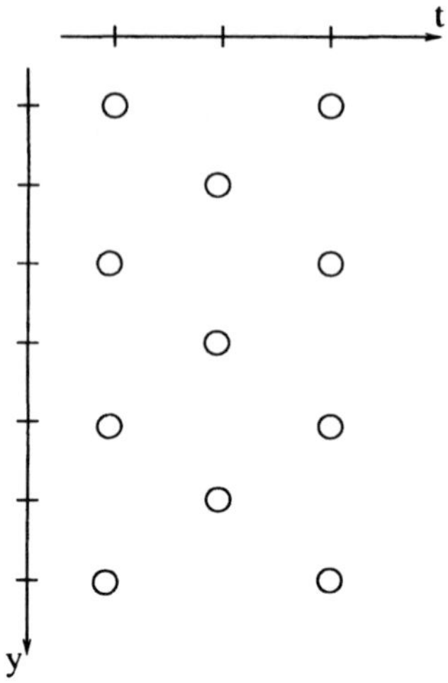

Fig. 2. The interlaced sampling grid. Each dot corresponds to a line in the horizontal dimension

Figure 2 shows the interlaced sampling pattern. Fields containing odd-numbered or even-numbered lines are alternated in time. Interlacing artifacts are in fact caused by aliasing since high temporal frequencies are mapped into high vertical frequencies and the other way around [9,25]. De-interlacing techniques fill up the missing lines of each field. Notice this problem is underdetermined, e.g., one cannot tell if the interlaced sequence in Fig. 3 (a) originates from the non-interlaced versions (b) or (c). Several assumptions about the video signal, such as the presence or absence of motion, are used to handle this problem.

Let's represent the luminance of an interlaced video signal by a discrete function $I(x, y, t)$ which is only known on the sampling grid, i.e., for certain values of x, y and t. Let the number of pixels of a line be X and the number of lines Y. The number of fields per time unit (T) is normalized to 1. Then the sampling grid consists of those (x, y, t) for which

$$\begin{cases} 0 \leq x < X \\ 0 \leq y < Y \ , \ y \text{ and } t \text{ even;} \\ 0 \leq y < Y \ , \ y \text{ and } t \text{ odd.} \end{cases} \tag{10}$$

Motion detection is based on the assumption that motion causes variations in the luminance of pixels as a function of time. The simplest motion detector is the one-point detector which calculates

$$H(x, y, t) = \frac{|I(x, y, t + 1) - I(x, y, t - 1)|}{2} \tag{11}$$

and compares the result to a threshold value to detect the absence or presence of motion at pixel (x, y) at time t (see Fig. 4). The function $H(x, y, t)$ of

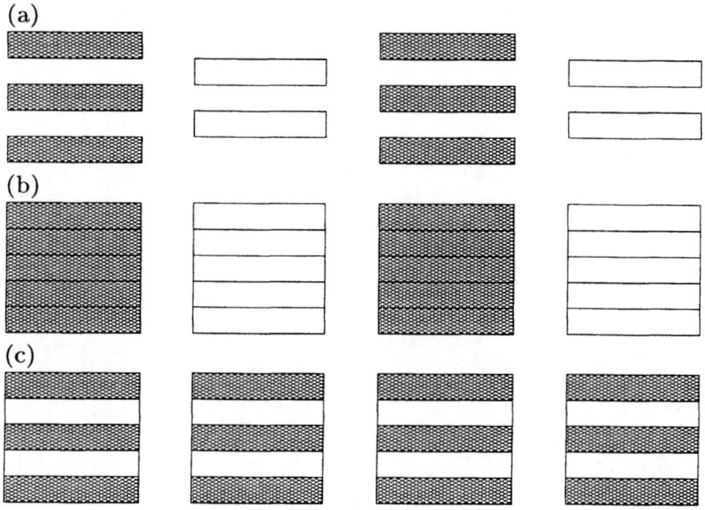

Fig. 3. The interlaced sequence (a) could both be originating from (b) or (c)

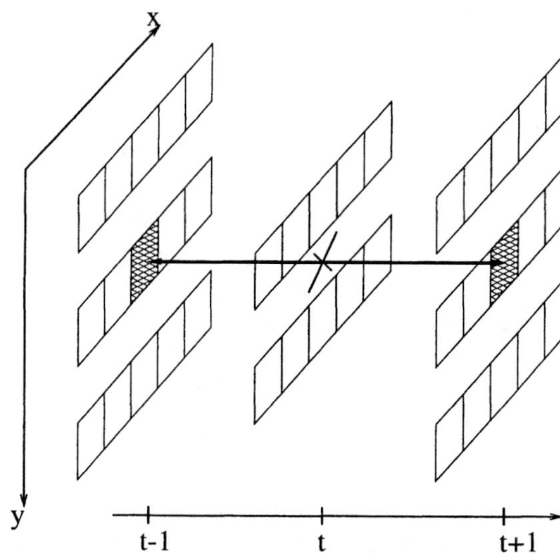

Fig. 4. The frame difference signal $H(x, y, t)$ takes the difference between two pixels on the same position, but different points in time

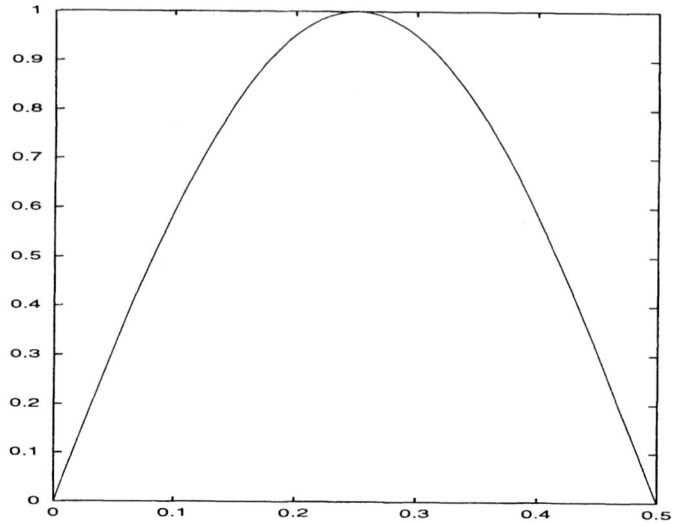

Fig. 5. Temporal amplitude frequency response of the frame difference signal $H(x, y, t)$ (field rate is normalized to 1)

Eq. (11) is the frame difference signal, which is the result of a rectified linear filter operation on the original video signal.

Using the two-sided $\mathcal{Z}$-transform

$$\mathcal{Z}\left\{W(\cdot)\right\}(z) = W_z(z) = \sum_{n=-\infty}^{\infty} W(n) z^{-n}, \tag{12}$$

one can easily calculate that the temporal frequency response of the filter in Eq. (11) is given by

$$W(f_t) = \frac{H_z(x, y, \exp(j2\pi f_t))}{I_z(x, y, \exp(j2\pi f_t))} = j\sin(2\pi f_t). \tag{13}$$

Figure 5 shows the amplitude frequency response $|W(f_t)|$. This response is zero at zero temporal frequency, corresponding to stationary regions, but also at the temporal Nyquist frequency (one half of the field sampling rate). On the positive side, this means that artifacts of the interlaced video signal like line flicker, which are caused by aliasing of high vertical frequency components into high temporal frequency components and which do not correspond to real motion, are not detected as motion by this detector [21,25]. However, on the negative side, moving fine details like the vertical bar of Fig. 6, or a fast moving object which is only present near the current pixel location in the field at time t, remain undetected [4]. The quality of a motion detector can be improved by combining several one-point detectors. Examples are the three-point and seven-point motion detectors of Haavisto [8]. Specifically, the

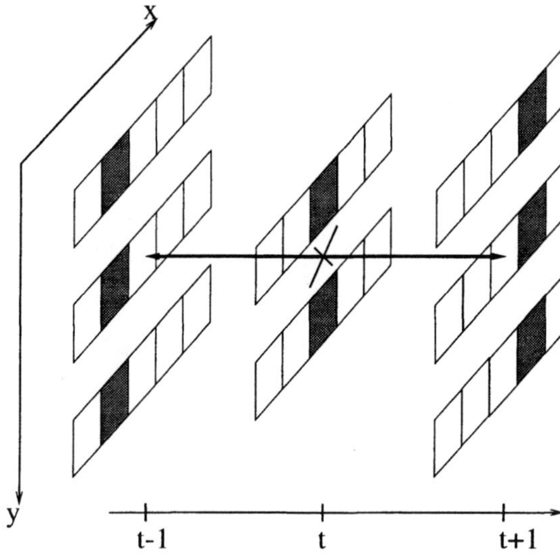

Fig. 6. Moving vertical bar stays undetected by the one-point motion detector

three-point detector uses the results of

$$H_3(x,y,t) = \max\left(H(x,y,t), H(x,y-1,t-1), H(x,y+1,t-1)\right), \quad (14)$$

and the seven-point detector

$$\begin{aligned} H_7(x,y,t) = \max(\ & H(x,y,t), H(x,y-1,t-1), H(x,y+1,t-1), \\ & H(x-1,y-1,t-1), H(x+1,y-1,t-1), \\ & H(x-1,y+1,t-1), H(x+1,y+1,t-1)), \end{aligned} \quad (15)$$

to compare to a single threshold, several thresholds [8], or a soft threshold [21], to obtain a binary of multi-level signal indication of the presence of motion.

2.3 Fuzzification

The fuzzification stage can be viewed as an interface from the real-world input signals to the FLC; it fuzzifies these inputs, i.e., it converts them to fuzzy set representations. In our application, the input is derived from the interlaced video signal.

We propose to use an FLC to combine the results of several frame difference signals. This FLC is a MISO-system, which evaluates the state (the presence of motion) for a pixel using $6K+3$ frame difference signals, where K is a free parameter. The fuzzification stage takes several frame difference signals and calculates their membership values towards two fuzzy sets *SMALL* and *LARGE*. The membership functions of these fuzzy sets are trapezoid-shaped, which are employed by many of FLCs because they are easy to implement in

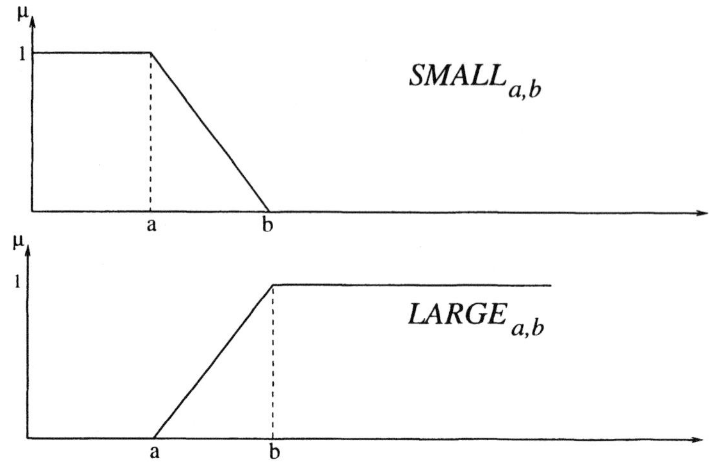

Fig. 7. Membership functions *SMALL* and *LARGE*

both hardware and software. Specifically, the membership functions *SMALL* and *LARGE* are shown in Fig. 7. They are dependent on two parameters, namely a and b.

2.4 Fuzzy rule base

Fuzzy rules characterize the behaviour of the fuzzy controller. A rule is a conditional statement which consists of an antecedent (the condition) and a consequent (the control decision). The truth level of the consequence is given by the result of the fuzzy evaluation of the antecedent. This simple mode of operation is possible because the inputs can be considered as fuzzy singletons and the output membership functions are spike functions. In particular, when we have

- an input value x_0 considered as a fuzzy singleton $\mu_{X'}(x_0) = 1$,
- a fuzzy set F represented by a membership function μ_F,
- a spike output membership function, e.g., $\mu_Y(\mathit{true}) = 0, \mu_Y(\mathit{false}) = 1$[3],
- a rule "IF x is F THEN y is *false*",

then the truth values (plausibilities) $\pi_Y(y)$ of the consequence are given by application of the general modus ponens:

$$\begin{aligned} \pi_Y(\mathit{true}) &= \sup_x (\mu_R(x, \mathit{true}) \star \mu_{X'}(x)) \\ &= \sup_x (\mathcal{I}(\mu_F(x), \mu_Y(\mathit{true})) \star \mu_{X'}(x)) \\ &= \mathcal{I}(\mu_F(x_0), \mu_Y(\mathit{true})) \\ &= 0, \end{aligned} \tag{16}$$

[3] *true* and *false* represent the truth values 1 and 0, respectively

$$\begin{aligned}\pi_Y(\mathit{false}) &= \sup_x (\mu_R(x, \mathit{false}) \star \mu_{X'}(x)) \\ &= \sup_x (\mathcal{I}(\mu_F(x), \mu_Y(\mathit{false})) \star \mu_{X'}(x)) \\ &= \mathcal{I}(\mu_F(x_0), \mu_Y(\mathit{false})) \\ &= \mu_F(x_0). \end{aligned} \tag{17}$$

This compositional operation holds for both the Mamdani minimum-operation rule and the Larsen product-operation rule listed in Table 1, as for all the fuzzy conjunction operators listed in Table 2.

When the fuzzy rule base is specified in its canonical form as in Eq. (9), the antecedents only use the fuzzy conjunction operator. However, for this application, it is easier to initially describe the fuzzy rule base in a non-canonical form, allowing the usage of antecedents with both fuzzy conjunction (AND) and fuzzy disjunction (OR) operators.

The fuzzy motion detector fuzzifies the results of several frame differences signals in the neighbourhood of each pixel by the membership functions *SMALL* and *LARGE*. At each side of the pixel, K frame difference signals are considered, thus in total $2K + 1$ frame difference signals are combined by several fuzzy rules.

Table 4 shows the initial fuzzy rule base. The consequents of the rules imply either $M(x, y, t) = \mathit{true}$ ("motion is present") or $M(x, y, t) = \mathit{false}$ ("motion is absent").
Rule 1 asserts, in a fuzzy way, no motion is present when all frame difference signals are small. The antecedent therefore uses the *SMALL* membership function. The second and third rule reject the assumption of motion when only frame differences at one side of the current pixel are large, but not the others. These rules try to improve the spatial accuracy of the motion detector along the borders of moving objects. The next rules state there is motion when at least one large frame difference signal occurs at each side of the current pixel or at the current pixel itself. These five rules use $2K + 1$ frame difference signals.

The rules are easy to specify and understand independent of the value of K using this non-canonical form. However, most software and hardware implementations require the fuzzy rule base to be specified in its canonical form. Once the parameter K is fixed, we can easily extract rules with antecedents only using the fuzzy conjunction by applying distributivity laws. The fuzzy disjunction of the antecedents is shifted to the "also-sentence connective" which unifies rules with the same consequent.[4] The first rule and the fifth rule are already canonical. The second and third rule will give rise

[4] The minimum and maximum implementation of Table 2 and 3 for the fuzzy conjunction and disjunction obey the distributivity laws. The other implementations only obey weakened distributivity laws or none at all [11].

to K rules each, while the fourth rule leads to K^2 canonical rules. Therefore, the canonical rule set contains $2 + 2K + K^2$ rules[5]. Table 5 shows the canonical rule base for $K = 2$. Each box of the antecedents stands for an evaluation of a frame difference signal at the corresponding pixel position. The current pixel position is the middle box. The symbols 'S' and 'L' stand for "*SMALL*" and "*LARGE*", while 'X' stands for "*DON'T CARE*". For example, the antecedent

$$\boxed{X}\boxed{L}\boxed{X}\boxed{X}\boxed{L} \tag{18}$$

of the fourth rule means "IF $H(x-1,y,t) = LARGE \wedge H(x+2,y,t) = LARGE$, THEN $M(x,y,t) = true$".

Table 4. The initial fuzzy rule set

Rule	Antecedent	Consequent
1	$\bigwedge_{i=-K}^{K} H(x+i,y,t) = SMALL$	$M(x,y,t) = false$
2	$(\bigwedge_{i=0}^{K} H(x+i,y,t) = SMALL) \wedge$ $(\bigvee_{i=-K}^{-1} H(x+i,y,t) = LARGE)$	$M(x,y,t) = false$
3	$(\bigwedge_{i=-K}^{0} H(x+i,y,t) = SMALL) \wedge$ $(\bigvee_{i=1}^{K} H(x+i,y,t) = LARGE)$	$M(x,y,t) = false$
4	$(\bigvee_{i=1}^{K} H(x+i,y,t) = LARGE) \wedge$ $(\bigvee_{i=-K}^{-1} H(x+i,y,t) = LARGE)$	$M(x,y,t) = true$
5	$H(x,y,t) = LARGE$	$M(x,y,t) = true$

2.5 Defuzzification

The final.stage of our fuzzy logic controller produces a numerically precise value in the output space of the controller. The defuzzication stage also incorporates a delayed version $M'(x,y,t)$ of M, in particular $M'(x,y,t)$ is computed as the combination of $M(x,y-1,t-1)$ and $M(x,y+1,t-1)$:

$$(M'(x,y,t) = false) = (M(x,y-1,t-1) = false) \vee (M(x,y+1,t-1) = false), \tag{19}$$

$$(M'(x,y,t) = true) = (M(x,y-1,t-1) = true) \vee (M(x,y+1,t-1) = true), \tag{20}$$

[5] The maximum number of rules equals the number of fuzzy sets powered to the number of inputs: 2^{2K+1}.

Table 5. The canonical fuzzy rule set for $K = 2$

Rule	Antecedent	Consequent
1	S S S S S	$M(x, y, t) = false$
2	L X S S S	
	X L S S S	$M(x, y, t) = false$
3	S S S L X	
	S S S X L	$M(x, y, t) = false$
4	L X X L X	
	L X X X L	
	X L X L X	
	X L X X L	$M(x, y, t) = true$
5	X X L X X	$M(x, y, t) = true$

which is consistent with the "also-sentence connective" used to unify rules which have the same consequent. Note that the results of $M(x, y-1, t-1)$ and $M(x, y+1, t-1)$ do not need to be recalculated and can be stored in an intermediate memory. The combined plausibility of motion is calculated as

$$\begin{aligned}\pi_{M(x,y,t)}(true) &= (M(x,y,t) = true \vee M'(x,y,t) = true)\\ \pi_{M(x,y,t)}(false) &= (M(x,y,t) = false \wedge M'(x,y,t) = false),\end{aligned}$$

such that in total $6K + 3$ frame difference signals contribute to determine the plausibility of motion for each pixel. Finally, a numerically precise or "crisp" value $\gamma(x, y, t)$ in the interval $[0, 1]$ is obtained using the "fuzzy mean" defuzzification method [16]:

$$\gamma(x,y,t) = \frac{\pi_{M(x,y,t)}(true)}{\pi_{M(x,y,t)}(true) + \pi_{M(x,y,t)}(false)}, \tag{21}$$

which is the multi-level output of our fuzzy motion detector.

2.6 Example

In Sect. 3, we will consider an application of the fuzzy motion detector which will enable us to evaluate the performance of it. At this moment, we already show some qualitative results of applying the motion detector to a test-sequence. Figure 8 shows four consecutive frames of the "salesman"-sequence. Figure 9 shows the output γ of the motion detector for frames 34 and 35. Note that the output is interlaced since we applied the motion detector as if the test-sequence was interlaced, as it will be in the next section.

Fig. 8. Four consecutive frames out of the "salesman"-sequence

3 Application to de-interlacing

Scan-format conversion problems include de-interlacing, line rate conversion and field rate conversion. Here, we present a motion adaptive linear de-interlacing algorithm that relies on the output of the fuzzy motion detector.

3.1 Adaptive interpolation

As we mentioned in the introduction, de-interlacing algorithms must compute pixels of the missing lines of each field. That way, a non-interlaced or progressive scanned video signal is generated from an interlaced input signal. The underlying idea of motion adaptive resampling is to use spatial interpolation for moving regions and temporal interpolation for static regions. Line-averaging is usually satisfactory in moving regions of the scene, where fine details are perceived as less important by the human visual system due to motion. However, as shown in Fig. 10, small differences between two consecutive scenes in a static part causes annoying flicker artifacts. These artifacts can be prevented by using a temporal interpolation technique such as field insertion; this restores fine details of static scenes very well but introduces ghosting artifacts in moving regions (see Fig. 11).

frame #34

frame #35

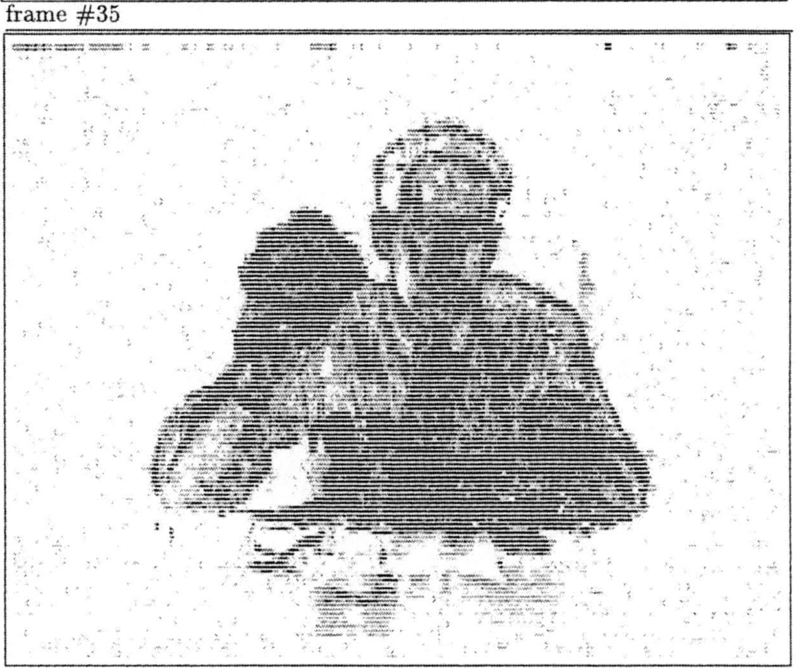

Fig. 9. Two consecutive frames of the output of the fuzzy motion detector

The output $\gamma(x, y, t)$ of the fuzzy motion detector indicates the presence of motion and will be used as weighting factor. We propose a linear combination of line-averaging (intra-field) and field insertion (inter-field):[6]

$$I(x,y,t) = (1-\gamma(x,y,t))\, I(x,y,t-1) + \gamma(x,y,t)\frac{I(x,y-1,t)+I(x,y+1,t)}{2}, \tag{22}$$

Prodan [21] showed how the frequency characteristics of such a combined interpolation filter alter properly when the linear weighting factor changes.

(a) Part of frame #7

(b) Part of frame #8

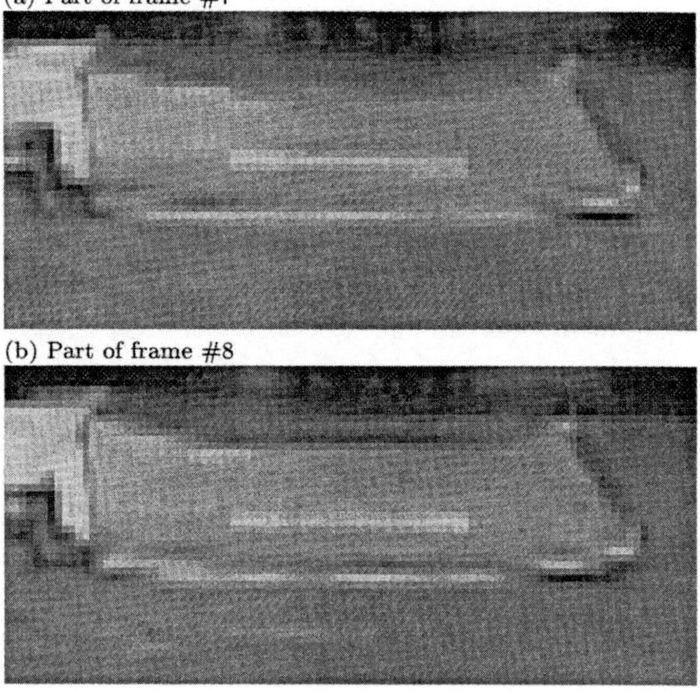

Fig. 10. Flicker artifacts result from small differences between two consecutive frames (a) and (b) when using intra-field interpolation techniques

3.2 Results

The quality of de-interlacing algorithms can be tested by generating interlaced versions of progressively scanned video sequences, de-interlacing these

[6] Since $I(x, y, t)$ represents the luminance, Eq. (22) can be used directly for grayscale video sequences. Color sequences use the same equation for each color plane using the results of the motion detector applied on the luminance.

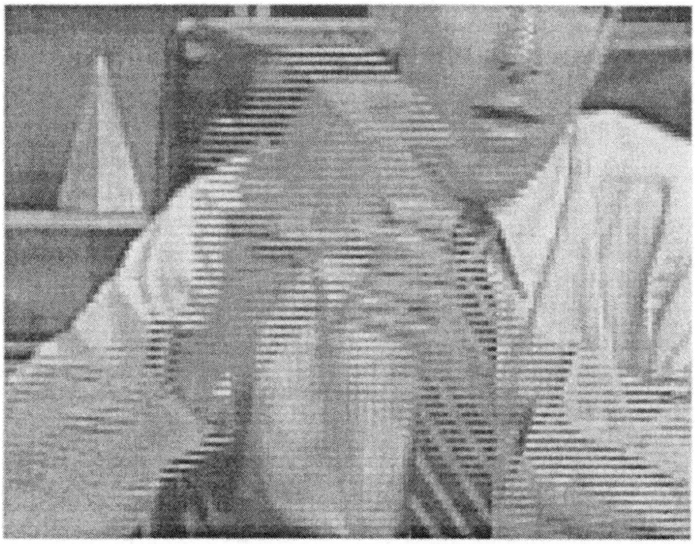

Fig. 11. Ghostings artifacts occur when two field with motion are merged

by some algorithm and comparing the result to the original. This comparison can be qualitative (by visual inspection of the sequences) or quantitative (by computing a numerical measure for the difference between the sequences). We already introduced the "salesman"-sequence to take a qualitative look at the output of the fuzzy motion detector. Because the performance of a de-interlacing algorithm needs to be evaluated in particular on mainly static and moving regions, we will consider two different parts of the "salesman"-sequence. Figure 12 shows two rectangular regions of the sequence which are used to evaluate respectively moving and static regions. The main goal is to obtain good results for each type of region. We will also consider the results of other test-sequences. A representative frame of these other sequences is shown in Fig. 13.

The next figures show the MSE (mean squared error) measurements, defined as

$$E = \frac{\sum_{t=0}^{N-1} \sum_{x=0}^{X-1} \sum_{y=0}^{Y-1} (I_1(x,y,t) - I_2(x,y,t))^2}{NXY}, \tag{23}$$

for two video sequences I_1 and I_2 containing N frames of resolution $X \times Y$. We also calculated MAE (mean absolute error) and PSNR (peak signal to noise ratio) values but these did not add information to the MSE measurements.

The value of the parameter K determines the number of frame difference signals that is taken into account for each pixel. From Fig. 14, we can see the MSE results for the moving part of "salesman" for different values of a, b (parameters of the membership functions), and K. The best result (lowest MSE) is obtained for $K = 2$ and $0 \leq a \leq 1$, $5 \leq b \leq 6$. Note that such values

Fig. 12. The rectangular regions $(120, 90) \rightarrow (200, 210)$ (framenumber 34 to 44) and $(270, 225) \rightarrow (350, 285)$ (framenumber 10 to 20) of the "salesman"-sequence contain respectively many motion and no motion

(a) "foreman"

(b) "mobile"

(c) "suzie"

(d) "deadline"

Fig. 13. Frame of the other test-sequences used to compare de-interlacing methods

of a and b correspond to membership functions which are more "fuzzy" than when $a = b$ since the truth levels have more chance to be different from 0 and 1. The results show performance drops when $b \geq 6$: the rules which imply $M(x,y,t) = true$ get too tolerable. In this example, motion artifacts starts become noticable when the MSE is larger than 16. The average MSE decreases for larger K, which indicates the motion detector is more robust against variations of the parameters a and b when more frame differences signals are taken into account. Figure 15 shows the MSE results of the static region of "salesman". The value of K has little influence on these results. Performance improves as a and b increase: the motion detector gets more tolerable against motion and field insertion (which restores static regions) is used. Good values of the parameters are $a \geq 1$ and $b \geq 3$. Note that the scale of the MSE results of the still region is much larger than the scale of the MSE results of the moving region. Artifacts in still regions (typically flicker artifacts) give rise to larger MSE than motion artifacts (typically ghosting artifacts). A complete sequence consists of both moving and static regions, so the MSE results are an average of performance on both types of regions. Figure 16 shows the MSE results for the whole "salesman"-sequence. The different magnitudes of MSE of artifacts in moving and still regions and the proportion of both types of regions in the video sequences, give larger values of b as optimal. However, visual inspection shows for all sequences that motion artifacts become visible when $b \geq 8$.

It is interesting to investigate other implementations of the fuzzy conjunction and disjunction operators than the minimum/maximum and to compare their results. The charts in Fig. 17 and 18 show the MSE measurements of the moving region of "salesman" for these different implementations. An important difference between these implementations are the results for small values of a ($a = 0, 1$). Performance clearly degrades for other implementations than minimum/maximum. This difference is less remarkable for larger a. When a is small, the *SMALL* membership-function is only exactly 1 when the frame difference signal is smaller than a too. The antecedent of a rule combines several membership values, thus when some components are not exactly 1, the truth value of the rule will decrease according to the sensibility of the fuzzy conjunction operator to such small differences. The different conjunction implementations can be ranked according to this sensitivity. Therefore, consider the fuzzy set

$$C_\delta : \mathbb{R} \mapsto [0,1],\ x \to \mu_{C_\delta}(x) = 1 - \delta, \tag{24}$$

where δ is a very small positive number ($\delta < 1$). We calculate the conjunction of a membership value x with the fuzzy set C_δ for each different implemen-

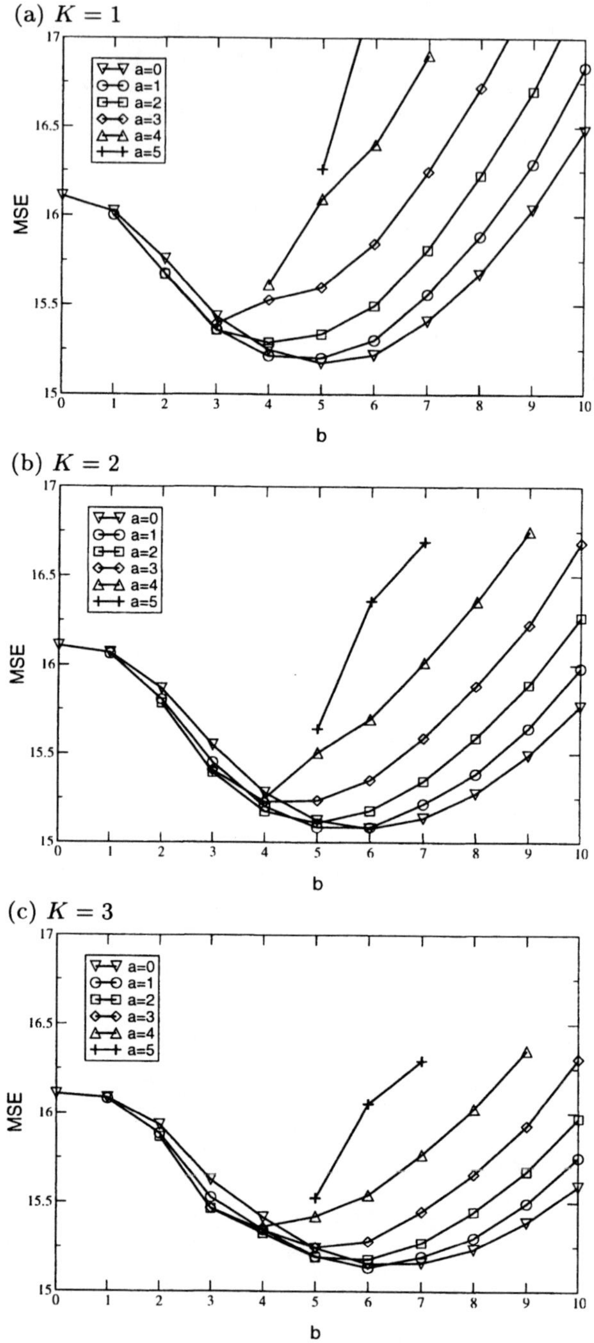

Fig. 14. Moving region of "salesman": MSE for different values of a and b for (a) $K = 1$, (b) $K = 2$, (c) $K = 3$

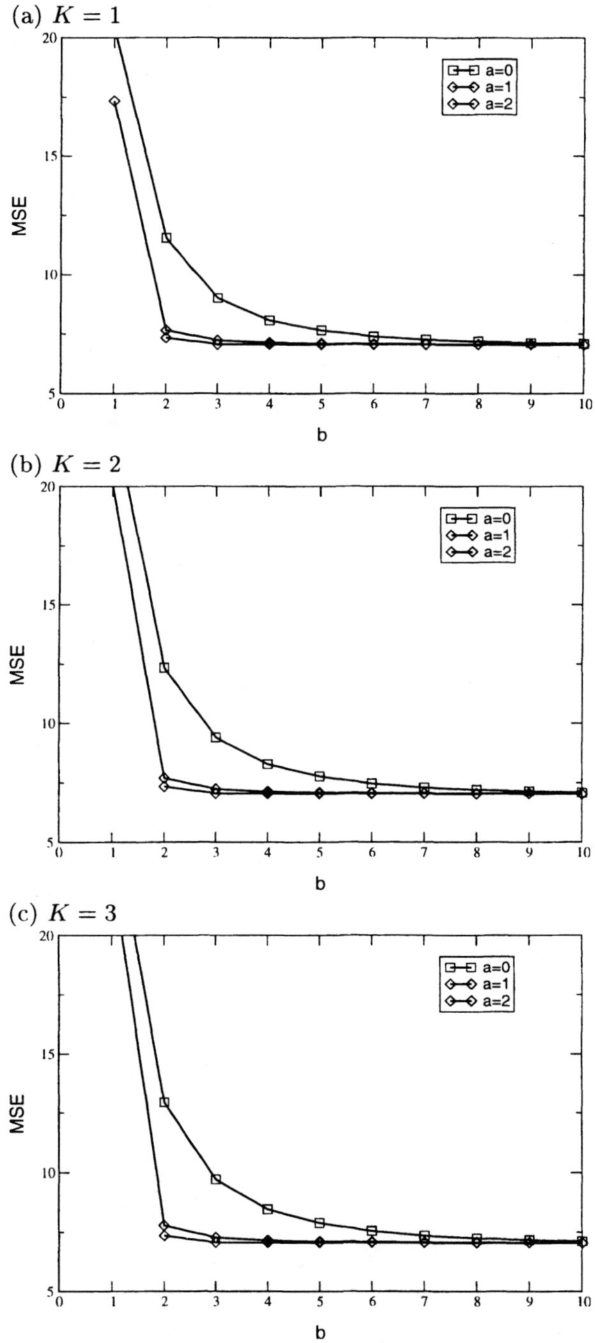

Fig. 15. Static region of "salesman": MSE for different values of a and b for (a) $K = 1$, (b) $K = 2$, (c) $K = 3$

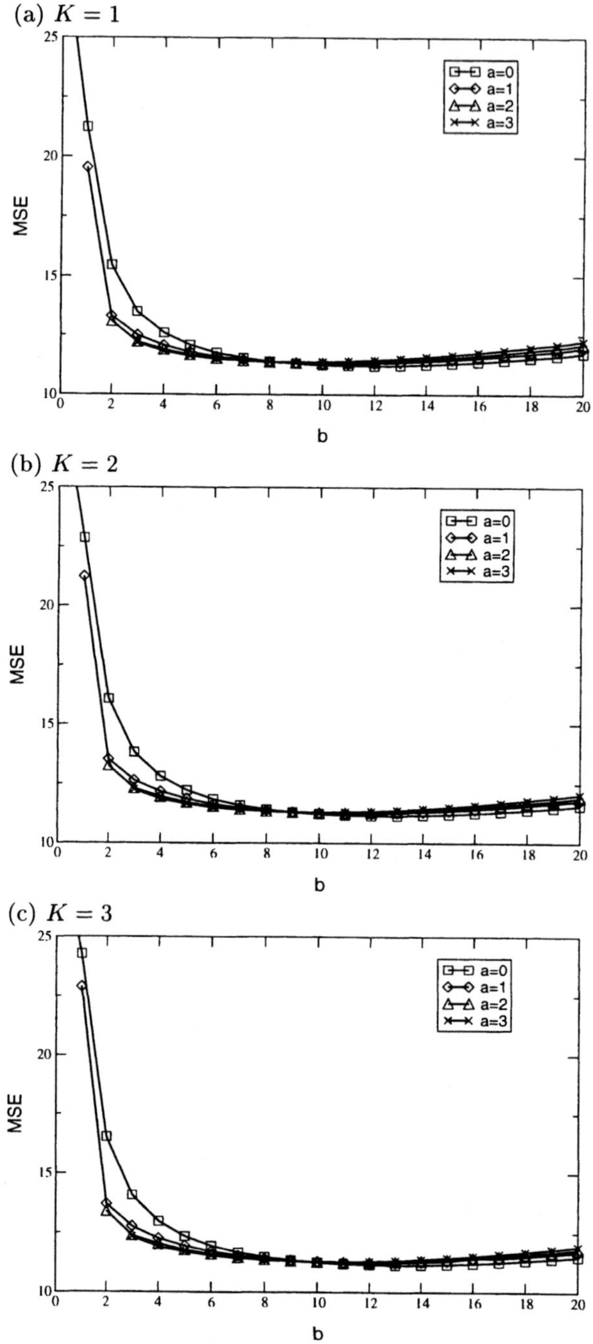

Fig. 16. "Salesman": MSE for different values of a and b for (a) $K = 1$, (b) $K = 2$, (c) $K = 3$

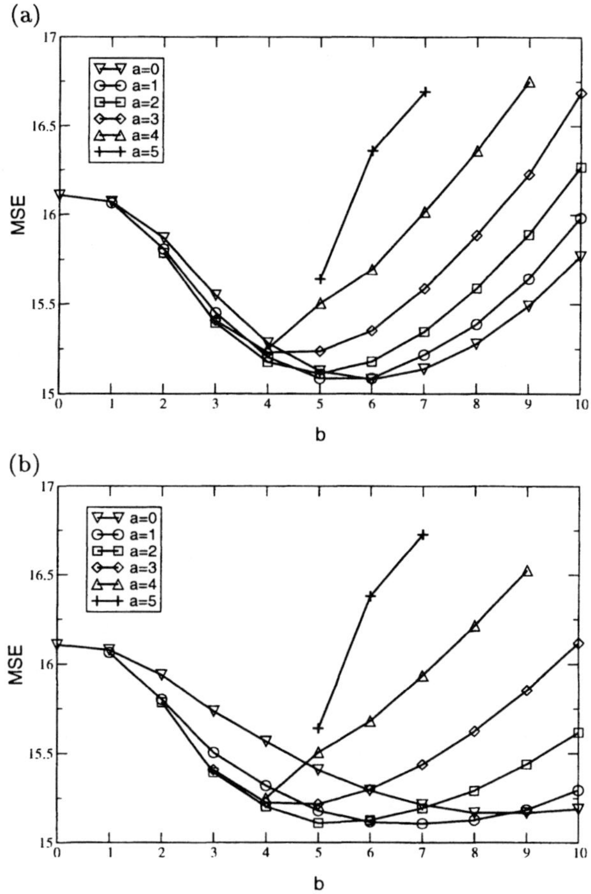

Fig. 17. MSE when fuzzy operators are implemented by (a) minimum/maximum and (b) algebraic product/sum ($K = 2$)

tation of the conjunction operator:

$$x \bigtriangleup (1-\delta) = \min(x, 1-\delta), \tag{25a}$$

$$x \,\hat{\cdot}\, (1-\delta) = x(1-\delta), \tag{25b}$$

$$x \odot (1-\delta) = \max(0, x-\delta), \tag{25c}$$

$$x \sqcap (1-\delta) = 0. \tag{25d}$$

A compound antecedent consists of several components, so we calculate the cumulated sensitivity using the shorthand notation

$$x \wedge_k y = x \wedge \underbrace{y \wedge y \wedge \ldots \wedge y}_{k \text{ times}}. \tag{26}$$

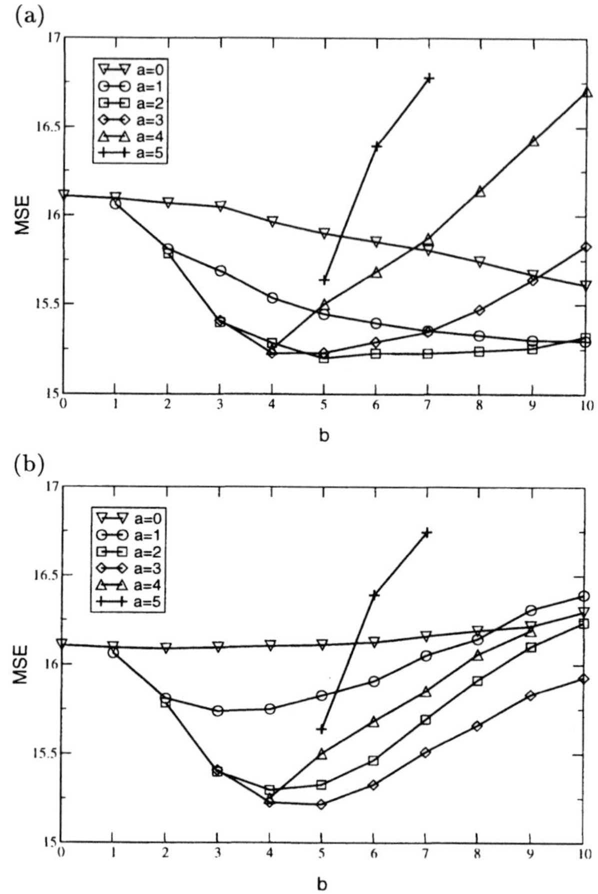

Fig. 18. MSE when fuzzy operators are implemented by (a) bounded product/sum and (b) drastic product/sum ($K = 2$)

The conjunction of a membership value x after k conjunctions with C_δ equals:

$$x \bigtriangleup_k (1 - \delta) = \min(x, 1 - \delta) \approx x, \tag{27a}$$

$$x \,\hat{\cdot}_k (1 - \delta) = x(1 - \delta)^k, \tag{27b}$$

$$x \odot_k (1 - \delta) = \max(0, x - k\delta), \tag{27c}$$

$$x \sqcap_k (1 - \delta) = 0. \tag{27d}$$

Figure 19 shows the results obtained with Eqs. (27a-27d) based on this sensitivity. The different implementations can be ranked according to the highest residual value of x after k conjunctions with C_δ. This ranking is the same as when ranking the performance of the different implementations for $a = 0, 1$.

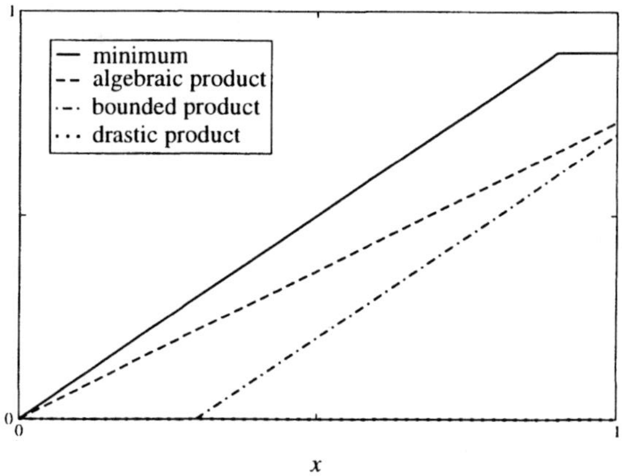

Fig. 19. Result of $x \wedge_k (1-\delta)$ when $k = 3, \delta = 0.1$

These results show the minimum/maximum and algebraic product/sum implementations yield the best results and are most robust regarding variations of the values a and b.

It is also interesting to compare the fuzzy algorithm to some other motion detectors, i.e., the three-point and seven-point motion detector of Haavisto. Haavisto compares the values of the signals $H_3(x, y, t)$ and $H_7(x, y, t)$ of Eq. (14) and (15) to several thresholds and uses the result to steer a median filter for frame rate up doubling. We will use these signals to perform motion adaptive de-interlacing. First of all, the values of $H_3(x, y, t)$ and $H_7(x, y, t)$ were calculated. Then, these values were put through a soft threshold similar to the *LARGE* membership function to get values in the interval $[0, 1]$ which are used for the interpolation. The best values of a and b were obtained to compare with our fuzzy algorithm.

Figure 20 shows MSE results for the fuzzy motion detector, the three-point detector and the seven-point detector. The results of the moving part are best for the fuzzy motion detector. Note that even a small improvement is important because most artifacts are ghosting artifacts. As b increases from 0 to 5, the results of the fuzzy motion detector improve a lot. The three-point detector does a better job on the static scene than the seven-point detector. Figure 21 shows the results of the static and the moving part of "salesman" on a frame basis. The fuzzy algorithm yields the best results, especially when motion gets large as in frames 7 and 8 of the moving part. Note once more that the three-point motion detector outperforms the seven-point motion detector in the static scene. It is interesting to explain why this happens. Consider the three-point detector after the soft threshold, which is the evaluation of

$H_3(x, y, t) = LARGE$. This can be further formulated as a fuzzy expression

$$\begin{aligned} H(x,y,t) &= LARGE \vee \\ H(x,y-1,t-1) &= LARGE \vee \\ H(x,y+1,t-1) &= LARGE, \end{aligned} \tag{28}$$

where the disjunction operator corresponds to the maximum implementation. The complement of this expression corresponds to our fuzzy motion detector which only uses the first rule and $K = 0$. This way we will compare our fuzzy motion detector for different values of K against a stripped version which only uses the first rule. Figure 22 shows the average results for both the static and the moving part of the test-sequence. It's clear the performance of the first rule only gets worse as K increases above 1. Also, the static part can't profit from larger values of K. On the other hand, using the full rule set gets advantage of the extra pixels that are taken into account to determine the presence of motion.

Table 6. MSE measurements for moving and static region of "salesman"

	moving region	static region
Line-replication	53.06	69.84
Line-averaging	16.09	29.33
ELA	24.40	38.60
3-taps median	49.41	73.28
9-taps median	35.41	43.30
Three-point	15.78	7.16
Seven-point	15.77	7.24
Fuzzy method	15.09	7.13

Table 6 shows the results of our algorithm against those obtained with other de-interlacing methods for the two types of regions. Line-replication (a.k.a. line-doubling), line-averaging, a spatially edge adaptive technique (enhanced ELA by Kuo *et al.* [13]) are all spatial intra-field interpolation techniques. The 3-taps median, 9-taps weighted median [10], three-point and seven-point motion detector, and our new fuzzy-based technique are listed as inter-field interpolation methods. We didn't optimize the values a and b of the fuzzy-based approach for each sequence but choose the values $a = 1$, $b = 5$, $K = 2$ fixed. Table 7 summarizes the average MSE results for the whole sequences. The line-replication method and 3-taps median perform the worst. The median techniques are not satisfactory and the results indicate these techniques are very dependent on the particular kind of sequence that is

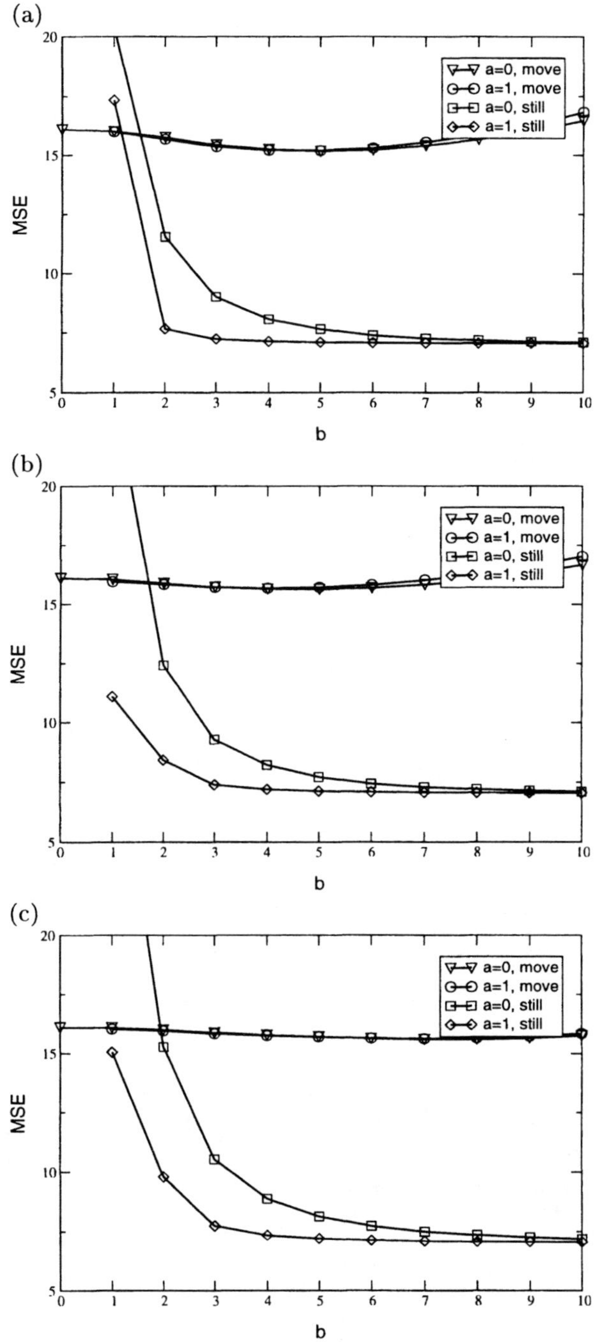

Fig. 20. MSE for different values of a and b for (a) fuzzy motion detector ($K = 1$, minimum/maximum), (b) three-point detector and (c) seven-point detector

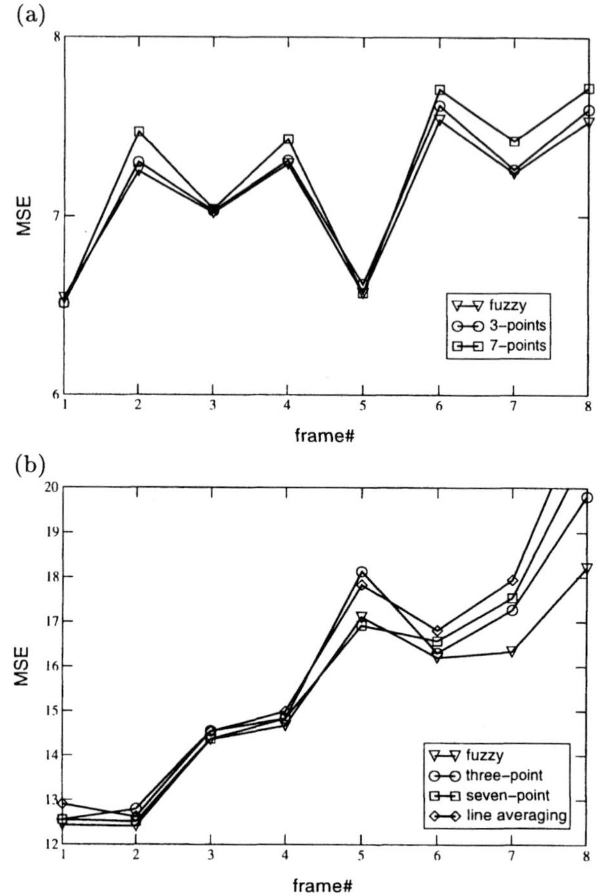

Fig. 21. Comparison between several de-interlacing methods for (a) static and (b) moving part of the "salesman"-sequence

used. Also notice the ELA method can't improve the result of line-averaging, which indicates too many false edge detections occur[7]. It seems that the average MSE of the three-point detector is lower than the seven-point detector. Small ghosting artifacts however are more likely to appear using the three-point detector. The fuzzy-based motion detector performs best for all the test-sequences.

[7] It is well known interlaced video complicates image processing tasks such as edge detection.

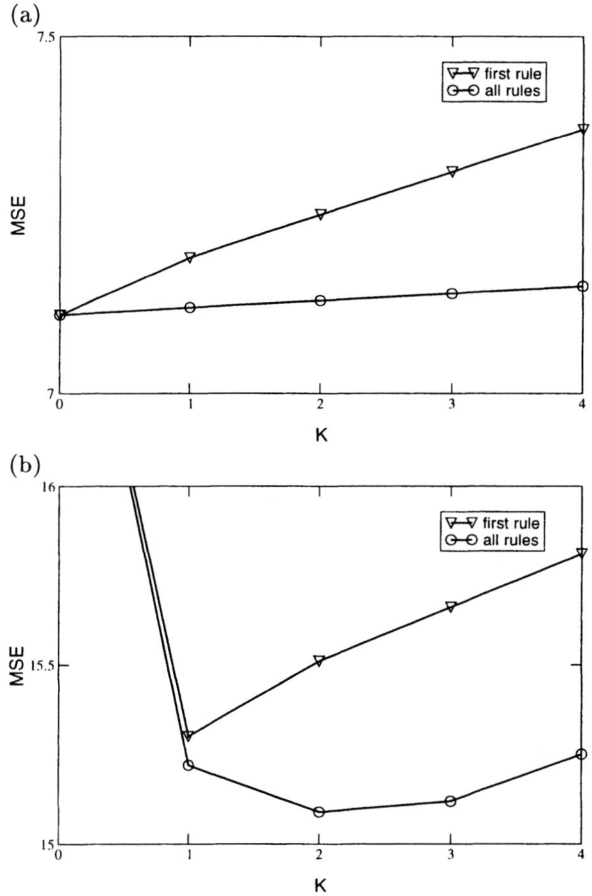

Fig. 22. Comparison between application of only the first rule and the whole rule set for (a) static and (b) moving part of the "salesman"-sequence

4 Conclusions

De-interlacing algorithms fill up the missing lines of fields of an interlaced video signal. They can be used to enhance picture quality and reduce interlacing artifacts, or can be necessary to use interlaced video on devices that prefer or require the progressive scan format. Good de-interlacing techniques should adapt to motion. The choice of threshold values can be critical for the performance of classical motion detectors. Fuzzy logic control provides a framework which allows to incorporate knowledge and takes care of levels of uncertainty. The numerical results show the trade-off between good performance for both static and moving regions is more easier to be made using the fuzzy motion detector. The influence of the parameters is made clear. We showed that both the classical Zadeh min / max and algebraic product/sum

Table 7. MSE measurements for different test-sequences

	"salesman"	"foreman"	"mobile"	"suzie"	"deadline"
Line-replication	71.94	112.3	61.20	28.79	127.9
Line-averaging	29.47	43.73	26.19	9.76	58.48
ELA	43.49	39.83	32.29	12.37	95.22
3-taps median	67.31	112.4	60.95	29.29	127.9
9-taps median	39.88	101.7	73.71	30.05	26.78
Three-point	12.49	39.98	23.54	8.51	11.44
Seven-point	12.95	41.43	24.42	8.89	12.80
Fuzzy method	11.93	37.20	22.69	7.89	10.51

implementations of the fuzzy conjunction/disjunction provide satisfactory results on several test-sequences.

Acknowledgments

This work was financially supported by the FWO (Fund for Scientific Research - Flanders), through a mandate of Research Assistant (Dimitri Van De Ville), the IWT-project (Institute for the Advancement of Scientific-Technological Research in Industry - Flanders) 980155, and GOA-project (Ghent University) 12.0513.98.

The test-sequences used in this chapter, can be found on the internet. Most of them are available on the ftp-site `ftp://ipl.rpi.edu/pub/image/`.

References

1. Blume H., Franzen O. and Schmidt M., *Optimizing video signal processing algorithms by evolution strategies*, Computational Intelligence, No. 1226, pp. 547–548, 1997
2. Booth S., *Digital TV in the US*, IEEE Spectrum 36, No. 3, pp. 39–46, 1999
3. Clarke C., *Future television systems: Comparison of sequential and interlaced scanning*, BBC Research and Development Report, No. 1987/18, 1987
4. Connor D.J., Haskell B.G. and Mounts F.W., *A Frame-to-Frame Picturephone Coder for Signals Containing Differential Quantizing Noise*, The Bell System Technical Journal, Vol. 52, No. 1, pp. 35–51, 1973
5. Cox E., *Fuzzy Fundamentals*, IEEE Spectrum, Vol. 29, No. 10, pp. 58–61, 1992
6. De Haan G. and Bellers E., *De-interlacing – An Overview*, Proceedings of the IEEE, Vol. 86, No. 9, pp. 1839–1857, 1998
7. Haavisto P., Juhola J. and Neuvo Y., *Fractional frame rate up-conversion using weighted median filters*, IEEE Transactions on Consumer Electronics, Vol. 35, No.3, pp. 272–278, 1989

8. Haavisto P. and Neuvo Y., *Motion Adaptive Scan Rate Up-conversion*, Multidimensional Systems Signal Processing, No. 3, pp. 113–130, 1992
9. Huang T. S., *"Image Sequence Analysis"*, Springer, Heidelberg, 1981
10. Karlsson M., Pohjala P., Rantanen H. and Kalli S., *Evaluation of Scanning Rate Up Conversion Algorithms; Subjective Testing of Interlaced to Progressive Conversion*, IEEE Transactions on Consumer Electronics, Vol. 38, No. 3, pp. 162–167, 1992
11. Kerre E., *Introduction to the basic principles of fuzzy set theory and some of its applications*, Communication & Cognition, Ghent, 1991
12. Koivunen T., *A Noise-insensitive Motion Detector*, IEEE Transactions on Consumer Electronics, Vol. 38, No. 3, pp. 168–173, 1992
13. Kuo C.J., Liao C. and Lin C.C., *Adaptive Interpolation Technique for Scanning Rate Conversion*, IEEE Transactions on Circuits and Systems for Video Technology, Vol. 6, No. 3, pp. 317–321, 1996
14. Larsen P.M., *Industrial applications of fuzzy logic control*, J. Man Mach. Studies, Vol. 12, No. 1, pp. 3–10, 1980
15. Lee C.C., *Fuzzy Logic in Control Systems: Fuzzy Logic Controller*, IEEE Transactions on Systems, Man, and Cybernetics, Vol. 20, No. 2, pp. 404–435, 1990
16. Van Leekwijck W. and Kerre E., *Defuzzification: criteria and classification*, Fuzzy Sets and Systems, Vol. 108, pp. 159-178, 1999
17. Mamdani E.H. and Gaines B.R., *"Fuzzy Reasoning and its Applications"*, Academic, London, 1981
18. Marsh D., *TV and the PC, State of the Union*, WinHEC 99 White Paper, Microsoft, 1999
19. Michaud F., Dinh C., Lachiver G., *Fuzzy Detection of Edge-Direction for Video Line Doubling*, IEEE Transactions on circuits and systems for video technology, Vol. 7, No. 3, pp. 539–542, 1997
20. Poynton C.A., *"A Technical Introduction to Digital Video"*, Wiley, New York, 1996
21. Prodan R.S., *Multidimensional digital signal processing for television scan conversion*, Philips Journal of Research, Vol. 41, No. 6, pp. 576–603, 1986
22. Russo F., *FIRE operators for image processing*, Fuzzy Sets and Systems, Vol. 103, No. 2, pp. 265–275, 1999
23. Takada S., Ohsawa M. *et al.*, *Video signal-processing technique for video printer*, Sharp Technical Journal, No. 62, pp. 5–9, 1995
24. Tabatabai A., Jasinschi R. and Naveen T., *Motion Estimation Methods for Video Compression – A Review*, Journal of the Franklin Institute, Vol. 335B, No. 8, pp. 1411–1441, 1998
25. Tekalp A.M., *"Digital Video Processing"*, Prentice Hall, New York, 1995
26. Thomas G.A., *A comparison of motion-compensated interlace-to-progressive conversion methods*, BBC Research and Development Report, No. 1996/9, 1996.
27. Tsang D., Bensaou B. and Lam S., *Fuzzy-Based Rate Control for Real-Time MPEG Video*, IEEE Transactions on Fuzzy Systems, Vol. 6, No. 4, pp. 504–516, 1998
28. Van De Ville D., Rogge B., Philips W. and Lemahieu I., *De-interlacing using fuzzy-based motion detection*, in: "Proceedings of KES'99 – the Third International Conference on Knowledge-Based Intelligent Information Engineering Systems" (Adelaide, Australia), pp. 263–267, 1999
29. Van Someren N., *"High Quality De-interlacing of Television Images"*, PhD Thesis. Trinity College, University of Cambridge, 1994

Chapter 14

Object Recognition and Visual Servoing: Two Case Studies of Employing Fuzzy Techniques in Robot Vision

Alois Knoll, Jianwei Zhang, Thorsten Graf, and André Wolfram

University of Bielefeld, Faculty of Technology
PO-Box 10 01 31, D-33501 Bielefeld, Germany
email: {knoll,zhang,graf,andre}@techfak.uni-bielefeld.de

Summary. The capabilities of observing the world and manipulating objects based on visual information are basic requirements in robotic applications. Typically, for manipulating objects in real environments it is necessary to recognise and locate the substantial objects robustly. Due to external influences, e.g. partial occlusions of objects and illumination changes, as well as to internal influences, e.g. noisy imaging hardware, inaccurate measurements and quantization effects, the recognition systems have to cope with incomplete, uncertain and inaccurate information.

In the first part of this chapter we present the general framework of a robust approach for recognising partially occluded objects. It combines the popular concept of using invariant shape descriptions, i.e. descriptions of objects which remain unaffected by certain variations of the intrinsic and extrinsic camera parameters, with the flexibility and readability of rule-based fuzzy systems by applying invariant object shape descriptions in fuzzy if-then classification rules.

In the second part, we propose a fuzzy control approach for learning fine-positioning of parallel-jaw robot gripper using visual sensor data. The first component of the used model can be viewed as a perceptron network that projects high-dimensional input data into a low-dimensional eigenspace. The second component is a fuzzy controller serving as an interpolator whose input space is the eigenspace and whose outputs are the motion parameters. Instead of undergoing cumbersome hand-eye calibration processes, our system is trained in a supervised learning procedure using systematical perturbation motion around the optimal grasping pose.

1 Introduction

Vision may aid robots (both mobile and fixed) in many tasks such as navigation, location and inspection of assembly parts, tracking objects, avoiding collisions, detecting errors, determining distances or even learning from a human instructor by analysing hand gestures. Unfortunately, unlike human vision, machine implementations of vision systems tend *not* to be particularly robust, i.e. they are susceptible to variations in lighting, to unexpected shadows, lens and perspective distortions, specular reflections etc. Moreover, these systems often cannot deal with more complex scenes in which objects occlude each other or in which parts change their orientation with respect to a reference image.

These uncertainties seem to lend themselves naturally to be dealt with by fuzzy techniques. Interestingly, such techniques have not met with much acceptance in the computer vision community even though they promise to alleviate two of the main methodological problems in computer vision: the ubiquitous application of crisp thresholding and (probabilistic) model matching (see [11,27])[1].

Both thresholding and model matching result in a more or less drastic loss of information that is not recoverable in higher processing stages of a vision system – data are irretrievably discarded either when they do not exceed a certain threshold or do not lie within a certain distance to the model. The obvious advantage of fuzzy techniques is that they do not necessarily discriminate sharply between data that are below and above the threshold. Instead, the threshold can be replaced by a membership function and valuable information retained for higher level processing stages. The same applies to models (of object form, pose, invariants, etc.) and clustering: while (probabilistic) models are normally based on Bayesian prior distributions with few degrees of freedom, fuzzy methodology easily combines the notion of membership with complex rule bases that make it easy to express and incorporate human expert knowledge. It is also underpinned by powerful learning or adaptation algorithms whose learning results are transparent, sometimes even human readable.

Examples of typical complete vision systems that have successfully incorporated fuzzy techniques are:

- path tracking of autonomous indoor vehicles through fuzzy control [4]. The main advantage of the fuzzy controller was considered to be its ability to extract heuristics from experiences. An outdoor mobile platform that is also controlled by a fuzzy rule base is presented in [17].
- visual inspection of assembly parts (integrated circuits) for their correctness with respect to their specification [6]. It was noted that both the fuzzy algorithm used there and expert systems represent human domain knowledge in the form of production rules; the former, however, does not run the risk of a combination explosion.
- identification of objects in a robotics scene based on a verbal description [8]. The noisy high-level features of an object are compared with a natural language expression.
- object extraction for navigation through fuzzy feature matching [14]. The main goal here is to recognise office chairs under varying viewing angles or in the case of occlusions by evaluating local features. Similarly, [15]

[1] These two papers contain references to other survey papers; [23] discusses some further issues related to uncertainty.

uses corners as local features for the recognition of transistor packages on an assembly line.

- recognition of occluded objects [25] using fuzzy linguistic statements as input for the training of a neural network. The classification of the partially hidden objects is then performed based on adequate local features.

In this chapter we address two issues in robot vision: the recognition of partially occluded objects in complex scenes of (known) objects and the fine-positioning of a robot gripper for grasping an object. We demonstrate the performance of our methods for a specific domain: a set of the wooden toy objects of a construction kit for children (Fig. 1, for details see [13]). Our experiments show that a robust recognition of occluded objects is possible even under a high degree of uncertainty (object type, object pose, highly structured background, change of perspective, lighting variations). The same is true for our "near-field" recogniser that guides the robot towards its gripping position.

Fig. 1. Typical test scenario

The rest of the chapter is organised as follows: in Section 2 we describe in detail a recognition system for the extraction of objects from images taken of a robotics scene. The images are recorded by a standard camera with a large area of view. Section 3 is devoted to the hand-camera based fine-positioning system, which "takes over" once the position of the objects in the scene has been determined and the gripper has been moved into the vicinity of the object to be grasped. Section 4 describes the whole "run" from the first image of the scene to the grasping. Finally, in Section 5, we conclude with some remarks on the qualities and deficiencies of the systems and possible lines of future research.

2 Recognition through fuzzy invariant indexing

2.1 Motivation

The recognition of partially occluded objects is undoubtedly one of the most challenging tasks in computer vision. Recent research has indicated that the use of invariants as shape descriptors is a promising and powerful approach to tackle this problem. Mathematically, invariants are functions of geometric configurations remaining unaffected under particular classes of transformations (for good introductory papers see [7,19]), e.g. the class of projective transformations modelling the camera mappings of a vision system. Since these invariants are independent of the viewpoint of the camera, the measured projective invariant values of an object can be used efficiently in the hypothesis generation as an index into an object-lookup table. This technique is called invariant indexing.

Several recognition systems based on invariant theory have been developed, e.g. an early system based on geometric hashing technique [16], the LEWIS-system [24] or the MORSE-system [18]. Since images taken from real-world scenes (and using real-world equipment) are generally discrete, cluttered and noisy, the observed projective invariant values fluctuate when different perspective views of an object are recorded. This problem must be handled within the indexing stage of every recognition system based on invariants. In our context, indexing means to assign image features to corresponding model features and therefore to generate object hypotheses.

Usually, invariant indexing hashes into a discrete index space, where all points belonging to an object are marked. For indexing, a hashing function is evaluated for the measured invariant values of a geometric configuration part of an object. The number of the independent invariants depends on the underlying geometric configuration. For example, the planar geometric structure of a conic and three straight lines has three independent projective invariants (see Section 2.2). To overcome the fluctuation, not only a single point of the index space is marked but also the neighbouring ones. Invariant values of a certain neighbourhood are hence mapped to the same object with equal weight.

Contrary to this, we utilize an invariant indexing technique based on fuzzy if-then-classification-rules and fuzzified invariant values modelling the fluctuation. This technique is called Fuzzy Invariant Indexing (FII).

2.2 The fuzzy invariant indexing technique

The basis of the fuzzy invariant indexing technique are disjunctively connected fuzzy if-then-rules that incorporate fuzzified invariant values. These classification rules have the following form:

$$\text{IF } i^k_{m1} = \widetilde{I}^k_{m1} \text{ AND ... AND } i^k_{mN^k_m} = \widetilde{I}^k_{mN^k_m} \text{ THEN } o^k_m = \widetilde{O}^k \tag{1}$$

$$\text{with} \begin{array}{l} k=1,2,\ldots,K \\ m=1,2,\ldots,M^k \\ n=1,2,\ldots,N^k_m \end{array}$$

where i^k_{mn} denotes the n-th input variable of subrule m for the k-th object, $\widetilde{I}^k_{mn}$ the corresponding fuzzy invariant value, o^k_m the output variable of subrule m and $\widetilde{O}^k$ the k-th object class modelled as a fuzzy singleton. The total amount of antecedents (N^k_m) depends on the number of independent invariants of the underlying geometric configuration of subrule m for object k and the total amount of subrules (M^k) depends on the number of different geometric configurations for object k.

The main problem with the fuzzy if-then-rules is to find appropriate membership functions to model the fuzzy invariant values $\widetilde{I}^k_{mn}$ in (1) for a given object. Our investigation of invariant values measured in views of different perspectives has indicated that the fluctuations can be adequately approximated by bell-shaped membership functions $\mu_{\widetilde{I}^k_{mn}}$:

$$\mu_{\widetilde{I}^k_{mn}}(u) = e^{-\frac{(u-\alpha^k_{mn})^2}{2\beta^{k\;2}_{mn}}}, \quad u \in \mathbb{R} \tag{2}$$

where the parameters $\alpha^k_{mn}, \beta^k_{mn}$ that shape the function are chosen as follows:

- The parameter α^k_{mn} determines the position of the maximum of the bell-shaped function (2). Therefore, this parameter should be the mean of the fluctuating invariant values: $\alpha^k_{mn} = \frac{1}{N}\sum_l I_l$, where I_l, $1 \leq l \leq N$ are the invariant values for an object taken from N different views.
- The parameter β^k_{mn} determines the position of the inflexions of (2), which are located at $\alpha \pm \beta$. This parameter should be the standard deviation of the invariant values: $\beta^k_{mn} = \left(\frac{1}{N}\sum_l (I_l - \alpha^k_{mn})^2\right)^{\frac{1}{2}}$.

For example, consider the well-known invariant of a conic and two lines under plane projective transformations [19]:

$$I(\mathbf{C}, \mathbf{l}_1, \mathbf{l}_2) = \frac{\left(\mathbf{l}_1{}^t\mathbf{C}^{-1}\mathbf{l}_2\right)^2}{\left(\mathbf{l}_1{}^t\mathbf{C}^{-1}\mathbf{l}_1\right)\left(\mathbf{l}_2{}^t\mathbf{C}^{-1}\mathbf{l}_2\right)} \tag{3}$$

where $\mathbf{C}$ is the conic coefficient matrix and $\mathbf{l}_1, \mathbf{l}_2$ denote lines expressed in homogeneous coordinates. Figure 2 shows the distribution of invariant values for a test object 'nut' measured in 30 images. To provide a better discrimination we apply Eq.(3) to feature groups of a conic $\mathbf{C}$ and three lines $\mathbf{l}_1, \mathbf{l}_2, \mathbf{l}_3$

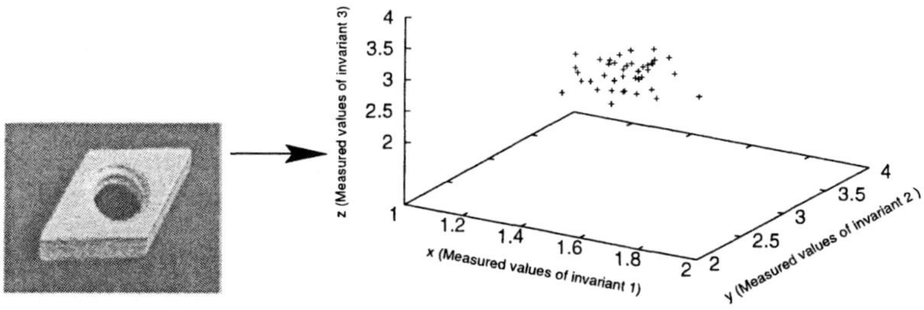

Fig. 2. Distribution of measured invariant values for test object 'nut' (30 images)

by determining the three independent invariant values:

$$I_1(\mathbf{C}, \mathbf{l_1}, \mathbf{l_2}, \mathbf{l_3}) = I(\mathbf{C}, \mathbf{l_1}, \mathbf{l_2}) \tag{4}$$

$$I_2(\mathbf{C}, \mathbf{l_1}, \mathbf{l_2}, \mathbf{l_3}) = I(\mathbf{C}, \mathbf{l_1}, \mathbf{l_3}) \tag{5}$$

$$I_3(\mathbf{C}, \mathbf{l_1}, \mathbf{l_2}, \mathbf{l_3}) = I(\mathbf{C}, \mathbf{l_2}, \mathbf{l_3}) \tag{6}$$

In Fig. 2, the invariant values on the x-axis are calculated using Eq. (4), the invariant values on the y-axis are calculated using Eq. (5) and the invariant values on the z-axis are calculated using Eq. (6). The distributions of these invariant values are depicted in the histograms shown on the left hand side of Figure 3. Thus, for the test object 'nut' we get the values $\alpha_{11}^k = 1.4$, $\beta_{11}^k = 0.086$ for the parameters of the first fuzzy invariant value, $\alpha_{12}^k = 3.2$, $\beta_{12}^k = 0.145$ for the second and $\alpha_{13}^k = 2.5$, $\beta_{13}^k = 0.14$ for the third fuzzy invariant value, which leads to the fuzzy invariant values shown on the right hand side in Figure 3. Note that the (fuzzy) model of an object may be composed of many such invariants. Finally, the fuzzy invariant values are incorporated into the following if-then-classification rule:

$$\text{IF (inv1} \approx 1.4) \text{ AND (inv2} \approx 3.2) \text{ AND (inv3} \approx 2.5) \quad \text{THEN (object is NUT)} \tag{7}$$

Object hypotheses are generated through the FII-technique by evaluating the fuzzy rules using standard fuzzy inference techniques:

$$\mu_{o_m^k} := \min_{1 \le n \le N_m^k} \mu_{\tilde{I}_{mn}^k}(i_{mn}^k) \tag{8}$$

where $\mu_{o_m^k}$ is the output of m-th subrule for object k and i_{mn}^k are the measured invariant values. These subresults are combined disjunctively:

$$\mu_{o^k} = \max_{1 \le m \le M^k} \mu_{o_m^k} \tag{9}$$

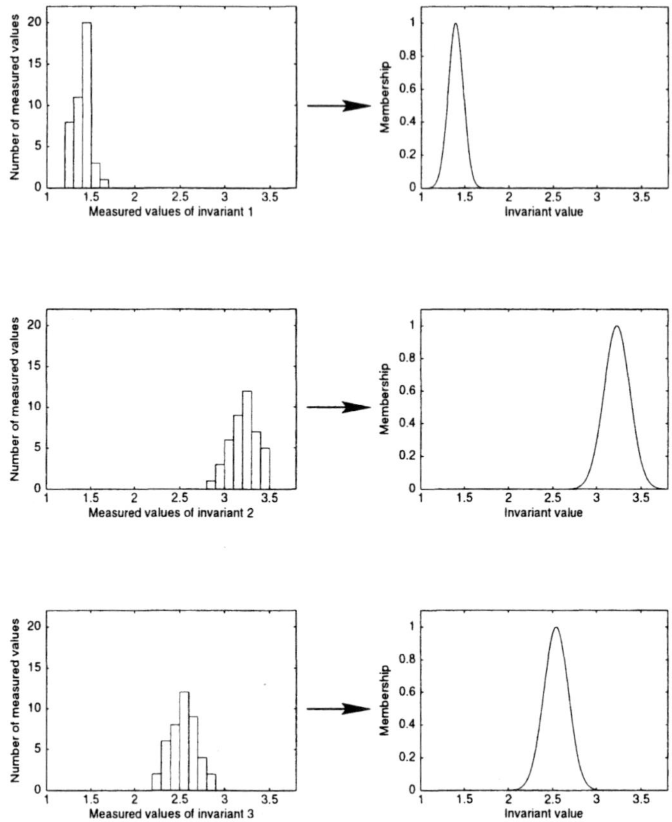

Fig. 3. Example for the generation of fuzzy invariant values

The final result is the indexed k-th object model with the measured credibility μ_{o^k}.

2.3 Recognition system

The fuzzy invariant indexing technique outlined above has been integrated into an object recognition system for partially occluded (quasi-)planar objects. The structure of the system is similar to other systems ([16,24]) but differs completely in applying a fuzzy rule base in the hypothesis generation stage.

As indicated in Tab. 1 the system provides two different processing phases: an off-line acquisition process and an on-line object recognition process.

Acquisition process The acquisition process is capable of learning the rules of the fuzzy invariant indexing automatically. The first stage of the acquisition process is the edge detection stage. In the implemented system we use

Table 1. Acquisition / Recognition Process

	Acquisition (offline)	Recognition (online)
1	Edge detection	
2	Feature extraction	
3	Computation of invariants	
4	Generation of fuzzy invariant values	Hypothesis generation
5	Generation of fuzzy rules	Hypothesis verification

the Canny edge detector [5], which takes a greyscale or color image as input, and generates as its output linked edge points. Next, in the feature extraction stage, geometric primitives are fitted to the extracted edge points, where the primitives that are used depend on the objects to be recognised. For the objects shown in Fig. 1 straight lines and ellipses are suitable. The features are grouped into configurations for which invariants can be computed. In the implemented system we use the invariants of two geometric configurations: the invariants of a conic and three lines (see Eqs. (4),(5),(6)), and the invariants of a pair of coplanar conics [21].

The last and most expensive stage is the model and rule generation, in which new objects are learned automatically, including both the object model and the fuzzy if-then classification rules. The object model is stored in a model base and consists of an object name, the extracted features and the computed invariant values. The fuzzy rules are generated as described in Section 2.2.

Recognition process The first three steps of the recognition process are equivalent to those of the acquisition process: the edge points are extracted in an image, features are fitted and invariants are calculated.

Next, in the hypothesis generation step, the classification rules of the fuzzy rule base are evaluated as described in Section 2.2. If the resulting credibility μ_{o^k} of an indexed object is above a threshold[2], a new object hypothesis is generated. This hypothesis consists of the object name, the credibility and the features used to compute the invariant values. The recognition process ends in the verification of the generated object hypotheses. This is done as usually: The hypothesized object model is mapped into the image and verified against the extracted features. Although this system is implemented for recognising (quasi-)planar objects only, this is no principle limitation.

2.4 Recognition examples

The performance of the FII-recognition system is demonstrated for the aforementioned object domain of quasi-planar, colored wooden toy objects, such as rims, tyres, nuts and slats as shown in Fig. 1.

The first scene, Figure 4, consists of four three-hole-slats, two seven-hole-slats, two orange nuts, two red rims, two white tyres and one "unknown"

[2] The threshold is used to rule out the very unlikely hypotheses only.

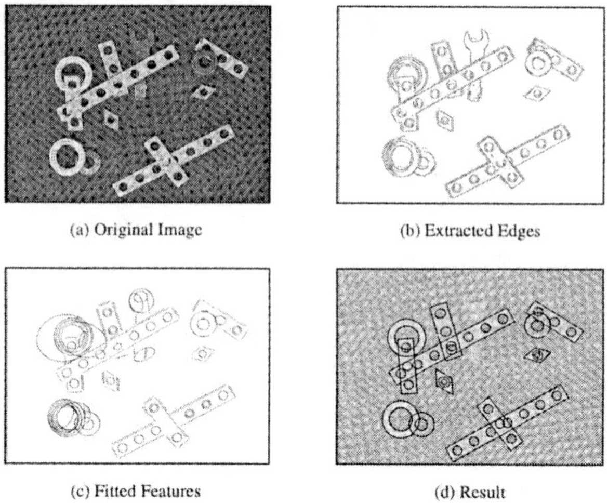

Fig. 4. Example scene 1

(i.e. unmodelled) spanner, which partially overlap each other. Since the extracted edge points (Figure 4b) as well as the fitted features (Figure 4c) provide a reliable image description, the system recognises all of the known objects (4d).

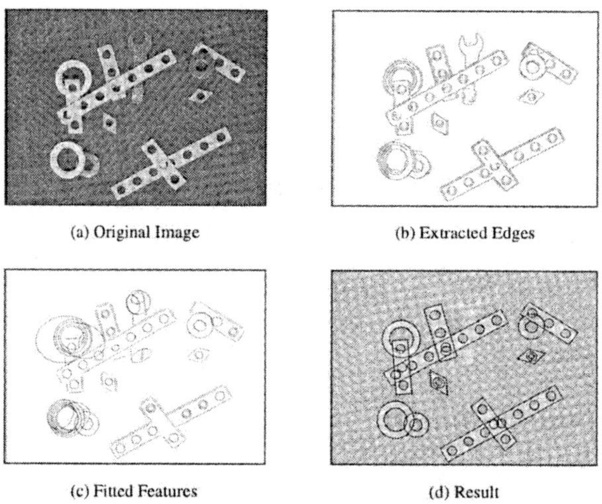

Fig. 5. Example scene 2

In the second scene (Figure 5a) several slats, three rims, one tyre, one nut and three unknown objects on a highly textured background are used. Figure 5b shows the detected edge points and Figure 5c the fitted features.

Although the complexity of this test scene is very high, the recognition system performs well (see Fig. 5d). The system detects all of the known objects except for two 3-hole-slats and one rim. The problems here are a consequence of an inaccurate feature extraction. Since the system fails to extract the topology of these objects correctly, no invariant values can be computed. False positives, however, are not made.

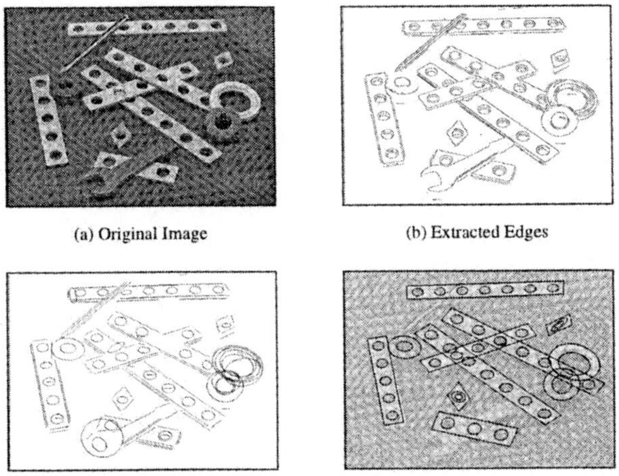

(a) Original Image (b) Extracted Edges

(c) Fitted Features (d) Result

Fig. 6. Example scene 3

Since the utilized invariants remain unaffected by the intrinsic and extrinsic camera parameters, the recognition system can be applied to different imaging conditions. Figure 6a shows a test scene taken at a viewing angle of 45°. Again, despite the resulting perspective distortion, the recognition system performs well. Just one 5-hole-slat has been misclassified as a 7-hole-slat (Fig. 6d). Further recognition results are shown in Fig.14 for hand-camera images.

To demonstrate how the fuzzy rules can easily be extended by integrating further attributes, we added color attributes to the fuzzy rules learned before. We measure the RGB color information of an object along the underlying geometric structures of the fuzzy rules and transform it into the HSV color space. Depending on the saturation of the object color we use the hue or the intensity for generating and evaluating the fuzzy rules, e.g. the rule for the nut (7) changes to:

$$\begin{aligned} &\text{IF (inv1} \approx 1.4) \text{ AND (inv2} \approx 3.2) \text{ AND (inv3} \approx 2.5) \\ &\qquad \text{AND (hue} \approx 283) \\ &\qquad \text{THEN (object is NUT)} \end{aligned} \tag{10}$$

Experimental results show that this extension generally reduces the number of generated object hypotheses by 25%, which further reduces the likelihood of false matches. For example, the extended fuzzy rules decrease the number of hypotheses for Fig. 4a from 4078 to 3119, for Fig. 5a from 5840 to 4385 and for Fig. 6a from 4094 to 3444. The integration of further attributes enhances the performance of the recognition system in two ways: It speeds up the recognition process because fewer object hypotheses must be investigated into in the time consuming verification stage and, secondly, the robustness of the system is increased, because fewer false positives are established.

Furthermore, we have compared the FII-technique to a crisp invariant indexing technique (where we have replaced the membership functions with intervals). It turns out, that the FII-technique provides better recognition results than the crisp one; this is true, especially in the difficult case of very similar objects (for details, see [9]).

We conclude this section by noting, that the average time for recognising the objects in Fig. 4a is 49 seconds, in Fig. 5a is 77 seconds and in in Fig. 6a is 50 seconds on a standard PC (K6-300MHz) with the potential of a straightforward distribution on multiple processors and a resulting drastic reduction in time.

We now turn to our second fuzzy robot vision system that directly controls the movement of a robot arm based on visual input.

3 Fine-positioning and object grasping: turning visual observations into action

3.1 Motivation

The task is the fine-positioning of a manipulator once the coarse positioning has been completed. The object to be grasped is visible in the image of a "self-viewing" eye-in-hand camera (Fig. 7), which sees an area of about 11 cm × 9 cm of the x-y-plane. The aim is to move the robot hand from its current position (Fig. 8 left) to a new position so that the hand-camera image matches the optimal grasping position (Fig. 8 right). Some of the objects in the image have the same shape but different colors. It is therefore mandatory that a general image processing technique be applied, which needs *no specialised algorithm for each object* and shows stable behaviour under varying object brightness and color. In other words: for dealing with the general case of handling objects whose geometry and features are not precisely modelled or specially marked, it is desirable that a general control model can be found which, after an initial learning step, robustly transforms raw image data *directly into action values*.

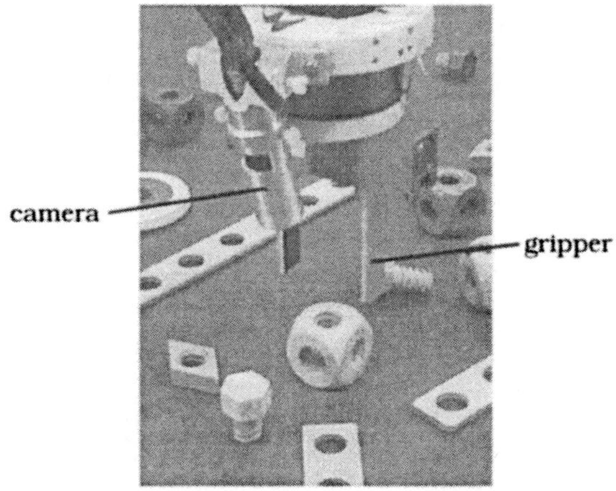

Fig. 7. The end-effector of the manipulator with a hand-camera (positioned optimally over the yellow cube)

3.2 The neuro-fuzzy model

One approach to developing such techniques is neural network-based learning, which has also found applications in grasping: [20,28,12] use geometric features as input to the position controller.

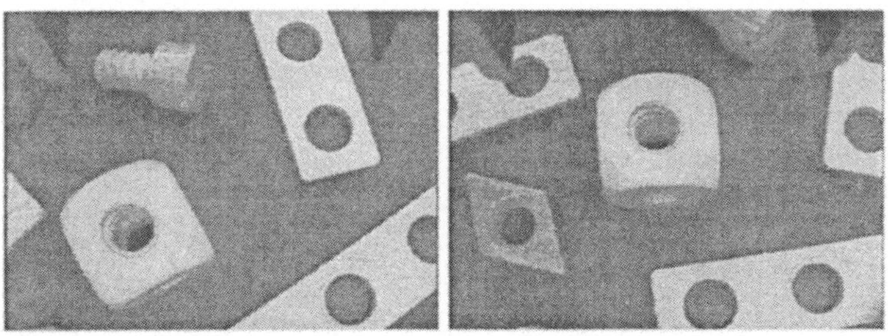

Fig. 8. A cube viewed from the hand-camera – before and after fine-positioning

Our idea to solve the fine-positioning control problem is to use a direct, linear method to reduce the input dimension and then apply the non-linear B-spline model [30] to map the projection on the subspace further to the control output.

Depending on how "local" the measuring data are and, therefore, how similar the observed sensor patterns appear during variations within a given situation, a more or less small number of eigenvectors calculated by a principle component analysis (PCA) [32] can provide a sufficient summary of the state of all input variables (see the left part of Fig. 9). Our experimental results show under the most diverse conditions that it is very likely that three or four eigenvectors provide all information indices of the original input space necessary for the positioning task. Therefore, in the case of very high input dimensions, an effective dimension reduction can be achieved by projecting the original input space into the eigenspace.

Eigenvectors can be partitioned by covering them with linguistic terms (the right part of Fig. 9). In the following implementations, fuzzy controllers constructed according to the B-spline model are used [30]. This model provides an ideal implementation of CMAC proposed by Albus [1]. We define linguistic terms for input variables with B-spline basis functions and for output variables with singletons. Such a method requires fewer parameters than other set functions such as trapezoid, Gaussian function, etc. The output computation is very simple and the interpolation process is transparent. We also achieved good approximation capabilities and rapid convergence of the B-spline controllers.

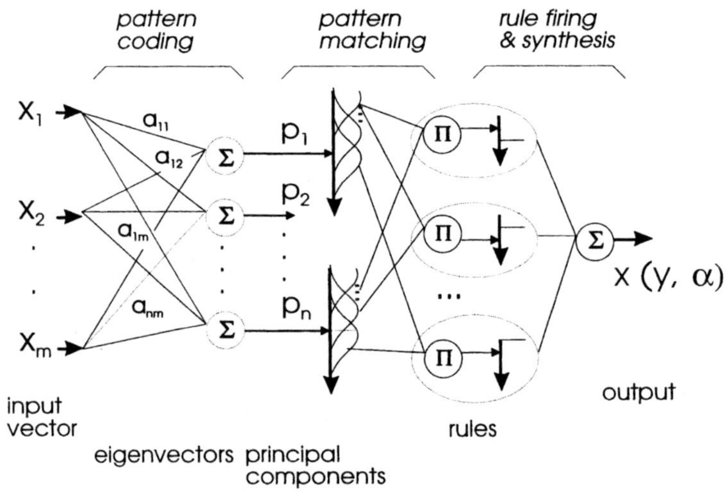

Fig. 9. The task-based mapping can be interpreted as a neuro-fuzzy model. The input vector consists of many thousands pixels of a grey-scale image

3.3 Implementation

The working system implements two phases: off-line training and on-line evaluation. In the off-line phase, a sequence between 10 and 100 training images showing the same object in different positions is taken automatically, i.e. without human intervention. For each image, the position of the manipulator in the plane and its rotation about the z-axis, both with respect to the optimal grasp position for the current object, is recorded.

In the on-line phase, the camera output is transformed into the eigenspace and is then processed by the fuzzy controller. The controller output is the end-effector's position and angle correction (Fig. 10).

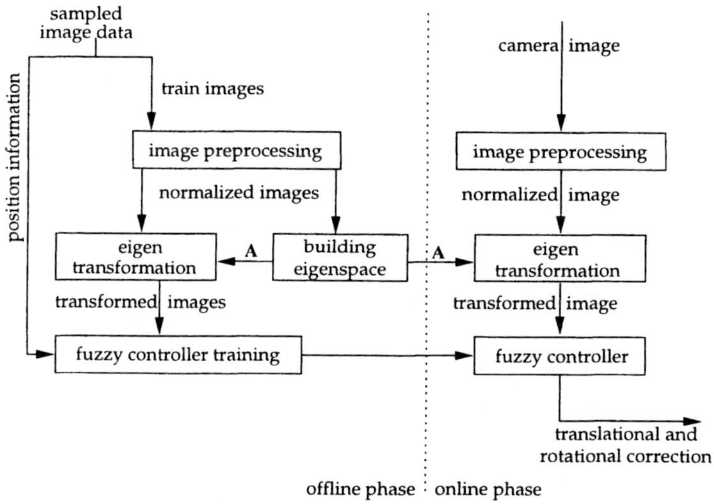

Fig. 10. The training and the application of the PCA neuro-fuzzy controller

Preprocessing Fig. 14 (left) shows typical pictures taken by the hand-camera. Fig. 14 (right) shows the images after a clipping process utilising the FII recognition system (Section 2). This clipping process leaves only the object of interest in the images. After clipping, all images are normalised with respect to their "energy" [22]:

$$x_j^i = \frac{\tilde{x}_j^i}{\sqrt{\sum_{l=1}^{dim} \left(\tilde{x}_l^i\right)^2}}$$

where $\tilde{x}_j^i$ is the intensity of the j-th pixel in the i-th image, x_j^i is the intensity of the j-th pixel in the corresponding normalised image and dim is the number of pixels in the image.

For detecting the rotation of an object, one more preprocessing step is necessary: since most of the variance in the images is caused by translations, the rotation cannot be learned properly from the eigen-transformed images. To eliminate the variance caused by changes in the position, we shift the region of interest to the centre of the image. As this removes the translational information from the images, two eigenspaces must be computed: one based on the original images and one based on the shifted versions.

Fuzzy controller training With the image intensity values and the corresponding desired action values, a B-Spline fuzzy controller is trained. We use third order splines as membership-functions and between 3 and 5 knot points for each linguistic variable. The distribution of these points is equidistant and constant throughout the whole learning process. The coefficients of the B-Splines (de Boor points) are initially zero. They are modified by the rapid gradient descent method during training [30].

On-line phase In the on-line phase, the same image preprocessing as in the off-line phase is applied. Then, the stacked image vector $\mathbf{x}$ is transformed into the eigenspace. The resulting vector is fed into the fuzzy controller, which, in turn, produces the position and angle of the object in the image. These values are then used to move the robot closer to the target object. This sequence is repeated several times; normally no more than 3 steps are necessary until all parameters (i.e. deviation in x and y direction and residual angular deviation) are below a specific threshold (e. g. 0.5 mm and 1 degree).

To improve the raw algorithm outlined above several aspects were refined:

Color images: Instead of the gray-scale images, the saturation parts of color images in the *Hue-Saturation-Intensity* color-space may be used. For objects with full colors ("rainbow"-colors) the saturation part is high; for colors like teal, pink or light blue this component is low and for all grey-tints including black and white it is zero. This increases the contrast between objects and background when compared with the intensity image. Thus, in the case of colored objects, the controller becomes highly independent of the hue of the objects.

Boosting image vectors: The complexity reduction method is not limited to one image per vector. For example, the vector $\boldsymbol{x}$ could consist of the intensity image, the saturation image, and a Sobel-filtered intensity image. This can help to suppress inaccuracies due to unusual lighting conditions. Obviously, further (possibly object-dependent) improvements can be achieved with specialised feature detectors (lines, angles, etc.).

Hierarchy: If, for a very difficult object, the discrimination accuracy of the neuro-fuzzy controller is not sufficient, a hierarchical system may be built. The camera images are separated into regions, then an appropriate classifier detects in which region in the image the object to be grasped is located, and, based on this information, the robot moves approximately to the optimal grasping position. After this movement, a neuro-fuzzy controller is trained. The training images for it need only show the object near the optimal position. Such a system is even more accurate than the neuro-fuzzy controller alone.

Optimal choice of training images Appearance-based vision is frequently criticised for the fact that the *training images* must be chosen manually, which often leads to simple trial-and-error. To cope with this problem, we developed a method for automatically determining the positions where the camera images should be taken. Since the robot is allowed to do several steps, high accuracy is only needed near the optimal grasp position $\boldsymbol{d} = (x_0, y_0, \alpha_0) = (0, 0, 0)$.

Rotation: The angles at which the images are taken depend on the object symmetry S. For objects with an S of less than 360 degrees there is more than one optimal grasp position. That is because it makes no difference whether a cube is grasped by the front and rear side or at the left and right side. So near the angles $0, S, 2S, \ldots$ more images are needed. The objects in Fig. 12 possess the following symmetries: For the slat S is 180 degrees, for the cube S is 90 degrees and for the screw head S is 60 degrees. To limit the number of images for objects with a small S, the following changes are made: If S is smaller than 90 degrees, then it is multiplied by the smallest integer that produces a value of greater than or equal to 90 degrees. This leads, for example, to an S of 120 degrees for the screw head. The following heuristic formula produced acceptable results:

$$\mathbf{W} = \bigcup_{\substack{i \in \mathbf{N_0} \\ j = 0, 1, \ldots, 360/S - 1}} \left\{ \left\lfloor \frac{S}{2} \frac{1}{2^i} \right\rfloor + j \cdot S,\ S - \left\lfloor \frac{S}{2} \frac{1}{2^i} \right\rfloor + j \cdot S \right\}$$

For the cube, this formula gives the set of angles $\mathbf{W} = \{45, 23, 67, 11, 79, 6, 84, 3, 87, 1, 89, 0, 90, 45{+}90, 23{+}90, \ldots\}$(in degrees), with $\mathbf{W}$ containing 48 elements. Due to the clipping described in Section 3.3 for rotation, only training images near the optimal grasping position are taken, at the points with coordinates $(0, 1)$, $(1, 0)$, $(0, 0)$, $(0, 1)$, and $(1, 0)$. Long objects like the slat can lie partly outside the image. In this case, images with 0, 90, 180 and 270 degrees are added at the 4 positions ($\pm 25\,\text{mm}, \pm 25\,\text{mm}$).

Translation: Images at the learning positions are taken with 0 degrees rotation. In most cases the resulting accuracy for the x- and the y-controller is satisfying with these images. If not, either the controller for x or that for y can be selected. If the y-placement is not correct, then we rebuild the y-controller with images at those positions where $x = 0$.

Preparation of continuous output for learning Since the fuzzy controller learns to approximate a function, it works correctly only if the function to be learned is continuous, i.e. a differential change of the input will result in a differential change of the output. The correction angle α of the objects to be grasped has different rotation symmetry (lying screw: 360°, slat: 180°, block: 90°, standing screw with six-edge head: 60°). Therefore, we need to find a set of functions which meet the following conditions: a) continuous output values can be generated for fuzzy controller learning; b) the original correction angle can be uniquely reconstructed given the values of these functions. We propose the following two learning functions (Fig. 11):

$$\mathrm{L}_a = \sin\left(\frac{1}{2}\alpha\right), \qquad \mathrm{L}_s = \sin(\alpha)$$

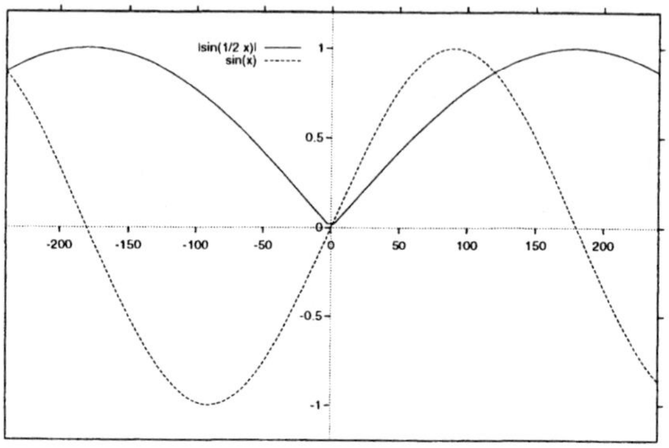

Fig. 11. The two functions which are used for fuzzy controller learning

Two fuzzy controllers are needed to learn L_a and L_s separately. The correction angle can be reconstructed as follows:

- The function arcsin supplies a value between $-90°$ and $+90°$. $|2\arcsin(\mathrm{L}_a)|$ supplies the absolute value of the correction angles.
- The sign of $\arcsin(\mathrm{L}_s)$ provides the information on whether the object is rotated clockwise or counter-clockwise with respect to the gripper.

In the application phase, the gripper motion should be corrected in the reverse direction of the object rotation. Therefore, the correction angle α can be calculated:

$$\alpha = -\mathrm{sign}(\mathrm{L}_s) \cdot |2\arcsin(\mathrm{L}_a)| \tag{11}$$

These two functions can be extended for objects with the symmetry S:

$$\mathrm{L}_a = \sin\left(\frac{360°}{S}\frac{1}{2}\alpha\right); \qquad \mathrm{L}_s = \sin\left(\frac{360°}{S}\alpha\right)$$

The reconstruction of the angle is then:

$$\alpha = -\frac{S}{360°}\mathrm{sign}(\mathrm{L}_s) \cdot |2\arcsin(\mathrm{L}_a)|$$

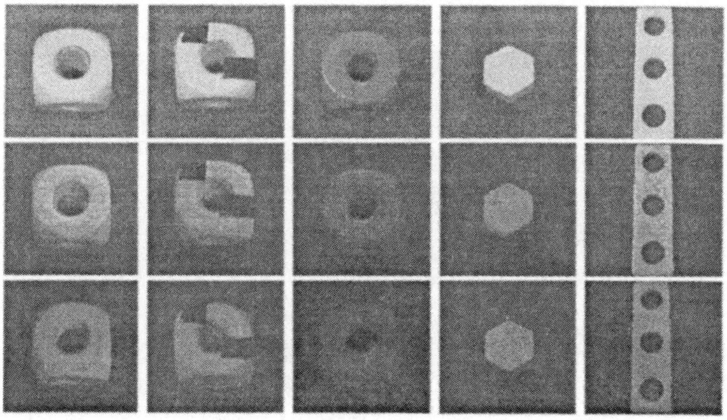

Fig. 12. 15 grasping scenarios; from left to right: yellow cube, partly covered yellow cube, blue cube, yellow screw head, 3-hole-slat; from top to bottom: optimal, worse and poor illumination

3.4 Experimental results

The approach was applied to the grasping of different objects: a yellow cube, a partly covered yellow cube, a blue cube, a yellow screw head, and a 3-hole-slat (Fig. 12). All training images were taken under optimal lighting conditions. For each object a specific controller was trained, except for the three cubes, where training (not grasping!) was restricted to the yellow cube. For the slat, different training images for x and y were used.

Only the eigenvectors corresponding to the three largest eigenvalues were used as input to the fuzzy controllers. The four largest eigenvalues for rotation/translation and the corresponding eigenvectors, which have the same dimension as the training images and can hence be interpreted as images. The eigenspace and the fuzzy controller that were derived from these data were applied to 15 different scenarios: the manipulator was to be positioned over the five objects, each with optimal, worse, and poor illumination (Fig. 12) and from the most remote starting position. The accuracy of the controllers was determined as the average error of 50 positioning sequences for each scenario.

Table 2 shows the *RMS error* for x, y, and the rotation angle α for positioning above the objects. Obviously, the positioning is correct even for the blue cube with the controller trained on the yellow one. It is easy to see that for the translation it makes hardly any difference whether the illumination is optimal or less optimal. The performance deteriorates under poor lighting conditions but it is still good enough to grasp the object. The rotation is more dependent on the illumination, in particular with the blue cube. That is because the vertical edges of the cube are practically invisible.

Table 2. RMS-errors for the three objects under different lighting conditions. Controllers with three input dimensions and four linguistic terms for each dimension were used.

yellow cube, completely visible			
illumination	x[mm]	y[mm]	α[degree]
optimal	0.399	0.665	0.608
worse	0.595	1.525	2.606
poor	3.126	1.038	6.059

yellow cube, 20% covered			
illumination	x[mm]	y[mm]	α[degree]
optimal	0.832	1.093	0.997
worse	0.524	2.373	1.141
poor	6.395	4.728	19.786

blue cube			
illumination	x[mm]	y[mm]	α[degree]
optimal	1.658	0.946	1.481
worse	0.494	2.020	1.979
poor	1.006	0.928	10.803

screw head			
illumination	x[mm]	y[mm]	α[degree]
optimal	0.630	0.535	1.850
worse	0.323	0.851	1.897
poor	0.610	0.751	1.281

3-hole-slat			
illumination	x[mm]	y[mm]	α[degree]
optimal	0.272	0.728	0.452
worse	0.940	0.704	0.386
poor	1.198	0.612	0.404

3.5 Linguistic interpretation of the controller

One main advantage of the neuro-fuzzy system in comparison with other adaptive systems like the multi-layer perceptron is the interpretability of the controller's function. Since we can transform the projections in the eigenspace back into the original input image space, the control rules can be given an interpretation as follows:

IF Antecedent THEN Consequent

where *Antecedent* is a back-transformed image and the *Consequent* (the controller output) is the x-, y- value or the correction angle α.

The following example illustrates the rules for a two-dimensional controller, each input variable with four linguistic terms. Therefore there are $4 \cdot 4 = 16$ rules altogether. The rotation control looks as follows:

if  then $|\Delta\alpha| = 2.2°$

if 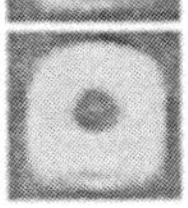 then $|\Delta\alpha| = 5.8°$

if 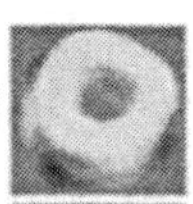 then $|\Delta\alpha| = 6.7°$

if 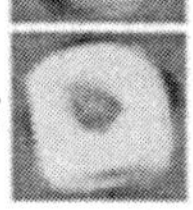 then $|\Delta\alpha| = 7.6°$

if  then $|\Delta\alpha| = 7.8°$

if  then $|\Delta\alpha| = 7.9°$

if  then $|\Delta\alpha| = 11.3°$

if  then $|\Delta\alpha| = 13.6°$

if 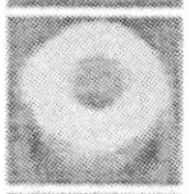 then $|\Delta\alpha| = 14.9°$

if 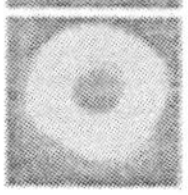 then $|\Delta\alpha| = 17.8°$

if  then $|\Delta\alpha| = 19.7°$

if  then $|\Delta\alpha| = 22.6°$

if  then $|\Delta\alpha| = 24.8°$

if 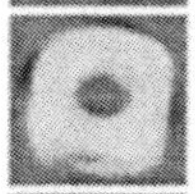 then $|\Delta\alpha| = 28.2°$

if  then $|\Delta\alpha| = 29.3°$

if 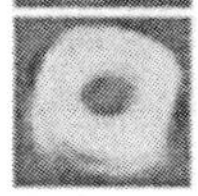 then $|\Delta\alpha| = 34.3°$

4 A complete recognition-grasping example

We now show a complete sample run of the hybrid system composed of the subsystems of Section 2 and Section 3. For the scene shown in Fig. 1 all steps are performed in an integrated way: a top view image is taken (Fig. 13a); the FII-recognition system recognises the objects of interest (Fig. 13b); the manipulator moves approximately above the object to be grasped; the evaluation of hand-camera images guides the gripper directly to the grasp position; the object is grasped.

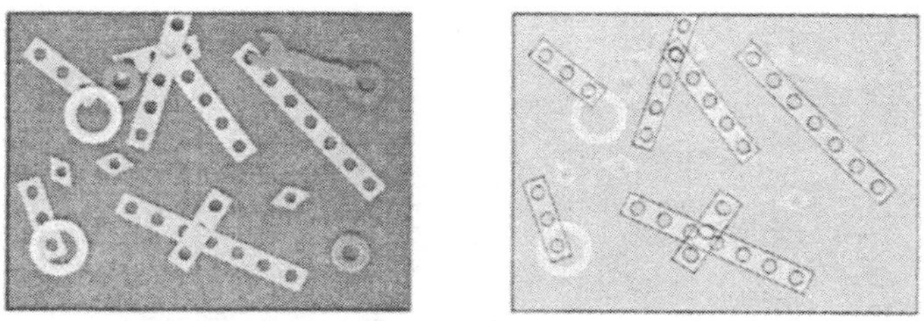

(a) Original Image (b) Result

Fig. 13. Test Scene (left) and recognised slats (right)

The task to be solved is the grasping of a slat (Fig. 13a). The FII-recognition system provides all the slats in the image (occluding each other or not), see Fig. 13b.

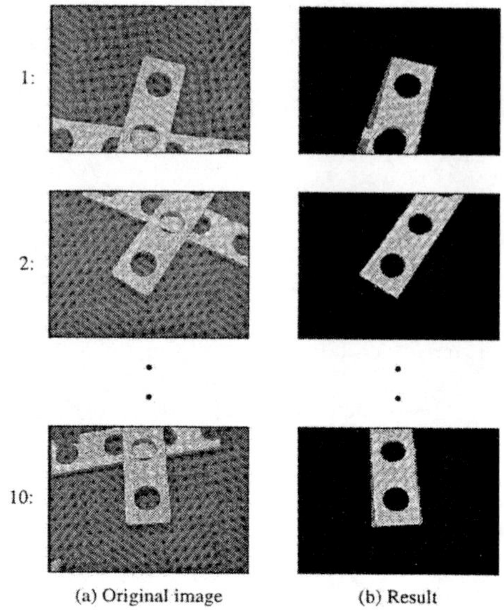

Fig. 14. Images of the hand camera taken at different time stamps

As we have not yet implemented heuristics that automatically pick a slat according to some given criteria, we manually choose the one that is not difficult to grasp: the 3-hole-slat lying on top of the 7-hole-slat. Figure 14 shows a part of the image sequence taken by the hand camera; the right row shows the results with the 7-hole-slat clipped based on the position information obtained by the FII-recogniser.

Fig. 15. Grabbed 3-hole-slat

Finally, as shown in Fig. 15, the slat is grasped successfully.

5 Conclusions

In this chapter we have shown that fuzzy rule based methodologies provide an added level of capabilities for robotic vision. We combined fuzzy rule systems with classic vision algorithms (invariants, PCA). This makes some challenging tasks like handling occlusion and calibration-free visual servoing feasible.

The object recognition system that utilizes fuzzy invariant values and fuzzy if-then-rules for the hypotheses generation step combines the approach of using invariants as object shape descriptors with the strength of fuzzy set theory. It is capable of recognising partially occluded objects from different viewpoints robustly, without the need of time-consuming and difficult camera-calibration.

The PCA in conjunction with neuro-fuzzy control is a practical and fast technique for performing multi-variant task-oriented image processing tasks. It is a general method, which needs learning. It is also a calibration-free approach and works robust even when the camera focus is not correctly adjusted or objects are soiled.

A complete recognition-grasping example has demonstrated the combined capabilities of both algorithms. It started with the recognition of partially occluded objects in a complex real robotic scenario and ended with the grasping process of an object of interest.

In sum the systems work without calibration and geometric models can be learned automatically. To a high degree they are:

- immune to uncertainties (illumination, perspective, ...)
- flexible, i.e. it easily adapts to new object poses, object types
- capable of recognising occluded objects in complex scenes

Future research directions will concentrate on some deficiencies of the presented systems:

As mentioned in Section 2, the implemented FII-recognition system is able to recognise (quasi-)planar objects only. Therefore, future research will focus on the recognition of three dimensional objects. Additionally, the recognition system will be distributed on multiple processors to reduce the recognition time.

The proposed neuro-fuzzy control method for fine-positioning is based on supervised learning. The further development of the approach will be on extending the approach to reinforcement learning which is life-long learning. The similar representation of robot state for fuzzy control can be used for reinforcement learning. The next challenging task is to use vision system to automatically evaluate the quality of grasping after each trial in order to supply the learning correct reward value. That task will demand on integration of active vision, multiple-view and diverse image processing algorithms. Fuzzy methodology can play an important role in the development.

References

1. Albus J.S., *A New Approach to Manipulator Control: The Cerebellar Model Articulation Contorller (CMAC)*, Transactions of ASME, Journal of Dynamic Systems Measurement and Control, Vol. 97, pp. 220–227, 1975
2. Binford T.O. and Levitt T.S., *Quasi-Invariants: Theory and Experiments*, in: "Proceedings of ARPA Image Understanding Workshop" (Washington, DC, USA), pp. 819–829, 1994
3. Black M.J. and Jepson A.D., *Eigen-Tracking: Robust Matching and Tracking of Articulated Objects Using a View-Based Representation*, in: "Proceedings of the European Conference on Computer Vision" (Cambridge, Great Britain), pp. 329–342, 1996
4. Blöchl B., *Fuzzy Control in Real-time for Vision Guided Autonomous Mobile Robots*, in: "Fuzzy Logic in Artificial Intelligence – Proceedings of the Austrian Artificial Intelligence Conference (Klement E.P. and Slany W., eds.)" (Linz, Austria), pp. 114–125, 1993
5. Canny J.F., *A Computational Approach to Edge Detection*, IEEE Transactions on Pattern Analysis and Machine Intelligence, Vol. 8, No. 6, pp. 679–698, 1986
6. Chen Y.H., *Computer Vision for General Purpose Visual Inspection: A Fuzzy Logic Approach*, Optics and Lasers in Engineering, Vol. 22, pp. 181–192, 1995
7. Forsyth D.A., Mundy J.L., Zisserman A.P., Coelho C., Heller A. and Rothwell C.A., *Invariant Descriptors for 3-D Object Recognition and Pose*, IEEE Transactions on Pattern Analysis and Machine Intelligence, Vol. 13, No. 10, pp. 971–991, 1991
8. Farreny H. and Prade H., *On the Problem of Identifying an Object in a Robotics Scene from a Verbal Imprecise Description*, in: "Advanced Software in Robotics (Danthine A. and Géradin M., eds.)", Elsevier Science, pp. 343–351, 1984
9. Graf T., Knoll A. and Wolfram A., *Recognition of Partially Occluded Objects through Fuzzy Invariant Indexing*, in: "Proceedings of the IEEE International Conference on Fuzzy Systems & IEEE World Congress on Computational Intelligence" (Anchorage, Alaska, USA), Vol. 2, pp. 1566–1571, 1998
10. Graf T., Knoll A. and Wolfram A., *Fuzzy Invariant Indexing: A General Indexing Scheme for Occluded Object Recognition*, in: "Proceedings of the International Conference on Signal Processing" (Beijing, China), pp. 908–911, 1998
11. Keller J.M., *Fuzzy set theory in computer vision: A prospectus*, Fuzzy Sets and Systems, Vol. 90, No. 2, pp. 177-182, 1997
12. Kamon I., Flash T. and Edelman S., *Learning to Grasp Using Visual Information*, in: "Proceedings of the IEEE International Conference on Robotics and Automation", pp. 2470–2476, 1996
13. Knoll A., Hildebrandt B. and Zhang J., *Instructing Cooperating Assembly Robots through Situated Dialogues in Natural Language*, in: "Proceedings of the IEEE International Conference on Robotics and Automation", (Albuquerque, NM), pp. 888–894, 1997
14. Kosako A. and Ralescu A.L., *Feature Based Parametric Eigenspace Method for Object Extraction*, in: "Proceedings of the IEEE International Conference on Fuzzy Systems" (Yokohama, Japan), pp. 1273–1278, 1995
15. Lee K.-J. and Bien Z., *A Model-Based Machine Vision System Using Fuzzy Logic*, International Journal of Approximate Reasoning, Vol. 16, pp. 119–135, 1997

16. Lamdan Y., Schwartz J.T. and Wolfson H.J., *Object Recognition by Affine Invariant Matching*, in: "Proceedings of Computer Vision and Pattern Recognition", pp. 335–344, 1988
17. Li W., Jiang X. and Wang Y., *Road Recognition for Vision Navigation of an Autonomous Vehicle by Fuzzy Reasoning*, Fuzzy Sets and Systems, Vol. 93, pp. 275–280, 1998
18. Mundy J.L., Huang C., Liu J., Hoffman W., Forsyth D.A., Rothwell C.A., Zisserman A., Utcke S. and Bournez O., *MORSE: A 3D Object Recognition System Based on Geometric Invariants*, in: "Proceedings of ARPA Image Understanding Workshop" (Monterey, California), pp. 1393–1402, 1994
19. Mundy J.L. and Zisserman A., *Introduction - Towards a New Framework for Vision*, in: "Geometric invariance in computer vision", Cambridge, Mass. MIT Press, 1992
20. Miller W.T., *Real-Time Application of Neural Networks for Sensor-Based Control of Robots with Vision*, IEEE Transactions on System, Man and Cybernetics, Vol. 19, pp. 825–831, 1989
21. Mundy J.L. and Zisserman A., *"Geometric invariance in computer vision"*, Cambridge, Mass. MIT Press, 1992
22. Nayar S.K., Murase H. and Nene S.A., *Learning, Positioning, and Tracking Visual Appearance*, in: "Proceedings of the IEEE International Conference on Robotics and Automation", pp. 3237–3244, 1994
23. Pal S.K., *Uncertainty Management in Space Station Autonomous Research: Pattern Recognition Perspective*, Information Sciences, Vol. 72, pp. 1–63, 1993
24. Rothwell C.A., *"Object recognition through invariant indexing"*, Oxford University Press, 1995
25. Ray K.S. and Ghoshal J., *Neuro-Fuzzy Reasoning for Occluded Object Recognition*, Fuzzy Sets and Systems, Vol. 94, pp. 1–28, 1998
26. Sanger T., *An Optimality Principle for Unsupervised Learning*, in: "Advances in Neural Information Processing Systems", Morgan Kaufmann, San Mateo, CA, 1989
27. Walker E.L., *Perspectives on Fuzzy Systems in Computer Vision*, in: "Proceedings of the Annual Conference of the North American Fuzzy Information Processing Society", pp. 296–300, 1998
28. Wei G.-Q., Hirzinger G. and Brunner B, *Sensorimotion Coordination and Sensor Fusion by Nneural Networks*, in: "Proceedings of IEEE International Conference on Neural Networks" (San Francisco, USA), pp. 150–155, 1993
29. Zadeh L.A., *Fuzzy sets*, Information and Control, Vol. 8, pp. 338–353, 1965
30. Zhang J. and Knoll A., *Constructing Fuzzy Controllers with B-Spline Models – Principles and Applications*, International Journal of Intelligent Systems, Vol. 13, pp. 257–285, 1997
31. Zhang J., Schmidt R. and Knoll A., *Appearance-Based Visual Learning in a Neuro-Fuzzy Model for Fine-Positioning of Manipulators*, in: "Proceedings of the IEEE International Conference on Robotics and Automation" (Detroit, USA), 1999
32. Zhang J. and Knoll A., *Situated Neuro-Fuzzy Control for Vision-Based Robot Localisation*, Journal of Robotics and Autonomous Systems, Elsevier Science, Vol. 28, pp. 71–82, 1999

Chapter 15

Topology-Preserving Deformations of Fuzzy Digital Pictures

Akira Nakamura[1] and Azriel Rosenfeld[2]

[1] Hiroshima-Denki Institute of Technology
Department of Computer Science
Hiroshima 739-0321, Japan
email: akira668@urban.ne.jp

[2] University of Maryland, Center for Automation Research
College Park, MD 20742-3275, USA
email: ar@cfar.umd.edu

Summary. This chapter considers the topology of two-dimensional fuzzy digital pictures, and discusses topology-preserving deformations of these fuzzy pictures that generalize deformations of two-valued digital pictures. It is shown that an arbitrary fuzzy picture can be transformed by this type of deformation into a coherent fuzzy picture. As another application, it is shown that the genus of a fuzzy picture is a linear combination of local property values.

1 Introduction

In [7] we defined topology-preserving deformation of two-valued digital pictures by repeatedly changing the values of (single) simple pixels (called "simple points" in this chapter), and proved some theorems about such deformations. In particular, we showed that such deformations can be used to magnify any picture by any integer factor, and we proved that any two topologically equivalent pictures differ by such a deformation. In this chapter we consider simple points in fuzzy (digital) pictures, as defined in [3], and discuss topology-preserving deformation of fuzzy pictures by changing the values of such simple points. This type of deformation (called "simple deformation", or SD for short) is a fuzzy version of the two-valued case treated in [7]. After reviewing some basic facts about fuzzy pictures and simple points, we show that an arbitrary fuzzy picture σ can be transformed by SD into a coherent fuzzy picture σ' that is topologically equivalent to σ. (Coherent fuzzy pictures have been studied in [2,6]; their definition will be given in Section 2.) We generalize the adjacency graph of a two-valued picture [4] to fuzzy pictures; using the fact that the adjacency graph of a coherent fuzzy picture is a tree, we show that an arbitrary fuzzy picture can be transformed by SD into a coherent fuzzy picture. As another application, we show that the genus of a fuzzy picture is a linear combination of local property values; this provides a solution to a problem posed in [5].

2 Basic definitions

Let Σ be a rectangular array of integer-coordinate points. Thus a point P of Σ has four horizontal and vertical neighbors, and it also has four diagonal neighbors. We say that the former points are 4-adjacent to, or 4-neighbors of, P; and we say that both types of neighbors are 8-adjacent to, or 8-neighbors of, P. Note that if P is on the border of Σ, some of these neighbors may not exist. For any point P, $N_8(P)$ means the set of 8-neighbors of P.

For all points P, Q of Σ, by a *path* ρ from P to Q we mean a sequence of points $P = P_0, P_1, \ldots, P_n = Q$ such that P_i is adjacent to P_{i+1}, $1 \leq 1 \leq n$. Note that this is two definitions in one ("4-path" and "8-path"), depending on whether "adjacent" means "4-adjacent" or "8-adjacent".

Let S be any subset of Σ. We say that two points P, Q of S are *connected* in S if there is a path from P to Q consisting entirely of points of S. Note that there are two kinds of connectedness, depending on whether "path" means 4-path or 8-path. It is easily shown that "connected" is an equivalence relation. This relation partitions S into equivalence classes, which are maximal subsets S_i of S such that every P, Q belonging to a given S_i are connected. These classes are called the (connected) *components* of S.

Let $c(S)$ be the *complement* of S (i.e., $c(S) = \Sigma - S$). It is standard practice to use opposite types of adjacency (4- or 8-) for a set and its complement. We assume, for simplicity, that the border points of Σ are all in $c(S)$. Thus one component of $c(S)$, called the *background* component, always contains the border of Σ. The other components, if any, are called *holes* in S. If S has no holes, it is called *simply connected.*

The above concepts can be extended to fuzzy sets. For convenience, to avoid the need for two types of adjacency we use a hexagonal array rather than a rectangular one. The neighborhood of a point P in a hexagonal array is illustrated below:

$$\begin{array}{ccccc} & A & & B & \\ C & & P & & D \\ & E & & F & \end{array}$$

The set $\{A, B, C, D, E, F\}$ is the neighborhood of P and is denoted by $N(P)$. This corresponds to $N_8(P)$ in a rectangular array. Note that $N(P)$ doesn't contain P.

We recall that a fuzzy subset of Σ is a function $\sigma : \Sigma \rightarrow [0,1]$. Such a function will sometimes be called a *fuzzy picture.* For $P \in \Sigma$, the value $\sigma(P)$ is called the *degree of membership* of P in σ. The function $1 - \sigma$, which takes each $P \in \Sigma$ into $1 - \sigma(P)$, is called the *complement* of σ. We assume that for every point P on the border of Σ we have $\sigma(P) = 0$. A fuzzy picture is called *crisp* if σ takes on only the values 0 and 1. In this case we usually take S to be the set of points P such that $\sigma(P) = 1$.

Let σ be a fuzzy subset of Σ, and let $\rho : P = P_0, P_1, \ldots, P_n = Q$ be any path between two points of Σ. We define the *strength* $s_\sigma(\rho)$ of ρ (with respect to σ) as $\min_{0 \leq i \leq n} \sigma(P_i)$ — "a path is as strong as its weakest link". We define the *degree of connectedness* of P and Q (with respect to σ) as $c_\sigma(P, Q) \equiv \max_\rho s_\sigma(\rho)$, where the max is taken over all paths from P to Q. For example, in the four-point fuzzy picture

$$\begin{array}{ccc} & P & \\ Q & & R \\ & S & \end{array}$$

whose σ values are

$$\begin{array}{ccc} & 0.8 & \\ 0.5 & & 0.3, \\ & 0.7 & \end{array}$$

the two paths between P and S have strengths 0.5 and 0.3, so that $c_\sigma(p, s) = 0.5$. We say that P and Q are *connected* in σ if $c_\sigma(P, Q) = \min(\sigma(P), \sigma(Q))$; in the example just given, P and S are not connected in σ. For any subset $T \subseteq \Sigma$, we call T *connected* with respect to σ if all P, Q in T are connected in σ. It is not hard to see that if σ is crisp, this concept reduces to the concept of connectedness defined above for ordinary pictures.

Although c_σ is not an equivalence relation when σ is not crisp, because it does not satisfy the transitivity property, we can define a notion of "connected component" with respect to σ. By a *plateau* in σ we mean a maximal connected subset of Σ on which σ has constant value. In other words, $\Pi \subseteq \Sigma$ is a plateau iff

(a) Π is connected;
(b) $\sigma(P) = \sigma(Q)$ for all P, Q in Π;
(c) $\sigma(P) \neq \sigma(Q)$ for all pairs of neighboring points $P \in \Pi, Q \notin \Pi$.

Note that a plateau can consist of only one point P, if all the points of $N(P)$ have values different from that of P. We call the plateau Π a *top* if its σ value is a local maximum. Similarly, we call Π a *bottom* if its σ value is a local minimum. The σ value of a plateau will be called its *height*.

We define two types of *level sets* of a fuzzy subset σ of Σ. The first one is a $\lambda(\geq)$-level set of σ, which is a non-fuzzy set consisting of the points $P \in \Sigma$ such that $\sigma(P) \geq \lambda$. The second is a $\lambda(>)$-level set of σ, which is a non-fuzzy set consisting of the points $P \in \Sigma$ such that $\sigma(P) > \lambda$. The $\lambda(\geq)$-level set of σ and the $\lambda(>)$-level set of σ are denoted by $\sigma_{\geq\lambda}$ and $\sigma_{>\lambda}$, respectively. The $\lambda(\geq)$-level set of σ is said to be obtained from σ by *thresholding* σ at λ.

The following fact is well known [5].

Theorem 1. *σ is connected w.r.t. σ iff there exists a unique top in σ.*

Proof. If P, Q are points belonging to two tops, any path between P and Q must leave these tops; hence it must have points whose σ values are less than both $\sigma(P)$ and $\sigma(Q)$, so that P and Q are not connected in σ. Conversely, if σ has only one top, say of height λ, then for any point P (or Q) there is a path of points having monotonically increasing σ values between P and a point of height λ; hence there is path between P and Q consisting of points whose σ values are all $\geq$ min $(\sigma(P), \sigma(Q))$. □

As in ordinary digital topology, we define the number of components of σ as the number of its tops. Also, the *genus* $g(\sigma)$ of σ is defined as the number of its tops minus the number of its bottoms (excluding the plateau that contains the border of Σ, which is evidently a bottom).

As in [2,6], a fuzzy set is called *coherent* if, for any plateau Π, exactly one plateau is adjacent to Π along each of its borders. In particular, Π is immediately surrounded by just one plateau along its outer border, and immediately surrounds just one plateau along the borders of each of its holes. For example, the fuzzy picture

$$\begin{matrix} & P & \\ Q & & R \\ & S & \end{matrix}$$

is coherent iff $\sigma(Q) = \sigma(R)$.

3 Simple points

In this section we define simple points of fuzzy pictures. Before giving the definition, let us review the concept of a simple point in the nonfuzzy ("crisp") case for a hexagonal array. A black point P (having value 1) is said to be *simple* iff

- (b1): P is adjacent to just one black (having value 1) component in $N(P)$;
- (b2): P is adjacent to just one white (having value 0) component in $N(P)$.

Let S be a subset of Σ, and let P be a simple point of S. Let S^- be a subset of S obtained from S by deleting P from S (changing the value of P from 1 to 0). Then it is well known that the numbers of components and holes in S^- are the same as those in S, respectively.

The above definition of simple point was for a black point, but dual to the black case we can also define a white simple point. A white point P (having value 0) is said to be simple iff

- (w1): P is adjacent to just one black component in $N(P)$;
- (w2): P is adjacent to just one white component in $N(P)$.

Let S be a subset of Σ and $P \notin S$, i.e. the value of P is 0. When we consider the subset $S \cup \{P\}$, the value of P changes to 1. If P is a simple point in the sense of (w1) and (w2), then P is said to be a *white simple point*. To distinguish the usual simple point from this white simple point, a simple point satisfying (b1) and (b2) will be called a *black simple point*.

Let S be a subset of Σ and $P \notin S$, and let S^+ be a subset obtained from S by adding a white simple P to S (changing the value of P from 0 to 1). Then it is easily shown that the numbers of components and holes of S are the same as those of S^+, respectively.

We now define simple points for a fuzzy picture σ. Let P be a point of Σ, and let the extended neighborhood $N(P) \cup P$ of P be

$$\begin{array}{ccccc} & A & & B & \\ C & & P & & D \\ & E & & F & \end{array}$$

and let the membership values at A, B, C, D, E, F, P be a, b, c, d, e, f, p, respectively; these values are denoted by $\sigma(N(P) \cup \{P\})$ (Hereafter, the lower case letter x means the value of point X). P is said to be *negative simple* iff P is a black simple point of $(\sigma(N(P) \cup \{P\})_{\geq p}$, and P is said to be *positive simple* iff P is a white simple point of $(\sigma(N(P) \cup \{P\})_{>p}$.

Let P be a negative simple point and let V be the set $\{x | x$ is a value of $N(P)$ and $x < p\}$. Then max V is called the *negative value* of P. Similarly, let U be the set $\{x | x$ is a value of $N(P)$ and $x > p\}$. Then min U is called the *positive value* of P. If P is a negative simple point, the replacement of p by the negative value of P is called the *negative simple point operation*. Similarly, if P is a positive simple point, the replacement of p by the positive value of P is called the *positive simple point operation*.

Let σ be a fuzzy subset of Σ. Let σ^- be a fuzzy subset which is obtained from σ by applying the negative simple point operation to a point of Σ, and let σ^+ be a fuzzy subset which is obtained from σ by applying the positive simple point operation to a point of Σ.

Example 1:

$$\text{(a)}\ \begin{array}{ccccc} & 0.8 & & 0.9 & \\ 0.8 & & 0.7 & & 0.3 \\ & 0.3 & & 0.4 & \end{array} \qquad \text{(b)}\ \begin{array}{ccccc} & 0.8 & & 0.5 & \\ 0.8 & & 0.7 & & 0.4 \\ & 0.3 & & 0.8 & \end{array}$$

In (a), the center is a negative simple point as well as a positive simple point, and in (b) the center is neither a negative nor a positive simple point. Further, in (a) 0.4 is the negative value and 0.8 is the positive value. Let (a) be σ; then σ^- and σ^+ are as follows:

$$\begin{array}{ccccc} & 0.8 & & 0.9 & \\ 0.8 & & 0.7 & & 0.3 \\ & 0.3 & & 0.4 & \\ & & \sigma & & \end{array} \qquad \begin{array}{ccccc} & 0.8 & & 0.9 & \\ 0.8 & & 0.4 & & 0.3 \\ & 0.3 & & 0.4 & \\ & & \sigma^- & & \end{array} \qquad \begin{array}{ccccc} & 0.8 & & 0.9 & \\ 0.8 & & 0.8 & & 0.3 \\ & 0.3 & & 0.4 & \\ & & \sigma^+ & & \end{array}$$

Theorem 2. *[3] Let us consider the neighborhood $N(P)$ of a point P in a fuzzy picture. If P is a negative simple point then the degrees of local connectedness of the pairs of points in $N(P)$ do not decrease after applying the negative simple point operation to P. Also, if P is a positive simple point then the degrees of local connectedness of the pairs of points in $N(P)$ do not increase after applying the positive simple point operation to P. Thus both simple point operations do not change the degrees of connectedness of the pairs of points in $N(P)$.*

Proof. We give the proof for a negative simple point; the proof for a positive simple point is analogous. Let Q, R be two points in $N(P)$. If they are both in $N(P)_{\geq p}$, the result is immediate, since every point of $N(P)_{\geq p}$ has value at least p. If neither of them is in $N(P)_{\geq p}$, their values are both less than p, and the result is again immediate. Suppose Q is not in $N(P)_{\geq p}$ but R is in it. If $c_\sigma(Q, R) = s_\sigma(\rho)$ for a path ρ that does not pass through P, the result is also immediate. Finally, if $c_\sigma(Q, R) = s_\sigma(\rho')$ where ρ' passes through P, the result is still true, because the negative value of P is the largest value x of a point of $N(P)$ such that $x < p$. □

In [1] a simple point of a fuzzy picture was defined as a point such that, if its value is replaced by the min of the values of its neighbors, the local connectedness of the pairs of points in its neighborhood does not decrease. In this chapter, we have defined positive and negative simple points in terms of level sets, and have proved that local connectedness does not decrease (increase) when we apply the (negative) positive simple point operation to such a point; note that these operations replace the value of the point by its (negative) positive value, rather than by the min of the values of its neighbors.

4 Simple deformations

Let σ and τ be fuzzy subsets of Σ. We say that τ is a *local deformation* of σ if $\tau = \sigma^-$ or σ^+ for some negative or positive simple point P of σ. We say that τ differs from σ by *simple deformation* (in short: SD) if there exists a sequence $\sigma = \sigma_0, \sigma_1, \ldots, \sigma_n = \tau$, $n \geq 0$, such that σ_i is a local deformation of σ_{i-1}, $1 \leq i \leq n$. Evidently, "differs by SD" is an equivalence relation. Note that each local deformation changes the value of only a single point; we do not consider "parallel" deformations.

Theorem 3. *[3] The numbers of tops and bottoms of σ and σ^- or σ^+ are the same.*

Proof. We give the proof (which is straightforward) for the number of tops in σ^-; the proofs in the other three cases are similar. Evidently, the negative simple point operation cannot cause a top to disappear, cannot merge two tops, and cannot split a top into two tops. □

Corollary 1. *The genus of σ^+ or σ^- is the same as that of σ.*

Corollary 2. *If σ and τ differ by SD, they have the same numbers of tops and bottoms and the same genus.*

As a generalization of the two-valued case [4], we define the *adjacency graph* of a fuzzy picture σ as a graph whose nodes correspond to the plateaus of σ, and where two nodes are joined by an arc iff the plateaus are adjacent. It is well known [4] that the adjacency graph of a two-valued picture is a tree. This evidently need not be true for a fuzzy picture; for example, if three plateaus are mutually adjacent, they form a cycle in the graph. If a fuzzy picture σ is coherent [2,6], a plateau of σ can only be adjacent to one other plateau along each of its borders. Evidently, this implies that the adjacency graph of σ is a tree. In the remainder of this section we show that any fuzzy picture σ differs by SD from a coherent fuzzy picture.

Note first that, as shown in [7], SD can be used to magnify any picture by any integer factor. The proof in [7] is for crisp pictures on the square grid, but a similar proof can be given for fuzzy pictures on the hexagonal grid; see Appendix A.

Let σ be a fuzzy picture, and let Π be any top of σ, say of height h. Let β be a border of Π; since Π is a top, it is adjacent along β to plateaus of heights $< h$. Let h' be the greatest of these heights. We will show that SD can be used to erode all the plateaus of heights less than h' until they are no longer adjacent to Π along β; when this has been done, Π is adjacent along β only to a single plateau of height h'. We first use SD to magnify σ by a factor of 2, to ensure that all the plateaus that meet Π along β have thickness at least 2. If a plateau of height $k < h'$ is adjacent to Π along β, there must exist adjacent points H', K along β having values h', k. Since all the plateaus have thickness at least 2, K is evidently positive simple, and we can replace k by its positive value h'. Repeating this process, we can replace the values of all the points along β by h'; when this has been completed, Π is adjacent along β only to a single plateau of height h'.

To show that this can be done for every border of every plateau of σ, let the heights of the plateaus of σ be $a > b > \ldots > k$. Let A be any plateau of height a; since A is a top, the method in the preceding paragraph can be used to modify σ so that every plateau of height A is adjacent, along each of its borders, to only one other plateau. (To ensure that the necessary erosions at this and the following stages of the proof are all possible, we first use SD to magnify σ by a sufficiently large integer factor.) This can evidently be done for every plateau of height a. Now let B be any plateau of height b. If B is adjacent, along any of its borders, to a plateau A of height a, evidently A and B can be the only two plateaus that meet at that border. Suppose B is adjacent to more than one plateau along one of its borders; then the highest of these plateaus has height $b' < b$. Then, using the same argument, by repeated replacement of positive simple points by their positive values we can erode all the lower plateaus away from that border until B is adjacent along that border only to a single plateau B' of height b'. Thus at the end of this step, every plateau of height B is adjacent, along each of its borders, to only one other plateau. Repeating this argument for the successive heights $a, b, c \ldots$ shows that we can transform σ into a fuzzy picture in which every plateau is adjacent, along each of its borders, to only one other plateau; in other words, σ differs by SD from a coherent fuzzy picture. We have thus proved

Theorem 4. *Any fuzzy picture σ differs by SD from a coherent fuzzy picture.*

5 Genus

In this section we show that the genus of a fuzzy picture is a linear combination of local property values. We first give a simple formula for the genus of a crisp picture on a hexagonal grid.

Theorem 5. *Let u be the number of "unit" equilateral triangles of points*

$$\begin{matrix} & Q & \\ R & & S \end{matrix}$$

or

$$\begin{matrix} Q & & R \\ & S & \end{matrix}$$

in which exactly one of Q, R, S is 1, and let t be the number of such triangles in which exactly two of them are 1. Then the genus g of the picture is given by the formula

$$6g = u - t$$

(This can be proved by induction on the number of 1's in the picture; the proof is given in Appendix B.)

We recall that the genus of a fuzzy picture is equal to the number of its tops minus the number of its bottoms (not counting the "background" region B of 0's connected to the border of the picture, which is a bottom). We shall show that the number of tops (and similarly for the number of bottoms) in a fuzzy picture can be computed by counting local patterns in fuzzy pictures derived from the given picture by local operations. Note first that we can assume that the fuzzy picture is coherent, since as we saw in Section 4, the picture can be transformed by SD (hence by local operations) into a coherent fuzzy picture.

Let Π be a plateau, say of height $p > 0$, in a coherent fuzzy picture; thus Π is immediately surrounded by a plateau Π', say of height p'. We call Π a *quasitop* if Π' is connected to B by a path whose points all have values $< p$ (so that in particular, $p' < p$).

Proposition 1. *If Π_1 and Π_2 are quasitops of heights p_1 and p_2, and Π_2 surrounds Π_1, then $p_1 > p_2$.*

Proof. Let Π_1' be the plateau (of height p_1') immediately surrounding Π_1; then $p_1' < p_1$, and there is a path from Π_1' to B whose points all have values $< p_1$. But this path must intersect Π_2; hence we must have $p_2 < p_1$. □

Proposition 2. *A quasitop is a top if it surrounds no other quasitop.*

Proof. If the quasitop Π (of height p) is not a top, it is adjacent to some other plateau Π^* of value $p^* > p$. Since Π is a quasitop, Π^* cannot immediately surround Π; hence Π immediately surrounds Π^*. Since Π is a quasitop, it is connected to B by a path whose points all have values $< p$; hence Π^* is connected to B by a path whose points have values $< p^*$, so that Π^* is also a quasitop. Thus we have proved that if a quasitop is not a top, it surrounds another quasitop. □

Evidently, if the fuzzy picture σ is thresholded at $p > 0$, the components of 1's in the thresholded picture $\sigma_{\geq p}$ that are adjacent to B coincide with the quasitops of value p in σ. In $\sigma_{\geq p}$, 0's connected to B can be identified by marking (say with b's) the 0's on the border and then repeatedly marking 0's that are adjacent to marked 0's; this involves only local operations.

Points whose values are greater than p can also be marked, say with h's. Points not marked with b's that are adjacent to points marked with h's can then be repeatedly marked with h's. If a quasitop Π of height p is not a top, it follows from Proposition 2 that this process will mark all the points surrounded by Π with h's.

The number of tops of height p in σ can then be counted by applying the formula $6g = u - t$ to the crisp picture whose 1's are the points that have value 0 and are not marked b or that have value 1 and are not marked h, and whose 0's are the points marked b.

By successively thresholding σ at each $p > 0$ and performing these processes on $\sigma_{\geq p}$ we can thus count all the tops in σ. The number of bottoms (other than B) can be counted similarly. We have thus proved the following theorem.

Theorem 6. *The number of tops, the number of bottoms, and the genus of a fuzzy picture can all be determined by performing local operations and counting local patterns.*

Appendix A: Magnification using simple point operations

In this appendix we show that a fuzzy picture on a hexagonal grid can be magnified by any positive integer factor by repeatedly performing simple point operations.

Let the extended neighborhood $N(P) \cup P$ of point P be

$$\begin{array}{ccccc} & A & & B & \\ C & & P & & D \\ & E & & F & \end{array}$$

We will describe how to magnify the picture "upward" in the direction PB; magnification in other directions is analogous. With respect to this direction, the picture can be divided into "rows". Five of these rows intersect $N(P)$; the intersections are $\{E\}, \{C,F\}, \{P\}, \{A,D\}$, and $\{B\}$. Let the nonzero points of the picture be contained in n rows, numbered "upward". Note that if P is in row i, B is in row $i+2$ and E in row $i-2$.

As in [7], our method of magnification is based on "upward" dilation of the constant-value runs of points (i.e., the maximal sequences of points in the PB direction that have the same values) in the PB direction. Let r_i be a run whose uppermost point is in row i. We will dilate each r_i by the amount $[id/2]$; we will do this first for all the runs r_n, then for all the runs r_{n-1}, and so on. Let the run below r_i have its uppermost point in row h, so that the length of run r_i is $(i-h)/2$ (note that $i-h$ must be even). When we dilate r_i by $[id/2]$, its length becomes $(i-h)/2+[id/2]$. When we later dilate r_h by hd, this erodes the dilated r_i so that its length becomes $(i-h)/2+[id/2]-[hd/2] = (i-h)/2+(i-h)d/2 = (i-h)(d+1)/2$, so that r_i is magnified by the factor $d+1$.

We now show that the dilations can be accomplished by repeated simple point operations. If P is the uppermost point of a run r_i, then when we dilate r_i, the runs that contain A, B, and D have already been dilated by greater amounts, or are infinite runs of 0's. Thus A, B and D belong to long runs of a's, b's, and d's in the PB direction. It is easily verified that, no matter what the values of a, b, d, and p are (note that $p \neq b$, since P is the uppermost point of a run), B is either positive simple or negative simple (or both). Suppose $p < b$. If $a \leq p$ and $d \leq p$, p is the negative value of B, so performing the negative simple point operation on B dilates r_i upward by one step. If $p < a < b$ or $p < d < b$ (or both), performing the negative simple point operation on B gives it the value a or d; but B is still simple, and performing the operation again (twice, if we have $p < a < d < b$ or $p < d < a < b$) gives B the value p, as desired. Similarly, if $p > b$, performing the positive simple point operation on B (once, twice, or three times) gives B the value p. Thus in any case, r_i can be dilated upward by repeatedly performing simple point operations.

Appendix B: Proof of the formula $6g = u - t$

If only one point of the picture has value 1, evidently we have $u = 6$, $t = 0$, and $g = 1$, so the formula is correct. Suppose it is correct for all pictures that have exactly $n-1$ points with value 1, and consider a picture that has

n such points. Let the neighborhood of the leftmost of the uppermost 1's in the picture be

$$\begin{array}{ccc} & 0 & 0 \\ 0 & 1 & A \\ & B & C \end{array}$$

If $A = B = C = 0$, changing the 1 to a 0 reduces g by 1 (since it eliminates a singleton component of 1's); it also reduces u by 6 and does not change t, so the formula remains correct. If $A = 0$ and B or C (or both) $= 1$, or $B = 0$ and A or C (or both) $= 1$, or $A = B = C = 1$, changing the 1 to 0 changes neither the number of components of 1's nor the number of components of 0's, so that it does not change the genus. In this case, if $A = B = C = 1$, changing the 1 to 0 does not change either u or t; if $A = 0$ and $B = C = 1$, or $B = 0$ and $A = C = 1$, changing the 1 to 0 decreases both of them by 1; and if $A = B = 0$ and $C = 1$, or $A = C = 0$ and $B = 1$, or $B = C = 0$ and $A = 1$, it decreases both of them by 2; in all these cases the formula remains correct. Finally, if $A = B = 1$ and $C = 0$, changing the 1 to 0 either splits a component of 1's (if A and B are not connected outside the neighborhood of the 1) or merges two components of 0's (if they are so connected, so that C is in a hole), so that it increases g by 1. In this case changing the 1 to 0 decreases t by 4 and increases u by 2, thus increasing $u - t$ by 6, so that once again the formula remains correct.

References

1. Dyer C.R. and Rosenfeld A., *Thinning algorithms for gray-scale pictures*, IEEE Transactions on Pattern Analysis and Machine Intelligence, Vol. 1, pp. 88-89, 1979
2. Nakamura A. and Aizawa K., *Connectedness of coherent fuzzy pictures*, Information Sciences, Vol. 61, pp. 123–133, 1992
3. Nakamura A. and Rosenfeld A., *Deformations of fuzzy pictures*, in: "Proceedings of JCIS'97 – Joint Conference on Information Sciences", Vol. 3, pp. 273–276, 1997
4. Rosenfeld A., *"Picture Languages"*, Academic Press, New York, 1979
5. Rosenfeld A., *Fuzzy digital topology*, Information and Control, Vol. 40, pp. 76–87, 1979
6. Rosenfeld A., *On connectivity properties of grayscale pictures*, Pattern Recognition, Vol. 16, pp. 47–50, 1983
7. Rosenfeld A., Kong T.Y. and A. Nakamura A., *Topology-preserving deformations of two-valued digital pictures*, Graphical Models and Image Processing, Vol. 60, pp. 24–34, 1998

Appendix

Color Images of Chapters 9 and 10

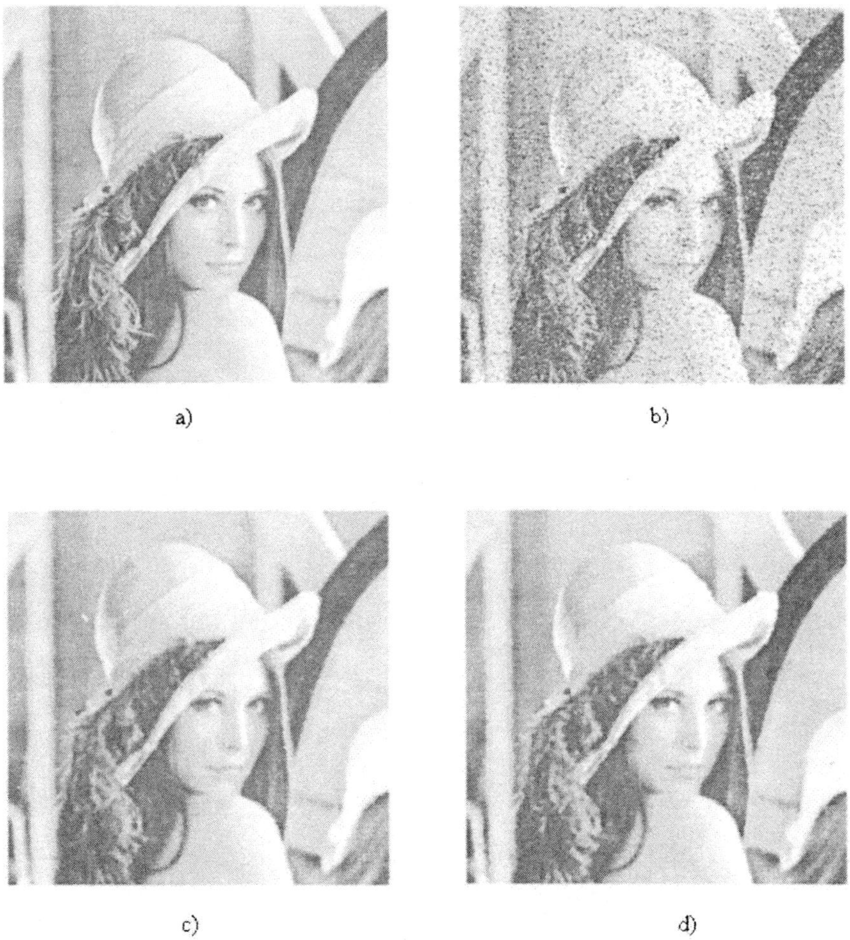

Fig. 1. Chapter 9, Figure 2

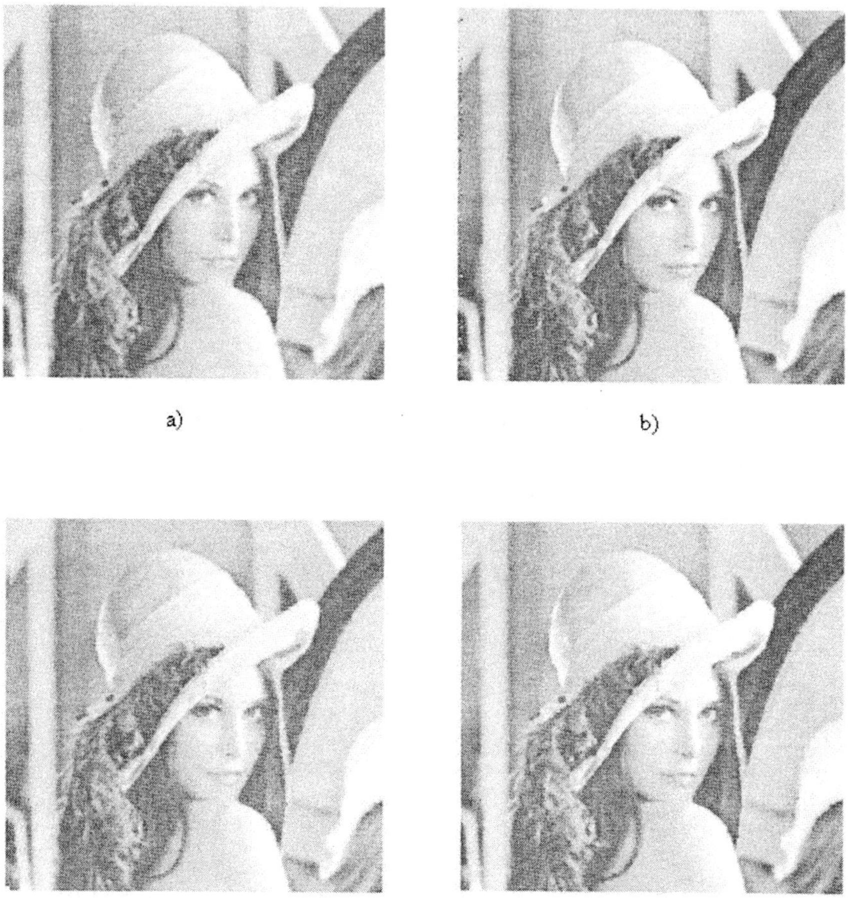

Fig. 2. Chapter 9, Figure 3

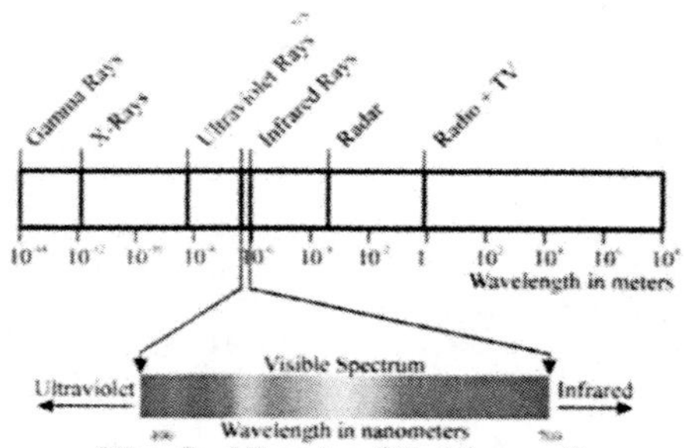

Fig. 3. Chapter 10, Figure 2

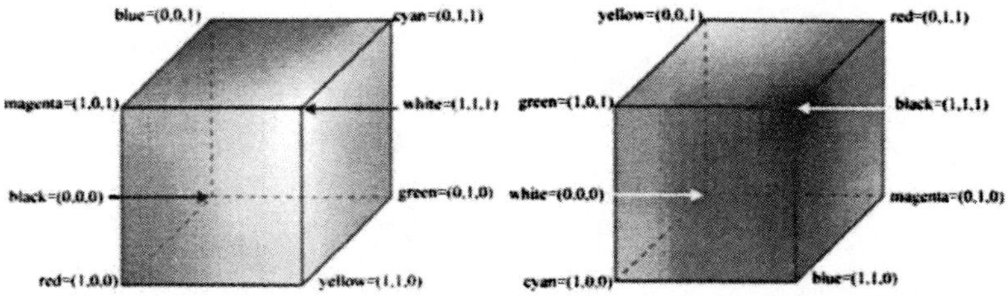

Fig. 4. Chapter 10, Figure 3 (left) and Figure 4 (right)

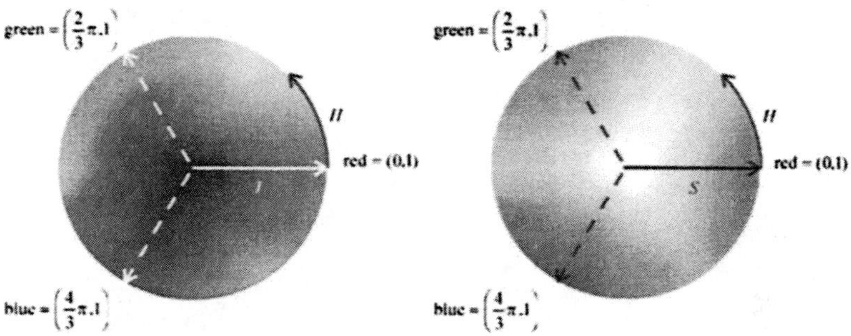

Fig. 5. Chapter 10, Figure 5 (left) and Figure 6 (right)

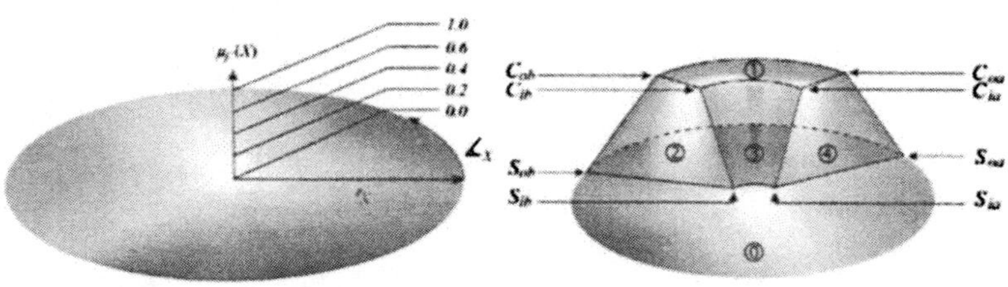

Fig. 6. Chapter 10, Figure 7 (left) and Figure 8 (right)

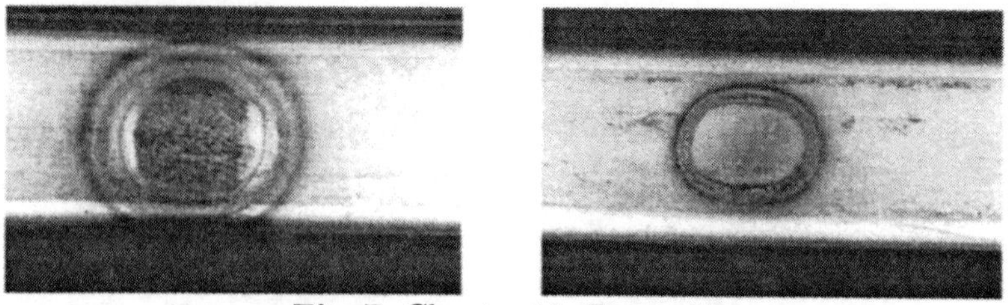

Fig. 7. Chapter 10, Figure 10

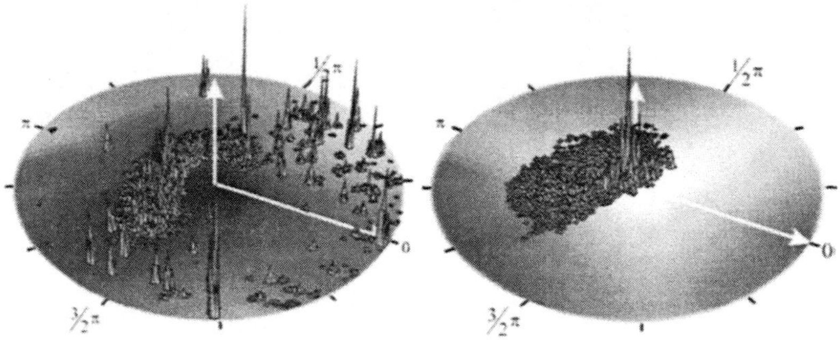

Fig. 8. Chapter 10, Figure 11 (left) and Figure 12 (right)

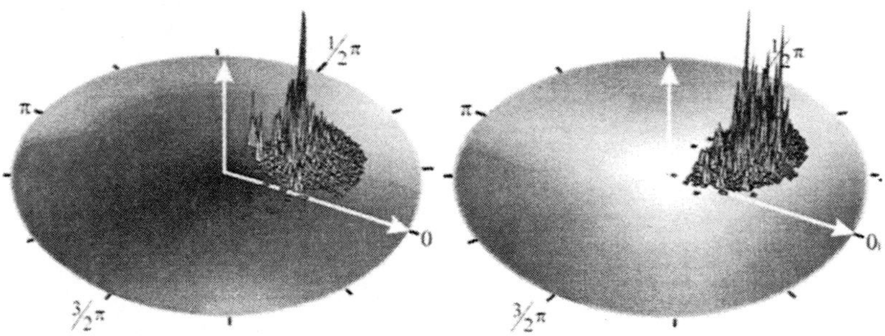

Fig. 9. Chapter 10, Figure 13 (left) and Figure 14 (right)

Index

ACFCF filter, 213
activity degree, 198
adaptive
- filtering, 152, 172
- neighborhood filter, 255
- prototype, 313
adjacency
- crisp, 121
- fuzzy, 120
- graph, 400
adjunction, 14, 41, 78, 87
AFCF filter, 213
approximate convexity, 97
AWFM filter, 178

B-spline model, 381
binary morphology, 4
boundary
- crisp, 121
- fuzzy, 122
breakdown probability, 186
breast cancer, 308, 325

C-average, 214
C4.5 algorithm, 291
centroid defuzzification, 301
CIELAB color space, 261
classification, 313, 322
closing, 78
- binary, 6
- fuzzy, 30, 62, 88
- threshold, 17
- umbra, 23
clustering
- filter, 255
- hierarchical, 257
- possibilistic, 257
- probabilistic, 257

CMY color space, 269
coherence, 397
color
- images, 248, 267
- models, 268
-- artistic, 270
-- conversion, 271
-- technical, 269
- processing, 248, 267
-- linguistic, 271, 281
- spaces
-- CIELAB, 261
-- CMY, 269
-- HI, 273
-- HS, 273
-- HSI, 260, 271
-- RGB, 260, 269
comparison measure, 319, 320
complete lattice, 78
computer-aided diagnosis, 325
conjunctor, 61
connectedness, 396
contrast, 140
convexity
- approximate, 97
correspondence matrix, 330
curvature method, 303

de-interlacing, 337, 352
decision tree, 327
- ID3, 291
deformation, 394
defuzzification, 259, 301, 350
degree of activity, 198
Dempster rule, 166
difference, 320
dilation, 78
- algebraic, 9

- binary, 5
- fuzzy, 29, 83, 108, 110
- threshold, 16
- umbra, 22

dimension reduction, 382
dissimilarity measure, 321
distance
- fuzzy, 113
-- Hausdorff, 117
-- nearest point, 116
- fuzzy set to fuzzy set, 116
- point to fuzzy set, 114

duality, 8, 35
dynamic selector, 178

EAWFM filter, 181
edge detection, 15, 20, 26, 41, 182, 222, 238
EIFCF filter, 204
EM-algorithm, 315
- hierarchical, 316
- modified, 317

enhancement, 137
erosion, 78
- algebraic, 10
- binary, 5
- fuzzy, 29, 83, 108, 110
- threshold, 16
- umbra, 22

extension principle, 312
extensivity, 12, 38
eye, 267
- cones, 268
- retina, 268
- rods, 268

FFCF filter, 212
filter
- ACFCF, 213
- adaptive neighborhood, 255
- AFCF, 213
- AWFM, 178
- clustering, 255
- EAWFM, 181
- EIFCF, 204
- FFCF, 212
- fuzzy
-- aggregative, 257
-- crude, 251
-- Gaussian, 156
-- inferential, 259
-- mean, 159, 174
-- median, 156
-- paradigm based, 255
- IFCF, 197
- L-filter, 249
- median, 232
- MIFCF, 201
- nearest-neighbor, 255
- SFCF, 205
- SSFCF, 210
- vector, 248
- weighted-averaging, 223
- WFM, 174

filtering, 137, 172, 194, 222, 248
fine-positioning, 372
fuzzy
- adjacency, 120
- aggregation, 258
- aggregative filter, 257
- attribute, 311
- closing, 30, 62, 88
- complement, 145
- contour, 310
- control, 194, 383
- decision tree, 327
- detector, 178
- dilation, 29, 83, 108, 110
- distance, 113, 114, 116
-- Hausdorff, 117
-- nearest point, 116
- edge region, 182
- erosion, 29, 83, 108, 110
- estimator, 176
- expected value, 143
- inclusion, 45, 76
- inferential filter, 259
- integration, 165
- interval, 175
- invariant indexing, 373
- k-means, 255
- logic, 194
- measurement, 311
- Minkowski addition, 44
- morphology, 4, 27, 58, 61, 76, 101
- motion detection, 337, 339
- normed operator, 182

– number, 174
– opening, 30, 62, 88
– prototype, 323
– relaxation, 142
– segmentation, 310
– set
– – comparison, 320
– – generation, 279
– signal space, 179
– smooth region, 182
– Sobel method, 181

generalized idempotence, 58, 60, 71
genus, 397, 401
gradient, 228
– morphological, 80, 89
grasping, 380
gray-scale morphology, 4, 15, 20

HI
– color space, 273
– point, 275
hierarchical EM-algorithm, 316
histogram
– equalization, 140
– fuzzy infinite norm, 182
– hyperbolization, 144
– parametrization, 314
hit-or-miss
– topology, 11
– transform, 80, 90
homogenity, 151
HS
– color space, 273
– point, 275
HSI color space, 260, 271
human vision, 267

ID3 decision tree, 291
idempotence, 12, 38, 58
– generalized, 58, 60, 71
IFCF filter, 197
image
– enhancement, 137, 172
– filtering, 137, 172, 194, 222, 248
implicator, 61, 340
impulse noise, 178
– long-tailed, 178
– median-tailed, 178
– short-tailed, 178
inclusion
– Bandler & Kohout, 53
– indicator, 82
– Kitainik, 50
– measure, 322
– Sinha & Dougherty, 48
– Zadeh, 46
indexing, 373
inference system
– fuzzy normed, 181
interlacing, 337, 341
invariant
– indexing, 373
– projective, 374

JND, 261

kernel representation, 92

L-filter, 249
local knowledge, 14, 40

magnification, 402
mammography, 308
mean
– fuzzy filter, 159, 174
– opinion score, 164
measure
– comparison, 319, 320
– dissimilarity, 321
– fuzziness, 139
– inclusion, 322
– resemblance, 321
– satisfiability, 322
– similitude, 321
median filter, 232
– fuzzy, 156
membership plane, 138
microcalcification, 309
MIFCF filter, 201
minimization of fuzziness, 140
Minkowski addition, 7, 43
modified
– u-dilation, 34
– u-erosion, 34
morphological
– gradient, 80, 89
– operation, 3

morphology
- binary, 4
- fuzzy, 4, 27, 58, 61, 76, 101
- gray-scale, 4, 15, 20
motion, 337, 339
- seven-point detection, 347
- three-point detection, 347
MSEE criterion, 207
multiscale edges, 239

nearest neighbor filter, 255
noise removal, 152, 178, 194, 222, 231, 248
- Gaussian, 231
- impulse, 232

object recognition, 370
opening, 78
- binary, 6
- fuzzy, 30, 62, 88
- threshold, 17
- umbra, 23
ordering property, 60, 69

P-EM algorithm, 317
pattern recognition
- model-based, 120
- structural, 124
plateau, 396
- bottom, 396
- quasitop, 401
- top, 396
position
- relative, 124
projective invariant, 374
prototype, 319

recognition, 370, 376, 377
relative position, 124
resemblance measure, 321
residual operators, 63
RGB color space, 260, 269
Robinson's operator, 241
robot vision, 370

satisfiability measure, 322
segmentation
- background-thinning-based, 288
- path, 287, 296
semicontinuity, 11, 86
servoing, 370
SFCF filter, 205
sharpening coefficient, 211
similitude measure, 321
simple
- deformation, 399
- point, 397
soft fusion, 159
spot welding, 279
SSFCF filter, 210
step-like approximation, 228, 230
subjectivity, 162
sup-star composition, 341

t-conorm, 340
- weak, 111
t-norm, 61, 340
- weak, 111
t-operation, 15
template matching, 216
three-dimensional (3D)
- reconstruction, 329
- visualization, 333
time-variant system, 223
top surface, 21
topology, 394
typicality, 324

u-operations, 21
umbra, 21, 24

video format, 337
- interlaced, 337, 341
- progressive, 337
visual servoing, 370

weak
- t-conorm, 111
- t-norm, 111
weighted-averaging filter, 223
WFM filter, 174
windowed operator, 96

Studies in Fuzziness and Soft Computing

Vol. 25. J. Buckley and Th. Feuring
Fuzzy and Neural: Interactions and Applications, 1999. ISBN 3-7908-1170-X

Vol. 26. A. Yazici and R. George
Fuzzy Database Modeling, 1999
ISBN 3-7908-1171-8

Vol. 27. M. Zaus
Crisp and Soft Computing with Hypercubical Calculus, 1999
ISBN 3-7908-1172-6

Vol. 28. R.A. Ribeiro, H.-J. Zimmermann, R.R. Yager and J. Kacprzyk (Eds.)
Soft Computing in Financial Engineering, 1999
ISBN 3-7908-1173-4

Vol. 29. H. Tanaka and P. Guo
Possibilistic Data Analysis for Operations Research, 1999. ISBN 3-7908-1183-1

Vol. 30. N. Kasabov and R. Kozma (Eds.)
Neuro-Fuzzy Techniques for Intelligent Information Systems, 1999
ISBN 3-7908-1187-4

Vol. 31. B. Kostek
Soft Computing in Acoustics, 1999
ISBN 3-7908-1190-4

Vol. 32. K. Hirota and T. Fukuda
Soft Computing in Mechatronics, 1999
ISBN 3-7908-1212-9

Vol. 33. L.A. Zadeh and J. Kacprzyk (Eds.)
Computing with Words in Information/Intelligent Systems 1, 1999
ISBN 3-7908-1217-X

Vol. 34. L.A. Zadeh and J. Kacprzyk (Eds.)
Computing with Words in Information/Intelligent Systems 2, 1999
ISBN 3-7908-1218-8

Vol. 35. K.T. Atanassov
Intuitionistic Fuzzy Sets, 1999
ISBN 3-7908-1228-5

Vol. 36. L.C. Jain (Ed.)
Innovative Teaching and Learning, 2000
ISBN 3-7908-1246-3

Vol. 37. R. Słowiński and M. Hapke (Eds.)
Scheduling Under Fuzziness, 2000
ISBN 3-7908-1249-8

Vol. 38. D. Ruan (Ed.)
Fuzzy Systems and Soft Computing in Nuclear Engineering, 2000
ISBN 3-7908-1251-X

Vol. 39. O. Pons, M.A. Vila and J. Kacprzyk (Eds.)
Knowledge Management in Fuzzy Databases, 2000
ISBN 3-7908-1255-2

Vol. 40. M. Grabisch, T. Murofushi and M. Sugeno (Eds.) *Fuzzy Measures and Integrals, 2000*
ISBN 3-7908-1255-2

Vol. 41. P. Szczepaniak, P. Lisboa and J. Kacprzyk (Eds.) *Fuzzy Systems in Medicine, 2000*
ISBN 3-7908-1263-4

Vol. 42. S. Pal, G. Ashish and M. Kundu (Eds.)
Soft Computing for Image Processing, 2000
ISBN 3-7908-1217-X

Vol. 43. L.C. Jain, B. Lazzerini and U. Halici (Eds.)
Innovations in ART Neural Networks, 2000
ISBN 3-7908-1270-6

Vol. 44. J. Aracil and F. Gordillo (Eds.)
Stability Issues in Fuzzy Control, 2000
ISBN 3-7908-1277-3

Vol. 45. N. Kasabov (Ed.)
Future Directions for Intelligent Information Systems on Information Sciences, 2000
ISBN 3-7908-1276-5

Vol. 46. J.N. Mordeson and P.S. Nair
Fuzzy Graphs and Fuzzy Hypergraphs, 2000
ISBN 3-7908-1286-2

Vol. 47. E. Czogała† and J. Łęski
Fuzzy and Neuro-Fuzzy Intelligent Systems, 2000
ISBN 3-7908-1289-7

Vol. 48. M. Sakawa
Large Scale Interactive Fuzzy Multiobjective Programming, 2000
ISBN 3-7908-1293-5

Vol 49. L.I. Kuncheva
Fuzzy Classifier Design, 2000. ISBN 3-7908-1298-6

Vol. 50. F. Crestani and G. Pasi (Eds.)
Soft Computing in Information Retrieval, 2000
ISBN 3-7908-1299-4

Vol. 51. J. Fodor, B. De Baets and P. Perny (Eds.)
Preferences and Decisions under Incomplete Knowledge, 2000
ISBN 3-7908-1303-6

Druck: Strauss Offsetdruck, Mörlenbach
Verarbeitung: Schäffer, Grünstadt